WITHDRAWN

STAFFORD LIBRARY
COLUMBIA COLLEGE
COLUMBIA, MO 65216

AMERICAN
LAW
YEARBOOK
2000

ISSN 1521-0901

AMERICAN LAW YEARBOOK 2000

AN ANNUAL SOURCE PUBLISHED
BY THE GALE GROUP AS A
SUPPLEMENT TO
WEST'S ENCYCLOPEDIA OF
AMERICAN LAW

Detroit
New York
San Francisco
London
Boston
Woodbridge, CT

STAFFORD LIBRARY
COLUMBIA COLLEGE
COLUMBIA, MO 65216

Jeffrey Lehman, *Editor*
Allison McClintic Marion, *Contributing Editor*
Brian J. Koski, *Associate Editor*
Jeffrey Wilson, *Assistant Editor*
Shelly Dickey, *Managing Editor*

Maria Franklin, *Permissions Manager*
Mark Plaza, *Permissions Assistant*

Mary Beth Trimper, *Composition and Electronic Prepress Manager*
Evi Seoud, *Assistant Composition and Electronic Prepress Manager*

Kenn Zorn, *Product Design Manager*
Barbara J. Yarrow, *Imaging/Multimedia Content Manager*
Randy Bassett, *Image Database Supervisor*
Pamela A. Reed, *Imaging Coordinator*
Robert Duncan, *Imaging Specialist*

This publication is designed to provide information on the subjects covered. It is sold with the understanding that the publisher, Gale Group, is not engaged in rendering legal or other professional advice. If legal advice or other professional assistance is required, the services of a competent professional person should be sought.

While every effort has been made to ensure the reliability of the information presented in this publication, Gale does not guarantee the accuracy of the data contained herein. Gale accepts no payment for listing; inclusion in the publication of any organization, agency, institution, publication, service, or individual does not imply endorsement of the publisher. Errors brought to the attention of the publisher and verified to the satisfaction of the publisher will be corrected in future editions.

This publication is a creative work fully protected by all applicable copyright laws, as well as by misappropriation, trade secret, unfair competition, and other applicable laws. The authors and editors of this work have added value to the underlying factual materials herein through one or more of the following: unique and original selection, coordination, expression, arrangement, and classification of the information.

All rights to this publication will be vigorously defended.

Copyright © 2001
Gale Group
27500 Drake Rd.
Farmington Hills, MI 48331-3535
http://www.galegroup.com
800-877-4253
248-699-4253

All rights reserved, including the right of reproduction in whole or in part in any form.

ISBN 0-7876-4788-8
ISSN 1521-0901

Printed in the United States of America

CONTENTS

Preface vii

Acknowledgments xi

Abandonment 1
Abortion 2
Acquired Immune Deficiency Syndrome 4
Adoption 5
Affirmative Action 8
Age Discrimination 10
Agricultural Law 12
Airlines 13
Albert, Carl (biography) 16
Aliens 17
Antitrust Law 19
Bankruptcy 23
Banks and Banking 24
Baseball 25
Bates, Daisy Lee Gatson (obituary) 27
Bird, Rose Elizabeth (biography) 27
Boundaries 28
Brennan, William Joseph, Jr. (obituary) . . . 29
Bribery 29
Buergenthal, Thomas (biography) 31
Capital Punishment 33
Carmichael, Stokely (obituary) 37
Carter, Rubin "Hurricane" (biography) . . . 38
Center to Prevent Handgun Violence 39
Clifford, Clark McAdams (obituary) 41
Commerce Clause 41
Commerce, Electronic 42
Competent 43
Computer Crime 44
Confrontation 45
Conspiracy 47
Criminal Procedure 48
Deportation 51
Disabled Persons 52

DNA Evidence 59
Drugs and Narcotics 60
Elections 63
Employment Law 65
Environmental Law 68
Equal Protection 71
Espionage 72
Evidence 74
Ex Post Facto Laws 76
Extradition 77
Family Law 81
Federalism 82
Fifth Amendment 87
First Amendment 88
Fourth Amendment 93
Freedom of Information Act 94
Freedom of Speech 95
Gay and Lesbian Rights 97
Gigante, Vincent "Chin" (biography) 105
Gun Control 106
Habeas Corpus 111
Hate Crime 113
Health Care Law 115
Health Insurance 118
Homeless Person 120
Immigration 123
Immunity 124
Inheritance 125
Intellectual Property 126
International Law 128
Internet 130
Johnson, Frank Minis, Jr. (obituary) 137
Jury 137
Juvenile Law 139

v

In Focus,
    Why is the Number of Juveniles
        Tried as Adults Increasing? 138
Kidnapping 143
Kleindienst, Richard Gordon
    (obituary) 144
Lewis, John R. (biography)......... 145
Libel and Slander 146
Manslaughter 153
Marshall, Margaret Hilary (biography) ... 154
Medicare....................... 156
Mezvinsky, Edward (biography) 157
Murder........................ 158
Native American Rights............ 161
Page, Alan Cedric (biography) 165
Pardon 166
Parks, Bernard C. (biography) 167
Parole......................... 169
In Focus,
    Is the Human Genome Patentable? ... 172
Patients' Rights 171
Police 174
Police Brutality 176
Pornography 178
Prior Restraint................... 181
Prisons 182
Privacy 183
In Focus,
    What Have Lawmakers Done to
    Regulate Human Cloning
    Research? 184
Product Liability 188
Racketeer Influenced and Corrupt
    Organizations Act 191
In Focus,
    Have Three-Strikes Laws Worked
        to Reduce Recidivism? 194
Recuse 192
Religion 193
Reparation 201
Richardson, Elliot Lee (obituary) 202
Riot 202
Robinson, Spottswood William, III
    (obituary) 204
Scheck, Barry (biography) 205
Schools and School Districts 206
Search and Seizure................. 209
Self-Incrimination 210
In Focus,
    Cruel and Unusual Punishment? 214

Sex Discrimination 213
Sex Offenses 215
Sexual Harassment................. 217
Sheppard, Samuel H................ 218
Sixth Amendment 219
In Focus,
    Why Do Athletes' Legal Problems
        Attract Attention? 224
Statehood 223
Stop and Frisk................... 226
Stout, Juanita Kidd (obituary)......... 228
Telecommunications 229
Terrorism 231
Tobacco 232
Trademarks..................... 235
Treaty......................... 236
Voting 239
Voting Rights Act of 1965 240
Welfare........................ 243
Women's Rights 244
Wrongful Death 246

Appendix:
    Nebraska's Partial-Birth Abortion
        Statute 249
    Utah Child Welfare Amendments 250
    FCC Rules to Implement § 255 of
        the Telecommunications Act
        of 1996...................... 250
    Executive Order 13145 (Barring
        Genetic Discrimination in Federal
        Employment) 252
    Weatherhead Letter 254
    Driver's Privacy Protection Act
        of 1994...................... 255
    Michigan's "Cussing Canoeist" Law... 257
    Ohio's Anti-Pornography Law....... 257
    Colorado's "Bubble" Law 259
    Jimmy Carter's Speech at the
        Transfer of Panama Canal
        Ownership 259

Abbreviations 263

Index to the Milestones 283

Table of Cases Cited................ 285

Index by Name and Subject 289

PREFACE

The need for a layperson's comprehensive, understandable guide to terms, concepts, and historical developments in U.S. law has been well met by *West's Encyclopedia of American Law* (*WEAL*). Published at the end of 1997 by the foremost legal professional publisher, *WEAL* has proved itself a valuable successor to *The Guide to American Law: Everyone's Legal Encyclopedia* from the same publisher, West Group, in 1983.

Now, in cooperation with West Group, Gale Group, a premier reference publisher, extends the value of *WEAL* with the publication of *American Law Yearbook*. The *Yearbook* both adds entries on emerging topics not covered in the main set and provides updates through July 2000, on cases, statutes, and issues documented there. A legal reference must be current to be authoritative, so the *Yearbook* is a vital companion to a key reference source. Uniform organization and cross-referencing make it easy to use the titles together, while inclusion of key definitions and summaries of earlier rulings in supplement entries, whether new or continuations, make it unnecessary to refer constantly to the main set.

Understanding the American Legal System

The legal system of the United States is admired around the world for the freedoms it allows the individual and the fairness with which it attempts to treat all persons. On the surface, it may seem simple. Yet, those who have delved into it know that this system of federal and state constitutions, statutes, regulations, and common law decisions is elaborate and complex. It derives from the English common law, but includes principles older than England, along with some principles from other lands. Many concepts are still phrased in Latin. The U.S. legal system, like many others, has a language all its own. Too often it is an unfamiliar language.

West's Encyclopedia of American Law (*WEAL*) explains legal terms and concepts in everyday language. It covers a wide variety of persons, entities, and events that have shaped the U.S. legal system and influenced public perceptions of the legal system.

FEATURES OF THIS SUPPLEMENT

Entries

This supplement contains 180 entries covering individuals, cases, laws, and concepts. Entries are arranged alphabetically and, for continuation entries, use the same entry title as in *WEAL*. There may be several cases discussed under a given topic. Entry headings refer to decisions of the U.S. Supreme Court by case name; other cases are identified by their subject matter.

Profiles of individuals cover interesting and influential people from the world of law, government, and public life, both historic and contemporary. All have played a part in creating or shaping U.S. law. Each profile includes a timeline highlighting important moments in the subject's life.

Definitions

Each entry on a legal term is preceded by a definition, which is easily distinguished by its sans serif typeface.

Cross References

To facilitate research, two types of cross-references are provided within and following entries. Within the entries, terms are set in small capital letters (e.g. DISCLAIMER) to indicate that they have their own entry in WEAL. Cross references at the end of an entry refer readers to additional relevant topics in WEAL.

In Focus Pieces

In Focus pieces present complex and controversial issues from different perspectives. These pieces, which are set apart from the main entries with boxed edges and their own logo, examine some of the difficult legal and social questions that confront attorneys, judges, juries, and legislatures. The human genome and sentencing of juveniles as adults are among the high-interest topics in this yearbook.

Appendix

The appendix to this volume features the full text of documents that complement the entries, such as Colorado's "Bubble Law," Nebraska's partial-birth abortion statute, and Jimmy Carter's speech upon the return of the Panama Canal to Panamanian control.

Index of WEAL's Appendix and Milestones in the Law

This section indexes a number of primary documents included in the main set. Primary documents included in the *Yearbook* are included in the name and subject index.

Table of Cases Cited and Index

These features make it easy for users to quickly locate references to cases, people, statutes, events, and other subjects. The Table of Cases Cited traces the influences of legal precedents by identifying mentions of cases throughout the text. In a departure from WEAL, references to individuals have been folded into the general index to simplify searches. Litigants, justices, historical and contemporary figures, as well as topical references are included in the Index.

Citations

Wherever possible, *American Law Yearbook* includes citations to cases and statutes for readers wishing to do further research. The citation refers to one or more of the series called "reporters" that publish court opinions and related information. Each citation includes a volume number, an abbreviation for the reporter, and the starting page reference. Underscores in a citation indicate that a court opinion has not been officially reported as of publication. Two sample citations, with explanations, are presented below.

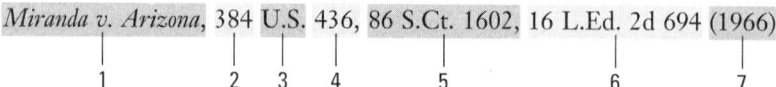

1. *Case title.* The title of the case is set in italics and indicates the names of the parties. The suit in this sample citation was between Ernesto A. Miranda and the state of Arizona.

2. *Reporter volume number.* The number preceding the reporter abbreviation indicates the reporter volume containing the case. (The volume number appears on the spine of the reporter, along with the reporter abbreviation.)

3. *Reporter abbreviation.* The suit in the sample citation is from the reporter, or series of books, called *U.S. Reports,* which contains cases from the U.S. Supreme Court. (Numerous reporters publish cases from the federal and state courts; consult the abbreviations list at the back of this volume for full titles.)

4. *Reporter page.* The number following the reporter abbreviation indicates the reporter page on which the case begins.

5. *Additional reporter citation.* Many cases may be found in more than one reporter. The suit in the sample citation also appears in volume 86 of the *Supreme Court Reporter,* beginning on page 1602.

6. *Additional reporter citation.* The suit in the sample citation is also reported in volume 16 of the *Lawyer's Edition,* second series, beginning on page 694.

7. *Year of decision.* The year the court issued its decision in the case appears in parentheses at the end of the cite.

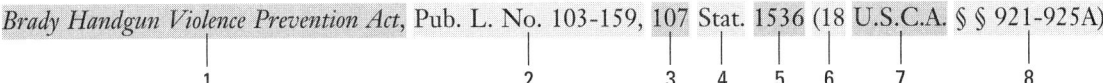

1. *Statute title.*

2. *Public law number.* In the sample citation, the number 103 indicates this law was passed by the 103d Congress, and the number 159 indicates it was the 159th law passed by that Congress.

3. *Reporter volume number.* The number preceding the reporter abbreviation indicates the reporter volume containing the statute.

4. *Reporter abbreviation.* The name of the reporter is abbreviated. The statute in the sample citation is from *Statutes at Large.*

5. *Reporter page.* The number following the reporter abbreviation indicates the reporter page on which the statute begins.

6. *Title number.* Federal laws are divided into major sections with specific titles. The number preceding a reference to the U.S. Code stands for the section called Crimes and Criminal Procedure.

7. *Additional reporter.* The statute in the sample citation may also be found in the *U.S. Code Annotated.*

8. *Section numbers.* The section numbers following a reference to the *U.S. Code Annotated* indicate where the statute appears in that reporter.

COMMENTS WELCOME

Considerable efforts were expended at the time of publication to ensure the accuracy of the information presented in *American Law Yearbook 2000.* The editors welcome your comments and suggestions for enhancing and improving future editions of this supplement to *West's Encyclopedia of American Law.* Send comments and suggestions to:

American Law Yearbook
Gale Group
27500 Drake Rd.
Farmington Hills, MI 48331-3535

ACKNOWLEDGMENTS

SPECIAL THANKS

The editor wishes to acknowledge the contributions of the writers who aided in the compilation of *American Law Yearbook*. In particular, the editor gratefully thanks Geraldine Azzata, Daniel E. Brannen, Jr., Halle I. Butler, Richard J. Cretan, Aaron D. Ford, Frederick K. Grittner, Lauri R. Harding, Anne Kevlin, Kathleen M. Knisely, Melynda M. Neal, Berna L. Rhodes-Ford, Mary Hertz Scarbrough, Scott D. Slick, and Lauren Zupnick for their writing contributions.

PHOTOGRAPHIC CREDITS

The editor wishes to thank the permission managers of the companies that assisted in securing reprint rights. The following list acknowledges the copyright holders who have granted us permission to reprint material in this edition of *American Law Yearbook*:

AP/Wide World Photos: pages 2, 3, 6, 8, 9, 13, 14, 16, 18, 20, 26, 27, 27, 30, 35, 37, 38, 41, 44, 47, 52, 57, 61, 65, 66, 68, 69, 71, 77, 78, 82, 91, 93, 96, 99, 102, 104, 105, 107, 109, 113, 115, 116, 117, 120, 127, 129, 134, 137, 140, 144, 145, 147, 153, 154, 158, 163, 165, 167, 167, 174, 175, 177, 178, 179, 181, 186, 193, 200, 202, 203, 205, 207, 208, 212, 213, 216, 219, 226, 228, 233, 237, 240, 245, and 247; **Corbis Corp.**: pages 34 and 202; **Courtesy Supreme Court**: page 29.

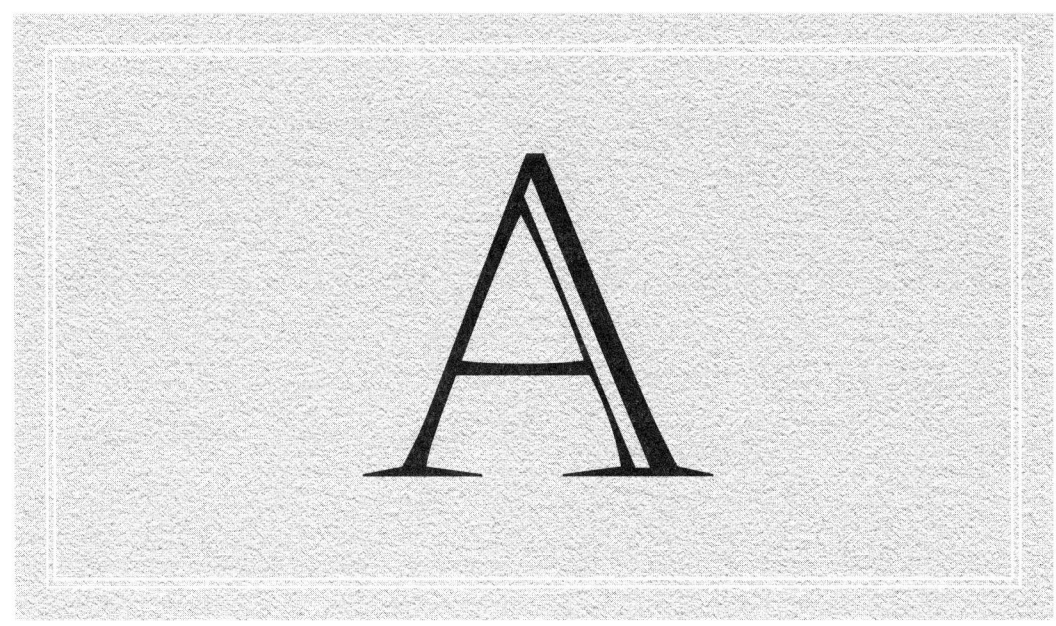

ABANDONMENT

The surrender, relinquishment, DISCLAIMER, or CESSION of PROPERTY or of rights. Voluntary relinquishment of all RIGHT, TITLE, CLAIM, and POSSESSION, with the intention of not reclaiming it.

Safe Haven Laws Passed to Protect Newborns from Abandonment

One of the most controversial legislative initiatives to manifest in the year 2000 is that which addresses the abandonment of newborn babies. By mid-2000 at least twenty-eight states were considering new laws that would permit mothers to give up their unwanted newborn babies without criminal prosecution for abandonment. Texas became the first state to pass such a law in late 1999, and several other states intended to follow close behind, including Alabama, Arkansas, California, Florida, Georgia, Kansas, Michigan, Minnesota, New York, Oklahoma, and Pennsylvania.

The rash of new bills attempt to address an "epidemic" rise in the number of newborn babies found abandoned in public places: from sixty-five in 1991, to more than one hundred in 1998. Nearly one-third of these babies did not survive. Public outcry has been intense, from grass-roots movements to emergency legislative measures.

While there has also been a steady increase in the number of newborns abandoned at hospitals (31,000 in 1998, according to the U.S. Department of Health and Human Services), most of those infants survived the trauma. For that reason, states considering "safe abandonment" laws are developing statutes that require that, in order to avoid prosecution, a parent must leave the newborn at a hospital or other designated "safe haven" within a specified number of hours or days after birth.

The most notorious and highly-profiled case was that of New Jersey teenagers Brian Peterson and Amy Grossberg, serving prison terms for killing their newborn infant after he was delivered in a Newark motel room in 1996. In Wichita, Kansas, sixteen- and seventeen-year-old parents of a newborn were also sentenced to prison for letting their newborn infant die in November 1999. Another example was the infamous "prom night" abandonment, which involved placing the newborn in a garbage receptacle. According to statistics, the only demographic factors that those who have abandoned their newborns have in common are youth and immaturity. Drug addiction appears to be a recurring factor in hospital-birth abandonments.

In most states, child abandonment is a FELONY, even if the child is left in a safe place. Penalties are graduated according to the condition of the child when found. The new safe abandonment laws are designed to allow mothers to place their babies in good hands without the fear of prosecution. The real focus, however, is on saving the lives of the unwanted newborns.

While many applaud the legislative efforts as intelligent public policy, criticism also mounted. Many believe that "decriminalizing" newborn abandonment will lead to social desensitization of the issue and a rising incidence of irresponsible parenthood. Critics are wary of the wrong message being sent: that abandonment is

Florida state representative Murman (right) and state senator Grant announce their sponsorship of a bill to allow legal forms of child abandonment.
FOLEY/AP/WIDE WORLD PHOTOS

"okay" as long as it is done in a safe place. As Congresswoman Tracy Stallings (D-GA) told Associated Press reporters, "We live in a throwaway society. We eat off paper plates . . . use plastic knives and forks and we toss them away. . . . And now, in this year 2000, we are incredibly talking about throwaway babies. . . ." Maureen Hogan, president of Adopt America is critical of the moral message. Interviewed by *Human Events* writer Joseph A. D'Agostino, she stated, "I think that a part of it is the growing acceptance of abortion. What's the difference between [aborting] an unborn baby and dumping it in a trashcan? Why should the former be legal and the latter, done a few days later, put you in jail for life?"

Another criticism is that it deprives the infant of the opportunity to "trace his roots" in later life, if so desired, and also deprives the child—and any adoptive parents—of knowledge about important genetic issues and medical histories. Many also believe the legislation is a "band-aid" addressing the problem too late in the process. Opponents seek, instead, more focus on educating persons about abstention, birth control, and adoption. Still others are critical of the resultant deprivation to the father and grandparents of the infant: their collective interest in the child can be unilaterally severed by the abandonment act of the mother. Finally, the fiscal and pecuniary responsibility of raising unwanted children rather than preventing pregnancies shifts from individuals to the government.

Notwithstanding, as evidenced by the spread of legislative efforts across the nation, a program that needs refinement may be better than no program at all, if it will save the lives of some newborns. As Debi Faris of Calimesa, California, told a *Human Events* reporter, "This bill is for the children. It's really hard to hold a baby who's cold and lifeless." Faris has started a grassroots movement in California by purchasing a group of cemetery plots for her non-profit corporation, Garden of Angels, Inc. The company will bury any abandoned newborn who is found dead. In Pittsburgh, Pennsylvania, more than 600 volunteers have put baby baskets lined with warm blankets on their porches at night, hoping to provide another option. As of May 2000 Georgia was working on a new bill to assist pregnant women with pre-natal care and adoption but still kept its Safe Place for Newborns bill in effect.

Far reaching consequences of the new laws are yet untested. For example, some believe that permitting young mothers to abandon their unwanted infants under safe haven programs will ultimately lead to fewer cases of child abuse and neglect. State intervention on behalf of mistreated children has always been a sensitive issue, however. Authorities are alternatively accused of interfering with family privacy and child rearing on the one hand, and with failing to prevent harm on the other. In general, a state's protective interest in the lives of children theoretically begins to vest when they are viable fetuses within the womb, and continues through the age of MINORITY. Both statutory language and interpretive case law have declared that children have a substantial interest in being free from physical and emotional harm, as well as an interest in stability.

CROSS REFERENCES
Children's Rights; Guardian and Ward; Parent and Child

ABORTION

The spontaneous or artificially induced expulsion of an embryo or fetus. As used in legal context, usually refers to induced abortion.

Stenberg v. Carhart

Abortion has dominated the American legal and political landscapes for more than thirty years. The Supreme Court's decision legalizing abortion in ROE V. WADE, 410 U.S. 113, 93 S.Ct. 705, 35 L.Ed. 2d 147 (1973), has remained controversial. Congress and the states have enacted laws that restrict public funding of abortions, and states have established procedures for minor females who seek an abortion without the consent of their parents. Despite numerous court attempts, the Supreme Court has not retreated from the essential right to have an abortion as announced in *Roe*.

In the late 1990s, anti-abortion leaders focused on a procedure they labeled "partial-birth abortion." They succeeded in having legislation passed in twenty-nine states that bans physicians from performing what doctors call dilation and extraction (D&X). The procedure, which is rarely performed, involves partially extracting a fetus, legs first, through the birth canal, cutting the skull, and draining its contents. It is used most commonly late in the second trimester, between twenty and twenty-four weeks of pregnancy, when a woman suffers from a life-threatening disease. A more common procedure, dilation and evacuation (D&E), involves taking an arm or leg of a live fetus and pulling the fetus into the birth canal during an abortion operation.

The state of Nebraska enacted a law that made it a crime for a physician to perform a D&X abortion. The procedure could only be used to preserve the life of the woman. It could not be used to preserve the *health* of the woman. Dr. Leroy Carhart, a Nebraska physician who performed abortions, filed a lawsuit in federal court asking that the court declare the Nebraska law unconstitutional. He argued that the statute was overbroad and could be used to prohibit most second-trimester abortions, and under *Roe*, abortion is an absolute right through the second trimester. Moreover, Carhart feared that the criminal sanctions tied to the law—loss of medical license, up to twenty years in prison, and a $25,000 fine—would force the state's three abortion providers to end their services. The federal district found the law unconstitutional, and the Eighth Circuit Court of Appeals affirmed the decision.

The Supreme Court, on a 5-4 vote, upheld the lower courts and found that the law violated a woman's constitutional right by imposing an "undue burden" on her decision to end her pregnancy. *Stenberg v. Carhart*, __ U.S. __, __ S.Ct. __, __ L.Ed.2d __ 2000 WL 825889 (2000). Justice STEPHEN G. BREYER, writing for the majority, restated the basic principles of *Roe*:

> before fetal viability, a woman has a right to terminate her pregnancy; state laws that impose an "undue burden" on a woman's decision are unconstitutional; once a fetus is viable, the state may regulate or even prohibit abortion except when it is necessary to preserve the woman's life or health.

Stenberg (2d from right) listens to Planned Parenthood President Gloria Feldt after he sought reinstatement of Nebraska's ban on partial-birth abortions.
KHUE/AP/WIDE WORLD PHOTOS

Justice Breyer noted that during the second trimester (12-24 weeks), the most common abortion procedure is D&E. He found evidence in the trial record, however, to indicate that Carhart's use of D&X was safer than D&E with certain patients.

Breyer found the Nebraska law deficient because it did not provide an exception to preserve the health of the woman. The state, he concluded, may promote but not endanger a woman's health when it regulates the methods of abortion. Nebraska had argued that other procedures were available and that banning D&X would not create a risk to women's health. Breyer rejected these arguments, finding that D&X reduced health risks in certain circumstances. In addition, Nebraska could not point to any controlled medical studies that demonstrated that the procedure created greater risks than other procedures. Therefore, the Court ruled that the law required a health exception.

The need for such an exception became moot, though, after Breyer examined whether the law imposed an undue burden on a woman's ability to choose an abortion. He pointed out that the statutory definition of the D&X procedure was broad enough to encompass the very common D&E procedure. In his view, the statute's language "does not track the medical differences between D&E and D&X, but covers both." Nebraska claimed that there were differences between the procedures in the statute, but Breyer rejected this claim. He concluded that "using this law, some present prosecutors and future attorneys general may choose to pursue physicians who use D&E procedures, the most commonly used method for performing previability second-trimester abortions." This prospect would create a fear of prosecution for those who perform abortion procedures. Therefore, the "result is an undue burden upon a woman's right to make an abortion decision."

Chief Justice WILLIAM H. REHNQUIST and Justices ANTONIN SCALIA, ANTHONY M. KENNEDY, and CLARENCE THOMAS each filed a dissenting opinion. Justice Scalia characterized the majority's decision as "absurd." Justice Kennedy argued that the states should retain the role of legislating on the subject of abortion in defined circumstances. The statute did not deny a woman's right to an abortion but rather prohibited an abhorrent medical procedure.

CROSS REFERENCES
Reproductive Rights; Roe v. Wade

ACQUIRED IMMUNE DEFICIENCY SYNDROME

Segregation of Prisoners Who Test HIV Positive

In January 2000 the U.S. Supreme Court denied CERTIORARI of an Eleventh Circuit Court of Appeals decision that upheld the state of Alabama's policy of segregating prison inmates who have the AIDS virus. The effect of such a policy may serve to bar the inmates from participation in some prison activities.

The litigation began ten years ago, when Alabama legislators effected an AIDS-protection program in Alabama's prison system. Under the program, all inmates entering the prison system are tested for the Human Immunodeficiency Virus (HIV), which causes AIDS. Inmates who test positive for HIV are then segregated from the general inmate population into separate living units for each gender. As a result, the HIV-positive (HIV+ or seropositive) inmates are prohibited from participating in most activities involving the prison's HIV-negative population. Restricted activities include educational, vocational, rehabilitative, religious, and recreational programs.

The procedural history of the case has been convoluted. The appellant class, consisting of Alabama inmates who are HIV+, sued the Alabama Department of Corrections (DOC) (Thigpen, Commissioner), claiming that excluding them from such activities violated the Rehabilitation Act of 1973, § 504 (29 U.S.C. 794). Following a bench trial in 1994, the federal district court ruled in favor of the DOC, but the case was appealed. It was then remanded back to the district court "for additional findings and clarification by the district court." *Harris v. Thigpen* 941 F.2d 1495, (11th Cir.1991).

On remand, the district court again found for the DOC, but it was again appealed. An Eleventh Circuit appellate panel agreed with most of the arguments raised by the plaintiffs in *Onishea v. Hopper*, 126 F.3d 1323 (11th Cir.1997). Again, the matter was appealed, this time requesting a hearing before the full court. The Eleventh Circuit, sitting *en banc*, vacated the appellate panel's decision, 133 F.3d 1377 (11th Cir.1998). The Eleventh Circuit later "revisited" its opinion in 1999, with a new briefing. In so doing, the court added that it "opted for the position of the Fourth, Fifth, and Sixth Circuits" (in other cases involving § 504). It is this 1999 opinion of the Eleventh Circuit that the U.S. Supreme Court let stand without review.

The substantive issues in the case involved an interpretation of § 504, which states in relevant part:

> No otherwise qualified individual with a disability . . . shall, solely by reason of her or his disability, be excluded from the participation in, be denied the benefits of, or be subjected to discrimination under any program, or activity receiving Federal financial assistance . . .

Accordingly, the plaintiff prisoners made four arguements in their PRIMA FACIE case. First, they were "handicapped" within the meaning of the Act. Second, they were "otherwise qualified." Third, they were excluded from programs or activities solely because of their handicap. And fourth, the programs/activities are operated by an agency that receives federal financial assistance.

The opinion of the district court alone was 475 pages long before the record reached the appellate level. The two key issues involved an interpretation of "otherwise qualified" under § 504 of the Act, and the requisite burden on the part of the DOC to provide "reasonable accommodation" of handicaps under the Act.

In the threshold case of *School Board of Nassau County, Fla. v. Arline*, 480 U.S. 273 (1987), the U.S. Supreme Court explained that in order for a person to be deemed "otherwise qualified" under the Act, he must be "able to meet all of a program's requirements in spite of his handicap." If the person has a contagious disease, however, then the district court is required to conduct an individualized inquiry and make appropriate findings of fact to determine whether integration with others would pose "significant health and safety risks." That is to say, if a significant risk would be imposed upon the health, safety, or welfare of others because of integration, then the person is not "otherwise qualified" under the Act.

Notwithstanding, if "reasonable accommodation" under the Act will render the risk no longer significant, a person is entitled to relief. The accommodation must not place undue burden upon the agency receiving the federal assistance.

Applying these precepts to the case at bar, the Eleventh Circuit concluded that denial of integration to the HIV+ inmates was not illegal under the Act:

> ... when transmitting a disease inevitably entails death, the evidence supports a finding of "significant risk" if it shows both (1) that a certain event can occur and (2) that according to reliable medical opinion the event can transmit the disease. This is not an "any risk" standard.... But this is not a "somebody has to die first" standard, either....

With respect to the issue of "reasonable accommodation," the appellate court found that, indeed, the district court had concluded that the proposed accommodations entailed the hiring of additional guards to prevent high-risk behavior. This, the court concluded, would impose an undue burden on the prison programs, and, as such, there was no reversible error on appeal as to the court's finding.

Plaintiffs had also proposed, as reasonable accommodation, that the DOC refine its classification system by separating HIV+ inmates according to the likelihood that they would engage in risk-spreading behaviors if integrated. The plaintiffs argued that the district court had erroneously excluded evidence relating to this proposed accommodation. While the Eleventh Circuit agreed that consideration of the accommodation was required, it held that plaintiffs were, in fact, permitted at trial to introduce substantial evidence about the proposed classification. Therefore, the district court "implicitly considered the feasibility of classification," and the plaintiffs' substantial rights were not affected by the trial court's evidentiary rulings. Other issues were argued on appeal, but the two discussed above were controlling.

CROSS REFERENCES
Prisoners' Rights; Segregation

ADOPTION

A two-step judicial process in conformance to state statutory provisions in which the legal obligations and rights of a child toward the biological parents are terminated and new rights and obligations are created in the acquired parents.

Annulment of Michael Chalek's Adoption

In a highly unusual adoption case, a Florida court granted 47-year-old Michael Chalek an ANNULMENT of his adoption, which had been illegally granted in the 1950s. Chalek was also granted a new birth certificate to reflect his mother's true name.

While separated from her husband, young waitress Winnie Faye Higginbotham Yarber became pregnant by another man. Yarber gave birth to a son, Michael, in January 1952. When the baby was eight-days old, he went home with Alex and Adela Chalek. The Chaleks were unable to have children. They arranged to adopt Michael through a baby dealer named Lenora Fielding, whom they paid $200. Although Florida law did not allow private adoption at this time, such services were rarely investigated.

Michael Chalek learned of his adoption when he was eleven-years old. In 1981 he discovered the name of the hospital where he was born. In 1995, he was able to obtain some information about his adoptive parents but not his birth parents. Finally, in 1998, Chalek obtained access to his personal adoption records. Normally Florida adoption records are sealed unless one can prove a compelling *medical* need. While reviewing them for information about his birth parents, Chalek discovered that his adoption had been illegally arranged. Notes indicated that the broker had coerced Chalek's birth mother into using a false name on adoption documents and that his birth mother asked a state worker if she could get him back.

After uncovering the truth about his adoption, Chalek decided to seek an annulment of his adoption, likening his situation to that of a couple seeking a divorce. His attorney acknowledged that she was unaware of similar cases elsewhere. In his request for annulment, Chalek alleged that he had been sexually and physically abused by his adoptive parents. His attorney also

Michael Chalek, who had his adoption annulled, holds a photo of the half-sister he has never known.
ROTHSTEIN/AP/WIDE WORLD PHOTOS

presented evidence that his adoptive parents had lied to adoption officials about previous marriages and that his adoptive mother suffered from a violent nature and promiscuity. At the time he sought the annulment, Chalek's adoptive parents and the baby broker were all deceased.

In ruling on Chalek's request, Circuit Judge Maurice Giunta of Gainesville recognized the extraordinary nature and the gravity of an annulment. He wrote that public policy in adoption matters "is to protect and respect the privacy" of the parties. In this case, however, Chalek's abusive parents had seriously misused the privilege of adoption and caused "profound harm," the judge concluded. He also found that Alex and Adela Chalek would not have been allowed to adopt had they been truthful in their application.

The judge also permitted Chalek to amend his birth certificate to indicate the name of his birth parents and his name at birth, Michael Edward Higginbotham Yarber.

Open Records in Tennessee

In a September 27, 1999, decision, *Doe v. Sundquist*, the Tennessee Supreme Court upheld a state law permitting adoptees over age twenty-one access to their sealed adoption records. Under the law, birth mothers must be notified of the request and may officially decline to see the child. The legislation provides that adoption records "shall be made available" without court order to an adopted person twenty-one years of age or older, or the legal representative of that person. It also provides for a "contact veto," where a parent, sibling, spouse, or lineal ancestor or descendant of the adoptee could register to prevent contact by the adopted person.

The contact veto may also prohibit the adoptee from contacting the spouse, sibling, lineal descendant or lineal ancestor of the person registering the veto. Violating the contact veto provision subjects the violator to civil or criminal liability. The veto provision does not prohibit any disclosure of identities.

Shortly before the legislation was to take effect on July 1, 1996, a lawsuit was filed in federal district court attempting to stop implementation of the law. One plaintiff, known as Promise Doe, alleged she had surrendered a child for adoption in 1990 with assurances that the information she provided could not be accessed by the child or the child's father. A federal district court judge granted a temporary restraining order preventing state officials from enforcing the statute. By February 1997 both the federal district court and the U.S. Court of Appeals for the Sixth Circuit refused to hold the law unconstitutional or forbid its implementation.

After the defeat in the federal court system, the plaintiffs brought suit in state court in Tennessee in March 1997. These birth parents argued that they had a "vested right" to have their identity remain confidential, and that to retroactively remove that right violated the Tennessee Constitution. They also argued that the law interfered with their right to familial and procreational PRIVACY.

The trial court initially granted a short reprieve, prohibiting disclosure of the records, but ultimately denied relief, determining that the legislation did not violate Tennessee's constitution. The Tennessee Court of Appeals overturned the decision of the trial court, determining that the law violated the state constitution. The appellate court found that the birth parents had a "reasonable expectation" that identifying information would remain confidential, and opined that this expectation "is a proper interest for the state to recognize and protect. Life-changing decisions were made based upon this expectation and to now deprive those who relied upon their legitimate expectation under the law would be to deprive them of a vested right."

The case was appealed again. The Tennessee Supreme Court began its review by examining Tennessee's adoption laws through the years. The first law, enacted in 1852, only provided for recording the names of the parties and terms of the adoption. A 1917 law granted a trial judge the discretion to "require" adoption records "be sealed and filed . . . to be unsealed only by judicial order." Later legislation preserved the requirement that the records be sealed, but allowed for disclosure in the discretion of the court.

Several amendments in the 1980s made it easier for adoptees to obtain information regarding their biological family. These changes made it possible for an adoptee to request and receive information through the Tennessee Department of Human Services (DHS), rather than by petitioning a court. A 1989 change permitted DHS to divulge birth parents' names, addresses, and identifying information to adoptees. DHS could provide the information, however, only after obtaining consent from the birth parents.

The court then focused on the plaintiffs' constitutional arguments. The Tennessee Constitution forbids "retrospective" laws that take away or impair vested rights. A vested right is one "which it is proper for the state to recognize and protect and of which [an] individual could not be deprived arbitrarily without injustice." Determining whether a new law impairs or destroys vested rights requires an examination of the public interest of the legislation, "the reasonable expectations of affected persons," and whether the statute surprises those who have long relied on a contrary provision of law.

The supreme court concluded that the challenged adoption law did not violate or impair any vested rights. The court determined that the law is in the public interest because it helps adoptees obtain information about themselves and because it recognizes the rights of birth parents and adopted persons to refuse contact. Furthermore, under Tennessee law, "[t]here simply has never been an absolute guarantee or even a reasonable expectation by the birth parent or any other party that adoption records were permanently sealed." Finally, the law "does not create new rights or allow access to any records that previously were not to be released," so the law does not surprise anyone.

The plaintiffs also argued that disclosure of the adoption information "invades the rights to familial privacy by impeding a birth parents' freedom to determine whether to raise a family and disrupting both biological and adoptive families by releasing identifying information previously sealed." A right to privacy is not specifically mentioned in either the Tennessee or the federal constitution, yet has been recognized as inherent in both. This legislation does not impede a constitutional right to privacy, the court ruled. The law does not permit "unfettered access" to adoption records, and the contact veto eliminates or reduces the risk of a disruptive effect upon the parties. Moreover, any risk of disruption only occurs a minimum of twenty-one years after the adoption.

Finally, the court disagreed with the plaintiffs' argument that "disclosure impedes the right to procreational privacy by impeding the birth parents' decision of whether to carry a child to term." The court noted that the decision whether to carry a pregnancy to term differs fundamentally from the decision to surrender a child for adoption. The court concluded that a possible event twenty-one years later is "far too speculative" to lead to the conclusion that the law interferes with the right of procreational privacy, and reiterated that disclosure was not a new concept in Tennessee adoption laws.

Utah House Bill 103

On March 14, 2000, Utah Governor Mike Leavitt signed a controversial new adoption law, House Bill 103. The new Utah law amends existing state adoption legislation. The law provides that "[a] child may not be adopted by a person who is cohabiting in a relationship that is not a legally valid and binding marriage under the laws of [Utah].... [C]ohabiting means residing with another person and being involved in a sexual relationship with that person." The law also applies, by definition, to children placed by the Utah Division of Child and Family Services (DCFS) in foster care. The law also orders the DCFS to "establish a policy providing that priority for foster care and adoptive placement shall be provided to families in which both a man and a woman are legally married under the laws" of Utah, but specifically did not prohibit "the placement of a child with the child's biological or adoptive parent."

In 1999 prior to passage of the new adoption legislation, the board of trustees of the DCFS adopted a rule very similar to House Bill 103. The Utah chapter of the American Civil Liberties Union immediately sued the DCFS, alleging that the rule violated constitutional EQUAL PROTECTION guarantees by denying adoption to certain categories of people, such as gay and lesbian couples. *Utah Children v. Utah Division of Child and Family Services* is currently pending in a Utah state court.

When House Bill 103 was signed in March, the DCFS reported that it planned to modify its rule to conform to the new law. New provisions of the law were to go into effect on May 1, 2000. A legal challenge is expected. For example, the Utah chapter of the American Civil Liberties Union drafted a letter to Governor Leavitt on March 7, 2000, urging him to veto the bill. The letter, signed by Utah Children's executive director Rosalind McGee and National Center for Youth Law attorney Martha Matthews, states, "The arbitrariness and the lack of fit between important state objectives and legislative means inherent in this bill invite a lawsuit on behalf of children and potential parents affected by its terms." Governor Leavitt clearly disagreed and claimed, "It may not meet the agendas of adults, but it is in the best interest of children."

CROSS REFERENCES
Equal Protection; Fourteenth Amendment; Privacy

AFFIRMATIVE ACTION

Employment programs required by federal statutes and regulations designed to remedy discriminatory practices in hiring minority group members; i.e. positive steps designed to eliminate existing and continuing discrimination, to remedy lingering cost effects of past discrimination, and to create systems and procedures to prevent future discrimination; commonly based on population percentages of minority groups in a particular area. Factors considered are race, color, sex, creed, and age.

One Florida Initiative

On February 22, 2000, Florida Governor Jeb Bush (Republican) and the state's independently elected CABINET voted to end affirmative action in college admissions, making Florida's state government the first to voluntarily ban af-

This lesbian couple cross-adopted each other's children to form a legal family.
PIZAC/AP/WIDE WORLD PHOTOS

firmative action in both college admissions and state contracts.

The concept of ridding the state's university system of affirmative action began when Governor Bush implemented his One Florida Initiative on November 9, 1999. The One Florida Initiative has an "Equity in Education" component as well as an "Equity in Contracting" component. The education plan requires the elimination of race and ethnicity as considerations in university admissions. The proposed alternative is being called the "Talented 20" plan, which allows for students who graduate in the top twenty percent of their class and who complete a college preparatory curriculum to be admitted into one of the ten state universities. The One Florida Initiative is designed to increase opportunity and diversity while ending racial preferences and set-asides. The plan was approved by the Board of Regents of the State University System ("Board of Regents"), the governing body of the state's public universities.

At the Cabinet meeting on February 22, Dr. Adam Herbert, Chancellor of the State University System, presented three admissions rules on behalf of the Board of Regents, which were unanimously adopted by the Board on February 17, 2000. Based on Governor Bush's One Florida Initiative, the Board of Regents developed rules for admission based on the guiding principal that "The Board affirms its commitment to equal educational opportunity, and to increasing student diversity in each of the State's universities." The Board attempted to clarify that "in supporting the Equity in Education Plan, it was mending, not ending, affirmative action . . . ."

Dr. Herbert further stated that although the rules eliminate the use of race, national origin, and gender as factors in the university admissions process, several elements of affirmative action remain:

1) outreach programs are expanded; 2) recruitment efforts for students from minority and low-income families will expand; 3) support services for these students will continue; 4) retention programs for these students also will continue; 5) partnerships will increase between higher educational institutions and low-performing schools, many of which are located in inner-city neighborhoods; 6) expanded mentoring programs will focus on students in low-performing schools; 7) admission into the State University System is guaranteed for all public high school students who complete the nineteen required high school units, and graduate in the top twenty percent of their class; 8) incentives are provided for minority students to prepare for college; and 9) need-based financial aid is increased to assist Talented 20 students.

Dr. Herbert noted that five of the ten universities in the System already do not use race, national origin, or gender in making admissions decisions. Further, he stated that none of the ten universities consider gender in making admissions decisions. Nevertheless, women constitute a majority of undergraduate and graduate enrollments in all ten universities.

In Florida, the voting population is thirty-eight percent non-white. Polls show, however, that as many as fifty-three percent of the voters who know about the One Florida Initiative also support it. Many, especially white males, feel that the old system does not work and that the special treatment is simply unfair. Of those who support the end of affirmative action, many feel that social conditions have improved to a point in America that affirmative action is no longer warranted and that it relies on "policies of the past."

Opponents of the ban on affirmative action argue that such a decision will divide the state along racial lines. Opponents also fear that there will be a drop in college enrollment of minority students like that in California after similar legislation was approved and like that in Texas after

Jesse Jackson speaks to demonstrators outside the Florida capitol who have gathered to protest the One Florida Initiative.
BURCHFIELD/AP/WIDE WORLD PHOTOS

a court-ordered end to the use of race in admissions decisions. To voice their disapproval of the governor's plan, opponents staged a twenty-five-hour sit-in in the lieutenant governor's office and a massive march in Tallahassee on March 7, the day that the state legislature opened. Coincidentally, March 7 marked the thirty-fifth anniversary of the civil rights march in Selma, Alabama. An economic boycott of Florida products has also been threatened.

Governor Bush defended the plan, arguing that it allows college admission committees to use criteria other than race to ensure access to disadvantaged and at-risk students of color. Bush contended that the new admission policy taken with the Talented 20 provision will result in the admission of 400 additional minority students who otherwise would not have attended college. The Talented 20 portion of the plan will not be implemented as a guarantee, however, because of an administrative rule challenge filed by the NAACP and joined by Florida NOW.

After public opposition, Governor Bush modified his plan and appointed a One Florida Accountability Commission, which is co-chaired by an African American and an Hispanic. The commission will examine minority student enrollment and minority business to gauge progress over the next three years under the plan.

CROSS REFERENCES
Education Law

AGE DISCRIMINATION

Kimel v. Florida Board of Regents

In a landmark decision that may affect other federal civil rights laws, the U.S. Supreme Court, in *Kimel v. Florida Board of Regents*, ___U.S.___, 120 S.Ct. 631, 145 L.Ed.2d 522 (2000), ruled that the Age Discrimination in Employment Act of 1967 (ADEA), 29 U.S.C. § 621 et seq., does not apply to state governments. The ADEA, which originally covered only private employers, was amended in 1974 to include state governments. It prohibits discrimination in employment based on the age of employees forty years or older. The Court concluded that although the ADEA contained a clear statement of Congress's intent to nullify the states' sovereign immunity, Congress did not have authority under Section 5 of the FOURTEENTH AMENDMENT to revoke sovereign immunity.

In 1995, a group of current faculty and librarians of Florida State University and Florida International University, including J. Daniel Kimel, Jr., filed an ADEA lawsuit against the Florida Board of Regents. The plaintiffs, all older than forty, alleged that the Florida Board of Regents refused to require the two state universities to allocate funds to provide previously agreed upon market adjustments to the salaries of eligible university employees. The plaintiffs contended that the failure to allocate the funds violated both the ADEA and the Florida Civil Rights Act of 1992, Fla. Stat. § 760.01 *et seq.*, because it had a disparate impact on the base pay of employees with a longer record of service, most of whom were older employees. The plaintiffs sought backpay, damages, and permanent salary adjustments in their lawsuit.

The Florida Board of Regents sought to have the lawsuit dismissed, arguing that it was immune under the ELEVENTH AMENDMENT. The federal district court denied the motion to dismiss and the defendants appealed to the Eleventh Circuit Court of Appeals. The appeals court affirmed the trial court and the board of regents asked the U.S. Supreme Court to review the case. The Court accepted the appeal to resolve a conflict within the circuit courts of appeal over whether the ADEA validly abrogated a state's Eleventh Amendment immunity.

The Supreme Court agreed with the Florida Board of Regents, ruling 5–4 that Congress could not take away the states' immunity in the ADEA legislation. Justice SANDRA DAY O'CONNOR, writing for the majority, noted that for Congress to subject states to suits by individuals, it must make its intention to do so "unmistakably clear in the language of the statute." O'Connor rejected Florida's claim that the statutory language was ambiguous on this point, concluding that the ADEA stated that its provisions could be enforced against any employer "including a state agency" in a state or federal court of competent jurisdiction. Such a "clear textual statement" could not be inferred to be ambiguous.

Justice O'Connor then turned to the essential issue: did Congress possess constitutional authority to make states liable for damages under the ADEA? Prior court decisions had found that Congress had validly exercised its power under the Constitution's Article I COMMERCE CLAUSE to enact the ADEA. Congress's powers, however, under Article I do not include "the power to subject States to suit at the hands of private individuals." Only § 5 of the Fourteenth

Amendment grants Congress the authority to abrogate the states' sovereign immunity.

Section Five is a broad grant of power to Congress to both remedy and deter the violation of the rights guaranteed under the Fourteenth Amendment. These rights include DUE PROCESS and equal protection of the law. Justice O'Connor stated that for remedial legislation to be appropriate under § 5, there must be a "congruence and proportionality between the injury to be prevented or remedied and the means adopted to that end." Using this standard, the Court found that the ADEA was not "appropriate legislation." Justice O'Connor noted that age is not a suspect classification under the EQUAL PROTECTION CLAUSE of the Fourteenth Amendment. Therefore, states may "discriminate on the basis of age without offending the Fourteenth Amendment if the age classification is rationally related to a legitimate state interest." The ADEA prohibits "substantially more state employment decisions and practices than would likely be held unconstitutional" under the equal protection, rational basis standard.

Despite these problems, the application of the ADEA against state governments could still be upheld if the legislative record demonstrated that Congress had good reasons to act. However, Justice O'Connor concluded that the legislative record revealed that "Congress had virtually no reason to believe that state and local governments were unconstitutionally discriminating against their employees on the basis of age." Therefore, the ADEA could not be applied against the states and the employees had to pursue their claims using state age discrimination statutes.

Justice JOHN PAUL STEVENS, in a dissenting opinion joined by Justices DAVID H. SOUTER, RUTH BADER GINSBURG, and STEPHEN G. BREYER, questioned the need of the Court to protect the states from "burdensome" laws. He argued that "Congress can use its broad range of flexible tools to approach the delicate issue of how to balance local and national interests in the most responsive and careful manner."

Reeves v. Sanderson Plumbing Products, Inc.

Employees who believe they have been the victims of racial, ethnic, religious, gender, disability, or age discrimination by their employers have the right to use federal anti-discrimination laws to seek redress. The Age Discrimination in Employment Act of 1967 (ADEA), 29 U.S.C.A. § 621 et seq, provides that an employer cannot discriminate against older workers (over the age of 40). Despite the statute, many employees find it difficult to prove intentional discrimination. The Supreme Court improved their chances, however, in *Reeves v. Sanderson Plumbing Products, Inc.*, ___ U.S. ___, 120 S.Ct. 2097, ___ L.Ed.2d ___ (2000), by ruling that employees can prevail in their lawsuits without direct evidence of an employer's illegal intent.

Roger Reeves had worked for forty years at the Sanderson Plumbing Products factory in Columbus, Mississippi. A supervisor in the hinge department of the toilet seat plant, Reeves recorded the attendance of workers and their hours of work, reporting these figures to his supervisor, Russell Caldwell. After Caldwell informed senior management of absenteeism and tardiness by many workers in the department, the company ordered an audit. The audit revealed numerous timekeeping errors and misrepresentations by Reeves, Caldwell, and another supervisor in the hinge department. Reeves, who was fifty-seven, and Caldwell, who was forty-five, were fired. The third supervisor, who was in his mid-thirties, was not.

Reeves filed a lawsuit under the ADEA alleging that the company's decision to fire him was based on his age. The trial court followed a three-step process mandated by the Supreme Court in *McDonnell Douglas v. Green*, 411 U.S. 792, 93 S.Ct. 1817, 36 L.Ed.2d 668 (1973). Reeves first had to prove that he was over the age of forty and that he had performed satisfactorily but had been dismissed while a similarly situated—but significantly younger—person had been retained. This disparate treatment creates an inference of employer decision-making motivated by age and establishes a PRIMA FACIE case of DISCRIMINATION. Having done that, Sanderson then had the burden of presenting a legitimate, nondiscriminatory reason for its actions. Sanderson's management told the jury that Reeves had been fired due to his failure to maintain accurate attendance records.

The burden then shifted back to Reeves to show that Sanderson's decision was motivated by age factors and that the reasons the company gave were merely pretexts. Reeves introduced evidence that he had accurately recorded the attendance and hours of the employees under his supervision. He also provided evidence that showed a senior executive had made derogatory comments about Reeves's age. The jury sided with Reeves and awarded him $70,000 in damages and more than $28,000 in back pay.

The Fifth Circuit Court of Appeals reversed the decision. The court ruled that Reeves may have introduced enough evidence to show that the company's reasons for his firing were only a pretext, but he had failed to prove that the company fired him because of his age.

Because the federal circuit courts of appeal were split over the type of evidence needed to overcome the employer's reasons and establish LIABILITY, the Supreme Court heard the case. In a unanimous decision, the Court reversed the Fifth Circuit ruling. Justice SANDRA DAY O'CONNOR, writing for the Court, stated that the appeals court had erroneously relied on "the premise that a plaintiff must always introduce additional, independent evidence of discrimination." A plaintiff's *prima facie* case, combined with sufficient evidence for a reasonable jury to reject the employer's nondiscriminatory reason for its decision "may be adequate to sustain a finding of liability for intentional discrimination under the ADEA."

Justice O'Connor examined the evidence Reeves put forward to discredit Sanderson's reasons for firing him. She noted that Reeves had produced substantial evidence to refute Sanderson's claim that he kept shoddy time records. In addition, Reeves had offered evidence that cast doubt on whether he was responsible for any failure to discipline late and absent employees. The Fifth Circuit ignored this and other evidence, focusing its review on evidence that would show that a Sanderson executive had made derogatory, age-based comments at Reeves and had singled him out for harsher treatment than younger employees. The appeals court, however, had "misconceived the evidentiary burden borne by plaintiffs who attempt to prove intentional discrimination through indirect evidence." In appropriate circumstances, the jury can reasonably infer that the reason offered by the employer is a smokescreen for a discriminatory purpose. Therefore, courts must assess on a case-by-case basis whether there is sufficient evidence to sustain a finding of liability solely by the discrediting of the employer's reasons.

The impact of this decision goes beyond age discrimination. The ruling will likely apply to claims of intentional discrimination based on race, ethnicity, gender, and disability, as the same three-part process is used in these areas.

CROSS REFERENCES
Employment Law; Fourteenth Amendment

AGRICULTURAL LAW

The body of law governing the cultivation of various CROPS and the raising and management of livestock to provide a food and fabric supply for human and animal consumption.

Rally for Rural America

More than one-thousand farmers and ranchers met in Washington, D.C., in March 2000 for the Rally for Rural America. They told lawmakers that low prices, corporate agribusiness, and subsidized foreign growers threatened to run family farms out of business. The farmers and ranchers sought price controls, fair competition, and fair trade policies to stave off elimination.

Price controls were the biggest concern at the Rally. In 1996, a Republican led Congress passed the Freedom to Farm Act, which is phasing out New Deal era price supports for agricultural commodities by 2002. According to small farmers, that has driven prices down, making it impossible for small farmers to cover their costs of production when they sell their harvests. To make their point, Rally participants said farmers get only thirty-nine cents of the eight dollars it costs to buy lunch—a roast beef sandwich, cole slaw, potato salad, baked beans, and milk—in the nation's capital.

Farm income nationwide dropped from $53 billion in 1996 to $48 billion in 1999. Meanwhile, corporate agribusinesses in the late 1990s and early 2000s continued to enjoy handsome profits along with the rest of America's booming economy. Because corporate farms buy or produce more seeds, fertilizers, and other farm inputs than small farms, they enjoy lower costs per unit of production and can make money on lower commodity prices. Canadian and many European growers also can compete at lower prices: their countries provide generous subsidies to make farming profitable.

Livestock ranchers also bemoaned the effects of corporate farming. They pointed to Smithfield Foods, which as of early 2000 was America's largest producer of pork products with more than twenty percent of the market. Smithfield Foods owes its success in large part to vertical integration, which means owning both the farms that raise hogs and the factories that butcher and package them for consumption.

Small ranchers said such arrangements make it hard for them to find fairly-priced markets for their livestock.

Small U.S. farmers and ranchers warned that the end result of low prices and unfair competition would be the extermination of small family farms. That would lead to the disappearance of specialty products such as livestock raised without antibiotics and produce grown without chemical fertilizers and pesticides.

The response from corporate agribusiness was that agriculture is simply following the same trend of consolidation as the rest of America's economy, including bookstores, airlines, and petroleum companies. According to Smithfield chairman and chief executive Joseph W. Luter III, "Vertical integration gives you high quality, consistent products with consistent genetics. And the only way to do that is to control the process from the farm to the packing plant." As for small farmers, Luter said, "The bottom line is [they] have been disappearing for 100 years."

Politicians at the Rally for Rural America promised to change that. President BILL CLINTON sent a letter to the Rally praising family farmers as "the backbone of our economy and the lifeblood of our land" and promising to help them survive. Senator Byron Dorgan, a Democrat from North Dakota, said, "Family farmers have been the victim of bad public policy in this country, and it's time to straighten it out." Agriculture Secretary Dan Glickman agreed, saying, "It is time to rewrite that 1996 Freedom to Farm bill."

Whether that will happen before 2002 is uncertain. Senator Richard Luger, a Republican from Indiana and chair of the Senate Agriculture Committee, suggested that farmers *wanted* the Freedom to Farm Act and would have to live with it until 2002. Since 1996, Congress has responded to agriculture's financial woes with annual emergency appropriations. In April 2000, Congress repeated this measure by setting aside $7.1 billion for income assistance incentives for farmers and ranchers.

As of May 2000, Congress was considering four bills to address concerns about mergers and competition in agriculture. The Farmers and Ranchers Fair Competition Act of 1999 would craft more stringent standards for agriculture mergers, enhance enforcement of antitrust laws, and increase penalties for violations of those laws. The Agriculture Competition Enhancement Act would outlaw unfair practices and al-

Family farmers from across the country protest the 1996 Freedom to Farm law during the Rally for Rural America.
BOITANO/AP/WIDE WORLD PHOTOS

low the Department of AGRICULTURE to review proposed mergers. Two other bills would regulate packer ownership of livestock and the interstate transportation of state-inspected meat.

AIRLINES

Death on the High Seas Act and TWA Flight 800

In March 2000, the 2d U.S. Circuit Court of Appeals upheld U.S. District Court Judge Robert W. Sweet's 1998 decision that the 1996 crash of TWA 800 was not governed by the Death on the High Seas Act. The significance of the decision relates both to damages available for recovery and to the appropriate forum for bringing suit. Earlier in the same suit involving the same air crash, Judge Sweet ruled in October 1999 that the surviving families of 45 crash victims who were citizens of France may maintain their suits in the U.S. courts. This decision also affects available damages and remedies since the maximum damages claims are lower in France.

On July 17, 1996, the Boeing 747 left New York for Paris, France. Just minutes into its ascent, however, the plane exploded and crashed off the coast of Long Island. All 230 persons aboard died. Most of the debris was found between eight and ten miles offshore. The exact cause of the crash has never been determined. The NATIONAL TRANSPORTATION SAFETY BOARD has ascertained that neither bomb nor missile was a factor in the crash, and the FBI has

A U.S. judge ruled that French families of TWA Flight 800 victims can sue in the United States.
LENNIHAN/AP/WIDE WORLD PHOTOS

ruled out any terrorist activity. What is known is that the center fuel tank exploded. While the exact ignition point or source remains unidentified, suspicion surrounds the fact that the plane sat on a hot tarmac for more than two hours with the air conditioning unit running full force below the center tank.

The plaintiffs' suit claims that Boeing, TWA, and Hydro-Aire Inc. (the manufacturer of the fuel pumps) were negligent in the design, construction, and operation of the plane. Court documents also alleged defective wiring combined with other failures to cause an explosion in the fuel tank. Defendants Boeing and Hydro-Aire are facing claims for PUNITIVE DAMAGES. Trial is not expected to begin until February 2001 in the Manhattan, New York, federal district court.

As Flight 800 was intended to carry passengers from New York to Paris, at stake in this legal battle were the millions of dollars of potential damages (for pain and suffering caused by the loss of their loved ones) claimed by the victims' families. In 1998 trial court judge Sweet ruled in favor of the plaintiffs who claimed exception under the Death on the High Seas Act because Flight 800 exploded in mid-air over territorial waters.

The 79-year-old act was originally designed to help widows who lost their husbands at sea. Damages under the Act are limited to pecuniary (economic) losses. Thus, to recover any damages under the Act, plaintiff survivors needed to establish that they relied upon the deceased victim's income. The law was enacted four years before the first commercial air flight in the United States and, therefore, did not contemplate application to international flights. Defendants in the TWA Flight 800 suit, however, intended to invoke it to avoid liability for non-economic damages.

In its 2–1 decision, the 2d Circuit Court of Appeals noted that in 1988, President RONALD REAGAN extended the U.S. territorial seas out to twelve miles offshore. Thus, it upheld the trial court's decision that the Death on the High Seas Act was not invoked. Victims' families can now seek non-economic damages, including loss of companionship and the pain and suffering of the victims. Also in March 2000, the Senate passed an aviation bill officially changing the definition of international waters from three miles offshore to twelve miles offshore. The bill also expands the scope of damages and remedies available to families of crash victims for non-economic losses. The law would be retroactive to July 1996.

Ruling on the French plaintiffs' *forum non conveniens* (Latin for "forum not convenient") issue, Judge Sweet balanced private and public interests in his decision, as required by law. He found no compelling private interest factors that would warrant either retaining or dismissing the French claims. Under factors affecting *public* interest, however, he found that if he were to dismiss the claims and have the parties submit to French courts, it would set a precedent for other foreign claims stemming from the deaths of other foreign nationals. Thus there would be "the prospect of several trials simultaneously taking place in different countries around the world." Judge Sweet also expressed that "local interest in having localized controversies decided at home, and avoiding unnecessary problems with conflict of law or application of foreign law" were important factors.

The judge conceded in his opinion that France is an adequate alternative legal forum, but also noted that even if he dismissed the French claims, it would not cause the entire case to be dismissed. Ultimately the judge ruled that he had little reason to force the French plaintiffs to pursue their claims in France. He denied defendants' motion to dismiss the French plaintiffs unless defendants offered to concede liability and transfer the case only on the issue of damages.

Spielberg v. American Airlines

On June 26, 1995, American Airlines Flight 58 was four hours into its flight from Los Angeles to New York when it ran into severe weather. At a cruising altitude of 37,000 feet, the DC-10 was flying over Minnesota when it was struck by 50 mph vertical winds, causing the plane to drop suddenly. During an estimated 28 seconds of ensuing air turbulence, several passengers were tossed about the cabin area of the plane. The pilots made an emergency landing in Chicago, where 13 of the 101 passengers onboard were hospitalized. None suffered serious injury, and only one passenger suffered any physical trauma at all. The remaining eleven passengers were badly shaken by the incident and treated accordingly.

Notwithstanding, fourteen passengers filed suit, one settling early on for a modest amount. The remaining thirteen, including Nancy Spielberg—sister to filmmaker Steven Spielberg—and her two daughters, sued in U.S. District Court for the Southern District of New York (*Nancy Spielberg v. American Airlines Inc.*, 96 Civ. 4763). Since only one person was physically injured by the incident, the plaintiffs sought DAMAGES for emotional trauma and mental anguish caused by the harrowing experience.

In lawsuits involving domestic air flights, federal courts have applied state law in ascertaining what damages may be compensable. Most state courts permit the recovery of damages for emotional trauma and mental anguish, although in certain types of cases, such damages are allowed only if accompanied by physical injury. Several states also permit compensable damages for such non-physical injuries as the subjective "fear of dying," "fear of cancer," and "fear of harm." In most cases, however, the alleged fear must be the result of manifest *objective* physical exposure to such a risk and not just based on an unreasonable or unfounded personal fear.

Damages for injuries occurring on international flights are usually controlled by the Warsaw Convention, which does not mention the issue of emotional trauma. The U.S Supreme Court, however, has ruled that emotional damage claims without accompanying physical injury are not compensable for international passengers. The Montreal Accord, which is scheduled to take effect in mid-2001, updates the language to certain provisions of the Warsaw Convention and expressly eliminates these damages.

On October 7, 1999, a Manhattan federal jury awarded $2.22 million in damages to the thirteen passengers in the American Airlines case. Of this total, $165,000 went to the physically-injured plaintiff. The other plaintiffs, alleging to the jury that they thought they were going to die, were awarded damages for their emotional distress. The jury awards ranged from $150,000 to $215,000 per plaintiff. By comparison, past suits involving similar charges have netted verdicts closer to $25,000 and $50,000 per plaintiff. Hence, this was the largest verdict ever awarded for emotional trauma from air turbulence. Notwithstanding, Spielberg called the verdict "a slap on the wrist" for American Airlines. Spielberg and her two daughters received a total of $540,000 for their non-physical trauma.

While the media focused on the damages, less attention was given to the fact that American Airlines had conceded liability early on and was only contesting the damages. Pre-trial evidence had established that the plane's pilots admitted to having sufficient advance warning of the storm to avoid it. They continued to fly through it, however, and also failed to post seat belt warning signs for the passengers. For this negligence and alleged recklessness, the jury spoke.

In early 2000, the NATIONAL TRANSPORTATION SAFETY BOARD conducted hearings into an American Airlines crash in June 1999 (Flight 1420 at Little Rock, Arkansas), which also involved flying in turbulent weather. Surprisingly, aeronautical research indicates that airplanes fly into severe thunderstorms with astonishing frequency. Because passengers are generally as irritated about flight delays as they are frightened of flying in storms, the constant tension between efficiency and safety creates a moveable fulcrum for air carriers on a daily basis. Airline industry officials have announced that the Spring/Summer 2000 Program will feature a daily national plan of thunderstorm avoidance. The creation of a policy of avoiding thunderstorms in airport terminal areas is expected to significantly reduce the number of such dangerous incidents.

CROSS REFERENCES
Damages

Carl Bert Albert
AP/WIDE WORLD PHOTOS

ALBERT, CARL BERT

Carl Bert Albert, nicknamed the "Little Giant from Little Dixie," rose from poverty in rural Oklahoma to become a thirty-year member of the U.S. Congress. While serving as Speaker of the House in the early 1970s, he presided over the WATERGATE hearings, and twice he became next in line for the presidency while the country had no vice president. Wes Watkins, the successor to Albert's Oklahoma congressional seat, remembered him as a man who "sought to unite our country instead of divide it."

Carl Albert was born on May 10, 1908, in a mining camp near McAlester, Oklahoma. His mother, Leona Ann, persuaded his father, Ernest Homer, to leave the dangerous job of coal miner. The family moved to neighboring Bug Tussle, where their log cabin lacked any modern conveniences such as running water or electricity. Albert—soon thereafter the oldest of five surviving children—heard the local U.S. congressman, Charles Carter, speak at his school, and decided that he, too, would be in Congress some day.

In high school Albert first acquired the nickname "Little Giant" because he never grew taller than five feet eleven inches. He also became an outstanding public speaker, winning a national oratorical contest in 1928. After graduating from the University of Oklahoma in 1931, Albert was named a Rhodes Scholar and spent three years at Oxford University. After his return to Oklahoma, he worked for the Federal Housing Administration, was admitted to the Oklahoma bar, and practiced law for several years. When World War II broke out, Albert enlisted in the U.S. Army, eventually becoming a lieutenant colonel in the Judge Advocate General Corps. In 1942 he married Mary Harmon, with whom he would spend almost sixty years.

CARL BERT ALBERT

1908	Born near McAlester, Oklahoma
1947	Elected to U.S. House of Representatives
1971	Elected Speaker of the House
1977	Retired from the House
2000	Died

Albert returned to Oklahoma after the war ended, planning to work as an attorney. Instead, he found himself running for Congress in Oklahoma's Third District when the incumbent retired. The region was known as "Little Dixie" since most of its residents had come from the Deep South and farmed cotton and peanuts. The "Little Giant from Little Dixie" barely won the Democratic primary, with a 329-vote margin in a runoff election, but he won the general election easily and remained the district's representative for the next thirty years. His "freshman class" in Congress included future presidents JOHN F. KENNEDY and RICHARD NIXON.

During his fifteen terms as a representative, Albert was a strong advocate for the interests of his largely rural constituents, many of whom were on the edge of poverty as his own family had been. He backed public works projects, agricultural subsidy programs, and antipoverty legislation. He was urged by the numerous hunters in his district to repeal gun control legislation. On some occasions, however, his votes in Congress did not match the views of the people from his home state. Although Albert had voted against civil rights legislation in the 1950s, he became a strong supporter of the civil rights laws proposed by LYNDON JOHNSON a decade later. Originally in favor of Johnson's Vietnam policies, by 1973 he had become a leader in calling for an end to U.S. involvement in the conflict. In his autobiography, *Little Giant*, he wrote that, even while he was publicly supporting Johnson, he "had no great enthusiasm for the Vietnam War." In 1968 Albert was presiding officer at the Democratic National Convention in Chicago, where confrontations between antiwar demonstrators and the Chicago police turned violent.

In 1962 Albert was chosen as Majority Leader by the Democrats in Congress, and in 1971 he was elected Speaker of the House, a position he held until 1976. Albert followed the custom of not introducing any original legislation as Speaker. The "Little Giant" served at a time of great turmoil during the Nixon presidency, however, and his part in guiding the nation through this crisis was crucial. After Vice President Spiro Agnew was forced to resign, the Constitution placed Albert next in line for the presidency. Rather than persuade Nixon to appoint him as Vice President, Albert recommended to Nixon that he choose GERALD FORD. Then Albert presided over the Congressional hearings into the Watergate break-in, which led to Nixon's resignation from the presidency in 1974. On the night before he resigned, Nixon asked Albert—who had known him for almost thirty years—to come to the White House and talk. Nixon's resignation, raising Ford to the presidency, once again left Albert second in line for that office.

In 1976 Albert decided not to run for re-election. After officially retiring from the House in January 1977, he rejected lucrative offers to become a lobbyist. Instead, he returned to his home state of Oklahoma, where he lived in a simple house with his wife, Mary, took correspondence courses, and translated literary works into English. He received numerous honors from his fellow Oklahomans, with statues, highways, and a junior college named for him. In his final years Albert became increasingly frail, suffering two heart attacks, undergoing bypass surgery, and receiving radiation therapy for cancer. He died on February 4, 2000, at the age of 91. The House quickly passed a resolution in his memory.

ALIENS

Foreign-born persons who have not been naturalized to become U.S. citizens under federal law and the Constitution.

Elian Gonzalez Case

In late 1999 the rescue of a Cuban boy led to an international CHILD CUSTODY battle. Saved from drowning by Florida fishermen, five-year-old Elian Gonzalez was the survivor of a capsized boat containing thirteen Cubans fleeing their homeland for the United States. He quickly became the prize in a tug-of-war between his Miami-based relatives and his father in Cuba: the former wanted to keep him in the United States, and the latter to repatriate him. As the drama unfolded in court, across diplomatic channels, and in angry public protests, it led to a standoff between the Miami relatives and the JUSTICE DEPARTMENT. In late April federal agents seized the boy at gunpoint in a predawn raid and delivered him to his father. The resulting furor provoked rioting and calls for congressional hearings. By the end of June, the Supreme Court refused to grant an ASYLUM hearing for Elian, which allowed his return to Cuba.

On November 25, two fishermen found five-year-old Elian clinging to an inner tube with two adults in the waters off Fort Lauderdale. Cuban Americans Donato Dalrymple and Sam Ciancio were hailed as heroes for rescuing the trio from drowning, a fate that had claimed the lives of the boy's mother, stepfather, and eight other Cubans who had illegally set sail from Cuba days before in a small boat. Like many Cubans before them, they had hoped to begin a new life in the United States under the terms of the Cuban Readjustment Act of 1966. Enacted during the heyday of Cold War tensions between the two countries, the law creates a special exception to otherwise strict U.S. immigration quotas by allowing any Cuban who reaches the country the ability to stay.

The boy's fate quickly became controversial in personal and political terms. U.S. officials granted temporary custody of Elian to his paternal great-uncle, Lazaro Gonzalez, a member of Miami's expatriate Cuban American community. Gonzalez announced his intention to give the boy a better life in the United States than would be possible under Communism in Cuba, and Cuban Americans made the boy's future a cause celebre. Within days, however, Elian's father, Juan Miguel Gonzalez, pleaded for the return of his son, whom he accused his ex-wife of having kidnapped.

Blasting U.S. officials for holding the child, Cuban authorities demanded his repatriation. As thousands of Cubans took to Havana's streets for the first of several demonstrations, President Fidel Castro and the U.S. STATE DEPARTMENT exchanged harsh words in the media. Although initially declining to intervene in what it called a matter for the courts, President BILL CLINTON's administration met in early December with Cuban authorities to explain what steps Juan Miguel Gonzalez would have to take in U.S. immigration court and then paved the way for his visit. As throughout the crisis, U.S. public opinion sided with Elian's father: a December

18 ALIENS

This early morning raid to take Elian Gonzalez from his relatives' home sparked protests.
LEE/AP/WIDE WORLD PHOTOS

ABCNews.com poll found that forty-three percent favored returning the boy to his father, and only thirty-three percent favored the Miami relatives. Meanwhile, the case drew criticism from Haitian Americans, who argued that U.S. policy favored Cuban refugees while summarily rejecting Haitians attempting to flee injustice in their country.

On January 5, the Immigration and Naturalization Service (INS) refused the Miami relatives' request for custody and granted it to the father. INS Commissioner Doris Meissner set a deadline of January 14 for Elian's return. Protests by furious Cuban Americans paralyzed downtown Miami, leading to hundreds of arrests, but this did less to frustrate authorities than events over the next few days. First, in a measure of the increasing politicization of the case, a U.S. congressman tried to block the INS ruling. On January 7, Representative Dan Burton (R-IN) issued a SUBPOENA requiring the boy to testify before a House committee in March, hoping to delay Elian's repatriation.

Then a Florida family court intervened. Granting temporary PROTECTIVE CUSTODY to a relative, Judge Rosa Rodriguez ordered that the child not be removed from the United States until a full hearing in March. Rodriguez's apparent conflict of interest came to light the following day; she had previously hired Elian's spokesperson for her election campaign.

As the case moved back to the federal level, the Justice Department and federal lawmakers entered the fray. Attorney General JANET RENO asserted that only the INS—and not the family court—held jurisdiction over the boy's fate. Calling the INS ruling correct, Reno twice refused to grant the relatives a hearing for their claim of political asylum for Elian. When the relatives sued to force the government to grant such a hearing, Reno postponed the January 14 repatriation deadline. Her position was vindicated on March 21, when Federal Judge K. Michael Moore dismissed the relatives' suit, holding that the attorney general had sole discretion to decide whether or not to grant asylum. The relatives appealed. Lawmakers, meanwhile, proposed special federal legislation to end the dispute by making Elian a U.S. citizen.

Through late April, following visits by Elian's Cuban grandmothers, the Justice Department increasingly pressured the Miami relatives for the child's return. The relatives pressed for mediation. But when they refused to sign an agreement to hand over Elian if they lost, negotiations soured, and INS officials threatened to revoke his temporary immigration status. With much fanfare, Juan Miguel Gonzalez arrived in Miami on April 6, demanding his son's return. As the relatives canceled a negotiation session and missed deadlines, Reno flew to Miami for an eleventh-hour meeting on April 12. On April 13, the relatives ignored a 2 P.M. deadline to surrender Elian, just as a federal court issued a temporary order for the child to remain in the United States until resolution of the custody question. The order was upheld by an appeals court on April 19.

Three days later Reno ordered INS agents to raid the relatives' home. Newspapers carried the shocking photo of an armed federal officer taking the crying Elian from the arms of Dalrymple, the fisherman who had rescued him. Dalrymple subsequently filed suit claiming violation of his constitutional rights. Newspapers also ran a photo of Elian smiling hours later after being reunited with his father. Outraged Cuban Americans protested nationwide. As police arrested hundreds of rioters against a backdrop of burning tire heaps in Miami's Little Havana, critics on Capitol Hill blasted Reno's decision as heavy-handed and possibly illegal. President Bill Clinton defended the attorney general, and polls showed a majority of Americans supported the action.

Between late April and June, the custody battle appeared to be winding down as fallout from the raid heated up. Elian remained in the United States in the custody of his immediate family, while federal authorities refused to grant visitation privileges to the Miami relatives. On April 27, a federal court also turned down their request for visits. On June 1, the 11th Circuit Court of Appeals ruled against the relatives' bid to force the government to grant Elian an asylum hearing, *Gonzalez v. Reno* (No. 00–11424).

The court required Elian to remain in the country for fourteen days pending appeal to either the U.S. Supreme Court or the full panel of the appeals court. While the justices decided whether to intercede, congressional critics, who had been threatening to hold hearings since the raid, moved closer to taking that step. On June 8, the Senate Judiciary Committee subpoenaed Justice Department records, ostensibly to determine if hearings would be justified. Since the committee is dominated by Republicans, most observers regarded it as a political move. Shortly after the Supreme Court denied CERTIORARI on June 28, Elian and his father boarded a privately chartered airplane and returned home, bringing closure to the months-long tug-of-war.

CROSS REFERENCES
Immigration; Protective Custody

ANTITRUST LAW

Legislation enacted by the federal and various state governments to regulate trade and commerce by preventing unlawful restraints, price-fixing, and monopolies, to promote competition, and to encourage the production of quality goods and services at the lowest prices, with the primary goal of safeguarding public welfare by ensuring that consumer demands will be met by the manufacture and sale of goods at reasonable prices.

United States v. Microsoft

The antitrust lawsuit filed in May 1998 by the U.S. Department of JUSTICE (DOJ) and nineteen state attorneys general against Microsoft Corporation moved closer to resolution in federal district court during 1999 and 2000. In November 1999, Judge Thomas Penfield Jackson, U.S. District Court for the District of Columbia, issued findings of fact that found that Microsoft had engaged in anticompetitive behavior and had wielded MONOPOLY power. *U.S. v. Microsoft*, 84 F.Supp.2d 9 (D.D.C. 1999). Although the judge appointed a mediator to conduct settlement discussions following the issuance of his findings, the discussions broke down on April 1, 2000. Two days later Judge Jackson issued rulings of law that concluded that Microsoft had violated federal antitrust laws by leveraging its monopoly position in operating systems to capture the INTERNET web browser market for its product, Internet Explorer. By the

Bill Gates and Microsoft attorneys participate in a news conference as the company faces antitrust litigation.
MILLS/AP/WIDE WORLD PHOTOS

end of April, the DOJ and seventeen of the nineteen states proposed to the court that it divide Microsoft into two corporations.

The judge's November 1999 findings of fact came after a lengthy nonjury trial that began in October 1998. The DOJ and the state attorneys general argued in their complaint that Microsoft had monopolistic power, that it employed predatory practices to prevent manufacturers of computers from installing Netscape Communication Corporation's Navigator web browser, that it engaged in illegal arrangements by bundling nonintegrated products (Windows operating system and Internet Explorer) together, and that it tried to split markets with its competitors. In his findings, Judge Jackson concluded that the facts demonstrated the truth of the plaintiffs' contentions in all four areas.

Judge Jackson then appointed Chief Judge RICHARD A. POSNER of the Seventh Circuit Court of Appeals to mediate the case. Judge Posner, who as a law professor was an influential proponent of the relationship between law and economics, appeared to possess the experience and knowledge required to mediate such an extremely complex case. The parties worked through the winter of 2000 with Posner. Legal commentators speculated that Microsoft would settle the case before Judge Jackson issued his conclusions, as the findings of fact had been very favorable to the government position. On April 1, 2000, however, Judge Posner announced that almost twenty drafts of a consent decree had circulated during his mediation. Despite the many attempts, the parties failed to reach an agreement.

Judge Jackson, who had delayed in hopes of encouraging a settlement, moved quickly after Judge Posner's announcement. On April 3, 2000, he issued conclusions of law that addressed whether the facts he had established in his November 1999 order meant that Microsoft had violated antitrust laws. *U.S. v. Microsoft*, 87 F.Supp.2d 30 (D.D.C. 2000). He stated, "The court concludes that Microsoft maintained its monopoly power by anticompetitive means and attempted to monopolize the Web browser market." Jackson also found that Microsoft could be held liable under state anticompetition laws. He accepted twenty-three of the twenty-six arguments presented by the nineteen states. He did not accept a claim that Microsoft used exclusive arrangements with computer manufacturers and other parties to prevent Netscape Communications from marketing its web browser.

In his ruling, Jackson cited Microsoft's dominance in operating systems. He stated, "There are currently no products—and there are not likely to be any in the near future—that a significant percentage of computer users worldwide could substitute for Intel-compatible PC operating systems without incurring substantial costs." Jackson concluded that manufacturers of personal computers did not believe there was a "single, commercially viable alternative to licensing Windows for pre-installation on their PCs." Moreover, Jackson found that Microsoft had used its control of word processing, spreadsheet, and other programs to protect its monopoly position in the operating system market.

The stock market reacted negatively to the decision, resulting in a steep decline in the price of Microsoft and other technology companies' stock. During the first four months of 2000, the value of Microsoft stock declined $250 billion. The market watched closely as the DOJ and the states prepared to file a set of proposed remedies with Judge Jackson. On April 28, 2000, the DOJ and seventeen of the state attorneys general filed their proposal. In it, the government proposed several major changes in Microsoft and its business practices. The major proposal called for dividing Microsoft into two companies, one that would produce operating systems, the other to produce software applications. Illinois and Ohio disagreed with the proposed breakup of Microsoft. The companies would not be allowed to recombine for ten years. In addition, Microsoft would be required to disclose its software code to all software makers. The proposal also would require Microsoft's new products to have the ability to be included in or removed from Windows. Computer makers would be allowed to configure Windows as they wished and display competitors' products. Finally, Microsoft would be banned from using retaliatory practices against those who did not comply with its wishes.

Microsoft announced after the release of the conclusions of law that it would appeal the decision. The final outcome likely will be delayed for several years.

CROSS REFERENCES
Monopoly

BANKRUPTCY

A federally authorized procedure by which a DEBTOR—an individual, corporation, or municipality—is relieved of total LIABILITY for its DEBTS by making court-approved arrangements for their partial repayment.

Innes v. Kansas State University

Federal bankruptcy laws give persons who have substantial debts the opportunity to discharge these financial obligations. They also provide creditors with the right to challenge the discharge of their debts. Student loans have emerged as a particularly troublesome area, as colleges and universities, as well as the federal government, have resisted the discharge of these debts. Under the law, however, a person can seek to have student loans discharged if they can prove undue hardship. Kansas State University (KSU) challenged the undue hardship provisions in *Innes v. Kansas State University*, 184 F.3d 1275 (10th Cir.1999), contending that under the ELEVENTH AMENDMENT, the university was immune from the bankruptcy proceedings. Under this theory, a bankruptcy court could never discharge student loans made by a public college or university. The federal courts concluded that the university had waived its sovereign immunity when it agreed to participate in the federal student loan program.

Mark and Genevieve Innes received student loans from the federally funded aid program while attending KSU. After graduation, they filed for bankruptcy in Topeka, Kansas, alleging that loan debts should be wiped out because of undue hardship. The Inneses based their undue hardship claim on a provision of the federal Bankruptcy Code, 11 U.S.C.A. §§ 523 (a)(8) and 1328. KSU replied by filing a motion to dismiss the bankruptcy proceedings, claiming it was immune from suit in federal court under the Eleventh Amendment. The Eleventh Amendment prohibits persons from suing a state in federal court. Congress can abrogate this immunity if it has constitutional authority. In addition, a state can voluntarily waive its immunity.

The question in this case was whether KSU waived its Eleventh Amendment immunity in the bankruptcy proceeding by entering into a contract with the U.S. Department of EDUCATION (DOE) for obtaining federal student loan funds. The DOE contract required colleges and universities, including KSU, to perform certain actions in case of the bankruptcy of the borrower. The Kansas bankruptcy court rejected KSU's immunity claim and a federal district court upheld this decision.

The Tenth Circuit Court of Appeals affirmed the lower court rulings. Judge Monroe G. McKay, writing for a unanimous three-judge panel, rejected KSU's arguments that nothing in Kansas law or in the DOE contract showed that KSU had waived its Eleventh Amendment immunity. Judge McKay noted that a valid waiver required an "unequivocal indication" that the state intended to consent to federal jurisdiction that otherwise would be barred by the Eleventh Amendment. The test for determining a valid waiver is a stringent one: the waiver must be indicated by express language or by an "overwhelming implication from the text" that leaves "no room for any other reasonable construction."

Judge McKay first examined Kansas's statutes. He concluded that no Kansas law expressly waived Eleventh Amendment immunity. In addition, the Kansas Constitution did not contain a waiver provision. Therefore, KSU had not waived its immunity by these methods.

The court then examined KSU's participation in the federally funded student loan program. KSU had argued that waiver could not be found in the context of a federal program. Judge McKay acknowledged that neither receipt of federal funds, participation in a federal program, nor an agreement to recognize and abide by federal laws, regulations, and guidelines was alone sufficient to waive Eleventh Amendment immunity. The court could find, however, a waiver based on the contract between the DOE and KSU, along with the supporting federal regulations referenced in the contract.

Judge McKay pointed to a provision in the contract explicitly providing that KSU "agrees to perform the functions and activities set forth in 34 CFR [§] 674." This federal regulation deals with the bankruptcy of the borrower. The regulation states that the educational institution, upon receiving notice of the petition for bankruptcy, shall suspend collection efforts outside the bankruptcy proceeding. Judge McKay found this to mean that KSU had subjected itself to the mandatory stay provision of federal bankruptcy law. Second, the institution must file a proof of claim in the proceeding, listing the borrower's outstanding debts. Finally, if the debtor claims the loan debt should be discharged because of undue hardship, the institution must follow procedures in the regulation.

The court concluded that the contract explicitly stated that KSU had agreed to perform the obligations imposed by this regulation. By including this regulation in the contract, KSU consented to perform certain functions in bankruptcy court. Judge McKay stated that to "conclude that KSU intended anything other than a waiver would defy logic, contract law, and the equitable principles of bankruptcy." The "overwhelming implication" of the contract and the federal law and regulations reflected an unequivocal intent by KSU to waive Eleventh Amendment immunity.

CROSS REFERENCES
Eleventh Amendment; Federalism

BANKS AND BANKING

Authorized financial institutions and the business in which they engage, which encompasses the receipt of money for deposit, to be payable according to the terms of the account; collection of checks presented for payment; issuance of loans to individuals who meet certain requirements; discount of commercial paper; and other money-related functions.

Gramm-Leach Financial Services Modernization Act

In November 1999, Congress enacted legislation that will dramatically change the face of the U.S. financial services industry. The Financial Services Modernization Act (PL 106–102, November 12, 1999, 113 Stat. 1338), also known as the Gramm-Leach Act after its principal authors, Senator Phil Gramm (R-Texas) and Representative James Leach (R-Iowa), rewrites banking laws dating from the 1930s and 1950s that prevented commercial banks, securities firms, and insurance companies from merging their businesses. Under the act, banks, brokers, and insurance companies will be able to combine and share customer transaction records as well as other sensitive information. The law, which the financial industries wanted, was hailed by its authors for removing government restrictions on the functioning of free markets. Critics, however, raised concerns about loss of privacy as banks share customer information with their brokerage and insurance divisions. In addition, some worried that the repeal of the GLASS-STEAGALL ACT of 1933 (48 Stat. 162) would reintroduce the financial instability that led to the stock market crash of 1929 and the Great Depression of the 1930s.

The Glass-Steagall Act, also known as the Banking Act of 1933, was enacted as a response to the failure of nearly 5,000 banks during the Great Depression. The law gave tighter regulation of national banks to the Federal Reserve System, prohibited bank sales of securities (stocks and bonds), and created the FEDERAL DEPOSIT INSURANCE CORPORATION, which insures bank deposits with a pool of money appropriated from banks. In the years leading up to the 1929 stock market crash, commercial banks established security affiliates that underwrote corporate stock issues. (In underwriting, a bank guarantees to furnish a definite sum of money by a definite date to a business or government entity in return for an issue of stocks or bonds.) Some bank failures of the 1930s were attributed to the activities of these security affiliates, which created artificial conditions in the markets. The use of the banking system for financial speculation led to banking reform. The Glass-Steagall Act forced a separation of commercial and investment banks by preventing commercial banks from underwriting non-government securities. Banks could offer advisory services regarding investments for their customers, as well as buy and sell securities for their customers. Banks could not use the information gained from providing these services when it acted as a lender, however.

Though the Glass-Steagall Act restored public confidence in banking practices during the Great Depression, many historians and bank reformers believed that commercial bank securities had little effect on the economic depression. Efforts to repeal Glass-Steagall intensified in the 1980s and the 1990s as the global economy put U.S. banks at a disadvantage. For example, European banks did not have restrictions placed on the financial services they could provide.

Reform efforts culminated with President BILL CLINTON signing the Financial Services Modernization Act on November 12, 1999. The U.S. TREASURY DEPARTMENT worked closely with the Republican leadership in Congress and the banking industry to craft a bill that would gain bipartisan support. The new law allows banks to offer brokerage and insurance services to their customers.

Gramm-Leach goes far beyond simply repealing Glass-Steagall, however. One section seeks to streamline the supervision of banks. It directs the FEDERAL RESERVE BOARD to accept existing reports that a bank has filed with other federal and state regulators, thus reducing time and expense for the bank. Moreover, the Federal Reserve Board may examine the insurance and brokerage subsidiaries of a bank *only* if reasonable cause exists to believe the subsidiary is engaged in activities posing a material risk to bank depositors. The new law contains many more such provisions that restrict the ability of the Federal Reserve Board to regulate the new type of bank that the law contemplates. The Gramm-Leach Act also breaks down barriers for foreign banks wishing to operate in the United States by allowing foreign banks to purchase U.S. banks.

Another component of the law is reforming bank ATM (automated teller machine) practices. The law now requires banks to disclose the fees it charges for use of their ATMs. If the consumer is not provided with proper fee disclosure, an ATM operator cannot impose a service fee concerning any electronic fund transfer initiated by the consumer. Furthermore, the law requires that possible fees be disclosed to a consumer when an ATM card is issued. Finally, Congress directed the GENERAL ACCOUNTING OFFICE to conduct a study to assess the feasibility of requiring disclosure of transaction fees to ATM users before the transaction is concluded.

The provisions of the new law went into effect on March 1, 2000. Financial analysts predict that large national banks will move quickly to acquire stock brokerage firms and insurance companies, or in some cases, insurance companies will do the buying. Such activity concerns critics of the law, who fear that deregulation and the consolidation of the financial services industry into a small group of banks could lead to financial instability in the future. The failure of one large conglomerate could jeopardize the national economy. Other critics note that the various divisions of a new "super-bank" will now be able to share customer credit histories with each other, compromising the privacy rights of consumers.

CROSS REFERENCES
Glass-Steagall Act

BASEBALL

Minnesota Twins Partnership v. State of Minnesota

Professional sports teams play an important part in shaping the identity of U.S. cities. However, a number of professional sports franchises have rejected allegiance to their city and moved to another city that promised a more lucrative financial package. Congress has looked into these relocations, but no federal legislation has been passed that restricts such movement.

Of all professional sports, Major League Baseball (MLB) enjoys the greatest legal protection: exemption from federal ANTITRUST LAWS. In *Federal Baseball Club of Baltimore, Inc. v. National League of Prof'l Baseball Clubs, Inc.*, 259 U.S. 200, 42 S.Ct. 465, 66 L.Ed. 898 (1922), the U.S. Supreme Court first announced this exemption. In his decision, Justice OLIVER WENDELL HOLMES wrote that that the SHERMAN ANTI-TRUST ACT did not apply to baseball because baseball did not involve interstate commerce. Over the years this conclusion became more tenuous as major league baseball added more franchises throughout the United States. Yet the Supreme Court reaffirmed *Federal Baseball* in *Toolson v. New York Yankees, Inc.* 346 U.S. 356, 74 S.Ct. 78, 98 L.Ed. 64 (1953) and *Flood v.*

Minnesota failed to prove that its baseball team was involved in a "taxpayer exploitation conspiracy" to boycott cities without taxpayer-financed stadiums.
AP/WIDE WORLD PHOTOS

Kuhn, 407 U.S. 258, 92 S.Ct. 2099, 32 L.Ed.2d 728 (1972). In *Flood*, the Court considered whether preventing a player from becoming a free agent through a league "reserve clause" violated the antitrust laws. It held, however, that the 1922 precedent would still be followed. The Court acknowledged that the legal foundations for the exemption were no longer valid, stating that "[p]rofessional baseball is a business and it is engaged in interstate commerce." However, the ruling had been based on a "recognition and an acceptance of baseball's unique characteristics and needs." If changes needed to be made, it was up to Congress to fashion them.

In *Minnesota Twins Partnership v. State of Minnesota* ex rel, 592 N.W.2d 847 (Minn. 1999), Major League Baseball again prevailed in a dispute by invoking the Court's antitrust exemption. The Minnesota Supreme Court ruled that Minnesota's attorney general did not have the legal authority to demand documents from the Minnesota Twins and Major League Baseball. The court decided that the U.S. Supreme Court decisions barred the attorney general from any state enforcement action. Therefore, the baseball organizations did not have to turn over the documents.

Michael Hatch's predecessor as Minnesota attorney general, Hubert H. Humphrey III, began the investigation of the Minnesota Twins and Major League Baseball in December 1997. In October 1997, Carl Pohlad, the Twins owner, announced that he had signed a letter of intent to sell the Twins to a North Carolina businessman. The sale was contingent on the Minnesota Legislature's refusal to authorize public funding for a new baseball stadium by November 30, 1997. After the announcement of the proposed sale, a delegation from Minnesota, including the governor and key legislators, met with then-Acting Commissioner of Major League Baseball Allan "Bud" Selig. Selig told the delegation that if a publicly-funded stadium was not authorized and built, the other team owners would approve the Twins' move from Minnesota. Nevertheless, the Minnesota Legislature rejected all stadium bills introduced in a special legislative session.

Humphrey served the Twins with civil investigative demands (CIDs) as part of a probe into possible violations of state antitrust laws. The CIDs requested a broad array of documents concerning, among other things, the financial viability of the the Twins' current stadium, the methods used by other professional baseball teams to obtain new stadiums, the potential purchase of the Twins by the North Carolina investors, and the 1961 relocation of the Washington Senators to Minnesota. The CIDs also sought information on the Twins' efforts to procure a new stadium, as well as information on the structure, governance, and revenues of MLB. The Twins and MLB challenged the CIDs in state district court, claiming they were immune from suit because of the antitrust exemption. The judge upheld the issuance of the CIDs, however, ruling that under the reasoning of *Piazza v. Major League Baseball*, 831 F.Supp. 420 (E.D.Pa.1993), MLB's exemption was limited to the "narrow area of the reserve clause."

On appeal, the Minnesota Supreme Court reversed the district court. Justice Paul H. Anderson, writing for a unanimous court, found that the antitrust exemption covered all aspects of baseball, not just the reserve clause. Justice Anderson admitted the peculiar position granted to MLB and acknowledged that the *Flood* decision could be construed as limited to the reserve clause and free agency. In *Piazza*, however, Vincent Piazza and a group of investors signed a letter of intent with the owner of the San Francisco Giants to purchase the Giants and move the franchise to Tampa, Florida. MLB then stepped in, directed the Giants' owner to negotiate with other potential purchasers, and refused to approve the purchase by Piazza's group. Piazza then sued MLB on a number of grounds, including federal antitrust law. The federal district court ruled that the *Flood* legal precedent did not apply. The case was settled out of court one day after a congressional committee voted to strip baseball of its antitrust exemption. Thus, the Supreme Court never had a chance to examine this ruling.

Justice Anderson characterized *Piazza* as a "skillful attempt to make sense of the Supreme Court's refusal to override *Federal Baseball*, an opinion generally regarded as 'not one of Mr. Justice Holmes' happiest days.'" Nevertheless, Anderson concluded that the *Flood* decision unequivocally upheld the broad antitrust exemption and placed the responsibility on Congress to change the law. Therefore, the Minnesota Supreme Court deferred to the U.S. Supreme Court's ruling and allowed the antitrust exemption to apply in the Twins case. Because the attorney general had no authority to prosecute the Twins or MLB, he had no authority to issue the CIDs.

CROSS REFERENCES
Antitrust Law; Commerce Clause

BATES, DAISY

Obituary notice

Born on November 10, 1920 (some sources say 1914), in Huttig, Arkansas; died November 4, 1999. Bates is most widely known for her involvement in the 1957 struggle to integrate Central High School in Little Rock, Arkansas. She founded the Arkansas *State Press* newspaper with her husband, Lucius Christopher Bates, in 1942, and wrote a National Book Award winning autobiography, *The Long Shadow of Little Rock*. In 1952 she became president of the Arkansas NAACP chapter. Upon her death, President BILL CLINTON honored her by allowing her body to lie in state at the Capitol.

BIRD, ROSE ELIZABETH

Rose Elizabeth Bird served as the first woman on the California Supreme Court, becoming the chief justice of one of the most prominent appellate courts in the United States. Bird became a controversial figure during the 1980s, as her adamant opposition to the death penalty drew fire from political conservatives. In 1986, these views led voters to remove her from office. In her nine years on the court, however, Bird led a liberal majority that strengthened environmental laws, consumer rights, and women's rights.

Bird was born on November 2, 1936, in Tucson, Arizona. She spent her childhood in Arizona and New York, where she graduated from Long Island University in 1958. She attended graduate school in political science at the University of California at Berkeley in 1960 but switched her career path to law when she entered Berkeley's Boalt Hall School of Law in 1962. After graduation in 1965, Bird was admitted to the practice of law in California.

Following graduation, Bird served a one-year term as a law clerk for the chief justice of the Nevada Supreme Court. In 1966 she joined the Santa Clara County, California, public defenders office. Bird remained in the public defenders office until 1974, serving successively as deputy public defender, senior trial deputy, and chief public defender of the appellate division. As head of the appellate division, Bird oversaw all public defender criminal appeals to the California Courts of Appeal and the California Supreme Court. In addition to these duties, Bird served as an adjunct professor of law at Stanford University Law School from 1972 to 1974.

Bird's eventual rise to the California Supreme Court began when she became the chauffeur during Democrat Jerry Brown's campaign for the governorship in 1974. Following his election, Brown appointed Bird to his cabinet as secretary of agriculture. She spent most of her time in that office working to settle a series of ongoing disputes between growers and farm unions. Moreover, she drafted reforms to the state's farm labor law and to consumer legislation.

In 1977, after twenty-two months in the cabinet, Governor Brown appointed Bird, then age 40, as chief justice of the California Supreme Court. She gained immediate national prominence because she was the first woman to serve on the state's high court. As a member of a liberal majority, Bird established herself as a brilliant and combative judge. During her tenure, the court issued decisions that promoted environmental regulation and civil rights for racial minorities and women. Other decisions gave tenants more rights and poor women the right to have a state-funded abortion.

Coming from the public defenders office, the large corporate law firms and influential bar associations viewed her as an outsider. Bird signaled her disdain for the "old boys" system of privilege by selling the chief justice's Cadillac and by staying at inexpensive motels rather than at expensive hotels while on state business. She also confirmed this view by exercising strong leadership over the administration of the courts. Bird promoted racial and gender diversity on the bench. During her tenure, more than one-thousand judges were appointed who were either

Daisy Lee Gatson Bates
AP/WIDE WORLD PHOTOS

Rose Elizabeth Bird
AVERY/AP/WIDE WORLD PHOTOS

ROSE ELIZABETH BIRD

1936 Born in Tucson, Arizona
1965 Graduated from Law School
1977 Appointed Chief Justice
1986 Defeated in Retention Election
1999 Died

persons of color or female. In addition, she led the court system to change its rules to allow cameras in the courtroom. Finally, she initiated a study of gender bias in the courts, a groundbreaking effort that was adopted by many other state courts during the 1980s and 1990s.

It was Bird's opposition to the death penalty that had the greatest effect on her judicial career. California reinstated the death penalty in 1977 over the veto of Governor Brown. Thus, Bird took the bench at the same time that death penalty appeals would return to the state supreme court. Although Bird never discussed her personal views while on the court, she voted to overturn all sixty-four death sentences under her consideration.

By the mid-1980s, conservative political leaders began attacking Bird and members of the liberal majority who regularly voted against the death sentence. In 1986, Republican Governor George Deukmejian, along with local prosecutors, led a hard-hitting campaign to remove Bird and fellow Justices Cruz Reynoso and Joseph Grodin from the court. They became the first judges in state history to be removed from office in a retention election. A retention election allows citizens to vote to retain or oust the judge in which there are no opposing candidates. Governor Deukmejian then appointed three justices to fill the vacancies.

Following her defeat, Bird dropped from the public scene. She volunteered at a Palo Alto legal aid office, doing clerical work because she let her bar registration dues lapse. She also worked at a local food bank, taught for a short time in Australia at the University of Sydney, and lectured occasionally around the country. She died on December 4, 1999, in Palo Alto from complications related to breast cancer.

CROSS REFERENCES
Capital Punishment

BOUNDARIES

Natural or artificial separations or divisions between adjoining properties to show their limits.

New Hampshire v. Maine

On March 6, 2000, New Hampshire officials filed a lawsuit asking the U.S. Supreme Court to decide whether the Portsmouth Naval Shipyard is located in New Hampshire or Maine. At stake is approximately $3 million a year in income taxes that Maine assesses against the nearly 1,400 New Hampshire residents who work at the shipyard. New Hampshire has no state income tax, and its residents who work at the shipyard assert that the assessment constitutes TAXATION without representation.

The shipyard sits on Seavey Island, a 272-acre tract in the Piscataqua River between Kittery, Maine, and Portsmouth, New Hampshire. New Hampshire contends that the island's border lies along the Maine bank of the river, putting the shipyard in New Hampshire. Maine contends that the border is in the middle of the river, putting the shipyard in Maine. In 1976 the U.S. Supreme Court set the ocean boundary between the two states at a point in the mouth of the Piscataqua [*New Hampshire v. Maine*, 426 U.S. 363, 371, 96 S.Ct. 2113, 2118, 48 L.Ed.2d 701 (1976)], but the Court's opinion left unclear how that boundary extends up river to Seavey Island.

The present dispute began in 1969 when Maine first assessed the income tax against the shipyard workers. In levying the tax, the Maine legislature relied on precedent recognizing its prerogative to tax income that is earned within state's borders. Since New Hampshire does not challenge this prerogative, but only questions whether Seavey Island falls within Maine's borders, the two states have spent the last thirty years accumulating evidence on this issue.

Maine points out that the only public road to the shipyard comes from Kittery, which has also provided municipal services to the naval outpost for decades. Maine's Attorney General Drew Ketterer relies on an historical agreement under which he claims that his state and the federal government have retained parallel jurisdiction over the island since the 1800s. Ketterer has also alluded to a number of modern maps and treaties that place the shipyard in Maine.

New Hampshire also relies on maps in support of its position. State Governor Jeanne Shaheen says she has discovered an 18th-century English map that places Seavey Island in New Hampshire. The governor also observes that during the American Revolution and the War of 1812, New Hampshire residents defended the harbor. Shaheen cites an 1886 Census that says the island belongs to Portsmouth. Finally, Shaheen reminds her neighbors that in 1991 New Hampshire invested $5 million to repair the Portsmouth harbor and its basin.

The states are not just fighting over income taxes. Should the U.S. Navy decide to close the base or even part of it, the state found to have jurisdiction over the island stands to profit by opening the area to commercial development. Maine fishermen worry that they may lose their rights to fish the contested waters were the island awarded to New Hampshire, where angling licenses are scarce. On the other hand, environmentalists in both states have expressed concern over toxic waste problems at the shipyard and the related clean-up costs that might eventually be assessed.

The legal aspect of the border dispute has been heating up over the last ten years. In 1992 New Hampshire shipyard workers filed a CLASS-ACTION lawsuit in Maine Superior Court. While that suit was pending, New Hampshire's Senators Bob Smith and Judd Gregg urged Congress to exempt those workers from Maine's income tax. Hearings were held before the Senate Governmental Affairs Committee in October 1997. Testimony was inconclusive, however, and the Committee Chairman Fred Thompson (R-Tenn.) rejected the proposed exemption. The next summer Maine Superior Court Justice Donald Alexander dismissed the class action for want of prosecution, ruling that the plaintiffs' claim had grown stale from inactivity.

The lawsuit New Hampshire filed with the U.S. Supreme Court has attracted interest among legal scholars because it invokes the Court's seldom-used ORIGINAL JURISDICTION. The most typical path to the nation's High Court is by appeal, either from a federal court of appeals or a state supreme court. Article III, Section 2 gives the Court original jurisdiction to try cases "affecting Ambassadors, other public Ministers and Consuls, and those in which a State shall be Party." In 1999 the Court exercised its original jurisdiction in ruling that most of Ellis Island in New York Harbor is New Jersey property [*New Jersey v. New York*, 526 U.S. 589, 119 S.Ct. 1743, 143 L.Ed.2d 774 (1999)].

CROSS REFERENCES
Taxation

BRENNAN, WILLIAM JOSEPH, JR.

Obituary notice

Born on April 25, 1906, in Newark, New Jersey; died on July 24, 1997, in Arlington, Virginia. Brennan was an associate justice of the U.S. Supreme Court from 1956 until he retired in 1990. He was a strong believer in expanding individual rights and liberties protected by the U.S. Constitution. The liberal Democrat played an influential role in key decisions by the Court during a period of unparalleled judicial activism, including *Furman v. Georgia*, which originally prohibited CAPITAL PUNISHMENT but was later overturned, ROE V. WADE, establishing a woman's right to an abortion, and NEW YORK TIMES V. SULLIVAN, which protects the press from LIBEL lawsuits brought by public officials unless actual malice is proved. Brennan continued his activism for individual rights from his retirement until his death.

William Joseph Brennan, Jr.
OAKES/SUPREME COURT

BRIBERY

The offering, giving, receiving, or soliciting of something of value for the purpose of influencing the action of an official in the discharge of his or her public or legal duties.

Al Lipscomb Trial

In May 1999, 73-year old Al Lipscomb was re-elected to his seventh term as a councilman for the city of Dallas, Texas. One month later, he was charged with accepting more than $90,000 in bribes, including $36,000 in cash from Floyd Richards, a local taxi cab company owner. Lipscomb pleaded not guilty to the charges, telling the media that he fully expected to be completely exonerated. That did not happen. On January 25, 2000, a federal jury convicted Lipscomb of sixty-five counts of federal bribery and CONSPIRACY.

Federal indictments handed down on March 4, 1999, alleged that Lipscomb and Richards entered into a criminal conspiracy in 1995. It was further charged that Richards paid Lipscomb $36,000 in monthly payments and also channeled almost $60,000 into two businesses run by Lipscomb's son-in-law. In return, the indictment charged, Lipscomb voted on matters

Al Lipscomb answers questions in March 1999 after being accused of receiving bribes.
OTERO/AP/WIDE WORLD PHOTOS

before the council that would favor Richards's cab interests.

To establish a conspiracy, prosecutors needed to prove that one or more persons combined or communicated to accomplish an unlawful end or purpose. Conspiracy requires an *intent* to commit a specific unlawful act through the combination of persons. Bribery includes the giving or accepting of valuable consideration by a public official or one performing a public duty (e.g., a juror, witness, or voter), with the corrupt intention of creating influence in the exercise of the legal duty.

Prosecutors argued at trial that Lipscomb had accepted monthly payments of $1,000 or more from co-defendant Richards. In exchange for this, Lipscomb was said to have voted in the company's favor on taxi-related issues before the city council. For example, Lipscomb voted to allow an increase in fleet sizes for Yellow and Checker cabs but limited the number of vehicles operated by other taxi companies or owners. Lipscomb also supported enhanced insurance requirements, which the prosecution alleged were intended to run smaller cab competitors out of business.

Evidence also established—and Lipscomb freely admitted—a long-time personal and business relationship with Richards. From 1993 to 1995, Lipscomb had taken a break from public office, serving during that time as Richards's "front man" for his cab company in the black community. Lipscomb retained that role and relationship with Richards after returning to public office in 1995. The alleged monthly payments began at about the same time. During this period, Lipscomb's apparent income came from sales at the Dallas Farmers Market and $50 for each attended city council meeting.

Lipscomb, a black civil rights activist, admitted during the two-week trial that he did not report the money or gifts on his campaign finance reports ("financial involvement statements") as required. Instead, he left blank the lines on the form or wrote "N/A" (not applicable). Lipscomb also admitted to the jury that he accepted food, money, clothing, and other benefits as a way to enable other people to support his civil rights struggles. He acknowledged that the blank lines on his campaign finance reports cast a cloud of suspicion over him. He told the jury that the reason he did not report the money was to shield his white contributors from criticism. He also testified that he did not report the money in order to protect *himself* from other blacks who might be critical of his accepting contributions from whites.

Defense counsel produced evidence that Lipscomb sometimes took positions adverse to Richards's interests. They further argued that even if bribes were intended, the bribes did not influence council votes on taxicab issues because most of the votes were unanimous or nearly unanimous. This was not, however, an element that the prosecution needed to prove or overcome. If evidence showed that Lipscomb accepted something of value in return for favored treatment, it did not matter what any other councilman did. Further, Floyd Richards testified that he expected Lipscomb to vote in his favor after receiving money and other goods from him. Richards pleaded guilty to charges of conspiracy in exchange for his testimony against Lipscomb.

When the verdict came down, defense counsel immediately declared that they would appeal to the 5th U.S. Circuit Court of Appeals. They cited racial bias on the part of the all-white jury. They also claimed error on the part of the trial judge for transferring the case to Amarillo, Texas, 300 miles away, because of Lipscomb's local prominence. Prosecution also had to fight the local prominence. During the 1960s and 1970s, Lipscomb served as a field organizer for the War on Poverty partnership program. He was a plaintiff in the 1971 federal lawsuit that forced Dallas to abandon at-large voting for city council seats. The city now votes by single member districts, resulting in more minority candidates gaining council seats.

In April 2000, at time of sentencing, 74-year-old Lipscomb suffered from diabetes and a limp following two hip surgeries. In January 2000, the trial was postponed after Lipscomb was hospitalized with heart problems. In April he missed two sentencing hearings because of pneumonia and congestive heart failure. Lipscomb was sentenced to more than three years of house arrest because of his medical conditions. He was also ordered to pay $14,000 in fines. Lipscomb could have received 265 years in prison and $16.2 million in fines. The rules of house arrest meant that Lipscomb could leave his house only to receive medical care.

CROSS REFERENCES
Conspiracy

BUERGENTHAL, THOMAS

After he survived internment in the concentration camp at Auschwitz as a child, Thomas Buergenthal devoted his life to advocacy for human rights and became an international authority in the field. He led a long career as a professor, author, judge, and member of international commissions, and then became a judge on the UNITED NATIONS INTERNATIONAL COURT OF JUSTICE (ICJ).

THOMAS BUERGENTHAL

1934	Born in Lubochna, Czechoslovakia
1944–45	Held in Nazi concentration camps
1979–91	Judge on Inter-American Court of Human Rights
1980–85	Dean of American University Law School
1989–	Law professor at George Washington University
1992–93	Member of El Salvador Truth Commission
2000	Elected World Court judge

Thomas Buergenthal was born in 1934 in Lubochna, Czechoslovakia, to Jewish parents. The family fled to Poland after their homeland was invaded by Adolph Hitler. When Buergenthal was only ten-years old, his family was seized as part of a roundup of local Jews, and sent to a work camp in Kielce, Poland. He was transferred to the camps at Auschwitz and then Sachsenhausen. As a result of the forced march to Sachsenhausen, he was separated from his parents and lost two frostbitten toes. Children routinely were killed on arrival at Auschwitz, but Buergenthal credited his survival to the fact that he had been sent there from the Polish work camp. When his group arrived at Auschwitz, the guards assumed that everyone was an able-bodied worker. Buergenthal was liberated from Sachsenhausen by Allied troops in April 1945. His father, Mundek, had died in Germany's Flossenburg camp only a few days before the war ended, but his mother Gerda lived through imprisonment at several camps and eventually was liberated from Germany's Ravensbruck camp.

Following the liberation, Gerda Buergenthal was unable to find her son for more than a year. Thomas had been sent to a Polish orphanage and then was on his way to Palestine. Zionists smuggled him back into Germany, where a reunion with his mother took place at a train station. The two came to the United States in 1951, first settling in New York. Buergenthal became a naturalized citizen six years later. He graduated from Bethany College in West Virginia and then received a J.D. from New York University Law School. Later he earned advanced international law degrees (L.L.M. and S.J.D.) from Harvard University Law School. With this extensive training, Buergenthal began his lifelong work as an academic and a human rights advocate.

Two highlights of Buergenthal's human rights work have been his twelve-year tenure as a judge on the Inter-American Court of Human Rights and his membership on the Truth Commission on El Salvador. While serving on the Inter-American Court from 1979 to 1991, Buergenthal became its president, and was largely responsible for the groundbreaking "disappearance" cases in which the government of Honduras was ordered to pay the families of people who had been abducted by government forces and presumably killed. Although Honduras objected to paying the victims' families, it eventually delivered a check to Buergenthal, who personally handed it over to the families. From 1991 to 1993 Buergenthal was a member of the Truth Commission on El Salvador, which investigated human rights violations committed during that country's 12-year-long civil war. The commission found the Salvadoran military responsible for perhaps thousands of civilian deaths, and blamed senior officers for the deaths of six Jesuit priests. Buergenthal also was the first American to be appointed to the U.N.'s Human Rights Committee.

In addition to his work as a human rights advocate and investigator, Buergenthal is a noted author and academic. Among his dozen books and numerous articles, his *International Human Rights in a Nutshell* is considered a classic legal textbook. From 1980 to 1985 Buergenthal was dean of the American University Law School, and since 1989 he has been the Lobingier Professor of International and Comparative Law at George Washington Law School. He became Chairman of the Committee on Conscience of the U.S. Holocaust Memorial Council. Furthermore, he is on the editorial boards of several prestigious law publications, including *American Journal of International Law*, *Encyclopedia of Public International Law*, and *Human Rights Law Journal*.

Despite his distinguished career as an author, scholar, and activist in the field of human rights, Buergenthal continued to be haunted by his own childhood. He once admitted that, for many years, he could not see the connection between his work and his concentration camp experience. He could not even read about the Holocaust.

In 1999, Buergenthal was appointed to the Claims Resolution Tribunal in Switzerland, which was attempting to match Swiss bank accounts of the Holocaust era with survivors and their heirs. The following year, he was selected as a judge of the International Court of Justice (WORLD COURT), the chief legal body of the United Nations. In a rare show of agreement, Buergenthal ran unopposed, and all 15 members of the U.N. Security Council and 117 of 124 members of the General Assembly voted in favor of his appointment (with seven abstentions).

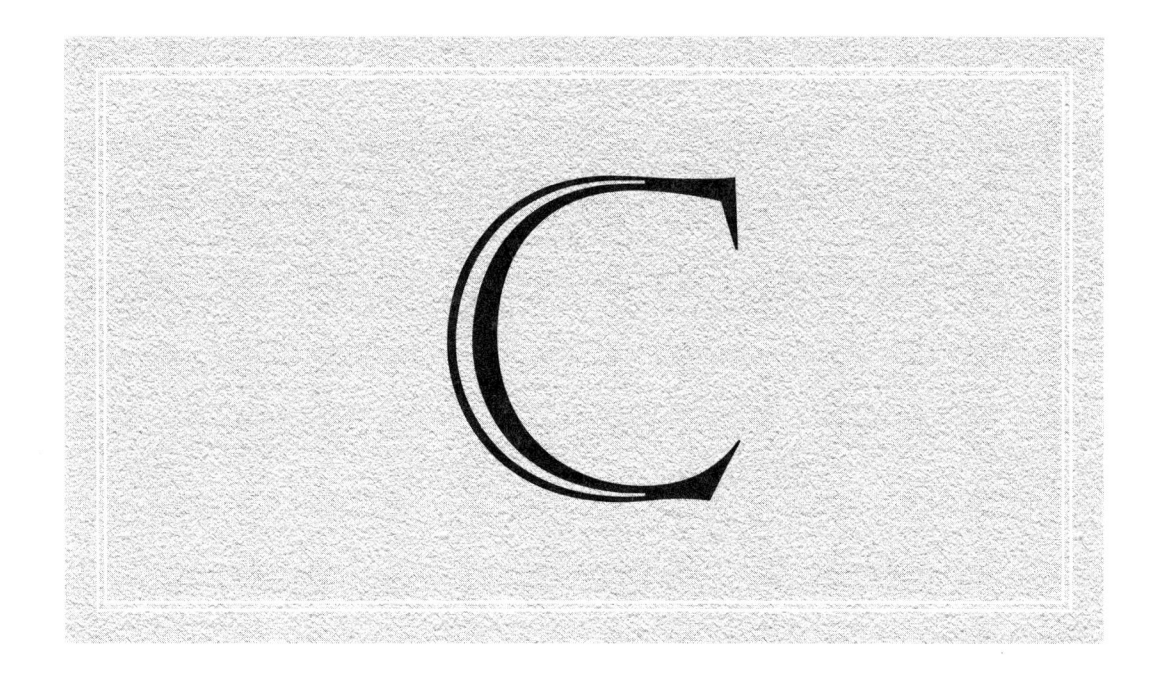

CAPITAL PUNISHMENT

The lawful infliction of death as a punishment; the death penalty.

Constitutional Challenge to the Electric Chair

Opponents of capital punishment have been unsuccessful in persuading the U.S. Supreme Court that application of the death penalty is CRUEL AND UNUSUAL PUNISHMENT under the EIGHTH AMENDMENT. Recently, however, opponents have focused on one particular mode of execution—electrocution—as being cruel and unusual. Although only a few states use the electric chair as the sole means of execution, the debate over electrocution appeared headed for resolution by the Supreme Court. Nevertheless, circumstances arose that led to the dismissal of the most recent APPEAL, leaving the issue unresolved.

In October 1999, the Supreme Court accepted an appeal from a Florida inmate sentenced to die in the electric chair. The question on appeal was whether execution by electrocution violated the Eighth Amendment's ban on cruel and unusual punishment by raising a constitutionally unacceptable risk of physical violence, disfigurement, and torment. Florida, along with Alabama, Georgia, and Nebraska, were the only states to use the electric chair as the sole means of execution. The thirty-five other states that permit capital punishment have abandoned electrocution, the gas chamber, and hanging as the sole means of execution. These states either use lethal injection or let the inmate choose the method of execution.

The controversy in Florida over electrocution grew more pointed after it was disclosed that during recent executions, flames shot from inmates' hoods, filling the execution chamber with smoke. In September 1999, Florida Associate Supreme Court Justice Leander J. Shaw, Jr., posted three photos on the court's website with his dissent in a death penalty case. The photos documented the July 8, 1999, execution of Allen Lee Davis. One photo showed Davis's body strapped to the electric chair with a belt around his head discoloring his face and causing what one expert said was partial asphyxiation. Another picture showed blood running from his nose down his neck and chest. The third photo showed burns to his head. Justice Shaw concluded that Davis had been "brutally tortured" by the state of Florida. Florida Governor Jeb Bush's press secretary refused to comment on the photos but stated the governor's belief that the U.S. Supreme Court would see this is "so much argument over a nosebleed."

The U.S. Supreme Court's decision to review the use of electrocution was the Court's first consideration of the method since its 1890 decision *In Re Kemmler*, 136 U.S. 436, 10 S.Ct. 930, 34 L.Ed. 519. The *Kemmler* decision came with the introduction of electrocution as a new technology for executing inmates. Proponents argued that electrocution was more humane than hanging, which was characterized as being barbarous and a remnant of the dark ages. The New York Legislature became the first state to authorize the use of the electric chair. The state court concluded "that it is within easy reach of electrical science at this day to so generate and apply to the person of the convict a current of

Claims of "cruel and unusual punishment" often stem from the form of execution, such as older models of electric chair.
CORBIS CORP.

electricity of such known and sufficient force as certainly to produce instantaneous, and therefore painless, death." The U.S. Supreme Court refused to overturn the law authorizing electrocution, finding that it did not have authority to do so.

After 110 years, however, the electric chair no longer seemed so progressive. Death by lethal injection has replaced electrocution as the modern and humane way to execute a person. In light of the controversy over executions, Florida rethought its methods. In January 2000 the Florida Legislature gave overwhelming approval to a bill that allows inmates to choose to die by lethal injection or electrocution. Governor Bush signed the bill, shortly before the Court's scheduled oral argument. Death penalty foes urged the Court to hear the case anyway, as three other states still use the electric chair. However, the Court agreed to dismiss the case when it became clear that all Florida death row inmates would be allowed to choose their method of execution, not just those inmates sentenced to death after the new law went into effect.

Robert Lee Tarver, an Alabama inmate convicted of murder, was scheduled to be executed in Alabama's electric chair in early February 2000. Tarver had filed numerous appeals of his conviction and sentence, but the Eleventh Circuit Court of Appeals denied his HABEAS CORPUS petition. *Tarver v. Hopper*, 169 F.3d 710 (11th Cir. 1999). In a last appeal to the Supreme Court, Tarver's attorneys raised for the first time the Eighth Amendment argument concerning electrocution. The Court granted a stay of Tarver's execution on February 3 to consider whether to hear his appeal, indicating that some of its members wished to review the issue of electrocution. Yet, within weeks, the Court voted against hearing his case, leaving the issue unresolved.

Illinois's Execution Moratorium

The use of capital punishment in Illinois is currently under close investigation. This close scrutiny arises in the context of several convictions being overturned by the courts, sometimes years after inmates have awaited their executions on death row. The State of Illinois re-enacted the death penalty in 1977. Since that time, twelve inmates have been subject to execution by lethal injection under Illinois law. Thirteen inmates, however, have been *freed* from death row in Illinois for various reasons.

One of thirteen men released from death row, a man named Anthony Porter, was discovered to be wrongfully convicted just two days prior to his scheduled execution. Another man, Verneal Jimerson, was freed from death row only after Northwestern University journalism students, investigating his case as a class project, discovered an old police file that contained evidence that other individuals may have committed the crime. After this discovery, the real perpetrators confessed to the crime and DNA EVIDENCE conclusively proved that Jimerson was innocent.

Unfairly sentencing inmates to death in Illinois has come with a high cost to inmates and taxpayers alike. Of the thirteen individuals sentenced to death and subsequently released, several served at least a decade of their lives in prison anticipating their execution. In addition, upon their release from prison, taxpayers assumed the cost of multi-million dollar settlements awarded to wrongly convicted inmates. Moreover, taxpayers also paid heavily throughout the litigation process for multiple trials, sentencing hearings, and appeals conducted at various levels of the court system.

Among the reasons for wrongful imprisonment were prosecutorial misconduct, defense attorney incompetence, and judicial error. Many of the improper sentences also resulted from unreliable evidence. In particular, several inmates were freed due to testimony given at their original trial by untrustworthy informants or eyewitnesses and unreliable forensic evidence, such as a visual comparison of hairs found at the crime scene. Some inmates were released from death row due to evidence that arose after their convictions, such as a confession by the real perpetrator or DNA evidence that proved that the individual could not have committed the crime.

In the State of Illinois, the governor has authority to exercise CLEMENCY, or leniency, toward any offender of a crime. Stated another way, the governor has the power to delay, postpone, or suspend the execution of any inmate in Illinois. A three-member panel known as the State Prisoner Review Board makes non-binding recommendations to the governor to aid him in determining whether to exercise clemency in a particular case.

The current governor of Illinois is Republican George Ryan, a supporter of the death penalty. Despite his pro-death penalty stand, Ryan has publicly expressed concern about the troubled death penalty system in Illinois. In fact, he was so concerned about the prospect of innocent people being placed on death row that on January 31, 2000, he declared a moratorium, or a stoppage, of any executions of inmates on death row in Illinois for an indefinite period of time.

Ryan is the first governor in history to establish such a moratorium on the death penalty. The governor made this decision against a backdrop of growing public concern about the accuracy of the death penalty system. In an official press release issued by his office on January 31, 2000, Ryan stated, "I cannot support a system, which, in its administration, has proven to be so fraught with error and has come so close to the ultimate nightmare, the state's taking of an innocent life." Despite his institution of the moratorium, the governor has made clear that he is still a supporter of the death penalty. He explains that although capital punishment is an appropriate punishment for the most severe of crimes, the release of thirteen inmates in Illinois is proof that the administration of the death penalty needs to be examined.

In order to undertake such an examination, Ryan established the Commission on Capital Punishment. The commission is comprised of thirteen members charged with the responsibility of conducting an exhaustive study of the implementation of the death penalty in Illinois. Commission members include former Senator Paul Simon, former U.S. Attorney Thomas Sullivan, and best-selling author Scott Turow. Former U.S. District Court Judge Frank McGarr serves as the commission's chair. When asked about the responsibility of the commission,

Governor George Ryan announces the Illinois moratorium on executions.
CARRERA/AP/WIDE WORLD PHOTOS

Judge McGarr explained that the commission's first responsibility is to focus on the problem, to completely understand it, and to gather all of the relevant evidence. Only after doing so would the commission undertake to find a solution to the problem.

North Carolina v. Thomas Richard Jones

America's intolerance of drunken driving, and the consequences thereof, has escalated in recent years. Since 1990, more than six states have changed their laws to permit prosecutors to seek first-degree felony MURDER charges against drunk drivers whose driving while under the influence lead to the death of another person. It has long been established that drunk drivers who cause the death of another could be charged with numerous crimes—including negligent HOMICIDE and MANSLAUGHTER—but the addition of a charge of first-degree felony murder raises other issues. As of 1999, thirty-eight state governments, as well as the federal government and the military, have death penalties in effect for first degree felony murder. This means that a drunk driver may receive the death penalty as a result of his drunken operation of a motor vehicle. North Carolina is such a state, and the first in the nation to have prosecutors seek the death penalty against a drunken driver, Thomas Richard Jones.

North Carolina law, like that of several other states, defines felony murder as a killing "committed in the perpetration or attempted perpetration of any arson, rape or a sex offense, robbery, kidnapping, burglary, or other felony committed or attempted with the use of a deadly weapon...." North Carolina law also includes motor vehicles under the definition of "deadly weapon." The North Carolina Supreme Court, in 1981, had defined a deadly weapon as any "article, instrument, or substance which is likely to produce death or great bodily harm." As early as 1922, state law had found instances where automobiles were deemed to be deadly weapons (e.g., *State v. Sudderth*, 184 N.C. 753, 114 S.E. 828 [N.C.1922]). Therefore, an automobile driven in a dangerous manner can be a deadly weapon. It stands to follow that, under the law, a drunken driver may be charged with first degree felony murder if he operates a vehicle so dangerously as to cause the death of another.

On September 4, 1996, at 10:30 p.m., Jones crossed the dividing line on Polo Road in Winston-Salem, North Carolina, and crashed his vehicle into another vehicle containing six college students. Two nineteen-year-old students were killed instantly, and three others were seriously injured. Jones himself suffered only minor injuries and was released from a local hospital emergency room within hours of admission.

As the facts of the tragic accident began to unfold, investigative reports revealed that Jones had been drinking alcohol and had also consumed three kinds of narcotic, which had been legally prescribed to him. Moreover, evidence further revealed that just minutes prior to the fatal crash, Jones had also struck another car at an intersection, yelled obscenities at the occupants of the car, and sped around them through a red light.

Jones had been convicted of driving while intoxicated (DWI) in 1992, and, at the time of the fatal accident, was waiting for trial on yet another pending DWI. The public was outraged, not only because innocent lives were lost at the hands of a drunk driver, but also because, again and again, a drunk driver with previous DWI convictions was still on the road. With public sentiment running high, the stage was set for the prosecutors: they charged Jones under North Carolina's felony murder statute and requested the death penalty.

In April of 1997, a full jury found Jones guilty of (1) "ASSAULT with a deadly weapon inflicting serious injury" on the three surviving students, and (2) first degree murder under the felony murder rule for the deaths of the other two students. The families of the two deceased students requested that the jury choose life imprisonment without parole instead of the death penalty, however, so that Jones could "live with his guilt." On May 5, 1997, the jury sentenced Jones to life without PAROLE. Jones then appealed his convictions.

In *State of North Carolina v. Thomas Richard Jones*, pending order, 351 N.C. 189, ___ S.E.2d ___, (1999), the North Carolina Court of Appeals affirmed the trial court's conviction, holding that "all the elements to sustain a conviction of first-degree murder by application of the felony murder rule are present." The appellate court then went on to address the other legal and technical arguments made by the defense.

One of the main arguments made by defense counsel—and an important one—was the lack of INTENT on the part of Jones to commit murder. The state, on the other hand, argued that Jones's intent was established by his purposeful reckless operation of his vehicle. Jones was not convicted of felony murder based upon intent to commit murder. Instead, he was convicted of using a deadly weapon—his car—while committing the felony of "assault with a deadly weapon inflicting serious injury" on the three surviving students. Since Jones used a "deadly weapon" in committing the assault felony, he met the requirements of the felony murder rule: a killing which occurs during the perpetration of some "other felony committed or attempted with the use of a deadly weapon...."

As of mid-June 2000, the North Carolina Supreme Court had not yet ruled on the case.

Williams v. Taylor

Congress enacted parts of the Antiterrorism and Effective Death Penalty Act of 1996 (AEDPA), 28 § 2254, to limit the ability of prisoners to file petitions seeking writs of HABEAS CORPUS in federal court. These provisions directed the federal courts to reject habeas requests if any claims had already been adjudicated in state court proceedings. However, Congress created an exception, allowing federal courts to grant writs of habeas corpus if the state court's decision "was contrary to, or involved an unreasonable application of, clearly established Federal law, as determined by the Supreme Court of the United States." One of Congress's goals in enacting these provisions was to shorten the appeal time of death-row inmates, who have fought their convictions and death sentences through a string of habeas applications.

The Supreme Court, in *Williams v. Taylor*, ___ U.S. ___, 120 S.Ct. 1495, 146 L.Ed.2d 389 (2000), upheld these provisions of the AEDPA, ruling that Congress had the authority to limit the powers of federal judges to review appeals by death-row and other inmates. In addition, the Court held that the law's one exception must be strictly construed. This means that prisoners will have a much more difficult time obtaining writs of habeas corpus that would give them an opportunity for a new trial. In this case, however, inmate Terry Williams did prevail because the Virginia Supreme Court acted both contrary to law and unreasonably in rejecting his appeal.

Williams was convicted and sentenced to death in 1985 for the murder and robbery of an elderly neighbor in Danville, Virginia. Williams had written a statement and turned himself in for the crimes. After he had exhausted his direct appeals of the conviction and sentence, Williams filed a claim in state court that his lawyer had been ineffective during the sentencing phase of the trial. The lawyer had failed to introduce evidence that Williams had been severely beaten as a young boy and that he was of borderline intelligence. These and other shortcomings led the trial court to grant a rehearing on the sentencing phase of the trial. The Virginia Supreme Court overturned this decision, however, concluding that the trial judge had misapplied the law.

Williams then sought a writ of habeas corpus in federal court. The federal district court agreed with the state trial judge that Williams's lawyer had failed to introduce five categories of mitigating evidence. Although the court granted habeas, the Fourth Circuit Court of Appeals reversed. The appeals court concluded that the Virginia Supreme Court's application of U.S. Supreme Court decisions was not unreasonable.

The Supreme Court, in a 6–3 decision, reversed the Fourth Circuit and granted Williams habeas relief. Justice JOHN PAUL STEVENS, writing for the majority, found that the Virginia Supreme Court had acted unreasonably and contrary to the Court's case law on ineffective counsel. The broader question, the constitutionality of the AEDPA provisions limiting habeas relief, produced a closer vote. On this issue, the Court split 5–4 in upholding the new limitations. Justice SANDRA DAY O'CONNOR wrote this part of the opinion, basing her ruling regarding Williams's case on this new, more stringent standard.

Justice O'Connor noted that Williams filed his petition in 1997 and, therefore, the new law governed his case. Turning to the act, O'Connor pointed out that before the 1996 law, the federal courts had conducted independent reviews of state prisoner habeas claims. Congress enacted the change to curb delays, to prevent "retrials" of state cases in federal courts, and to give effect to state convictions to the extent possible under law. Justice O'Connor grounded her analysis of these new provisions on the common meanings of the words contained in the statute.

The phrases in the exception clause, "contrary to" and "unreasonable application" were the key to her analysis. The word "contrary" meant "diametrically different." Thus, the first clause of the exception had to be interpreted to mean that a federal court may grant habeas relief if the state court (1) reaches a conclusion of law opposite to that of the Supreme Court or (2) decides a case differently than the Supreme Court on a set of "materially indistinguishable facts."

Under the "unreasonable application" clause, a federal court may grant habeas relief if the state court identifies the "correct governing legal principle" from the Supreme Court's decisions but unreasonably applies that principle to the facts of the prisoner's case. Although Justice O'Connor admitted that the word "unreasonable" was difficult to define, she pointed out that an unreasonable application of federal law is different from an incorrect application of federal law. Therefore, a federal court cannot grant habeas relief because it concludes that the state court decision applied clearly established federal law erroneously or incorrectly. The federal court must also find that the application was unreasonable. Finally, O'Connor reiterated that the source of clearly established law could only be the Supreme Court's decisions.

CROSS REFERENCES
Cruel and Unusual Punishment; Eighth Amendment; Habeas Corpus; Prisoners' Rights

CARMICHAEL, STOKELY

Obituary notice

Born on June 29, 1941, in Port of Spain, Trinidad; died November 15, 1998, in Conakry, Guinea. Carmichael was a militant activist for civil rights during the 1960s known for coining the phrase "Black Power." He had been both chairman of the STUDENT NON-VIOLENT COORDINATING COMMITTEE (SNCC) and prime minister of the BLACK PANTHER PARTY. Carmichael later moved to Guinea to work for Pan-Africanism, the uniting of Africa under socialist leadership. He died of prostate cancer in 1998.

Stokely Carmichael
AP/WIDE WORLD PHOTOS

CARTER, RUBIN "HURRICANE"

Rubin Carter, once a noteworthy prizefighter, was convicted and imprisoned for nearly two decades for murders that he did not commit. The son of a Baptist minister, Rubin Carter was born on May 6, 1937, in Clifton, New Jersey. He grew up in Paterson, New Jersey, where he had several encounters with the law at an early age. In his 1974 autobiography, Carter stated, "The kindest thing that I can say about my childhood is that I survived it."

At the age of twelve, the police arrested Carter for stabbing a man with his Boy Scout knife. Carter claimed that he acted in self-defense, asserting that the man tried to sexually ASSAULT him. As a result of this incident, a judge sentenced Carter to a six-year term in the Jamesburg State Home for Boys. Before he fully served his sentence, however, Carter escaped and joined the U.S. Army.

While in the Army, Carter began his boxing career. He won several boxing championships and had dreams of becoming a professional boxer. His dreams fell short of reality, however, when authorities discovered his escape from the Jamesburg State Home for Boys. In 1956, the Army discharged Carter and returned him to serve the remaining ten months of his term in the Annandale, New Jersey, Reformatory.

Shortly after Carter completed his sentence, he had yet another encounter with the law. Police arrested Carter in 1957 for purse snatching. A judge sentenced Carter to a four-year term to be served in the Trenton State maximum security prison for this crime. Upon his release from prison, Carter finally pursued his dream of becoming a professional boxer. He did so with much success, despite standing only five feet, eight inches tall. Carter is well-known for his first round knockout victory against Emile Griffith on December 20, 1963. Just prior to the fight against Carter, boxing writers awarded Griffith the title of fighter of the year. Based upon his reputation as a tough contender, a boxing promoter gave Carter the nickname of "Hurricane," likening him to a fierce force of nature. By 1966, Carter was at the peak of his boxing career and was the number-one contender for the U.S. middleweight boxing title.

Before he could earn that title, however, Carter's life took a tragic turn. On June 17, 1966, at approximately 2:30 A.M., two armed African American men entered the Lafayette Bar & Grill in Paterson, New Jersey. They opened fire, instantly killing the bartender and a patron. Another patron died later from gunshot wounds. A third patron survived but was partially blinded after being shot in the head. Following the shooting, police arrested Carter and John Artis, a nineteen-year-old college-bound track star who was in Carter's vehicle at the time.

After the prosecution presented evidence that a court would later refer to as "often conflicting and sometimes murky," *Carter v. Rafferty*, 621 F. Supp. 533, 534 (D.N.J. 1985), both Carter and Artis were found guilty by a jury for the triple MURDER. Both men were given sentences of life imprisonment. Throughout the trial and even after the jury rendered its verdict, both men insisted upon their innocence and claimed that they were victims of racism and a police frame-up.

Carter appealed his conviction and sentence in the New Jersey state courts. The state courts let Carter's conviction and sentence stand. While serving his time in prison, Carter wrote his autobiography, *The Sixteenth Round: From Number 1 Contender to Number 45472*. *Sixteenth Round* became a best-seller in the United States and brought considerable attention to Carter's case. Most notably, Carter received an outpouring of support from celebrities such as singer Bob Dylan, who recorded the song "Hurricane" about Carter in 1975, and Muhammad Ali, who dedicated a fight to Carter.

This publicity, in addition to a continuing defense investigation, led to a motion for a new trial filed on Carter's behalf. In 1976, the New Jersey Supreme Court granted the motion for a

---

Rubin "Hurricane" Carter
AP/WIDE WORLD PHOTOS

RUBIN "HURRICANE" CARTER

- **1937** Born in Clifton, New Jersey
- **1966** Became number-one contender for U.S. middleweight boxing title
- **1967** Convicted of triple murder
- **1974** Published autobiography
- **1976** Granted new trial; convicted again
- **1985** Writ of habeas corpus issued; Carter released

new trial, finding that the prosecution violated its duty under *Brady v. Maryland*, 373 U.S. 83, 83 S.Ct. 1194, 10 L.Ed.2d. 215 (1963), which permits defendants to inspect any evidence that might prove their innocence. On October 12, 1976, the new trial began in the lower court. A jury convicted Carter and Artis for the triple murder once again. On December 22, 1981, Artis was released on parole. Carter remained in prison.

After Carter's state court appeals were exhausted, and just as he was beginning to lose hope, things took a turn for the better. With the help of lawyers doing PRO BONO work, Canadians who became acquainted with Carter after reading his book, and a young boy named Lesra Martin, Carter and Artis filed a petition for a WRIT of HABEAS CORPUS in the U.S. District Court for the District of New Jersey. The writ of habeas corpus, which calls for a testing of the legality of an imprisonment, gives a court the power to release a prisoner after he has been fully processed through the criminal justice system. On November 7, 1985, Judge H. Lee Sarokin issued the writ and overturned the convictions. In doing so, the Judge stated that "[t]he extensive record clearly demonstrates that petitioner's convictions were predicated upon an appeal to racism rather than reason, and concealment rather than disclosure." Based upon this ruling, on November 8, 1985, Carter was released after nineteen years of wrongful imprisonment.

Upon his release, Carter moved to Canada. Carter heads the Association for the Defense of the Wrongly Convicted and is a public speaker. On April 11, 1996, Canadian narcotics officers arrested Carter and took him into custody for allegedly selling cocaine to an undercover police officer. The officers ultimately realized that it was a case of mistaken identity and set Carter free. In January 2000, Universal Pictures released *The Hurricane*, a movie about Carter's struggle to prove his innocence in the American justice system.

CROSS REFERENCES
Habeas Corpus

CENTER TO PREVENT HANDGUN VIOLENCE

The Center to Prevent Handgun Violence (CPHV) and its sister organization Handgun Control, Inc., (HCI) are dedicated to education and legal change to reduce gun deaths and injuries. HCI, a grassroots organization, was started in 1974 by a victim of gun violence, Dr. Mark Borinsky. His goal was to create common sense gun laws. He was joined in 1975 by N. T. Shields, who had lost a son to a serial killer. In 1985, current chairperson Sarah Brady joined the group after her husband, Jim Brady, was shot and seriously wounded during the 1981 assassination attempt on President RONALD REAGAN.

In 1983, the CPHV was formed by Shields to focus on education and research in GUN CONTROL while the HCI remained a LOBBYIST group. A subdivision of CPHV is the Legal Action Project. Its goal is to reform the sales and marketing practices of the gun industry. One of its most effective tools has been the use of lawsuits against gun manufacturers and distributors. The CPHV provides free legal assistance to victims in lawsuits against gun manufacturers, dealers, and owners in its effort to force the gun industry to improve the safety in gun design and sales.

CPHV has been successful in several landmark court cases in seeking court awarded DAMAGES not only to shift the cost of gun violence from innocent victims to negligent gun sellers and owners but also to reform the practices of gun manufacturers and owners. Until these recent cases, gun makers and sellers had not been held responsible for gun-related deaths and injuries. The logic was that only the individual shooter was responsible.

In *Merrill v. Navegar, Inc.*, 89 Cal. Rptr.2d. 146 (Cal. App. 1999) the CPHV obtained a major victory in its fight for more responsible gun controls. On July 1, 1993, a lone gunman, Gian Luigi Ferri, entered a high rise office building in San Francisco, California, with two semi-automatic assault weapons manufactured and sold by Navegar, Inc., plus another gun. He opened fire in the hallways and offices of the lower floors of the building, killing eight people and wounding six others before he shot and killed himself in a stairwell of the building. The survivors and relatives of the deceased brought suit against Navegar, Inc., on three legal theories: common law NEGLIGENCE, negligence per se, and STRICT LIABILITY for engaging in an ultrahazardous activity. The trial court dismissed the case on all three legal theories holding that the victims could not sue the gun manufacturer for the actions of the gunman Ferri. They appealed to the Court of Appeals of California. The court reversed on the single issue of common law negligence. Navegar, Inc., owed a duty to exercise reasonable care not to create risks over and above the risks inherent in the presence of firearms in society. Issues of fact supported the claim that Navegar had increased the risk to society through its method of advertising and promotion of its weapons. This ruling was the first appellate court decision to hold that a gun manufacturer can be held liable for its negligence in designing and selling a gun for use in crime and promoting it so that it would appeal to individuals with violent intentions. Judge J. Anthony Kline, writing for the court, held that, "Fundamental fairness requires that those who create and profit from commerce in a potentially dangerous instrumentality should be liable for conduct that unreasonably increases the risk of injury above and beyond that necessarily presented by their enterprise." The court referred to Navegar's manufacture and marketing of the TEC-9 semi-automatic weapons used in the killings. The TEC-9 has the maximum legally available firepower and is equipped with high capacity magazines and other features that make it able to be spray-fired from the hip so as to quickly inflict the maximum damage on large numbers of people at close range. Navegar advertised the TEC-9 as being "tough as your toughest customer," "paramilitary," and providing "excellent resistance to fingerprints." The Court of Appeal held that the gun had no legitimate civilian purpose such as self-defense or sporting. It was deemed a weapon solely designed for the efficient killing of large numbers of people and was advertised in a manner to appeal to persons with violent or criminal tendencies. The Supreme Court of California has agreed to review the case.

The CPHV received another legal victory in 2000 in *Hamilton v. Accu-tek* 62 F.Supp.2d 802 (E.D.N.Y.1999). Twenty-six handgun manufacturers were sued for negligence in their indiscriminate marketing and distribution practices. The plaintiffs—including the relatives of six handgun violence victims and one handgun attack survivor and his mother—argued that the companies' manufacturing and sales created an underground market for handguns and provided easy access for youths and criminals to handguns for violent use. The defendants supply most of the guns for the U.S. market in handguns. The plaintiffs alleged that the handgun manufacturers must exercise reasonable care in the marketing and distribution of handguns to protect against the risk that their products will be involved in criminal use. While selling guns is not unlawful, the method of sale and distribution can be unlawful. After a four week trial, fifteen of the defendants were found negligent and nine of them were found to have contributed to the injuries of the plaintiffs. After a lengthy analysis of the law, a review of the history of TORT LAW, and analysis of criminal and other gun-related statistics, the court refused to set aside the jury verdicts against the gun manufacturers. The decision was appealed to the Second Circuit Court of Appeal.

In addition to supporting negligence lawsuits against gun manufacturers, the HCI and CPHV encourage local legislatures to enact new gun control laws. A federal district court for the Northern District of Texas, San Angelo Division, rejected gun control legislation on the basis of the "right to bear arms" provision of the SECOND AMENDMENT in *United States v. Emerson* 46 F.Supp.2d 598 (N.D.Tex.1999). Timothy Joe Emerson was indicted on December 8, 1998, in violation of a federal law prohibiting firearm possession while under a civil PROTECTIVE ORDER. Emerson had two 9 mm pistols, a military-issue, semi-automatic M1 carbine, a semi-automatic SKS assault rifle with bayonet, and a semi-automatic M-14 assault rifle in violation of the order. He waved a weapon in front of his wife and child, then threatened to shoot his wife and her boyfriend. The federal judge dismissed the indictment against Emerson because it violated the SECOND AMENDMENT and the FIFTH AMENDMENT of the U.S. Constitution. The government has appealed the decision to the Fifth Circuit Court of Appeals. The CPHV has filed an AMICUS CURIAE brief in support of the government's position.

In 2000 the CPHV was representing twenty-four municipal agencies and was assisting others to prevent the unlawful sale of handguns and irresponsible, negligent distribution practices of gun manufacturers to criminals and juveniles. Unlike the other lawsuits, these cases allege that the gun manufacturers have violated the state business and professions code with their sales practices. The lawsuit against gun manufacturer Smith and Wesson ended in settlement. Their guns may only be sold by authorized dealers who must comply with specific terms and conditions on where and to whom the guns can be sold. Smith and Wesson also agreed to add a number of safety features to their weapons to prevent accidental injury or use by children.

CPHV has garnered enough publicity to prompt the federal government to consider its own lawsuit against gun manufacturers. The U.S. Depatment of HOUSING AND URBAN DEVELOPMENT would seek to recover millions of dollars spent on security and other programs needed to minimize gun violence in public housing.

The CPHV has become a significant force in the battle for gun control by encouraging legislative reforms, initiating lawsuits, and educating the public about the need for gun control.

CROSS REFERENCES
Gun Control; Second Amendment

CLIFFORD, CLARK MCADAMS

Obituary notice

Born on December 25, 1906, in Fort Scott, Kansas; died October 10, 1998, in Bethesda, Maryland. Clifford was an advisor to four Democratic presidents: White House counsel to HARRY S TRUMAN, personal legal advisor to JOHN F. KENNEDY, secretary of defense to LYNDON JOHNSON, and foreign policy advisor to JIMMY CARTER. He played a key role in the establishment of the DEFENSE DEPARTMENT, CENTRAL INTELLIGENCE AGENCY, U.S. Air Force, and NATIONAL SECURITY COUNCIL under Truman and in the de-escalation of the Vietnam War under Johnson. Clifford will also be remembered for being indicted—though not convicted—by both federal and New York state grand juries as part of the Bank of Credit and Commerce International (BCCI) scandal.

COMMERCE CLAUSE

The provision of the U.S. Constitution that gives Congress exclusive power over trade activities between the states and with foreign countries and Indian tribes.

Hunt-Wesson, Inc. v. Franchise Tax Board of California

The drafters of the U.S. Constitution sought to create a system of interstate commerce in which states could not enact TARIFFS, taxes, and other protectionist devices to insulate local economies. The states *are* entitled, however, to regulate and tax persons and entities within their borders. Throughout U.S. history, attempts by states to tax out-of-state businesses when they do business in the state have been challenged as infringing the Commerce Clause. The Supreme Court has generally upheld the taxation of out-of-state businesses as long as the tax is proportionate to the income that the business earned within the state. In *Hunt-Wesson, Inc. v. Franchise Tax Board of California*, 528 U.S. ___, 120 S.Ct. 1022, 145 L.Ed.2d 974 (2000), the Court struck down a California tax law that had been in place for more than 40 years. It concluded that California violated the Commerce Clause by unfairly taxing business income outside its jurisdiction.

Hunt-Wesson is one of the nation's largest and most successful food companies. It markets and manufactures a wide range of brand name grocery and foodservice products through its independent operating companies. Hunt-Wesson operates more than twenty manufacturing plants, fourteen distribution and customer service centers, and forty-five grocery retail and foodservice sales offices in twenty-four U.S. states. It filed a lawsuit in California state court challenging the $400,000 that one of its subsidiaries had to pay California in business taxes for the years 1980–1982. The corporation, which is now headquartered in California, had its headquarters in Illinois during the early 1980s, and thus was subject to California law on the taxation of out-of-state businesses. Cal. Rev. & Tax Code Ann. § § 25128 et seq. The California Court of Appeals found the statute constitutional and the California Supreme Court denied review. Hunt-Wesson then appealed to the U.S. Supreme Court.

The Supreme Court, in a unanimous decision, ruled the statute unconstitutional. Justice STEPHEN G. BREYER, writing for the Court, used numerous examples to help clarify a highly technical set of accounting issues that lay at the heart of the dispute. He noted that a state may tax a proportionate share of the income of an out-of-state corporation that conducts business both inside and outside the state. However, the state may not tax income received by the corporation from an "unrelated business activity" that constitutes a "discrete business enterprise." The core issue before the Court was whether California could limit Hunt-Wesson's deduction of interest expenses involving business activities outside of California. A smaller deduction meant Hunt-Wesson paid more taxes.

Justice Breyer concluded that the California law unconstitutionally restricted the out-of-state corporation's ability to claim interest paid as a business expense. Under the law, these deductions were offset dollar-for-dollar against the interest and dividend income a corporation received from its subsidiaries located outside California. Justice Breyer pointed out that California was barred from taxing this income.

For example, if an Illinois company sells canned goods in California, that portion of its total income attributable to its sales in California would be taxable by California. If the company has a subsidiary in North Dakota that sells

Clark McAdams Clifford
AP/WIDE WORLD PHOTOS

clothing that is not marketed in California, the income from this discrete business activity could not be included in the total business income subject to taxation by California. The California limitation on interest expense deductions worked this way. Suppose the Illinois canned good company had interest expenses of $150,000 and it received $100,000 in dividend income from its North Dakota subsidiary. California's rule authorized an interest deduction not of $150,000 but of $50,000. The deduction was allowed only insofar as the interest expense exceeded this other unrelated income.

In the Court's view, this restriction violated the Commerce Clause. Justice Breyer stated that a state cannot tax income arising from interstate activities unless there is a "minimal connection" or "nexus" between the interstate activities and the taxing state. The relevant income in dispute was income like that of the North Dakota clothing subsidiary example above; it had no "rational relationship" to California. Under Supreme Court case precedent, this income could only be taxed by the state of North Dakota.

Although California did not directly impose a tax on business income unrelated to California, the limitation on how much the corporation could deduct from its California income amounted to a tax. Hunt-Wesson had more gross income attributable to California because it could not deduct interest expenses, thus subjecting it to a higher tax. Justice Breyer noted that neither the federal government nor any other state had taken California's approach. These jurisdictions allow the corporation to allocate interest expenses between the in-state and out-of-state income. Breyer believed that "over some period of time, the ratios used will reflect approximately the amount of borrowing that firms actually devoted to generating each type of income." Because California's offset provision did not reasonably allocate expense deductions to the income that the expense generated, it unconstitutionally taxed income outside its jurisdiction.

CROSS REFERENCES
Taxation; States' Rights

COMMERCE, ELECTRONIC

Uniform Computer Information Transactions Act

The computer industry scored its first success in a controversial campaign to revise state laws. In summer 1999, several states began to consider adopting the Uniform Computer Information Transactions Act (UCITA), a model law designed to broadly reform regulation of electronic commerce and SOFTWARE licensing. UCITA represented the culmination of years of lobbying in which the software industry has argued that its products are not adequately covered by current law. Staunch opposition to UCITA came from a coalition that included consumer protection groups, libraries, computer scientists, major corporations, and twenty state attorneys general. They argued that it gives too much power to the software industry at the expense of consumer rights. In March 2000, Virginia became the first state to enact it into law as other state legislatures heard testimony from both sides.

UCITA applies chiefly to the licensing agreements that come with the purchase of proprietary software programs. In one important respect, commercial software is unique from other products. When consumers pay for software, they do not acquire it outright in the same way that they do clothing or furniture, for example. Instead, they buy a LICENSE to use the program in particular ways and under certain terms; the software maker retains ownership of the program itself. Traditionally, these terms have limited the consumer's ability to share, copy, distribute, or alter the software, among other restrictions.

Generally speaking, UCITA belongs to the modern effort to promote fairness in commercial transactions across state jurisdictions. For nearly half a century, the National Conference of Commissioners on Uniform State Laws (NCCUSL) has sought to establish uniform state laws, the best known of which is the UNIFORM COMMERCIAL CODE (UCC). In the late 1990s, the ideas in UCITA first emerged as various amendments to the UCC. The computer industry wanted standardized laws in all states governing commercial licensing agreements. When the amendments did not pass, however, industry trade groups increased their lobbying efforts. Groups such as the Business Software Alliance and leading companies such as Microsoft lobbied the NCCUSL for a distinct law, which ultimately took shape as UCITA. On July 29, 1999, the commissioners voted forty-three to six to send it in bill form to state legislatures.

UCITA replaces and changes consumer protection provisions of the UCC. Covering a wide range of issues from CONTRACTING and WARRANTIES to responsibilities, rights, and

LIABILITIES, the law delineates the roles of software makers and licensees. It particularly emphasizes the legality of the so-called shrink-wrap or click-on license—the legalese found inside boxes of computer software and commonly presented on screen for approval when a consumer installs software for the first time. The law also establishes rules for handling disputes between makers and buyers, empowers makers to take so-called "self-help" steps to disable software when buyers violate licenses, and creates a right-of-return for consumers who refuse to enter into licensing terms.

Views on UCITA's merits are sharply divided. The computer industry has hailed UCITA for attempting to eliminate time and money expenditures that result from the differences in law from state to state, bringing antiquated law up to date in the digital age, and building much-needed protections for businesses into electronic commerce. Opponents have criticized the law as being made for a powerful industry that seeks special treatment and as a wholesale surrender of consumer rights. They claim that shrink-wrap contracts are rarely read in full and, therefore, do not receive sufficient attention from consumers. Moreover, the licenses amount to a "take it or leave it" proposition, with the software industry dictating terms to consumers. Among opponents' chief complaints are UCITA provisions that prohibit transfer of software from one company to another in the course of mergers, or even from one person to another as a GIFT.

The self-help provision has engendered the greatest controversy, however. According to the software industry, state law currently does not allow a software company to take appropriate, timely action when it is aware that its licenses are being violated. Under UCITA, a company could remotely disable its software on a consumer's computer—essentially, pulling the plug. Critics have scorned this provision as an invasion of privacy that could destroy data and cripple businesses, government, or even hospitals. Proponents stress that such intervention would come only after a fifteen-day warning period that would allow for restitution or contingency plans.

Two groups have raised unique complaints against UCITA. First, the nation's library associations and their 80,000 members have lined up against it. Summarizing their position, James G. Neal, the dean of libraries at Johns Hopkins University, gave four reasons to the Maryland legislature in February 2000 for opposing the law: the restrictiveness of shrink-wrap licenses, the likelihood that librarians could relinquish valuable rights by entering such licenses, the danger of software makers holding the self-help threat over licensees, and the fact that only a few major software companies dominate the research market and can lord their terms over libraries. Second, opposition has come from computer scientists in the so-called "open source movement." This recent trend in software development advocates that programmers collaborate without restrictive trade secrets in the creation and free distribution of software. Furthermore, users of open source programs do not have to sign a license agreement that prohibits them from modifying that program for their own benefit. Open source advocates fear that their liability will increase under UCITA while the commercial software industry will avoid liability almost entirely.

Proponents of UCITA have decried these arguments as distortions and matched their opponents' intense lobbying of state lawmakers. In March 2000, they won their first major victory by convincing the Virginia legislature to enact UCITA as law. Virginia Governor James Gilmore publicly expressed his hope that the new law would attract more computer business to his state, where UCITA will go into effect in mid-2001. The Business Software Alliance praised him for setting a precedent for other states to follow. Maryland also weighed enactment of UCITA, while Hawaii, Illinois, and Oklahoma planned to consider it during their 2000 sessions.

CROSS REFERENCES
License; Software

COMPETENT

Possessing the necessary reasoning abilities or legal qualifications; qualified; capable; sufficient.

Kenneth Curtis Trials

Kenneth Curtis was convicted of first-degree manslaughter in a Connecticut court in December 1999, twelve years after he shot and killed his former girlfriend. In 1988, Curtis was charged with MURDER in the shooting death of 21-year-old Donna Kalson. He was also charged with the attempted murder of Kalson's companion. The shootings took place outside a Stratford, Connecticut, restaurant on October 30, 1987.

After shooting Kalson and her companion, Curtis shot and wounded himself with his .32-caliber pistol. The bullet lodged in Curtis's

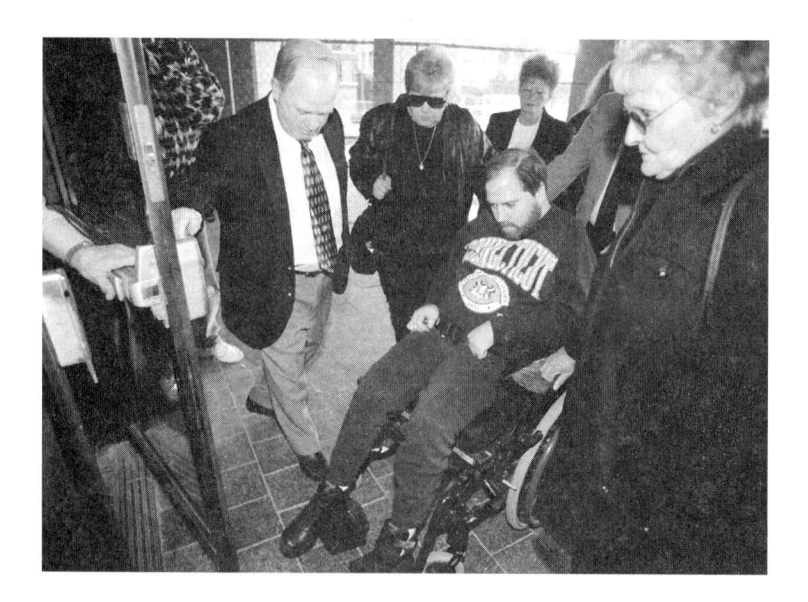

In 1999 Kenneth Curtis (in wheelchair) was found competent to stand trial for the death of his former girlfriend in 1987.
HEALEY/AP/WIDE WORLD PHOTOS

TENCING hearing, Curtis's attorney argued for leniency, contending that his client had suffered sufficiently from the severity of his injuries. The court disagreed. Kenneth Curtis was sentenced to the maximum manslaughter sentence, twenty years. As part of the plea agreement, Curtis agreed to waive his right to appeal.

COMPUTER CRIME

Denial of Service Web Site Attacks

In February 2000 a computer hacker stunned the world by paralyzing the INTERNET's leading U.S. web sites. Three days of concentrated assaults upon major sites crippled businesses like Yahoo, eBay, and CNN for hours, leaving engineers virtually helpless to respond. When the dust had settled, serious doubts were raised about the safety of Internet commerce, an international manhunt was underway, and web sites claimed losses in the hundreds of millions of dollars. After pursuing several false leads, investigators ultimately charged a Canadian teenager in March in one of the attacks. As authorities tried to calm fears at a time when the Internet represents the fastest growing sector of the economy, the White House held a security summit and called for creation of a national cyber security center.

brain and left him with partial paralysis and brain damage. Following his arrest in 1988, he underwent competency hearings to determine whether he could understand the proceedings against him. In 1989 Curtis was ordered discharged from custody after findings that he was incompetent to stand trial. As a condition of his discharge from custody, he was ordered to undergo an annual psychiatric evaluation. A Connecticut appellate court overturned that requirement in 1990, ruling that state law did not permit conditions to be imposed on his release.

A New Haven, Connecticut, television station investigated a tip that Curtis was in college and earning good grades. The tip was accurate. Police determined Curtis had earned forty-eight credits at several colleges between 1992 and 1995, with a respectable grade-point average. He was rearrested in November 1997. At the time of his arrest he was a pre-med psychiatry student at Southern Connecticut State University in New Haven.

Following his rearrest, Curtis endured another round of competency hearings after his attorney's claims of DOUBLE JEOPARDY were dismissed. Videotaped evidence showed Curtis behaving normally at school and conversing lucidly about his future, but in court he remained silent and kept his head down. In August 1999 a judge ruled that Curtis had willfully amplified his symptoms to avoid prosecution and determined that Curtis was capable of understanding the charges against him.

In September 1999, pursuant to a plea bargain, Curtis pled guilty to a charge of first degree MANSLAUGHTER. At his December SEN-

On February 7, engineers at Yahoo, the popular portal web site, noticed traffic slowing to a crawl. Initially suspecting faulty equipment that facilitates the thousands of connections to the site daily, they were surprised to discover that it was receiving many times the normal number of hits. Buckling under exorbitant demand, the servers—the computers that receive and transmit its Internet traffic—had to be shut down for several hours. Engineers then isolated the problem: remote computers had been instructed to bombard Yahoo's servers with automated requests for service.

Over the next two days, several other major web sites suffered the same fate. Hackers hit the auction site eBay, the bookseller Amazon.com, the computer journalism site ZDnet, stock brokerages E*Trade and Datek, the computer store Buy.com, the web portal Excite At Home, and the flagship site of news giant CNN. As each site ground to a halt or went offline, engineers tried vainly to determine where the digital bombardment originated. While they struggled for answers, U.S. Attorney General JANET RENO appeared at a press conference appealing for calm and vowing to bring the attackers to justice.

Experts expressed amazement at the attacks' simplicity as well as the inherent technical vulnerabilities they exposed in the Net's architecture. Hackers had launched what quickly came to be known as a distributed Denial-of-Service (DOS) attack—essentially, a remote controlled strike using multiple computers. First, weeks or months in advance, they had surreptitiously installed commonly-available hacking programs called "scripts" on fifty or more remote computers, including university systems chosen for their high speed connections to the Internet. Later, they activated these scripts, turning the remote computers into virtual zombies that were ordered to send unfathomably large amounts of data—up to one gigabyte per second—continuously to their victims. This data asked the target web sites to respond, just as every legitimate connection to a web site does. The sheer multitudes of requests and responses overwhelmed the victim sites. To escape detection, the "zombies" forged their digital addresses.

Surprisingly, the attacks seem not to have been unexpected. The scripts used to bombard the web sites had been readily available for several months under names such as TFN, trinoo, and *Stacheldraht* (German for "barbed wire"). In December 1999 the FEDERAL BUREAU OF INVESTIGATION (FBI) had issued warnings about a possible DOS attack after uncovering installations of the scripts on several computers. And in January 2000, the Carnegie Mellon University Computer Emergency Response Team released its own advisory. The warnings went largely unheeded.

Responding to concerns a few days later about the safety of Internet commerce, the White House held a highly-publicized summit on cyber crime. Attending were academics, electronic security analysts, major computer manufacturers, and even a celebrated hacker known as "Mudge." Calling the web site attacks "very disturbing," President BILL CLINTON asked consumers not to panic and called for the creation of a national cyber security center that would thwart such attacks in the future. With federal government computers having come under repeated attack in 1999, Clinton's initiative had a broader context.

In the hacker hunt, federal investigators initially were stymied. They had legal authority to act under 18 U.S. § 1030 (a) 5a, which criminalizes "knowingly transmit(ting) a program information code or command" that "intentionally causes damage." Sleuthing was difficult, however. Not only had the hackers covered the trail well, but the FBI had suffered numerous personnel losses to private industry. This meant that the bureau had to hire consultants and develop special software to assist in its manhunt. Moreover, as FBI official Ron Dick told reporters, the proliferation of common hacking tools meant that even a teenager could have orchestrated the crime. Computer security experts guessed that the best hope was that someone in the hacker underground would provide a lead by bragging publicly. Unfortunately, too many did: as investigators looked for a mysterious suspect nicknamed "Mafiaboy," Internet chat rooms filled with dozens of people calling themselves by that name.

In early March authorities arrested seventeen-year-old New Hampshire resident Dennis Moran, allegedly known online as "Coolio." The lead proved false. In mid-April, claiming to have found "Mafiaboy," Canadian Royal Mounties arrested a fifteen-year-old Montreal hacker. The youth, whose real name was not divulged, allegedly had boasted of his exploits online while trying to recruit helpers. Officials charged him with a misdemeanor for launching the attack upon CNN's web site. The JUSTICE DEPARTMENT expressed satisfaction with the arrest but said its investigation was ongoing.

As summer approached, popular consensus viewed the Internet as remaining vulnerable. While Justice Department officials lobbied Congress for broader cyberterrorism laws in April, government and industry leaders met in May in California at what was billed as the Internet Defense Summit. This gathering attracted participants from companies such as Microsoft and Visa International as well as the U.S. Postal Service and local authorities. Participants agreed that hackers currently held the upper hand, with solutions still elusive.

CROSS REFERENCES
Internet

CONFRONTATION

A fundamental right of a defendant in a CRIMINAL ACTION to come face to face with an adverse witness in the court's presence so the defendant has a fair chance to object to the TESTIMONY of the witness and the opportunity to cross-examine the witness.

Lilly v. Virginia

The SIXTH AMENDMENT to the U.S. Constitution contains the Confrontation Clause, which states that a criminal defendant must be "confronted with the witnesses against him" at trial. Through CROSS-EXAMINATION, defendants may test the CREDIBILITY and reliability of witnesses by probing their recollection and exposing any underlying prejudices, biases, or motives to distort the truth or lie. Confrontation and cross-examination are important components of the U.S. ADVERSARIAL SYSTEM.

There are circumstances, however, under which defendants are disallowed confronting and cross-examining their accusers under the rules of HEARSAY evidence. Hearsay is a written or verbal statement made out of court by one person that is later repeated in court by another person who heard or read the statement. The law generally treats hearsay as unworthy and courts will not admit such evidence into a trial. Nevertheless, the courts have made exceptions to the rule that allow the admission of hearsay evidence without violating the Sixth Amendment's Confrontation Clause. The U.S. Supreme Court, in *Lilly v. Virginia*, 527 U.S. 116, 119 S.Ct. 1887, 144 L.Ed.2d 117 (1999), ruled that the Confrontation Clause was violated when a trial court used a hearsay exception to allow an unavailable witness's confession to police to be admitted into evidence. The Court overturned the murder conviction because the admitted statements were presumptively unreliable.

Benjamin Lilly, his brother Mark Lilly, and Gary Barker broke into a home, stole three bottles of liquor, three loaded guns, and a safe. The next day they drank the liquor and robbed a store. After their car broke down, they abducted Alex DeFilippis and drove his vehicle to a deserted location. One of the men then shot and killed DeFilippis. The trio committed two more robberies before police arrested them that night. The police questioned each of the three men separately. Mark Lilly and Gary Barker told police that Benjamin Lilly had masterminded the robberies and killed DeFilippis. Mark Lilly emphasized in his police interviews that he had been very drunk during the crime spree, but admitted he had stolen liquor during the first BURGLARY and beer during the robbery of the store. He also stated that he had handled a gun and had been present during the robberies and the MURDER.

The Commonwealth of Virginia charged Benjamin Lilly with the murder of DeFilippis. At his trial, the prosecutor called Mark Lilly to testify but he invoked his FIFTH AMENDMENT right against SELF-INCRIMINATION. Because Mark Lilly's statements were a vital part of the prosecution case, the prosecutor asked that the tape recordings and transcripts of the statements be introduced into evidence. The trial court agreed to the request, stating that the materials were admissible as "declarations of an unavailable witness against penal interest." Benjamin Lilly's attorney had objected to the admission because the statements were not against Mark's penal interest (i.e., Mark Lilly was not putting himself at risk of conviction of the crimes) because they shifted responsibility for the crimes to his brother and Barker. In addition, the attorney argued that the admission of the statements violated the Confrontation Clause. Nevertheless, the judge admitted the statements. Benjamin Lilly was ultimately found guilty of robbery, abduction, car jacking, firearms charges, and murder. He was sentenced to death for the murder of DeFilippis.

The Supreme Court of Virginia affirmed Lilly's convictions and death sentence. The court upheld the admission of Mark Lilly's statements, finding that they were declarations of an unavailable witness against penal interest, that other evidence confirmed their reliability, and that the statements fell within an exception to the Virginia hearsay rule. Based on this hearsay exception, the court rejected Lilly's Confrontation Clause argument.

The U.S. Supreme Court, in a unanimous decision, reversed the Virginia Supreme Court, finding that the decision of the state court represented a significant departure from its Confrontation Clause precedents. Justice JOHN PAUL STEVENS, writing for a majority of the court (the other four justices offered different reasons for the reversal), held that the admission of the "untested confession" violated Lilly's Confrontation Clause rights. Restating prior case law, Justice Stevens found that hearsay statements are sufficiently dependable to allow their admission only when the statements fall within a "firmly rooted hearsay exception" or they contain "particularized guarantees of trustworthiness" such that cross-examination would be expected to add little, if anything, to their reliability.

Using these two principles, Justice Stevens analyzed the "against penal interest" exception cited by the Virginia Supreme Court. He concluded that allowing accomplice statements into evidence under this exception is wrong, as these statements are "presumptively unreliable, even when the accomplice incriminates himself together with the defendant." Therefore, accomplice statements that shift the blame to a criminal defendant fall outside of those hearsay exceptions that the Court had previously judged trustworthy. Moreover, Justice Stevens rejected Virginia's argument that the U.S. Supreme Court should defer to the Virginia Supreme Court's determination that Mark Lilly's statements were supported by particularized guarantees of trustworthiness. Stevens held that the Court should independently review the record to see if the statements were reliable. Based on the record, Stevens found that there were many factors that contradicted the claim that Mark Lilly was trustworthy: he was in custody for a serious crime; responding to leading questions from the police; he was under the influence of alcohol during the interrogation; and he had a "natural motive" to blame his brother for the crime. Therefore, the Court reversed Benjamin Lilly's conviction.

CROSS REFERENCES
Fifth Amendment; Sixth Amendment

CONSPIRACY

An AGREEMENT between two or more persons to engage jointly in an unlawful or criminal act, or an act that is innocent in itself but becomes unlawful when done by the combination of its actors.

ValuJet Flight 592 Crash

ValuJet Flight 592 crashed into the Florida Everglades eleven minutes after takeoff on May 11, 1996. All 110 passengers were killed. A 1997 investigation by the NATIONAL TRANSPORTATION SAFETY BOARD (NTSB) directed fault toward three entities: SabreTech (an airlines maintenance company), ValuJet, and the Federal Aviation Administration (FAA). However, the true focus of LIABILITY—and blamed for the cargo fire that brought down the DC-9—was a case of 144 oxygen generators stored onboard. SabreTech employees took the generators off other ValuJet planes and placed them on Flight 592 without marking them as hazardous and without installing safety caps. Crash investigators concluded that these explosive-tipped materials probably caused the fire that caused the crash.

For the first time in aviation history, federal criminal charges in connection with a crash were filed against an airlines maintenance company. Also named as defendants were two individual employees of SabreTech. Eugene Florence, a maintenance mechanic, was charged with falsifying aircraft maintenance records for signing a work card stating that he had installed safety shipping caps on the generators. He later admitted that he had not. Florence and his supervisor, Daniel Gonzalez, were also charged with conspiracy to falsify government records with respect to the handling and shipment of hazardous materials. The company itself was also charged with seventeen counts of federal hazardous materials regulatory violations, including the failure to train employees in hazardous materials. ValuJet and the FAA were not named in the criminal charges. Separate from this, SabreTech faced 110 manslaughter charges in state court.

The defense focused on the lack of criminal intent, a necessary element for both conspiracy and intentional falsification of records. The crime of conspiracy requires specific intent. Not only must there be an intent to combine with another to accomplish an unlawful purpose, but there also must be an intent to commit a specific unlawful act through the combination. Defense argued that, while employees may have exercised bad judgment, they acted without the requisite criminal intent and did not realize how volatile the empty oxygen canisters were.

The defense also chipped away at "probable cause" by bringing into evidence the airplane's old age and history of electrical problems. During the course of the three-week trial, counsel for SabreTech further attempted to admit other evidence that directed blame toward the "empty-chair" defendant, ValuJet. This evidence was in the form of testimony from a teleconference operator regarding her recollection of statements made between ValuJet company executives, their attorneys, and their insurers ten days after the crash. U.S. District Court Judge James King dismissed the proposed evidence as

Daniel Gonzalez (left) and SabreTech employees were acquitted, but the company was convicted of mishandling hazardous materials that allegedly caused the ValuJet crash.
GUTIERREZ/AP/WIDE WORLD PHOTOS

"inflammatory hearsay and nothing more than rumor." Arguments for and against the admission of the testimony were heard by the judge outside of the jury's presence.

Defense counsel attacked the CREDIBILITY of one of the prosecution's key witnesses, Chris DiStefano. Under the cloak of immunity, DiStefano testified that Gonzalez had signed his name to work that he knew had never been performed. Counsel for Gonzalez forced the witness to admit that he had previously lied to a federal grand jury by stating that he had no criminal record, when he had once been court-martialed while in the military for stealing an airplane. DiStefano further testified that he intentionally got rid of a ValuJet maintenance log that federal agents sought in their investigation of ValuJet's role in the crash.

Finally, the defense argued that the findings of the NTSB, which led to these indictments, could not prove guilt "beyond a reasonable doubt," which is the minimum standard for conviction in a criminal case. The NTSB report that was admitted into evidence claimed "failures all up and down the line, from federal regulators to airline executives, from the boardroom to workers on the shop room floor." The jury agreed. It acquitted both maintenance employees and the company on all conspiracy charges. A member of the jury panel told reporters that the jury did not believe that the workers had done anything "intentionally." Notwithstanding, the jury did find SabreTech guilty of nine other charges—eight for the reckless mishandling of hazardous materials and one for the failure to train its employees in the proper handling of such materials. SabreTech immediately announced plans to appeal the verdict, arguing that the regulation they purportedly violated was not effective as good law until after the crash.

Further, counsel for SabreTech also argued that federal sentencing guidelines require that the eight similar counts be grouped together as one, resulting in a reduction of fines to $1 million. The separate count for failure to train employees would add another $500,000 to the fine. Defense counsel argued that the defendant company's financial resources also must be taken into consideration for sentencing. The company went out of business after the crash and its assets were sold to Aviation Management Systems of Orlando, Florida, in June 1999. The company retained its liabilities after the sale, but liabilities exceeded remaining assets. General liability insurance for the company does not cover criminal fines, but the company's insurers have settled 107 civil suits from victims' families, and two more were partially settled. SabreTech's parent company, SabreLiner, is not legally liable for the debts of its incorporated subsidiaries, despite its own profitability.

The pending state murder charges were not expected to go to trial until October 2000. While state prosecution continued to prepare for the trial, it was doubtful whether—considering the finances of the defunct defendant company—actual prosecution would continue.

There has been an increasing trend in recent years to incorporate criminal penalties into sanctions for violations of federal and some state regulations, particularly those involving the public welfare. These provisions usually make the highest-ranking official for a particular corporate activity the responsible party, even where that individual's direct responsibility in the violation cannot be shown. Furthermore, courts do not hold the prosecution responsible for establishing intent or even negligence to support such convictions. The court record is consistent in upholding convictions of these individuals under such public welfare statutes. Constitutional DUE PROCESS challenges to these convictions have been denied as well. (See, for example, U.S. Supreme Court case, *Hanousek v. United States*, 176 F.3d 1116 [9thCir. 1999]).

CROSS REFERENCES
Airlines

CRIMINAL PROCEDURE

The framework of laws and rules that govern the administration of justice in cases involving an individual who has been accused of a crime, beginning with the initial investigation of the crime and concluding either with the unconditional release of the accused by virtue of acquittal (a judgment of not guilty) or by the imposition of a term of punishment pursuant to a conviction for the crime.

New York v. Hill

Criminal defendants are entitled to speedy trials under the Constitution, statutes, and rules of criminal procedure. Statutes that set specific time periods provide the opportunity for a defendant to move for dismissal of the charges if the state fails to meet the trial deadline. A defendant may waive the speedy trial provision, however, and agree to a later trial date. The courts have had to examine speedy trial waivers to determine whether only the defendant may affirmatively agree to abandon this right or whether the defendant's attorney may agree to a trial date beyond the statutory time period.

The Supreme Court, in *New York v. Hill*, ___ U.S. ___, 120 S.Ct. 659, 145 L.Ed.2d 560 (2000), confronted this question in the context of the Interstate Agreement on Detainers (IAD), 18 U.S.C.A. App. § 2, which sets up a procedure for returning an incarcerated prisoner to another state to face criminal charges. The court concluded that the IAD allowed an attorney to waive the 180-day speedy trial provision on behalf of his client, thereby preventing dismissal of the criminal charges.

The IAD is a compact entered into by forty-eight states, the United States, and the District of Columbia that establishes procedures for resolution of one state's charges outstanding against a prisoner of another state. Because the IAD is a Congressionally sanctioned interstate compact based on the Constitution's COMPACT CLAUSE, Art. I, § 10, cl. 3, the IAD is a federal law subject to interpretation by the federal courts.

Michael Hill was a prisoner in Ohio. New York law enforcement officials filed a detainer under the provisions of the IAD against him with Ohio criminal justice authorities, requesting that Ohio hold Hill for New York or notify New York when Hill's release from custody was imminent. New York wanted Hill returned to New York to face MURDER and robbery charges. After the detainer had been lodged against Hill, he was permitted to file a request for a final disposition to be made of the indictment, information, or complaint. Once Hill filed this request, the IAD required that he be brought to trial within 180 days, unless the court found good cause for a reasonable continuance. If a defendant is not brought to trial within the 180-day period, the IAD requires that the indictment be dismissed with prejudice, which means the state cannot refile charges.

A court hearing was held in January 1995 in New York to set a trial date for Hill, but only the prosecutor and Hill's defense attorney were present. The prosecutor suggested a trial date of May 1 and the defense counsel told the court "that will be fine." The court then scheduled the trial for May 1. In mid-April, however, Hill moved to dismiss the indictment, arguing that the IAD's time limit had expired. The trial court found that on the day in January when the trial date was set, 167 days had already elapsed, so that if the state could not rebut Hill's motion, the 180 day time period had expired. The trial court concluded that the defense attorney's explicit agreement to the trial date set beyond the statutory period "constituted a waiver or abandonment of defendant's rights under the IAD." Therefore, the court denied Hill's motion to dismiss.

Hill went to trial, where a jury convicted him of second degree murder and first degree robbery. Hill appealed his conviction in New York state court, contending that the trial court should have dismissed the indictment because he did not receive a speedy trial as mandated by the IAD. Though the intermediate court of appeals rejected this argument, the New York Court of Appeals, the state's highest court, agreed with Hill, ruling that the conviction must be reversed and the indictment dismissed. It held that the waiver of speedy trial provisions could only be made by Hill.

The U.S. Supreme Court, in a unanimous decision, overturned the New York Court of Appeals decision. Justice ANTONIN SCALIA, writing for the Court, noted that various state courts had disagreed as to what is necessary to effect a waiver under the IAD. Some states allowed the defense attorney to waive a speedy trial, while other states required the defendant, either expressly or impliedly, to agree to a delay in the trial. Justice Scalia based his analysis on "the nature of the rights at issue." For certain fundamental rights, such as the right to plead not guilty, the defendant must personally make an informed waiver to plead guilty to the charges. The defense attorney, however, may waive other rights. Those matters that involve "the conduct of the trial" are within the authority of the defendant's attorney and the attorney's words bind the client.

Justice Scalia characterized the setting of a trial date as a scheduling matter, which the defense attorney has the right to control on behalf of the defendant. The defense attorney is in the best position to assess what is in the best interest of the defendant concerning a delay. Justice Scalia concluded that "requiring express assent from the defendant himself for such routine and often repetitive scheduling determinations would consume time to no apparent purpose." Although delay can lead to a less accurate outcome as witnesses become unavailable and memories fade, some social interests served by prompt trial were less relevant in Hill's case. Scalia pointed out that because Hill was already incarcerated in another jurisdiction, "society's interests in assuring the defendant's presence at trial and in preventing further criminal activity" were not at issue. The Supreme Court refused to adopt the "hypertechnical" waiver requirement of the state court. Justice Scalia stated that "such an approach would enable defendants to escape justice by willingly accepting treatment inconsistent with the IAD's time limits, and then recanting later on."

DEPORTATION

Banishment to a foreign country, attended with CONFISCATION of property and deprivation of CIVIL RIGHTS.

Hammer v. INS

When a person from another country seeks to enter the United States, that individual is subject to U.S. immigration laws. These laws bar the entry of individuals for numerous reasons. Under the Holtzman Amendment, the United States bars the entry of ALIENS who assisted or participated in the persecution of persons because of race, religion, national origin, or political opinion under the direction of the Nazi government of Germany between 1933 and 1945. 8 U.S.C.A. § 1182(a)(3)(E). Another provision authorizes the government to deport such aliens. If a person has concealed information about their Nazi past and has become a U.S. citizen, the government may go into court and seek to obtain a denaturalization order. This order strips a person of citizenship.

The workings of this process were demonstrated in the case of *Hammer v. INS*, 195 F.3d 836 (6th Cir. 1999). Ferdinand Hammer, a 78-year-old resident of Warren, Michigan, asked the Court of Appeals for the Sixth Circuit to overturn an immigration judge's ruling that he must be deported to Austria because he had served in several concentration camps, including Auschwitz, as a member of the Schutzstaffel (SS) during World War II. Hammer contended that he had been wrongly accused and that he had actually served on the Russian front. Nevertheless, the appeals court upheld the ruling, concluding that he had concealed his Nazi past when he entered the United States and must be deported.

In 1994 the federal government started a denaturalization proceeding in federal district court against Hammer. The government charged that Hammer had illegally obtained U.S. citizenship by concealing the fact that he had served in the notorious "Death's Head Battalion" of the Nazi Waffen-SS. Hammer, in contrast, claimed that he had served in an SS combat unit known as the Wiking Division that saw action on the Russian front. In its June 1996 order, the district court specifically found Hammer's testimony incredible. The district court concluded that Hammer had obtained his U.S. citizenship by willful, material misrepresentation and concealment of his service as an armed concentration camp guard and prisoner escort. It ordered his certificate of naturalization revoked. Hammer did not appeal this order, though he was entitled to seek higher review.

In 1996, the government began deportation proceedings against Hammer under the Holtzman Amendment and corresponding statutory sections. These proceedings were administrative, rather than judicial, and were conducted by the Immigration and Naturalization Service (INS). The immigration judge held a hearing, during which the government introduced more than 2,000 pages of exhibits, including most of the evidence that it had presented at the denaturalization proceeding. Hammer presented two witnesses who had briefly known him in Europe, gave his own testimony, and introduced an unauthenticated document stating that ethnic Germans in Croatia—where he had been

Ferdinand Hammer was deported after officials determined that he had lied about his activities during World War II.
PIDGEON/AP/WIDE WORLD PHOTOS

born and had lived—were automatically drafted into the Waffen-SS.

In 1997, the immigration judge ruled that the doctrine of COLLATERAL ESTOPPEL barred Hammer from relitigating issues relating to his date of birth, wartime service, and the conditions at the concentration camps where he served. Under the doctrine of collateral estoppel, which is also referred to as issue preclusion, once an issue is actually and necessarily determined by a court, that determination is conclusive in later lawsuits based on a different cause of action involving a party to the prior litigation. A party, therefore, cannot relitigate issues between the same parties that have been settled in a previous court case. The immigration judge also conducted an independent review of the evidence submitted at the denaturalization proceeding, concluding that the government had proven by unequivocal, clear, and convincing evidence that Hammer had assisted in persecutions on the basis of race, religion, national origin, or political opinion. He, too, found Hammer's testimony to be inconsistent and incredible. For example, Hammer could not recall the name of the SS Wiking Division officer under whom he had supposedly served or the name of a single battle in which he alleged he had fought.

Hammer was initially ordered deported to Croatia, but Croatia would not accept him. The deportation order was amended to make Austria the country to which Hammer was to be deported. After his appeal to the Board of Immigration Appeals was dismissed, Hammer petitioned the Sixth Circuit Court of Appeals to overturn the deportation order.

The court's three-judge panel denied the petition, ruling unanimously that Hammer had provided no grounds for a reversal. The court agreed with the immigration judge that Hammer could not relitigate issues that he addressed during his denaturalization proceedings in federal district court. The court noted that the issues of when he was born, where and when he had served, and what had happened at the concentrations camps were "extensively litigated in the denaturalization proceeding." The government had presented documentary evidence showing that Hammer was an armed SS guard at Auschwitz and Sachsenhausen, and served as a guard on prisoner rail transports between Nazi concentration camps. Included in this evidence were Nazi-regime documents identifying Hammer by name, rank, and date of birth. The government also presented the testimony of an expert witness and two Auschwitz survivors to prove the nature of the concentration camp.

Hammer also alleged that under the Holtzman Amendment he could not be deported unless the government proved that he had personal involvement in specific atrocities at the concentration camps. The court rejected this argument. As a guard, Hammer had standing orders to shoot anyone who tried to escape. More than one million people were murdered based solely on their religion or ethnicity at the camps where he had stood guard. This was enough evidence to satisfy the Holtzman Amendment. The government did not need to provide eyewitness testimony about Hammer's specific conduct, and Hammer's deportation to Austria was upheld.

CROSS REFERENCES
Immigration; War Crimes

DISABLED PERSONS

Persons who have a physical or mental impairment that substantially limits one or more major life activities. Some laws also include in their definition of disabled persons those people who have a record of or are regarded as having such an impairment.

Albertson's, Inc. v. Kirkingburg

The U.S. Supreme Court, in *Albertson's, Inc. v. Kirkingburg*, 527 U.S. 555, 119 S.Ct. 2162, 144 L.Ed.2d 518 (1999), continued to clarify the employment discrimination provisions of the Americans with Disabilities Act (ADA), 42 U.S.C.A. § 12101 et seq. The Court ruled that an employer who requires as a job qualification that an employee meet a federal safety regulation does not have to justify enforcing the regulation solely because it may be waived in an individual case.

In April 1990, Albertson's, Inc., a grocery-store chain with supermarkets in several states, hired Hallie Kirkingburg as a truck driver based at its Portland, Oregon, warehouse. Kirkingburg had more than ten years driving experience and performed well when Albertson's transportation manager took him on a road test. Before starting work, Kirkingburg was examined to see if he met federal vision standards for commercial truck drivers. The U.S. Department of Transportation (DOT) is responsible for devising the standards for individuals who drive commercial vehicles in interstate commerce. Since 1971, the basic vision regulation required corrected distant visual acuity of at least 20/40 in each eye and a combined distant acuity of at least 20/40. Kirkingburg, however, suffered from amblyopia, an uncorrectable condition that left him with 20/200 vision in his left eye, making him almost blind in that eye. Despite Kirkingburg's condition, the doctor erroneously certified that he met the DOT's basic vision standard, and Albertson's hired him.

In December 1991, Kirkingburg injured himself on the job and took a leave of absence. Before returning to work in November 1992, he went for a further physical as required by the company. This time, the examining physician correctly assessed Kirkingburg's vision and explained that his eyesight did not meet the basic DOT standards. The physician told Kirkingburg that to be legally qualified to drive, DOT would have to issue him a waiver of its basic vision standards.

The DOT permitted waivers to applicants with deficient vision who had three years of recent experience driving a commercial vehicle and a clean driving record. A waiver applicant had to agree to have his vision checked annually for deterioration and to report certain information about his driving experience to the Federal Highway Administration—the agency within the DOT responsible for overseeing the motor carrier safety regulations. Kirkingburg applied for a waiver, but because he could not meet the basic DOT vision standard, Albertson's fired him from his job as a truck driver. In early 1993, after he had left Albertson's, Kirkingburg received a DOT waiver, but Albertson's refused to rehire him.

Kirkingburg sued Albertson's, claiming that firing him violated the ADA. Albertson's filed a motion with the federal district court requesting that the lawsuit be dismissed on the ground that Kirkingburg was not "otherwise qualified" to perform the job of truck driver with or without reasonable accommodation. The ADA prohibits employers from discriminating against a "qualified individual with a disability" because of that disability. A disability is defined as a condition that "substantially limits a major life activity." A qualified person is defined as one who can perform a job when given reasonable accommodation.

The district granted the motion, ruling that Albertson's had reasonably concluded that Kirkingburg was not qualified without an accommodation because he could not meet the basic DOT vision standards. The court held that giving Kirkingburg time to get a DOT waiver was not a required reasonable accommodation because the waiver program was "a flawed experiment that has not altered the DOT vision requirements." On appeal, the Ninth Circuit Court of Appeals reversed the district court. The appeals court rejected Albertson's new argument that Kirkingburg did not have a disability within the meaning of the ADA. Kirkingburg had presented "uncontroverted evidence" that his vision was effectively monocular and had demonstrated that the way he sees was significantly different from the way in which most people see. That difference in manner, the court held, was sufficient to establish disability.

The Ninth Circuit also ruled that Albertson's could not use compliance with the DOT regulation as the justification for its vision requirement because the waiver program, which Albertson's disregarded, was "a lawful and legitimate part of the DOT regulatory scheme." The court conceded that Albertson's was free to set a vision standard different from that mandated by the DOT but held that under the ADA, Albertson's would have to justify its independent standard as necessary to prevent "a direct threat to the health or safety of other individuals in the workplace."

The Supreme Court, in a unanimous decision, rejected the reasoning of the Ninth Circuit and reversed its decision. Justice DAVID H. SOUTER, writing for the Court, found that the appeals court had made three mistakes in determining whether Kirkingburg's amblyopia met the ADA's definition of disability. First, ADA regulations define "substantially limits" as requiring a significant "restriction" on performing a major life activity. The Ninth Circuit incorrectly found a disability based on a significant "difference" between the way Kirkingburg and the general population see. Second, the appeals court had failed to note that Kirkingburg's brain compensates for the visual impairment. The ADA requires, however, that mitigating circumstances be taken into account. Finally, the appeals court had not made its determination on a case-by-case basis, as required by the ADA. Instead, it had made general conclusions beyond the facts of Kirkingburg's impairment.

Justice Souter then focused on the effect of the DOT safety regulation and the waiver provision on Kirkingburg's ADA claim. He concluded that an employer who requires as a job qualification that an employee meet a federal safety regulation does not have to justify the regulation solely because its standard may be waived experimentally in an individual case. For the waiver program, however, there would have been no basis for questioning Albertson's decision to follow the DOT regulations. As to the waiver program, Justice Souter characterized it as "simply an experiment proposed as a means of obtaining data" that would inform the DOT whether the safety regulations could be relaxed on a permanent basis. The ADA did not have to be read to require Albertson's to defend its decision not to participate in the waiver program.

FCC Rules to Improve Telecommunications for Disabled Persons

In 1990 Congress enacted the Americans with Disabilities Act (ADA). At that time some 43 million Americans had one or more physical or mental disabilities. The ADA was intended to combat the many forms of discrimination that individuals with disabilities face. Congress understood that, at the time of the ADA's passage, individuals with disabilities had been relegated to receiving lesser services, programs, activities, benefits, jobs, and other opportunities. To eradicate these discrepancies, the Act sought to end blatant and intentional exclusion of individuals with disabilities in many areas including architecture, transportation, and education. In addition to these areas, Congress also intended to affect the communication arena. On July 15, 1999, the ADA received some much needed help with the adoption of the rules and policies implementing § 255 of the Telecommunications Act of 1996 ("1996 Act") and § 251(a)(2) of the Communications Act of 1934 ("1934 Act").

Section 255 of the 1996 Act requires that manufacturers of telecommunications equipment or customer premises equipment ensure that their equipment is designed, developed, and fabricated to be accessible to and usable by individuals with disabilities. Section 255 further requires that providers of telecommunications service ensure that their services are accessible to and usable by individuals with disabilities. Where either of these requirements is not readily achievable, the 1996 Act requires that all manufacturers and providers ensure that their equipment and services are compatible with existing peripheral devices or specialized customer premises equipment commonly used by individuals with disabilities to achieve access, if readily achievable. The amendments to the 1934 Act place an affirmative responsibility upon telecommunications carriers not to install network features, functions, or capabilities that do not comply with the guidelines and standards established pursuant to section 255.

Since the enactment of the ADA, it has been declared that the proper goals regarding individuals with disabilities are to assure them equality of opportunity, full participation, independent living, and economic self-sufficiency. The rules established to implement the 1996 and 1934 Acts will provide individuals with disabilities a more equivalent amount of access to services and products as compared to the average person. Thus, individuals with disabilities will have greater access to telephones, pagers, cellular phones, call-waiting, and operator assistance. Moreover, the regulations will offer people with disabilities more independence and opportunities for expression. For example, the Federal Communications Commission (FCC) voted 5–0 to establish a nationwide service allowing users to talk directly to specially trained operators who recognize certain speech patterns of individuals with disabilities. These operators, in turn, will relay communications to an individual on the other end of the phone line. The regulations assist Congress in achieving its goal of providing people with disabilities greater and simpler access to employment, emergency services, and education.

Though the ADA was the first federal statute addressing discrimination against persons with disabilities in everyday life, and was designed to outlaw discrimination in many areas, including telecommunications, it has fallen short in many respects. Arguably, where the ADA lacks in the telecommunications area, the recent regulations implementing the 1996 and

1934 Acts compensate. These mandates will undoubtedly spur innovation and creativity in telecommunication companies that have heretofore been resistant to providing obvious necessities for individuals with disabilities.

As Supreme Court Justice THURGOOD MARSHALL noted in his dissenting opinion in *City of Cleburne v. Cleburne Living Center* 473 U.S. 432, 467 (1985), for the disabled "much has changed in recent years, but much remains the same; out-dated statutes are still on the books, and irrational fears or ignorance, traceable to the prolonged social and cultural isolation of the [disabled], continue to stymie recognition of the dignity and individuality of [disabled] people." With improved communication comes the possibility of improved education. Indeed, providing services in the most integrated setting appropriate to the needs of qualified individuals with disabilities will undoubtedly enlighten otherwise ignorant Americans as to the existence of our nation's invisible minority. It is this exposure and experience, on the part of mass of society, that might eliminate exclusion on the basis of disability. The FCC lauds its most recent attempt at improving telecommunication products and services as "the most significant opportunity for people with disabilities since the passage of the Americans with Disabilities Act."

Murphy v. United Parcel Service, Inc.

In *Murphy v. United Parcel Service, Inc.*, ___U.S.___, 119 S.Ct. 2133, 144 L.Ed.2d 484 (1999), the U.S. Supreme Court examined whether an employee could qualify as disabled under the Americans with Disabilities Act (ADA), 42 U.S.C.A. § 12101 et seq., for having high blood pressure that could be controlled with medication. The Court concluded that the employee's high blood pressure did not substantially limit his major life activities when he was medicated. The Court also found that the employee was not regarded as disabled by his employer despite the fact that the employer discharged the employee for failing to meet a federal health certification requirement. As in *Sutton v. United Airlines, Inc.*, ___U.S.___, 119 S.Ct. 2139, 144 L.Ed.2d 450 (1999), the Supreme Court made clear it would not expand the coverage of ADA to individuals who can take measures to correct the physical or mental impairment.

Vaughn Murphy was first diagnosed with hypertension (high blood pressure) when he was ten years old. With medication, however, Murphy's high blood pressure did not significantly restrict his activities and he functioned without problems while engaging in normal activities. In August 1994, United Parcel Service, Inc. (UPS) hired Murphy as a mechanic, a position that required him to drive commercial motor vehicles. Driving a commercial motor vehicle was an essential function of the mechanic's job at UPS. To drive such vehicles, however, Murphy had to satisfy health requirements imposed by the U.S. Department of Transportation (DOT). Under DOT regulations a person cannot drive a commercial motor vehicle unless the person is physically qualified to do so. The driver must obtain a medical examiner's certificate that states he or she is physically qualified to drive a commercial motor vehicle. One of the requirements is that the driver have "no current clinical diagnosis of high blood pressure likely to interfere with his/her ability to operate a commercial vehicle safely." 49 C.F.R. § 391.41(b)(6).

When UPS hired Murphy, his blood pressure was so high that he was not qualified for DOT health certification. Murphy was mistakenly granted certification, though, and he started work. A month later, a UPS medical supervisor discovered the error and requested that Murphy have his blood pressure retested. When the retest disclosed that Murphy's blood pressure remained high, UPS fired him on the grounds his blood pressure exceeded the DOT's requirements for drivers of commercial motor vehicles.

Murphy sued under Title I of the ADA in federal district court but the court granted UPS's request that the case be dismissed. The court held that, to determine whether Murphy was disabled under the ADA, his "impairment should be evaluated in its medicated state." It noted that when Murphy was medicated he could not lift heavy objects but otherwise functioned normally. Therefore, the court concluded that Murphy was not disabled under the ADA. The court also rejected Murphy's claim that he was "regarded as" disabled; it held that UPS did not regard Murphy as disabled, "only that he was not certifiable under DOT regulations." The Tenth Circuit Court of Appeals affirmed the district court.

The U.S. Supreme Court, on a 7–2 vote, affirmed the Tenth Circuit decision. Justice SANDRA DAY O'CONNOR, in her majority opinion, followed the same analysis set out in *Sutton*. O'Connor first stated that the determination of disability for Murphy must be made "with reference to the mitigating measures he employs." When medicated, Murphy's high blood pressure did not substantially limit him in any major life activity.

A second issue involved whether UPS regarded Murphy as disabled because of his high blood pressure. Justice O'Connor concluded that a person is "regarded as" disabled within the meaning of the ADA "if a covered entity mistakenly believes that the person's actual, nonlimiting impairment substantially limits one or more major life activities." Murphy had alleged that the manager who fired him stated that it was due to his hypertension; therefore, UPS believed that his high blood pressure substantially limited his ability to work. UPS, however, argued that it did not regard Murphy as substantially limited in the major life activity of working, but regarded him as unqualified to work as a UPS mechanic because he was unable to obtain the DOT health certification. Justice O'Connor sided with UPS, finding that UPS regarded him as unable to meet the DOT regulations. O'Connor pointed out that Murphy was only unable to perform mechanical repair work where driving a commercial vehicle was required. He was still generally employable as a mechanic and had, in fact, found a mechanic's job shortly after leaving UPS. In light of Murphy's skills and the "array of jobs" available to him, he was not regarded by employers as being unable to perform a class of jobs.

Justice JOHN PAUL STEVENS, in a dissenting opinion joined by Justice STEPHEN G. BREYER, concluded that Murphy had a disability within the meaning of the ADA. Without medication, Murphy would likely have to be hospitalized. Such severe hypertension "easily falls within the ADA's nucleus of covered impairments."

Olmstead v. L.C.

Title II of the Americans with Disabilities Act (ADA) prohibits discrimination in providing public services. 42 U.S.C.A. § 12132. Title II is aimed at providers of public transportation, including commuter railroads, passenger trains, bus services, and taxi services. However, Title II also is aimed at making state and local governments "mainstream" persons with disabilities who are under their supervision. When choosing a method of providing program access, a public entity must give priority to the one that results in the most integrated setting appropriate to encourage interaction among all users, including individuals with disabilities.

The U.S. Supreme Court examined Title II's requirements for the first time in *Olmstead v. L.C.*, ___ U.S. ___, 119 S.Ct. 2176, 144 L.Ed.2d 540 (1999). Two women housed in a psychiatric unit in a Georgia hospital sought to enter community-based programs. When the state refused to provide community placement, they sued under Title II. The Supreme Court ruled that states are required to place persons with mental disabilities in community settings rather than in state institutions. Though the Court affirmed Title II's goal of mainstreaming, it also recognized that states have to balance the needs of all the people under their care and make decisions on a case-by-case basis.

The case arose out the treatment of L.C. and E.W., two mentally retarded women with psychiatric disorders. Both women were voluntarily admitted to Georgia Regional Hospital at Atlanta (GRH), where they were confined for treatment in a psychiatric unit. Although their treatment professionals eventually concluded that each of the women could be cared for appropriately in a community-based program, the women remained institutionalized at GRH. L.C. and E.W. filed suit against the Georgia Department of Human Resources under the federal civil rights law 42 U.S.C. § 983 and Title II, seeking placement in community care. They alleged that the State violated Title II in failing to place them in a community-based program once professionals treating them determined that such placement was appropriate.

The federal district court ordered their placement in an appropriate community-based treatment program. In doing so, the court rejected Georgia's argument that inadequate funding—not discrimination against L.C. and E.W.—accounted for their retention at GRH. The court concluded that, under Title II, unnecessary institutional segregation constituted discrimination *per se*, which could not be justified by a lack of funding. The court also rejected the State's defense that requiring immediate transfers in such cases would "fundamentally alter" the State's programs. The Eleventh Circuit Court of Appeals affirmed the ruling, but ordered the district court to reassess the State's cost-based defense. The appeals court read the statute and regulations as allowing that defense but only in very limited circumstances. Therefore, the Eleventh Circuit instructed the district court to consider, as a key factor, whether the additional cost for treatment of L.C. and E.W. in community-based care would be unreasonable given the demands of Georgia's mental health budget. The state of Georgia then appealed to the Supreme Court.

By a 6–3 vote, the Supreme Court held that Title II of the ADA requires community placement of mentally disabled persons whenever appropriate. Justice RUTH BADER GINSBURG, writing for the Court, stated that such an action "is in order when the state's treatment professionals have determined that community placement is appropriate, the transfer from institutional care to a less restrictive setting is not opposed by the affected individual, and the placement can be reasonably accommodated, taking into account the resources available to the state and the needs of others with mental disabilities."

The Court agreed that Congress believed community placement is desirable and that segregation of persons with disabilities is a form of discrimination. Unjustified segregation of individuals who can benefit from community settings "perpetuates unwarranted assumptions that persons so isolated are incapable or unworthy of participating in community life." In addition, Justice Ginsburg found that institutional confinement "severely diminishes individuals' everyday life activities." Nevertheless, Ginsburg warned that nothing in the ADA or its regulations condoned the "termination of institutional settings for persons unable to handle or benefit from community settings." In this case, however, L.C. and E.W. were qualified for community placement.

Justice Ginsburg limited the scope of the ruling by concluding that a state's responsibility, once it provides community-based treatment to qualified persons with disabilities, is "not boundless." The Court recognized, as did the Eleventh Circuit, that states "can resist modifications that would fundamentally alter the nature of their services and programs." Justice Ginsburg concluded, however, that Georgia must have "more leeway" than either the Eleventh Circuit or the district court believed appropriate. For example, if Georgia could show that its waiting list for community care moved "at a reasonable pace" not controlled by its desire to keep institutions fully populated, then it could justify denying L.C. and E.W. community placement until they moved to the head of the list. Therefore, the Court remanded the case to the Eleventh Circuit, directing it to reexamine the appropriate relief for the two women, "given the range of facilities the State maintains for the care and treatment of persons with diverse mental disabilities, and its obligation to administer services with an even hand."

Justice CLARENCE THOMAS filed a dissenting opinion, which Chief Justice WILLIAM H. REHNQUIST and Justice ANTONIN SCALIA joined. Justice Thomas contended that temporary exclusion from community placement does not amount to discrimination "in the traditional sense of the word." In his view, L.C. and E.W. were not singled out for discriminatory treatment based on their disabilities.

Sutton v. United Airlines, Inc.

The Americans with Disabilities Act of 1990 (ADA) was a landmark piece of legislation, giving persons with disabilities legal protections against employment discrimination. 42 U.S.C.A. § 12101 et seq. Titles I and II of the ADA prohibit employers, employment agencies, labor organizations, and joint labor-management committees, in the private sector and in state and local governments, from discriminating because of disability. The act covers private employers with fifteen or more employees. All state and local government employers are covered, regardless of their number of employees. Because of the breadth and complexity of its provisions, the federal courts have begun to examine the ADA's application to claims of employment discrimination.

The U.S. Supreme Court, in *Sutton v. United Airlines, Inc.*, ___U.S.___, 119 S.Ct. 2139, 144 L.Ed.2d 450 (1999), placed a significant limitation on the scope of the ADA's coverage. The Court excluded more than 120 million persons in the United States from the law, ruling that the ADA generally does not cover people with poor eyesight or other correctable conditions. It concluded that persons with visual impairment who can correct the impairment by

Elaine Wilson and Lois Curtis are at the center of a case to decide how government care best attends to the needs of mentally disabled patients.
BAZEMORE/AP/WIDE WORLD PHOTOS

wearing eyeglasses or contact lenses are not disabled under the ADA.

The case arose when twin sisters Karen Sutton and Kimberly Hinton applied in 1992 to work as commercial airline pilots for United Airlines. They met United's basic age, experience, and Federal Aviation Agency (FAA) certification qualifications. United invited them to an interview and to flight simulator tests. During the interviews, however, they were informed that a mistake had been made in inviting them to the interviews. United told them that they did not meet the company's minimum vision requirement, which was uncorrected visual acuity of 20/100 or better. Therefore, United terminated the interviews and did not offer positions to Sutton and Hinton.

Both sisters had severe myopia, with uncorrected visual acuity of 20/200 or worse in their right eyes and 20/400 or worse in their left eyes. However, with the use of corrective lenses each woman had vision of 20/20 or better. Without corrective lenses, they could not conduct activities such as driving a car, watching television, or shopping in public stores. With eyeglasses or contact lenses they could function identically to individuals without a similar impairment.

Based on United's reason for rejecting their applications, Sutton and Hinton filed an ADA disability discrimination lawsuit in federal court against the airline. They alleged that due to their severe myopia they had a substantially limiting impairment or were regarded as having such an impairment, thus qualifying them as disabled under the ADA. The district court dismissed their action, concluding that because the sisters could fully correct their visual impairments, they were not substantially limited in any major life activity as required by the ADA. Without such a substantial limitation they could not claim that they were disabled within the meaning of the law. The court also found no evidence that the women were regarded by United as having an impairment that substantially limited a major life activity. United had only regarded them as unable to satisfy the requirements for the particular job of global airline pilot. The sisters appealed the dismissal but the Tenth Circuit Court of Appeals affirmed the decision on similar grounds.

The U.S. Supreme Court, in a 7–2 decision, agreed with the lower courts. Justice SANDRA DAY O'CONNOR, writing for the majority, stated that the determination of whether an individual is protected by the ADA "should be made with reference to measures that mitigate the individual's impairment, including, in this instance, eyeglasses and contact lenses." In reviewing the applicable provisions of the ADA, Justice O'Connor concluded that a disability exists only where an impairment "substantially limits" a major life activity, not where it "might," "could" or "would" be "substantially limiting if corrective measures were not taken." Second, Justice O'Connor noted that the question of whether a person has a disability under the ADA was an "individualized inquiry." The federal government's position that a person be judged in their uncorrected or unmitigated status ran counter to this mandated individualized inquiry.

Justice O'Connor also looked at the Congressional findings that supported the ADA provisions. Congress found that 43 million Americans have one or more physical or mental disabilities, yet the number would swell to over 160 million people if Congress had intended to include everyone with a correctable impairment. Therefore, the 43 million number "reflects an understanding that those whose impairments are largely corrected by medication or other devices are not 'disabled' within the meaning of the ADA."

The Court also rejected the sisters' contention that United Airlines regarded them as disabled. Justice O'Connor stated that such claims are protected under the act when an "employer *mistakenly* believes that an individual has a substantial limiting requirement." The sisters argued that United's vision requirement was based on myth and stereotype and that United mistakenly believed they were unable to work as global airline pilots. O'Connor noted that the ADA allows employers to prefer some physical attributes to others, "so long as those attributes do not rise to the level of substantially limiting impairments." In this case, United was entitled to prefer persons who met a minimum uncorrected vision requirement. Moreover, Sutton and Hinton were ineligible for just the global airline pilot position. They were qualified to work as regional pilots or pilot instructors. Therefore, they could not claim that they were restricted from a broad class of jobs.

Justice JOHN PAUL STEVENS, the only member of the Court with a pilot's license, filed a dissenting opinion that Justice STEPHEN G. BREYER joined. Justice Stevens accused the majority of having "crabbed vision" and adopting a "miserly construction of the law."

CROSS REFERENCES
Civil Rights; Employment Law; Telecommunications

DNA EVIDENCE

Unnamed Rape Suspects Identified by DNA

Science outpaced the law in 2000 as prosecutors in Milwaukee and New York City used DNA profiles to stop unsolved RAPE cases from expiring under STATUTES OF LIMITATIONS. In Milwaukee in October 1999, Assistant District Attorney Norman Gahn filed an arrest warrant for an unnamed man who raped a seven-year-old girl in an alley in 1993. In New York in March 2000, Manhattan prosecutors indicted an unnamed serial criminal known as the East Side rapist for three rapes committed between 1995 and 1997.

DNA fingerprinting has made this creative legal maneuver possible. DNA, shorthand for deoxyribonucleic acid, is the component of human chromosomes that transfers genetic information. In 1984 British geneticist Alec Jeffreys discovered that each person has a virtually unique DNA sequence. Scientists can identify a criminal's DNA sequence using semen, blood, skin, or hair samples taken from victims and crime scenes. If investigators can match the sequence to that of a known person, they have a high degree of certainty that they have pinpointed the right suspect.

That is where time becomes an enemy. Most states have a statute of limitations that requires prosecutors to file rape cases within certain time limits. In Wisconsin the limit is six years, while in New York it is five. Matching a DNA profile with a known person means using the FEDERAL BUREAU OF INVESTIGATION's newly-created Combined DNA Index System, or Codis. Codis, however, links the DNA databases of only twenty-two states, and those databases only contain DNA profiles for some convicted felons. Typically, if the statutory time limit passes before investigators find a match, the case cannot be prosecuted.

Assistant District Attorney Gahn decided not to let that happen. DNA profiles suggest that one man is responsible for three unsolved rapes in Milwaukee in 1993. After the statute expired for the first two, Gahn filed an arrest warrant for the one involving the seven-year-old girl. Under Wisconsin law, an arrest warrant must contain a name or other description identifying the person to be arrested with "reasonable certainty." Gahn filed a warrant that identifies the assailant as "John Doe, unknown male, with matching deoxyribonucleic acid [DNA] at genetic locations D2S44, D4S139, D5S110, D10S28, D1S7 and D17S79." According to Gahn, "genetic code goes well beyond reasonable certainty."

Manhattan District Attorney Robert Morgenthau agrees. In March 2000 Morgenthau announced the indictment of the East Side rapist, who purportedly has attacked sixteen women. The indictment charged three rapes, and Morgenthau expected another indictment for a fourth rape for which investigators have a DNA profile. While prosecutor Ty Kaufman in McPherson County, Kansas, used a DNA profile in an arrest warrant in 1991, Manhattan appeared to be the first jurisdiction to indict a criminal identified solely by his DNA.

Whether the legal tactic will work is uncertain. Investigators have not yet found a match for the DNA profiles in McPherson County, Milwaukee, or New York City. When they do, defense lawyers are likely to say that DNA profiles cannot stop the statute of limitations from expiring. According to Susan Hendricks, deputy attorney for the criminal defense division of the Legal Aid Society, DNA evidence is not foolproof. Hendricks says that as time passes and the statute of limitations expires, evidence that could exonerate a defendant disappears. Using only DNA profiles to identify rapists at that point might be inaccurate and unfair. Prosecutors will respond by saying DNA evidence is about as reliable as evidence gets. According to Morgenthau, the chance that another person has the same DNA profile as the East Side rapist is 1 in 240 billion.

Whatever the result of this legal issue, it already has sparked reform across the country. Investigators are calling for increased funding for various projects. Twenty-eight states remain unconnected to Codis, a system that will require $500 million to put in order. The nation needs more laboratories to construct DNA profiles from the estimated 500,000 crime scene samples that sit untested in police departments and to collect DNA samples from the one million convicts who should have given DNA samples but have not.

Meanwhile, lawmakers are considering two major reforms. One would require a greater pool of criminals to give DNA samples for entry into state databases. For example, Wisconsin collects DNA samples only from convicted sexual offenders. The legislature is considering a law to require all convicted felons to give DNA samples, as Alabama and Virginia do. Governor George E. Pataki of New York has proposed to collect DNA from people convicted of all crimes, including MISDEMEANORS.

In light of the reliability of DNA evidence, lawmakers also are considering legislation to eliminate the statute of limitations in rape cases. Florida, Nevada, and New Jersey already have done so. California is considering a law to replace its six-year limit with a limit of one year to file charges after a rapist is identified by a DNA test. New York is considering a law to eliminate time limits entirely for rape and fifteen other felonies.

According to Governor Pataki, "There should be no statute of limitation that allows a violent offender to walk away scot-free after five years, while the victim is still languishing in emotional pain." A 38-year-old New York woman who was raped in the early 1980s agreed, saying, "Other than murder there is no worse thing that someone can do to you than rape."

Civil libertarians, however, were concerned about these reforms. Some thought it would be unfair to force defendants to fight old cases in which exculpatory evidence had disappeared. Others said collecting DNA from entire groups of people violates the FOURTH AMENDMENT, which forbids unreasonable searches and seizures. Some warned that DNA collection could lead to routine DNA profiling in hospitals after birth. The end result could be discrimination based on DNA, which might reveal information about intelligence, longevity, or other personal characteristics.

CROSS REFERENCES
Statute of Limitations

DRUGS AND NARCOTICS

Drugs are articles intended for use in the diagnosis, cure, mitigation, treatment, or prevention of disease in humans or animals, and any articles other than food intended to affect the mental or body function of humans or animals. *Narcotics* are any drugs that dull the senses and commonly become addictive after prolonged use.

Juan Raul Garza: First Federal Execution Since 1963

On May 26, 2000, U.S. District Court Judge Filemon Vela scheduled an execution date for convicted killer Juan Raul Garza. He will be the first federal prisoner to be executed in almost forty years. The last federal execution was in 1963, when Victor Feguer was hanged for kidnapping and murdering a physician. All of Garza's appeals have been exhausted, and President BILL CLINTON has refused to grant CLEMENCY. Garza is slated to die by lethal injection August 5, 2000.

Garza's crimes are despicable but not notable. He is a convicted drug smuggler responsible for three MURDERS in Brownsville, Texas, all of which were drug related. He was also convicted of several other drug-related offenses, including money laundering and, for ten years, running a marijuana pipeline from Mexico to Louisiana and Michigan.

Under Texas state law, first degree murder is a capital offense. Garza was convicted in federal court under the Anti-Drug Abuse Act of 1988, which imposes a maximum penalty of CAPITAL PUNISHMENT for any murder resulting from large-scale illegal drug dealing. The act is often referred to as the drug-kingpin law. In 1994 Congress expanded the act to include more than sixty federal crimes now punishable by death, including use of a weapon of mass destruction, murder for hire, car jackings, fatal drive-by shootings, and sexual abuse.

In 1972 the U.S. Supreme Court ruled that state capital punishment laws, as written, were unconstitutional. Many persons believe the Supreme Court had ruled that capital punishment *per se* was unconstitutional, and then reversed itself in a later 1976 case. In fact the Supreme Court struck down state death penalty laws in 1972 because it found that they were random and aleatory in their application and effect. When state legislators rewrote the laws several years later, they withstood constitutional challenge and were upheld by the Supreme Court. However, the effect of the Supreme Court's 1972 ruling was that for several years, no executions took place, either under state or federal law. In fact, Congress did not rewrite the federal death penalty law until 1988.

Garza is one of twenty prisoners, all male, on federal death-row. All twenty have committed HOMICIDE in the act of some other federal crime: drug crime, KIDNAPPING, ROBBERY, witness killing, and killing a federal officer. Until 1999 no federal death row prison existed, and those sentenced to death under federal law were imprisoned and executed in the state where the trial was held. In the summer of 1999, the Bureau of Prisons established a fifty-cell federal death row unit in Terre Haute, Indiana, which now houses Garza and the others, including convicted Oklahoma City bomber Timothy McVeigh. Garza is the first inmate there to exhaust all his appeals and be scheduled for execution.

Sammy "The Bull" Gravano Charged with Drug Dealing

Salvatore "Sammy the Bull" Gravano allegedly was New York Gambino mobster John J. Gotti's second in command. In 1991 and 1992, he testified against Gotti and thirty-seven other mob members in New York's federal district court, in return for a sentence reduction and protection under the federal Witness Protection Program (WPP). Gravano was not prosecuted for the role he played in nineteen gangster murders. His boss, John Gotti, was convicted in 1992 and is now serving a life sentence for RACKETEERING and MURDER. Gravano, on the other hand, served five years in jail on the federal racketeering charges and was released in 1995. Upon his release, Gravano entered the WPP.

The Federal Witness Security Program, commonly called the Witness Protection Program, is administered by the U.S. Marshals Office. It has accommodated more than 6,700 witnesses since its inception in 1970, not including dependants or family members. The Witness Security Reform Act of 1984 expanded the program to cover "other serious offenses" outside of organized criminal activity, and established a victim compensation fund. Statistically, the government reports a conviction rate of eighty-nine percent in cases involving protected witness testimony.

Under the auspices of the WPP, Gravano underwent facial plastic surgery to change his identifying appearance, changed his name to Jimmy Moran, and moved to suburban Tempe, Arizona. There, notwithstanding an alleged $1 million bounty placed on his head by the Mafia, Gravano took up with the local lifestyle. He bought a sprawling ranch, opened a legitimate swimming pool installation company, and set his ex-wife up as owner of a small Italian restaurant in Scottsdale. His daughter Karen and son Gerard also joined him in Arizona and became employees in the family businesses.

Despite his protection under the WPP, Gravano reveled in his past, and enjoyed engaging in conversations with anyone who would listen to stories of his notorious history. In fact, shortly after being relocated to Phoenix, he partially left the WPP, finding it too cumbersome for his lifestyle. He retained the physical protective services of federal marshals under the program, but little else.

Gravano was in court on March 6, 2000, facing drug charges after years in the federal Witness Protection Program.
GING/AP/WIDE WORLD PHOTOS

No longer seeking to hide his identity, Gravano engaged in a controversial book deal about his mobster life, called *Underboss*, with writer Peter Maas. In 1997, the New York Crime Victim's Board sued Gravano, Maas, and publisher HarperCollins under New York's "Son-of-Sam Law," which was enacted to prevent criminals from profiting on the sale of stories or other "expressions" of their crimes to the public. The law requires any income derived for such "expressions" to be turned over to the New York State Crime Victim's Board to be paid to victims' families. Enraged by the rise of his book to the best-seller list, the daughter of one of Gravano's murder victims, Laura Garofalo, then filed a $50 million suit against him for the WRONGFUL DEATH of her father. Several other victims' suits followed, but lawyers for the plaintiffs were unable to serve process upon Gravano, who was physically protected from service by federal authorities under WPP. The suit brought by the Crime Victim's Board was dismissed by the New York State Appellate Division, essentially ruling that the statute was inapplicable to the type of crime Gravano pleaded guilty to—racketeering.

What Gravano apparently did not appreciate, however, was that he could be prosecuted for future crimes. In fact, federal DRUG ENFORCEMENT AGENCY officers and local police had been surveilling Gravano and intercepting telephone conversations for several months. This followed tips from local gangs that

Gravano's name was dropped to competing drug suppliers in order to intimidate them.

On February 24, 2000, Gravano, his ex-wife Debra, his son Gerard, his daughter Karen, her fiancé David Seabrook, and about forty others were arrested in a massive drug-dealing CONSPIRACY to route and supply the drug known as Ecstasy to area teens and rave dance clubs. At its height, the drug ring was selling about 10,000 pills per week and earning about $1 million per month.

Gravano and his family originally were arrested on a single count of conspiracy to distribute illegal drugs. Review of evidence obtained mostly through the WIRETAPPING of more than 16,000 conversations, in conjunction with police surveillance, resulted in the filing of a 181-count complaint against them. The charges, filed by Arizona Attorney General Janet Napolitano, include racketeering, conspiracy, money laundering, possession of dangerous drugs for sale, illegal enterprise, and participation in a criminal syndicate. Four of the charges are felonies carrying maximum twelve-year sentences even if the convicted has no prior convictions.

Gravano's son Gerard and family friend Michael Papa face serious charges for actual drug-dealing in conjunction with their involvement in local Phoenix gang activity. Papa, a premed student on the dean's list at Arizona State University, allegedly utilized former high school friends to distribute the drugs. Gravano's charges focus more on his role in masterminding and financing the drug ring.

Gravano and his immediate family pleaded not guilty to all charges on March 13, 2000. Held in the Maricopa County Jail on a $5 million cash bond, Gravano told court officers that New York law enforcement agents have promised to testify in his behalf for release on bail. As of July 2000, that has not happened.

CROSS REFERENCES
Capital Punishment; Protective Custody

ELECTIONS

The process of voting to decide a public question or to select one person from a designated group to perform certain obligations in a government, corporation, or society.

Gutierrez v. Ada

Election laws provide the rules for conducting elections and for determining what proportion of votes will decide who will be declared the winner for public office. In most cases involving the election of public officials, a simple majority of the votes cast for a specific office will suffice. Some states, however, require a runoff election when a race of three or more candidates prevents one candidate from winning more than 50 percent of the total votes cast for the office. The top two candidates participate in the runoff election, with one candidate reaching the required percentage needed to win.

The U.S. Supreme Court faced a similar issue involving just two slates of candidates in *Gutierrez v. Ada*, 528 U.S. ___, 120 S.Ct. 740, 145 L.Ed.2d 747 (2000). The Court had to determine whether a federal election law governing the territory of Guam required a governor and lieutenant governor to be elected by a majority of the voters who voted in this contest, or whether the successful slate needed to attain a majority of the total number of ballots that voters cast. The Court concluded that a simple majority of those who voted for governor and lieutenant governor was sufficient, overturning the lower federal courts' decisions that Guam should conduct a runoff election.

In the November 3, 1998, Guam general election, Carl T.C. Gutierrez and Madeleine Z. Bordallo were candidates running on one slate for Governor and Lieutenant Governor. They were opposed by the slate of Joseph F. Ada and Felix P. Camacho. Gutierrez received 24,250 votes, as against 21,200 for Ada. In addition, 1,294 voted for write-in candidates and 609 voted for both slates. Most importantly, 1,313 persons who cast ballots did not vote for either slate or any write-in candidate. Therefore, the total number of ballots cast in the general election was 48,666, and the Gutierrez slate's votes represented only 49.83 percent of that total. The Guam Election Commission certified the Gutierrez slate as the winner, finding it had received 51.21 percent of the vote, as calculated by deducting the 1,313 ballots left blank as to the gubernatorial election from the total number of ballots cast. Ada and Camacho sued in federal district court, asking the court to order a runoff election. They contended that Gutierrez and Bordallo had not received a majority of the votes cast, as required by the Organic Act of Guam, 48 U.S.C.A. § 1422.

The federal district court agreed with Ada and Camacho and ordered the runoff election. The Ninth Circuit Court of Appeals affirmed this decision, concluding that the territorial law required more votes than just a simple majority of those who actually voted for governor.

The Supreme Court, in a unanimous decision, disagreed with the lower courts and reversed the decision, thereby validating the election of Gutierrez and Ada. Justice DAVID H. SOUTER, writing for the Court, based the entire decision on a close reading of § 1422. This type of analysis, called statutory interpretation, employs various "rules of interpretation" to determine what the legislators meant when they passed the law.

In this case, Justice David H. Souter employed "plain meaning" rules of interpretation. The use of plain meaning analysis confines the Court to looking at how the words relate to each other on the page rather than reading legislative debates and inferring legislative intent. Ada and Camacho had argued that in § 1422 the phrase "majority of votes cast in any election" required that a slate of candidates for governor and lieutenant governor receive a majority of the total number of ballots cast in the general election, regardless of the number of votes for all gubernatorial slates by those casting ballots. Justice Souter rejected this analysis and concluded that the phrase refers "only to votes cast for gubernatorial slates." He found that the key to understanding the statute was the phrase "in any election." This phrase was used six times in § 1422, which clearly was written to deal with the election of the governor and lieutenant governor, not any other election. In this context, the majority vote requirement was based on the ballots of those who actually voted for a slate of candidates.

Justice Souter concluded that to rule otherwise would "impute to the Congress a strange preference for making it hard to select a Governor." The "unreality" of requiring a runoff election when one slate received a majority of "all those who cared to make any choice among gubernatorial candidates" made no sense. Moreover, another provision of the law permitted recall elections of the governor and lieutenant governor. Justice Souter noted that the recall provision looked at the total number of persons who actually voted for governor, not the total number who went to the polls. Thus, in a "rational world, we would not expect the vote required to oust a Governor to be pegged to a lower number than it would take to elect one."

Nixon v. Shrink Missouri Government PAC

Campaign financing has been a controversial topic in U.S. politics since the early 1970s. Allegations that large contributions by individuals corrupted the political system during the administration of President RICHARD NIXON led to a federal law that capped individual contributions at $1,000 per political candidate and placed restrictions on how much a candidate could spend on his or her campaign. Although the Supreme Court ruled in *Buckley v. Valeo*, 424 U.S. 1, 96 S.Ct. 612, 46 L.Ed.2d 659 (1976), that the limitation on how much candidates could spend was an unconstitutional restriction on free speech, it did uphold the cap on individual contributions. In the intervening years, almost two-thirds of the states have adopted similar measures that limit the amount of political contributions.

The Supreme Court was called upon in *Nixon v. Shrink Missouri Government PAC*, ___ U.S. ___, 120 S.Ct. 897, 145 L.Ed.2d 886 (2000), to examine a 1994 Missouri campaign finance law. The court ruled that state caps on political contributions did not violate the free speech rights of political candidates, political organizations, and private citizens. In so ruling, the court seemingly signaled to Congressional champions of new campaign finance reform that it is not hostile to restricting the potentially corruptive role of money.

In 1994, Missouri enacted a law that imposes limits ranging from $275 to $1,075 on contributions to candidates for state offices. Mo. Rev. Stat. § 130.032. The law was challenged by Zev David Fredman, an unsuccessful candidate for the 1998 Republican nomination for Missouri state auditor, and Shrink Missouri Government PAC, a group that wished to donate more money to Fredman than the law allowed. Fredman and the PAC filed suit in federal district court, alleging that the law violated the FIRST and FOURTEENTH AMENDMENTS. The PAC argued that it wished to contribute more money and Fredman contended that he needed more contributions than the law allowed in order to campaign effectively. The district court upheld the statute, but the Eighth Circuit Court of Appeals overturned it, applying a strict scrutiny test that required Missouri to show it had a compelling interest and that the contribution limits were narrowly drawn to serve that interest. The appeals court found that Missouri's claim that the law was needed to avoid corruption or the perception of corruption was not compelling.

On a 6–3 vote, the Supreme Court reversed the Eighth Circuit and upheld the Missouri statute. Justice DAVID H. SOUTER, writing for the majority, took issue with the strict scrutiny test applied by the appeals court. He noted that in *Buckley v. Valeo* the Court had referred generally to the "exacting scrutiny required by the First Amendment." The decision clearly allowed a lower justification than restrictions on expenditures. Therefore, under that decision, the standard involving the regulation of contributions required Missouri to show that the contribution limitation was closely drawn to match a "sufficiently important interest." Moreover, Souter pointed out that in *Buckley* the Court found that the prevention of corruption and the appearance of corruption were constitutionally sufficient justifications for the contribution limits.

Turning to the Missouri law, Justice Souter concluded that Missouri had espoused the same interests of preventing corruption and the appearance of it. Fredman and the PAC had argued that Missouri had failed to justify these concerns with empirical evidence of actual corrupt practices or of a perception by Missouri voters that the unrestricted contributions would exert a corrosive influence. In their eyes the law was based on sheer conjecture. Souter rejected this argument, finding that there was enough evidence in the legislative record to support the need for the law. He noted that "there is little reason to doubt that sometimes large contributions will work actual corruption of our political system and no reason to question the existence of a corresponding suspicion among voters."

Because the limitations imposed by Missouri were similar to those upheld in *Buckley*, the majority agreed that the law was tailored to meet its purpose. In addition, there was no evidence that the limits had produced a dramatic adverse effect on the funding of campaigns or political associations, or that candidates could not amass sufficient funds to run effective campaigns. Finally, the Court rejected the idea that the maximum amounts, which were close to the same amount allowed in 1976 in *Buckley*, should be adjusted upward for inflation. Justice Souter concluded that the Court had never set a constitutional minimum amount.

Justice ANTHONY M. KENNEDY wrote a vigorous dissenting opinion, which was joined by Justices ANTONIN SCALIA and CLARENCE THOMAS. Justice Kennedy challenged the majority, calling its legal reasoning weak and an affront to the First Amendment. He contended that the Missouri limits suppressed political speech and that the Court's decision "has lasting consequences for political speech in the course of elections, the speech upon which democracy rests." Kennedy pointed out that the *Buckley* decision had introduced "covert speech," driving "political speech underground as contributors and candidates devise even more elaborate methods of avoiding contribution limits, limits which take no account of rising campaign costs."

Missouri's Attorney General Jay Nixon discusses the Supreme Court's ruling on January 24, 2000.
BUTKUS/AP/WIDE WORLD PHOTOS

CROSS REFERENCES
First Amendment; Voting Rights

EMPLOYMENT LAW

The body of law that governs the employer-employee relationship, including individual employment contracts, the application of TORT and CONTRACT doctrines, and a large group of statutory regulation on issues such as the right to organize and negotiate COLLECTIVE BARGAINING AGREEMENTS, protection from DISCRIMINATION, wages and hours, and health and safety.

Executive Order to Ban Genetic Discrimination

Wary of abuses that may result from advances in genetic testing, President BILL CLINTON issued an executive order in February 2000 prohibiting the federal government from using genetic test results to discriminate against its employees. Executive Order No. 13145; and genetic discrimination, 65 FR 6877, affects the jobs of nearly 2 million federal workers. Clinton also urged Congress to pass a similar law covering workers in the private sector.

Clinton's executive act was largely in response to the Human Genome Project, a $250 million public project whose goal is to determine the exact chemical sequence contained in human DNA. A genome is the totality of DNA that exists in the cells of a species. With the

President Clinton signs executive order No. 13145 on February 8, 2000.
WALSH/AP/WIDE WORLD PHOTOS

exception of red blood cells, every cell in every human body contains a copy of the same DNA. Within DNA is a code, or sequence, of the molecules adenine, cytosine, guanine, and thymine. These molecules, grouped in sets of three, instruct human cells to perform certain functions. Some cells work to produce enzymes to digest food; other cells manufacture growth hormones; other cells release chemicals into the brain to alter mood. Scientists working on the Human Genome Project tracked the sequence of these molecules, which when added together occur in DNA about 3.2 billion times. The project began in 1988 and scientists finished sequencing work in late June 2000, ahead of schedule.

Armed with this knowledge, scientists believe they will be able to better diagnose diseases and even predict conditions such as heart disease and Alzheimer's disease. Scientists may learn which genes are responsible for triggering milestones in human development, such as when a baby learns to talk or when brown hair turns gray.

Some politicians fear that with increased ability to predict the health of an individual through DNA testing comes the risk that the testing may be used to discriminate. Employers could fire or refuse to hire people whose DNA shows them to be at risk for cancer, diabetes, Alzheimer's disease, or other health conditions—afflictions that *might* affect future job performance or lead to increased costs for the employer. In 1996 Congress outlawed genetic discrimination in group health insurance plans. Other bills before Congress have focused on private sector employers and individual insurance plans.

President Clinton's executive order places restrictions on attempts by federal agencies to collect genetic information, including family medical histories. Under the order, the federal government may not use genetic test results to hire, fire, promote, or demote employees. The government also cannot discriminate against employees with respect to compensation, terms, conditions, or privileges of employment due to protected genetic information or due to a request for—or the receipt of—genetic services by an employee. The EQUAL EMPLOYMENT OPPORTUNITY COMMISSION is responsible for coordination of the executive order's anti-discrimination policy.

Kolstad v. American Dental Association

Title VII of the Civil Rights Act of 1964 (42 U.S.C.A. § 2000e et seq.) prohibits employment discrimination based on gender. Congress amended Title VII in 1991 to permit plaintiffs to ask for up to $300,000 in punitive damages at trial when the employer has engaged in intentional discrimination and has done so "with malice or with reckless indifference to the federally protected rights of an aggrieved individual." 42, U.S.C.A. § 1981a(b)(1). PUNITIVE DAMAGES are designed to punish a defendant for the actions taken against the plaintiff. Since this amendment, the lower federal courts developed conflicting views on what standard of misconduct triggers a punitive damages claim.

The U.S. Supreme Court, in *Kolstad v. American Dental Association*, 527 U.S. 526, 119 S.Ct. 2118, 144 L.Ed.2d 494 (1999), resolved this conflict, ruling that victims of job discrimination can recover punitive damages without showing that their employer's conduct was "egregious." The Court also ruled, however, that an employer cannot be forced to pay punitive damages for a manager's discriminatory conduct if that conduct is "contrary to the employer's good faith efforts to comply" with the provisions of Title VII.

Carole Kolstad worked for the American Dental Association (ADA) in its Washington, D.C., office as director of federal agency relations. When the director of legislation and legislative policy announced his retirement, both Kolstad and Tom Spangler, the association's legislative counsel, applied for the position. Both Kolstad and Spangler had worked directly with the retiring director and both had received "distinguished" performance ratings by Leonard Wheat, the acting head of the Washington office. Although the executive director of the Chicago office was supposed to make the decision, Wheat recommended that Spangler be promoted. The Chicago official then named Spangler to the directorship.

Kolstad sued the association under Title VII, contending that the entire selection process was a sham. Her attorney asked the jury to conclude that the stated reasons for selecting Spangler were nothing more than pretexts for gender discrimination and that Spangler had been chosen for the position before the formal selection process began. Kolstad presented evidence that the Chicago director had modified the description of the vacant post in order to track aspects of the job description used to hire Spangler. Kolstad also testified that Wheat told sexually offensive jokes and that he had referred to certain prominent professional women in derogatory terms. In addition, Wheat allegedly refused to meet with Kolstad for several weeks regarding her interest in the position.

The federal district court denied Kolstad's request for a jury instruction on punitive damages. The jury concluded that the ADA had discriminated against her on the basis of sex and awarded her backpay totaling $52,718. Kolstad appealed to the Court of Appeals for the District of Columbia Circuit regarding the district court's failure to give the jury the punitive damages instruction, but the appeals court affirmed the decision. The majority concluded that, before the question of punitive damages could go to the jury, the evidence of the defendant's culpability must exceed what is needed to show intentional discrimination. Based on the structure and legislative history of the 1991 amendment to Title VII, the court held that a defendant must be shown to have engaged in some "egregious" misconduct before the jury is permitted to consider a request for punitive damages. The court refused, however, to define what factors would meet this "egregiousness requirement."

The Supreme Court, on a 7–2 vote, overturned the circuit court of appeals, rejecting the need for Kolstad and other Title VII plaintiffs to prove egregious misconduct by the employer. Justice SANDRA DAY O'CONNOR, writing for the majority, stated that evidence of egregious behavior might provide the plaintiff with a means of showing "malice" or "reckless indifference" required by the statute, but it was not an independent requirement. Looking at the 1991 amendment, O'Connor concluded that Congress intended to impose two standards of liability: malice and reckless indifference. Both standards focus on the employer's state of mind while the egregiousness standard looks at how outrageous the actual conduct appeared. Absent statutory language, the Court found that punitive damages can only be measured by malice and reckless indifference.

The Supreme Court went beyond this holding to reach another decision on punitive damages. On a 5–4 vote, the Court ruled that employers are not liable to pay the punitive damages for their managers "where these [discriminatory] decisions are contrary to the employer's good-faith efforts to comply with Title VII." Justice O'Connor stated that to rule otherwise would "reduce the incentive for employers to implement antidiscrimination programs." Therefore, if an employer can show that efforts were made to prevent the alleged actions that resulted in a Title VII action, the employer is immune from a punitive damages award.

CROSS REFERENCES
Damages; Discrimination; Punitive Damages

ENVIRONMENTAL LAW

An amalgam of state and federal statutes, regulations, and common-law principles covering air pollution, water pollution, hazardous waste, the wilderness, and endangered wildlife.

Gray Wolves Allowed to Remain in Yellowstone

In 1995 the U.S. Department of the Interior (DOI) reintroduced gray wolves to Yellowstone Park, where the wolves had not lived since being hunted to extinction in the 1920s and 1930s. Farmers and ranchers filed a lawsuit in opposition to the reintroduction because they feared the wolves would kill their livestock. A federal court in 1997 ordered the DOI to remove the wolves from the park because the program violated the ENDANGERED SPECIES ACT (ESA). In January 2000 the Tenth Circuit U.S. Court of Appeals reversed that decision and said the wolves may stay.

Congress enacted the ESA in 1973 to protect and restore endangered wildlife. In 1978, the DOI listed the gray wolf as endangered in the forty-eight contiguous states except Minnesota. That made it illegal to kill gray wolves. Over the next decade, the DOI made plans to reintroduce gray wolves into habitats where they once lived, including Yellowstone Park.

Livestock farmers and ranchers generally opposed such plans because they feared gray wolves would kill their animals. In 1982 Congress added section 10(j) to the ESA to create a special program for "experimental populations" of endangered species. Section 10(j) gives the DOI the power to move endangered species into new habitats but also allows ranchers to kill wolves in the experimental population if they roam from their new habitats and kill domestic livestock.

Under section 10(j), the ESA moved sixty-six gray wolves from Canada to Yellowstone Park and central Idaho in 1995 and 1996. As for lone wolves that migrated to those areas naturally from Canada and Montana, the DOI said it would treat them as part of the experimental populations. To make the program palatable to livestock ranchers, an environmental group called Defenders of Wildlife maintained a $100,000 fund to compensate ranchers for livestock killed by the wolves.

Ranchers objected to the plan despite the fund. Led by the American Farm Bureau (AFB), groups of ranchers from Idaho, Wyoming, and Montana filed a lawsuit against the DOI, charging the agency with violating the ESA in two ways. First, they said the DOI violated the ESA by allowing the experimental populations to overlap with naturally occurring wolf populations that migrated to the new areas. Second, they said that treating indigenous wolves as part of the experimental populations deprived them of full endangered species protection under the ESA.

In December 1997 U.S. District Court Judge William Downes reluctantly ruled in favor of the AFB. Judge Downes was reluctant because the wolf reintroduction program had been very successful. The program restored ecological balance to Yellowstone by reducing an overabundant elk population and allowing other rare species, such as the American bald eagle, to thrive. It also improved Yellowstone tourism during spring when the wolves are most visible. Because the DOI had violated the ESA, however, Judge Downes ordered the DOI to remove the wolves from the new areas.

The DOI appealed the decision amidst support from Defenders of Wildlife and other environmental groups. In January 2000 the Tenth Circuit U.S. Court of Appeals handed them a victory by reversing Judge Downes's decision. The court said the DOI had not violated the ESA with the reintroduction program. According to the Tenth Circuit, the ESA does not require experimental populations to be kept separate from lone wolves that wander from natural packs in other areas. The court also said that treating naturally migrating wolves as part of the experimental populations does not violate federal law because Congress did not write the ESA to protect individual, migrating wolves at the

In 1995 the DOI transferred gray wolves from Canada to Idaho and Wyoming in hopes of getting them off the endangered species list.
AP/WIDE WORLD PHOTOS

expense of reintroducing an entire population to their natural habitat.

The DOI and Defenders of Wildlife hailed the Tenth Circuit's decision and touted the success of the wolf reintroduction program. As of early 2000 there were about 300 wolves in Yellowstone and central Idaho. If the packs continue to thrive, the DOI may be able to take the gray wolf off the endangered species list in those areas. Defenders of Wildlife, which has raised its compensation fund to $200,000, said livestock losses have been minimal compared to the importance and success of the reintroduction program. According to one count, the program was responsible for the deaths of eighty-four sheep and seven cattle during its first three years.

AFB challenged those numbers, saying there were twenty times more livestock killed than ranchers reimbursed. Although the wolves are fearful of humans, AFB warned that it is only a matter of time before a person is attacked by one of these "vicious predators." Because of limited resources and the low likelihood of success, however, AFB decided not to appeal the Tenth Circuit's decision to the U.S. Supreme Court.

United States v. Locke

All levels of U.S. government have recognized the importance of protecting the natural environment. They have responded by enacting legislation that seeks to prevent or at least minimize the pollution of air, water, and land. However, disputes have arisen over whether the states may regulate activities that are the subject of federal legislation. The U.S. Supreme Court has developed the PREEMPTION doctrine, which declares that in certain situations, the federal government has the sole constitutional authority to regulate an activity. For example, the federal National Labor Relations Act preempts the states from enacting laws that seek to regulate labor unions.

The preemption doctrine and its application to environmental law came before the Supreme Court in *U.S. v. Locke*, 528 U.S. ___, 120 S.Ct. 1135, 146 L.Ed.2d 69 (2000), where the state of Washington sought to impose tougher conditions on oil tankers that use its ports than required by the federal Oil Pollution Act of 1990 (OPA), 33 U.S.C.A. § 2701. The Court ruled that the Washington regulations were preempted by the "comprehensive federal regulatory scheme governing oil tankers."

The history of oil tanker regulation in the United States began in the early 1970s, following a massive spill of crude oil off the coast of England in 1967 by the supertanker *Torrey Canyon*. Congress responded by enacting the Port and Waterways Safety Act of 1972 (PWSA), 33 U.S.C.A. §1223. The state of Washington passed even stricter regulations for tankers and provided greater remedies in the event of an oil spill. The Supreme Court struck down the Washington regulations dealing with tankers in *Ray v. Atlantic Richfield Co.*, 435 U.S.151, 98 S.Ct.988, 55 L.Ed.2d 179 (1978), holding that the PWSA preempted the state from imposing limitations on tanker size, design, and construction.

The state-federal tension over tanker regulation arose again following the 1989 incident in which the supertanker Exxon *Valdez* ran aground in Alaska. The resulting oil spill was the largest in U.S. history, causing massive ecological damage. Congress enacted the OPA, and in 1994, the state of Washington imposed a number of requirements on tankers that exceeded the federal law. Washington's regulations included standards for training, language, staffing, and drug testing of oil tanker crews. The state also required vessels to have certain navigation and towing equipment.

The International Association of Independent Tank Owners, known as Intertanko, filed a lawsuit in federal court challenging the Washington regulations. The district court upheld the regulations and Intertanko appealed to the Ninth Circuit Court of Appeals. The federal

The Exxon *Valdez* oil spill increased tension regarding tanker regulations.
AP/WIDE WORLD PHOTOS

government joined the appeal on Intertanko's behalf, but the Ninth Circuit upheld the regulations.

The Supreme Court, in a unanimous decision, overturned the Ninth Circuit. Justice ANTHONY M. KENNEDY, writing for the Court, stated that Washington had legislated "in an area where the federal interest has been manifest since the beginning of our republic and is now well established." Justice Kennedy noted that since 1936, Congress had enacted a series of laws that regulated tanker transports, and that the United States is party to TREATIES and international agreements concerning the LICENSING and operation of vessels. In addition, Congress in the OPA had preserved the states' authority to impose additional liability and penalties on tankers that spill oil. Congress had not agreed, however, to allow the states to impose additional regulations on the manner of enhancing tanker safety.

Justice Kennedy concluded that the *Ray* decision controlled the analysis of the case. In *Ray*, the Court ruled that states and localities could only regulate some matters of local concern—such as the depth and narrowness of local waters—as long as they did not conflict with federal regulations. The Court further held that Congress had mandated uniform federal rules on tanker regulation in the 1972 PWSA. Justice Kennedy reaffirmed *Ray*'s holding that only the federal government may regulate the design, construction, alteration, repair, maintenance, operation, equipping, personnel qualification, and manning of tankers. He declared, "Congress has left no room for state regulation of these matters."

Justice Kennedy examined several of the Washington regulations and found that they did not govern matters of local concern. For example, one regulation imposed a series of training requirements on a tanker's crew. These requirements would "control the staffing, operation, and manning of a tanker outside" of Washington's waters. Federal law clearly reserved to the federal government the right to regulate the operations of tankers and the personnel qualifications. Another Washington regulation imposed English language proficiency requirements on a tanker's crew. Again, this regulation was not limited to governing "local traffic or local peculiarities."

The Court sent the case back to the lower courts for a full consideration of all the Washington regulations based on the Court's preemption analysis. It directed that the federal government should be allowed to participate in these hearings. Justice Kennedy made clear, however, that Washington's chances of retaining any of the regulations were slim. He concluded that "it is largely for Congress and the Coast Guard to confront whether their regulatory scheme, which demands a high degree of uniformity, is adequate."

Wetlands Development Rules Change

In March 2000, the U.S. Army Corps of Engineers issued new rules to protect U.S. wetlands. The rules, which were to become effective June 2000, affect builders who discharge dredged or fill-in material into wetlands during construction projects. The rules make it harder for builders to construct homes, roads, and erosion protection near small streams and creeks.

The Corps's new rules changed a program called Nationwide Permit 26 (NWP 26). It allows builders to conduct discharge activities at construction sites across the United States. Under the new rules, builders must notify the Corps and get a permit if their discharge activities will affect more than one-tenth an acre of wetlands. The permit can be granted for nationwide or regional projects of one-half an acre or less. For larger projects, builders must get an individual permit, which costs ten times as much—and takes twice as long to get—as a nationwide permit.

This is the third time the Corps has tightened its rules since the early 1980s, when builders could discharge unlimited amounts of material into wetlands without notifying the Corps. In 1984 the Corps established a one acre notification threshold and a ten acre limit for nationwide permits. In 1996 it lowered the notification threshold to one-third an acre and the limit to three acres.

A lawsuit by the Natural Resources Defense Council (NRDC) spurred the adoption of the new rules, which the Corps said are necessary to stem the loss of U.S. wetlands to construction activities. Wetlands are areas that have water at or near the surface for varying periods of time each year, which includes building sites near many streams and creeks. Wetlands are important because they purify drinking water, provide flood protection, and house rare and endangered species. The Corps estimates that the United States loses 100,000 acres of wetlands annually. In 1999 NWP 26 was responsible for filling in (eradicating) 21,556 acres of wetlands.

Builders condemned the new rules, calling them unnecessary. The National Association for

Home Builders said there is no evidence that NWP 26 harms the environment. Indeed, builders said they create more wetlands than they destroy each year. In 1999 the Corps required builders to create, restore, or enhance 46,444 acres of wetlands to compensate for the loss caused by NWP 26. Data is not yet available on the extent to which builders satisfied those requirements. The Clinton administration advocates annual net gains for wetlands by the year 2005.

Builders also warned that enforcing and complying with the new rules would cost public agencies and developers an additional $300 million annually. Organizations such as the National Association of Counties and the Foundation for Environmental and Economic Progress suggested that the Corps issued the new rules just to enhance its annual operating budget. In contrast, the Corps estimated that it will need only $6 million more annually to process an approximate 20 percent increase in individual permits. The Corps also estimated that the new rules will cost the private sector only an additional $39 million annually.

Environmentalists praised the new rules, even though they originally asked for even stricter standards. NRDC attorney Daniel Rosenberg called NWP 26 "the biggest weapon of mass wetlands destruction." Another NRDC attorney, Drew Caputo, said builders object to the new rules because wetlands are inexpensive to buy for development.

Whether the new rules actually will save wetlands remains to be seen. In a press release announcing the new rules, the Corps said, "we do not believe that there will be a substantial increase in the number of permit requests that are denied by the Corps." To decide whether to grant a permit in a specific instance, the Corps considers a number of factors, including conservation, economics, aesthetics, cultural values, navigation, fish and wildlife values, water supply, water quality, and other factors important to people in the affected area.

CROSS REFERENCES
Endangered Species Act; Maritime Law; States' Rights

EQUAL PROTECTION

The constitutional guarantee that no person or class of persons shall be denied the same protection of the laws that is enjoyed by other persons or other classes in like circumstances in their lives, liberty, property, and pursuit of happiness.

Village of Willowbrook v. Olech

The Equal Protection Clause of the FOURTEENTH AMENDMENT has been a potent constitutional weapon for fighting unequal application of the law. In most CIVIL RIGHTS cases where a violation of equal protection is asserted, the plaintiff contends that he or she is a member of a historically vulnerable group to which the U.S. Supreme Court has given special protection. Therefore, victims of racial and gender discrimination readily use the Equal Protection Clause. In *Village of Willowbrook v. Olech*, 528 U.S. ___, 120 S.Ct. 1073, 145 L.Ed.2d 1060 (2000), the Supreme Court ruled that anyone who claims to have been singled out for adverse, irrational government action may bring a lawsuit based on the violation of the Equal Protection Clause. In effect, a person can become a "class of one."

The case began when Grace Olech filed a federal lawsuit against the Village of Willowbrook, Illinois. Olech alleged that she and her now-deceased husband used to get their water from a well on their property. When the well broke, they asked the village to connect their home to the municipal water system. The village agreed but the Olechs had to agree to pay for the cost of the hook-up and to grant a 33-foot easement so the village could widen the road on which they lived. The Olechs refused to grant the easement, as the village normally asked for a 15-foot easement to enable servicing of the water main. After three months the village agreed to the smaller easement and hooked up

Rules for construction on and near wetlands—like these in Delaware—changed again in 2000.
CHERRY/AP/WIDE WORLD PHOTOS

the water. During this period, however, the Olechs suffered damages from not having water.

In the lawsuit, Grace Olech alleged that she was denied equal protection of the law. She based this claim on a previous lawsuit she had filed against the village. In that suit, she had obtained damages for flood damage caused by the village's negligent installation and enlargement of culverts located near her property. Olech claimed that the first lawsuit generated "substantial ill will" from angered village officials and caused the village to depart from its normal easement policy and demand she give 33 feet for a widened road. The demand was, she alleged, "irrational and wholly arbitrary." Therefore, she alleged she had been denied equal protection of the laws.

The federal district court granted the village's motion to dismiss the case. The court ruled that Olech had failed to allege that the village had "orchestrated" a campaign of official harassment motivated by "sheer malice." On appeal, the Seventh Circuit Court of Appeals reversed the district court. 160 F.3d 386 (1998). Judge Richard Posner, writing for the appeals court, found that Olech had alleged sufficient facts for the lawsuit to go forward. Judge Posner stated that if the village refused to perform its obligation to provide water to its residents "for no reason other than a baseless hatred, then it denies that resident equal protection of the laws." Olech's failure to allege an orchestrated campaign against her was legally irrelevant.

Willowbrook appealed to the Supreme Court. The Court, in a unanimous decision upheld the Seventh Circuit's decision. In a PER CURIAM opinion (an opinion not signed by any of the justices), the Court agreed that Olech should be allowed to proceed with her lawsuit based on an equal protection claim. The key issue was whether an individual who is not a member of a traditionally protected class or group could use the provisions of the Fourteenth Amendment.

The Court noted that it had recognized successful equal protection claims brought by a "class of one" where the plaintiff alleged she had been treated differently from others in a similar situation and where there was no rational basis for the difference in treatment. In addition, the purpose of the Equal Protection Clause is to secure every person within a state against "intentional and arbitrary discrimination." This reasoning applied to Olech's complaint.

The Court ruled that the allegations were sufficient for Olech to move forward with her equal protection claim. In contrast to the lower courts, it found no need to inquire into the subjective motivations of the village officials at this early stage of the lawsuit. Therefore, the case was remanded to the district court where Olech could proceed with her action.

However, as the Seventh Circuit pointed out, Olech' s type of claim requires proof that the cause of the different treatment by village officials was based on "totally illegitimate animus." If the village would have taken the same action, even if it did not have a hatred of Olech, the ill will would not make the village action a breach of equal protection.

CROSS REFERENCES
Civil Rights

ESPIONAGE

The act of securing information of a military or political nature that a competing nation holds secret. It can involve the analysis of diplomatic reports, publications, statistics, and broadcasts, as well as spying, a clandestine activity carried out by an individual or individuals working under a secret identity for the benefit of a nation's information gathering techniques. In the United States, the organization that heads most activities dedicated to espionage is the CENTRAL INTELLIGENCE AGENCY.

Chinese Scientist Accused of Leaking Nuclear Secrets

In December 1999 Wen Ho Lee was arrested and charged with mishandling classified nuclear secrets at Los Alamos National Laboratory. The charge followed months of controversial investigations by the FEDERAL BUREAU OF INVESTIGATION (FBI) and the JUSTICE DEPARTMENT into what some government officials believed was a spy operation with China. Considered a security risk, Lee was placed in solitary confinement in a Santa Fe, New Mexico, county jail cell.

Unable to prove that Lee revealed nuclear secrets to anyone, the FBI pointed to Lee's mishandling of sensitive nuclear codes by downloading them from a secure computer to a nonsecure computer on several occasions. Doing this made the secret codes accessible by a third party, presumably Chinese agents. FBI officials suspected that Lee systematically changed the classification status on the files he downloaded, creating portholes for Chinese spies to hack into the Los Alamos computers and collect the information. The FBI found evidence of one computer intrusion, but could not prove that it came from a foreign government.

Lee denied wrongdoing, indicating that he destroyed seven missing computer tapes, and that he began downloading nuclear codes as a backup after the laboratory's classified computer system crashed in 1994. He said that he created three separate passwords to protect the codes he downloaded. Lee's adult children testified to a grand jury that they accessed the non-secure computer from remote locations to play high-speed Internet games, so the computer intrusion may have been innocent. Supporters of the veteran mechanical engineer argued that the government was pursuing Lee because of his Asian heritage.

Wen Ho Lee was born in 1939, one of ten children of farmers in Nantou, a rural community in Taiwan. He graduated from college in Taiwan in 1963 with a mechanical engineering degree, then won a student visa to attend Texas A&M University, where he completed a doctorate in mechanical engineering in 1969. Lee became a U.S. citizen in 1974. After marriage and the birth of a son and daughter, Lee started working at Los Alamos National Laboratory in 1978. In the early 1980s, Lee and his wife, Sylvia, were FBI informants during the investigation of a Taiwan-born scientist working at the Lawrence Livermore National Laboratory in California. Sylvia Lee allowed FBI agents to monitor her conversations with visiting scientists from mainland China, even providing the agents with translated copies of her correspondence with the scientists. Wen Ho Lee, however, was the subject of two counter-intelligence investigations in the early 1980s—on both occasions he was cleared of wrongdoing.

The recent investigation of Lee dates back to 1995, when U.S. authorities determined that Beijing weapons designs so closely mirrored designs of U.S. bombs that the technology must have been leaked by agents for the Chinese. Officials believed the leaks to have occurred in the mid 1980s. Lee, as an employee of the Los Alamos National Laboratory, made trips to Beijing in 1986 and 1988 where he admitted he met with Chinese weapons researchers, his professional counterparts. The trips were approved, and even paid for, by Los Alamos Lab.

The investigation continued until April 1999, when agents searched Lee's Los Alamos home and discovered 400,000 to 800,000 pages of classified documents containing information about the entire U.S. nuclear arsenal. Agents said that Lee had copied the information from classified to unclassified computers, a task that would have required numerous hours. Lee then allegedly downloaded the data to portable tapes. Some of these tapes remain unfound. Lee testified that he destroyed them.

With a presidential election nearing, the political climate in 1999 focused on the declining relations between the United States and China. Republicans accused the administration of President BILL CLINTON of being soft on China. The Clinton administration blamed nuclear security breaches on the RONALD REAGAN and GEORGE BUSH administrations of the 1980s. The pressure to find the security leak intensified, and the FBI settled on Lee as the prime suspect. Still unable to prove that Lee had committed espionage, or even that his actions had resulted in a security leak, federal officials were forced to lessen the charge against Lee to fifty-nine counts of mishandling classified material.

Lee's supporters accuse the U.S. government of racial motivation in pursuing these allegations. They point out a double standard. Former CENTRAL INTELLIGENCE AGENCY director John Deutch accessed classified files remotely from a non-secure home computer. His breach left CIA secrets open to computer hackers, yet he was not prosecuted. Government officials have, over the years, documented similar computer violations and have declined to take action.

Lee's trial has been scheduled for November 2000.

Cuban Espionage

Tensions between Cuba and the United States flared at the turn of the twentieth century as U.S. officials cracked down on a surge in Cuban spy activity. In 1998 authorities rounded up the largest number of Cuban spies since Fidel Castro became the leader of Cuba in 1959. Linda and Nilo Hernandez, a married couple living in Miami, were among the twelve-member spy ring and pleaded guilty to being unregistered agents of a foreign government. In February 2000 a U.S. District Court judge in Miami sentenced the Hernandezes to seven years in prison. Some of the other accused members of the spy ring, who used short-wave radios to communicate with Cuba, faced possible life sentences for espionage CONSPIRACY.

Linda Hernandez was born in New York City but spent her childhood in Cuba before moving back to the United States with her husband in 1983. Nilo Hernandez was born in Havana, where he met his wife. The couple became sub-lieutenants in the Cuban military before moving to the United States. At their sentencing hearing, Linda Hernandez explained that she and her husband had begun working as spies for Cuba not for financial gain, but because they thought it was the right thing to do. She testified that after living in the United States, they grew to enjoy its freedoms and tried to stop spying for Cuba. Their efforts were unsuccessful. The Cuban government put pressure on the couple's relatives in Cuba, and the Hernandezes felt forced to continue their espionage activities. They helped the Castro government by counting airplanes at Homestead Air Reserve base in Florida, tracking U.S. troop activities at Fort Bragg in North Carolina, monitoring boats on the Miami River, and attempting to infiltrate a group of Cuban exiles. The Cuban government also asked the couple to investigate a telecommunications company in Miami and to develop a friendship with a former U.S. Navy employee to gauge his reaction to providing them classified information. Attorneys for the couple told the court that the Cuban government did not pay the Hernandezes directly for their spy activities but did forward money to their relatives in Cuba.

Another Havana-born American, Mariano Faget, was close to retiring from his thirty-four year career with the U.S. Immigration and Naturalization Service (INS) when he was arrested at his Miami home and charged with espionage in February 2000. A twelve-member jury convicted him May 30, 2000, on four counts of violating the Espionage Act. As a supervisor in the Miami office of the INS, he had access to highly sensitive information about defectors from Cuba. His duties involved overseeing naturalization decisions and requests for political ASYLUM. Investigators from the FEDERAL BUREAU OF INVESTIGATION (FBI) secretly observed Faget in meetings with known Cuban intelligence officers. To confirm their suspicions, the FBI fabricated a story, telling Faget that a high ranking Cuban intelligence officer was planning to defect to the United States. In keeping with his job description, Faget agreed to keep silent about the sensitive information. Twelve minutes later, though, the FBI recorded the first of two telephone calls Faget made to another Cuban intelligence operative advising Cuba about the planned defection. Federal agents arrested Faget six days later. He is the first INS official to be charged with spying and faces a possible ten-year prison sentence. Sentencing is scheduled for August 18, 2000.

One of the Cuban officials to whom Faget was accused of releasing sensitive information was Jose Imperatori, a Cuban diplomat who lived in Washington, D.C., until being expelled by the U.S. STATE DEPARTMENT in February 2000. Acting on information from the FBI that Imperatori had served as a Washington contact for Faget, the State Department asked that he leave the United States within a few days. Cuban leader Fidel Castro initially refused to withdraw Imperatori from the United States, calling the State Department's action a "desperate and spectacular maneuver." Castro requested that Imperatori be allowed to remain in the United States to defend his name and to testify on behalf of Faget. U.S. officials refused, giving Imperatori a deadline of February 29, 2000. Imperatori agreed to fly to Canada that night and to return to Havana the following day, but instead he flew to Canada and sought refuge in the Cuban Embassy there, going on a hunger strike while Castro attempted to negotiate for his return to the United States. Five days later, Imperatori boarded a plane and flew to Havana, where he received a hero's welcome from Castro. Cuba announced that it had satisfactorily negotiated a deal with the United States that would permit Imperatori to return to the United States and testify for himself and Faget. State Department officials, however, insisted that there had been no negotiations. Under specified conditions, the State Department agreed that Imperatori would be allowed to return to Washington to speak to law enforcement agents about the accusations against him.

EVIDENCE

Any MATTER OF FACT that a party to a lawsuit offers to prove or disprove an isse in the case. A system of rules and standards used to determine which facts may be admitted, and to what extent a JUDGE or JURY may consider those facts, as proof of a particular issue in a lawsuit.

Ohler v. United States

Under the FIFTH AMENDMENT, criminal defendants have the right not to testify at their trials, however, there are many times when a defendant's only chance to overcome the evidence is to testify. If the defendant has prior criminal convictions, the prosecutor may be able to CROSS-EXAMINE the defendant about these convictions and seek to discredit the defendant's testimony. The trial judge must determine, usually before trial, if the prosecutor can introduce past convictions as evidence. Such evidence is normally admitted only if its relevance is greater than the PREJUDICE it may raise with jurors.

The Supreme Court resolved a troubling issue involving the introduction of prior conviction evidence in *Ohler v. United States*, ___ U.S. ___, 120 S.Ct. 1851, ___ L.Ed.2d ___ (2000). The Court ruled that criminal defendants who volunteer evidence on their prior criminal convictions during their direct examination have waived their right to appeal the judge's decision to allow the convictions into evidence. The decision presents defendants with a dilemma: either forgo testifying so the prosecutor cannot introduce past convictions, or testify, allow prosecutors to tell the jury the evidence, and then appeal the introduction of the evidence if convicted.

Maria Ohler drove a van from Mexico to the border crossing at San Ysidro, California, in 1997. U.S. Customs inspectors searched her van and found eighty-one pounds of marijuana. Ohler was charged with importation of marijuana and possession of marijuana with the intent to distribute. Before her trial, the federal prosecutor asked permission from the judge to introduce Ohler's 1993 conviction for possession of methamphetamine as character evidence. The judge declined to grant permission but ruled on the first day of trial that if Ohler testified, the prosecutor could cross-examine her about the 1993 conviction. Ohler testified in her own defense and admitted the conviction during the direct examination by her attorney. Despite her testimony, the jury convicted her on both counts.

Ohler appealed her conviction, contending that the judge's decision to admit the prior conviction if she testified was wrong. The Ninth Circuit Court of Appeals affirmed her conviction, concluding that Ohler had waived her objection by introducing the 1993 conviction evidence during her direct examination. The appeals court decision conflicted with a Fifth Circuit decision, which allowed defendants in Ohler's position to appeal.

The Supreme Court, in a 5–4 decision, resolved the conflict by siding with the Ninth Circuit. Chief Justice WILLIAM H. REHNQUIST, writing for the majority, noted that generally, a party who introduces evidence "cannot complain on appeal that the evidence was erroneously admitted." He summarily rejected Ohler's claim that the Federal Rules of Evidence gave her the right to appeal the judge's decision. The larger issue that concerned the Court was whether the waiver rule was unfair to criminal defendants.

Ohler claimed that the waiver was unfair because it compelled her to "forgo the tactical advantage of preemptively introducing the conviction in order to appeal" the trial judge's evidentiary ruling. In her view, if a defendant is forced to wait until the prior conviction is introduced during cross-examination, the jury will believe that the defendant has tried to conceal the conviction and is less credible. The government argued that Ohler's conclusion was shaky, contending that jurors do not see defendants as more credible if they introduce the convictions themselves.

Justice Rehnquist looked past the merits of these arguments, concluding that both sides in a criminal trial must make choices as the trial moves forward. The defendant must decide whether to testify. In Ohler's case, she testified that she did not know that the marijuana was in her van. She had the choice of volunteering the past conviction "to remove the sting" or to "take her chances with the prosecutor's possible elicitation of the conviction on cross-examination." The government also had choices. It could introduce the conviction on cross-examination to discredit her, but its introduction might be found reversible error on appeal.

Rehnquist acknowledged that prosecutors have an "inherent advantage" because cross-examination comes after direct examination. They can defer their decision to use prior convictions until the defendant has testified. He ruled that Ohler's argument would deny prosecutors this advantage. Her attempt "to short-circuit that decisional process by offering the conviction herself" and then appeal its admission had no merit. There was nothing unfair about putting Ohler "to her choice in accordance with the normal rules of trial."

Justice DAVID H. SOUTER, in a dissenting opinion joined by Justices JOHN PAUL STEVENS, RUTH BADER GINSBURG, and STEPHEN G. BREYER, argued that the decision "is without support in precedent, the rules of evidence, or the reasonable objectives of trial." Ohler should have been allowed to appeal, as her introduction of the 1993 conviction "tends to promote fairness of trial without depriving the Government of anything to which it is entitled."

CROSS REFERENCES
Cross-Examination; Fifth Amendment

EX POST FACTO LAWS

[*Latin, "After-the-fact" laws.*] Laws that provide for the infliction of punishment upon a person for some prior act that, at the time it was committed, was not illegal.

Carmell v. Texas

The Ex Post Facto Clause of the Constitution, Article 1, Section 10, Clause 1, prevents the government from retroactively changing the definition of a crime, retroactively increasing the punishment for a criminal act, punishing conduct that was legal when committed, or retroactively changing the rules of evidence in a criminal case. The Supreme Court revisited the scope and meaning of the clause in *Carmell v. Texas*, ___ U.S. ___, 120 S.Ct. 1620, ___ L.Ed.2d ___ (2000). In this case, the Court ruled that several criminal convictions of a sex offender could not stand because the state of Texas had changed the rules of evidence after he had committed the offenses.

In 1996, a Texas grand jury indicted Scott Carmell on fifteen counts that involved various sexual offenses against his stepdaughter. The alleged acts took place over more than four years, from February 1991 to March 1995. The victim was twelve- to sixteen-years old during this period. A jury convicted Carmell on all fifteen counts and he was sentenced to life imprisonment on two of the counts. For the thirteen other counts, he received concurrent sentences of twenty years.

In September 1993, the Texas legislature changed its rules of evidence concerning sexual offenses. Until the law changed, a person could not be convicted based only on the testimony of the victim, unless the victim was less than fourteen-years old at the time of the offense. The amended law raised the age to eighteen. Carmell challenged four of his convictions, arguing that they occurred after the stepdaughter turned fourteen but before the amended law went into effect. Therefore, her uncorroborated testimony alone could not support these convictions. Carmell did not contest the other charges, either because the victim was under fourteen when they occurred, or because they took place after the amended law became effective. The Texas Court of Appeals upheld the convictions, concluding that applying the 1993 law retroactively did not violate the Ex Post Facto Clause. The court noted that the statute did not increase his punishment or change the elements of the offense that the state had to prove. The court characterized the change as removing restrictions on the competency of certain classes of witnesses. The Texas Court of Criminal Appeals denied review of Carmell's case. He then appealed to the U.S. Supreme Court.

The Court, in a 5–4 decision, reversed the Texas state courts. Justice JOHN PAUL STEVENS, writing for the majority, relied on a 1798 decision, *Calder v. Bull*, 3 U.S. (3 Dall.) 386, 1 L.Ed. 648, as the basis for the ruling. In *Calder*, the Court prohibited "every law that alters the legal rules of evidence, and receives less, or different, testimony, than the law required at the time of the commission of the offence, in order to convict the offender." Justice Stevens noted that Joseph Story and James Kent—both distinguished nineteenth century legal scholars—had agreed that retroactive alterations of the rules of evidence violated the Ex Post Facto Clause.

Justice Stevens concluded that "fundamental justice" was served by the Court's recognition that the Ex Post Facto Clause applied to retroactive changes in the rules of evidence. The U.S. government had filed a friend of the court brief in support of Texas, arguing that the Court should abandon the *Calder* position on the rules of evidence. Stevens rejected this, pointing out that later decisions had always included this category within the Ex Post Facto Clause.

Stevens also rejected Texas's argument that the evidence category applied only to laws that retrospectively altered the burden of proof. In the majority's view, "laws that lower the burden of proof and laws that reduce the quantum of evidence necessary to meet the burden are indistinguishable in all meaningful ways relevant to concerns of the Ex Post Facto Clause." Stevens concluded that the prosecutor's case was legally insufficient unless Texas could produce both the victim's testimony and corroborative evidence. Under the 1993 law, Carmell "could be (and was) convicted on the victim's testimony alone . . . ." A law that reduces the amount of evidence "required to convict an offender is grossly unfair as, say, retrospectively eliminating an element of the offense."

Justice RUTH BADER GINSBURG wrote a dissenting opinion, which was joined by Chief Justice WILLIAM H. REHNQUIST, and Justices SANDRA DAY O'CONNOR and ANTHONY M. KENNEDY. Ginsburg argued that "retroactive changes to rules concerning the admissibility of evidence and the competency of witnesses to testify" does not violate the Constitution. She contended that the majority had misread the Texas law and the Court's precedents on the Ex Post Facto Clause. Ginsburg agreed with the Texas courts that the law merely dealt with a witness competency rule that was not an ex post facto violation.

CROSS REFERENCES
Evidence; Witness

EXTRADITION

The transfer of an ACCUSED from one state or country to another state or country that seeks to place the accused on TRIAL.

Augusto Pinochet's Extradition Case

Augusto Pinochet was the Chilean head of state from 1973–1990. During his rule he oversaw a regime that murdered and tortured thousands of people. In 1998 he was arrested in Britain on a Spanish WARRANT. Spain requested that Pinochet be extradited to Spain where he would face trial for the atrocities that occurred during his dictatorship. These events led to a series of appeals and decisions from the British Courts. On March 2, 2000, British officials ruled against EXTRADITION and Pinochet was free to return to his homeland of Chile.

Augusto Pinochet Ugarte was born in Santiago, Chile, and educated at Chile's National Military Academy. He graduated from the military academy in 1936 as a second lieutenant and steadily rose through the army's ranks to eventually become Commander in Chief of the Army. On September 11, 1973, Pinochet used Chile's armed forces to stage a *coup d'etat* against President Salvador Allende. Chile's armed forces overthrew Salvador Allende, who was killed in the process. Pinochet was appointed president two days later. The coup had terminated Chile's long tradition of constitutional government and started an era of military rule.

Once Pinochet was in power, he immediately took action to eliminate opposition. His new regime conducted raids, executions, and kidnappings—more commonly referred to as "disappearances." Thousands of Chilean citizens were arrested and tortured. An official Chilean report indicates that 3,197 people died or disappeared during Pinochet's seventeen-year rule. Many of his victims were also people from other countries, including Spain. Amnesty International and the United Nations Human Rights Commission reported that approximately 180,000 Latin Americans were arrested and tortured during Pinochet's first year in power, and 250,000 people were also detained for political reasons.

Pinochet's government drafted and adopted a new constitution for Chile. The new constitution enabled Chile to have a gradual return to a democratic government and allowed for an elected president. The new constitution also provided for past presidents to become senators for life, which shielded them from being prosecuted for crimes carried out during their reign. Pinochet continued to rule until 1988 when he was denied the right to continue as president beyond 1990. He did, however, retain his position as head of the armed forces. In March of 1998, Pinochet ended his career with the army and started his position of "senator for life."

Although Pinochet had absolute IMMUNITY in Chile, other countries were still free to charge Pinochet for his crimes. Baltasar Garzon, a Spanish magistrate compiled evidence of HUMAN RIGHTS violations committed by Pinochet. He issued a warrant in the United Kingdom for Pinochet's arrest. The first warrant was considered invalid, and therefore, Garzon was required to issue a second one. The second warrant for Pinochet alleged the offenses of GENOCIDE, MURDER, torture, hostage-taking, and CONSPIRACY to commit those crimes. In October of 1998, while Pinochet was in England for back surgery, the then eighty-three-year-old Chilean senator was arrested for the deaths of Spanish

General Augusto Pinochet, former leader of Chile, was not extradited to Spain where he would have faced human rights abuse charges.
LLANQUIN/AP/WIDE WORLD PHOTOS

nationals by the Chilean armed forces. After his arrest, Garzon issued an extradition request from Spain. The issue then arose as to whether Pinochet's immunity would preclude his extradition.

On November 25, 1998, the highest British Court ruled that Pinochet was not entitled to immunity from prosecution for the alleged torture and hostage taking. The judges found that a former head of state is only immune for all "official" acts performed while in office. They held that torture and hostage taking could not be considered within the scope of governing. In effect, the court's decision was that Pinochet could potentially be extradited to Spain on the charges of torture and hostage taking—and, presumably, genocide. The British House of Lords issued a second ruling on March 24, 1999, finding that Pinochet could only be extradited for the allegations of torture and conspiracy to torture after December 8, 1998. All of the other charges were eliminated.

After more than sixteen months of debates over whether Augusto Pinochet would be extradited to Spain, the British Home Secretary, Jack Straw, ruled on March 2, 2000, that Augusto Pinochet would not be extradited for trial in Spain. While the legal battle ensued, Pinochet was on house arrest in London. After sixteen months, Augusto Pinochet was free to return to Chile. Straw stated that he was inclined to free Pinochet after medical tests revealed that he was not fit to face trial. Reports indicated that Pinochet had suffered brain damage as a result of two strokes, and might have difficulty remembering details from when he ruled.

The response in Chile was split. Upon his return, Pinochet was greeted with a hero's welcome from the country's military. On the other hand, angry opponents openly demanded justice for the thousands of people who died or disappeared during Pinochet's reign. The Spanish government stated it would not take any other action with regard to Britain's decision. Garzon, however, indicated that he would have Pinochet arrested again if he ever left Chile. Pinochet is also not completely clear of any charges, as he could still potentially face trial in Chilean courts if he is stripped of his immunity. On June 5, 2000, a Chilean appellate court stripped Pinochet of his immunity by a 13–9 vote. Pinochet and his lawyers can appeal the decision to the Chilean Supreme Court and have stated that they will.

The Weatherhead Letter

The desire of the U.S. government to retain confidentiality of information exchanged between it and foreign governments has meant that it will vigorously contest any effort to make the information public. This attitude was born out in the lengthy litigation involving the release of a letter from the British Foreign Office to the U.S. JUSTICE DEPARTMENT. The lower federal courts were divided over the letter's release, with the Ninth Circuit Court of Appeals ruling in *Weatherhead v. U.S.*, 157 F.3d 735 (1998) that it should be released. The U.S. government appealed to the Supreme Court, but just before oral argument, new disclosures led to the voluntary release of the letter, the dismissal of the Supreme Court case, and the vacating of the Ninth Circuit decision.

In November 1994, Leslie Weatherhead, an attorney, made identical requests under the FREEDOM OF INFORMATION ACT (FOIA), 5 U.S.C.A. § 552 to the Justice and the STATE DEPARTMENTS. He sought a letter dated July 28, 1994, from the British Foreign Office to George Proctor, Director of the Office of International Affairs, Criminal Division, Department of Justice. The letter was related to the extradition of two women, Sally Croft and Susan Hagan, from Great Britain to the United States to stand trial for conspiracy to murder the U.S. attorney for Oregon. Weatherhead, who represented Croft, believed that the letter contained an official British request that the Justice Department take measures to avoid PREJUDICE to Croft and Hagan in the district where the Croft

The extradition of Sally Croft—seen here walking to court for sentencing in 1995—lead to the Weatherhead case.
YOUNG/AP/WIDE WORLD PHOTOS

case was pending. He intended to provide the letter to the district judge presiding over the case.

The requests moved slowly. The State Department wrote the British government asking if it would object to releasing all or part of the letter. In October 1995, the British government responded that it was "unable to agree" to the letter's release because "the normal line in cases like this is that all correspondence between Governments is confidential unless papers have been formally requisitioned by the defence." Based on this response, the State Department classified the letter as confidential and refused Weatherhead's FOIA request. He then sued in federal district court for the letter's release.

The district court initially agreed with Weatherhead's position but then reconsidered. The court reviewed the letter IN CAMERA, which meant that the judge looked at it privately and that Weatherhead could not see its contents. After reading it, the judge issued an order in September 1996, which upheld the government's position. The judge stated that he "knew without hesitation or reservation that the letter could not be released" because "there is no portion of it which could be disclosed without simultaneously disclosing injurious materials." Weatherhead filed a motion to reconsider this decision. He submitted an affidavit in which he included information from a phone conversation between an acquaintance of his and an English government official who had disclosed the letter's contents. Nevertheless, the court rejected his motion.

Weatherhead found the Ninth Circuit Court of Appeals more sympathetic to his point of view. The appeals court, in a 2–1 decision, noted that the FOIA mandates a policy of broad disclosure of government documents. The court focused on the government's claim that the letter was exempt from FOIA disclosure based on EXECUTIVE ORDER No. 12958, 60 Fed. Reg. 19825 (April 20, 1995). One of the conditions required under this order is that the State Department must determine "that the unauthorized disclosure of the information reasonably could be expected to result in damage to the national security" and must be "able to identify or describe the damage." Chief Judge Proctor Hug, writing for the majority, pointed out that the government had the burden of showing that the letter met the exemption requirement. Moreover, the government had to give a "particularized explanation" of how disclosure would injure national security.

Judge Hug ruled that the government had failed to meet its burden of identifying any damage to national security that would result from the release of the letter. The government had submitted declarations from three State Department officials. The gist of the declarations was that disclosure of a letter between foreign governments, regardless of its particular content, would damage national security in general. In particular, disclosure would impair international extradition proceedings.

The appeals court rejected these declarations because they were not particularized. The court characterized the statements as being of a "general and conclusory nature." In addition, the court examined the letter and "failed to comprehend" how the release of the letter would harm national defense or foreign relations. Judge Hug thought the letter so "innocuous" that the court ordered it be released to Weatherhead.

The government appealed to the Supreme Court, which set oral argument for December 1999. Weatherhead's brief to the court, filed in November 1999, however, mentioned a separate letter Weatherhead had received in 1994 from the British consul. The British official disclosed some of the contents of the classified letter to Weatherhead. The government immediately sought to dismiss the case as moot. In light of this letter, the British government dropped its objections to the release of the classified letter. The government attorney even filed a copy of the long-requested letter in its motion to the Supreme Court to dismiss the case. In its motion, the government asked the Supreme Court to vacate the Ninth Circuit decision, as it did not want that decision applied to future cases. The Supreme Court agreed, dismissing the appeal and vacating the appeals court decision. As for the letter itself, it turned out to be as innocuous as the Ninth Circuit described it.

CROSS REFERENCES
Appendix: Weatherhead Letter; Freedom of Information Act; Immunity; International Law

FAMILY LAW

Statutes, court decisions, and provisions of the federal and state constitutions that relate to family relationships, rights, duties, and finances.

Troxel v. Granville

With so many marriages ending in divorce, child custody and visitation issues have become contentious areas of family law. The visitation rights of grandparents have also been recognized, as all fifty states have enacted laws that give them the right to seek court-ordered visitation. Such laws have come under attack by parents, who argue that giving grandparents visitation rights infringes on their right to raise their children as they see fit. The U.S. Supreme Court, in *Troxel v. Granville*, ___ U.S. ___, 120 S.Ct. 2054, ___ L.Ed.2d ___ (2000), addressed this issue for the first time. The court ruled that the state of Washington's grandparent visitation statute violated the FOURTEENTH AMENDMENT's DUE PROCESS Clause, as it interfered with the rights of parents to make decisions concerning the care, custody, and control of their children. The Court made clear, however, that it struck down this particular law and not all fifty.

The State of Washington, under § 26.10.160(3) of its Revised Code, permitted "any person" at "any time" to petition a state family court for visitation rights whenever "visitation may serve the best interest of the child." Jenifer and Gary Troxel used this statute to petition a Washington court in 1993 for the right to visit their grandchildren, Isabelle and Natalie Troxel. Tommie Granville, the mother of the children, opposed the petition. Brad Troxel, the son of Jenifer and Gary, had shared a relationship with Tommie that ended in 1991. Though they never married, they had Isabelle and Natalie. After they broke up, Brad brought his daughters to his parents for weekend visits. When Brad committed suicide in early 1993, his parents sought to continue the weekend visitations. Tommie refused, however, allowing them one short visit per month. This led to the filing of the visitation petition in which the Troxels asked for two weekends of visitation per month and two weeks of visitation per summer. The family court ultimately ordered visitation one weekend per month and one week during the summer, along with four hours on each grandparent's birthday.

Granville appealed the decision to the Washington Court of Appeals, which reversed the lower court order and dismissed the petition. The Washington Supreme Court upheld this decision, holding that the law unconstitutionally infringed on the fundamental right of parents to rear their children. It noted that the U.S. Constitution allows the state to interfere with this right only to prevent harm to the children. The Washington statute did not require a showing of harm. In addition, the statute permitted "any person" to file a visitation petition. The court found that this provision was too broad. In its view, parents have a right to limit visitation of their children with third persons.

The Troxels appealed to the U.S. Supreme Court. In a 6–3 decision, the Court upheld the Washington Supreme Court. Justice SANDRA DAY O'CONNOR, writing the main opinion for the Court, acknowledged that the demographics of the American family had changed in the past

Jenifer and Gary Troxel are at the Supreme Court petitioning for visitation rights to see their granddaughters.
BOWMER/AP/WIDE WORLD PHOTOS

one hundred years. In 1998, almost 4 million children lived with their grandparents and twenty-eight per cent of all children under eighteen lived in single-parent households. Though she noted that these changes helped explain the extension of statutory visitation rights, there were "obvious costs" that came with these changes. The primary cost was the "substantial burden" placed on the "traditional parent-child relationship."

Justice O'Connor based her legal analysis on the Due Process Clause of the Fourteenth Amendment. She invoked "substantive due process," which guarantees heightened protection against government interference with certain fundamental rights and liberty interests. The liberty interest in this case involved the "interest of parents in the care, custody, and control of their children." O'Connor pointed out that since 1925 the Court had upheld this liberty interest. Therefore, the government could not interfere with this interest except for good cause, which generally has meant harm or potential harm to children. The Washington statute did not require a showing of harm.

O'Connor concluded that as long as a parent adequately cared for his or her children "there will normally be no reason for the state to inject itself into the private realm of the family to further question the ability of that parent to make the best decisions concerning the rearing of that parent's children." Therefore, the Washington law was too broad in its terms and its application. However, the Court declined to endorse the Washington Supreme Court's ruling that the Due Process Clause required all nonparental visitation statutes to include a showing of harm or potential harm to a child as a condition for granting visitation. O'Connor indicated that the standard for awarding visitation is made on a case-by-case basis. It made more sense for each state to examine its nonparental visitation statute rather than have the Supreme Court issue a blanket ruling of unconstitutionality.

In a dissenting opinion, Justice JOHN PAUL STEVENS argued that the Washington statute merely gave an individual, acting in the best interests of the child, the procedural right to ask a state court for visitation rights. The state had a right to intervene as a neutral arbiter to decide what was best for the child.

CROSS REFERENCES
Custody; Due Process

FEDERALISM

Alden v. Maine

The division of political power between the federal government and state governments has been a source of friction since the ratification of the U.S. Constitution. The federal system of government established by the Constitution recognized the sovereignty of state governments and the federal government by giving them mutually exclusive powers as well as concurrent powers. This allocation of power is known as federalism. In the first half of the nineteenth century, slavery became the context for federalism. From the 1870s to the 1930s, economic issues shaped the debate. In the 1950s, racial SEGREGATION and the CIVIL RIGHTS MOVEMENT renewed the issue of state power. By the 1970s, economic and political conservatives began calling for a reduction in the power and control of the federal government and the redistribution of responsibilities to the states.

The U.S. Supreme Court followed this conservative trend in the late 1990s. In *Alden v. Maine*, 527 U.S. 706, 119 S.Ct. 2240, 144 L.Ed.2d 636 (1999), the Court ruled that a group of state employees could not sue their state employer using a federal labor law because the state was immune from suits for damages. The Court concluded that the states enjoyed SOVEREIGN IMMUNITY under the original Constitution and the ELEVENTH AMENDMENT. In so ruling, the Court indicated that it would look closely at federal laws that purported to revoke a state's sovereign immunity.

The case arose in 1992, when a group of probation officers sued their employer, the state of Maine, for violating the overtime provisions of the Fair Labor Standards Act of 1938 (FLSA). 19 U.S.C.A. § 201 et seq. The employees sought compensation and other damages for the violation. While the case was pending in the federal district court, the Supreme Court ruled in *Seminole Tribe of Fla. v. Florida*, 517 U.S. 44, 116 S.Ct. 1114, 134 L.Ed.2d 252 (1996), that Congress lacked the power under Article I of the Constitution to invalidate a state's sovereign immunity from suits started or prosecuted in the federal courts. Based on this ruling, the district court dismissed the officers' action, and the Court of Appeals affirmed. The officers then filed the same action in state court. The state trial court dismissed the suit on the basis of sovereign immunity and the Maine Supreme Judicial Court affirmed this ruling.

The officers then appealed to the U.S. Supreme Court, arguing that under these rulings no court could force the state to pay them the time-and-one-half they were guaranteed by the FLSA. The Supreme Court, in a 5–4 decision, upheld the state court decision, restating its belief that Congress could not abrogate a state's sovereign immunity. Justice ANTHONY M. KENNEDY, writing for the majority, stated that "the powers delegated to Congress under Article I of the United States Constitution do not include the power to subject non-consenting States to private suits for damages in state courts." Because the state of Maine had not consented to the lawsuit for overtime pay damages under the FLSA, the state courts properly dismissed the lawsuit.

Justice Kennedy based his ruling on the structure of the Constitution, constitutional history, and prior interpretations by the Court. Based on these sources, the majority concluded that the states' immunity from suits "is a fundamental aspect of the sovereignty which the States enjoyed before the ratification of the Constitution, and which they retain today" except as altered by the original Constitution or certain constitutional amendments.

Kennedy pointed out that the belief in state sovereign immunity was reaffirmed by the ratification of the Tenth and Eleventh Amendments. The TENTH AMENDMENT was added to insure ratification of the Constitution. It stipulates that "powers not delegated to the United States by the Constitution, nor prohibited by it to the States, are reserved to the States respectively, or to the people." When the Supreme Court, in *Chisholm v. Georgia*, 2 U.S. (2 Dall.) 419, 1 L.Ed. 440 (1793), allowed a state to be sued, it was promptly overruled by the ratification of the Eleventh Amendment, which prohibits a person from suing a state in federal court.

Justice Kennedy extended the prohibition to prevent a person from suing a state in *state* court to vindicate a federal right. Prior Court decisions had upheld the right of states to bar lawsuits in their courts based on state laws and rights. Kennedy concluded that these decisions "suggesting that the States retain an analogous constitutional immunity from private suits in their own courts support the conclusion" that Congress lacked the power to subject the states to private suits in state courts. Therefore, "Congress must accord states the esteem due to them as joint participants in federal system."

Justice DAVID H. SOUTER, in a scathing dissenting opinion joined by Justices JOHN PAUL STEVENS, RUTH BADER GINSBURG, and STEPHEN G. BREYER, argued that the majority had misinterpreted the structure and history of the Constitution. In Souter's view, "Congress exercising its conceded Article I power may unquestionably abrogate such immunity."

Florida Prepaid Postsecondary Ed. Expense Bd. v. College Savings Bank

The U.S. Supreme Court continued its tilt toward STATES' RIGHTS in *Florida Prepaid Postsecondary Education Expense Board v. College Savings Bank*, 525 U.S. ___, 119 S.Ct. 2199, 144 L.Ed.2d 575 (1999) and its companion case, *College Savings Bank v. Florida Prepaid Postsecondary Education Expense Board*, 525 U.S. ___, 119 S.Ct. 2219, 144 L.Ed.2d 653 (1999). The Court ruled that the state of Florida could invoke its sovereign immunity to block federal lawsuits against it by a bank charging it with PATENT and TRADEMARK law violations. In holding federal patent and trademark law inapplicable to the states, the Court also signaled a willingness to examine other federal statutes that seek to abrogate the states' sovereign immunity. The Court made clear that Congress must respect the doctrine of federalism and that it cannot easily impose federal regulations on the states by invoking the FOURTEENTH AMENDMENT.

Beginning in 1987, the College Savings Bank, a New Jersey-chartered savings bank, marketed and sold certificates of deposit known as CollegeSure CDs. They were annuity contracts for financing future college expenses. College Savings obtained a patent for its financing method designed to guarantee investors sufficient funds to cover the costs of college tuition. In 1994 College Savings filed lawsuits against the Florida Prepaid Postsecondary Education

Expense Board (Florida Prepaid), which the state of Florida created to administer similar tuition prepayment contracts available to Florida residents and their children. College Savings claimed that, in the course of administering its tuition prepayment program, Florida Prepaid directly and indirectly infringed College Savings's patent under the terms of the federal Patent and Plant Variety Protection Remedy Clarification Act of 1992. 35 U.S.C.A. § 271(h). Moreover, College Savings charged Florida Prepaid with false advertising, which violated the federal Trademark Remedy Clarification Act of 1992. 15 U.S.C.A. § 1125(a). In these two laws, Congress had amended the patent and trademark statutes to expressly abrogate the states' sovereign immunity from claims of patent and trademark infringement.

Florida Prepaid challenged the lawsuits, arguing the 1992 acts were unconstitutional because the Constitution's ELEVENTH AMENDMENT bars suits by private citizens against state governments brought in federal court. Florida Prepaid based its argument on the Supreme Court's 1996 decision in *Seminole Tribe of Fla. v. Florida*, 517 U.S. 44, 116 S.Ct. 1114, 134 L.Ed.2d 252 (1996), that Congress lacked the power under Article I of the Constitution to invalidate a state's sovereign immunity from suits started or prosecuted in the federal courts. College Savings Bank contended the laws were constitutional because Congress properly exercised its authority under § 5 of the Fourteenth Amendment to enforce the guarantees of the DUE PROCESS Clause. The federal district denied Florida Prepaid's motion to dismiss the patent claim and the Third Circuit Court of Appeals affirmed this decision. The district court dismissed the trademark claim, however. The Third Circuit affirmed this decision as well, and both sides appealed to the U.S. Supreme Court.

The Supreme Court, in a 5–4 vote, sided with Florida Prepaid, reversing the patent law decision and affirming the trademark ruling. Chief Justice WILLIAM H. REHNQUIST wrote the majority opinion in the patent law appeal and Justice ANTONIN SCALIA wrote the majority opinion in the trademark appeal. Though the Court issued separate opinions, the legal reasoning was the same.

Chief Justice Rehnquist posited two basic questions: did Congress unequivocally express its intent to abrogate the states' sovereign immunity and did it have the authority to exercise this power? As to the first issue, Congress, in its 1992 amendments to the patent and trademark laws made known its intent to abrogate sovereign immunity. As to Congress's authority to withdraw sovereign immunity, Rehnquist noted that § 5 of the Fourteenth Amendment provides the *only* basis for Congress to do so. Because Congress's enforcement power is remedial under § 5, "Congress must identify conduct transgressing the Fourteenth Amendment's substantive provisions, and must tailor its legislative scheme to remedying or preventing such conduct."

In reviewing the legislative record, Chief Justice Rehnquist found that Congress had not identified a pattern of patent infringement by the states or a pattern of constitutional violations. A legislative report made in connection with the law provided only two examples of patent infringement suits against states; the circuit courts of appeal identified only eight such lawsuits in 110 years. In the Court's view, there was no evidence that "unremedied patent infringement by States had become a problem of national import." Justice Scalia reached a similar conclusion regarding trademark violations by the states.

Turning to the Fourteenth Amendment's Due Process Clause, Rehnquist pointed out that a state's infringement of a patent would violate the Constitution only if the state provided no remedy, or only inadequate remedies, to injured patent owners. Congress had "barely considered the availability of state remedies for patent infringement." The limited testimony on this issue revealed that the state remedies were less convenient than federal remedies and might undermine the uniformity of patent law. Because of this lack of legislative support for Congress's conclusion, the patent law's provisions were "out of proportion to the supposed remedy or preventive object." Therefore, Congress did not meet the standards to justify the abrogation of sovereign immunity under the Fourteenth Amendment. Justice Scalia made the same ruling regarding the trademark law.

Justices JOHN PAUL STEVENS, DAVID H. SOUTER, RUTH BADER GINSBURG, and STEPHEN G. BREYER dissented in both cases. Justice Stevens contended that the two laws should have been upheld and continued to dissent from "the Court's aggressive sovereign immunity jurisprudence." He noted that the Court appeared to be intent on guaranteeing "rights the States themselves did not express any particular desire in possessing."

Norfolk Southern Railway Co. v. Shanklin

There are approximately 160,000 public railroad crossings in the United States today. According to the Association of American Railroads (AAR), a "public crossing" is where a railroad track crosses a road that is both open to and paid for by the public. Annual federal funds of more than $150 million are available for warning devices to be posted at highway-rail grade crossings.

The 1970 Federal Railroad Safety Act, administered by the TRANSPORTATION DEPARTMENT's Federal Highway Administration, sets safety standards for railroads, including minimum requirements for public railroad crossings. Any state laws that also address railroad safety measures and responsibilities at public crossings are thus preempted by federal regulation.

In the 1993 case of *CSX Transportation, Inc. v. Easterwood*, the U.S. Supreme Court held that a railroad's obligations to state laws regarding warning devices were preempted by federal law if federal funds were used for the devices. This ruling did not affect state law obligations of railroads where federal funds were not used.

Coincidental for that year, motorist Eddie Shanklin was killed on October 3 when struck by a train at a railroad crossing in Gibson County, Tennessee. The crossing had a reflective warning sign but no gates or flashing lights. His widow, Dedra Shanklin, sued Norfolk Southern Railway Company under Tennessee state law, claiming that the devices at the crossing were insufficient.

Defense counsel for the railroad sought to have the case dismissed by way of federal PREEMPTION. Counsel argued that the warning sign at the crossing had been part of a state project which had Federal Highway Administration approval and funding. Therefore, the argument continued, the Tennessee state court did not have jurisdiction on the matter. Notwithstanding, the trial court denied the motion for dismissal and the case proceeded to trial. Ultimately, the jury awarded $430,000 in DAMAGES to the widow. The railroad appealed.

The U.S. Circuit Court of Appeals for the 6th Circuit in Cincinnati upheld the jury verdict. Siding with a 7th Circuit ruling in a similar case, the 6th Circuit held that, in order for federal preemption to apply, states must fully comply with all applicable federal regulations. In addition to federal funding, the crossing and its warning devices must be evaluated and approved by federal officials for federal preemption to occur. Another factor in the appellate court's decision was that victims cannot sue under federal law.

The 6th and 7th Circuit opinions seemed to flesh out the *Easterwood* decision. Other circuit courts had used a more narrow interpretation of the *Easterwood* decision. Again, Norfolk Southern appealed, this time to the U.S. Supreme Court. Because of conflicting opinions at the circuit court level, the Supreme Court accepted the case for review.

In its appellate brief, Norfolk Southern argued that railroads should not be held liable for warning devices that they neither chose or funded themselves. Its appellate counsel posed the question for the Supreme Court as:

> Whether the court of appeals properly applied this Court's decision in *CSX Transportation, Inc. v. Easterwood*, 507 U.S. 658 (1993), when it held, in acknowledged conflict with decisions of three other circuits, that claims of negligence based on inadequate warning devices at a railway grade crossing are not preempted even though the warning devices at the crossing were installed with federal funds under a project approved by the federal government.

More simply put, as AAR attorney Dan Saphire stated, "Do federal funds used to erect rail-highway grade crossing warning devices equal preemption, or does the use of federal funds plus something else equal preemption?" In addition to the AAR, the Supreme Court granted review of AMICI CURIAE briefs filed by several groups, including the solicitors general of Texas and Kansas, arguing for the railroads, and Railwatch and other safety organizations on behalf of the Shanklin family.

On April 17, 2000, the U.S. Supreme Court reversed both the 6th Circuit and the trial court on a 7–2 vote, dismissing the case against the railroad. The Court held that if federal regulations are applicable, as Justice SANDRA DAY O'CONNOR wrote in the majority opinion, they establish "a federal standard [for adequacy of warning devices] that displaces state law addressing the same subject." The Court further found, as it had in *Easterwood*, that the subject federal regulations were mandatory for all such devices. As Justice Stephen G. Breyer noted in his concurring opinion:

> once federal funds are requested and spent to install warning devices at a

grade crossing, the regulations' standards of adequacy apply across the board and pre-empt state law seeking to impose an independent duty on a railroad with respect to the adequacy of warning devices installed.

Reno v. Condon

Citizens have become interested in protecting their PRIVACY in a world where government and business trade and sell information. A person's state driver's license application contains a wealth of information, including the registrant's name, address, telephone number, Social Security number, vehicle description, medical information, and photograph. State governments have freely sold this information to businesses and provided it to private citizens seeking information on an individual.

In 1994 Congress decided to restrict access to this information when it enacted the Driver's Privacy Protection Act (DPPA), 18 U.S.C.A. § § 2721–2725. The state of South Carolina sued the federal government, arguing that the law violated the TENTH and ELEVENTH AMENDMENTS to the Constitution by infringing on the principles of federalism that give states the sole authority to regulate driver's license information. The Supreme Court, in *Reno v. Condon*, __ U.S. __, 120 S.Ct. 666, 145 L.Ed.2d 587 (2000), ruled that the DPPA did not violate principles of federalism because Congress properly based its authority on the Constitution's COMMERCE CLAUSE.

The DPPA regulates the disclosure and resale of personal information contained in the records of state motor vehicle departments (DMVs). State DMVs require drivers and automobile owners to provide personal information as a condition of obtaining a driver's license or registering an automobile. Congress found that many states sold this personal information to individuals and businesses, reaping substantial revenue. For example, the Wisconsin Department of Transportation received approximately $8 million each year from the sale of motor vehicle information.

The law regulates the states' ability to disclose a driver's personal information without the driver's consent. The DPPA prohibits any state DMV, or officer, employee, or contractor from "knowingly disclos[ing] or otherwise mak[ing] available to any person or entity personal information about any individual obtained by the department in connection with a motor vehicle record." The law defines "personal information" as any information "that identifies an individual, including an individual's photograph, social security number, driver identification number, name, address (but not the 5-digit zip code), telephone number, and medical or disability information."

The ban on disclosure of personal information does not apply if drivers have consented to the release of their data. States may not imply consent from a driver's failure to take advantage of an opportunity to block disclosure. Instead, they must obtain a driver's affirmative consent to disclose the driver's personal information for use in surveys, marketing, solicitations, and other restricted purposes. The DPPA does provide exceptions to these restrictions, allowing disclosure of personal information to law enforcement officials, courts, government agencies, and licensed private investigators. A state agency that violates the law may be fined $5,000 a day until it comes into compliance with the DPPA.

The restrictions also apply to private persons who have obtained personal information from the state DMV. If a state has obtained consent from drivers to disclose their personal information to private persons, the private person may re-disclose the information for any purpose. In addition, a private citizen or business that has obtained drivers' information from DMV records specifically for direct marketing purposes may resell that information for other direct marketing uses, but not otherwise. Any person who re-discloses or resells personal information from DMV records must, for five years, maintain records identifying to whom the records were disclosed and the permitted purpose for the resale or re-disclosure.

South Carolina challenged the DPPA because it conflicted with its policies on the disclosure of DMV records. The state contended that under the Constitution, including the Tenth and Eleventh Amendments, government power is divided between the federal government and the states. This doctrine, which is known as federalism, gives to the states the exclusive authority to regulate its citizens on local matters such as drivers license registration. The federal district court and the Fourth Circuit Court of Appeals agreed with South Carolina, concluding that the DPPA violated constitutional principles of federalism.

The Supreme Court disagreed. Chief Justice WILLIAM H. REHNQUIST, writing for a unanimous court, found that the DPPA was constitutional, for Congress found its authority to act in the Commerce Clause. Congress justified this authority on the fact that the personal, identifying information that the DPPA regulates is a "thin[g] in interstate commerce," and that the sale or release of that information in interstate commerce is therefore a proper subject of congressional regulation. Rehnquist accepted this argument, finding that "the motor vehicle information which the states have historically sold is used by insurers, manufacturers, direct marketers, and others engaged in interstate commerce to contact drivers with customized solicitations. The information is also used in the stream of interstate commerce by various public and private entities for matters related to interstate motoring." Therefore, the link between the sale of information and interstate commerce was clear.

South Carolina had argued that the DPPA would force it to spend time and effort administering its complex provisions. This was not proper because it forced the state to administer a federal law under threat of civil fines for noncompliance. Chief Justice Rehnquist acknowledged South Carolina's concerns but noted that any federal law or regulation "demands compliance." Chief Justice Rehnquist concluded, however, that the DPPA "does not require the States in their sovereign capacity to regulate their own citizens." Moreover, the law "does not require the South Carolina Legislature to enact any laws or regulations, and it does not require state officials to assist in the enforcement of federal statutes regulating private individuals." Therefore, the DPPA was constitutional and South Carolina must abide by its provisions.

CROSS REFERENCES
Commerce Clause; Eleventh Amendment; Fourteenth Amendment; Labor Law; Patent; Preemption; Privacy; States' Rights; Tenth Amendment; Trademark

FIFTH AMENDMENT

Portuondo v. Agard

Criminal defendants are entitled to a fair trial, but this simple statement has been the subject of countless court cases. Under the Fifth Amendment, a defendant has the right *not* to testify. The Supreme Court has ruled that prosecutors may not suggest to the jury that the defendant's silence can be construed as evidence of guilt. The Supreme Court, in *Portuondo v. Agard*, 528 U.S. __, 120 S.Ct. 1119, 146 L.Ed.2d 47 (2000), refused to extend this prohibition to include general attacks on the CREDIBILITY of a defendant who does testify, simply because the defendant has the benefit of being present during trial and hearing all the testimony. No other witness is allowed into the courtroom before testifying. The Court ruled that prosecutors are free to inform jurors that a defendant's presence in the courtroom allows him to tailor his testimony to fit the evidence.

A New York City jury convicted Ray Agard of sodomy and weapons possession. Agard testified at his trial that he had consensual sex with the woman who accused him of sexual assault. During her final argument to the jury, the prosecutor attacked the credibility of Agard's testimony. She noted that unlike other witnesses, he was allowed to be in court and hear all of the testimony before he testified. The prosecutor asked rhetorically, "That gives you a big advantage, doesn't it? You get to sit here and think 'What am I going to say... how am I going to fit it into the evidence?'"

After Agard exhausted his state court appeals, he filed a petition for HABEAS CORPUS in federal court alleging that the prosecutor's comments violated his Fifth and SIXTH AMENDMENT rights to be present at trial and to confront his accusers. Though the district court denied his petition, the Second Circuit Court of Appeals reversed this decision.

The Supreme Court reversed the Second Circuit ruling. The Court, in a 7–2 decision, held that the prosecutor's remarks did not violate the Fifth and Sixth Amendments. Justice ANTONIN SCALIA, writing for the majority, noted that Agard's argument "boils down" to a request that the Court extend its ruling in *Griffin v. California*, 380 U.S. 609, 85 S.Ct. 1229, 14 L.Ed.2d 106 (1965). In *Griffin*, the defendant refused to testify. The judge instructed the jury that it was free to take the defendant's failure to deny or explain facts within his knowledge as tending to indicate the truth of the prosecution's case. The Supreme Court ruled that the judge's comment turned "the silence of the accused into evidence against him." Such a comment was unconstitutional because it "cuts down on the privilege [against self-incrimination] by making its assertion costly."

Justice Scalia refused to extend the *Griffin* ruling. In *Griffin*, the Court prohibited the prosecution from "urging the jury to do something the jury is not permitted to do"—that is, infer guilt from a defendant's silence. In Agard's case, however, the jury was entitled to evaluate the "relative credibility of a defendant who testifies last" with the knowledge that the defendant had heard all the previous testimony. In contrast to the facts in *Griffin*, the prosecutor did not argue that Agard's testimony was evidence of guilt. Instead, she questioned his credibility as a witness. Once Agard took the stand in his defense, the prosecutor was entitled to attack his credibility. Justice Scalia noted that the Court had a long-standing rule that once a defendant testifies, his credibility "may be assailed like that of any other witness." This rule served the trial's "truth-seeking function."

Agard also contended that the prosecutor's comments were unfair because they came not during her cross-examination of Agard, but in her final argument, when his attorney was powerless to respond. In addition, Agard argued that the prosecutor's comments were generic. She did not point to one instance where Agard specifically tailored his testimony to fit the evidence already admitted at trial. Justice Scalia rejected both arguments. First, U.S. trial structure requires the defense to close its case before the prosecution. This means the defense must predict what the prosecution will say. Therefore, it was up to Agard's attorney to anticipate the prosecutor's remark and attempt to reduce its effect on the jury. As to the claim that the comments were generic, Scalia held that the Court had previously approved general comments that were not based on specific evidence, such as how the personal interest of a defendant may affect the credibility of the defendant's evidence. These types of comment merely put forward a point of view for the jury to consider when deliberating the weight and credibility of the evidence.

Justices JOHN PAUL STEVENS and STEPHEN G. BREYER, while agreeing that the prosecutor's comments were constitutional, argued that such comments should be "discouraged rather than validated." They expressed their disagreement with the majority's "implicit endorsement" of the comments.

Justice RUTH BADER GINSBURG, in a dissenting opinion joined by DAVID H. SOUTER, argued that the "generic accusation" was unconstitutional. The defendant was required under New York law to be present at his trial and hear all the evidence. It followed that after this case, "every defendant who testifies is equally susceptible to a generic accusation about his opportunity for tailoring" testimony, whether guilty or not.

CROSS REFERENCES
Jury; Trial

FIRST AMENDMENT

Board of Regents of the University of Wisconsin System v. Southworth

Public college and university campuses are home to many student organizations with differing political, religious, and social viewpoints. This diversity has long been viewed as one of the strengths of higher education. Nevertheless, some students have objected to having part of their mandatory student fees distributed to organizations whose views they find repugnant to their own. They argued that the First Amendment gives them the right not to contribute to these organizations. The U.S. Supreme Court resolved this issue in *Board of Regents of the University of Wisconsin System v. Southworth*, ___ U.S. ___, 120 S.Ct. 1346, 142 L.Ed.2d 624 (2000), holding that as long as the funding program is "viewpoint neutral" it does not offend the First Amendment. If the publicly funded college or university does not prefer one group over another, students may be assessed fees to help fund these groups.

The Board of Regents of the University of Wisconsin System required students at the University's Madison campus to pay an activity fee. The fee supported various campus services and extracurricular student activities. The university believed such fees enhanced students' educational experience by promoting extracurricular activities, stimulating advocacy and debate on diverse points of view, enabling participation in campus administrative activity, and providing opportunities to develop social skills. All of these goals were consistent with the university's broad educational mission.

Registered student organizations (RSOs) were eligible to receive a portion of the fees, whose allocation was administered by the student government, subject to the university's approval. The process for reviewing and approving RSO applications for funding was administered in a viewpoint-neutral fashion. RSOs could also obtain funding through a student referendum. RSOs included the Future Financial Gurus of America, the International Socialist Organization, the College Democrats, the College Republicans, and the American Civil Liberties Union Campus Chapter.

A group of current and former Madison campus students sued the university, alleging that the fee violated their First Amendment rights. They argued that the university must grant them the choice not to fund RSOs that engage in political and ideological expression offensive to their personal beliefs. The federal district court agreed with the students and declared the fee program invalid. It issued an INJUNCTION that prohibited the university from using the fees to fund any RSO engaging in political or ideological speech. The Seventh Circuit Court of Appeals affirmed the district court's decision, ruling that the program was not relevant to the university's mission, did not further a vital University policy, and imposed too great a burden on respondents' free speech rights.

The Supreme Court, in a unanimous vote, reversed the lower courts. Justice ANTHONY M. KENNEDY, writing for six justices, ruled that the First Amendment permits a public university to charge its students an activity fee used to fund a program to facilitate extracurricular student speech. However, the program must be viewpoint neutral to pass constitutional muster. Justice Kennedy made clear that students who object to the fee "may insist upon certain safeguards with respect to the expressive activities they are required to support."

The Court examined several of its previous First Amendment cases to illustrate the necessary safeguards. These cases held that a required service fee paid by nonunion employees to a union and fees paid by lawyers who were required to join a state bar association could be used to fund speech "germane" to those organizations' purposes. These fees could not be used, however, to fund the *organizations'* political expression. Justice Kennedy concluded that this germane speech standard was unworkable in the context of student speech at a university. This standard provided inadequate protection both to the objecting students and to the university program itself. Even in the union context, the Supreme Court had "encountered difficulties in deciding what is germane and what is not." The standard was all the more unmanageable in the public university setting where the state "undertakes to stimulate the whole universe of speech and ideas."

Justice Kennedy acknowledged "the high potential for intrusion on the objecting students' First Amendment rights, for it is all but inevitable that the fees will subsidize speech that some students find objectionable or offensive." A university was free to protect those rights by allowing an optional or refund system, but this was not a constitutional requirement. As long as the university determined that wide-ranging debate over issues was part of its mission, it could impose a mandatory fee to sustain the debate. The best way to preserve each student's First Amendment rights was to require viewpoint neutrality in the allocation of funding support. This meant that the university could not "pick and choose" organizations to receive funding based on the organizations' views.

The Wisconsin system generally maintained viewpoint neutrality in its funding of RSOs. However, the university did permit a referendum that allowed students to either authorize funding or take away funding from an RSO. Justice Kennedy stated that this mechanism was unconstitutional, as the "referendum substitutes majority determination for viewpoint neutrality."

Justice DAVID H. SOUTER, in an opinion joined by Justices JOHN PAUL STEVENS and STEPHEN G. BREYER, agreed that the funding of organizations was constitutional. Souter believed, however, that the majority went too far in its viewpoint neutrality standard, characterizing it as a "cast-iron" requirement.

Erie v. Pap's A.M.

The U.S. Supreme Court has made a distinction between expression that is fully protected by the First Amendment and expressive *conduct* that is not. For example, during the Vietnam War, protesters burned their draft registration cards at antiwar demonstrations. The government prosecuted them because it was illegal to destroy a draft card. The Court upheld the ban on burning the cards because the government sought to prevent the means of the expression and not the expression of antiwar sentiment itself. In *City of Erie v. Pap's A.M. tdba "Kandyland,"* ___ U.S. ___, 120 S.Ct. 1382, 146 L.Ed.2d 245 (2000), the Supreme Court applied the same reasoning to a city ordinance banning nude dancing. The Court's decision could have an impact on the more than 3,000 adult clubs that operate in the United States.

In 1994, Erie, Pennsylvania, enacted an ordinance that made it a crime to knowingly or intentionally appear in public in a "state of nudity." Pap's A.M., a Pennsylvania corporation, operated Kandyland, an Erie club that featured totally nude erotic dancing by women. To comply with the ordinance, the dancers had to wear, at a minimum, pasties on their breasts and a G-string. Pap's filed a suit in state court challenging the constitutionality of the ordinance. The trial court struck down the ordinance as unconstitutional but the intermediate court of appeals reversed. The Pennsylvania Supreme

Court reversed the appeals court, finding that the ordinance's public nudity sections violated Pap's freedom of expression as protected by the First and FOURTEENTH AMENDMENTS. Although the court noted that one stated purpose of the ordinance was to combat negative secondary effects, such as crime around the adult entertainment establishments, another unmentioned purpose was to limit the "erotic message of the dance." This purpose involved the suppression of expression and therefore violated the First Amendment.

While on appeal to the Supreme Court, Pap's attempted to have the appeal dismissed because it had sold the club to a new owner who had closed Kandyland. Such a dismissal would have preserved the Pennsylvania Supreme Court's ruling in Pap's favor. The Supreme Court, in a 6–3 decision, rejected this argument and went on to hold that the ordinance was not unconstitutional. Justice SANDRA DAY O'CONNOR, in the main opinion for the Court, first held that the case was not moot because the club could reopen. In addition, the Court did not want to allow persons who won a lower court ruling from seeking to "insulate a favorable decision from review."

As to the merits of the Erie ordinance, Justice O'Connor held that nude dancing is "expressive conduct" that "falls only within the outer ambit" of First Amendment protection. She based her analysis on the framework for content-neutral restrictions on symbolic speech set forth in the draft registration card case, *United States v. O'Brien*, 391 U. S. 367, 88 S.Ct.1673, 20 L.Ed.2d 672 (1968). The first factor of the *O'Brien* test is whether the regulation is within the constitutional power of the government to enact. O'Connor concluded that Erie had the power to protect public health and safety.

The second factor is whether the regulation furthers an important or substantial government interest. The city established its public nudity ban as a way of combating the harmful secondary effects associated with nude dancing. Justice O'Connor found this an important government interest and ruled that the city did not have to produce new evidence about these secondary effects but merely cite relevant evidence from other cities. The preamble to the ordinance stated that Erie City Council had for over 100 years expressed "its findings that certain lewd, immoral activities carried on in public places for profit are highly detrimental to the public health, safety and welfare, and lead to the debasement of both women and men, promote violence, public intoxication, prostitution and other serious criminal activity." In O'Connor's view, this confirmed the right of local government to assess harmful secondary effects associated with nude dancing establishments.

The ordinance also satisfied *O'Brien*'s third factor, that the government interest is unrelated to the suppression of free expression. Justice O'Connor emphasized that Erie sought to combat the secondary effects of nude dancing and did not attempt to suppress the erotic message of nude dancing. The ordinance was a "content-neutral restriction that regulates conduct, not First Amendment expression." The fourth *O'Brien* factor—that the restriction is no greater than is essential to the furtherance of the government interest—was satisfied as well. Any "incidental impact" on the expressive content of the nude dancing was minimal. The requirement to wear the pasties and G-string left "ample capacity to convey the dancer's erotic message."

Justice ANTONIN SCALIA, in a concurring opinion joined by Justice CLARENCE THOMAS, cited different grounds for upholding the Erie ordinance. Scalia argued that government had "the traditional power to foster good morals." In his view, the ordinance could be upheld simply on "the acceptability of the traditional judgment ... that nude public dancing itself is immoral."

Justice JOHN PAUL STEVENS, in a dissenting opinion joined by Justice RUTH BADER GINSBURG, contended that the alleged secondary effects asserted by Erie could not "justify the total suppression of protected speech."

Greater New Orleans Broadcasting Association, Inc. v. United States

The U.S. Supreme Court has stringently limited government regulation of noncommercial expression, citing the First Amendment's guarantee of freedom of expression. Prior to the mid-1970s, however, the Court regarded the regulation of commercial speech—a broad category including but not limited to the advertising of services and products—as simply an aspect of economic regulation and entitled it to no special First Amendment protection. Since that time the Court has made it more difficult for government to restrict advertising. For example, in the case of *44 Liquormart, Inc. v. Rhode Island*, 517 U.S. 484, 116 S.Ct. 1495, 134 L.Ed.2d 711 (1996), the Court ruled that a state could not prohibit the public advertising of liquor prices, as the state law abridged the liquor retailers their freedom of speech. After *Liquormart*, the ability of government to restrict truthful, non-deceptive advertising appeared extremely limited.

The Court confirmed this view in *Greater New Orleans Broadcasting Association, Inc. v. United States*, 527 U.S. 173, 119 S.Ct. 1923, 144 L.Ed.2d 161 (1999). In this case the Court ruled that a federal law that prohibited television stations from broadcasting advertising of casino gambling in states where it was legal violated the First Amendment. It rejected the federal government's contention that the ban sought to reduce the social costs caused by compulsive gamblers, finding that the growing popularity of all types of government-sponsored or endorsed gambling undercut this argument.

A long-standing provision of the Federal Communications Act prohibited broadcast advertising for "any lottery, gift enterprise or similar scheme offering prizes dependent in whole or in part upon lot or chance." 18 U.S.C.A. § 1304. Congress amended the law to allow radio and television ads for casinos run by Indian tribes, state lotteries, and charity gambling. The growth in legalized gambling has been considerable, with most states participating in lotteries. Twenty-two states allow tribal-operated casinos, while ten states permit gambling at private casinos.

Since 1988, § 1304 has been primarily used against privately owned casinos. In the 1990s some federal appeals courts ruled the provision unconstitutional, while others upheld it, creating a patchwork enforcement scheme. The Greater New Orleans Broadcasting Association challenged the provision, arguing that Louisiana's and Mississippi's legalization of private casino gambling made the prohibition an illegal restraint of free speech. Both the federal district court and the Fifth Circuit Court of Appeals rejected the association's arguments, concluding that the government's interest in discouraging gambling justified the ban on advertising.

The U.S. Supreme Court disagreed. In a unanimous decision, the Court ruled that the statute unconstitutionally restricted commercial speech. Justice JOHN PAUL STEVENS, writing for the Court, based his analysis on a test announced in *Central Hudson Gas & Elec. Corp. v. Public Serv. Comm'n of N.Y.*, 447 U.S. 557, 100 S.Ct. 2343, 65 L.Ed.2d 341 (1980). In *Central Hudson*, the Court noted that commercial speech serves the economic interests of the speaker, but also helps consumers and society overall. It outlined a four-part test for evaluating regulation of commercial speech. To begin with, commercial speech must concern a lawful activity and must not be misleading if it is to receive First Amendment protection. Second, it must be determined whether the asserted governmental interest is substantial. If the answer is yes, the court must then determine if the regulation directly advances the asserted governmental interest. Finally, the court decides if the regulation is more extensive than is necessary to serve that purpose.

Justice Stevens found that the proposed broadcasts constituted commercial speech, that they concerned lawful activities (private casino gambling in Louisiana and Mississippi), and that the contents of the ads were not misleading. He also agreed that the government's asserted interest in discouraging gambling was substantial. Justice Stevens concluded, however, that the government could not meet the third and fourth parts of the *Central Hudson Gas & Elec. Corp. v. Public Serv. Comm'n of N.Y. Central Hudson* test. Section 1304 did not directly advance the interest in discouraging gambling because the law "is so pierced by exemptions and inconsistencies that the government cannot hope to exonerate it." He pointed out that the law permitted state-run and Indian-run casinos to broadcast advertisements. Therefore, the government was not interested in banning all "commercial enticements" but rather sought to prevent certain brands of casino gambling from advertising. Justice Stevens could find no compelling reason to

The Supreme Court ruled that the Mississippi law prohibiting casino advertising in states where gambling was legal violated the First Amendment.
HABER/AP/WIDE WORLD PHOTOS

justify limiting the free speech of government and tribal competitors.

Turning to the fourth part of the test, Justice Stevens concluded that § 1304 was more extensive than could be justified by the government's interest in preventing compulsive gambling. The law "sacrifices an intolerable amount of truthful speech about lawful conduct when compared to the diverse policies at stake and the social ills that one could reasonably hope such a ban to eliminate."

LAPD v. United Reporting Publishing Corporation

The First Amendment protects both public and commercial speech. When government seeks to limit the use of public information, the press and other businesses interested in marketing this information usually challenge the law in court. This was the case in *Los Angeles Police Department v. United Reporting Publishing Corporation*, ___ U.S.___, 120 S.Ct. 483, 145 L.Ed.2d 451 (1999), where the U.S. Supreme Court examined the constitutionality of a California statute that limited public access to the addresses of persons arrested for crimes. United Reporting, a private publishing service, sued in federal court, arguing that the law would drive it out of business. Though the lower federal courts agreed, the Supreme Court reversed these decisions, ruling that these courts had misapplied an exception to a general rule of First Amendment analysis.

United Reporting is a private publishing service that provides names and addresses of recently arrested individuals to its customers, who include attorneys, insurance companies, drug and alcohol counselors, and driving schools. These customers then used the information to contact these persons and offer their services. Before July 1996, United Reporting routinely received names and addresses of those arrested. California law generally required state and local law enforcement agencies to make public the name, address, and occupation of every individual arrested by the agency. The California legislature amended the law effective July 1, 1996, to limit public access to this information (Cal. Govt. Code § 6254[f]). The amended law limited release of the current address of every individual arrested to those persons who declare that the request was made for a scholarly, journalistic, political, or governmental purpose, or that the request was made for investigation purposes by a licensed private investigator. In addition, the law banned the use of this address information, directly or indirectly, to sell a product or service to any individual or group of individuals.

Once the law went into effect, United Reporting stopped receiving the address information. It challenged the law in federal district court, as the law clearly prevented it or its clients from obtaining or using an arrestee's address information. The company filed a CIVIL RIGHTS lawsuit under 42 U.S.C.A. § 1983, contending that the statute violated the First Amendment on its face and in its application. A facial challenge to a statute means that the statute is unconstitutional by its own terms, without recourse to any outside evidence of its effect on the plaintiff. In contrast, an attack on the law's *application* requires proof that the law has actually injured the plaintiff.

The federal district court and the Ninth Circuit Court of Appeals agreed with United Reporting that on its face the California law unconstitutionally restricted commercial speech. The Supreme Court, in a 7–2 vote, disagreed. Chief Justice WILLIAM H. REHNQUIST, in his majority opinion, concluded that the Ninth Circuit had mistakenly allowed a facial challenge of the California statute. He noted that the traditional rule is that a person to whom a statute may constitutionally be applied may not challenge that statute on the ground that it may conceivably be applied unconstitutionally to others in situations not before the court. There are exceptions to this rule, including challenges of overly broad statutes that restrict a person's First Amendment rights. However, Rehnquist stated that "the overbreadth doctrine is not casually employed."

Turning to the issues in dispute, Chief Justice Rehnquist agreed with the view of the Los Angeles Police Department. The department had argued that the law was not an abridgment of anyone's right to engage in speech, commercial or otherwise, but a law regulating access to information in the hands of the police department. In the majority's view, this was not a case in which the government prohibited a speaker from conveying information that the speaker already possessed. California "merely requires" that those who seek the address information qualify for it under the statute. This amounted to "nothing more than a governmental denial of access to information in its possession." Moreover, California could decide to withhold all arrestee information without violating the First Amendment. Based on this view of the case, Rehnquist concluded that United Reporting's facial challenge relied on the effect of the law on its potential customers, who were not parties to the lawsuit. Under prior case law, such a facial challenge was not allowed. Therefore, the decision was reversed.

Justice ANTONIN SCALIA, in a concurring opinion joined by Justice CLARENCE THOMAS, agreed that a facial challenge of the law could not be sustained. Scalia noted, however, that the decision did not address the "as-applied" challenge to the statute. In his view, United Reporting had a better case for showing how the application of the law denied access to persons who wished to use the information for speech purposes. On remand to the lower courts, United Reporting would have a chance to make its case using this type of analysis.

Justice JOHN PAUL STEVENS, in a dissenting opinion joined by ANTHONY M. KENNEDY, contended that the majority had mischaracterized the case as based solely on a facial challenge of the law. He argued that the record was filled with references to how the law injured United Reporting in its application, including statements from the corporation that it had lost prospective clients and sales and would ultimately be put out of business. Turning to the merits, Justice Stevens found that the statute was overly broad, violating the First Amendment. In his view, the law sought to keep the names and addresses of criminal defendants out of the hands of lawyers, to prevent them from soliciting law business.

CROSS REFERENCES
Education Law; Freedom of Expression; Gaming; Obscenity; Police Powers

FOURTH AMENDMENT

Illinois v. Wardlow

Since the 1960s, the U.S. Supreme Court has examined many cases involving claims by criminal defendants that the police did not have a reasonable suspicion to stop and question them. In these cases, the stops then led to an arrest. Under Fourth Amendment case law, a constitutional SEARCH AND SEIZURE must be based on PROBABLE CAUSE. Police can conduct a stop based on reasonable suspicion that a person has committed or is about to commit a crime, a somewhat lower standard than probable cause. A stop is different from an arrest. An arrest is a lengthy intrusion in which the suspect is taken to the police station and booked, while a stop involves only a temporary interference with a person's liberty. If, however, the officer uncovers further evidence, the stop may lead to an actual arrest; if no further evidence is developed, the person will be released.

The Supreme Court has made clear that police cannot indiscriminately stop people, yet it has increasingly given police the benefit of the doubt as to what constitutes "reasonable suspicion." This trend continued in *Illinois v. Wardlow*, ___ U.S. ___, 120 S.Ct. 673, 145 L.Ed.2d 570 (2000). The court ruled, on a 5–4 vote, that police can stop and question people who run away at the sight of a police officer. Police organizations hailed the decision, while civil libertarians worried that the decision gives too much discretion to the police to stop whomever they please, whether or not the person has done anything truly suspicious.

The case arose out of William Wardlow's response to the sight of police officers patrolling a Chicago neighborhood known for narcotics trafficking. The officers noticed Wardlow standing next to a building holding a bag. When he saw the officers, he ran; the officers pursued in their patrol car. They eventually cornered Wardlow. One officer got out of the car, stopped Wardlow, and immediately conducted a pat-down search for weapons. As the officer frisked Wardlow, he squeezed the bag the suspect was carrying and felt something that seemed like the shape of a gun. He opened the bag and discovered a .38-caliber handgun with five rounds of live ammunition. The officer arrested Wardlow, who was then charged with unlawful use of a weapon by a felon.

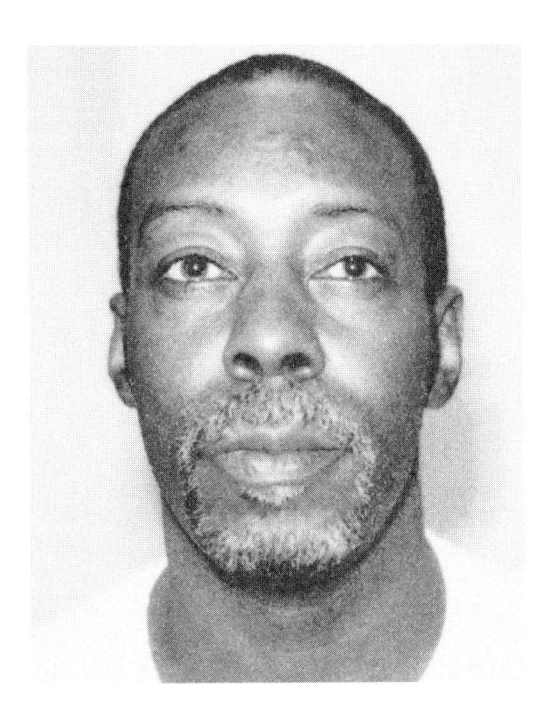

William Wardlow was arrested after he ran from police and was found to carry an unregistered firearm.
IL DEPT OF CORR./AP/WIDE WORLD PHOTOS

Wardlow was convicted of the crime, but the Illinois Appellate Court reversed his conviction, ruling that the gun should not have been allowed into evidence because the officer did not have reasonable suspicion sufficient to justify an investigative stop. The appeals court based its decision on *Terry v. Ohio*, 392 U.S. 1, 88 S.Ct. 1868, 20 L.Ed.2d 889 (1968). The Illinois Supreme Court agreed with the appeals court that the officer lacked the reasonable suspicion mandated by *Terry*. Instead, the court said that the officer had acted on "nothing more than a hunch."

The state of Illinois appealed this decision to the U.S. Supreme Court. A closely divided court reversed the state supreme court, ruling that the officers' actions did not violate Wardlow's Fourth Amendment right against unreasonable searches and seizures. Chief Justice WILLIAM H. REHNQUIST, writing for the majority, noted that the *Terry* reasonable suspicion standard requires "at least a minimal level of objective justification for making the stop." Rehnquist pointed out that the police officers were entering an area known for heavy narcotics trafficking and that they expected to encounter large numbers of people, including drug customers and individuals serving as lookouts. This was the context for the police officers' decision to pursue the fleeing Wardlow. Although an individual's presence in an area of expected criminal activity by itself is not enough to create a reasonable suspicion, Rehnquist declared that officers "are not required to ignore the relevant characteristics of a location in determining whether the circumstances are sufficiently suspicious to warrant further investigation."

Rehnquist concluded that it was Wardlow's flight, not his presence in a high crime area, that aroused the officers' suspicion. The Supreme Court had recognized in prior cases that "nervous, evasive behavior is a pertinent factor in determining reasonable suspicion." The court expanded the list of pertinent factors: "headlong flight—wherever it occurs—is the consummate act of evasion; it is not necessarily indicative of wrongdoing, but it is certainly suggestive of such." Therefore, the officer who pursued Wardlow was justified in suspecting that he was involved in criminal activity and in investigating further. Chief Justice Rehnquist pointed out that Wardlow had been free to go about his business when he saw police approaching, and he could have ignored them. If he had stayed and refused to cooperate, the police would not have had reasonable suspicion to stop him.

Justice JOHN PAUL STEVENS, in a dissenting opinion joined by Justices DAVID H. SOUTER, RUTH BADER GINSBURG, and STEPHEN G. BREYER, argued that the Chicago police did not have a reasonable suspicion to stop Wardlow. Stevens contended that there are many possible motivations for flight, not all of them criminal.

CROSS REFERENCES
Stop and Frisk

FREEDOM OF INFORMATION ACT

A federal law (5 U.S.C.A. § 552 et seq.) providing for the disclosure of information held by ADMINISTRATIVE AGENCIES to the public, unless the documents requested fall into one of the specific exemptions set forth in the statute.

Federation of American Scientists v. CIA

The U.S. fiscal budget for national intelligence was classified in 1947, ostensibly to protect national security. Since that time private persons and organizations have attempted repeatedly to access classified documents. Public access to some restricted documents was finally granted in 1966 when President LYNDON JOHNSON signed into existence Public Law 89487, the Freedom of Information Act (FOIA). Since this law only covers the EXECUTIVE BRANCH and since there are numerous exemptions, it does not assure the release of all federal records.

Thirty years after the signing of the FOIA, a 1996 intelligence commission chaired by former Defense Secretary Harold Brown concluded that disclosure served a worthwhile purpose, and to some degree, "[helped] restore the confidence of the American people in the intelligence function." Following the Brown Commission report, President BILL CLINTON authorized Congress to make public disclosure of the "bottom line" intelligence budget appropriation.

For the next two years, government officials voluntarily disclosed the 1997 and 1998 intelligence budgets ($26.6 billion and $26.7 billion, respectively), but only after being pressured with a request under the FOIA and threatened with a lawsuit. The lawsuit was filed by Steven Aftergood, a researcher for the Federation of American Scientists, an advocacy group. When Aftergood sought the 1999 figures along with those for thirteen other intelligence agencies, he was refused. In 1999 CENTRAL INTELLIGENCE AGENCY (CIA) Director George Tenet declared, "Disclosure of the budget request . . . [could] assist [foreign countries] in redirecting their own resources to frustrate the United States' intelligence collection efforts."

Aftergood, director of the Federation's government secrecy project, again sued in U.S. District Court in the District of Columbia. In November 1999 U.S. District Judge Thomas Hogan ruled that the Freedom of Information Act does not compel CIA Director Tenet to divulge the 1999 budget. Hogan commented in his opinion, "The fact that the president encouraged release of similar information in the earlier years is not determinative here." The judge then granted the government's motion to dismiss the lawsuit.

The court ruling only clarified that the CIA was not *required* under the FOIA to release the information. Full congressional hearings followed, addressing the appropriate posture to assume when confronted with future requests. In May 2000 the CIA informed Aftergood that his request for the 2000 budget under FOIA also had been denied.

Some have viewed the abrupt shift in policy as cautious, following U.S. failure to predict India's 1998 nuclear weapons testing and the bombing of the Chinese Embassy in Yugoslavia—blamed on an intelligence mapping mistake. In fact, the JUSTICE DEPARTMENT testified at the congressional hearings that recent international developments persuaded Clinton to support Director Tenet and return to secrecy. Tenet had successfully argued in court papers that since 1997 and 1998 budgets had been disclosed, the publication of more recent figures would divulge too much information about changes and trends in spending. On that point, Judge Hogan wrote:

> . . . The court must defer to . . . Tenet's decision that release of a third consecutive year, amidst information already publicly available, provides too much trend information and too great a basis for comparison and analysis for our adversaries . . .

Public access to government information has ebbed and flowed over the years, according to the crisis at hand. President GEORGE WASHINGTON deferred to federal agencies and gave them complete control of their records. THOMAS JEFFERSON, while following Washington's practice, favored disclosure that would assure the public that officials were conducting themselves in the public's interest. President WOODROW WILSON, during World War I, first invoked national security as a reason to deny disclosure. The trend of increasing restrictions and minimizing disclosure continued for the next fifty years. Subsequent abuse of the policy, such as classifying a document merely to preclude its disclosure to the public, prompted a twenty-year campaign led by the press and Congressman John E. Moss (D-CA). Their efforts culminated in the signing of the FOIA.

Attitudes of the chief executive have varied drastically over the past thirty years. President RICHARD NIXON signed EXECUTIVE ORDER 11652, which established levels of classifications based on the potential harm to national security that would result from unauthorized release of information. The WATERGATE scandal, however, prompted Congress to strengthen the FOIA in 1974, over the veto of President GERALD FORD. JIMMY CARTER signed Executive Order 12065, encouraging as little classification as possible. President RONALD REAGAN signed Executive Order 12356 in April 1982, reversing the prior approach. According to his policy, agencies were required to classify as much information as possible and at the most restrictive level. GEORGE BUSH followed suit. President Clinton's Executive Order 12958 returned to a more liberal disclosure policy, making it more expensive for agencies to maintain classification than to declassify. In 1996 Congress passed the Electronic Freedom of Information Act (Public Law 104–231), extending the freedom of information to electronic records. In 1997 the Commission on Protecting and Reducing Governmental Secrecy recommended legislation that would unify previous approaches by incorporating a philosophy of disclosure into the classification process.

FREEDOM OF SPEECH

The right, guaranteed by the FIRST AMENDMENT to the U.S. Constitution, to express beliefs and ideas without unwarranted government restriction.

The Cussing Canoeist

While on a canoe trip in Michigan with about forty friends, Timothy Boomer's craft hit a rock, knocking him into the water. When he surfaced, he screamed a string of profanity. His tirade was heard by several other canoeists including a deputy sheriff and a family with two small children. The sheriff was monitoring the

Timothy Boomer (right) and his lawyer speak to the press about the law against cursing before women and children.
OSORIO/AP/WIDE WORLD PHOTOS

river as a show of force to help keep the rowdier people under control. Upon hearing Boomer's loud and lengthy string of obscenities, the sheriff issued him a citation for violating a 101-year-old Michigan law prohibiting the use of "indecent, immoral, obscene, vulgar or insulting language" in the presence of women or children (MCL 750.337; MSA 28.569).

The U.S. Supreme Court has carved out two narrow exceptions to the freedom of speech clause of the First Amendment. The first area of unprotected speech is OBSCENITY. For the government to prohibit obscene speech or expression, the Court has stated "such expression must be in some way erotic, meaning that it appeals to the prurient interest or has a tendency to excite lustful thoughts." *Roth v. United States* (1957). The other exception is for "fighting words." In *Chapinsky v. New Hampshire* (1942), the Court described fighting words as "those which by their very utterance inflict injury or tend to incite an immediate breach of the peace." Historically, the Court has afforded profane speech a high level of constitutional protection. In *Cohen v. California* (1971), the Court held that offensiveness of speech furnishes no reason to regulate it, stating, "one man's vulgarity is another's lyric."

Defense attorney William Street from the AMERICAN CIVIL LIBERTIES UNION (ACLU) represented Boomer. Prior to trial, Street filed a motion to dismiss the case based, in part, on constitutional issues. He argued that Boomer's speech was protected under the First Amendment. He claimed that the law was overbroad and unclear as to what actions were prohibited. The trial court upheld the constitutionality of the law with the exception of an EQUAL PROTECTION challenge relating to the statute's reference to language used "in the presence or hearing of any woman." The judge held that while Boomer's language was not obscene in the legal sense, it *could* be construed as "fighting words" based on the circumstances and context.

After the jury had listened to all of the evidence, Street moved for a DIRECTED VERDICT, arguing that, on the facts presented, Boomer's speech was constitutionally protected. While Boomer's comments included repeated usage of unwelcome words, trial testimony showed that the two main responses of note were laughter from his friends and an urgent covering of a child's ears by a concerned canoeist. Judge Yenior determined that portions of Boomer's speech were not fighting words and were protected speech. In a novel legal approach, however, Yenior found that Boomer's continuous use of certain profane words—while not "obscene" or "fighting words"—were "non-speech" with "no communicative intent or anything" and, thus, not entitled to constitutional protection as *speech*. He instructed the jury, "If you find, beyond a reasonable doubt, that any portion of the words spoken by the defendant were not intended to convey any idea, thought or concept, in other words, that they carried no meaning whatsoever, you may only then consider whether defendant used indecent language in the presence of children."

Based on this interpretation of the law, the jury convicted Boomer. He was sentenced to four days of community service and a seventy-five dollar fine. The ACLU has taken the case to a higher court, urging that it reject Judge Yenior's distinction between speech and non-speech and arguing that everything Boomer said was entitled to First Amendment protection. The court suspended the penalty enforcement until Boomer argues his case in front of a Michigan appellate court.

A trial court in a different Michigan jurisdiction previously found this statute to be unconstitutional on vagueness grounds. The trial judge, in *People v. Prak* (1991), stated "the drafters might just as well have prohibited 'bad' language and they would have achieved the same level of notice to a potential offender."

CROSS REFERENCES
First Amendment

GAY AND LESBIAN RIGHTS

The goal of full legal and social equality for gay men and lesbians sought by the gay movement in the United States and other Western countries.

Anti-Gay and Lesbian Legislation

In 1996 the U.S. Supreme Court invalidated a Colorado constitutional amendment that prohibited, among other things, antidiscrimination legislation benefitting gays, lesbians, and bisexuals. The Court's decision prompted divergent responses from state and local governments. Some state and local lawmakers expanded homosexuals' CIVIL RIGHTS, guaranteeing them EQUAL PROTECTION of the laws in various sectors of society, but others passed laws barring homosexuals from exercising certain "special rights" traditionally exercised by heterosexuals, including the right to marry and the right to adopt children. One city even amended its charter to prohibit the city from enacting any laws *protecting* homosexuals from DISCRIMINATION. The Supreme Court has generally upheld these laws, creating two lines of seemingly conflicting precedent governing so-called anti-gay legislation. At the same time, politicians and the public continue to debate whether civil rights laws protecting gays and lesbians from discrimination create a group of "special rights" or merely guarantee equal protection.

In *Romer v. Evans*, 517 U.S. 620, 116 S.Ct. 1620, 134 L.Ed.2d 855 (1996), the U.S. Supreme Court rendered what was then considered a landmark decision for the gay and lesbian rights movement. The case stemmed from an amendment to the Colorado state constitution that prohibited state and local governments from enacting laws that would allow discrimination claims by gays, lesbians, and bisexuals based on their sexual orientation. Known as Amendment 2, the amendment also would have prohibited laws granting minority status, quota preferences, or protected status to gays, lesbians, and bisexuals while preventing them from making such claims.

The Supreme Court declared that Amendment 2 violated the Equal Protection Clause of the FOURTEENTH AMENDMENT. The Court said that Amendment 2 constituted an unprecedented attempt to identify persons by a single trait and then deny them any protection from the legal system. Amendment 2 did not merely deny homosexuals "special rights," the Court emphasized, but rather imposed upon them a "special disability" that deprived them of their fundamental right to participate in the state's political process.

State and local governments did not respond uniformly to *Romer*. A large number of governmental entities expanded the legal rights of gays and lesbians. By the year 2000, ten states, the District of Columbia, twenty-seven counties, and more than 150 cities had passed laws protecting gays and lesbians from discrimination. Most laws were limited to prohibiting discrimination against homosexuals in the workplace. A few laws went further, however, barring gay discrimination by public accommodations, credit institutions, healthcare providers, educational facilities, and landlords.

Conversely, a large number of state and local governments enacted measures restricting homosexuals' civil rights. Unlike Amendment 2 in Colorado, these measures did not generally attempt to completely exclude gays and lesbians from seeking legal redress for discrimination. Instead, some state and local governments tried preventing gays and lesbians from exercising particular legal rights traditionally exercised only by heterosexuals. The right to marry and the right to adopt children were the two most frequent targets of these "anti-gay" laws.

In 1996 Congress passed the Defense of Marriage Act, which denied federal recognition of homosexual marriages and allowed states to ignore same-sex unions licensed elsewhere. President BILL CLINTON signed it into law. PL 104–199, September 21, 1996, 110 Stat 2419. Many states followed suit, passing laws affirmatively denying legal recognition of gay marriages in their jurisdictions. By the year 2000, more than thirty states had banned gay marriages and ten states were considering such legislation. No state currently sanctions gay marriages, though Vermont passed a bill that creates "civil unions" similar to marriage. A few states recognize domestic partnerships for same-sex couples. California, for example, instituted a domestic partnership registry that allows gays and lesbians to register with their partners as a couple so they can have hospital visitation rights and certain healthcare benefits.

As of May 2000, Florida, Mississippi, and Utah enacted laws prohibiting homosexuals from adopting children. Three other states are debating such legislation: Hawaii, Oklahoma, and South Carolina. In 1999 New Hampshire repealed its ban on gay adoptions. About half the states allow unmarried individuals—including gays and lesbians—to adopt children, but domestic partners must petition separately for joint-custody rights in those jurisdictions.

In 1993 voters in Cincinnati, Ohio, passed an initiative amending its city charter to prohibit the city from adopting or enforcing any ordinance, regulation, rule, or policy that entitles gays, lesbians, or bisexuals to claim minority or protected status. Gay and lesbian groups challenged the constitutionality of the amendment in court, arguing that it denied them equal protection of the laws.

In *Equality Foundation of Greater Cincinnati v. Cincinnati*, 860 F.Supp. 417 (S.D.Ohio 1994), the U.S. District Court for the Southern District of Ohio agreed with the plaintiffs, granting them a permanent INJUNCTION that precluded the charter amendment from going into effect. The District Court's decision was overturned on appeal in *Equality Foundation of Greater Cincinnati v. City of Cincinnati*, 128 F.3d 289 (6th Cir.1997). The U.S. Court of Appeals for the Sixth Circuit said that Cincinnati's charter amendment was different from Colorado's Amendment 2 because the charter amendment did not deprive gays and lesbians of all legal redress in the entire state. The Sixth Circuit found that the charter amendment's scope was limited to the confines of the city, and that homosexuals' fundamental right to participate in the state's political process was not affected by the local law. Thus, the Sixth Circuit concluded that the charter amendment was rationally related to the city's valid interest in conserving public costs that are incurred from investigating and adjudicating sexual orientation discrimination complaints.

The Supreme Court surprised many legal observers when it let the Sixth Circuit's decision stand. *Equality Foundation of Greater Cincinnati, Inc. v. City of Cincinnati*, 525 U.S. 943, 119 S.Ct. 365, 142 L.Ed.2d 302 (1998). Though the Court denied CERTIORARI without any recorded vote or statement from the majority, three of the Justices wrote separately to stress that not too much should be read into the High Court's decision to reject the appeal. Justices JOHN PAUL STEVENS, DAVID H. SOUTER, and RUTH BADER GINSBURG observed that the intended scope of the Cincinnati charter amendment was not clear. The Sixth Circuit had found that the charter "merely removed municipally enacted special protection for gays and lesbians." The justices said that this finding differed significantly from the interpretation of the charter amendment advanced by the plaintiffs, who argued that it barred antidiscrimination protections only for gays, lesbians, and bisexuals.

Armed with Supreme Court precedent that arguably supports opposing views, opponents and proponents of laws protecting homosexuals from discrimination continue to debate the propriety of such measures when they are proposed by state and local lawmakers. Opponents of such laws contend that the legal system should not afford "special rights" to gays and lesbians. Homosexuals, they say, are different from other classes of individuals who are legitimately protected from discrimination because of some inherent or genetic trait like skin color or ethnic origin. Under this theory, a person's sexual orientation is a choice, not a genetically determined or influenced characteristic. Some religious people who oppose equal protection laws for gays and lesbians argue that homosexuals should be denied "special rights" because they are immoral sinners. Others worry that granting homosexuals equal protection of the law would adversely change the basic family unit in the United States, destabilizing traditional two-parent heterosexual families.

Proponents of equal protection laws for gays and lesbians argue that sexual orientation is an essential aspect of the human personality, as immutable as skin color and essential as one's religious preference. The right to be free from discrimination in employment, housing, and public accommodations is not a "special right" that only gays and lesbians seek, they say, but a fundamental aspect of a full and genuine citizenship that outweighs any competing liberty interest of another person to be free from associating with homosexuals. They contend that, to a large extent, America is already accommodating homosexuals' demands for equal treatment in the workplace, observing that almost 3,000 American businesses confer full benefits to the domestic partners of their gay and lesbian employees.

Leaders from the gay and lesbian communities are predicting that the year 2000 will be a pivotal one for homosexuals' civil rights. Democrats have pledged to pass a federal law barring anti-gay employment discrimination if they regain control of Congress in the November elections, while Republicans have vowed to fight any such legislative proposals. At the state level, Kentucky lawmakers are debating a bill much like Colorado's Amendment 2. Meanwhile, Vermont lawmakers passed a bill that confers upon homosexual couples an assortment of benefits, including the rights to inherit from their partners, sue for their partner's WRONGFUL DEATH, collect their partner's workers' compensation survivor benefits, and invoke the marital privilege not to testify about communications with one's spouse.

Baehr v. Miike

The state of Hawaii, which in the early 1990s appeared to be the first state likely to legalize gay marriages, reversed course and stopped the possibility of same-sex unions in a series of legislative, constitutional, and court actions. Gay marriage plaintiffs lost their legal battle when the Hawaii Supreme Court issued an unpublished summary disposition order on December 9, 1999, ruling that a 1998 constitutional amendment had removed all legal grounds for the plaintiffs' case. Nevertheless, advocates of same-sex marriage contended that the court's order in *Baehr v. Miike* would not end the national debate over this controversial issue.

Because no state recognizes gay/lesbian unions as marriages Jon and Michael Galluccio have a "holy union," recognized by their church in New Jersey.
JACOBSON/AP/WIDE WORLD PHOTOS

The Hawaii case began when a gay male couple and two lesbian couples filed suit in 1991, claiming that the Hawaii Marriage Law was unconstitutional because it justified the Department of Health's (DOH) refusal to issue a marriage license on the sole basis that the applicants were of the same sex. This, the plaintiffs argued, constituted a violation of the rights to PRIVACY, EQUAL PROTECTION of the laws, and DUE PROCESS OF LAW under the Hawaii Constitution. They sought a permanent injunction that would prohibit the DOH from withholding marriage licenses solely because couples were of the same sex.

This case of "same-sex marriage" reached the Hawaii Supreme Court in *Baehr v. Lewin*, 74 Haw. 530, 852 P.2d 44 (10th Cir.1993). The court ruled that the state must have a compelling state interest in order to ban same-sex marriages. The plaintiffs succeeded in convincing the court that the trial judge had used the wrong standard of constitutional review in assessing the constitutionality of the marriage statute. The Hawaii Constitution, Article I, Section 5, stated that no "person shall ... be denied the equal protection of the laws, nor be denied the enjoyment of the person's civil rights or be discriminated against in the exercise thereof because of race, religion, sex, or ancestry." The inclusion of "sex" made the provision similar to the failed EQUAL RIGHTS AMENDMENT to the U.S. Constitution.

The critical issue was whether the denial of same-sex marriages qualified as SEX

DISCRIMINATION under Section 5. The trial judge concluded that the denial was not sex discrimination and therefore the DOH only had to show that the legislature had a "rational basis" for restricting marriages to male-female couples. The rational basis test is the least difficult standard for upholding the constitutionality of a statute.

The Hawaii Supreme Court, however, reasoned that the prohibition on same-sex marriages appeared, on the skimpy record before it, to be sex discrimination prohibited by the Hawaii Constitution. Equal protection of the laws came into play because the state maintains a monopoly on the "business of marriage." It alone confers the legal status of marriage, from which many benefits flow.

Because the plain language of the marriage statute restricted the marriage relation to male and female, the Hawaii Supreme Court concluded that the statute must be examined using the "strict scrutiny" test. This test requires the state to show that it has a "compelling interest" to justify the ban on same-sex marriages. Having ruled that this issue was sex discrimination deserving "strict scrutiny," the court returned the case to the trial court. On remand, the DOH would have to overcome the presumption that the marriage law is unconstitutional by "demonstrating that it furthers compelling state interests and is narrowly drawn to avoid abridgments of constitutional rights."

Political reaction to the decision led to state and congressional legislation. U.S. Congress passed the Defense of Marriage Act, which denies certain federal benefits and entitlements to same-sex marriage partners by defining marriage as a union between a man and a woman. It also allows states to ban same-sex marriages within their borders and to refuse to recognize such marriages performed in other states. Thirty states responded by passing laws banning gay marriage. In Hawaii the legislature sought to blunt the decision, enacting in 1994 a law that said marriage can only be a union of opposite-sex couples. In 1997, the legislature enacted a bill that gave lesbian and gay couples some of the same benefits as those in traditional marriage. Same-sex couples were permitted to obtain benefit certificates that give them the right to share medical insurance, joint property ownership, and inheritance.

More importantly, the Hawaii legislature placed on the 1998 election ballot a proposed constitutional amendment that, while not banning same-sex marriage, gave the legislature the power to restrict marriages to opposite-sex couples. In November 1998 the voters of Hawaii adopted the amendment, which garnered 69 percent of the vote.

The constitutional amendment set the stage for the December 1999 Hawaii Supreme Court order dismissing the case. The court, in its two-page order, took judicial notice of the amendment and held that the amendment placed the marriage law on "new footing." The amendment removed the equal protection argument and gave the marriage law "full force and effect."

Baker v. Vermont

In the 1990s, gay and lesbian couples have fought for the right to marry through civil litigation. Following a 1993 state supreme court ruling, there appeared to be a good possibility that the state of Hawaii would legalize same-sex marriages. In 1998, however, Hawaiian voters passed a constitutional amendment that had the effect of preventing gay marriage. After this setback, supporters of gay marriage looked to a pending court case in the Vermont state courts. After thirteen months of deliberation, the Vermont Supreme Court, in *Baker v. Vermont*, 744 A.2d. 864, 1999 WL1211709, decided in December 1999 that homosexual couples were entitled to the same benefits and protections as married couples. The court stopped short, however, of mandating the legality of same-sex unions, leaving it up the Vermont legislature to either legalize same-sex marriages or create a domestic partnership status that would guarantee equal benefits to both same-sex and opposite-sex couples. Because the court based its ruling on the state's constitution, the ruling was final and could not be appealed to the U.S. Supreme Court.

Three same-sex couples, Stan Baker and Peter Harrigan, Nina Beck and Stacy Jolles, and Lois Farnham and Holly Puterbaugh, filed suit in 1997 in Vermont state court, charging that the clerks in three towns had violated state law and the state constitution by refusing to issue marriage licenses to the three couples. Two of the couples had raised children together and one couple had lived together for twenty-five years. The state and local governments moved the trial court to dismiss the lawsuit. The trial court granted the motion, finding that the marriage statutes could not be interpreted to permit the issuance of a license to same-sex couples. In addition, the court ruled that the marriage laws were constitutional because they rationally advanced the state's interest in promoting "the link between procreation and child rearing."

The plaintiffs appealed the dismissal to the Vermont Supreme Court. The court unanimously agreed that gay and lesbian couples are entitled to the same benefits as opposite-sex married couples. Justice Denise R. Johnson dissented from the court's decision to turn the final resolution of the issue over to the legislature. Instead, she argued that the court should have ordered the state to issue marriage licenses to same-sex couples.

Chief Justice Jeffrey Amestoy, writing for the court, rejected the plaintiffs' claim that they were eligible for marriage licenses under the marriage statutes. Amestoy stated that there was "no doubt that the plain and ordinary meaning of 'marriage' is the union of one man and one woman as husband and wife." The understanding of the term marriage was "well-rooted in Vermont common law." He pointed out that the license must be issued by the clerk "where either the bride or groom resides," 18 V.S.A. § 5131(a), and that the terms "bride" and "groom" are gender-specific terms. Thus, taken as a whole, the Vermont laws reflected the common understanding that marriage consists of a union between a man and a woman.

The court was persuaded, though, by the plaintiffs' constitutional claims. The plaintiffs contended that their ineligibility for a marriage license violated their rights to the common benefit and protection of the law guaranteed by Chapter I, Article 7 of the Vermont Constitution. By denying them access to a civil marriage license, the law effectively excluded them from a wide array of benefits and protections, including access to a spouse's medical, life, and disability insurance, hospital visitation and other medical decision-making privileges, spousal support, the ability to inherit property from the deceased spouse without a will, homestead protections, and more than 200 other statutory items.

Chief Justice Amestoy agreed that the Equal Benefits Clause mandates that same-sex couples receive the same benefits and protections as conferred on opposite-sex married couples. The court stopped short of legalizing gay marriage, stating that it was up to the legislature to modify the marriage laws, create a parallel domestic partnership system, or devise some "equivalent statutory alternative." It made clear, however, that the system "must conform with the constitutional imperative to afford all Vermonters the common benefit, protection, and security of the law." The court gave the legislature a "reasonable period of time" to act, but did not specify what that meant.

Democratic Governor Howard Dean predicted that the Vermont legislature would pass a domestic partnership law. Under these laws, a couple registers as domestic partners with the local government and receives paperwork that allows them to claim the same benefits that married couples receive. Other political leaders, however, supported same-sex marriage. The plaintiffs, while happy with the outcome, indicated that a domestic partnership law would not satisfy them. They vowed to renew their legal challenge, claiming that domestic partnership is not equal to marriage.

Dale v. Boy Scouts of America

Tradition and CIVIL RIGHTS came into conflict when a New Jersey Boy Scout troop expelled a scoutmaster because he was gay. In a groundbreaking decision, the New Jersey Supreme Court, in *Dale v. Boy Scouts of America*, 160 N.J. 562, 734 A.2d 1196 (1999), ruled that the gay scoutmaster could not be expelled for of his sexual orientation because the Boy Scouts of America (BSA) and its New Jersey council were public accommodations under New Jersey's Law Against Discrimination (LAD). N.J.S.A. 10:5–1 et seq. LAD prohibits discrimination based on several categories, including affectional or sexual orientation, which encompasses male or female heterosexuality, homosexuality, or bisexuality. In so ruling, the New Jersey Supreme Court rejected the BSA's contention that it was a private association entitled under the FIRST AMENDMENT to regulate the type of boys and men admitted into its ranks.

James Dale became a Cub Scout at the age of eight and went on to become an exemplary member, eventually achieving the status of an Eagle Scout, the highest rank to which a scout can aspire. In 1989, after he turned eighteen, Dale applied for adult membership and was approved. He then served as an assistant scoutmaster in a Matawan, New Jersey, troop during the periods he was not away at Rutgers University attending college. On August 5, 1990, Dale received a letter from the Monmouth scout council, informing him that his registration had been revoked. Registration was a prerequisite for service as an adult volunteer.

After Dale asked for the grounds of the decision, he was told that the BSA forbids "membership to homosexuals." The Monmouth scout director noted that Dale had been in a newspaper photograph taken at Rutgers,

James Dale (left) and lead attorney Evan Wolfson won their case against the Boy Scouts in 1999 but lost on appeal in 2000.
RAMSON/AP/WIDE WORLD PHOTOS

where he was co-president of the university gay and lesbian campus organization. He was also quoted in the newspaper as "only admitting his homosexuality during his second year at Rutgers." According to the scout director, Dale had demonstrated his inability to live by the Scout Oath and Law by publicly avowing that he was homosexual.

Dale filed suit in New Jersey state court, charging that his expulsion as an assistant scoutmaster violated the LAD. He asked for reinstatement and damages. The trial court, however, dismissed his suit, ruling that the BSA had consistently excluded any self-declared homosexuals. It found that homosexuality, from a Biblical and historical perspective, was not only morally wrong, but also criminal. The BSA had implicitly subscribed to this historical view since its inception. The LAD did not apply in Dale's case because the BSA was not a place of public accommodation and because the BSA, as a private association, could not be compelled to accept a gay scoutmaster because this would violate the FREEDOM OF ASSOCIATION guaranteed by the First Amendment.

On appeal, the New Jersey Superior Court rejected the assumptions and legal reasoning of the trial court. The appeals court concluded that the BSA was a "place of public accommodation" under the LAD. The court rejected a narrow interpretation of the concept, noting that the LAD was a remedial statute that must be "read with an approach sympathetic to its objectives" It noted that the BSA invited the public at large to join its ranks, and it was dependent upon the broad-based participation of its members. There were more than 100,000 members in New Jersey alone, demonstrating its mass public appeal. In addition the BSA used advertising and public promotion to encourage new membership.

The New Jersey Supreme Court, in a unanimous decision, affirmed the basic holdings of the Superior Court. Chief Justice Deborah T. Poritz, writing for the court, held that the BSA was a "place of public accommodation" within the meaning of the LAD and that the BSA was not exempt from the LAD. In addition, the court found that the BSA violated the LAD and that it was not sufficiently personal or private to warrant constitutional protection under freedom of intimate association. The court also ruled that the enforcement of the LAD did not violate BSA's freedom of expressive association or FREEDOM OF SPEECH.

The New Jersey Supreme Court's rejection of the BSA's claims to free speech rights was based on *Roberts v. United States Jaycees*, 468 U.S. 609, 104 S.Ct. 3244, 82 L.Ed.2d 462 (1984), which distinguished between freedom of intimate association and freedom of expressive association. Freedom of intimate association shields against unjust government intrusion into an individual's choice to maintain intimate or private associations with others. Intimate associations include marriage, child bearing, education, and cohabitation with relatives. Chief Justice Poritz concluded that intimate association was not implicated in this case because the BSA had a national membership of five million.

Freedom of expressive association is linked to the right of freedom of speech. Generally, overtly political organizations or organizations formed to advance gender or race-based interests are most likely to demonstrate successfully a genuine relationship between their discriminatory practices and their objectives. Though freedom of association presupposes a freedom not to associate, the *Roberts* decision made clear that the government could regulate an association if the state had a compelling interest, unrelated to the suppression of ideas, that could not be achieved in a less restrictive way.

The BSA appealed the decision to the U.S. Supreme Court, arguing that the state supreme court had mistakenly applied the *Roberts* decision when it should have applied *Hurley v. Irish-American Gay, Lesbian and Bisexual Group of Boston*, 515 U.S. 557, 115 S.Ct. 2338, 132 L.Ed.2d 487 (1995). In *Hurley*, the Court ruled that the sponsor of Boston's St. Patrick's Day parade could not be forced to let a group of gays and lesbians participate. The Court held that parades are a form of expression and that the sponsors could not be forced to include "a group imparting a message the organizers do not wish to convey."

On January 14, 2000, the U.S. Supreme Court granted review of *Boy Scouts of America v. Dale*, __ U.S. __, __ S.Ct. __, __ L.Ed.2d __ 2000 WL 826941 (2000). Two weeks later, the Court ruled in favor of the BSA. The Court, in a 5–4 decision, held that forcing the organization to accept gay troop leaders would violate the BSA's rights of free expression and free association under the First Amendment. Thus, it accepted the BSA's argument and rejected the New Jersey Supreme Court's application of public accommodations law to the case.

Visitation Rights Granted in Massachusetts

On June 29, 1999, the Supreme Judicial Court (SJC) of Massachusetts ruled in a 4–2 decision that a lesbian who helped raise her former partner's biological son had become the child's *de facto* parent, and thus was entitled to temporary visitation rights. *E.N.O. v. L.M.M.*, 429 Mass. 824, 711 N.E.2d 886 (Mass.1999). Five months later the U.S. Supreme Court let that decision stand when it denied the biological mother's petition for CERTIORARI. *L.M.M. v. E.N.O.*, __U.S.__, 120 S.Ct. 500, 145 L.Ed. 386 (2000). The Suffolk County Probate Court (SCPC) will now make a final order regarding custody, visitation, and child support.

The case stemmed from a thirteen-year relationship between two same-sex partners, known only as E.N.O. and L.M.M. In 1994 the couple decided to start a family. L.M.M. was artificially inseminated, and she gave birth to a son. The couple separated in 1998. E.N.O. then filed a motion asking the SCPC to grant her visitation rights, permission to adopt the child, and the right to assume joint custody. The SCPC ordered temporary visitation pending trial, and L.M.M. appealed. A single justice from the Appeals Court vacated SCPC's order, and the matter was taken to the SJC.

L.M.M. argued that the SCPC lacked jurisdiction to issue the temporary visitation order. She maintained that authority to grant visitation rights may arise from divorce proceedings and paternity actions. The legislature also allows PROBATE courts to grant visitation rights to grandparents of unmarried MINOR children, L.M.M. asserted. Nevertheless, she said, no statute existed authorizing any Massachusetts court to grant same-sex partners visitation rights under the circumstances of this case.

Conceding that no such statute existed, the SJC held that SCPC's authority was derived from its broad EQUITY jurisdiction. The SJC

Lesbian and gay couples in Pennsylvania receive a Certificate of Life Partnership, granting them certain rights and privileges that married couples have.
KENNEDY/AP/WIDE WORLD PHOTOS

said that a probate "court's duty as PARENS PATRIAE necessitates that its equitable powers extend to protecting the best interests of children in actions before the court, even if the legislature has not determined what the best interests require in a particular situation." In applying the best interests standard, the SJC found that E.N.O. was a *de facto* parent of her ex-partner's son.

The SJC explained that a de facto parent is one who has no biological relation to a child but has participated as a member of the child's family. A de facto parent, the SJC continued, resides with the child and performs a share of the caretaking functions with the consent and encouragement of the legal parent. The SJC distinguished a de facto parent from a babysitter or other paid caretaker who fulfills their duties primarily for financial compensation. A de facto parent, the SJC wrote, shapes a child's daily routine, addresses developmental needs, administers discipline, provides educational and medical assistance, and serves as a moral guide. In short, a de facto parent serves as a parent "in fact," if not in law.

The SJC observed that the record was replete with evidence of E.N.O. acting as a de facto parent. During the pregnancy, the two partners attended doctor's visits and workshops together. E.N.O. served as L.M.M.'s birthing coach and cut the child's umbilical cord. The couple sent out birth announcements naming both as parents. The child's last name consisted of each partner's last name. E.N.O. supported the family financially and was the child's primary caretaker when L.M.M was ill. The child called E.N.O "Mommy" and told people he had two mothers.

The SJC also emphasized the importance of a co-parenting agreement signed by the partners before birth and reexecuted after birth. The agreement stated the partners' intent to raise the child together. It reflected their wish that the child could continue his relationship with E.N.O. should the couple ever separate. L.M.M. authorized E.N.O. to make medical decisions for the child and designated E.N.O. to serve as the child's guardian in the event of L.M.M.'s death or incapacity.

Two justices dissented, criticizing the majority for deviating from other jurisdictions that have denied visitation rights to lesbian ex-partners who have helped nurture a child with whom they have no biological tie. The dissenting opinion accused the majority of "judicial lawmaking" by establishing the previously unrecognized COMMON LAW principle of de facto parenthood. The dissent said that only the legislature has the power to create a new category of paternity. The dissenting justices also suggested that the majority had infringed on the biological mother's fundamental right to parent the child as she saw fit.

The majority of justices on the SJC acknowledged that such a fundamental right exists but said it must be balanced with the best interests of the child. It is to be expected, the majority said, that children of nontraditional families form parent relationships with both parents, whether those parents are legal or de facto. "The recognition of de facto parents is in accord with the notions of the modern family," the majority concluded.

CROSS REFERENCES
Civil Rights; Discrimination; Equal Protection; Family Law; First Amendment; Marriage; Parent and Child

GIGANTE, VINCENT "THE CHIN"

He wandered through New York City for years, a disoriented old man dressed in a robe and slippers and talking to himself, always accompanied by a group of concerned companions. To federal prosecutors, however, Vincent "The Chin" Gigante was the head of the largest organized crime family in the country, faking senility to avoid prosecution. After a seven-year struggle to bring "The Oddfather" to trial on conspiracy to murder and racketeering charges, he was convicted and sentenced to twelve years in prison in 1997. His appeal to the Supreme Court was rejected in January 2000.

Vincent Gigante, known to associates as "The Chin" and to the outside world as "The Oddfather," began his climb on the criminal career ladder in the early 1950s. As a young Mafioso in Don Vito Genovese's family, he reportedly was appointed to murder mob boss Frank Costello. The "hit" was unsuccessful, but Gigante rose within the Genovese family and, by the early 1980s, had become its leader.

The Genovese family, founded by Charles "Lucky" Luciano in the early 1930s, was renowned for being more educated and less violent than other Mafia clans and is the only family never to lose a leader to a hit. Part of this success stemmed from a long held Genovese tendency to secrecy. Gigante continued this insistence on privacy and supposedly was deeply concerned about the attention-getting behavior of John Gotti, leader of the Gambino family. A 1987 hit attempt on Gotti, according to the prosecution's charges in Gigante's later trial, was ordered by Gigante personally.

Under Gigante's leadership, the Genovese family continued their domination of business operations on the New York and New Jersey waterfront. Despite federal racketeering crackdowns, he even managed to get his son Andrew elected vice president of the longshoremen's union in the mid-1980s. The Genovese family also reportedly controlled millions of dollars of contracts for windows in New York's public housing. Meanwhile, Gigante had adopted his public garb of robe and slippers and the senile behavior that his attorneys claimed made him incompetent to stand trial. This defense first kept him out of prison in 1970, when he was accused of bribing all five officers of the Old Tappan, New Jersey, police force.

By the mid-1980s, the Genovese family was feeling pressure from federal prosecutors, losing a dozen top members to prison sentences. Even worse, informers began to turn on the family. In 1990, prosecutors tried to bring Gigante to trial on charges related to racketeering, gangland murders, and the attempted murder of Gotti. For several years, his attorneys managed to delay the trial. "The Oddfather" finally was indicted in 1996, but the trial had to be postponed so that he could undergo heart surgery.

The trial finally began in 1997 and became a media circus as attention moved to the various Gigante relatives crowding the courtroom. The main diversion was Gigante's brother, Father Louis Gigante, who had been in prison for refusing to answer grand jury inquiries about mob activities. Despite such distractions, in July 1997 Gigante was convicted of racketeering and conspiracy to murder, largely due to the testimony

Vincent "The Chin" Gigante
DEBLAKER/AP/WIDE WORLD PHOTOS

> **VINCENT "THE CHIN" GIGANTE**
>
> | | |
> |---|---|
> | 1928 | Born |
> | 1970 | Unsuccessful attempt to bring Gigante to trial |
> | c. 1981 | Became head of Genovese family |
> | 1997 | Tried and convicted |
> | 2000 | Lost final appeal to Supreme Court |

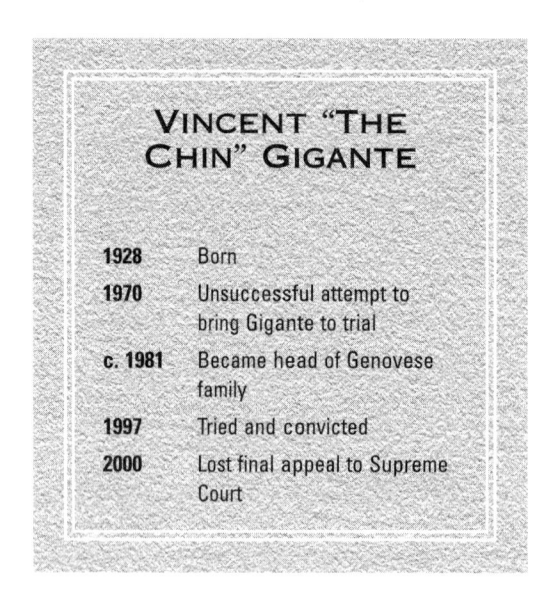

of former family members and videotapes that showed him behaving normally when he thought he was not being observed. The court rejected his attorneys' request that he be kept under house arrest or sent to a mental hospital. In December 1997, Gigante was sentenced to twelve years in prison and fined $1.2 million.

After Gigante was convicted, his attorneys continued working to free him. First, they claimed that there had been jury misconduct during the trial, based on the testimony of a woman hired to coax stories from the court driver who had transported the jurors. After a May 1999 hearing at which the driver said he had made up the stories about the jurors' conversations to impress the woman, the judge rejected the misconduct claims.

Gigante's attorneys next argued that the conviction had been improper on three other grounds. First, they claimed that the testimony of a government witness over closed-circuit television had violated Gigante's SIXTH AMENDMENT right to confront witnesses. Secondly, they alleged that the former Mafia members who testified were Gigante's co-conspirators and that their testimony should not have been allowed. Finally, they reiterated that Gigante had not been competent to stand trial. Six former Mafia members had testified against Gigante, including Peter Savino. One of the convictions against Gigante was for conspiring to murder Savino in 1990, via a bomb placed under a car in his driveway. During the trial, prosecutors had used televised testimony because, they said, Savino could not travel to New York: he was dying of cancer and had entered a witness protection program. The U.S. Second Circuit Court of Appeals rejected Gigante's arguments in *United States v. Gigante* 166 F.3d 75 (2nd Cir.1999). Without comment, the U.S. Supreme Court rejected Gigante's appeal in January 2000.

CROSS REFERENCES
Organized Crime

GUN CONTROL

Government regulation of the manufacture, sale, and possession of firearms.

The Brady Bill in Lower Court Decisions

The SECOND AMENDMENT of the U.S. Constitution states that "[a] well regulated Militia, being necessary to the security of a free State, the right of the people to keep and bear Arms, shall not be infringed." Though this Amendment was proposed to the Legislatures of the several States by the First Congress on September 25, 1789, and ratified on December 15, 1791, it has long been recognized that the right to bear arms preexisted our nation and its Constitution. The U.S. Supreme Court informed us of this fact in 1875, when it stated that the right to bear arms of a lawful purpose "is not a right granted by the Constitution." *United States v. Cruikshank*, 92 U.S. 542 (1875). Moreover, said the Supreme Court, the prohibition against infringing on the right to bear arms is limited to acts of Congress.

Notwithstanding the Supreme Court's interpretation in *Cruikshank*, Congress enacted the Brady Handgun Violence Prevention Act ("Brady Bill" or the "Act"), 18 U.S.C. § 922, on November 30, 1993. The Brady Bill was named after James Brady, the former White House Press Secretary who was shot in the assassination attempt on President RONALD REAGAN on March 30, 1981. Secretary Brady was left partially paralyzed as a result of the shooting. Both he and his wife Sarah became gun control advocates and lobbyists for the Brady Bill.

The Act attempts to limit handgun purchases and initially required that up to five business days pass between the time an individual seeks to buy a handgun and the time that the purchase transpires. Not surprisingly, the Act has come under attack on constitutional grounds several times. For example, *Gillespie v. City of Indianapolis*, 185 F.3d 693 (7th Cir.1999), involved the Act's prohibition against persons convicted of domestic violence offenses possessing firearms in or affecting commerce. Gerald Gillespie was convicted of domestic violence and, as a result, lost his job as a police officer. Gillespie filed suit against the city of Indianapolis seeking to have the statute declared unconstitutional. He also sought to have his employment with the Indianapolis Police Department preserved.

The U.S. Court of Appeals for the Seventh Circuit noted at the outset that Gillespie had standing to bring suit under the Second Amendment because the Brady Bill "deprived him of the ability to possess a firearm and, consequently, . . . cost him his job as an Indianapolis police officer." Thus, the court continued, Gillespie "has suffered a cognizable injury as a result of the statute's enactment, and that injury is one that would be redressed through a favorable ruling on his Second Amendment challenge."

The court noted, however, that the Second Amendment protects a limited right belonging to the people collectively, not to the individual. The Seventh Circuit further noted that, according to the jurisprudence of the U.S. Supreme Court, the Second Amendment's broad range was necessary to ensure protection by a militia for the people as a whole. Indeed, declared the Seventh Circuit, absent "some reasonable relationship" between a particular gun and "the preservation or efficiency of a well regulated militia," the Second Amendment did not guarantee the right to keep and bear such an instrument. Moreover, "the viability and efficacy of state militias" would not be undermined by prohibiting those convicted of perpetrating domestic violence from possessing weapons in or affecting interstate commerce. Thus, Gillespie's claim failed.

In a similar case, the Western District of Texas also found that the Brady Bill did not violate the Second Amendment right to bear arms. In *United States v. Spruill*, an illiterate individual signed a form admitting to participating in domestic violence against his wife. Spruill claimed that he did not know that his signing the form served as a waiver of his right to carry a gun under the Brady Bill.

Sometime after signing the form, Spruill allegedly informed a friend that he intended to shoot his estranged wife. Since the friend knew that Spruill possessed a firearm, and since the friend apparently believed Spruill, he contacted the authorities. The friend and several federal agents set up a transaction involving the exchange of one gun for another. The federal agents were present when the actual transaction took place. Immediately after the trade and while Spruill was in possession of a firearm that had traveled in interstate commerce, the federal agents arrested him.

Noting that no appellate courts had yet rendered an opinion on the particular provision of the Brady Bill at issue, the district court chose to follow "the majority path" and held that the Second Amendment did not prohibit the federal government from imposing some restrictions on private gun ownership. Both the *Gillespie* and *Spruill* decisions represent the position taken by most lower courts. Indeed, this position seems to advocate the proposition that the Second Amendment does not confer individual rights upon the citizens of this country.

However, the Supreme Court has remained quite silent regarding the Second Amendment. As the *Spruill* court noted, "Someday there will undoubtedly be a clear cut opinion from the Supreme Court on the Second Amendment." Until that day arrives, however, the lower courts will continue to forge the path for gun control.

School Shootings and Ensuing Legislation

In 1999 a rash of school shootings led lawmakers to grapple anew over gun control. Between April and December, the shootings, which followed four such incidents the previous year, claimed fourteen lives and wounded thirty-three. The first and deadliest of the incidents, the Columbine High School massacre in Littleton, Colorado, on April 20, brought numerous calls for legislative action. Amid intense lobbying, some states passed limited legislation, but

Students and others pray in Springfield, Oregon, one year after the 1998 shooting that left two students dead.
RYAN/AP/WIDE WORLD PHOTOS

far-reaching efforts fell victim to the perennial controversy over enacting gun reforms at the federal level. Meanwhile, new school shootings occurred in the spring of 2000, even as national opinion polls showed support for more vigorous law enforcement and a Mother's Day rally for stricter gun laws in Washington, D.C., drew an estimated 750,000 protesters.

On April 20, 1999, a stunned nation learned that Columbine High School had become the deadliest scene of school violence in U.S. history. At the high school, located in a town of 35,000 near Denver, two senior students went on a killing spree armed with semi-automatic weapons. They killed twelve students and a teacher, wounded twenty-three other students, and finally committed suicide. Bombs intended to kill hundreds more in the school cafeteria failed to explode. No sooner had the tragedy provoked national soul-searching about school safety than it was followed, exactly one month later, by a new assault. In Conyers, Georgia, a 15-year-old boy armed with a handgun and rifle wounded six students. In November and December, more school tragedies heightened fears and outrage. First, a 12-year-old boy killed a classmate in Deming, New Mexico, and, then, a 13-year-old boy wounded four classmates in Fort Gibson, Oklahoma.

As the eighth school shooting incident nationwide in two years, Columbine struck a nerve with the public and lawmakers. In May the White House blamed school shootings on the easy availability of weapons and called upon Congress to enact new gun control legislation. President BILL CLINTON's proposals included several regulations aimed at children and teens: requiring child-proof locks on all guns; raising the minimum age for handgun ownership from eighteen to twenty-one; requiring background checks on sales of weapons at gun shows; banning juveniles from owning semi-automatic assault weapons; and barring violent juvenile offenders from gun ownership for life. Among other controls, the legislation called for establishing three-day waiting periods for all handgun purchases, limiting buyers to one handgun purchase per month, and banning the import of large-capacity ammunition clips.

At first, the outlook for reform was mildly promising, but it soon hit snags. In May and June, the Senate and House each passed different versions of the legislation—S.R.254 and H.R.1501—which were then sent to a conference committee where differences in the bills were to be hammered out. Lawmakers quarreled, however, over one provision in the Senate bill to close a loophole in existing federal law: under the 1994 Brady Bill, firearms purchases in gun shops are subject to background checks for felony convictions, but purchases at gun shows are not. The Senate bill sought to close the loophole in response to federal data showing an increase in purchases of weapons by youths at the shows. Opponents declared the background checks an onerous burden on gun show participants. Neither side would compromise, the bills remained stalled in committee, and no further action was taken in 1999.

Throughout early 2000, as election year politics heated up, those in favor of increased gun control and those in favor of increased enforcement of existing gun control laws grappled over the direction of reform. The National Rifle Association (NRA), the nation's leading enforcement lobbying organization, derided new legislative efforts and called for Washington to increase enforcement efforts in existing law. It pointed to the small number of federal prosecutions since enactment in the mid-1990s of tougher gun control laws: in each case, the JUSTICE DEPARTMENT had undertaken less than ten prosecutions per law. In response, the White House blamed a lack of funding. In January the president requested $280 million from Congress for enforcement of existing laws, gun interdiction, research, and public education. As Congress delayed consideration, hundreds of thousands of women favoring gun control staged the Million Mom March in Washington on May 14, where they were addressed by the Clintons, activists, and celebrity speakers including comedian Rosie O'Donnell and singer-actress Courtney Love. Following the protest, U.S. Attorney General JANET RENO blasted lawmakers for stalling on pending 1999 legislation as well as the president's request for funding enforcement activities.

In the states, lawmakers produced a small amount of new legislation in 1999. Six states—California, Connecticut, Idaho, Illinois, Kentucky, and Nevada—passed laws to fund grants for school violence prevention activities. Other states tightened existing laws. In some respects, this was not unusual given the busy school violence agenda in state legislatures since the mid-1990s. In particular, states responded to Congress's passage of the Gun-Free Schools Act of 1994, requiring all federally-funded school districts to adopt no-gun policies, establish penalties of one-year expulsion for students who bring a gun to school, and make reports of all violations to state authorities.

Tightening of these laws began in 1997 as lawmakers increased penalties for weapon possession and violent behavior. Virginia, with the most severe penalty, established a minimum of six months incarceration for students who use a gun or other weapon at school (1999 Va. Acts, H.B. 2445). As the Justice Policy Industry has noted, about two-thirds of the states also enacted legislation reducing confidentiality provisions for sharing information about juvenile offenders. Thus Arkansas, under a 1999 law, requires school districts to report violent offenses to law enforcement officials (1999 Ark. Act, S.B. 259). In imitation of sex offender notification laws, Tennessee and Washington passed laws requiring parents of students convicted of violent crimes to notify new school districts of the offenses when their children enroll. 1999 Tenn. Pub. Acts, S.B. 1888; 1999 Wash. Laws, H.B. 1153.

In response to the Columbine tragedy, Colorado lawmakers made numerous proposals, ranging from using local police to enforce a federal ban on gun sales to teenagers to posting the Ten Commandments in school classrooms. As elsewhere in the nation, gun control in Colorado not only inflamed passions but gave birth to deep ambivalence. In February, Governor Bill Owens vetoed the police enforcement scheme, but in April he signed legislation reauthorizing background checks on gun purchases. A month later he refused to join President Clinton at a rally in the state for tougher national gun control. Shortly thereafter, a national poll by the Pew Research Center showed a gender gap growing on the issue of gun control: about half of men said gun-owners' rights were more important than gun control, whereas two-thirds of women said gun control was more important than rights.

One state required manufacturers to make safer guns, while another passed similar legislation. On April 11, Maryland Governor Parris Glendening signed the first legislation in the nation to require gun makers to personalize guns for use only by their authorized owner. The law takes effect in January 2003. In May, New Jersey lawmakers passed the nation's first-ever mandatory childproof gun legislation, which, if enacted, would require safety mechanisms on all handguns sold in the state.

Update of Lawsuits Filed by Cities

Many cities across the country have begun to engage in what has become the most recent attempt in ridding communities of death and violence. Cities such as Miami, Atlanta, San Francisco, Cleveland, Chicago, and Cincinnati have brought suit against the gun manufacturing industry to recover what the cities maintain are DAMAGES wrought by the industry's negligent manufacturing and sale of firearms.

Courts throughout the nation have come down on both sides of the issue. Some courts have found that, in some instances, gun manufacturers negligently fail to include safety features that they know will aid in reducing HOMICIDES, SUICIDES, and accidental shootings in cities, towns, and communities. Other courts have found that gun manufacturers are not responsible for the acts of individuals with whom they have no relationship and over whom they have no control.

On December 13, 1999, a judge dismissed Miami-Dade County's lawsuit against gun manufacturers. A week prior to Miami's defeat, Bridgeport, Connecticut, also saw the courts turn away its claims against gun manufacturers. Two months before, the city of Cincinnati also lost its suit against gun manufacturers and trade associations on a motion to dismiss for failure to state a claim for which relief could be granted. Oral arguments were heard in the Ohio Court of Appeals for Cincinnati's suit on May 17, 2000. Courts in both Chicago and Atlanta have allowed suits to continue against the same entities.

Miami's mayor, Alex Panelas, announces that his city is filing suit to force gun makers to childproof their products.
LEE/AP/WIDE WORLD PHOTOS

The cities engaged in suits have waged their claims against numerous defendants. Miami-Dade, for example, sought damages from twenty-six companies involved in the industry. It also included three trade associations in the suit. Similarly, Cincinnati sued a number of gun related entities. The city of Chicago filed a $433 million suit against thirty-eight gun retailers, distributors, and manufacturers. Indeed, across the country, gun manufacturers such as Smith and Wesson, Sturm Ruger, Glock, and Beretta have had attributed to them the ills of violent deaths, both intentional and accidental.

The claims asserted against the gun manufacturing industry and the trade associations include: negligent manufacturing, negligent distributing, STRICT LIABILITY for products, UNJUST ENRICHMENT, and public nuisance. The cities claim that the industry owes the cities a duty to manufacture and distribute their products in a responsible manner. Responsible manufacturing and distributing, the cities argue, would include, for example, installing fingerprint identification and chamber warning devices on handguns. The cities further claim that handguns possess inherently dangerous characteristics that are not open and obvious. As a result, the argument continues, strict product liability should apply. The municipalities also assert that, because gun manufacturers benefit from cities expending funds on tending to incidents involving gun violence, the industry is unjustly enriched by its own failure to act. Finally, the cities argue that the manufacturing and distribution practices of the industry result in a public nuisance to communities.

The primary defense asserted by the industry has been that all of the claims by the municipalities are derivative of those of individuals actually injured, and, as a result, are too remote to be adjudicated in the courts. Without injury to the city's citizens, the argument goes, the city itself actually has no claim against the industry. Gun manufacturers say that, for this reason, the municipalities are not able to maintain actions against them.

The gun manufacturers also assert that there can be no negligence on their parts because they do not owe the cities a duty of any sort. Absent either a statutory obligation or a special relationship between the actual gun manufacturers and the cities suing them, the law says that a claim for negligence in the manufacturing or distributing of firearms is nonexistent. Similarly, the industry maintains that with no claim for negligence possible, there can be no claim of public nuisance. Finally, the gun manufacturers and trade associations argue that the municipalities' claims of unjust enrichment must be discarded, because cities cannot recover expenditures spent on services that are inherent to and required of the municipal enterprise.

As mentioned earlier, some of our nation's courts have agreed with the cities, while others have concurred with the gun manufacturers and trade associations. Regardless of which side the courts come down on, however, the impact of these suits is already being felt by the industry. For example, Colt, one of the major firearm manufacturers, has decided to discontinue its production of handguns. Similarly, Smith and Wesson has agreed to a list of restrictions if the lawsuits were dropped, which includes safety locks on all of its handguns. Settlements of this kind might lead to the outcome the cities desire.

CROSS REFERENCES
Civil Liberties; Schools; Second Amendment

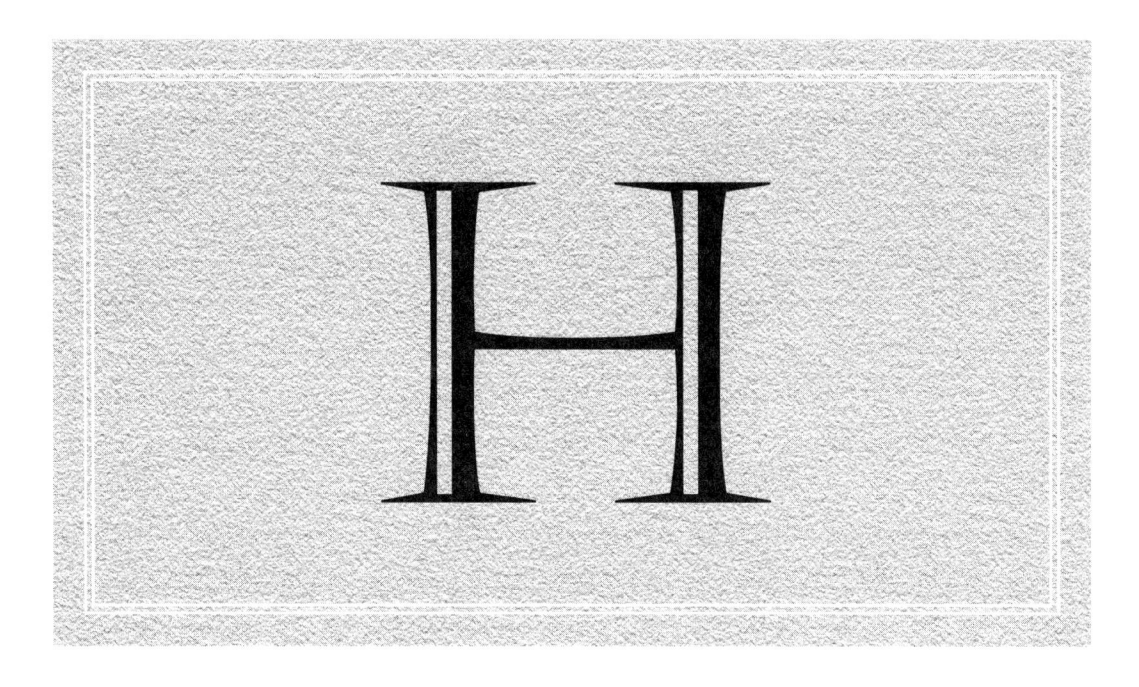

HABEAS CORPUS

[*Latin, You have the body.*] A WRIT (court order) that commands an individual or a government official who has restrained another to produce the prisoner at a designated time and place so that the court can determine the legality of CUSTODY and decide whether to order the prisoner's release.

Edwards v. Carpenter

The legal rules governing habeas corpus have continued to grow more technical and complex. The Supreme Court regularly issues decisions that attempt to resolve some of the more ambiguous questions about when a federal court may grant a writ of habeas corpus. In *Edwards v. Carpenter* ___ U.S. ___, 120 S.Ct. 1587, ___ L.Ed.2d ___ (2000), the Court limited federal access for state prisoners who claim that their lawyers gave them constitutionally inadequate help.

Robert Carpenter pleaded guilty to murder and robbery charges in exchange for the prosecutor's agreement that the plea could be withdrawn if the death penalty was imposed. The Ohio Court of Appeals affirmed his conviction and imposed a sentence of thirty years imprisonment. Carpenter did not appeal to the Ohio Supreme Court. After pursuing state post-conviction relief without an attorney, Carpenter retained a new lawyer. This lawyer petitioned the Ohio Court of Appeals to reopen Carpenter's direct appeal, claiming that Carpenter's original appellate lawyer was constitutionally ineffective in failing to challenge the sufficiency of the evidence supporting his conviction and sentence. The court dismissed the application as untimely under Ohio Rule of Appellate Procedure 26(B). This rule states that claims of ineffective legal counsel must be filed within ninety days of the appeals court's final judgment in the case. Carpenter's claim had been filed years beyond the final judgement. Therefore, Carpenter had procedurally defaulted on the sufficiency of evidence and ineffective counsel claims. The Ohio Supreme Court affirmed this decision.

Carpenter then petitioned the federal district court for a writ of habeas corpus. In his petition, he argued that there was insufficient evidence to support his sentence and that his original appellate lawyer had been constitutionally ineffective in not raising that claim on direct appeal. The federal district court found that the ineffective counsel claim served as good cause to excuse the procedural default of his sufficiency-of-the-evidence claim. The court ruled that Rule 26(B) was not an adequate procedural ground to bar federal review of the ineffective assistance claim. Turning to the merits of the claim, the judge ruled that Carpenter's lawyer had been constitutionally ineffective and granted a writ of habeas corpus conditional on the state court of appeals reopening Carpenter's direct appeal of the sufficiency-of-the-evidence claim.

Ohio appealed to the Sixth Circuit Court of Appeals. The federal appeals court upheld the district court's issuance of the writ. The court ruled that the ineffective assistance claim served as cause to excuse the default of the sufficiency-of-the-evidence claim, whether or not the former claim had been procedurally defaulted. The Sixth Circuit concluded that Carpenter had exhausted the ineffective assistance claim by presenting it to the state courts in his application to reopen the direct appeal.

The Supreme Court disagreed with the lower courts. In a 7–2 decision, the Court held that a procedurally defaulted ineffective assistance claim can serve as cause to excuse the procedural default of another habeas claim only if the habeas petitioner can satisfy the "cause and prejudice" standard with respect to the ineffective assistance claim itself. Justice ANTONIN SCALIA, writing for the majority, stated that it is not enough to say "the ineffective-assistance claim was 'presented' to the state courts, even though it was not presented in the manner that state law requires. That is not a hard question."

Justice Scalia concluded that state courts should be given the opportunity to correct their own mistakes. This purpose would be frustrated "were we to allow federal review to a prisoner who had presented his claim to the state court but in such a manner that the state court could not . . . have entertained it." The Court sent the case back to the Sixth Circuit to allow Carpenter the chance to show that the Ohio deadline for filing ineffective-assistance claims is not sufficient to bar federal review of that claim. He can also try to show that he had adequate cause to default the ineffective-assistance claim in state court.

Justice STEPHEN G. BREYER, in a concurring opinion joined by Justice JOHN PAUL STEVENS, agreed that the case should be returned to the Sixth Circuit, but he argued that the majority decision unnecessarily complicated an already complex set of rules for prisoners trying to appeal their state court convictions in federal court. Breyer asked "Why should a prisoner . . . lose his basic claim because he runs afoul of state procedural rules governing the presentation to state courts of the 'cause' for his not having followed state procedural rules?"

Slack v. McDaniel

The U.S. Supreme Court continued to define the rules governing habeas corpus in *Slack v. McDaniel*, ___ U.S. ___, 120 S.Ct. 1595, ___ L.Ed.2d ___ (2000). In the Antiterrorism and Effective Death Penalty Act of 1996 (AEDPA), 28 § 2253(c), Congress sought to restrict the ability of inmates to appeal dismissal of their habeas petitions to the federal courts of appeal. Before an appeals court may accept a habeas appeal, it must issue a certificate of appealability (COA). In *Slack*, the Supreme Court clarified the rules and procedures governing appealability under the new 1996 act.

Antonio Slack was convicted of second-degree murder in Nevada, and his direct appeal in state court was unsuccessful. In 1991, he filed a federal habeas corpus petition, seeking to litigate claims he had not yet presented to the Nevada courts. Under Supreme Court precedents, however, he could not do so until he completely exhausted his state remedies. Therefore, the federal district court ordered the habeas petition dismissed without PREJUDICE, which meant that Slack was entitled to file an application to renew his petition upon exhausting state remedies. After unsuccessful state post-conviction proceedings, Slack again filed his petition in the federal court in 1995, presenting fourteen claims for relief.

The district court granted the state of Nevada's motion to dismiss the case. The court found that Slack's 1995 petition was a "second or successive" petition, even though his 1991 petition had been dismissed without prejudice. The court also ruled that Slack's action was an abuse of the WRIT of habeas corpus and dismissed with prejudice the claims Slack had not raised in the 1991 petition. This meant that Slack could not raise these issues again.

The dismissal order was filed in 1998. Slack tried to appeal the dismissal, but the Ninth Circuit Court of Appeals refused to allow the appeal, finding that under the version of § 2253 that existed before enactment of AEDPA, he was not entitled to a certificate of probable cause (CPC). Slick then appealed to the Supreme Court.

In a 7–2 decision, the Court reversed the lower federal courts and clarified the rules governing the appeal of a denial of habeas corpus. Justice ANTHONY M. KENNEDY, writing for the majority, made three rulings. First, when a habeas corpus petitioner seeks to start an appeal of the dismissal of a habeas corpus petition after April 24, 1996 (the effective date of AEDPA), the right to appeal is governed by the certificate of appealability (COA) requirements, not the CPC requirements. The lower courts had, in Slack's case, incorrectly applied the pre-1996 version of the statute to his attempted appeal. Under the AEDPA, an appellate case is begun when the application for a COA is filed. Because Congress stated that the application of the AEDPA is triggered by the commencement of a case, "the relevant case for a statute directed to appeals is the one initiated in the appellate court." Justice Kennedy saw "no indication that Congress intended to tie application of the provisions to the date a petition was filed in the district court."

The second ruling involved clarifying the standards a district court judge must use in granting or denying a COA when the judge has dismissed the habeas petition on procedural grounds without examining the constitutional claims of the prisoner. Justice Kennedy held that the court should issue a COA, allowing an appeal of the court's order, if the prisoner shows, at minimum, two things: (1) "jurists of reason would find it debatable whether the petition states a valid claim of the denial of a constitutional right" and (2) "jurists of reason would find it debatable whether the district court was correct in its procedural ruling." The Court concluded that Congress had expressed no intention to "allow trial court procedural error to bar vindication of substantial constitutional rights on appeal."

Justice Kennedy's third ruling addressed whether the district court committed procedural error in Slack's case. Kennedy found that the district court had been wrong in classifying Slack's 1995 petition as a "second or successive petition" that was barred by federal law. The Court stated that a habeas petition that is filed after an initial petition was dismissed without adjudication on the merits for failure to exhaust state remedies is not a second or successive petition. Therefore, the Court sent the case back to the lower courts to determine whether Slack was entitled to a hearing on the merits of his appeal.

Justice ANTONIN SCALIA, in a dissenting opinion joined by Justice CLARENCE THOMAS, argued that Slack should not be permitted to address claims that he did not include in his original 1991 habeas petition.

CROSS REFERENCES
Appeal; Prisoners' Rights

HATE CRIME

A crime motivated by racial, religious, gender, sexual orientation, or other PREJUDICE.

Apprendi v. New Jersey

The growth in crimes motivated by bias against persons because of their race, religion, nationality, or sexual orientation has led to the enactment of criminal statutes that target bias. Some statutes criminalize the hate crime itself, while others increase the criminal penalty if the crime was motivated by bias. The U.S. Supreme Court has upheld laws that enhance the penalties for bias-motivated crimes. Almost all states have enacted hate crime laws.

The states have not adopted uniform hate crime laws, however. As a consequence, some states mandate that a jury decide whether a defendant was motivated by bias, while others authorize the trial judge to decide bias motivation. In *Apprendi v. New Jersey*, __ U.S. __, __ S.Ct. __, __ L.Ed.2d __ 2000 WL 807189 (2000), the Supreme Court examined a New Jersey statute that gave judges the power to decide bias. The Court ruled this practice unconstitutional, requiring that a jury decide the issue based on the REASONABLE DOUBT standard of proof.

Police in Vineland, New Jersey, arrested Charles C. Apprendi, Jr. in December 1994 after he fired eight shots into the home of an African American family in his otherwise all white neighborhood. No one was injured in the shooting and Apprendi admitted that he fired the shots. He confessed to the police that he wanted to send a message to the black family that they did not belong in his neighborhood. Later, however, Apprendi claimed that police had pressured him into making that statement. He contended that he had no racial motivation for the shooting but rather fired into the house when its purple front door attracted his attention.

Apprendi pleaded guilty to a firearm violation and processing a bomb in his house. Though the offenses carried a maximum sentence of ten years in prison, the prosecutor

Charles Apprendi stays at a boarding house while waiting to hear how the Supreme Court will rule on his appeal.
PIERCE/AP/WIDE WORLD PHOTOS

invoked the New Jersey hate crime law and asked that the judge increase the sentence. The judge agreed and imposed a twelve-year prison term, stating that prosecutors had shown by a preponderance of the evidence that Apprendi's act was racially motivated.

Apprendi appealed the sentence, arguing that he could be given such an enhanced sentence only if prosecutors presented evidence to a jury that proved beyond a reasonable doubt that he had fired the weapon out of racial bias. The prosecutor contended that the hate crime law punished MOTIVE, which has been regarded as a SENTENCING issue for the judge to resolve. After the New Jersey Supreme Court rejected his appeal, Apprendi appealed to the U.S. Supreme Court.

The Supreme Court, on a 5–4 vote, reversed the New Jersey Supreme Court and found the hate crime provision unconstitutional. Justice JOHN PAUL STEVENS, writing for the majority, stated that any factor, except for a prior conviction, "that increases the maximum penalty for a crime must be charged in an indictment, submitted to a jury, and proven beyond a reasonable doubt."

Justice Stevens based the Court's decision on the FOURTEENTH AMENDMENT's DUE PROCESS CLAUSE and the SIXTH AMENDMENT's right to trial by a jury. Taken together, these two provisions entitle a criminal defendant to a jury determination that "[he] is guilty of every element of the crime with which he is charged, beyond a reasonable doubt." Though judges do have the right to exercise discretion in sentencing, they must comply with sentencing provisions contained in state criminal statutes. Justice Stevens noted the "novelty of the scheme that removes the jury from the determination of a fact that exposes the defendant to a penalty exceeding the maximum he could receive if punished according to the facts reflected in the jury verdict alone."

The Court also examined the effect of the New Jersey law on a defendant. A defendant charged with a second-degree crime could be punished identically to a defendant charged with a first-degree crime. In addition, the standard of proof—preponderance of the evidence—employed by the hate crime law was less than the "beyond a reasonable doubt" standard. Therefore, it took less evidence to *increase* the criminal penalty. Justice Stevens concluded that the New Jersey procedure was "an unacceptable departure from the jury tradition that is an indispensable part of our criminal justice system."

Justice SANDRA DAY O'CONNOR, in a dissenting opinion joined by Chief Justice WILLIAM H. REHNQUIST and Justices STEPHEN G. BREYER and ANTHONY M. KENNEDY, argued that the majority had misread the court's prior cases. She contended that "not every fact that bears on a defendant's punishment need be charged in an indictment, submitted to a jury, and proved by the government beyond a reasonable doubt." The dissenters believed that the legislature can define the elements of a criminal offense.

Courts-Martial for the Killing of Private Barry Winchell

Early in the morning on July 5, 1999, Private Calvin N. Glover attacked Private First Class Barry Winchell with a baseball bat as Winchell slept on his cot in the barracks at Fort Campbell on the Kentucky-Tennessee border. Winchell died the next day in a civilian hospital, a victim of anti-gay animus. The murder ended the promising career of a capable U.S. soldier. Winchell enjoyed the physical and mental training that went with being in the Army. He was the best in his company at firing a .50-caliber machine gun and vowed to be one of the best helicopter pilots in the Army.

Winchell's murder culminated months of harassment. Six months earlier, Specialist Justin R. Fisher told Sergeant Michael Kleifgen that he saw a soldier at the Connection, a gay nightclub sixty miles from Fort Campbell. Under federal law, military personnel are forbidden from engaging in homosexual relations. After investigating the claim with a staff sergeant, Kleifgen established that it was Winchell who had been at the club. Winchell had been dating Cal "Calpernia" Addams, a performer at the nightclub.

In apparent violation of President BILL CLINTON's "Don't ask, don't tell" policy, Kleifgen asked Winchell if he was gay. Winchell denied it. Rumors circulated despite the denial, and soon Winchell was the target of anti-gay harassment. According to Kleifgen, everyone in the company began calling Winchell derogatory names, including "faggot." Fisher once got into a scuffle with Winchell and hit him with a dustpan, giving Winchell a cut that required stitches. When Winchell reported the harassment to his superiors, the Army refused to stop or punish anyone.

The night before the murder, Glover, who had been drinking alcohol, picked a fight with Winchell. Winchell beat Glover easily. Soldiers in the company teased Glover, saying he got his "butt kicked by a gay man." Some soldiers said Glover vowed to "get even, kill [Winchell]."

The next night, soldiers in the company celebrated the Fourth of July by drinking a keg of beer. Winchell, Glover, and Fisher all drank heavily that day. Toward the end of the evening, Fisher and Glover were talking about the fight. Fisher handed Glover a baseball bat and urged him to get revenge. When Glover found Winchell sleeping in his cot, he beat Winchell as many as five times with the bat. The blows were so hard that blood spattered onto the ceiling and onto a wall fifteen feet away.

At 3 A.M., the fire alarm in the barracks clanged as Glover fled the scene and Fisher alerted other soldiers that Winchell was dying. Private First Class Nikita Sanarov and Private First Class Jonathon Joyce saw Winchell lying motionless in the hallway. Sanarov also saw Glover running to a trash bin with clothes in his arms. Investigators later found Glover in his room with blood on his shirt and the door.

Five months later, Glover faced a COURT-MARTIAL for premeditated MURDER. Before his trial, Glover pleaded guilty to unpremeditated murder in hopes of getting a light sentence. Glover cried during his plea as he recalled beating Winchell "at least two or three times." Glover blamed the incident on his inebriation and Fisher's prodding. He never addressed the allegation that he hates gays.

Prosecutors proceeded with their case against Glover anyway and secured a conviction for premeditated murder. Glover received a sentence of life in prison with the possibility of parole, a reduction in rank, and a dishonorable discharge.

For his role in Winchell's murder, Fisher faced charges of murder, accessory after the fact, and lying to investigators. Before the court-martial, Fisher pleaded guilty to reduced charges of lying to investigators and OBSTRUCTING JUSTICE by wiping blood from the bat Glover used to kill Winchell. In exchange for the plea, the Army dropped the murder and accessory charges. Fisher's sentence was twelve and a half years in prison.

Winchell's parents, Pat and Wally Kutteles, called the plea bargain a travesty. They said Fisher was as responsible for their son's death as Glover. Mostly, however, they blamed Defense Secretary William S. Cohen and Major General Robert Clark, who was in charge of Fort Campbell, for failing to protect Winchell.

Justin R. Fisher approaches his court martial on January 8, 2000, for his role in the murder of Barry Winchell.
ROSHAN/AP/WIDE WORLD PHOTOS

Winchell's parents considered filing a lawsuit against the Army and called for an end to the military policy on homosexuals. "'Don't ask, don't tell, don't pursue' did not protect our son," said Pat Kutteles. "It won't protect anyone else's child. This policy must end."

CROSS REFERENCES
Fourteenth Amendment; Gay and Lesbian Rights; Sixth Amendment

HEALTH CARE LAW

Patients' Bill of Rights

In 2000 Lawmakers again failed to pass the so-called Patients' Bill of Rights—legislation to improve patients' rights under private health insurance plans, which cover as many as 169 million Americans. Divided sharply over the scope and content of those rights, Democrats and Republicans seemed destined to reserve the issue for their November 2000 election campaigns.

Managed care plans, also called health maintenance organizations, or HMOs, were the main focus of dispute. HMOs usually must approve non-routine, expensive, and often critical medical care before a patient receives treatment. When an HMO delays or denies coverage, patients' sole recourse may be an internal review process that is stacked against them. If the patient dies or is seriously injured because his HMO delays or mistakenly denies treatment, he typically cannot sue the HMO for damages.

Senators Collins (left) and Gregg claim Senator Ted Kennedy's plan (diagram) for the Patients' Bill of Rights is too complicated.
MARQUETTE/AP/WIDE WORLD PHOTOS

Democrats in both houses of Congress pushed for legislative reform to correct these and other shortcomings. They sought an appeals process to allow patients to challenge HMO decisions before a board of independent doctors. They also fought to give patients the right to sue HMOs in state court for damages resulting from delays and improper denials of treatment. Polls suggested that as many as seventy percent of Americans favored such reforms.

Senate Republicans and most House Republicans, however, feared the reforms would increase the cost of health care, drive up insurance premiums, and thus add to the already 43 million Americans who are uninsured. Republicans accused Democrats of appeasing trial lawyers, who are big contributors to Democratic political campaigns and who would benefit from increased state court litigation. Democrats accused Republicans of kowtowing to the health care and insurance industries, which contribute heavily to Republican campaigns and might experience lower profits under the Democratic reforms.

On July 15, 1999, Senate Republicans passed their own version of a patients' rights bill. It would create an appeals process for the approximately 124 million Americans enrolled in employer-sponsored health plans. The appeals board, however, would be limited to determining whether the insurance company or HMO followed its own internal procedures, including its definition of "medically necessary," when it denied a claim. The board would not be allowed to review whether the insurance company or HMO denied medical care required by the *best* medical practices.

The Senate bill did not contain a right to sue. Barbara Boxer (D-CA) said, "If. . .H.M.O.'s cannot be held accountable in court of law, what it means is if they kill you, if they maim you, if they hurt you or your family or your children due to callous or uncaring bureaucrats they cannot be held accountable."

The Senate bill contained some other protections, including the right to consumer information, hospital stays after mastectomies, and emergency room care outside the health plan network. Many of these rights, however, would apply only to the 48 million Americans enrolled in self-financed health insurance plans. Vice President AL GORE called the bill "a charade," and President BILL CLINTON promised to veto it if it reached his desk.

Three months later, lawmakers in the House of Representatives debated various patients' rights bills, including one sponsored by Charles Whitlow Norwood, Jr. (R-GA) and John Dingell (D-MI). Unlike the Senate bill, the Norwood-Dingell bill had bipartisan support. During debate over the bill, Greg Ganske (R-IA) told the story of James Adams, a seven-year-old boy from Georgia who lost his legs and hands to gangrene after cardiac arrest when his mother's HMO ordered her to take him to a hospital seventy miles away instead of to a local hospital for a high fever. Nancy Pelosi (D-CA) told the story of Stephen Parrino, who died after brain tumor surgery when his HMO failed to approve post-surgical therapy.

On October 7, 1999, sixty-eight Republicans crossed party lines to help the House pass the Norwood-Dingell bill with a vote of 275–151. The bipartisan measure would protect all 161 million Americans who have private health insurance. It would allow patients to appeal health care denials to an independent review panel of doctors. The panel would be allowed to consider factors outside the health plan's own definition of "medically necessary." The bill also would allow patients to sue health plans for injuries caused by delays and improper denials.

Patients under the House bill would have an easier time getting coverage for emergency-room visits, pediatricians, obstetrician-gynecologists, and other specialists. HMOs would be forbidden from preventing doctors from discussing expensive options with patients, and from giving bonuses to doctors who limit their care recommendations. E. Clay Shaw (R-FL) said the bill "puts medical decisions in the hands of doctors, not in the hands of Wall Street investors." President Clinton praised the bill as "a Patients' Bill of Rights not just in name but in reality."

In a possible effort to defeat the bill, House Republicans tacked on a package of health care tax breaks. The package was similar to one passed by Senate Republicans in its bill in July, which would create $13 billion in tax breaks through deductions for health insurance premiums and long-term care costs and expansion of tax-free savings accounts for medical expenses. House Republicans said the tax breaks would drain a portion of the Social Security surplus.

After the House vote, the Senate and House bills went to a conference committee, where negotiators tried to work out a compromise bill. Bill Thomas (R-CA) likened reaching a compromise to "mating a Chihuahua with a Great Dane," difficult but not impossible. While negotiators seemed to reach agreement on easy issues, such as access to emergency rooms, pediatricians, and obstetrician-gynecologists, both sides were unwilling to budge on the appeals process and the right to sue. This led President Clinton to summon ten members of Congress to the White House in May 2000 to urge them to resolve this important issue.

Pegram v. Herdrich

The dramatic growth of health maintenance organizations (HMOs) since the early 1970s has transformed the practice of medicine in the United States. Designed to emphasize preventive care and reduce health care costs, HMOs have also proven to be profitable businesses. The tension between cutting costs for profitability and providing professional medical care grew in the 1990s. Congress and state legislatures have debated, among a number of solutions, the need for a patient's bill of rights.

Trial lawyers have sought to hold HMOs accountable for cost-based decisions that have affected patients by filing lawsuits in state and federal courts. However, the U.S. Supreme Court, in *Pegram v. Herdrich*, ___ U.S. ___, 120 S.Ct. 2143, ___ L.Ed.2d ___ (2000), restricted these efforts. The Court ruled that patients cannot sue HMOs under the federal EMPLOYEE RETIREMENT INCOME SECURITY ACT of 1974 (ERISA), 29 U.S.C.A. § 1109(a), because the HMOs give doctors financial bonuses to hold down treatment costs. The Court found that to allow such suits would contradict Congress's intent to promote the creation of HMOs.

Cynthia Herdrich sued the Carle HMO and Lori Pegram—the physician who treated her—in federal court over a medical episode. Pegram had examined Herdrich after she complained of pain in her groin. Six days later she discovered Herdrich had an inflamed mass in her abdomen. Dr. Pegram could have ordered an ultrasound diagnostic procedure at a local hospital but instead she told Herdrich she would have to wait

Cynthia Herdrich alleges that her doctor failed to diagnose appendicitis in a timely manner.
KOSSOFF/AP/WIDE WORLD PHOTOS

eight days for an ultrasound that would be performed at a Carle facility fifty miles away. Before she went for the ultrasound, Herdrich's appendix ruptured, causing peritonitis.

In her suit, Herdrich alleged medical MAL-PRACTICE on Pegram's part and claimed that Carle HMO had breached its duty under ERISA by giving doctors financial incentives to keep the costs of medical treatment low. ERISA mandates that health plan managers act in the patients' best interest. The judge dismissed the claim against Carle, but a jury awarded Herdrich $35,000 for Pegram's medical malpractice. The Seventh Circuit Court of appeals reversed the trial court and reinstated the ERISA claim. The appeals court reasoned that the financial incentives offered to doctors could be a breach of duty where doctors delay or withhold treatment for the sole purpose of increasing their bonuses.

The Supreme Court, in a unanimous decision, reversed the Seventh Circuit. Justice DAVID H. SOUTER, writing for the Court, concluded that the decisions that HMOs make through their doctors are not FIDUCIARY decisions under ERISA. Justice Souter reviewed the history, purpose, and structure of HMOs, noting that the "defining feature" of an HMO is the receipt of a fixed fee for each person enrolled under the terms of a contract for health care. Cost control measures, which all businesses must employ, are part of an HMO. Moreover, providing financial incentives to doctors as a reward for decreasing the use of health care services was also an important part of the HMO structure. In Souter's view, an "HMO physician's financial interest lies in providing less care, not more." Therefore, if the essence of HMOs is the rationing of health care, Herdrich's lawsuit was an invitation to open the floodgates to HMO litigation.

The Court refused to open the floodgates. Justice Souter pointed out that Congress had passed legislation in 1973 that encouraged the formation of HMOs, predating ERISA by one year. Since 1973, Congress had continued to promote HMOs. Judicial restraint mandated that the Court not undercut this policy by allowing a claim "portending wholesale attacks on existing HMOs solely because of their structure."

As to the merits of the ERISA argument, the Court found that the HMO had not violated its fiduciary duty to administer the health plan funded by Herdrich's husband's employer. ERISA referred to the management of a "plan." Justice Souter concluded that the common understanding of the word "plan" is "a scheme decided upon in advance." Under this definition, the basic elements of the health care contract between the HMO and the employer meant that the HMO had a fiduciary duty to see that the contract was carried out. However, the HMO was not a fiduciary when it acted through its doctors in their day-to-day decisions.

The proper course was to allow patients to sue their doctors for malpractice. If the Court found a fiduciary duty, it would allow recovery against for-profit HMOs simply because they had a general business purpose to ration medical services. Souter stated that this "would be nothing less than elimination of the for-profit HMO." The value to patients such as Herdrich was that such an action was not allowed in most state malpractice laws. The availability of such an action was outweighed by the desire of Congress to ensure that HMOs succeeded in providing healthcare in an economical way.

CROSS REFERENCES
Employee Retirement Income Security Act; Fiduciary; Malpractice; Patients' Rights

HEALTH INSURANCE

Doe v. Mutual of Omaha Insurance Co.

In a 2–1 decision written by Chief Judge Richard Posner, the U.S. Court of Appeals for the Seventh Circuit ruled that the Americans with Disabilities Act (ADA) does not prohibit insurance companies from capping the amount of benefits paid for the treatment of ACQUIRED IMMUNE DEFICIENCY SYNDROME (AIDS) or AIDS-Related Conditions (ARC), even when those caps are lower than for other conditions under the same policy. *Doe v. Mutual of Omaha Insurance Co.*, 179 F.3d 557 (1999). The U.S. Supreme Court denied *certiorari* and let that decision stand on January 10, 2000, rejecting without comment an appeal from the two plaintiffs, anonymous policyholders with Mutual of Omaha Insurance Company (Mutual). *Doe v. Mutual of Omaha Insurance Co.*, ___U.S.___, 120 S.Ct. 845, ___L.Ed. ___(2000).

Both plaintiffs in the case are infected with human immunodeficiency virus (HIV). One plaintiff, identified as John Doe, purchased an insurance policy from Mutual that places a lifetime limit of $100,000 on benefits recoverable for treatment of AIDS and ARC. The other plaintiff, identified as Richard Roe, purchased a policy from Mutual with a $25,000 lifetime limit on benefits recoverable for such treatment.

The lawsuit alleged that the caps are discriminatory when compared to the $1 million worth of coverage offered for other serious, non-AIDS related illnesses in the same policies. Mutual argued that the caps were not discriminatory, but simply provided different levels of benefits for different illnesses. The U.S. District Court of the Northern District of Illinois agreed with the plaintiffs, finding that the two anonymous policyholders stated a cognizable claim for discrimination under the ADA. *Doe v. Mutual of Omaha Insurance Co.*, 999 F.Supp. 1188 (1998). The District Court observed that the insurance policies provided $1 million worth of coverage to treat pneumonia, but far less than that amount to treat AIDS-related pneumonia. Both Mutual and the Plaintiffs stipulated that AIDS constitutes a disability for the purposes of the ADA.

Title III of the ADA provides that "no individual shall be discriminated against on the basis of disability in the full and equal enjoyment of the goods, services, facilities, privileges, advantages, or accommodations of any place of public accommodation." 42 U.S.C.A. 12182(a). In overturning the District Court's decision, the Seventh Circuit explained that this provision has two core meanings. First, it means that places of public accommodation cannot exclude disabled persons from initially entering their facility. Second, it means that once a disabled person has entered a place of public accommodation, he or she must be allowed to use it in the same way other non-disabled people do.

In the case at hand, the Seventh Circuit wrote, Mutual did not refuse to sell the plaintiffs a policy or deny coverage to them. Instead, the insurance company placed a ceiling on how much it was willing to pay for the treatment of AIDS and ARC. The Seventh Circuit analogized the services provided by Mutual to those provided by a camera store owner. The ADA prohibits camera stores from closing its doors to the disabled or from refusing to sell them cameras once in the door, the Seventh Circuit wrote. The ADA, however, does not require camera stores to stock products specially designed for the disabled. In the same vein, the Seventh Circuit reasoned, the ADA does not regulate the content of insurance policies that are offered to disabled persons on the same terms as non-disabled persons.

The Department of JUSTICE (DOJ) filed a brief in support of the plaintiffs' claim. The District Court had relied in part on the DOJ's interpretation of the ADA to reach its decision for the anonymous policyholders. The Seventh Circuit agreed that the DOJ's interpretation deserved deference, but the Seventh Circuit said that it had to pay more deference to any discernible congressional intent underlying the ADA, since Congress passed the law and Congress was accountable to the electorate. The Seventh Circuit concluded that nothing in the ADA's legislative history would allow a federal court to regulate the terms and conditions of an insurance contract between the insurer and the insured.

Even if the ADA compelled the opposite conclusion, the Seventh Circuit said that the McCarran-Ferguson Act (MFA) would still prevent the plaintiffs from prevailing. 15 U.S.C.A. 1012(b). The MFA generally reserves insurance regulation to the states, and in most instances bars federal courts from interfering with a state's administrative regime. The Seventh Circuit said that requiring a federal judge to decide whether an insurance policy is actuarially sound and consistent with state law would "obviously" interfere with the administration of state law. The Seventh Circuit conceded that such questions were not presently before it. At the same time, however, the Seventh Circuit did not want to establish a precedent that might allow litigants to bring these questions before federal courts in the future.

Judge Terrance T. Evans wrote a dissenting opinion. He rejected the majority's analogy to camera shops, stating that a better analogy would be to a store that lets disabled customers in the door, but then refuses to sell them anything but inferior cameras. Evans said that the issue was not whether federal courts can regulate the content of insurance policies, but whether an insurer may discriminate against people with AIDS by refusing to pay for the same expenses it would pay if they did not have AIDS.

The Seventh Circuit's decision allows Mutual to enforce the policy caps that it had agreed not to enforce during the lawsuit. A spokesperson for the insurer said the company had not decided if it would put the limits back into place. Lawyers for the plaintiffs said they were not sure if they would pursue remedies available through the Illinois Insurance Commission.

CROSS REFERENCES

Acquired Immune Deficiency Syndrome; Disabled Persons

HOMELESS PERSON

An individual who lacks housing, including an individual whose primary residence during the night is a supervised public or private facility that provides temporary living accommodations, an individual who is a resident in transitional housing, or an individual who has as a primary residence a public or private place not designed for, or ordinarily used as, a regular sleeping accommodation for human beings.

New York's Homeless Cannot Be Forced to Accept Workfare Jobs

For several years New York City has continued to enforce a workfare program that requires WELFARE recipients to maintain city jobs in return for their benefits. The program has periodically undergone considerable criticism in that the jobs proffered by the city are often menial or custodial in nature, and do not promote the enhancement of marketable skills. Nonetheless, such programs have passed muster on constitutional EQUAL PROTECTION challenges and boast modest successes in reducing welfare fraud and long-term dependence upon public assistance.

In 1999 New York's Department of Social Services attempted to implement a 1995 regulation extending the workfare program to persons seeking public shelter in New York City. The largest group affected by this policy is that of the estimated 7,100 single adults and 4,600 families who are homeless and use the shelters regularly.

More than 1,000 people gather to hear speeches opposing Mayor Giuliani's plan for keeping homeless people off the streets.
MECEA/AP/WIDE WORLD PHOTOS

Latinos and African Americans make up ninety percent of the shelter population.

In February 2000 Manhattan Supreme Court Judge Stanley Sklar ruled that the city cannot force homeless persons to accept workfare jobs in exchange for city shelter. Although the Coalition for the Homeless claimed a substantive victory, the court's decision had less to do with homeless rights than it did with previous case precedent. In settlement of a pending 1979 case, *Callahan v. Carey*, the city had signed consent decrees guaranteeing shelter to every man and woman who asked for it. Sklar ruled that the consent decree was still controlling. The Judge's decision was being appealed to the state's Court of Appeals as of May 2000. (The Supreme Court in New York is a trial court, not an appellate court.)

Notwithstanding the pending legal issues, the program had other vociferous critics. Some members of the city council referred to the policy as "morally wrong" in its ultimate mandate to put homeless persons on the street if they did not comply with the program's requirements. One of the most sensitive issues surrounding the contentious program was the separation of children and parents if the parents were removed from the shelter for non-compliance. Under such circumstances, the children would be put into the foster care system on grounds of parental neglect. In the eyes of many, this was merely transferring problems from one system to another.

Criticism from public advocates also proliferated through the media. A busload of homeless persons from Philadelphia, along with their organized advocates, traveled to New York City for a much-publicized rally in Union Square Park. Their general position was that the regulations placed undue hardship upon families and persons already struggling to survive.

Finally, and in connection with the program, Mayor Rudolph Giuliani's administration had been under increasing criticism for what many saw as a harsh approach to the homeless situation. There were several claims of undue harassment and arrests of homeless persons who refused social services. Advocates for the homeless viewed the program as a reflection of the administration's fundamental misunderstanding about the true nature of homelessness in New York City. City Council Speaker Peter Vallone remarked to the media that such laws and programs were supposed to help the homeless, not punish or hurt them. According to the advocates, what the homeless need are more housing, more services, and more employment—not rejection and criminalization.

The administration was quick to point out, though, that free services do not come without a price. There is no constitutional right to shelter or to welfare benefits. Under the U.S. Constitution, states reserve "police powers" to regulate matters pertaining to the protection and promotion of the public health, safety, welfare, and morals. Thus, states may, in their discretion and under the moral obligation of social contract, choose to allocate monies or services to certain classes, such as the homeless. Though public aid may benefit a certain class, if its ultimate purpose is to contribute to the welfare of the people of the whole state, it does not constitute a special privilege or otherwise offend the Constitution. That some members of the public may derive more benefit than others is immaterial if the chief objective is to minister to the public good and welfare.

Notwithstanding, once a state has deemed a person eligible to receive welfare benefits, it cannot then remove or terminate the benefits without DUE PROCESS OF LAW. Collateral to this issue is whether the state, having established welfare benefits, may otherwise restrict benefits or impose additional criteria—such as work requirements—upon the intended recipients. They can, as long as the criteria or qualifiers do not offend other constitutional provisions, such as those that protect against arbitrary or discriminatory application of qualifying criteria.

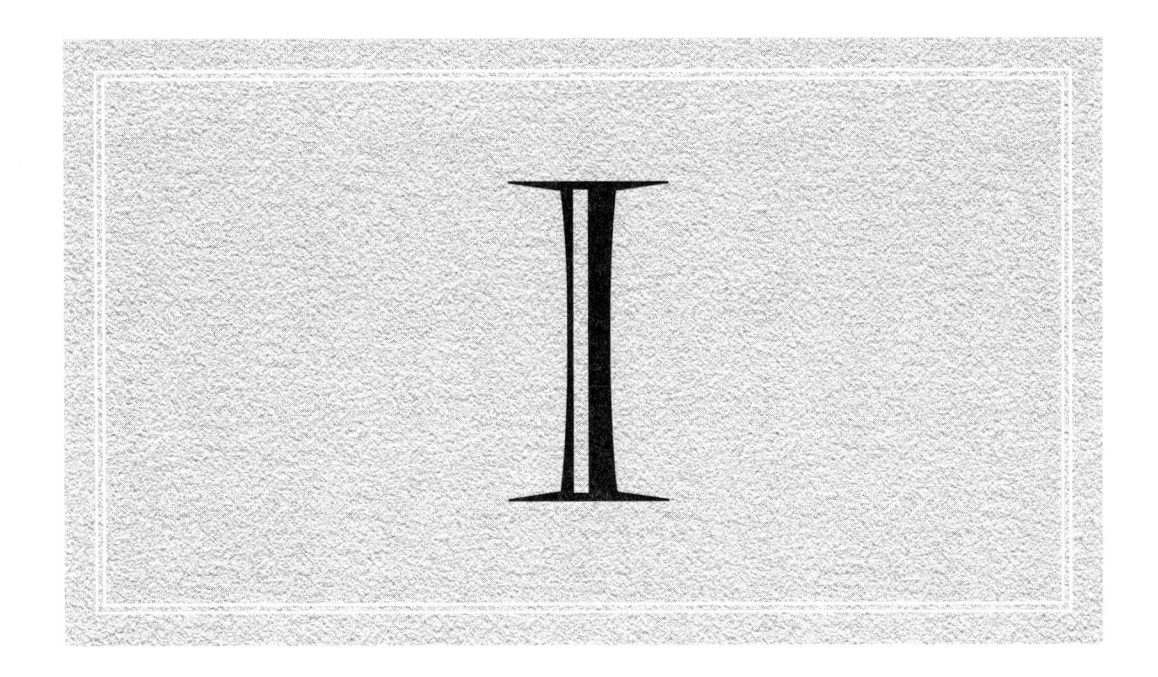

IMMIGRATION

The entrance into a country of foreigners for purposes of permanent residence. The correlative term *emigration* denotes the act of such persons in leaving their former country.

Richardson v. Reno

When Congress enacted the Illegal Immigration Reform and Immigrant Responsibility Act of 1996 (IIRIRA), 110 Stat. 3009–546, it sent a strong message to the federal courts to stay out of immigration proceedings until the Immigration and Naturalization Service (INS) had entered final administrative orders. The IIRIRA removed jurisdiction of the federal courts in a number of areas, including HABEAS CORPUS proceedings. The full extent of these restrictions became clearer after the Eleventh Circuit Court of Appeals issued its decision in *Richardson v. Reno*, 180 F.3d 1311 (1999). The appeals court ruled that an ALIEN could not appeal the legality of his detention or the denial of his request to post BOND and be released, pending the final INS ruling on his case. The court made clear that aliens would have to remain jailed until the final disposition of the case. In addition, an alien has virtually no avenue to file a court action until the INS issues its final order.

Ralph Richardson emigrated to the United States from Haiti in 1968 as a young child with his family, living most of the time in Georgia. In 1990, he was convicted on cocaine-related drug charges and sentenced to five years in prison. After his release from prison, Richardson remained in the United States as a legal permanent resident alien. In October 1997, he returned to Haiti for a brief visit. When he returned to the United States, the INS detained him. The INS initiated removal proceedings to have Richardson deported as an immigrant "seeking admission into the United States." Because of his drug conviction, he was deemed inadmissible. The INS placed Richardson in Miami's Krome Detention Center and denied his request to post BAIL.

Richardson sued in federal court, seeking a writ of habeas corpus that would require the INS to release him from custody pending the outcome of the removal proceeding. The Eleventh Circuit Court of Appeals ruled in 1998 that the IIRIRA's amendments to the Immigration and Naturalization Act (INA) precluded the habeas corpus jurisdiction of the court. The appeals court cited § 242(g) of the INA to support its ruling.

While Richardson's case was on appeal to the Supreme Court, the Court issued its decision in *Reno v. American-Arab Anti-Discrimination Committee*, 525 U.S. 471, 119 S.Ct. 936, 142 L.Ed.2d 940 (1999). In this case, the Supreme Court ruled that § 242(g) did not apply to the "universe" of DEPORTATION or removal claims. The Supreme Court later vacated the Eleventh Circuit decision and remanded it for reconsideration in light of the *American-Arab* decision.

On remand, the Eleventh Circuit readopted and reaffirmed its reasoning in the first decision except for its reliance on § 242(g). Judge Frank M. Hull, writing for a unanimous three-judge panel, emphasized that its first ruling had not rested exclusively on § 242(g). The extensive revisions to the judicial review of removal proceedings enacted by the IIRIRA repealed the court's jurisdiction to consider petitions challenging removal proceedings. Judge Hull pointed to § 242(b)(9), which stated that judicial review in removal proceedings "shall be available only in judicial review of a final order under this section." This provision provided "clear evidence" of Congress's desire to "abbreviate judicial review to one place and one time: only in the court of appeals and only after a final removal order and exhaustion of all administrative remedies."

The appeals court noted that § 242(b)(9) was intended to assure that issues of law and fact were not subject to separate rounds of litigation. The IIRIRA instituted a "sufficiently broad and general limitation on federal jurisdiction" that prohibited the federal courts from asserting jurisdiction in pending deportation and removal proceedings.

Richardson had argued that the IIRIRA's limitation on habeas corpus jurisdiction was unconstitutional because it prevented him from obtaining judicial review. Judge Hull rejected this argument because Richardson did have a right to judicial review of a final removal order. He pointed to a recent Eleventh Circuit case, *Lettman v. Reno*, 168 F.3d 463 (1999), where the court had reviewed a deportation order and concluded that the alien should not be deported. Therefore, the "constitutional adequacy of judicial review" would not be decided "unless or until Richardson attempts to pursue a petition for judicial review" after the INS enters a final removal order. The appeals court concluded that at this "interim stage," Richardson had failed to establish that he would not secure "full and adequate judicial review."

The court also rejected Richardson's assertion that the appeals court had jurisdiction to examine whether he should be released on bond. Judge Hull read § 242(g) as applying to any action taken to remove an alien. Moreover, congressional findings in support of IIRIRA disclosed that criminal aliens often failed to show for their immigration proceedings. Therefore, the INS had the authority to hold Richardson in custody until the completion of the removal proceeding.

CROSS REFERENCES
Aliens; Due Process; Jurisdiction

IMMUNITY

Exemption from performing duties that the law generally requires other citizens to perform, or from a penalty or burden that the law generally places on other citizens.

LaLonde v. County of Riverside

Society recognizes that police officers perform difficult and often dangerous work. The law acknowledges this as well, providing rules that minimize a police officer's exposure to CIVIL ACTIONS for deeds performed while on duty. Nevertheless, the U.S. Supreme Court has not granted absolute immunity to police officers. Instead, the Court has adopted the "qualified immunity" test. Under this two-part test, a police officer will be granted immunity if (1) the constitutional right which allegedly has been violated was not clearly established, and (2) the officer's conduct was "objectively reasonable" in light of the information that the officer possessed at the time of the alleged violation. The qualified immunity test is usually employed during the early stages of a lawsuit. If the test is met, the court will dismiss the case.

Although police officers generally can meet the qualified immunity test, there are times when the courts will find their conduct unreasonable. Such was the case in *LaLonde v. County of Riverside (CA)*, 204 F.3d 947 (9th Cir.2000), where the Ninth Circuit Court of Appeals overturned the trial court's grant of immunity to two members of the Riverside County Sheriff's Department. The court concluded that the trial judge had erred by dismissing an illegal entry claim against the officers before trial and dismissing an EXCESSIVE FORCE claim after the plaintiff presented his case to the jury. In light of the facts and the law, the appeals court found that the plaintiff had the right to argue both claims to a jury.

John LaLonde lived in an apartment in Hemet, California, with Monica Jones and her three young children. Around 1:00 A.M. one night, two sheriff's deputies arrived at the apartment building. LaLonde's next door neighbor had called police to complain about his allegedly noisy behavior. LaLonde, who was eating a sandwich and playing a video game at the time, later claimed that any noise came from the neighbor herself. Three times she had called police to complain about noise in the apartment complex and all three times the police found the charges groundless. The officers that night, however, did not have this background information. Moreover, the neighbor warned the officers that LaLonde had a rifle and that he was hostile to law enforcement officers.

The two officers went to LaLonde's apartment. Monica Jones opened the door and spoke with one of the officers. LaLonde soon appeared, remaining inside the apartment and away from the doorway. The officer asked LaLonde to step outside but he refused, saying he would talk to him from inside his apartment. When LaLonde angrily denied the neighbor's charges, the office reached into the apartment and tried to grab him. As LaLonde stepped back, the officer advanced into the apartment. The officer told him he was being arrested for obstructing a police investigation and knocked LaLonde to the floor when he refused to cooperate. They got into a scuffle, and the officer shot pepper spray into LaLonde's face. The second officer then entered the apartment and handcuffed the now passive LaLonde, forcefully putting his knee into LaLonde's back, causing significant pain. The officers then let LaLonde sit handcuffed on a couch for almost thirty minutes while the pepper spray burned his face. When two other officers arrived, they immediately wiped LaLonde's face with a wet towel. LaLonde was not taken to the police station, and he did not receive any citation that night.

LaLonde filed a federal CIVIL RIGHTS suit alleging that the officers had violated his constitutional rights and had caused painful injuries to his back and wrist. He alleged that the officers had violated his FOURTH AMENDMENT rights by: (1) illegally entering his home without a WARRANT; and (2) using excessive force, in particular the knee in his back, the tight handcuffing, and the unnecessarily prolonged exposure to pepper spray. LaLonde also claimed that the County was liable for his back injury because the method of handcuffing him—which allegedly caused his back injury—was pursuant to the official policy of Riverside County Sheriff's Department.

The district judge dismissed all of LaLonde's claims. On the issue of illegal entry, the court conducted a pre-trial evidentiary hearing and granted SUMMARY JUDGMENT to the officers on the ground of qualified immunity. A jury heard LaLonde's excessive force claims, but, after LaLonde's final witness, the court granted the defendants' motion to dismiss the case.

The Ninth Circuit Court of Appeals reversed. Judge Stephen Reinhardt, in his majority opinion, held that the trial court had mistakenly granted qualified immunity to the officers.

Judge Reinhardt concluded that a reasonable officer would have known that the conduct at issue was unlawful under clearly established law. Under the Fourth Amendment, a police officer cannot make a warrantless entry into a person's home unless the officer has PROBABLE CAUSE that a crime has been committed and there are exigent circumstances that require immediate action. In this case, the court found that there was no probable cause and no exigent circumstances.

As to the excessive force claim, the Fourth Amendment permits police to use such force as is objectively reasonable under the circumstances. LaLonde asserted that the excessive force while handcuffing him, along with the tight handcuffs and the prolonged exposure to the pepper spray, were unreasonable and unnecessary applications of force. Judge Reinhardt ruled that the claims had merit and that the jury, not the judge, should have decided the factual issue. Therefore, the court ruled that the officers were not entitled to qualified immunity and that LaLonde was entitled to have a jury evaluate his complaints against the officers and the county. The court remanded the case for trial.

CROSS REFERENCES
Excessive Force; Fourth Amendment; Section 1983

INHERITANCE

Property received from a DECEDENT, either by WILL or through state laws of INTESTATE SUCCESSION, where the decedent has failed to execute a valid will.

Charles Kuralt's Mistress Sues for Right to Inherit His Montana Estate

A clear majority of states have adopted the UNIFORM PROBATE CODE (UPC), which, among other things, creates consistency in the handling of distributive inheritances and other ESTATE matters. Notwithstanding, most state courts maintain full dockets of cases involving will contests and other estate controversies. These matters seldom reach appellate court levels, and rarely gain media attention unless they involve public figures. The April 2000 court decision involving the estate of legendary television journalist, Charles Kuralt, was one such case. At stake were ninety acres of fishing retreat along the Big Hole River in the state of Montana. At issue was whether the property belonged to Kuralt's wife or to his mistress.

Kuralt, at the time of his death in July 1997, was married to Suzanne "Petie" Baird Kuralt, his wife of thirty-five years. Other heirs included his two daughters from a previous marriage. In a will he executed on May 4, 1994, Kuralt left everything to his wife and daughters. The will was contested, however, in a suit filed by Patricia Shannon, who claimed to have been his lover and significant other since the 1960s. Shannon, through her attorney, alleged that she and Kuralt had hidden their relationship, but that Kuralt regularly visited and became "Pop" to her children. She also alleged that he had purchased a house for her in Ireland and had sent monthly checks of at least $5,000 until his death. She further produced multiple writings, letters, photographs, and other indicia of a bona fide relationship with Kuralt. Shannon testified that she and Kuralt had restored an old schoolhouse on the Montana property, and the two of them had built a cabin on the shores of the stream. She was still using the cabin as a residence at the time of her suit in Montana district court. Of significance—and apparently uncontested in the suit—was the fact that Kuralt had given Shannon the cabin and twenty acres of the 110-acre Montana ranch just four months prior to his death. The remaining ninety acres, valued at $600,000, were the subject of the suit between Shannon and Kuralt's wife.

Central to the argument on both sides was a letter admitted into evidence by Shannon. Apparently uncontested as to authenticity, the letter was written by Kuralt from his hospital bed in New York, just sixteen days before he died. In the letter, Kuralt wrote to Shannon, "I'll have the lawyer visit the hospital to be sure you inherit the rest of the place in MT, if it comes to that."

Because the letter was written *after* the only known last will and testament, the quintessential issue for the district court was whether the letter qualified as a CODICIL, HOLOGRAPH, or will substitute. Letters may, in a minority of states, satisfy the requirements of ordinary wills, and may therefore be admitted to PROBATE. Generally speaking, however, statements of intention to prepare a certain will in the future do not evidence the necessary DISPOSITIVE, TESTAMENTARY intent to qualify as a will or will substitute. Because they are seldom witnessed or notarized, they are often dismissed as mere statements of INTENT, insufficient to effect a BEQUEST or DEVISE of property or interest.

Kuralt's widow argued exactly that. When she died in October 1999, the two step-daughters substituted as parties to the ongoing litigation. Their attorney argued that the letter in question expressed only Kuralt's intention to draft a new will. Shannon produced a purported holographic will (handwritten by Kuralt) dated in 1989, in which he willed to her the Montana ranch. Again, the family's lawyer argued that even if, IN ARGUENDO, the 1989 document was a valid will, it was revoked by his subsequent 1994 will, leaving everything to his wife and daughters.

Under a theory of "integration of a will," many states acknowledge that a TESTATOR may have prepared several different documents, each separately executed, which, when read together, constitute his will. This is particularly common where realty is owned in a state other than that of the testator's domicile. The partial will, relating to the out-of-state property, will be probated in the state where the property is located, utilizing IN REM jurisdiction.

On March 22, 2000, Montana district court judge John Christensen ruled that Kuralt's letter written to Shannon two weeks before he died constituted a valid will giving her the remaining ninety acres of the ranch. Weighing the totality of evidence, the judge concluded that the express language in Kuralt's note made his intentions clear. Judge Christensen made note that Kuralt had gone to great lengths to conceal his relationship with Shannon, a factor the judge found significant in explaining why Kuralt may not have immediately contacted an attorney to draft a new formal will. Judge Christensen thus concluded, "Kuralt was anxious to transfer the remaining properties to Shannon."

INTELLECTUAL PROPERTY

Internet Music Piracy

In 1999 the Internet continued to give fits to the owners of COPYRIGHTED intellectual property. The Net's popularity led to a soaring increase in the illegal copying of music, movies, television, and even sports broadcasts. Once an underground activity, PIRACY of this material moved brazenly into the light of everyday practice as it became an easy task for Net users worldwide. Decrying the practice, the entertainment industry took legal action against commercial businesses that it said had sprung up to abet piracy. It scored some early victories, but even with the U.S. Congress holding hearings, the digital future for intellectual property looked murkier than ever.

Music has quickly become the most visible form of copyright INFRINGEMENT on the Internet. In large part this is owed to recent technological advances. First, the development in the late 1990s of new data compression techniques created the so-called "MP3" file—popular shorthand for Mpeg Layer-3 compression. MP3s are digital copies of songs squeezed into computer files that are much smaller than commercial recordings: whereas the typical music compact disc (CD) holds only fifteen to twenty songs, a CD-ROM can hold hundreds of MP3s. At the same time, the rise of high speed Internet access has made transmitting and receiving the files easy for many.

Although the music industry has blasted this trend, its efforts to curtail it have failed. Tracking down illegal MP3 distribution has proved an endless quest for the Recording Industry Association of America (RIAA), the trade group and watchdog organization leading the industry's anti-piracy campaign. And it has been helpless to stop a not-too-subtle cultural transformation. In late 1999 universities and colleges reported seeing their computer networks slow to a crawl under the weight of MP3 downloading traffic, while students told reporters they had few ethical qualms about stealing music. Meanwhile, the computer hardware industry capitalized on the MP3 trend by issuing a stream of portable players, CD-burners, and larger data storage devices.

The music industry had greater success fighting online businesses. On April 28, several major record labels won their infringement case against the website MP3.com, a San Diego, California-based online digital storage service that allowed subscribers who own commercial CDs to listen to MP3 versions of those songs from its database of more than 80,000 albums. The complaint said the database constituted unauthorized, and hence illegal, copying of the labels' intellectual property. The website countered that it was merely offering consumers the means to play music they had already paid for. As most legal observers had predicted, U.S. District Court Judge Jed Rakoff of Southern District of New York issued a terse order siding with the music industry and holding the website liable for infringement. A few days later, MP3.com removed all major label music from its website and then entered negotiations with the plaintiffs. In July, the company reached a settlement with two labels, Warner Music and BMG Entertainment, that appeared to allow it to continue offering their songs. The undisclosed agreement reportedly called for the website to pay the labels between $15 and $25 million each, while also establishing ongoing fees when users of the service access the labels' CDs and songs.

With even more fanfare, the music industry battled an online service called Napster. From its inception in the fall of 1999, Napster provided an easy conduit for trading MP3s. Net users could connect via its software to thousands of other users, search for particular songs, and exchange them in a sort of anonymous, freewheeling bazaar with the songs passing through Napster's server en route to their computers. So popular was it on college campuses that more than 135 schools nationwide blocked its usage in order to reduce the strain on their networks, sometimes provoking student protests. Usage continued nevertheless. In May 2000 a survey of ten New England colleges by the research firm Webnoize Inc. found that 73 percent of students used Napster at least once a month.

While the recording industry viewed Napster as its gravest threat to date, Napster officials promoted their service as a means for artists without recording contracts to distribute their music. After the RIAA filed suit, Napster sought refuge in a legal defense under the Digital Millennium Copyright Act. The law's so-called "safe harbor" provision states that Internet Service Providers are not liable for criminal activity committed by users—essentially an outgrowth of the traditional immunity granted to telephone carriers, who are not responsible when people use telephones to break the law. On May 5, 2000, a federal judge shot down Napster's defense, rejecting its motion that the case be dismissed. The ruling set the stage for a

Gene Kan's company, Gnutella, has created a way for people to easily find free digital versions of copyrighted music on the Internet.
SAKUMA/AP/WIDE WORLD PHOTOS

full trial later in the year in which the company is expected to argue that it is protected by the decision in Sony Corporation of America v. Universal City Studios, Inc., 464 U.S. 417, 104 S. Ct. 774, 78 L. Ed. 2d 574 (1984), in which the U.S. Supreme Court held that no liability for copyright infringement existed when a product has non-infringing uses as well.

Napster's legal problems multiplied as recording artists launched their own suits. Heavy metal rockers Metallica and the rapper Dr. Dre sued the service and, while their litigation was pending, each performed digital surveillance on Napster users. Both artists presented lists of hundreds of thousands of Napster users whom they alleged were illegally trading their songs. Napster banned users in response, but hackers found ways to reinstate banned users, and some 30,000 users filed reinstatement appeals with Napster. Meanwhile, alternative music and file-sharing programs like the Gnutella appeared, suggesting to some observers that a digital genie had escaped the bottle. Yet Napster, if down, was not out. It received an infusion of $15 million in investment capital in late May, just as the U.S. House of Representatives Small Business Committee began holding hearings into its impact on music sales.

By summer, the controversy heated up. In a surprise move, Napster retained the noted antitrust attorney David Boies, fresh from successfully prosecuting Microsoft as lead attorney for the Justice Department. Boies announced a new weapon in its legal strategy for the forthcoming trial: Napster would argue that, based on music industry documents unearthed during the pretrial discovery process, the major record labels are in violation of antitrust law. Dramatically, Boies contended that they therefore lack legal standing to enforce their copyrights. The music industry countered with full-page ads in major newspapers denouncing music piracy.

As a fact-finding exercise, the U.S. Senate Judiciary Committee held three hours of hearings on July 11. Testifying were representatives from the RIAA, along with Metallica drummer Lars Ulrich, who argued that legislative intervention was necessary to stop MP3 downloading from destroying the viability of the industry. Also present were Napster and MP3.com executives, who argued that their technology increases music sales. The hearing had moments of excitement: senate aides downloaded and played an MP3 version of a song by the band Creed, and the impassioned Ulrich personally confronted Napster chief executive Hank Barry. But despite making some critical remarks about Napster, lawmakers again demonstrated their longstanding reluctance to regulate Internet commerce. Committee chairman Senator Orrin G. Hatch (R.-Utah) merely endorsed the view that fair and reasonable licensing of copyrighted music should occur.

Meanwhile, a coalition of major league sports organizations, movie studios, and television networks sued a Canadian company that was transmitting television broadcasts over the Internet. The infringement action came against Toronto-based iCraveTV.com, a $13 million venture capital start-up. On January 28, 2000, the plaintiffs won a temporary restraining order forcing the company to stop allowing U.S. Internet users to view its content, and a month later, the company agreed in a settlement with the plaintiffs to shut down permanently. Observers viewed the case as the first in what is expected to be a series of legal battles between purveyors of traditional and online media.

CROSS REFERENCES
Copyright; Music Publishing

INTERNATIONAL LAW

The body of law governing the legal relations between states or nations.

Former Hostage Terry Anderson Wins $341 Million Verdict Against Iran

Terry Anderson was KIDNAPPED and confined in Lebanon from 1985 to 1991 by a group of Islamic extremists called Hezbollah, or Party of God. In March 1999, Anderson filed a federal lawsuit accusing Iran of financing, training, and otherwise supporting Hezbollah's TERRORIST activities. One year later, after Iran refused to appear to defend itself, Judge Thomas Penfield Jackson awarded Anderson and his family $341 million for their ordeal.

The ordeal began in March 1985, when Anderson was stationed in Beirut, Lebanon, as chief Middle East correspondent for the Associated Press to cover a civil war. At the time, Anderson's wife, Madeleine Bassil, was pregnant with their first child, Sulome. On his way home from a tennis game with AP photographer Don Mell one Saturday morning, Anderson was abducted by terrorists, who told him, "Don't worry, it's political."

The words of encouragement turned out to be unwarranted. Anderson spent most of the next 2,454 days in captivity shackled by a chain,

Terry Anderson greets his sister in Wiesbaden, Germany, shortly after his release.
KIENZLE/AP/WIDE WORLD PHOTOS

blindfolded, and banished from sunlight. His captors, including a guard Anderson called "the Ghost," frequently beat him and threatened to kill him. He and seventeen fellow hostages ate bread and cheese and had to communicate secretly with sign language because they were forbidden from speaking. While in captivity, Anderson missed the first six years of his daughter's life.

After his release in December 1991, Anderson said his Catholicism required him to forgive his captors. In March 1999, however, Anderson and his wife and daughter sued Iran and the Iranian Ministry of Information and Security to hold that country accountable for the ordeal. They asked the federal court in the District of Columbia for $100 million in damages.

The lawsuit became possible when Congress passed the Antiterrorism and Effective Death Penalty Act of 1996. The Act allows American victims of terrorism abroad to sue foreign countries in federal court if the U.S. STATE DEPARTMENT has classified those countries as sponsors of terrorism. The State Department has designated Iran as a sponsor of terrorism since 1984.

Iran refused to appear to defend itself against Anderson's lawsuit. Iran's United Nations Ambassador, Seyed Mohammed Hadi Nejad, said Iran condemns terrorism and did not support any hostage-taking activities in Lebanon. Nejad also insisted that U.S. courts lacked JURISDICTION over Iran in the case. Iran's failure to appear led Judge Jackson to enter a default judgment in favor of the Andersons.

In February 2000 Judge Jackson held a hearing to determine the Andersons' damages. Terry Anderson, now a journalism professor at Ohio University, told about the conditions in captivity and the trauma he suffered after being released. Anderson described how relations with his wife were strained and how it took years to establish a functional relationship with his daughter. The whole family said it nearly fell apart in the process.

On March 24, 2000, Judge Jackson issued an order finding that Anderson was "imprisoned under deplorable, inhumane conditions" that were "savage and cruel by any civilized standards." Judge Jackson ordered Iran to pay $24.5 million to Terry Anderson, $10 million to Madeleine Bassil, and $6.7 million to Sulome. He also awarded the family $300 million in punitive damages. Judge Jackson said punitive damages were necessary to punish Iran's conduct and to protect the right of journalists to cover dangerous world events. While Terry Anderson praised the award, saying "terrorism should be expensive," he insisted that holding Iran accountable for its wrongdoing was more important than the money.

Whether the Andersons will ever collect that money is uncertain. Because Iran will not submit to the court's jurisdiction, the Andersons need to find Iranian assets for the court to seize to apply to the judgment. In 1998 Congress passed a measure asking the State and TREASURY DEPARTMENTS to help victims of terrorism find money for judgments. The law, however, allows President BILL CLINTON to decline support in the interest of national security. Until February 2000 the Clinton administration declined to proceed against Iran, a country that recently made overtures regarding diplomatic relations with the United States.

In February 2000, U.S. Secretary of State MADELEINE K. ALBRIGHT told a congressional committee that the Clinton administration was prepared to help victims of terrorism locate Iranian assets in the United States. In addition to the Andersons, three of Terry Anderson's fellow hostages are trying to collect a $65 million court award, and the family of Alisa M. Flatow, a college student killed in a 1995 bombing in Israel, is trying to collect a $247.5 million award. The Clinton administration wants to make sure the United States seizes only non-diplomatic Iranian assets in order to avoid seizure of American diplomatic assets in foreign disputes.

CROSS REFERENCES
Terrorism

INTERNET

A worldwide telecommunications network of business, government, and personal computers.

Anticybersquatting Act Strengthens Trademark Owner Rights

On November 29, 1999, President BILL CLINTON signed into law the Anticybersquatting Consumer Protection Act (ACPA). Title III, Public Law 106–113. The act's title is somewhat misleading, however, as the new law is designed to strengthen the INTELLECTUAL PROPERTY rights of TRADEMARK owners and not consumers. It gives owners a cause of action against so-called "cybersquatters" or "cyberpirates," individuals who register a third-party's trademark as a domain name for the purpose of selling it back to the owner for a profit.

ACPA adds subsection (d)(1)(A) to § 43 of the Lanham Trademark Act of 1946. 15 U.S.C.A. 1125. This subsection enables trademark owners to sue any person who registers, traffics in, or uses a domain name that is identical to or confusingly similar to a distinctive or famous mark, and does so with "a bad faith intent to profit" from the mark. Liability may also be imposed on any person whose bad faith use of a domain name dilutes a famous mark.

Courts are provided with a list of nine non-exclusive factors for determining whether a domain name has been used in bad faith. The list attempts to balance the rights of trademark owners with the interests of entrepreneurs using the Internet for legitimate business purposes. The list also attempts to provide courts with a uniform starting point in their analysis of cybersquatting cases, so that both trademark owners and web entrepreneurs are treated the same without regard to JURISDICTION.

Evidence of bad faith under ACPA includes an attempt to tarnish or disparage an owner's mark, an offer to sell a domain name back to the owner for financial gain without first having used it at a web site, the commercial use of a domain name to divert consumers away from a trademark owner's web site, and the acquisition of multiple domain names that are confusingly similar to federally registered trademarks. Evidence of good faith includes the registration of a domain name that is the registrant's legal name; the noncommercial, fair, or prior use of a mark at a web site that is accessible under the domain name; and the use of a mark that is neither "famous" nor "distinctive" under the Federal Trademark Dilution Act. 15 U.S.C.A. 1125(c). Persons who register and use a domain name under the belief that it was lawful to do so may not be found to have committed bad faith acts of cybersquatting, but a court determines whether the person had reasonable grounds for the belief.

ACPA creates several remedies for aggrieved trademark owners. Owners may seek injunctive relief, including a court order to have the offending mark forfeited, canceled, or transferred to them. DAMAGES, profits, costs, and attorney fees are recoverable to the same extent as under the Lanham Act. Statutory damages of not less than $1,000 and not more than $100,000 per domain name may be awarded in lieu of actual damages and profits. Domain name registration authorities, such as Network Solutions Inc., are immunized from liability under the act, unless they act with a bad faith intent to profit from their role, willfully disregard a court order, or fail to provide documents expeditiously to a court.

The new law also gives trademark owners the right to bring an IN REM action (a lawsuit against an item of property, not a person or owner of that property) against the domain name itself, in a contradistinction to a personal action against the registrant of the domain name. Before an *in rem* action may be filed, however, a court must determine that (1) IN PERSONAM jurisdiction over the domain name registrant could not be obtained or (2) the domain name registrant could not be located through the exercise of "due diligence," a phrase that ACPA equates with actions constituting service of process.

An owner would be deemed to have acted with due diligence by first sending the domain name registrant notice of the alleged violation accompanied by an intent to proceed. The notice and intent must be mailed to the postal and email addresses provided by the registrant to the domain name registration authority. The owner would then have to publish notice of the proceeding as directed by the court. An *in rem* action can only be filed in the judicial district where the domain name registration authority is located, which ACPA defines as its place of business. Remedies for an *in rem* action are limited to forfeiture, cancellation, or transfer of the domain name.

Individuals who have trademarked their names are afforded the same rights under ACPA as other people who have trademarked terms to promote a commercial enterprise. ACPA also affords a certain measure of protection to individuals who have *not* trademarked their names. The act adds § 1129 to Title 15 of the United States Code. This section makes liable any person who registers a domain name that is "substantially and confusingly similar" to the name of another living person, if done without that person's consent and with the specific intent of selling it for financial gain. Record companies and copyright owners who lawfully exploit the work of recording artists and entertainers are exempted from this provision, unless a contract provides otherwise.

ACPA serves as the basis for two pending lawsuits filed shortly after its enactment. On December 2, 1999, actor Brad Pitt filed suit in the U.S. District Court for the Central District of California, alleging that the registrants of the domain names bradpitt.net and braddpitt.com violated ACPA by using the actor's name to market merchandise related to him. The operators of bradpitt.com—two men living in the United Arab Emirates—allegedly offered to sell the plaintiff the domain name for $20,000. On December 5, 1999, the National Football League brought an action in the U.S. District Court for the Southern District of New York against a web site operator who used the domain names NFLtoday.com, NFLtoday.net, and NFLtoday.org to promote gambling on professional football games. According to the complaint, the defendant offered to sell the names to plaintiff for $120,000.

Children's Online Privacy Protection Act

As PRIVACY issues continued to be a focus of Internet safety, the federal government moved to protect children. In April 2000 the FEDERAL TRADE COMMISSION (FTC) began enforcing provisions of a 1998 law designed to shield children from excessive intrusion by web site operators. Under the terms of the Children's Online Privacy Protection Act (COPPA) (15 U.S.C. § 6501 et seq.)—not to be confused with the mainly anti-pornography Child Online Protection Act, 47 U.S.C. § 231—the FTC established rules ranging from publicizing web site privacy guidelines to verifying the age of web visitors. Internet content providers, who helped shape the rules, largely praised the effort, but some protested that the regulations imposed expensive costs and were too hard to follow. Noting that many web operators were far from achieving full compliance, the FTC promised vigorous enforcement and threatened costly fines.

Privacy concerns are not new on the Internet. During the mid-1990s, civil liberties groups led campaigns to raise public awareness regarding the ability of companies to track, record, and use data about consumer web browsing. In particular, new attention was paid to the previously arcane technologies that run web sites and make a great range of potentially intrusive behaviors possible, especially invisible "cookies" that record web site visits along with data about users' geographic locations, ages, tastes, and so on. While business defended the technology as merely a new marketing tool, critics noted the tendency to casually look over private citizens' shoulders. Much to the consternation of critics but to the delight of industry, the administration of President BILL CLINTON took a hands-off approach to Net regulation.

Congress had other ideas. Lawmakers took interest in the issue in June 1998, when the FTC concluded its three-year study of online privacy protections. Based on surveying 1,400 web sites, the blistering report said the industry had failed to protect consumers through voluntary self-regulation. According to the agency, eighty-five percent of the web sites it surveyed collected personal information about consumers, but only fourteen percent told them about doing so. Fully ninety-eight percent of the sites neglected to publicize a comprehensive privacy policy.

Particularly at risk, according to the agency, were children. The commission found that eighty-nine percent of the 212 children's sites it visited were siphoning off data about kids, but nearly half did so without formally explaining the practice. FTC Chairman Robert Pitofsky warned that parents were being excluded from decision making: only one in four kids' sites even sought parental permission before directly soliciting information from children. Some web sites disguised marketing questions in the form of games. The report asked Congress to intervene with regulations.

In October 1998 lawmakers passed COPPA, designed to protect children under the age of thirteen and to promote parental involvement in their Internet usage. The law regulated collection of a broad range of personal data from children, including names, e-mail and home addresses, telephone numbers, and Social Security numbers. It required web sites to provide notice of their data collection activities and to obtain verifiable parental consent for the collection, use, or disclosure of personal information from children. Finally, it prohibited making participation in online games or contests contingent upon a child's providing such data. COPPA gave enforcement power to the FTC, decreed violations to be illegal forms of unfair or deceptive trade, and delayed enforcement for a year while businesses prepared for compliance.

Throughout 1999 FTC regulators and businesses hammered out compromises on enforcement. Although business generally supported the aim of the law, it wanted to escape onerous costs for compliance. The most contentious area was parental notification, which the FTC initially considered requiring in the form of letters or faxes in order to prevent children from impersonating their parents' consent electronically. In a compromise sought by business lobbyists, the commission agreed to allow parental consent to be delivered over toll-free phone numbers, through credit-card numbers, and in digitally-signed e-mail that is harder to spoof. The FTC said it would review the system in two years to see if it was working.

The FTC issued several specific rules, some of which govern the intent of the data collection. Businesses do not need to obtain parental consent for one-time offers such as coupons, but they must do so if they intend to collect, sell, or trade the data. One retroactive rule orders companies that have already collected data to seek parental consent now if they wish to keep storing it. In all instances the rules give parents broad control over what is stored. Parents have the right to review and delete any details held regarding their children as well as to forbid collection of any further data. Violators face a fine of $11,000 per violation.

As the rules took effect in April 2000, some initial grumbling was heard. While major sites such as Yahoo and the Disney-owned Go.com reported little trouble, a few businesses told reporters that costs were soaring. San Francisco-based eCrush.com complained that it lacked the manpower to verify parental consents, and the Freezone Network said it had spent $96,000 in order to reach compliance. For its part, the FTC observed that it was discovering web sites that mistakenly thought they were not regulated, when in fact all web sites now fall under the regulations' purview.

Domain Name Sales Ruled Legal

In January 2000 the U.S. Supreme Court rejected a challenge to federal fees for Internet domain names. The dispute centered on who had the power to license the so-called "dot coms," or URLs—the addresses assigned to the owners of web pages. Declining to hear an appeal from the ruling in *Thomas v. Network Solutions* (176 F.3d 500 (D.C. Cir. [1999]), the Court affirmed the constitutionality of a unique registration scheme that had existed in the mid-1990s. Several plaintiffs had sued the National Science Foundation and a private company to which the foundation contracted out registration. The case, which had resulted in a temporary ban on domain name registration fees in 1998, reached into a murky area that ultimately provoked Congressional intercession the following year. Its resolution settled doubts about several millions of dollars in fees collected from Internet web site registrants.

Internet domain names are a common feature of the World Wide Web. With suffixes commonly ending in ".com," ".net," and ".org," the names are stored in huge databases known as registries that serve as central directories for the Net. Applied to web site names like www.galegroup.com, they function to direct traffic on the Web to its proper destination.

By the 1990s, these names became part of a complex registration scheme. The National Science Foundation (NSF), which was charged with overseeing the domain system, paid Network Solutions, Inc. (NSI), a private company, to register domain names in its database. The names were free to individuals. As the Internet experienced a massive surge in growth, though, the NSF established registration fees and a new deal with NSI. Between 1993 and 1995, the company charged $100 for a two-year registration, kept $70 for itself, and paid $30 to the foundation. The government amassed $39 million during this time, which went into the Intellectual Infrastructure Fund for future Internet development. As the sole registrar of domain names and keeper of the Internet's vital directory, NSI reaped millions more. After 1995 the government stopped collecting its $30 cut.

In October 1997 nine individuals and companies calling themselves the American Internet Registrants Association sued both parties. The group's class-action suit made ten allegations, chief among which were that NSI acted as an illegal MONOPOLY and that NSF's infrastructure fee constituted an illegal, unauthorized tax. On April 8, 1998, the lawsuit scored a partial success. Although U.S. District Judge Thomas Hogan dismissed nine of the counts, he accepted the plaintiffs' argument that Congress never explicitly sanctioned the Intellectual Infrastructure Fund fee and hence it was illegal, in *Thomas v. Network Solutions, Inc.*, 2 F. Supp.2d 22, 31–32 (D.D.C. 1998). Although lawmakers may have intended to do so, Hogan wrote, they had yet to grant the NSF authority to collect the tax. The ruling led many observers to expect government refunds.

Less than a month later, Congress intervened. Lawmakers swiftly approved a retroactive tax on the domain names on April 30, 1998, by inserting language into an emergency appropriations bill (H.R. 3579) earmarked for defense spending and disaster relief. This essentially authorized the NSF to collect the taxes it already had collected. Among other reasons, lawmakers had ample financial motivation: the money was already spent. In 1997, they had allocated $23 million to President BILL CLINTON's plan to build a second, faster Internet for scholars and scientists.

In light of Congress's action, Judge Hogan revisited the case in September, affirmed the tax's constitutionality, and dismissed the lawsuit. The plaintiffs appealed. On May 14, 1999, they received another defeat when a three judge panel of the circuit court of appeals upheld Hogan's decision to dismiss the suit entirely. In the majority opinion, Judge A. Raymond Randolph concluded that the plaintiffs had failed to explain why Congress had lacked authority to impose the tax. Additionally, the panel held that the plaintiffs lacked standing—legal grounds to bring suit—for their ANTITRUST claims against NSI. The panel left one legal question dangling, however. Although noting that the NSF, as a government body, was traditionally immune from antitrust prosecution, it declined to say whether a government contractor also automatically had immunity.

With the Supreme Court's refusal to hear the case, the tax question was settled and the immunity question left for another day. In some ways, the case was seen as a leftover dispute from the Internet's adolescence: intervening events in the governance of the Net, even more than the lawsuit, had altered the way domain names are registered. By November 1999 NSI no longer enjoyed a monopoly on domain registration. In negotiations with the U.S. Department of COMMERCE as well as a new standards-setting body called the Internet Corporation for Assigned Names and Numbers, NSI had agreed to compromises on the issue of control over the key directory of domain names. Furthermore, with the registrar field opened to competition, new private businesses had appeared, offering consumers choices.

Internet Crime Update

From computer viruses to web site hacking and financial FRAUD, Internet crime became a larger concern than ever in the 1990s. In one sense, this was less a measure of growing pains than of the increasing importance of the Net in daily life. More users surfing the Web, greater business reliance upon e-mail, and the tremendous upsurge in electronic commerce have raised financial stakes. A single virus outbreak in 1999 was blamed for more than $80 million in damage, while web site hacking in early 2000 purportedly cost hundreds of millions more. Adding new wrinkles were complaints about rampant fraud on popular online auction sites. Together, the problems drew tough rhetoric from U.S. officials, who announced new initiatives, deployed cyber-crime units, made numerous arrests, and even pursued international manhunts.

In March 1999 the FEDERAL BUREAU OF INVESTIGATION (FBI) became involved in a highly publicized hunt for a computer virus author. Electronic viruses are malicious software programs written to cause harm to unsuspecting computer users. They are designed to spread from computer to computer. Their propagation traditionally relied upon computer users sharing disks or software. On March 26, 2000, the appearance of the Melissa virus announced a new, dangerous breed of viruses delivered by e-mail,

Notorious hacker Kevin Mitnick (right) leaves his press conference after being released from prison on January 21, 2000.
DOVARGANES/AP/WIDE WORLD PHOTOS

and it prompted heightened interest from federal law enforcement.

The virus was less deadly than those that erase data on a computer's hard drive. At heart, Melissa was an e-mail that contained a list of pornography web sites, along with programming code that sent up to fifty copies of itself to names found in a victim's e-mail address book. This self-replicating behavior had the potential to strain and disable computer networks, as the FBI warned on March 28 in an alert issued through its National Infrastructure Protection Center (NIPC). Within days, these fears were realized as dozens of corporate e-mail servers slowed under a flood of Melissa e-mail. In all, the infection reached nearly nineteen percent of U.S. corporations and an estimated 1.5 million computers.

Less than a week later, the FBI nabbed the virus author. David L. Smith, a thirty-year-old, Aberdeen, New Jersey, computer programmer, had unintentionally left his name in similar virus code. Charged with CONSPIRACY, theft of computer services, and interruption of public communications, he pleaded innocent. After striking a plea bargain with state and federal prosecutors on December 11, however, he pleaded guilty to a single state count of computer theft along with a single federal count of sending a damaging computer program. Smith acknowledged that the virus had caused upwards of $80 million worth in clean-up costs. With sentencing expected in mid-2000, he faced up to fifteen years in prison.

The FBI issued a second virus advisory in June 1999, and then, in May 2000, U.S. and Philippine officials cooperated in a manhunt for a third virus author. Like Melissa, the so-called Love Bug worm transmitted and replicated itself via e-mail, but it differed by damaging files on victims' computers. As authorities deemed it the fastest-spreading virus in history, the NIPC traced its origins to Manila. Prompted by U.S. officials, the Philippine National Bureau of Investigation arrested twenty-seven-year-old Reomel Ramones. The case hit snags, however, as authorities were at a loss to find physical evidence and even to know what to charge Ramones with, since virus writing is not a criminal offense under Philippine law.

Hackers also launched assaults on U.S. government systems. For several years, hackers penetrated federal computers belonging to the Pentagon and other agencies, often eluding authorities. They occasionally publicized government data in works such as *2600: The Hacker Quarterly* and created a daring image celebrated in popular culture. In 1999 the White House declared war. President BILL CLINTON targeted hackers in get-tough speeches in January and May. An FBI dragnet culminated in the arrest of twenty suspected hackers in six states. Apparently as retaliation, hackers defaced web sites belonging to the FBI, the INTERIOR DEPARTMENT, the U.S. Senate, and even the White House, forcing some to shut down for hours. A few days later, on June 2, White House press secretary Joe Lockhart announced a government-wide review of computer security and vowed to punish the responsible parties. Yet the government's effectiveness came into question in early 2000 as high-profile attacks crippled major web sites.

As the government grappled with hackers, a famous hacker was released from prison. Kevin Mitnick, held in federal custody without bail or a trial since 1995, entered a plea bargain with the Los Angeles District Attorney's office on charges pending from his arrest for intrusion into several corporate computer systems. A cause celebre in the computer underground since fleeing a manhunt in the early 1990s, Mitnick's case had prompted public protests and even hacks of web sites proclaiming the message, "Free Kevin." On August 9, U.S. District Judge Mariana Pfaelzer sentenced the thirty-five-year-old hacker to forty-six months in federal prison and ordered him to pay $4,125 in restitution. He was released on January 21, 2000. Mitnick's parole terms forbid him to use computers in any way for another three years. When authorities subsequently barred him from accepting lucrative speaking engagements, Mitnick retained famed FIRST AMENDMENT attorney Floyd Abrahms, filed suit, and successfully proved that the terms of his parole violated his right to FREEDOM OF SPEECH.

As Internet auction sites gained popularity, fraud also attracted federal attention. In February 2000 the FEDERAL TRADE COMMISSION (FTC) announced a multi-agency effort to combat what it said was a one hundred-fold increase in complaints about Web-based fraud. The FTC reported that complaints had soared from 107 in 1997 to 10,700 in 1999. In response, it announced plans to work with the Department of JUSTICE, the U.S. Postal Inspection Service, and other federal and state authorities to increase the number of cases it files in court, which to date amounted to only thirty-five. The leading Internet auction site eBay separately announced that it would cooperate with authorities to sniff out con artists.

CROSS REFERENCES
Antitrust; Computer Crime; Federal Trade Commission; Fraud; Intellectual Property; Privacy; Taxation; Trademark

J

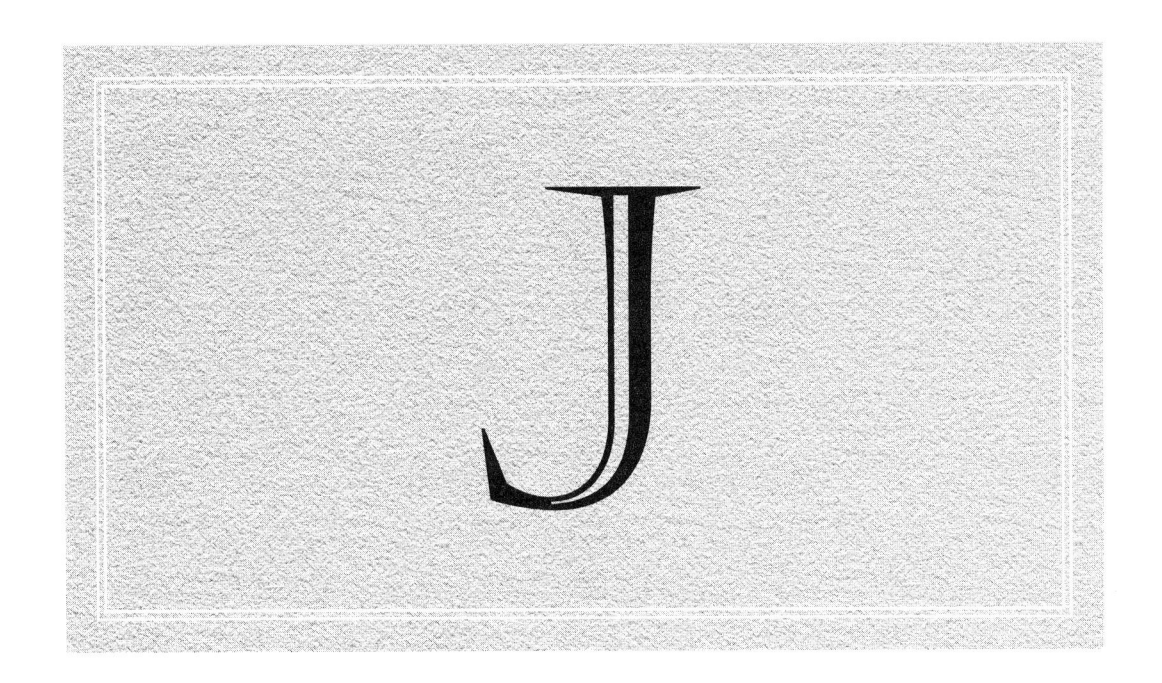

JOHNSON, FRANK MINIS, JR.

Obituary notice

Born on October 30, 1918, in Delmar, Alabama; died on July 24, 1999. Johnson served as a federal judge for the majority of his life and made a name for himself as a defender of civil rights. He ruled against the Montgomery, Alabama, ordinance that required segregated city buses in *Browder v. Gayle* (1956); he developed the "freeze" doctrine, which allowed African Americans to vote as long as they were as qualified as the least qualified white voter; and he wrote an opinion declaring a Georgia sodomy statute was unconstitutional (though this ruling was overturned by the Supreme Court). Johnson received the Presidential Medal of Freedom in 1995.

JURY

In trials, a group of people selected and sworn to inquire into matters of fact and to reach a VERDICT on the basis of the EVIDENCE presented to it.

United States v. Martinez-Salazar

One of the fundamental requirements in criminal law is that a defendant is entitled to a trial by a jury that is unbiased and impartial. A defendant has two important tools to remove prospective jurors who may not be impartial: challenges for CAUSE and PEREMPTORY CHALLENGES. In *U.S. v. Martinez-Salazar*, ___ U.S. ___, 120 S.Ct. 774, 145 L.Ed.2d 792 (2000) the U.S. Supreme Court considered the interplay between these two types of challenges and the effect of the failure of a judge to remove a juror for cause.

A defendant may challenge a potential juror for cause if there is evidence of bias, partiality to law enforcement, or other factors that suggest the person would not be neutral when considering the evidence. The trial judge has the sole discretion to remove the potential juror for cause and may disagree with the defendant's claims of bias. A defendant can still remove the person from the jury by exercising a peremptory challenge. A peremptory challenge permits a party to remove a prospective juror without giving a reason for his or her removal. This type of challenge has had a long history in U.S. law and has been viewed as a way to insure an impartial jury. A defendant cannot exercise an unlimited number of peremptory challenges, however. For example, in a federal criminal trial, the defendant can exercise up to eleven peremptory challenges if an alternate juror is chosen as well as twelve regular jurors.

In *Martinez-Salazar*, the Supreme Court ruled that a federal criminal defendant's conviction does not need to be thrown out because the judge mistakenly fails to exclude a potential juror. In doing so, the court applied a previous decision involving a state criminal defendant, reaffirming that peremptory challenges do not raise constitutional challenges but rather interpretations of statute and procedure.

Abel Martinez-Salazar was arrested in Phoenix, Arizona, and charged with a number of federal drug offenses. During the selection of the jurors, Martinez-Salazar twice challenged a man who said several times that he would favor

Frank Minis Johnson, Jr.
AP/WIDE WORLD PHOTOS

WHY IS THE NUMBER OF JUVENILES TRIED AS ADULTS INCREASING?

In 1999, the U.S. celebrated the 100th anniversary of the founding of the first juvenile court in the world. It was established in Chicago, Illinois, by individuals such as JANE ADDAMS, Lucy Flower, and Julia Lathrop, who believed that children should be treated differently than adults. To that end, they organized a juvenile court that recognized that children "are still young, immature and not fully developed. Thus character and behavior could still be molded and they could be rehabilitated."*In re Abraham*, No. 97 63787 FC, p.2 (Mich. Ct. App. January 13, 2000). This Illinois court served as a model for the extensive juvenile court system that exists today. Accordingly, the concepts of prevention and rehabilitation became the benchmarks of juvenile justice in America.

In recent years, however, the trend appears to be retreating into the last century when children accused of a crime were treated the same as adults. This change arises in the context of public outrage caused by increasingly violent crimes committed by children. The media has given extensive coverage to instances when children commit violent crimes, bringing both gruesome and sad images into living rooms across the nation.

One notorious example of a child committing a violent crime occurred when eleven-year-old Nathaniel Abraham shot and killed eighteen-year-old Ronnie Greene, Jr., in Pontiac, Michigan. He was one of the nation's youngest convicted murderers. Also widely publicized in the media, in Springfield, Oregon, fifteen-year-old Kip Kinkel shot and killed his parents and two classmates. Another fifteen-year-old pleaded guilty to participating in the purse snatching and death of 84-year-old Ida Mirel in West Palm Beach, Florida. In that case, the boys were in a stolen car when they drove their car over and dragged the elderly woman's body 2,000 feet down a busy road. In addition, in Minnesota, four children, all under the age of ten, were accused of raping an eight-year old girl. Moreover, the list of children opening fire at schools is only partially complete when citing those in Pearl, Mississippi; Paducah, Kentucky; Jonesboro, Arkansas; and Littleton, Colorado.

Although youth crime rates have been declining since 1995, such examples of violent crimes committed by children have led many states to adopt a "get tough" approach to juvenile justice. Each state, through its legislature, has the authority to establish its own laws concerning crimes committed by children. In response to the increasingly violent crimes committed by children, a majority of states have lowered the age at which a child can be tried and sentenced as an adult. In fact, since 1992, forty-four states have adopted legislation that permits more children to be tried and sentenced as adults. All states have a provision allowing prosecutors to try juveniles as young as fourteen as adults under certain circumstances. Moreover, in states such as Indiana, South Dakota, and Vermont, children as young as ten may be tried as adults. Approximately twenty states, such as Pennsylvania, have no minimum age at which a child can be tried as an adult for certain crimes.

An example of a "get tough" law exists in Michigan. In 1997 the Michigan legislature adopted a controversial law known as the Juvenile Waiver Law. The law lowered the age that juveniles could be automatically tried as

---

the prosecution. The trial judge refused to excuse the man from the jury. At that point Martinez-Salazar exercised one of his eleven peremptory challenges granted to him by Rule 24 of the Federal Rules of Criminal Procedure and removed the man from the jury. At the end of jury selection, the defendant had used all eleven peremptory challenges. Martinez-Salazar made no objection to the final set of jurors. This jury convicted him, and the court sentenced him to more than ten years in prison.

Martinez-Salazar appealed his conviction, arguing that the judge's failure to remove the potential juror for cause was an abuse of discretion. Even the federal prosecutor did not dispute this point. The Ninth Circuit Court of Appeals agreed that the judge abused his discretion but ruled that this error did not violate the SIXTH AMENDMENT because the potential juror was removed and the impartiality of the jury eventually seated was not challenged. The appeals court, however, concluded that the error resulted in a violation of Martinez-Salazar's FIFTH AMENDMENT DUE PROCESS rights because it forced him to use a peremptory challenge, thereby impairing his right to the full number of peremptory challenges to which he was entitled.

The Supreme Court disagreed and reinstated his conviction. In a unanimous decision, the Court rejected the Ninth Circuit's conclusion that the error required an automatic reversal. Justice RUTH BADER GINSBURG, writing for the court, held that a defendant's exercise of peremptory challenges under Rule 24 is not "denied or impaired when the defendant chooses to use such a challenge to remove a

adults and created a new process in which juveniles of any age could be charged, tried, and sentenced as adults within the juvenile court system. Such a law is a departure from traditional juvenile law, which typically permitted judges to use their discretion in weighing certain criteria in order to determine if a juvenile should be tried as an adult. Such criteria included the nature of the offender's actions, psychiatric evaluations, and previous criminal history.

Another controversial law, known as Proposition 21, was passed in California on March 7, 2000. The law permits prosecutors to send many juveniles accused of felonies directly to adult criminal court. As such, the prosecutors, not the judges, decide whether youths should be tried and sentenced within the adult criminal system. It also prohibits the use of a widely-used punishment known as "informal probation" in felony cases. This type of probation was allowed for first-time juvenile offenders who admitted guilt and attempted to make restitution. It permitted those individuals to remain free, with the knowledge that they would be subject to severe punishment if convicted again. The law also requires known gang members to register with police agencies and heightens the punishment for crimes such as vandalism.

The U.S. Department of JUSTICE (DOJ) statistics demonstrate that prosecutors have been putting these new "get tough" laws to use throughout the country during the last several years. A study released by the DOJ in 2000 states that violent juvenile offenders are more likely to serve their sentences in an adult prison today than their counterparts were fifteen years ago. Also according to the DOJ, by 1997, the juveniles under eighteen-years old who were serving their time in adult prisons amounted to 7,400 nationwide. That number is more than twice the amount of juveniles serving time in adult prisons in 1985. As a whole, however, juveniles only amount to a small percentage of the two million adults incarcerated in the nation's prisons.

The DOJ statistics also demonstrate that juveniles receiving adult sentences are typically convicted of a violent felony such as ROBBERY, MURDER, or aggravated ASSAULT. Furthermore, the DOJ states that minority youths are more likely to be affected by the laws that impose heightened standards upon juvenile offenders.

Some states, such as New Jersey, have more than doubled the number of juveniles being tried and sentenced as adults in the past few years. In New Jersey, the State's Juvenile Delinquency Commission statistics reflect that 198 juveniles were tried as adults in 1990, as opposed to the 86 juveniles tried as adults in 1987. To be tried as an adult in New Jersey, the offender must be at least fourteen years old. In addition, the offender must have an extensive criminal history or be charged with a violent FELONY.

Recent studies, however, have demonstrated that trying and sentencing juveniles as adults may be worsening the problem instead of making it better. In a study conducted by the University of Florida, statistics show that youths serving time in adult prisons are more likely to commit another crime more quickly than those serving time in a juvenile facility. The study also showed that the youths incarcerated in the adult prisons were likely to commit more serious crimes than those in juvenile detention centers.

Some human rights groups, such as the Human Rights Watch, attribute this result to the poor prison conditions for juveniles in adult facilities. Statistics demonstrate that youths in adult prisons are at a greater risk for assault, disease, and physical abuse than those doing time in juvenile facilities. Moreover, juveniles in adult prisons have less exposure to counseling, family services, and educational programs. They also have a higher rate of suicide. Based upon these statistics, critics of the "get tough" laws argue that trying and sentencing juveniles as adults fails to rehabilitate them and releases them into society without coping skills. As such, they argue that those offenders are more likely to become hardened criminals.

---

juror who should have been excused for cause." Justice Ginsburg noted that in *Ross v. Oklahoma*, 487 U.S. 81, 108 S.Ct. 2273, 101 L.Ed.2d 80 (1988), the Supreme Court decided that peremptory challenges are not based on the Constitution but are based on law and rules of procedure. Therefore, the question for the Court was not whether Martinez-Salazar's Fifth Amendment due process rights were denied but whether he was deprived of any right provided in Rule 24.

Justice Ginsburg concluded that Rule 24 was not violated in this case. Though Martinez-Salazar reduced his allotment of peremptory challenges by one when he removed the potential juror, it was his choice to do so. Ginsburg stated that a "hard choice is not the same as no choice." Martinez-Salazar, in exercising all of his peremptory challenges received everything that Rule 24 entitled him to receive. If he had let the juror sit on the jury, he then could have pursued a Sixth Amendment challenge to his conviction. The Court did not see that Martinez-Salazar had lost anything by using his peremptory challenge. Rather, Justice Ginsburg concluded that he used it for the principal reason for peremptories: "to help secure the constitutional guarantee of trial by an impartial jury."

CROSS REFERENCES
Fifth Amendment; Sixth Amendment

JUVENILE LAW

An area of the law that deals with the actions and well-being of persons who are not yet adults.

Thirteen-year old Nathaniel Abraham sits with his lawyers just before jury selection.
CORTEZ/AP/WIDE WORLD PHOTOS

Nathaniel Abraham

Two years after enacting controversial legislation, Michigan convicted a thirteen-year-old of second degree murder. In November 1999 Nathaniel Jamar Abraham became the first child to be tried under a 1997 law allowing criminal prosecutions of many juveniles as adults. Prosecutors had sought a first degree murder conviction. Jurors credited defense arguments that Abraham, who was only eleven when he shot eighteen-year-old Ronnie Lee Green, Jr., to death, did not intentionally commit MURDER. The case provoked outcries from civil rights activists, human rights groups, and even the trial judge, who criticized lawmakers for subjecting children to the harsh adult justice system.

As one of the youngest children tried for murder in the United States since the eighteenth century, Abraham's case provoked debate over whether Michigan was looking forward or backward with its law. From Amnesty International to the AMERICAN CIVIL LIBERTIES UNION (ACLU), observers blasted a return to archaic notions about children while the activists Martin Luther King III and the Reverend Al Sharpton led courtroom protests against the state for prosecuting an African American boy. Geoffrey Fieger, the outspoken left-wing attorney who joined the defense team as the trial began, called the prosecution "draconian," and said it was motivated by racism. Prosecutors replied that Abraham was precisely the type of violent young offender the law was designed to prosecute.

At trial, lead state prosecutor Lisa Halushka portrayed Abraham as an habitual criminal suspected in nearly two dozen previous crimes. Prosecutors told the jury that he had boasted of his intent to kill somebody, bought and practiced shooting a .22 rifle, and then killed Greene outside a store and bragged about the deed. They relied upon testimony from several of Abraham's friends and a man who claimed that Abraham menaced him with the rifle shortly before the crime. Prosecution also introduced rebuttal testimony from a psychologist who said that Abraham not only was old enough to form the intent to kill, but also had lied to prevent being caught.

The defense advanced three arguments. Co-counsel Fieger contended that Abraham had killed Greene accidentally, that the defendant's age and mental fitness made him incapable of forming the intent to kill, and that the prosecution failed to prove Abraham fired the fatal bullet. He introduced testimony from a world champion skeet shooter who said that, on the night of the killing, it was too dark and the distance from the defendant to the victim too far for even an expert shooter to hit. The defense also called two psychologists who deemed Abraham mentally incapable of forming intent to murder; one psychologist estimated the boy was borderline retarded, with a mental age of eight.

On November 16, after more than three days of deliberation, jurors returned a verdict of guilty on a reduced count of second degree murder. Afterwards they told reporters that they doubted Abraham's ability to form the intent to kill, yet found he shot Greene with the knowledge that shooting could seriously harm someone. They swept aside a charge of possessing a firearm while committing a felony, however. Fieger decried apparent inconsistencies in the verdict, questioning how his client could be guilty of murder yet innocent of possessing a firearm. Halushka praised what she called a fair outcome. Both sides then focused on SENTENCING. Prosecutors wanted Abraham to be held as a juvenile until the age of twenty-one, after which the court could decide to release him or sentence him to up to fifteen more years as an adult. Defense attorneys, in addition to appealing the conviction, called for juvenile incarceration only.

On January 13, 2000, Judge Eugene Moore rejected the prosecution's bid for a "blended sentence." Instead he sentenced Abraham to juvenile detention until the age of eighteen. Judge Moore said both the public and the child's interests would be best served by the rehabilitative goals of the juvenile justice system rather than the punitive ends of adult justice. Noting in his sentencing opinion to *State of Michigan v. Abraham* that it was not his place to make law, the judge nevertheless criticized state lawmakers as "short-sighted" for subjecting kids to "a failed adult system," and called for more resources to be devoted to preventing crime and rehabilitating young offenders.

CROSS REFERENCES
Sentencing

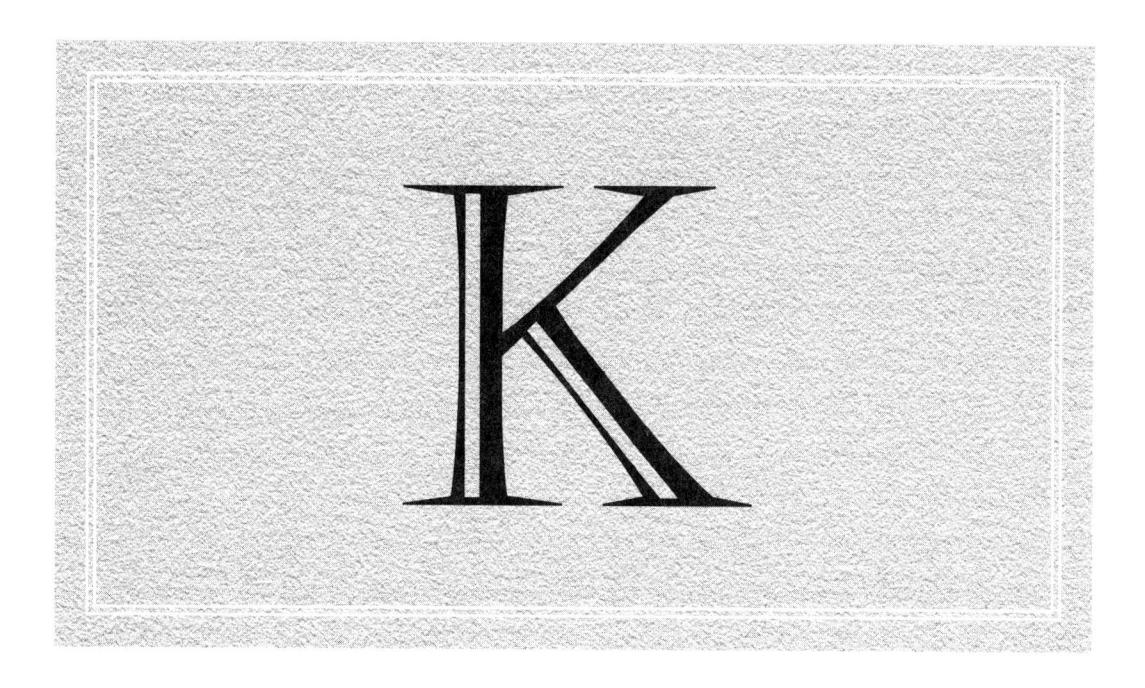

KIDNAPPING

The crime of unlawfully seizing and carrying away a person by force or FRAUD, or seizing and detaining a person against his or her will with an intent to carry that person away at a later time.

Parental Kidnapping

The National Incidence Studies of Missing, Abducted, Runaway, and Thrownaway Children (NISMART) reports that children abducted by family members (e.g., in a custody battle) account for almost half of all child abductions in the United States. Incidence of family abductions ranges from 150,000–400,000 reported cases per year.

A high-profile example of familial kidnapping is that of fifty-seven-year-old Stephen Fagan, who abducted his two young daughters in Massachusetts on October 25, 1979, and was not caught until 1997, while living in Palm Beach, Florida. By then, his daughters were college graduates who had been raised to believe their mother was deceased. When they discovered she was not, they had little or no desire to meet with their estranged mother, and supported their defendant father in the 1999 trial against him for kidnapping charges and CONTEMPT of court.

Mrs. Fagan (also known as Barbara Kurth) met Fagan when she was seventeen. He was a married twenty-five-year-old law student studying for the bar examination. They went to Haiti in 1973, where Fagan got a "quickie" divorce and they married. Their first daughter, Rachael, was born the following year. Wendy was born in 1977.

Neither side disputes that the marriage was unhappy. Kurth allegedly suffered from narcolepsy and developed an addiction to prescription amphetamines. She was admitted to a rehabilitation facility shortly after Wendy's birth. About six months later, Kurth admitted herself to a hospital for severe depression. When she came home for a weekend visit, Fagan allegedly refused to let her visit with her daughters. After release from the hospital, Kurth consulted with Jacob Atwood, a Boston divorce attorney.

A contested and bitter divorce followed, with Kurth ultimately settling for $45,000 cash and $500 monthly child support. During divorce proceedings, Fagan neither sought custody of his daughters nor did he challenge Kurth's fitness as a mother. Kurth moved into an apartment complex with her daughters and remarried. Fagan had weekend visits with the children.

According to court documents, Fagan alleged that in 1979 he received several telephone calls from his ex-wife's neighbors. They were concerned that his daughters were left unsupervised outside, often hungry and unkempt. Allegedly, the neighbors also complained to him that Kurth was frequently passed out drunk. When neighbors contacted the police, complaining that Kurth was passed out on the floor, an investigator was sent from Social Services. The report on file, however, indicates that the investigator found Kurth sober and alert; the children were eating pizza and showed no signs of mistreatment. After interviewing the neighbors, the investigator concluded that they had "gone overboard" in their claims.

Regardless, Fagan filed for custody at that time, alleging that his children were in jeopardy and that his wife was an alcoholic. A full investigation of Kurth by the state found that none of the charges from either the neighbors or Fagan were corroborated by medical or psychological experts. Shortly thereafter, the children disappeared. Fagan's parents also disappeared, and left no forwarding address. Prior to disappearing, Fagan's parents were questioned under oath, but denied any knowledge of the whereabouts of the children. His sister refused to cooperate with investigators.

Fagan changed his name to William Martin. Over the next several years he married two more times, ostensibly to wealthy women. He fabricated his past, posing at various times as a retired psychiatrist, an ex-CIA agent, a Harvard scholar, a former presidential advisor, and a chemist. A visible member of the Palm Beach society circuit, Fagan was known simply as an attentive parent of two charming girls whose brilliant mother, a surgeon, had been killed in a motor vehicle accident. The girls were raised with the best of everything.

Kurth herself remarried again, after exhausting all her legal, administrative, and governmental resources. She eventually earned her Ph.D. and became a medical school researcher. Her search for her daughters ended about six years prior to the telephone call announcing that they had been found.

Following his arrest, Fagan pleaded not guilty to the charges and asserted that his conduct was precipitated by the need to protect his daughters. In fact his investigators found two drunk driving convictions on Kurth's record from the year prior to the kidnapping. Fagan was released on $250,000 bail and subsequently agreed to a television interview with Diane Sawyer on ABC's *Nightline*. At his arraignment in Middlesex County Court in Massachusetts, both daughters appeared on his behalf, testifying to his excellent parenting and indicating that they had no wish to make contact with Kurth.

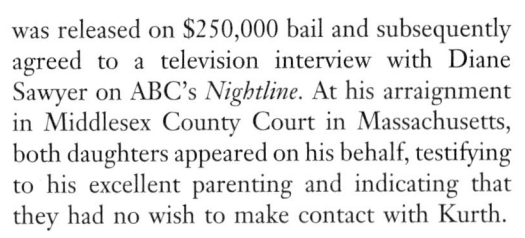

In June 1999 Fagan negotiated a plea with Middlesex County prosecutors and pleaded guilty. He was sentenced to probation and community service at the Department of Veterans' Affairs Medical Center in Massachusetts.

In most states, parental abduction is a felony. Studies indicate that men and women commit this offense in about equal proportions. The crime was not treated seriously until the passage of the Parental Kidnapping Prevention Act (PKPA) of 1980, enacted after Fagan's abduction of his daughters.

CROSS REFERENCES
Family Law

KLEINDIENST, RICHARD GORDON

Obituary notice

Born on August 5, 1923, near Winslow, Arizona; died of lung cancer on February 3, 2000, at his home in Prescott, Arizona. Kleindienst was elected to the Arizona state House of Representatives in 1953. He spent years aiding politicians such as BARRY GOLDWATER, John R. Williams, and RICHARD NIXON in their bids for office. In 1969 President Nixon appointed him as U.S. deputy attorney general. Only five days after becoming attorney general, the WATERGATE story broke. Kleindienst resigned less than a year later and returned to Arizona to practice law.

Richard Gordon Kleindienst
AP/WIDE WORLD PHOTOS

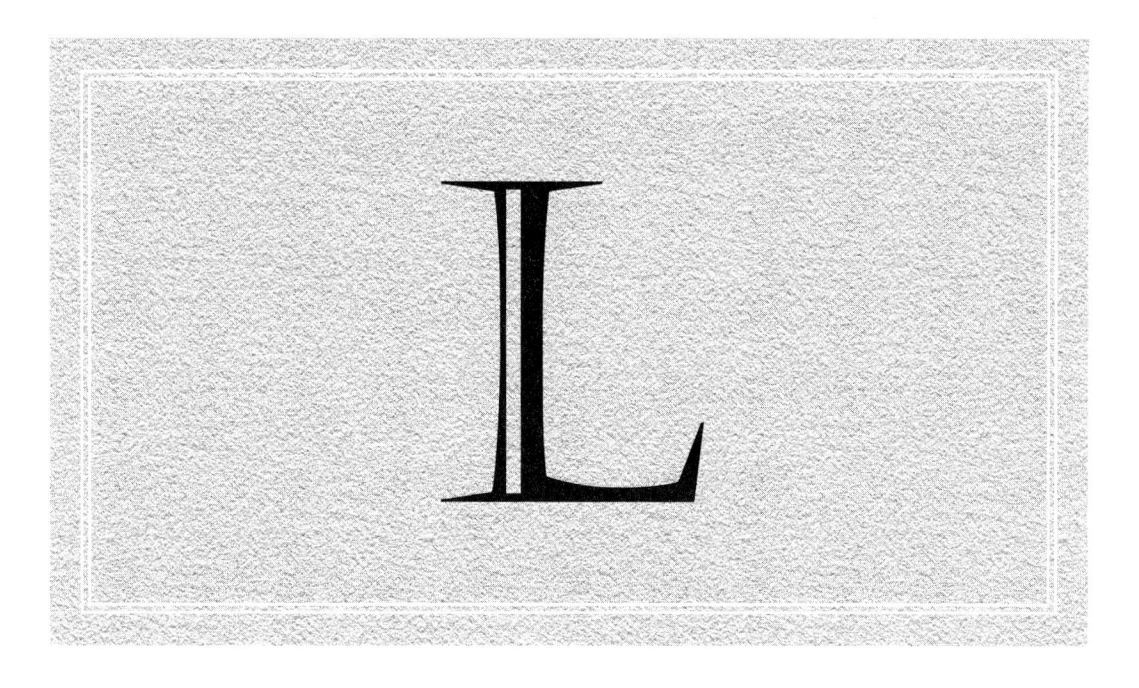

LEWIS, JOHN R.

John Robert Lewis first achieved national attention while he was chairman of the STUDENT NONVIOLENT COORDINATING COMMITTEE (SNCC) during the 1960s and was elected to the U.S. House of Representatives in 1986. Lewis was born on February 21, 1940, to Willie Mae and Eddie Lewis in Troy, Alabama.

While he was a teenager Lewis felt the call to the Christian ministry and began to preach periodically in local churches. He listened regularly to a radio gospel program presented by a young Boston-trained theologian, MARTIN LUTHER KING, JR., and was inspired because King, a southern African American man, was intelligent, articulate, and interesting. King also had thoughtful ideas about addressing the problems of racial injustice through passive resistance. When Lewis was fifteen, he learned of the Montgomery, Alabama, bus boycott led by King, RALPH DAVID ABERNATHY, and other members of the Montgomery Improvement Association (MIA). The MIA led the vast majority of the African Americans in the city in their decision to refuse to ride the segregated city buses unless they were treated more fairly by white drivers and passengers. It filled Lewis with pride to see the African American community of Montgomery acting in concert and with determination. After a year-long struggle, the bus company agreed to their demands.

Lewis was kept from actively participating in CIVIL RIGHTS agitation for a while by his parents who were frightened for his life. But in 1960, after four students from North Carolina A&T College in Greensboro sat down in the "whites only" section of the local Woolworth's lunch counter and refused to move, hundreds of African American and white students all over the South followed their example. Though Lewis's parents urged him to remain uninvolved, he joined the lunch counter sit-in demonstrations that were taking place in Nashville. Before the federal CIVIL RIGHTS ACT OF 1964 was passed, Lewis had been jailed and beaten many times and had suffered a fractured skull at the hands of an angry white mob in Selma, Alabama, during the 1965 Selma to Montgomery protest march.

Because of the spontaneity of the sit-ins, the students had no organizational body or any general affiliation with existing civil rights groups. ELLA BAKER, the executive secretary of the SOUTHERN CHRISTIAN LEADERSHIP CONFERENCE (SCLC, King's regional organization), called a meeting at Shaw University in Raleigh, North Carolina, in April 1960. The students refused to affiliate with any of the existing major civil rights groups such as the SCLC, the NATIONAL ASSOCIATION FOR THE ADVANCEMENT OF COLORED PEOPLE (NAACP), or the CONGRESS ON RACIAL EQUALITY (CORE), and formed their own organization. There, with Lewis as a co-founder along with about 200 other students, SNCC was formed.

After a 1961 Supreme Court decision declaring illegal all segregation in interstate bus depots and on buses, CORE leaders decided to stage a "freedom ride" from Washington, D.C., to New Orleans. Led by CORE director James Farmer, seven African American and six white freedom riders left Washington, D.C., on May 4, 1961. Lewis was among them. The riders, who had pledged themselves to nonviolence,

John R. Lewis
DIGGS/AP/WIDE WORLD PHOTOS

JOHN R. LEWIS

1940 Born in Troy, Alabama

1960 Co-founded Student Nonviolent Coordinating Committee (SNCC)

1961 Part of "Freedom Ride" from Washington, D.C., to New Orleans

1963 Unanimously elected chairman of SNCC

1963 Spoke at March on Washington rally

1965 Participated in Selma to Montgomery march

1986 Elected to U.S. House of Representatives

were brutally beaten during the ride. Lewis was the first to be attacked. Finally, when the Greyhound bus that some of the demonstrators were riding in was burned outside of Anniston, Alabama, the CORE volunteers were ready to discontinue their protest. SNCC members—including Lewis—refused to be dissuaded. Lewis also led marches against segregated movie theaters in Nashville, again prompting numerous arrests as well as physical and verbal abuse by local whites. Through it all Lewis maintained a path of nonviolence toward achieving civil rights.

Lewis was unanimously elected chairman of SNCC in 1963 and served until 1966 when STOKELY CARMICHAEL, the proponent of the more aggressive "Black power" strategy, won his seat. During the time that he was chairman, Lewis was one of the speakers during the August 28, 1963, March on Washington, when nearly 250,000 people converged on the U.S. capital to stage a peaceful protest for freedom and fairness in hiring practices. After he was ousted as SNCC chairman, Lewis went on to work for the Field Foundation. One of his most significant roles at the foundation was director of its Voter Education Project. From 1970 through 1977, Lewis led grass roots efforts to organize southern African American voters and politically educate the youth, among other things. In 1977 President JIMMY CARTER appointed Lewis to be director of U.S. operations for ACTION, a federal agency overseeing economic recovery programs on the community level.

In 1982 Lewis was elected to Atlanta City Council where he was known for his close attention to the needs of the poor and the elderly. Twenty years after he stepped down as the leader of SNCC, Lewis was elected to the U.S. House of Representatives after a hard fought battle with his former SNCC co-worker, Georgia state senator JULIAN BOND. Although, as a congressman, critics accused him of not adapting his positions to the changing needs of African Americans, he nonetheless remained a voice calling for a "sense of shared purpose, of basic morality that speaks to blacks and whites alike." In 1991, Lewis became one of the three chief deputy whips for the DEMOCRATIC PARTY, one of the most influential positions in the House. His criticism of House speaker NEWT GINGRICH brought him to the forefront of controversy in 1996, although he was considered a moderate by many African Americans. In 1994, during a speech to African Leaders in Ghana, Lewis summed up his experience and his commitment to civil rights for all peoples: "Do not give up, do not give out, and do not give in. We must hold on and we must not get lost in a sea of despair."

In 1998, Lewis published his autobiography: *Walking with the Wind: A Memoir of the Movement*. In 2000, Lewis participated in a gathering in Selma, Alabama, commemorating the thirty-fifth anniversary of the Selma to Montgomery protest march.

CROSS REFERENCES
Civil Rights Movement; Student Non-violent Coordinating Committee

LIBEL AND SLANDER

Two TORTS that involve the communication of false information about a person, a group, or an entity such as a corporation. Libel is any DEFAMATION that can be seen, such as a writing, printing, effigy, movie, or statue. Slander is any defamation that is spoken and heard.

Jewell v. Atlanta Journal-Constitution

Richard Jewell started out as a hero. One of thousands of security guards hired for the 1996 Summer Olympics in Atlanta, Jewell's claim to fame was in finding a knapsack containing a bomb that killed one person instantly and injured more than one-hundred. A second person later died of his injuries. Despite the sad toll, Jewell was praised for discovering the bomb and helping to evacuate the area, thus preventing countless other injuries and deaths.

In the days immediately following the bombing, Jewell granted interviews in eleven media forums. During the course of the interviews, Jewell rendered statements not only as a factual witness to the bombing, but also as a spokesperson for the training that he and others had received, commenting on the safety of the park and encouraging the general public to return. Those interviews helped lead the FEDERAL BUREAU OF INVESTIGATION (FBI) to include him as a primary suspect in the bombing, investigating whether he might have planted the bomb in order to appear a hero. He was not cleared as a suspect by the JUSTICE DEPARTMENT until three months later.

After his release as a suspect, Jewell sued or threatened suit against several components of the media for defamation. They included ABC, NBC, CNN, the *New York Post*, NBC anchor Tom Brokaw, and a local Georgia radio station. In January 1997 Jewell sued the *Atlanta Journal-Constitution* and its parent company, Cox Enterprises Inc., claiming that the newspaper libeled him "in a series of false and defamatory articles that portrayed him as an individual with a bizarre employment history and an aberrant personality who was likely guilty." *Jewell v. Cox Enterprises Inc.*, No 97- VS 0122804, Fulton County, GA. The newspaper had reported in an extra edition four days after the bombing that, according to anonymous sources, Jewell was the focus of the FBI's investigation. Although truth is the key defense in a defamation case and Jewell *was* a suspect in the bombing, the libel action was based on more than just a statement of his status as a suspect.

Jewell found himself in the spotlight a second time when Fulton County state court judge John R. Mather ruled on October 5, 1999, that Jewell was a "public figure" for purposes of his legal burden in the defamation case. The significance of this ruling is far-reaching. As a private individual in a defamation case, Jewell would simply need to prove that the newspaper acted with negligence or carelessness in reporting information that was false and defamatory in content.

In order for a *public* figure to prevail in a defamation action, the plaintiff must prove "actual MALICE" on the part of the media defendants. Actual malice in this context has been defined as having knowledge that the reported information was false or having a reckless disregard for the truth. The distinction between the two types of plaintiffs was made clear by the oft-cited 1964 U.S. Supreme Court ruling in *New York Times v. Sullivan*.

Designation as a public figure is usually reserved for the likes of celebrities or government officials. While news coverage alone would ordinarily be insufficient to convert Jewell into a public figure, Mather noted that Jewell nonetheless "used his credibility and new-found publicity to relieve the anxiety of the public" and in hope "of influencing the resolution of this public controversy." Thus, the judge found, Jewell chose to become a "limited purpose" public figure. Mather reasoned that by voluntarily appearing so often in the press, Jewell invited the media scrutiny of his background and personality.

Jewell's attorney filed an appeal, telling the media that there was "simply no evidence Richard agreed to interviews to influence the outcome of the debate. He thought his employers wanted him to do the interviews." The Georgia Court of Appeals has agreed to review the trial court's ruling.

Meanwhile, Jewell was getting his life back in order after all the publicity. The U.S. Department of Justice, in a surprise move, sent a formal letter of apology to him. Jewell also settled his libel suit against ABC for $5,000 in November 1999. He had previously settled his suits with CNN, NBC-TV, and former employer Piedmont College. As of May 2000, the *Atlanta Journal-Constitution* case was still pending, and Jewell's attorney told the media that he would be

Richard Jewell, under intense media scrutiny, August 4, 1996.
BAZEMORE/AP/WIDE WORLD PHOTOS

asking for "astronomical" dollars in damages. In early 2000 Richard Jewell was hired by the police department in Jefferson, Georgia.

Levan v. Capital Cities/ABC

Persons in the public eye face an uphill struggle if they are to prevail in a libel action. The Supreme Court, in *New York Times v. Sullivan*, 376 U.S. 254, 84 S.Ct. 710, 11 L.Ed.2d 686 (1964), set out a rule that reshaped libel law. A public official could recover in a libel action only if and when there was a finding that the libelous statement about the official was made with "'actual malice'—that is, with knowledge that it was false or with reckless disregard of whether it was false or not." As long as there is an "absence of malice" on the part of the press, public officials are barred from recovering damages for the publication of false statements about them. In *Curtis Publishing v. Butts*, 388 U.S. 130, 87 S.Ct. 1975, 18 L.Ed.2d 1094 (1967), the Court held that prominent public persons ("public figures") had to prove actual MALICE on the part of the news media in order to prevail in a libel lawsuit.

The workings of modern libel law were demonstrated in *Levan v. Capital Cities/ABC*, 190 F.3d 1230 (11th Cir. 1999). A jury awarded substantial damages for libel, but the appeals court reversed the verdict and dismissed the case. In so ruling, the Eleventh Circuit Court of Appeals reviewed the facts of the case and applied case law. The court concluded that the television network had not demonstrated actual malice.

BFC Financial Corporation ("BFC") and its president, chief executive officer, and controlling shareholder, Alan Levan, brought an action for defamation against Capital Cities/ABC, Inc. ("ABC") and one of its producers, Bill Willson. Levan and BFC based their case on a segment aired on ABC's television program *20/20*. The segment portrayed BFC and Levan as unfairly taking advantage of investors in real estate-related limited partnerships by inducing them to participate in transactions known as "rollups." BFC and Levan claimed that ABC had made numerous false or misleading statements with actual malice, and that ABC and Willson were liable for the injuries they suffered as a result of the story.

During the early 1980s, Levan and BFC organized and managed commercial real estate limited partnerships. These partnerships were made up of many small investors, who individually could not raise the millions of dollars needed to invest in commercial real estate. Instead, Levan pooled these small amounts of money—averaging between $5,000 to $20,000 dollars per investor—and purchased commercial properties. It was anticipated that the partnerships would hold the properties between four and nine years, sell them, and distribute the proceeds among the investors. By the mid-1980s, however, an economic downturn in the real estate market severely reduced the value of the limited partners' interests. BFC responded by offering the investors a "rollup" transaction. The limited partners would give BFC their shares in the real estate in exchange for corporate bonds known as debentures. The partners voted to approve the rollup and received debentures that would mature in twenty years. During this period the investors would receive interest payments from BFC. The rate of interest paid by BFC, however, was very low and the debentures would essentially be worthless if BFC filed for BANKRUPTCY. In addition, the investors who voted against the rollup were forced to take the debentures. Security analysts later labeled the debentures "junk bonds," as they were very risky investments.

ABC and its program *20/20* investigated an emerging national trend concerning rollups of limited real estate partnerships. It aired its results in November 1991. The segment included interviews with an unhappy BFC debenture holder, security analysts, and other experts. It contained congressional testimony that condemned rollups as well as Levan's appearance before the congressional committee. Levan and ABC could not agree to terms for an on-camera interview but ABC did show portions of a video statement recorded by Levan. Though the show noted that rollups were legal, it pointed out that Levan had greatly benefitted from the rollup. He had sold most of the property and placed the cash in a failing savings and loan institution that he controlled.

Levan sued, arguing that ABC had falsely implied that he had refused any contact with ABC, thereby suggesting he had something to hide. He also claimed that ABC had altered some of the lead-in questions to his videotaped statement and had taken some of his comments out of context. This, Levan contended, created false impressions about the rollup. Finally, he alleged that a statement by a member of Congress at the hearing had been used to create false impressions about events at the hearing. The underlying claim was that ABC had manipulated interviews and other footage to create the impression that Levan had deliberately set out to defraud his investors.

A Florida jury agreed with Levan. It awarded BFC $1.25 million and Levan $8.75 million in COMPENSATORY DAMAGES. The 11th Circuit overturned the verdict, however, and entered judgment in favor of the defendants. Judge Gerald B. Tjoflat, writing for a unanimous three-judge panel, applied the actual malice standard to the facts of the case. He concluded that Levan and BFC failed to prove that ABC "entertained serious doubts" that the underlying theme of the broadcast was untrue.

Judge Tjoflat pointed to the numerous "objective" experts ABC had interviewed, who all agreed that the rollup transactions were bad for the investors and very good for Levan and BFC. The court also noted that Levan had a conflict of interest, as he advised the investors to agree to the rollups and then reaped the benefits, selling the real estate for $16 million. As for ABC's alleged misuse of Levan's videotaped statement and congressional testimony, the court found that this evidence "pales in contrast" to the sources who told ABC that Levan had traded worthless junk bonds in return for valuable real estate. In sum, most of the evidence that related to actual malice all pointed to the lack of it by ABC.

Liddy v. Wells

On January 18, 2000, the U.S. Supreme Court rejected the appeal of WATERGATE burglary conspirator G. Gordon Liddy, who is being sued by Ida Maxwell Wells for allegedly defamatory remarks he made suggesting that she procured prostitutes for visitors in her role as secretary at the Democratic National Committee (DNC) during 1972. *Liddy v. Wells*, ___ U.S. ___, 120 S.Ct. 939, 145 L.Ed. 817 (2000). In denying Liddy's petition for CERTIORARI without comment, the Court let stand a federal court of appeals decision allowing Wells to procede with her lawsuit after it had been dismissed on a SUMMARY JUDGMENT motion by the federal district court.

Now a nationally syndicated radio talk show host, Liddy allegedly made the injurious remarks about Wells on several occasions, including once during a speech at James Madison University in Virginia and once on a cruise ship in the Mediterranean Sea. He made the remarks in connection with his revisionist explanation of the Watergate break-in and cover-up. The conventional explanation of the scandal is that in June 1972, five burglars broke into DNC headquarters at the Watergate hotel and office complex to fix a malfunctioning bugging device that had been installed to eavesdrop on Democratic politicians during that year's presidential race. Liddy contends, however, that the burglars were seeking to obtain compromising information about a call-girl service being run by DNC operatives.

One of the burglars, James McCord, worked for President RICHARD NIXON's reelection campaign. After he was arrested, he told authorities that he and the other burglars had been paid "hush money" to keep silent and perjure themselves at trial to protect officials in the Nixon administration. Liddy, then the chief lawyer in charge of the president's campaign, was implicated in the conspiracy and later convicted on various counts for arranging the burglary. He served four years and four months in prison. Ultimately, the cover-up led to the White House and resulted in Nixon's resignation.

Wells's lawsuit is expected to resume sometime during the year 2000 in the U.S. District Court for the District of Maryland. The plaintiff will bear the burden of demonstrating that Liddy's remarks were defamatory. Wells may rely on Virginia COMMON LAW, which defines defamatory words as those imputing to a person the commission of some criminal offense involving moral turpitude and for which the person could be indicted and punished. She may also rely on the Restatement (Second) of Torts § 614, which provides that words are capable of a defamatory meaning if they tend to PREJUDICE the plaintiff among a substantial and respectable minority of her associates.

One question that will not be at issue during trial is whether Wells is a "public figure." Under the FIRST AMENDMENT, a public figure may recover for injury to reputation only upon clear and convincing proof that the defamatory falsehood was made with "actual malice," which is a statement made with knowledge of its falsity or with reckless disregard of the truth. Private figures have a lower standard of proof. They may recover for injury to reputation by merely showing that a statement was defamatory, false, and negligently made.

The district court found that Wells was an "involuntary public figure," or someone who tries to stay out of a public controversy but nevertheless becomes a central figure in the event. *Wells v. Liddy*, 1 F.Supp.2d 532 (1998). The U.S. Court of Appeals for the Fourth Circuit overturned the District Court's finding, concluding that Wells was a "very minor figure" in Watergate. *Wells v. Liddy*, 186 F.3d 505 (1999). Liddy, the Fourth Circuit noted, was unable to cite more than a few published reports about Watergate that even mentioned Wells's name. As a result, Wells retained her status as a private figure who did not have to meet the higher "actual malice" standard of proof to prevail on her claims for $1 million in damages to reputation and $1 million in damages for mental suffering. She would still be required under the First Amendment to prove "actual malice" to prevail on her claim for $3 million in punitive damages.

Liddy has said that he will assert truth as a defense if the case ever comes to trial. This defense would allow the defendant to demonstrate that the facts underlying Wells's purported role in the call-girl ring were provably true or substantially correct. Liddy is likely to advance this defense by calling Phillip Mackin Bailley as a witness. The district court found Bailley to be unreliable during the earlier proceedings, observing that he was a substance-abusing, mentally-ill, convicted felon and disbarred attorney who had changed his story about the prostitution ring several times. The district court also determined that Bailley was the sole source of the prostitution ring theory.

Texas Beef Group v. Winfrey

A lawsuit by an association of Texas cattle ranchers against television talk show host Oprah Winfrey and a guest on her program highlighted the power of the mass media to influence opinion. The ranchers claimed that false statements about the safety of beef as broadcast on her program led to a sharp decline in the price of cattle for the two weeks after the show. The so-called "Oprah Crash" of 1996 led to a highly publicized 1998 trial in a Waco, Texas, federal district courtroom. In the end the judge dismissed most of the ranchers' charges and the jury found Winfrey not LIABLE on the one remaining charge. Two years later, a federal appeals court affirmed the lower court decision in *Texas Beef Group v. Winfrey*, 201 F.3d 680 (5th Cir. 2000).

The events at issue followed the 1996 outbreak in Great Britain of "Mad Cow Disease," the popular term for bovine spongiform ecephalopathy (BSE). Transmitted through beef to humans, it causes a fatal brain illness called Creutzfeld-Jakob disease. At least twenty people died in the British outbreak, and 1.5 million cows were destroyed in efforts to stop it. BSE is most likely to arise when cattle are fed contaminated ruminant-derived protein supplements, made from the ground up parts of cattle and sheep. At the time of the outbreak, the United States had a voluntary ban on this type of supplement. Moreover, no cases of the disease had been reported in the United States.

The mass media devoted many articles and news programs to the Mad Cow Disease outbreak and Oprah Winfrey's producers developed a show devoted to "dangerous food." One segment of the program was devoted to the British outbreak. One of Winfrey's guests was vegetarian activist Howard Lyman. Lyman, who was a program director for the Humane Society of the United States, attacked the voluntary ban on feeding cattle ground-up cattle parts and called for a mandatory ban on the practice. Lyman stated that if unchecked, this practice could lead to a U.S. epidemic that would "make AIDS look like the common cold." Other guests contended that the public had nothing to fear and that procedures had been in place for decades to prevent what had happened in Britain. The key comment, however, came from Winfrey, who said that Lyman's statements "just stopped me cold from eating another burger."

Beginning the day of the broadcast, the price of beef dropped drastically and remained low for two weeks. The Texas Beef Group filed a civil lawsuit in Texas state court against Winfrey, her company, and Lyman. The defendants had the case moved to federal court because all of them were from outside Texas. The plaintiffs based their case on a recent Texas "food disparagement law," which allows victims of false statements about their perishable food to sue for damages. The judge dismissed this part of the case but allowed the plaintiffs to use a business DISPARAGEMENT cause of action. The jury found Winfrey, her company, and Lyman not liable for damages.

On appeal, the Texas cattle ranchers argued that the case should not have been moved to federal court, that the judge had mistakenly dismissed the food disparagement law claim, and that the jury instruction on business disparagement was unfair. The Fifth Circuit, however, upheld the judge's decisions. In a PER CURIAM opinion (no judge signed as the author), the three-judge panel admitted that the trial judge should have allowed the case to be tried in state court. Nevertheless, the appeals court held that for reasons of finality, efficiency, and judicial economy, it would not reverse the federal court decision and send the case to state court for a new trial.

As for the trial court's dismissal of the food disparagement charge, the appeals court noted that the key issue was the statute's definition of a "perishable food product." At trial, the defendants argued that live cattle are not perishable food, but the appeals court declined to rule on this issue. Instead it focused on whether the defendants knowingly disseminated false information about beef. The court grounded its analysis on the legal precedent that the expression of opinion as well as fact is protected by the FIRST AMENDMENT, "so long as a factual basis underlies the opinion."

Using this framework, the court examined the "dangerous food" program in close detail. It held that while Winfrey, Lyman, and the show's employees had overdramatized the Mad Cow Disease scare, they had not knowingly disseminated false information. Winfrey's comment about not eating another hamburger was "neither actionable nor claimed to be so." The only issue was whether Lyman's AIDS comment and his assertion that the U.S. government was treating BSE as a public relations issue were false. The court found that at the time of the show the factual basis for Lyman's opinions was truthful. Although there was a ban on using ground-up cattle for livestock feed, the practice did continue on a limited basis. As for Lyman's AIDS comparison statement, the court characterized it as hyperbole, and, in its view, exaggeration did not equal defamation. Because the challenged comments had a factual basis, Winfrey and Lyman had a First Amendment right to say them.

Finally, the cattle ranchers had challenged the jury instruction on the business disparagement charge. The appeals court rejected it out of hand, as the ranchers forfeited their right to appeal this issue during the trial. Under rules of procedure, their failure to object on the record at the time eliminated their right to appeal.

CROSS REFERENCES
First Amendment; Watergate

M

MANSLAUGHTER

The unjustifiable, inexcusable, and intentional killing of a human being without deliberation, premeditation, and MALICE. The unlawful killing of a human being without any deliberation, which may be involuntary, in the commission of a lawful act without due caution and circumspection.

Pit Bull Owner Held Responsible for Deadly Attack

More than one million dog bites occur each year in the United States, approximately 12–14 of which are fatal. The majority of them come from family pets rather than stray dogs. Historically, the most serious bites are from pit bulls, German shepherds, and rottweilers. Civil lawsuits for dog bites are so common that many insurance companies no longer insure dog owners for losses caused by bites, or, at a minimum, exclude from coverage all owners of certain breeds of dogs considered vicious.

Increasingly, states are imposing criminal charges against owners whose vicious dogs attack others. Since 1987, there have been at least five cases in which owners have been convicted of criminal charges for their pet's conduct. The latest of these involves the filing of involuntary manslaughter charges against a Winnsboro, South Carolina man after his two pit bulls killed a 45-year-old man in December 1999. The dogs' owner, 22-year-old Frank Speagle, was charged after authorities found John Mickle's body about 200 yards from Speagle's house. A coroner's report indicated that Mickle had been bitten more than 1,000 times and suffered a crushed windpipe.

The county in which Speagle lived did not require dogs to be leashed or fenced in. Such requirements change from state to state, and from county to county within each state. Notwithstanding, COMMON LAW requires an owner to keep a dangerous animal restrained or contained.

Authorities charged that Speagle knew or should have known that his dogs were potentially dangerous. The breed is generally known for its ferocity and was bred specifically to fight other animals and kill them for human sport. Pit bulls have been known to take down a bull weighing more than 1,000 pounds. While it is

One of the dogs who mauled John Mickle to death is penned by the Winnsboro, SC, sheriff's office.
KRASKY/AP/WIDE WORLD PHOTOS

true that many are gentle and loving, their unpredictability makes them frightening, and the stereotype prevails.

The reputation of the breed alone would have been insufficient evidence, however, to charge Speagle with involuntary manslaughter. Instead, authorities will rely on Speagle's knowledge of the dogs' previous conduct and temperaments. First, Speagle left the dogs loose in his yard at the time of the attack. Also, just a month earlier, another man had reported to Speagle that his dogs had bitten the man on the calf and thigh and would have continued their attack if he had not lashed out with his belt. Authorities also had reports that the dogs had flattened car tires with their teeth. As of July 2000, the Winnsboro, South Carolina, case was still pending.

Under common law, owners are not automatically LIABLE for a dog's bite in the absence of prior knowledge of the dog's propensities for attack. This is commonly referred to as the "one-bite rule." In other words, once the dog bites a human, strict liability for future bites attaches, as the owner then has notice of the dog's propensity. Many states have codified or incorporated the common law into their statutes, while others include strict liability as a matter of law. Most states permit defenses of provocation, lack of knowledge of previous propensity for attack, and the victim's status as trespasser upon the dog owner's property.

A violation of these laws resulting in a death, though, does not automatically amount to manslaughter. Manslaughter is a form of HOMICIDE, the killing of another person. Voluntary manslaughter, like murder, is an intentional killing, but unlike murder, contains an element of mitigating circumstance, such as overwhelming provocation. Conversely, involuntary manslaughter does not involve an "intentional" killing. The resultant death is most often caused by the reckless or grossly negligent conduct of the perpetrator.

Seized dogs that have attacked humans are usually quarantined for rabies, and then euthanized. In 1997 a Kansas woman was convicted of involuntary manslaughter following the death of an 11-year-old boy attacked by her rottweilers. As recently as May 2000, a five-year-old New York boy and his one-year-old brother were attacked by family pit bulls while having breakfast in their house. The pit bull brought down the older boy in his back yard, then ran into the kitchen and attacked the infant in his high chair. When medical assistance arrived, another of the family's pit bulls attacked, forcing animal control officers to kill it immediately. Both children were expected to recover from their injuries, albeit following several surgeries.

As in most states, a dog is deemed "personal property" of its owner. Authorities have no jurisdiction or control over a vicious dog if it is contained on the owner's property and warning signs are posted clearly for anyone approaching the property. Some states have been successful in prosecuting for "nuisance" if the dog is deemed a constant risk to the safety and welfare of the community or public at large.

MARSHALL, MARGARET HILARY

On October 13, 1999, Margaret Hilary Marshall became the first woman Chief Justice of the Supreme Judicial Court of Massachusetts. Marshall was born in 1944 in Newcastle, Natal, South Africa. Her mother, Hilary A.D. Marshall, was born in Richmond, England. Her late father, Bernard Charles Marshall, was a native of Johannesburg, South Africa, and was a chemist and production manager at the African Metals Corporation. She is married to *New York Times* columnist Anthony Lewis and has three stepchildren.

In 1966, Marshall received a bachelor of arts degree from Witwatersrand University in Johannesburg. At Witwatersrand, Marshall majored in English and art history. From 1966 to 1968, she was president of the National Union of South African Students, leading her fellow classmates in protests against apartheid. The National Union of South African Students was the only multi-racial national group in the country at the time.

Marshall immigrated to the United States in 1968 in order to pursue an education at the graduate level. She studied at Harvard University, where she was awarded a graduate scholarship by the Ernest Oppenheimer Trust. The following year, she received her master's degree in education from Harvard. After doing so, Marshall decided on a law career. She studied at Yale Law School from 1973 until 1975. Although she completed her last year of law school at Harvard, Yale awarded her a juris doctorate degree in 1976.

Marshall began her career as a lawyer in private practice, working as both an associate and a member in the Boston law firm of Csaplar & Bok from 1976 through 1989. In 1978, she became naturalized as a U.S. citizen. She then continued the private practice of law in Boston as a partner at the prominent law firm of Choate, Hall & Stewart from 1989 through 1992. During these years, Marshall's practice consisted primarily of civil litigation. She became regarded as an expert in the area of INTELLECTUAL PROPERTY, which includes PATENT, COPYRIGHT, and TRADEMARK LAWS that protect inventions, designs, artistic and literary products, and commercial symbols.

While pursuing her career in private practice, Marshall continued in the fight against apartheid in her native county. She urged the United States to impose sanctions against South Africa due to its continuance of racial segregation. At that time, advocating sanctions against South Africa was a treasonable offense in her native country. Consequently, she was not able to return to South Africa because of her activities in the United States.

Marshall returned to Harvard University in 1992, where she served as general counsel and vice president until 1996. In this position, Marshall was responsible for Harvard's legal and regulatory affairs. Furthermore, she served as an active member of the President's Academic Council.

In November 1996, Marshall became an Associate Justice of the Supreme Judicial Court of Massachusetts. Marshall was only the second woman ever to serve as a Justice on the highest Court in Massachusetts. The Massachusetts Supreme Judicial Court is the oldest court in continuous service in the United States.

As a Supreme Judicial Court Justice, Marshall is known for authoring opinions that strongly support CIVIL RIGHTS and liberties. For example, in one opinion, she supported the constitutional rights of SEX OFFENDERS by holding that they are entitled to a hearing before their names are entered on the sex offender registry in Massachusetts. Marshall is also known for opposing CAPITAL PUNISHMENT.

On March 9, 1998, Marshall authored an opinion in the widely publicized case of *Commonwealth of Massachusetts v. Woodward*, 694 N.E.2d 1277 (Mass. 1998). In that case, at the trial court level, a jury found Woodward, an au pair from England, guilty of the MURDER of Matthew Eappen, an eight-month-old child under her care. However, the trial judge reduced the jury's verdict from murder to involuntary MANSLAUGHTER and sentenced Woodward to time served. Both sides appealed and the case ultimately came before the Supreme Judicial Court for disposition. In the 46-page decision, Marshall stated that the reduced conviction of manslaughter, as well as the sentence imposed by the trial judge, were lawful. In making this ruling, Marshall explained that the trial judge merely invoked the commonly used right to reduce a jury verdict and to sentence a defendant to time served.

After Marshall served as an Associate Justice on the Supreme Judicial Court for three years, the Governor of Massachusetts, Paul Cellucci, nominated her to be the Court's first female Chief Justice and the first female to head one of the three branches of government in Massachusetts. On October 13, 1999, the Governor's Council approved Marshall's nomination. In December of the same year, Marshall was sworn in as Chief Justice of the Supreme Judicial Court. As such, she is the first naturalized U.S. citizen to become a Chief Justice.

As Chief Justice, Marshall designates which judges write opinions on particular cases, acts as the liaison to the Massachusetts governor and legislature, and has wide ranging authority over the administration of the state's courts. In a keynote address delivered to the Massachusetts Bar Association on January 2, 2000, Marshall stated, "Because of my experiences in South Africa, I value profoundly the central place of law in American society ... law in the true sense. An impartial judiciary. Equal justice under the law." Marshall's term on the Supreme Judicial Court could last until the year 2014, when she reaches the mandatory retirement age of seventy.

MARGARET HILARY MARSHALL

1944 Born in Newcastle, Natal, South Africa
1968 Immigrated to the United States
1976 Earned J.D. from Yale Law School
1978 Became a naturalized U.S. citizen
1996 Became Associate Justice of the Supreme Judicial Court of Massachusetts
1999 Sworn in as Chief Justice of the Supreme Judicial Court

MEDICARE

A federally funded system of health and hospital insurance for persons age sixty-five and older and for DISABLED PERSONS.

Fischer v. United States

Federal programs that provide funding to a variety of services and activities have improved the quality of life for many Americans. Federal funding also gives Congress the opportunity to regulate activities that would otherwise be within the jurisdiction of state governments. Congress has used this authority to federalize many crimes that would normally be tried in state courts. The Supreme Court, in *Fischer v. United States*, __ U.S. __, 120 S.Ct. 1780, 146 L.Ed.2d 707 (2000), reaffirmed this federalization of criminal law, ruling that a federal BRIBERY statute applied when an individual defrauded a hospital that received federal Medicare funds. In so ruling, the Court set out an analysis that can be applied to other federal programs.

Jeffrey Fischer was president and part owner of Quality Medical Consultants, Inc. (QMC), a corporation that provided financial accounting services to health care organizations. In 1993 Fischer negotiated on QMC's behalf a $1.2 million loan from West Volusia Hospital Authority (WCHA), a municipal agency that operated two hospitals in West Volusia County, Florida. Both of the hospitals participated in the Medicare program in 1993 and received between $10 and $15 million in Medicare funds. In 1994, an audit of QMC revealed that Fischer had used the loan to repay creditors, raise his salary, and speculate in securities. Moreover, the investigation found that Fischer had used $10,000 of the loan proceeds to pay a kickback to WCHA's chief financial officer, who had negotiated the loan with Fischer. Soon after the audit, QMC defaulted on the loan and declared BANKRUPTCY.

A federal GRAND JURY indicted Fischer on thirteen criminal charges for his actions. One charge was based on 18 U.S.C.A. § 666, which makes it a crime to defraud an organization that receives more than $10,000 in benefits from a federal assistance program. A jury convicted Fischer on all counts. Fischer then appealed, claiming that § 666 did not apply because WVHA did not receive $10,000 in "benefits" as defined by the statute. He contended that only individual Medicare recipients receive benefits; the hospitals received payments for services. The Eleventh Circuit Court of Appeals rejected this argument, finding that funds received by an organization constitute "benefits" within the meaning of § 666 if the source of funds is a federal program, like Medicare, which provides aid or assistance to participating organizations.

The Supreme Court, in a 7–2 decision, upheld the appeals court. Justice ANTHONY M. KENNEDY, writing for the majority, examined the nature and purpose of the Medicare program. He noted that Medicare employs an "elaborate funding structure" that is designed not only to compensate providers for the cost of their services to patients, but "also to enhance health care organizations' capacity to provide ongoing, quality services to the community at large." Kennedy also found it significant that Medicare payments are often provided to hospitals before they provide services. This is done to insure the hospital's liquidity.

Justice Kennedy then reviewed what the word "benefits" meant in relation to the Medicare program. He first defined "benefits" in its ordinary sense, as found in dictionaries. As a noun, "benefits" means something that promotes well-being, useful aid, or a cash payment for service. In this sense, Kennedy admitted that Fischer's claim that elderly and disabled persons are the primary beneficiaries of the Medicare program was true. However, the identification of one beneficiary of an assistance program did not, in Kennedy's view, "foreclose the existence of others." He concluded that Medicare had a "purpose and design above and beyond point-of-sale patient care," and therefore the benefits of the program extended in "a broader manner as well." Hospitals and other health care organizations derived significant advantages from participating in the Medicare program and these advantages constituted benefits within the meaning of the federal bribery statute. From the language of the statute, Kennedy found that Congress viewed many federal assistance programs as providing benefits to organizations. Therefore, the Court ruled that Congress's "expansive, unambiguous intent" showed that it wanted "to ensure the integrity of organizations participating in federal assistance programs."

Despite the ruling in this case, Justice Kennedy sought to limit its scope. Any receipt of federal funds could at some "level of generality" be called a benefit, which could turn "almost every act of FRAUD or bribery into a federal offense, upsetting the proper federal balance." Kennedy insisted, however, that a court must examine the structure, operation, and purpose of an organization participating in a federal assistance program to determine whether it receives "benefits." An essential question will be "whether the recipient's own operations are one of the reasons for maintaining the program." In this case, health organizations participating in the Medicare program satisfied this question.

Justice CLARENCE THOMAS, in a dissenting opinion joined by Justice ANTONIN SCALIA, agreed with Fischer that the two hospitals had received reimbursements for services but not benefits. Only elderly and disabled persons received Medicare "benefits." Thomas contended that the Court's analysis could easily be applied to other federal programs, resulting in the federalization of more crimes.

CROSS REFERENCES
Bribery; Fraud

MEZVINSKY, EDWARD MAURICE

Edward Maurice Mezvinsky, a former two-term U.S. Congressman from Iowa, went on to become the U.S. Representative to the U.N. Commission on Human Rights and later Pennsylvania's Democratic Party Chair. His wife Marjorie Margolies-Mezvinsky, a former newscaster who also entered politics, is perhaps best known for casting the deciding vote in favor of President BILL CLINTON's 1993 budget while a U.S. Congresswoman. Unfortunately, the couple later became embroiled in a financial scandal that threatened to overshadow their past accomplishments.

Born in Ames, Iowa, on January 17, 1937, Edward Maurice Mezvinsky displayed an early interest in politics. After graduating from the University of Iowa (1960), he received both an M.A in political science (1963) and a J.D. (law degree, 1965) from the University of California at Berkeley. He returned to Iowa and became a legislative assistant to U.S. Representative Neal Smith. In 1969 Mezvinsky was elected to the Iowa House of Representatives, and then to the U.S. Congress for two terms (1973–76). He was a member of the House Judiciary Committee, which in 1974 voted to impeach President RICHARD NIXON. Mezvinsky chronicled his congressional experiences in *A Term to Remember*.

While in Congress Mezvinsky was interviewed by a young television newswoman, Marjorie Margolies. She already had won broadcast awards for her stories on Southeast Asian war orphans and had adopted two Asian children as a single parent. Mezvinsky married Margolies in

EDWARD MAURICE MEZVINSKY

1937	Born in Ames, Iowa
1973–76	U.S. Congressman
1977–79	U.S. Representative to UN Commission on Human Rights
1981–86	Pennsylvania Democratic Party Chair
2000	Filed for bankruptcy

1975. Eventually they became parents to eleven children: a mixture of adopted children, biological children, and children for whom they served as guardians.

After being defeated in his attempt at a third term in 1976, Mezvinsky was appointed U.S. Representative to the U.N. Commission on Human Rights (1977–79). He and Margolies-Mezvinsky settled in Pennsylvania, where Mezvinsky again became politically active. By 1981 he had been selected as Pennsylvania's Democratic Party Chair, a position he held until 1986. After an unsuccessful bid to become Pennsylvania's lieutenant governor in 1990, Mezvinsky turned to international business ventures.

Meanwhile, Margolies-Mezvinsky decided to pursue a political career of her own. From 1971 to 1991 she had been a news correspondent for NBC, contributing to programs such as *Today* and *Real Life with Jane Pauley*. In 1992, she ran for Congress as a Democrat in Pennsylvania's affluent and heavily Republican 13th Congressional District. She won a surprising victory by only 1,400 votes and entered Congress in what became known as the "Year of the Woman." (Women occupied a record-shattering 48 seats in Congress, including 24 "freshman" seats.) Margolies-Mezvinsky later described the experiences of these women in *A Woman's Place: The Freshmen Women Who Changed the Face of Congress*. In 1993 she cast the deciding vote in favor of President Clinton's budget, which reduced the federal deficit but also raised taxes. This vote probably resulted in her defeat in the 1994 election. She then became co-chair of the U.S. delegation to the U.N. Fourth World Conference on Women in Beijing, and also worked with Women's Campaign International, a political training program for women in other countries. In 1998 she began a campaign to unseat Pennsylvania's Republican senator, Rick Santorum, in the upcoming 2000 election.

The seemingly charmed life led by Margolies-Mezvinsky and her husband collapsed in late 1999. He was sued for FRAUD in federal court by David G. Sonders, a Virginia businessman, who claimed that Mezvinsky had cheated him out of $500,000 in an elaborate business scheme. Sonders said that Mezvinsky had persuaded him to invest in a business transaction in Africa's Ivory Coast. Sonders placed $500,000 in an escrow account in Mezvinsky's name. Although Mezvinsky gave Sonders reports showing that the money was still in the account, Sonders discovered that Mezvinsky had withdrawn all but about $250. Sonders then sent an associate, Jeff Webb, to meet Mezvinsky in Spain. There Mezvinsky told Webb that instead of the Ivory Coast business, he had set up a deal with Zaire's President Mobutu, in which Mezvinsky would help to hide a half-billion dollars smuggled out of Zaire in Swiss bank accounts. Sonders's funds supposedly had been transferred to a Spanish bank as part of this deal. When Sonders sued Mezvinsky, it turned out that there was no such account and no arrangement with Mobutu. Allegedly almost all of the $500,000 had been used for Mezvinsky's personal expenses.

Sandra Murphy waves to her family at her arraignment.
RAUCH/AP/WIDE WORLD

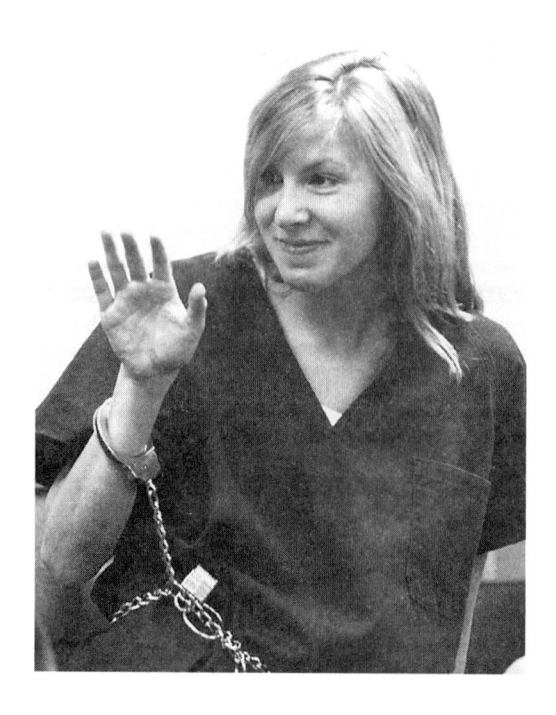

By early 2000 the couple had severe legal and financial problems. Citing personal reasons, including her elderly mother's health, Margolies-Mezvinsky dropped out of the Pennsylvania senatorial race. Only a few days later, however, her husband filed for BANKRUPTCY, and it was revealed that together they were responsible for millions of dollars of unpaid debt, ranging from mortgages to utility bills to tuition loans for one of their children. In early February, Margolies-Mezvinsky also filed for bankruptcy, claiming that she had let Mezvinsky handle all of their finances and had been unaware of any problems. Meanwhile, several lawsuits brought by their creditors were put on hold by the bankruptcy filings, and the U.S. Attorney's Office reportedly was investigating whether Mezvinsky had committed any crimes in his financial dealings.

MURDER

The unlawful killing of another human being without justification or excuse.

Casino Owner Ted Binion Killed for "Buried Treasure"

One of the more sensational murder trials in 2000 was that of 55-year-old Ted Binion. The wealthy Las Vegas casino owner and heir was found on the bedroom floor of his home, apparently the victim of a drug overdose. Various drug paraphernalia and an empty bottle of the sedative Xanax were nearby. His sister, Becky Behnen, immediately suspected foul play from Binion's live-in girlfriend, 27-year-old Sandy Murphy. A former topless dancer whom Binion had recently suspected of having an affair with his friend Rick Tabish, Murphy allegedly found Binion on the floor when she came home on the afternoon of September 17, 1999. A frenzied Murphy then phoned 911 and reported that Binion was not breathing. Paramedics on the scene thought he looked like he had been dead for some time. Binion's sister immediately told police, "Consider it a homicide until further notice."

It took nine months of investigation for prosecutors to feel comfortable that they had enough evidence to go forward against Murphy and Rick Tabish. Even so, their evidence was largely circumstantial. Little by little, the evidence fit together to create a collage of sex, violence, greed, power, thievery, drugs, and murder. The case became known as "the largest murder trial to hit Southern Nevada," and was the first trial ever televised live on the INTERNET, starting on April 19, 2000.

Binion was the youngest son of casino mogul Benny Binion, who owned the famous Horseshoe Hotel-Casino in Las Vegas. Described as bright and talented, Ted was the consummate big game casino operator. His drug habits, however, overcame his abilities and he lost his gaming license in 1987. Because random drug tests showed continued use, Nevada officials permanently revoked his license in 1998.

In the interim, Binion had lost his mother to death, and his wife and daughter to divorce. He plunged deeper into his vices and met Sandy Murphy on a visit to a topless nightclub. She moved into his house within weeks of their meeting. He showered her with clothes, credit cards, cash, and a $100,000 Mercedes.

After permanently losing his license in 1998, he again sank heavily into heroin and his relationship with Murphy became more abusive. Binion's sister took over control of the casino. Concerned about some valuables he had previously stored at the casino, Binion hired Tabish in 1998 to move $5 million in rare coins and silver bars to an underground vault on Binion's property, near a small town sixty miles from Las Vegas. Tabish, a contractor who was burdened with debt, struck up a friendship with Murphy and they began spending weekends together in places like Beverly Hills and Montana.

Prosecutors hoped to prove that the two began a secret affair in early 1998 and that Binion ordered Murphy to be removed from his will when he found out. This created the MOTIVE needed to tie together a circumstantial case. The prosecutors also hoped to prove to the jury that Murphy and Tabish plotted to kill Binion and steal his buried treasure, since Tabish was the one who buried it in Binion's secret vault.

Pieces of evidence presented to the jury began to build the case. For example, coroners had initially ruled Binion's death as an accidental overdose. Although he was not the suicidal type, defense counsel could create doubt by showing his depression following the loss of his license and his paranoia over Murphy's relationship with him. A more thorough autopsy concluded otherwise. Binion's stomach had twice the amount of heroin needed to kill a grown man. At trial, one key piece of evidence prevailed: Binion usually smoked his heroin. In this case, it seemed that someone had forced him to ingest it. Added to this was the coroner's testimony that Binion's body had bruises on it, and his body had been turned over after death. The coroner opined that the death was a homicide.

Even more damaging was testimony from a sheriff's deputy in the town of Pahrump, sixty miles from Las Vegas. He testified that two days after Binion's death, he came upon three men digging with a backhoe in an empty lot at 2:00 A.M. When the men responded that nothing was in their tractor-trailer, the deputy took a look inside and found millions of dollars in rare coins and silver bars. One of the men was Tabish, who told the deputy that he had been told by Binion to move the bounty to Binion's ranch.

Just days before his death, Binion had hired a private investigator to follow Murphy. He suspected she was having an affair, but did not know with whom. On September 12, 1999, a technician notified Binion that a household surveillance camera—set up to catch Murphy and Tabish together—had been sabotaged. Binion's attorney told police that on September 16, the night before his death, Binion contacted him and told him to remove Murphy from his will, "if she doesn't kill me tonight." He also intended to remove her from the house. Police on the scene at Binion's house found his personal safe emptied of all valuables. The vault that Tabish was found digging up was also empty.

Throughout the trial, Murphy and Tabish declared their innocence, telling the jury that their relationship was platonic. After proofs, the jury deliberated for eight days. It returned guilty verdicts against both Murphy and Tabish. The reconvened jury took only ninety minutes to recommend sentences of life in prison with possibility of parole after twenty years. Formal sentencing of the two was scheduled for August 2000.

Separate from the murder trial, Murphy had won her right to her share of Binion's estate, because Binion never signed a new will removing her. Binion's estate has appealed that to the Nevada Supreme Court. Another criminal trial is also pending against Tabish and his accomplices for the alleged theft of the vault contents. Murphy was added as a defendant in this case as well.

NATIVE AMERICAN RIGHTS

Cayugas and Northern Utes Win Large Land Claims

In January 2000 the federal government announced it will return more than 80,000 acres of land in Utah to the Northern Utes, a Shoshone-speaking tribe of Native Americans. The following month, a federal jury recommended that the Iroquoian-speaking Cayuga Indian Nation receive $37 million for more than 64,000 acres of land that New York purchased illegally in 1795 and 1807. These unrelated events were part of ongoing efforts by Native Americans to reclaim ancestral and traditional lands.

About 4,200 Northern Utes live on the 4.5 million acre Uintah and Ouray Reservation in eastern Utah, which got its name from the tribe. The federal government settled the tribe there in 1882. Then in 1916, the government seized 88,890 acres of the Ute reservation for oil reserves to fuel the U.S. Navy during World War I. Because the government never needed the reserves, it has not touched the oil at what is now called Naval Oil Shale Reserve No. 2.

Meanwhile, near Moab in another part of the state, Atlas Corporation operated a uranium mine from 1962 to 1984. Atlas has declared BANKRUPTCY and left behind 10.5 million tons of rock and soil containing radioactive uranium tailings. According to a study by the U.S. Fish and Wildlife Service, toxins are leaching from the Atlas site into the Colorado River just 750 feet away, threatening three endangered species of fish: the southwestern willow flycatcher, the razorback sucker, and the Colorado squawfish. Estimates say it will cost $300 million to clean up the Atlas site and move the radioactive waste to a safe location in the desert.

In January 2000 U.S. Energy Secretary Bill Richardson announced a deal to give land back to the Utes while cleaning up the Atlas mine site. In exchange for reclaiming 84,000 acres of Naval Oil Shale Reserve No. 2, the Utes agreed to pay 8.5 percent of royalties it receives from oil and gas mines to the federal government for Atlas mine clean-up costs. Current estimates say the 84,000 acres contain six trillion cubic feet of natural gas, equal to 30 percent of the annual usage in the United States. There are no estimates of how much oil the land contains.

Secretary Richardson called returning the land "the right thing to do." Tribe leader O. Roland McCook, Jr. called it "a moral issue," saying, "the government has finally returned to us what was taken from us without our consent." Congress still must approve the deal before it becomes final.

Meanwhile, the Cayuga Indian Nation and New York State are still fighting in court over 64,000 acres of land in Cayuga and Seneca Counties. At the beginning of the American Revolution in 1775, a large part of the tribe moved from those lands to Canada because they favored the British. In 1795 and 1807, the tribe sold its land to New York State and relocated among other Iroquoian tribes in Wisconsin, Ohio, and Ontario.

In 1980 the Cayugas filed a lawsuit saying New York violated the Federal Trade and Intercourse Act of 1790 by purchasing the land without permission from the federal government. In a related case involving another Native American tribe, the U.S. Supreme Court ruled in 1985 that New York had violated that law. The question then became whether the Native Americans should get their lands back or receive compensation for the true value of the land.

The true value of the Cayugas' land was a matter of great dispute. The Cayugas estimated that the land is worth $660 million, the federal government appraised it at $335 million, and New York State said it is worth only $51 million. In January 2000 New York offered the tribe $120 million to settle the case. The tribe rejected the offer and then was shocked in February when a jury decided the land is worth only $37 million.

Martin Gold, an attorney for the tribe, called the jury recommendation "ridiculous." Tribe spokesman Clint Halftown was less critical, saying, "We have always said this was not about money. So we have a little less to buy back our land, to begin rebuilding our nation. It is enough to start." U.S. District Judge Neal McCurn will make the final decision about what the Cayugas get for their land.

Kennewick Man DNA Tests Proceed

A 1996 lawsuit between eight scientists and the federal government concerning the 9,200-year-old "Kennewick Man" skeleton continued unresolved into 2000. At issue is whether the government must return the skeleton to Native Americans, or whether it may allow scientists to study it. Under federal law, the result depends on whether Kennewick Man was culturally related to the ancestors of any of the five Native American tribes who seek custody of his remains. To answer that question, federal scientists in 1999 and 2000 proceeded with radiocarbon and DNA tests, which Native Americans condemned as desecration.

Two boating enthusiasts discovered Kennewick Man's skull on July 28, 1996, in the Columbia River at Kennewick, Washington. Under a permit issued by the U.S. Army Corps of Engineers (ACE), which has jurisdiction over navigable waterways, local authorities and scientists recovered 380 bones, or about ninety percent of Kennewick Man's skeletal remains. The shape of the pelvic and other bones suggested Kennewick Man was a five-foot ten-inch tall male who died between forty and fifty-five years of age. A radiocarbon test in August 1996 indicated that he lived 9,200 years ago. That discovery set off the dispute between scientists, Native Americans, and the federal government.

Under the Native American Graves Protection and Repatriation Act (NAGPRA), the federal government must notify Native American tribes that are "likely to be culturally affiliated" with human remains found on federal land. On August 27, 1996, ACE notified the Umatilla tribe, who traditionally inhabited the region where Kennewick Man was found. Together with four other tribes, the Umatillas filed a claim for Kennewick Man to be returned for reburial.

The Umatillas' claim is simple. Their oral histories, which go back 10,000 years, say Native Americans have inhabited North America since the beginning of time. If Kennewick Man is 9,200 years old, then he was here before European settlers arrived with Christopher Columbus in 1492. That means he is a Native American. Because he died in the Umatillas' traditional homelands, he must be related to their ancestors. According to religious leader Armand Minthorn, "Our elders have taught us that once a body goes into the ground, it is meant to stay there until the end of time."

On August 30, 1996, ACE announced its intention to return Kennewick Man to the coalition of Native Americans. That launched a thirty-day waiting period to allow other groups to make competing claims. The Asatru Folk Assembly, a religious group that worships Viking deities, filed its own claim suggesting that Kennewick Man may have descended from Vikings who migrated to North America. The Asatru demanded DNA tests to ascertain Kennewick Man's true origin.

Before ACE could resolve the dispute, eight scientists sued ACE in 1996 in federal court. They said ACE violated NAGPRA by basing its determination of cultural affiliation solely on Kennewick Man's age and location. The scientists pointed to early reports by anthropologists who said Kennewick Man's skull does not resemble those of Native American ancestors. Anthropologists Douglas Owsley and Richard Jantz said, "If a pattern of returning [such] remains without study develops, the loss to science will be incalculable and we will never have the data required to understand the earliest populations in America."

Facing a lawsuit, ACE asked the U.S. Department of the INTERIOR (DOI) for advice on how to proceed. Francis P. McManamon, chief archaeologist of the National Park Service, decided there was not enough information about Kennewick Man to determine his cultural affiliation. McManamon ordered further studies and

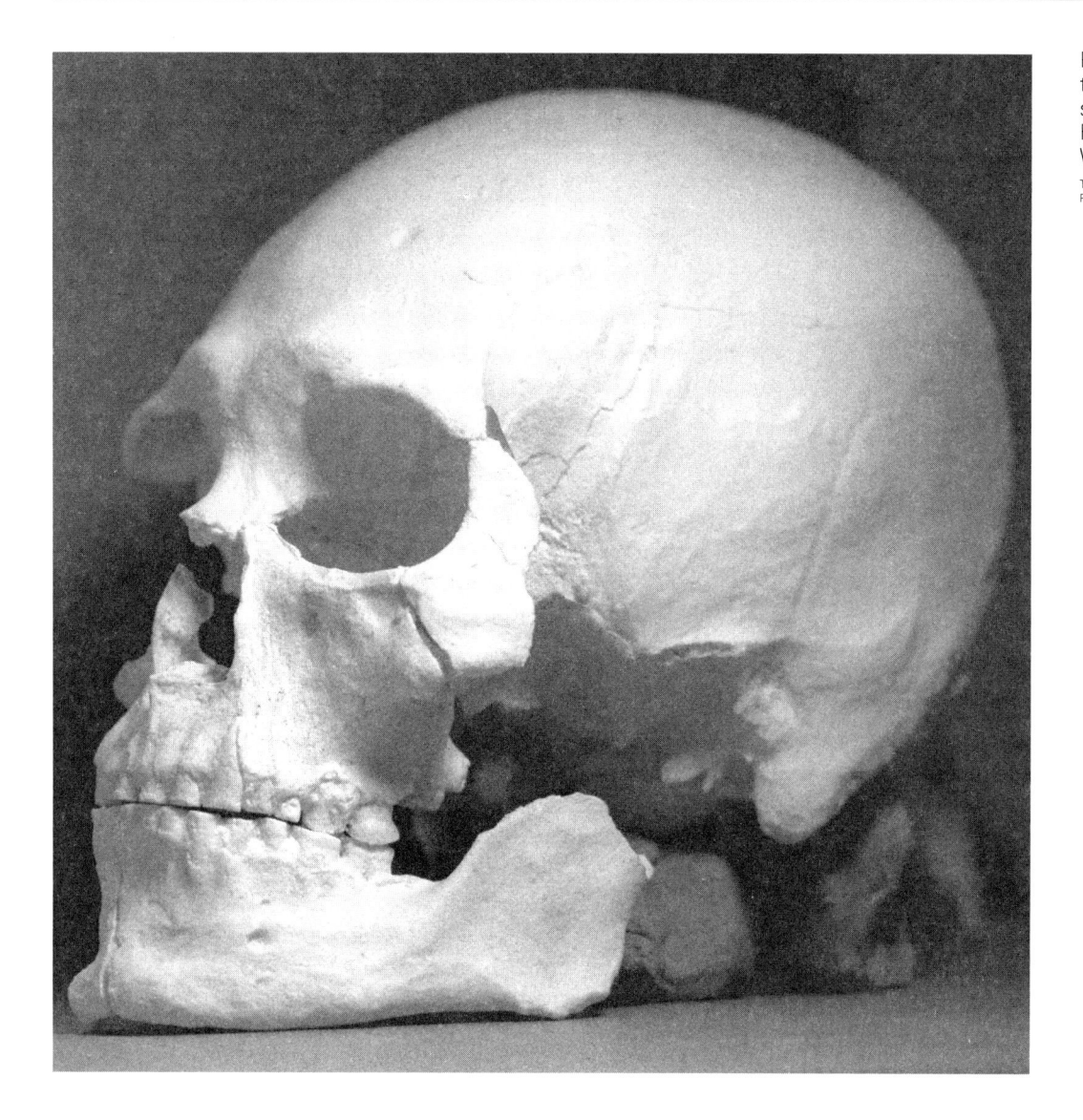

Plastic replica of the 9,200-year-old skull found in Kennewick, Washington.
THOMPSON/AP/WIDE WORLD PHOTOS

tests, exactly what the Native Americans wanted to avoid.

In July 1999 DOI scientists announced the results of an initial round of tests, including bone and teeth measurements, soil analysis, and analysis of a stone tip embedded in Kennewick Man's pelvis. They said Kennewick Man was formally buried when he died and may have been painted with a ceremonial red dye. Comparison of his skull measurements with those of 300 populations, however, resulted in no matches. With cultural affiliation still inconclusive, the scientists announced plans to conduct more radiocarbon tests.

That angered the Native Americans, who felt Kennewick Man had been dishonored enough already. It also angered the independent scientists, who filed a motion asking the court to put an end to the federal government's "intellectual censorship." U.S. Magistrate Judge John Jelderks, who had been allowing the government to proceed at its own pace, ordered the government to make a decision by March 24, 2000.

In October 1999 DOI scientists reported that Kennewick Man's skull most resembles Asian ancestors, such as Polynesians and the Ainu of Japan. That supports a prevailing theory that Native Americans descended from Asians who migrated to North America when an ice mass connected it with Siberia. Native Americans generally reject that theory.

In January 2000 the Asatru Folk Assembly dropped out of the lawsuit, saying it did not have time or money to pursue its claim for independent DNA testing. That same month DOI announced that two out of four additional radiocarbon tests indicated Kennewick Man lived about 9,200 years ago. Based on those results, DOI officially classified Kennewick Man as Native American under NAGPRA. The question still remained, however, whether he was culturally affiliated with Umatilla ancestors.

To answer that question, DOI asked Judge Jelderks for a six-month extension of time to conduct DNA tests. In theory, such tests could determine Kennewick Man's cultural affiliation by matching his DNA with data from known Native American ancestors. Native Americans pointed out, however—and federal scientists admitted—that DNA testing probably would confirm only whether Kennewick is Native American, not his tribal affiliation.

Lawyers for the eight scientists opposed the DNA tests, saying they had asked for such tests years before and it was time for the government to turn Kennewick Man over to the scientists. Native Americans condemned the DNA testing because it would destroy portions of Kennewick Man's bones. Suggesting that science must yield to human rights, anthropologist Jonathan Marks likened continued testing to Nazi experimentation on Jews during World War II. Legal scholar George Annas said standards of ethics require family consent for scientific testing of dead people. Judge Jelderks, however, granted the extension, giving DOI until September 2000 to complete the DNA tests and decide Kennewick Man's fate.

PAGE, ALAN CEDRIC

Alan Cedric Page, former Minnesota Vikings football star, has served as an associate justice of the Minnesota Supreme Court since 1993. Page gained athletic fame as one of four "Purple People Eaters" for the Minnesota Vikings' defense who were essential to the team's ten division titles and four Super Bowl victories. While still employed full-time as a professional football player, Page attended the University of Minnesota Law School full time and graduated in 1978. He is the first and only African American supreme court justice for Minnesota.

One of four children of Georgianna Umbles and Howard Felix Page, Alan Page was born on August 7, 1945, in Canton, Ohio. His mother, a country club attendant, and his father, a bar manager, always emphasized the importance of learning. They instilled strong values in him, and Page looked up to his parents as role models.

Page was an outstanding athlete in high school, but even at a young age, his fantasies went beyond the gridiron and into the courtroom. Page admired former Supreme Court Justice THURGOOD MARSHALL and was a fan of the *Perry Mason* television show. He told *Parade Magazine* in 1990, that he viewed sports not as a goal, but as a means to achieve an education: "Even when I was playing professionally, I never viewed myself as a football player. There's far more to life than being an athlete."

Page graduated from the University of Notre Dame in 1967 with a B.A. in political science. At Notre Dame, Page was an All-American defensive end. Chosen in 1967 by the Minnesota Vikings as their first-round draft pick, Page went on to earn the Most Valuable Player award in the National Football League in 1971. In the NFL, he played the position of a defensive tackle. He logged fifteen seasons with the Vikings and the Chicago Bears without missing a game. After graduating from law school, he joined the firm of Lindquist and Vennum in Minneapolis and specialized in employment and labor litigation (1979–84). Page was Assistant Attorney General in Minnesota (1987–93) when he was elected to the National Football Hall of Fame in 1988.

Page established the Page Education Foundation in 1988 to increase the participation of minority youth in postsecondary education and work-readiness activities. Scholarship recipients tutor kindergarten through eighth-grade students for eight to ten hours each month during the school year while attending post-secondary school, thus creating a pyramid influencing younger students of color as mentors and role models.

Page regularly speaks to minority students about the importance of education. He also encourages adults to influence children to look at the values and good examples of hard work that decent Americans provide every day for "creating and sustaining hope for the future." He went on to say, "These are not the heroes who offer hope with promises of winning the lottery, becoming a rap star or pulling down backboards and endorsement contracts in the NBA. These are simply men and women who get up every morning and do the things that citizens do."

Alan Cedric Page
BOUDRY/AP/WIDE WORLD PHOTOS

> **ALAN CEDRIC PAGE**
>
> **1945** Born in Canton, Ohio
> **1967** Began professional football career
> **1978** Graduated from the University of Minnesota Law School
> **1979** Entered private practice while still playing professional football
> **1987** Began stint as Assistant Attorney General
> **1993** Elected to Minnesota Supreme Court
> **1998** Reelected to Minnesota Supreme Court

In his 1998 reelection campaign, an opponent charged that Page's foundation activities violated canons regarding the judicial appearance of impartiality. The ETHICS complaint showed that donations to the scholarship fund had soared in recent years and that some of the contributors included companies and law firms with cases pending before the Supreme Court. Page and his lawyer said that he refused to help raise funds and intentionally avoided any knowledge of contributors. The complaint also charged that awarding scholarships only to minorities violated the judicial canon prohibiting any expressions of bias or prejudice. In February 1999 the Minnesota Board on Judicial Standards cleared Page of any ethics violations in the matter.

Page was in the news in 2000 when he was ticketed for driving with expired automobile tabs. He demanded a trial on the $57 fine, although the fine would have been reduced to $28, had he agreed to pay. In court, Page's attorney offered documentation that his client had mailed his check for the tabs weeks before he received the ticket. The Minneapolis City Attorney's office argued that Page had an obligation to stay off the road until he received his tabs. As an alternative to waiting for them via the mail, they argued he could have visited the driver and vehicle services office personally and purchased them on the spot; when the mail-ordered tabs arrived, he could have sought a refund for his previous payment. The court ruled in Page's favor, finding that Page should not be penalized for the state's delay.

While playing for the NFL, Page met and married Diane Sims. They have four children, Nina, Georgianna, Justin, and Khamsin. They all shared their father's interest in education beyond high school, but not his passion for sports.

PARDON

The action of the executive official of the government that mitigates or sets aside the punishment for a crime.

Preston King Returns to the United States After 39 Years

The power of federal and state executives to officially pardon their criminal constituents is generally derived from constitutional or statutory authority. Most executives wish to avoid the potential for releasing persons back into society who may cause harm again, so it is exercised infrequently. Some crimes seem more pardonable than others, however, and create less political backlash. Indeed, executives are often accused of invoking the CLEMENCY power for their own political gain.

President BILL CLINTON has followed a recent trend of cutting back on presidential pardons from the thousands of requests received each year. The decline began in 1988, when President GEORGE BUSH criticized Massachusetts Governor Michael Dukakis for temporarily releasing Willie Horton. While free, Horton committed further crimes, including rape.

During his tenure, Clinton has granted seventy-four pardons and sixteen commutations of sentences. In February 2000 he granted pardon to Dr. Preston King, a black educator who fled the United States in 1961 for refusing to be inducted into the U.S. Army during the VIETNAM WAR.

King alleged at the time that an all-white military draft board would not address him as "Mister." He had originally been granted several deferments by the board to pursue studies at the London School of Economics and Political Science. When the war intensified, however, he received correspondence from the board, addressed to "Preston King." Previous correspondence had addressed him as "Mr. Preston King," but according to King, the Albany draft board had since learned that he was black.

When he refused to report for his physical, he was tried for draft evasion. During the trial,

King denied accusations that his real intentions were draft-dodging. It was simply an act of civil disobedience. The jury unanimously disagreed and convicted him. The presiding judge sentenced him to eighteen months in prison. While out on bail during appeal of his conviction, he fled to England, where he has resided for thirty-nine years. After pursuing graduate studies in political philosophy, King taught in England, Ghana, Kenya, and Australia. He has been a political science professor at England's University of Lancaster since 1986.

King had originally aspired to a political career. He attributes his political activism to his parents, who taught their seven children to stand up for what they believed in, no matter the cost. The King family included prominent residents in the Albany, Georgia, community. In the 1940s, King's father, Clennon King, Sr., organized a voters' league for local black residents. King's oldest brother, Clennon Jr., was the first black person who attempted to enroll at the University of Mississippi in the 1950s. In 1976 Clennon Jr. tried to join an all-white Baptist church in Plains, Georgia, where President JIMMY CARTER was a member. In his work as an attorney, Clennon Jr. represented MARTIN LUTHER KING, JR. (no relation). It was Clennon Jr.'s death that indirectly helped bring about King's pardon, as Clinton granted Preston King's pardon in time for him to attend the funeral.

King visited President Clinton to thank him for the pardon, and sat in on one of Clinton's taped weekly radio addresses. He also visited with 97-year-old William Bootle, the judge who presided over King's original trial. Bootle has said that the trial would have ended the same way if King had been "white as snow." He added, however, that if King had been white, there would have been no case at all. Bootle was among many over the years who asked that King be pardoned. President Carter had granted a blanket pardon of all draft dodgers in 1976, and King could have been home several years sooner.

Clinton's pardon of King has not gone without criticism. Questioning King's earlier motives, J.R. Labbe wrote in the *Fort Worth Star-Telegram*, "[King] didn't have any problems with the manner in which his local draft board referred to the African American when it was granting those requests [for student deferments]...." Labbe, for one, believes that the true heroes are those blacks "who served in the Army for their country, and answered the call of duty when their local draft boards sent out those 'Dear Preston' letters." Labbe remarked in her article, "Too bad the draft-dodger didn't stick around long enough to visit the Korean War Memorial . . . or walk by The Wall, where the names of more than 58,000 of this nation's true heroes are inscribed,—none of them beginning with the word 'Mister.'"

Preston King received a pardon from President Clinton, allowing him to return home for the first time since 1961.
STONE/AP/WIDE WORLD PHOTOS

PARKS, BERNARD C.

Appointed in 1997, Bernard C. Parks is only the second African American police chief in the history of Los Angeles. He starred on his high school football team, then earned an associate degree at the Los Angeles City College. After graduation he found a job in a General Motors assembly plant. He applied to the Los Angeles Police Department after hearing an advertisement on the radio in 1965. His first job with the police department was directing traffic, but eventually he found a niche in a detective division.

While working for the LAPD, Parks earned a Bachelor of Science degree from Pepperdine University, and then a Master's Degree in Public Administration in 1976 from the University of Southern California. The following year Parks was promoted to the rank of captain. Only four years later, Parks became a commander in charge of the Operations/Headquarters Bureau. This group included the department's Robbery/Homicide Division, the Forgery Division, and the Narcotics and Metropolitan Divisions. Also under Parks's charge was the elite Special Weapons and Tactics (SWAT) platoon, acknowledged to be the most highly trained assault team

Bernard C. Parks
UT/AP/WIDE WORLD PHOTOS

> **BERNARD C. PARKS**
>
> **1943** Born
> **1965** Joins Los Angeles Police Department
> **1976** Earns Master's Degree in Public Administration from University of Southern California
> **1980** Promoted to Commander
> **1988** Selected as Deputy Chief
> **1997** Sworn in as Chief of Police
> **1999** Scandal emerges from Rampart Division in Los Angeles

in the world. By 1987 Parks had advanced further and was overseeing the daily activities of 1,300 officers and civilian staff members, running the police department's Records and Identification Division, its scientific laboratories, its communications and computer systems planning, and its research functions and jail units.

In February 1988 Police Chief Daryl Gates selected Parks for a newly created deputy chief's position. Chief Gates was forced out of office by June 1992, in large part because of the infamous incident in which a black construction worker, RODNEY KING, was severely beaten by four Los Angeles police officers after a high speed chase. Although a bystander captured the episode on videotape, the white officers were acquitted by an all-white jury, touching off full-scale riots throughout the city.

Parks was a candidate to succeed Gates. He lost by one vote to Willie Williams, an African American police chief from Philadelphia. Parks clashed with his new chief from the beginning. Williams found it impossible to trust Parks, and Parks charged that his superior lacked management skills. "If you don't give subordinates direction ... they certainly can't be criticized if they missed the mark, if they don't know what the mark is," he commented in the *Los Angeles Times*. In turn, Williams blamed Parks for a lack of progress in the matters of increasing arrests while minimizing racism and POLICE BRUTALITY. In October 1994 he demoted Parks to Deputy Chief and also tried to force him to take a pay cut.

In 1993 Parks spearheaded an audit into allegations of SEXUAL HARASSMENT at the West Los Angeles Division. Finding merit to some of these allegations, Parks decided to make senior officers responsible for the behavior of their subordinates—a move that did not enhance his popularity in the department. Later that year he clashed with the powerful Police Protective League, when he canceled a set of promotions in the Narcotics Group, claiming that the testing procedures had been improper. The League accused him of circumventing departmental rules of promotion by denying white male officers their rightful promotions in order to promote female and minority police officers in their stead. The City Council sided with Parks.

Parks began as the new police chief for Los Angeles on August 7, 1997, after Williams's contract was not renewed. Before entering office, Parks had submitted a written plan of reforms scheduled for immediate implementation. It included centralizing his authority by restructuring the hierarchy at police stations so that captains would be closer to patrol operations and investigative functions. A departmental OMBUDSPERSON was appointed to deal with complaints. The post of department commander was created to have someone responsible for running the LAPD during nights, weekends, or times when Parks himself was away or off-duty. Parks also abolished the plan whereby officers could work three twelve-hour days weekly and take the other four days off. This schedule change garnered him stiff criticism from the unions.

In 1999 Parks came under fire when allegations of serious misconduct in Los Angeles's Rampart Division were made public. Officers were accused of unjustified shootings, brutality, and framing innocent persons. The scandal began when Rampart officer Rafael Perez admitted he had stolen eight pounds of cocaine from evidence lockers and sold it to dealers. Pursuant to a plea agreement stemming from the stolen narcotics, Perez began implicating some of his fellow officers in serious misdeeds. Soon, twelve officers from Rampart had been suspended or relieved of duty.

In September 1999 Parks announced he was forming a board of inquiry to investigate not only allegations of misdeeds at the Rampart station, but throughout the entire Los Angeles Police Department. Parks and Los Angeles County District Attorney Gil Garcetti clashed frequently regarding the handling of the scandal. By late March 2000, fifty convictions had been overturned as a result of information stemming from Perez's charges of corruption, and at least twenty officers had been implicated in the scandal. In April 2000 the Los Angeles City Council passed a resolution requesting that the U.S. JUSTICE DEPARTMENT take over the investigation, which may eventually result in the reexamination of several thousand criminal cases.

CROSS REFERENCES
Police Brutality

PAROLE

The conditional release of a person convicted of a crime prior to the expiration of that person's term of imprisonment, subject to both the supervision of the correctional authorities during the remainder of the term and a resumption of the imprisonment upon violation of the conditions imposed.

Garner v. Jones

The EX POST FACTO Clause of the U.S. Constitution forbids the states from enacting laws that retroactively increase the punishment for a crime after its commission. In the 1990s the U.S. Supreme Court has reviewed claims by prison inmates that state laws that increased the time between parole hearings violate the ex post facto clause. In *Garner v. Jones*, ___ U.S. ___, 120 S.Ct. 1362, 146 L.Ed.2d 236 (2000), the Court rejected this argument, ruling that the states have the authority to change parole review rules as long as there is no sufficient risk of increasing the measure of punishment attached to the covered crimes.

In 1974 Robert Jones began serving a life sentence after his conviction for MURDER in Georgia. He escaped from prison in 1979 and committed another murder while he was a fugitive. He was arrested and convicted for the second murder, and in 1982, he was sentenced to a second life term. State law required the Georgia Board of Pardons and Paroles to consider inmates serving life sentences for parole after seven years. In addition, the rules of the pardon board mandate the interval between proceedings to reconsider those inmates for parole after its initial denial. At the time Jones committed his second murder, the rules required reconsideration of his parole to take place every three years. In 1985, after Jones had begun serving his second life sentence, the board amended its rules to provide that reconsideration of those inmates serving life sentences who have been denied parole would take place at least every eight years.

The board considered Jones for parole in 1989, seven years after the 1982 conviction. It denied release and, consistent with the 1985 amendment, set reconsideration for 1997, eight years later. In 1991, however, the Eleventh Circuit Court of Appeals ruled that retroactive application of the amended rule violated the ex post facto clause. *Akins v. Snow*, 922 F. 2d 1558 (11th Cir.1991). The board then reverted to its three-year review rule and reconsidered Jones's case in 1992 and in 1995. Both times parole was denied. The board based its decisions on Jones's multiple offenses and the circumstances and nature of the second offense.

In 1995 the Supreme Court, in *California Department of Corrections v. Morales*, 514 U.S. 499, 115 S.Ct. 1597, 131 L. Ed. 2d 588 (1995), rejected the reasoning contained in the Eleventh Circuit's decision in *Akins*. The board then began scheduling a parole reconsideration at least every eight years. Therefore, after Jones's 1995 review, his next parole hearing was set for 2003 rather than 1998. Jones then filed a federal CIVIL RIGHTS lawsuit, claiming the eight-year review rule violated the ex post facto clause. The federal district court dismissed the suit but the Eleventh Circuit reversed. The appeals court concluded that the Georgia rule differed from the California rule in *Morales*, and therefore it did not have to follow the *Morales* precedent. The court believed that the retroactive rule change covered many inmates who could expect to be paroled and would have the effect of extending their incarceration.

The Supreme Court, in a 6–3 decision, overturned the Eleventh Circuit decision. Justice ANTHONY M. KENNEDY, writing for the Court, noted that in its *Morales* decision it "did not adopt a single formula for identifying which parole adjustments would survive an ex post facto challenge." In addition, Kennedy declared that states must have the flexibility in handling parole matters. The key issue was what role the eight-year rule played in the whole context of the parole system.

In Kennedy's view, Georgia had given the parole board great discretion to decide whether an inmate should receive early release. Though the board had the discretion to lengthen the time between parole hearings to an eight-year maximum, the board had policies that permitted expedited reviews in case of changed circumstances or new information. These policies meant that the board could set a reconsideration date "according to the likelihood that a review will result in meaningful considerations as to whether an inmate is suitable for release." This resulted in the board setting an eight-year review interval for inmates, like Jones, whom the board did not expect to parole, and devoting more attention to those inmates who should receive parole.

Justice Kennedy examined Jones's criminal history and concluded that it was difficult to see how the board had increased his risk of serving a longer prison sentence because of the rule change. He also pointed out that Jones could seek an earlier review if he showed changed circumstances or new information. Based on the rule itself and the rule's "practical implementation," the Court found no evidence that the rule would result in longer periods of incarceration.

Justice DAVID H. SOUTER, in a dissenting opinion joined by Justices JOHN PAUL STEVENS and RUTH BADER GINSBURG, argued that the rule change would result in longer sentences. He noted that the parole board's web site included statements from the board and its chairman that the policies were intended to increase the time served in prison. Therefore, the rule was ex post facto and unconstitutional.

Roy Lee Johnson

Federal appellate courts have long been divided in their approach to determining the effective starting date for supervised release of convicted criminals. At least two jurisdictions have credited any extra time served in prison as fulfilling all or part of the sentence for supervised release following incarceration. Three other jurisdictions have taken the approach that supervised release does not begin until a prisoner is actually released from prison. The U.S. JUSTICE DEPARTMENT intervened and requested review of the issue by the U.S. Supreme Court, following a Sixth Circuit Court of Appeals decision in *United States v. Johnson*, 25 F.3d 1335 (Ca.6 1994).

Roy Lee Johnson was convicted in early 1990 on multiple counts of possessing and intending to distribute cocaine, as well as another charge for use of a firearm during a drug-trafficking offense, which under federal law, carries an enhanced sentence. He was sentenced to fifty-one months in prison for the drug charges and two five-year sentences for the gun-related conviction to be served concurrently over one five-year period. Pursuant to the Supreme Court's 1995 decision in *Bailey v. United States*, Johnson appealed his enhanced prison sentence, arguing that prosecutors had proved only that he had been in possession of a gun while drug-trafficking. Under *Bailey*, the Supreme Court now held that prosecutors must show "active employment" of a gun during the drug-trafficking.

In 1996 District Judge Horace Gilmore agreed with Johnson and vacated the two gun convictions. All that remained was the fifty-one month sentence for the drug offenses. Because Johnson had already served more time in prison than that provided for in the revised sentence, Judge Gilmore ordered Johnson's immediate release. Johnson then requested that the court apply the extra time served in prison toward fulfilling the three-year term of supervised release. Judge Gilmore refused, and Johnson appealed.

The relevant statute, 18 U.S.C. § 3624(a-e) reads in part:

> [A] term of supervised release commences on the day the person is released from imprisonment ... [and a] term of supervised release does not run during any period in which the person is imprisoned in connection with a conviction for a Federal, State, or local crime.

Johnson argued that the day he was "released from imprisonment" should not be considered the date he was *entitled* to be released from prison, being that he had served more time than necessary under his revised sentence. Therefore, his three-year sentence of supervised release should be reduced proportional to the number of excess months served in prison. The U.S. Circuit Court for the Sixth Circuit agreed. It held that Johnson's term of supervised release commenced at the end of the fifty-one-month sentence for drug offenses. That opinion was overturned by the U.S. Supreme Court, which ruled that it was bound by the statute. The statute's language does not reduce the length of a supervised release term by reason of excess time served in prison.

In the interim between opinions, Johnson violated two conditions of his supervised release. The district court revoked his supervised release and ordered him to serve an eighteen month prison term, followed by another twelve months of supervised release. Johnson appealed again.

By amendment in 1994, Section 3583(h) was added to the Sentencing Reform Act of 1984, which expressly authorized district courts to order a new supervised release period following re-imprisonment. The district court did not articulate in its opinion whether it relied on

§ 3583 for authority. Johnson argued on appeal, though, that applying the 1994 amendment to him constituted a violation of the EX POST FACTO clause of the U.S. Constitution. Because the district court was not allowed to devise a new supervised release period at the time that Johnson was initially sentenced, it had no authority to impose a new, additional sentence of supervised release after his re- imprisonment. On this point, the Sixth Circuit disagreed with Johnson and affirmed the district court's re-sentencing, inferring that the district court had presumably relied on the authority of § 3583(h). It reasoned that application of § 3583(h) was not retroactive because Johnson's violations of release conditions, as well as revocation of his supervised release and post-revocation issuance of a new sentence, occurred *after* the 1994 amendment.

The U.S. Supreme Court affirmed the Sixth Circuit result, but for different reasons. The high court held that, contrary to the Sixth Circuit's reasoning, post-revocation penalties are attributable to the *original* conviction, and not to new offenses of violating supervised release conditions. Therefore, had the district court sentenced Johnson under the auspices of § 3583(h), it would have constituted impermissible retroactive application. However, ruled the Supreme Court, § 3583(h) does not apply anyway, because it only applies where the original offense occurs after its effective date—in this case, after 1994. Since the section does not apply retroactively, there can be no *ex post facto* issue.

Instead, the district court had the authority to impose a new period of supervised release for a different reason. Section 3583(e), not (h), authorized the court to "revoke [the] release" and require a person to serve all or part of the time in prison without credit for time previously served on post-release supervision. In fact, the district court had revoked Johnson's initial supervised release and ordered him to serve eighteen months in prison, followed by a new supervised release. Under the statute, it is fair to reason that revocation of supervised release "was meant to leave open the possibility of further supervised release, as well."

CROSS REFERENCES
Ex Post Facto Laws; Prisoners' Rights

PATIENTS' RIGHTS

The legal interests of persons who submit to medical treatment.

Jesse Gelsinger Dies During Poorly Regulated Experiment

Jesse Gelsinger was an idealistic young man who wanted to help others learn more about—and find ways to cure—his rare disease. He had a serious genetic disorder that prevented his liver from properly processing ammonia, a by-product of a protein diet. While most individuals with this condition seldom escape coma and death during childhood, Gelsinger was able to control his disease by following a strict diet and taking medication. He was a fairly healthy eighteen-year-old from Tucson, Arizona.

Gelsinger volunteered to be a patient in a clinical trial in the highly experimental field of gene therapy at the University of Pennsylvania. The University of Pennsylvania is one of fifty research centers in the United States using clinical trials on human patients to further knowledge in gene therapy. Gene therapy has been viewed as an extremely promising area for advances in medical treatment. There are dozens of genetic defects that cause a variety of diseases. The research focuses on introducing normal DNA into the body using a virus, usually a cold virus (adenovirus), in an attempt to replace the defective gene. While research theory is promising, to date the results have been minimal.

The University of Pennsylvania research trials were unusual because, unlike other gene therapy research programs, this program used fairly healthy patients who were not facing imminent death and had other treatment alternatives. In addition, it used a novel method of introducing the gene therapy into the patient. Instead of a simple intravenous line, the Penn experiment used a catheter to insert the drug directly into the main artery of the liver. The federal Office of Recombinant DNA Activities is supposed to oversee patient safety on gene therapy experiments. It did not approve the catheter approach. At the time of Gelsinger's experiment, it had been stripped of its power due to lack of funding. The FOOD AND DRUG ADMINISTRATION (FDA) ultimately approved the experiment, however.

On September 17, 1999, Jesse Gelsinger died from complications from the gene therapy experiment. His death is the first in the field of gene therapy research. At first his liver stopped working properly, then other major organs began to fail, including much of his brain. After four days of progressive decline in his condition, Jesse's father, Paul Gelsinger, decided to disconnect the life support equipment. After Jesse's

IS THE HUMAN GENOME PATENTABLE?

Deoxyribonucleic acid (DNA) is often called the "blueprint of life." Over the last twenty years efforts have been made to patent the human genome, which contains the entire genetic code for the human species. These efforts have generated controversy, especially between members of the scientific and religious communities. In 1980 the U.S. Supreme Court contributed to the controversy by ruling that live, human-made micro-organisms are patentable subject matter under the federal Patent Act. Applying the Supreme Court's ruling to the human species, the U.S. PATENT AND TRADEMARK OFFICE (USPTO) has extended patent protection to isolated and purified strands of the human genome.

The U.S. Constitution gives Congress the power to "promote the Progress of Science and useful Arts, by securing for limited Times to Authors and Inventors the exclusive Right to their respective Writings and Discoveries." U.S.C.A. Const. Art. I Section 8, Clause 8. Pursuant to this authority, Congress enacted the Patent Act of 1952. July 19, 1952, c. 950, 66 Stat. 797. Section 101 of that act allows a patent to be obtained by anyone who "invents or discovers any new and useful process, machine, manufacture, or composition of matter, or any new and useful improvement thereof." 35 U.S.C.A. 101. Congress also created the USPTO to issue patents.

A patent is like a legally protected monopoly over a specific INTELLECTUAL PROPERTY. Patents grant inventors the exclusive right to make, use, or sell their inventions for a period of twenty years. 35 U.S.C.A. 154. Patent holders can prevent anyone else from using their invention, even someone who innocently infringes on the patent holder's intellectual property rights by subsequently developing the same invention independently. Alternatively, patent holders can require that subsequent users pay licensing fees, royalties, and other forms of compensation for the right to make commercial use of an invention. In exchange for this broad, exclusive right over an invention, patent holders must disclose their invention to the public in terms that are sufficient to allow others in the same field to make use of it. 35 U.S.C.A. 112.

The human genome represents a biological map of the DNA in a body's cells. The human body is made up of roughly one trillion cells. Every cell contains twenty-three pairs of chromosomes, and each chromosome houses a single DNA molecule. DNA's chief task is to provide cells with instructions for building thousands of proteins that perform most of the body's essential chores. Proteins contain amino acids and enzymes that catalyze hormones, biochemical reactions, and major structural development, a process known as protein synthesis.

Biological instructions for an individual cell are commonly referred to as genes, which are the fundamental units of heredity. Genes consist of long chains of chemical subunits known as nucleotides. There are four nucleotides, adenine (A), cytosine (C), guanine (G), and thymine (T). These four nucleotides form base pairs to hold together the familiar double-stranded, spiral ladder of the DNA molecule. Each rung of the DNA ladder consists of a single base pair, with A always pairing with T and G always pairing with C. Base pairs are arranged in an almost infinite variety of sequences up and down the DNA ladder. The sequence determines the specific instructions for each gene and makes nearly every person's genetic code unique. The human genome contains an estimated 3 billion base pairs in about 100,000 genes.

The battle over the patentability of the human genome is being fought on several levels. At its core, the battle is a legal one. Opponents question how DNA can be patented as a "novel" invention since the double-helical structure has encoded the human gene for as long as the human species has been around. Observing that DNA was first discovered in the 1950s, opponents claim that scientists have invented nothing new, but only identified something that is very old.

Similar arguments persuaded the U.S. Supreme Court to invalidate a patent on a mixed culture of bacteria strains that were used to inoculate the roots of certain plants. *Funk Brothers Seed Co. v. Kalo Inoculant Co.*, 333 U.S. 127, 68 S.Ct. 440, 92 L.Ed. 588 (1948). Previous efforts to mix the strains had failed because the different species of bacteria inhibited each other's effectiveness. The inventor discovered strains that were not mutually inhibitive and was the first to combine them in a mixed-culture inoculant. The Supreme Court said that patents cannot be issued for the mere discovery of natural phenomena. The qualities of the bacteria, the Court said, were like the sun's heat and the principles of electricity: "They are manifestations of the laws of nature, free to all men and reserved exclusively to none." The Court emphasized that the bacteria acted independently of any effort of the patent applicant.

The issue was revisited in *Diamond v. Chakrabarty*, 447 U.S. 303, 100 S.Ct. 2204, 65 L.Ed. 144 (1980). The USPTO rejected a microbiologist's

death, the FDA stopped all gene therapy research at Penn.

Later investigation by the FDA and the National Institutes of Health (NIH) into Gelsinger's death has shown that he should never have been a subject in the study. The University of Pennsylvania researchers failed to disclose to the FDA that two other patients in the experiment suffered liver damage severe enough to have terminated the research pro-application for a patent to protect a genetically engineered bacterium that was capable of breaking down multiple components of crude oil at an efficient rate. The USPTO found that the inventor had only discovered an unpatentable product of nature. The Supreme Court disagreed with the USPTO, holding that a living, genetically-altered organism may qualify for patent protection as a new "manufacture" or "composition of matter" under section 101 of the Patent Act. The Court said patentable organisms may be distinguished from unpatentable products of nature by determining whether a claimed invention is the result of human intervention.

The USPTO has applied this standard to issue patents for a single gene that has been isolated and purified and offers some utility over a naturally-occurring, impure gene. A gene is "isolated" when, through controlled experiments, the inventor can describe it with sufficient particularity to distinguish it from other genes. *Amgen Inc. v. Chugai Pharmaceutical Co. Ltd.*, 927 F.2d 1200, 18 USPQ.2d 1016 (Fed.Cir. 1991). A "purified" gene performs the same function as its naturally occurring counterpart, but can be identified and sequenced more easily, is shorter and simpler to clone, and is more likely to be translated into a protein by bacterial cells.

The legal controversy surrounding DNA patenting intensified during 1988 when Congress initiated the Human Genome Project (HGP), a fifteen-year, $3 billion dollar research project designed to map and sequence the entire human genome. HGP's goal is to develop diagnostic tests and treatments for more than 5,000 genetically-based diseases. A rough draft of the entire genome was completed in June 2000.

These legal developments accelerated the number of applications seeking patents for genetic compounds based on novel DNA sequences. Between 1980 and 1997, biotechnology and genetic research companies filed approximately 5,000 patent applications with the USPTO, claiming complete gene sequences. Roughly 1,500 patents were granted, more than 400 of which were for human genes. In 1999 the USPTO reported that tens of thousands of such applications awaited approval.

These legal developments also helped spread the controversy surrounding the patentability of the human genome to other segments of society. In 1995 a group of more than 200 Catholic priests, Protestant ministers, Jewish rabbis, and other religious leaders gathered in San Francisco at the annual Biotechnology Industry Organization conference to attack the laws that have allowed scientists to patent the DNA of various organisms. They argued that such laws violate the sanctity of life by unlocking divine secrets and enabling scientists to patent god's creations. A variation of this criticism has been leveled by environmentalists, who assert that nature is devalued by laws enabling corporations to reduce a species and its molecules to ownership. Environmentalists question what will happen to society when its most basic notions about the distinctions between animate and inanimate objects are blurred, as human life becomes just another commodity to be bought and sold on the open market.

Genetic ethicists also have criticized the U.S. government sharply for granting patents on human DNA. They note that prenatal tests are being developed that will one day allow parents to diagnose genetic disorders and other undesirable traits in their unborn children. Some ethicists fear that upon learning such information, parents might choose to terminate a pregnancy to avoid raising a "feeble" child. Such ethicists sometimes invoke images of Nazi Germany, which implemented an infamous eugenics plan that called for involuntary sterilization of individuals who exhibited signs of hereditary disease. Genetic ethicists predict that so-called eugenic abortions could become widespread in the United States with the advent of noninvasive means for prenatal genetic testing.

Some of the strongest criticism has come from the scientific community itself. Certain members of that community have argued that patenting human DNA sequences hampers the free flow of information necessary to most research projects. They contend that having to invest time in tracking down a patent holder, entering into licensing agreements, and paying royalties drives up costs, slows down research, and provides disincentives for scientists to undertake research in the first place. They observe that two companies, Incyte Pharmaceuticals Inc. and Human Genome Sciences Inc., own more than half of the U.S. patents on human genetic structures, and thus can exact exorbitant fees from healthcare companies hoping to put their discoveries to use.

Proponents of DNA patenting acknowledge the pitfalls inherent in the system, but they answer their critics by pointing to the groundbreaking discoveries that have already been patented, including genetic links to breast cancer, colon cancer, multiple sclerosis, tuberculosis, diabetes, cystic fibrosis, Huntington's disease, and Alzheimer's disease. Proponents maintain that the speed at which these discoveries were made was dramatically increased by laws making them a commercially valuable, patentable invention. While mixing profit with human genetic research may produce some thorny ethical problems for society, proponents of DNA patenting are willing to work on these issues when they come to them, so long as the research may ultimately facilitate the treatment of serious health problems.

gram. In addition, researchers did not inform potential patients in the consent form that a monkey had died after receiving the gene therapy. The FDA ban on all gene therapy research at the University of Pennsylvania has been indefinitely extended.

Since Gelsinger's death, experiments in gene therapy faced intense public scrutiny and controversy. Federal regulators have learned that the University of Pennsylvania study is not unusual in its failure to follow federal regulations designed for patient safety. In another

Dr. Krishna Fisher feels that some of the experiments he helped conduct in the clinical trial that lead to Jesse Gelsinger's death were too hasty.
BOTTONI/AP/WIDE WORLD PHOTOS

highly publicized case, the FDA stopped gene therapy experiments by a Tufts University scientist at St. Elizabeth's Medical Center in Boston, Massachusetts. Several other institutions have been lax in reporting deaths and test failures to the FDA and are accepting patients who do not qualify for gene therapy. The FDA acknowledges that it has not enforced the rules for gene therapy research.

In response to these incidents, the FDA and NIH have announced new methods to secure patient safety in gene therapy experiments. Researchers will be required to give the FDA a specific plan of safety monitoring for gene therapy patients. In addition, the researchers will be required to hire independent, specially trained individuals to protect patients' rights and ensure compliance with FDA safety regulations and FDA reporting requirements. The FDA and NIH will hold quarterly meetings for the exchange of safety reports between gene therapy researchers. In spite of these steps, several researchers are calling for a moratorium on gene therapy research to address the safety and ethical concerns surrounding it. The CLINTON administration and members of Congress have requested that the FDA, NIH, and other branches of the government investigate the adequacy of the regulation of gene therapy. Currently, the FDA and NIH lack money and personnel to strictly supervise this research.

Another complication in monitoring the research is that safety reports to the FDA are not made public so that the results of the research can remain secret. The NIH has proposed that researchers be required to report any death or serious illness, even if not directly related to the gene therapy, within fifteen days to both the NIH and FDA. The biotechnology industry and researchers oppose this requirement, claiming that valuable commercial information or confidential patient information may become public.

CROSS REFERENCES
Food and Drug Administration

POLICE

Los Angeles Police Corruption Scandal

In 1999 one of the worst police corruption scandals in U.S. history engulfed the Los Angeles Police Department (LAPD). Allegations ranging from MURDER, drug dealing, and RAPE to perjured testimony and witness intimidation emerged as stunned officials probed the LAPD's Rampart precinct, a downtown police station known locally for its controversial anti-gang unit. As local and federal investigations continued into 2000, the fallout from the scandal began to take shape: the department dismantled the anti-gang unit, more than thirty officers were relieved of duty, and some seventy current and former officers were under investigation. Four officers faced criminal charges, and federal agents raided the homes of seventeen more. In California courts, more than seventy criminal convictions—out of thousands expected to be affected—had already been overturned by July 2000. Civil litigation against the city of Los Angeles also began in earnest, with estimates of DAMAGES as high as $300 million.

No stranger to controversy, the LAPD has seen numerous crises in the past century, ranging from corruption before World War II to criticism for racial intolerance in the 1960s. In 1991 RIOTS raged throughout Los Angeles after a jury acquitted four white police officers of aggravated ASSAULT in the videotaped beating of RODNEY KING, an African American motorist accused of resisting arrest. Although officials promised reforms after the King incident, civilian complaints against the department continued throughout the decade and, by May 1999, had reached such levels that the U.S. Civil Rights Commission recommended appointing a special prosecutor to investigate possible federal violations.

In September 1999 an arrest in the Rampart precinct pointed to a wider problem than was suspected. Officials caught police officer Rafael Perez stealing eight pounds of confiscated cocaine from an evidence locker. In return for a reduced sentence and limited IMMUNITY, Perez offered to turn STATE'S EVIDENCE against other members of his anti-gang unit, the high-profile, heavily-armed Community Resources Against Street Hoodlums (CRASH). Credited with cutting the murder rate and winning convictions in some of Los Angeles's toughest neighborhoods, CRASH had previously attracted criticism and, occasionally, lawsuits.

Officer Perez's revelations were staggering. He admitted to shooting a suspect in 1996 with his partner, and then planting a weapon on the paralyzed man, 19-year-old Francisco Ovando, to make it seem as if the officers had been in danger. Ovando received a 23-year prison sentence. He also confessed to covering up two other illegal police shootings—one in which a suspect allegedly bled to death while police concocted alibis, and another in which officers shot at and killed New Year's Eve revelers. Perez described a pattern of official misbehavior that included the rape, beatings, and shootings of suspects, along with routinely framing innocent parties by planting weapons and drugs and then lying at trial to win convictions.

The allegations set a vast legal machine in motion. First, parallel investigations began. One day after Perez's guilty plea was entered on September 15, the U.S. attorney's office launched its probe of the LAPD, whose officials appointed their own board of inquiry. Next, the court system began the task of reviewing cases in which convictions were obtained illegally by tainted police work and officer perjury. The first to be reversed was that of Ovando, who had already served three years for a crime he did not commit. In mid-October, he filed the first civil lawsuit stemming from the scandal.

The new year shined light on the human and fiscal costs of the scandal. In January, based on Perez's testimony, LAPD Chief Bernard Parks announced that the department had identified ninety-nine cases in which police illegally obtained convictions. Federal estimates ran higher: Los Angeles District Attorney Gil Garcetti said the true number might reach 4,000 cases. Meanwhile, in anticipation of paying out huge claims in civil suits, Los Angeles Mayor Richard Riordan proposed using the $300 million that the city had recently obtained from a tobacco litigation settlement.

In March the scandal broadened with new allegations that CRASH officers illegally used DEPORTATION as a weapon against immigrants whose testimony might harm them. Not only did the alleged roundups of illegal ALIENS violate department policy, but they pointed to a disquieting practice: CRASH allegedly made arrests by using a secret list of 10,000 area Latinos.

On March 12 the LAPD dismantled CRASH only days after the board of inquiry issued its 327-page report on corruption. Not surprisingly, the report concluded that Rampart

Los Angeles police witness a demonstration against corruption on March 15, 2000.
UT/AP/WIDE WORLD PHOTOS

officials exercised lax oversight over officers. It blamed the corruption on only a few individuals, however. In nine general areas, its recommendations ranged from better screening of police office candidates and ETHICS training to operational controls and anti-corruption inspections. One month later, in mid-April, the Los Angeles Police Commission appointed a new panel for the purposes of a department-wide review of the LAPD.

Subsequently, the federal probe intensified. In late April the District Attorney charged three Rampart officers—a sergeant, a detective, and a patrolman—with perjury, filing a false police report, and CONSPIRACY to commit a crime. In July the three officers had further charges added at the same time that a fourth officer was charged. On May 5, 2000, federal agents raided the homes of seventeen LAPD officers to seize papers and photographs. The raids brought fierce protest from the Los Angeles Police Protective League, which accused investigators of abusing police officers for political purposes. Meanwhile, the police chief and the district attorney feuded publicly.

As the scandal reverberated through the summer, tensions between city and federal officials worsened. Unimpressed by the board of inquiry report, the JUSTICE DEPARTMENT in early May threatened to sue the city for a pattern of constitutional violations. On May 8, Bill Lann Lee, head of the Justice Department's Civil Rights Division, surprised city officials with the threat of a police misconduct lawsuit if the city did not swiftly enter a settlement aimed at producing reforms. The Justice Department's proposed settlement called for the city to enter a consent decree—a legally binding agreement to enact reforms, monitored at regular intervals by a court. Federal officials wanted to model the agreement after one entered by Pittsburgh after a 1997 probe of its police department. In early June, however, Mayor Riordan vigorously refused the consent decree, calling the Pittsburgh model a failure. Federal officials repeated their threat of legal action.

POLICE BRUTALITY

The use of excessive force or deliberately cruel treatment by police officers.

New York Police on Trial for Abner Louima Abuse

Police Officers Justin Volpe, Charles Schwarz, Thomas Wiese, and Thomas Bruder from the 70th Precinct in Brooklyn, New York, were called to a disturbance outside a nightclub at 4:00 A.M. on August 9, 1997. Abner Louima, a legal immigrant from Haiti who worked as a security guard in Brooklyn, was present at the disturbance. During the disturbance, Louima's cousin sucker punched Volpe. Volpe mistakenly believed that it was Louima who had hit him. Louima was arrested by the officers and transported to the police station.

According to the prosecution, the officers took turns beating Louima in the police cruiser on the way to the police station. Louima was then brought to a bathroom where Volpe proceeded to SODOMIZE him with a broomstick or plunger handle. Louima suffered internal injuries that required a two month hospital stay and numerous surgeries to correct.

Officer Volpe was charged with the attack on Louima, while Schwarz was charged with restraining Louima during the attack. Both faced a maximum sentence of life if convicted. Volpe, Schwarz, Bruder, and Wiese were accused of beating Louima on the way to the police station. Sergeant Michael Bellomo, the patrol supervisor the night Louima was brought in, was charged with attempting to cover up the incident. Bruder, Wiese, and Bellomo, if convicted, could receive a maximum of ten years in prison.

On May 4, 1999, the trial of the five officers began. On May 25, 1999, Volpe plead guilty to violating Louima's CIVIL RIGHTS by sexually assaulting him and made a formal apology to Louima and to his own family. On June 8, 1999, two weeks after Volpe's plea of guilty, Charles Schwarz was found guilty of holding Louima down while Volpe sodomized him. Schwarz, as well as Wiese and Bruder, were acquitted of the charges of beating Louima on the way to the police station. Sergeant Bellomo was acquitted of the cover-up charges. Officers Wiese, Bruder, and Schwarz still faced CONSPIRACY and OBSTRUCTION OF JUSTICE charges for stating to investigators that Schwarz was not in the bathroom during the attack.

Volpe was sentenced to thirty years in prison on December 13, 1999. Afterward, the trial of Wiese, Bruder, and Schwarz on the obstruction charge began. Volpe testified on Schwarz's behalf, as he had done in the first trial, that Schwarz was not in the bathroom during the attack. Schwarz testified, which he had not done in the first trial, that he was neither in the station nor the station's bathroom. Schwarz insisted that he had no part in the attack, and he

Charles Schwarz **Thomas Wiese** **Justin Volpe**

The three men here were all tried for their alleged involvement in the 1997 torture of Abner Louima in a NYPD stationhouse.
AP/WIDE WORLD PHOTOS

could not remember details regarding numerous phone calls during that time between himself and officers Bruder and Wiese. The prosecution maintained that the phone calls indicated that the three officers conspired to cover up Schwarz's role in Louima's beating. Prosecutors also pointed out that Volpe had nothing to lose by testifying on Schwarz's behalf.

On March 6, 2000, all three officers were found guilty of conspiracy to obstruct justice. Schwarz's sentencing came on June 27, 2000. Despite Schwartz's continued and adamant insistance that he was not in the stationhouse at the time of the torture, U.S. District Judge Eugene Nickerson sentenced him to roughly half the time that Volpe received, fifteen years and eight months. Schwarz was also ordered to make monetary restitution in the amount of $277,495. Schwarz planned to appeal.

On March 10, 2000, Volpe appealed his thirty year sentence. Volpe claimed the sentence was excessive and felt that he should be given credit for having testified that Wiese and not Schwarz was the second officer in the bathroom during the attack.

Louima has filed a $155 million civil rights violation case against the city of New York, the Patrolmen's Benevolent Association, and individual officers. High-profile counsel JOHNNIE COCHRAN has been retained as his lawyer. No trial date had been set as of late June 2000.

New York Police on Trial for Amadou Diallo Shooting

Amadou Diallo, a twenty-two-year-old Muslim immigrant from Guinea, was a street vendor in New York City and lived in the Bronx. Diallo came from a middle-class family and by all accounts was a good, law abiding citizen. New York City police shot him in his own neighborhood on the night of February 4, 1999.

That night, four police officers from the New York City Street Crime Unit (SCU) were working undercover and patrolling the Soundview neighborhood for a serial rapist. Edward McMellon, Sean Carroll, Kenneth Boss, and Richard Murphy were in an unmarked car and wearing bulletproof vests under their plain clothes. The officers came across Diallo outside of his apartment. Because there were no eyewitnesses, details are sketchy as to what exactly transpired that night. What is known is that the officers fired forty-one shots at Diallo, hitting him nineteen times and killing him. Diallo was later found to have been carrying only his wallet, a pager, and a set of keys.

On March 26, 1999, all four officers were indicted on charges of second degree MURDER. If convicted, the officers faced up to twenty-five years to life in prison. Some argued that the Diallo case was indicative of police brutality carried out by the New York Police Department toward minorities. The four officers pleaded not guilty to the charges on March 31, 1999. The

Ahmed Amadou Diallo
AP/WIDE WORLD PHOTOS

officers served a thirty day suspension from police duties without pay, then were assigned to desk duty for the remainder of the trial.

After much pretrial publicity, with marches and demonstrations in support of both sides, on December 16, 1999, the trial was moved to Albany, New York. It was presided over by State Supreme Court Justice Joseph Teresi. Jury selection began on January 31, 2000, with the trial beginning on February 2, 2000. The prosecution attempted to focus the court's attention on the fact that Diallo was unarmed and the question of whether the officers had identified who they were. The defense, however, maintained that the officers identified themselves and feared their lives were in danger since they thought that Diallo was reaching for a gun.

Officers Carroll and McMellon were the first to approach Diallo, while Murphy and Boss remained behind. Carroll testified that McMellon identified himself and that Diallo backed up and reached into his pocket. Carroll shouted that Diallo had a gun and opened fire. McMellon then tripped when backing up and Diallo remained standing, appearing as though McMellon had been shot. Carroll assumed Diallo was wearing a bulletproof vest. Boss testified that he did not shoot until he thought McMellon had been shot. Murphy also testified. All four claimed that Diallo had been warned but he reached into his pocket, which they assumed was for a gun.

On February 16, 1999, the defense rested its case. The prosecution requested that, in addition to the second degree murder charges, the jury be able to consider MANSLAUGHTER and criminally negligent HOMICIDE charges against the officers. Protestors continued to gather outside the courthouse. Judge Teresi granted the prosecution's request but denied a defense motion to dismiss the second degree murder charges. Closing arguments were heard on February 22, 2000, and jury DELIBERATIONS began on February 23, 2000, after three hours of jury instructions.

On February 25, 2000, all four officers were acquitted of all charges. Soon after, the U.S. JUSTICE DEPARTMENT stated it would investigate whether evidence existed to warrant a federal CIVIL RIGHTS trial. On February 26, 2000, thousands of people marched in New York City to protest the verdict; on March 4, 2000, a rally was held in Washington, DC, to call for a civil rights trial.

On April 18, 2000, Diallo's parents sued the city of New York and the four police officers for the death of their son. The parents sued for $81 million: $1 million for every shot fired plus an additional $40 million for pain and suffering since February 4, 1999. Diallo's parents allege that the officers acted in a GROSSLY NEGLIGENT manner and in complete disregard for the rights and safety of their son. The parents further allege that the city was negligent in their supervision of the officers and that the New York City Police Department implemented a policy within the Street Crime Unit of racial profiling.

CROSS REFERENCES
Civil Rights; Murder

PORNOGRAPHY

The representation in books, magazines, photographs, films, and other media of scenes of sexual behavior that are erotic or lewd and are designed to arouse sexual interest.

Family Photographs Lead to Child Pornography Convictions

Family members are being charged criminally for taking nude photographs of their children. In late 1999 an Ohio mother was charged with the illegal use of a child in nudity-oriented material and pandering sexually explicit material for taking nude photographs of her daughter. Cynthia Stewart suffered several miscarriages prior to her current daughter which, she says, explains why she has taken 40,000 photographs of the daughter she considers to be a "miracle" child. The offending photographs depict her daughter posing in the shower. Police regarded the child's pose with the shower head as provocative. In a related case, the domestic relations magistrate found that Stewart's family was in need of supervision, but the decision has been appealed. Stewart, a school bus driver, was suspended by her employer pending trial.

A New Jersey woman, Marian Rubin, was arrested in March 2000 for taking nude pictures of her young granddaughters. A New Jersey father was charged in a similar case in 1994 but was exonerated of the charges. Despite the charges being dropped, the man's attorney insists that he and his family were traumatized by the ordeal.

In both the Stewart and Rubin cases, employees of photo labs notified the police of the photos, who in turn determined that they were inappropriate after applying a pornographic litmus test. Prosecutors contend that the women "crossed the line of decency" by making images of the young girls in provocative poses.

Stewart was charged with pandering sexually oriented matter involving a minor under Ohio Revised Code Section 2907.322. The statute prohibits a person from creating, recording, photographing, filming, developing, reproducing, or publishing any material that shows a minor participating or engaging in sexual activity, masturbation, or bestiality. The statute does not criminalize material created or presented for a bona fide medical, scientific, educational, religious, governmental, judicial, or other proper purpose. Mistake of age is not a defense to a charge under that section.

Stewart was also charged with illegal use of a minor in nudity-oriented material or performance under Ohio Revised Code Section 2907.323. This statute prohibits a person from consenting to or photographing the minor child in a state of nudity unless the material is used for a bona fide purpose. Violation of this section is a FELONY of the second degree.

Supporters argue that the women are being persecuted by a system that is paranoid about sexual exploitation. Supporters feel that, given the overzealous prosecution of ambiguous pornography laws, all parents are potential pedophiles. Many people argue that OBSCENITY is subjective and that pornography must be for the purpose of gratification of the person taking the picture or for the distribution to others for their gratification.

The AMERICAN CIVIL LIBERTIES UNION Ohio ("ACLU Ohio") agreed with supporters, filing an AMICUS CURIAE (friend of the court) brief on Stewart's behalf. The ACLU Ohio argued that the statute under which Stewart was charged is vague and overbroad. Christine Link, Executive Director of ACLU Ohio, stated that families are being prosecuted "under laws that are meant to protect children—not destroy families." The ACLU Ohio feels that prosecution of such cases fails to elicit assistance for children in legitimately dangerous situations.

After months of negotiation, Stewart avoided going to trial by agreeing to give up two photos that prosecutors found offensive. She was also required to complete a minimum of six months of counseling on adolescent sexuality and demonstrate an understanding of what constitutes sexually oriented material. The prosecutor requested a court order that the two photos in question be destroyed. As part of the settlement, Stewart had to admit that the pictures could be interpreted as sexually oriented, but she maintained that the pictures were an artistic documentation of her daughter's life. If convicted, Stewart could have been sentenced to as much as sixteen years in prison.

Several challenges have been made to the Ohio pornography statutes over the years. In *State v. Schmakel* (1989, Ohio App, Lucas Co) 1989 Ohio App LEXIS 3873, a man challenged the constitutionality of the statute, arguing that it violated his rights under the First and FOURTEENTH AMENDMENTS to the U.S. Constitu-

Cynthia Stewart hugs a supporter at a rally on April 17, 2000.
DUNCAN/AP/WIDE WORLD PHOTOS

tion and Section 14, Article I, of the Ohio Constitution. He argued that the statute chilled legitimate behavior, such as a parent photographing his child in the bathtub or running naked on the beach, and therefore, was constitutionally overbroad. The appellate court agreed with the parent in that case and remanded the proceedings to the trial court. The appellate court further noted that the statute's blanket prohibition against allowing parents to photograph their nude children, without mention of the parents' intentions, trampled on protected conduct. The court further commented that the statute could be revised so as to prohibit only unprotected conduct while allowing parents their FIRST AMENDMENT freedoms. The Ohio legislature has not amended the language of the statute, as parents continue to be charged under the same provision.

Man Accused of Internet Rape

Obtaining control of a minor for the purpose of creating child pornography is punishable by up to life in prison. With increased use of the INTERNET, pedophiles have a broader range of minors to target. Many times, the youths believe they are having conversations with their peers. In some cases, however, the teenagers understand that they are communicating with adults.

Catalin Buculei was one such adult who met his victim on the Internet. Buculei was eventually charged with child pornography after engaging in sexual relations with a teenager he met over the Internet. The MINOR child was fourteen-years old at the time of the incident. She met Buculei through an online chat room in December 1998, when she was only thirteen. They later communicated by e-mail and telephone, and Buculei began trying to meet with the girl. She refused the first meeting, but on January 23, 1999, the teen sneaked out of her home to meet Buculei in a motel room. While there, the teen stated that Buculei gave her an alcoholic drink and raped her. Buculei videotaped the sexual assault. After the sexual act, Buculei drove the teenager home.

Two weeks later, the crime was revealed after Buculei stalked his victim at a roller rink. She hid from him in a bathroom and revealed the relationship to an adult. Buculei was arrested in a Maryland motel in February 1999, during another trip to visit the minor. He was charged on five counts, including a federal child pornography law that prohibits persons from traveling across state lines to produce child pornography. Buculei had traveled from Maryland to New York to meet with the child. At the time of the arrest, police discovered a video camera, Polaroid camera, condoms, lubricants, and a bottle of the prescription drug Viagra. Buculei stated that he did not travel across state lines with the intent to have sex with the minor child. The items found in the motel room helped the jury return guilty verdicts on all the charges. The pornography charge was based on the fact that Buculei taped part of the encounter.

Buculei faces a maximum penalty of life imprisonment and a minimum mandatory sentence of twenty years incarceration. Producing, trafficking in, or possessing child pornography is criminalized by the Child Sexual Abuse and Pornography Act of 1986, as amended in 1988, 1990 and 1996 (18 U.S.C.A. § 2251, et. seq.). The U.S. Sentencing Guideline Sections 2G2.1 through 2G2.5 determine the punishment for those crimes.

A defendant's base offense level may be increased or decreased depending on certain factors. An example of an aggravating factor might be the appearance in the material of very young children. An offense level may also be increased if it can be proven that the defendant intended to gain financially from the distribution of the child pornography. A mitigating factor might be the defendant's acceptance of responsibility for the offense. In *United States v. Studley*, 907 F.2d 254 (1990), the U.S. Court of Appeals for the First Circuit cautioned that departures from the sentencing guidelines are only to be used in exceptional cases—that is, when the case involves aggravating or mitigating circumstances of a nature or to a degree not adequately considered by the Sentencing Commission. The court also pointed out that unless there is an express finding to the contrary, a defendant's circumstances are presumed not to be so unusual as to justify a deviation from the guideline. Furthermore, sentences are determined on a case-by-case basis. Therefore, Buculei's ultimate sentence will depend on the factors presented by his defense attorney and by the prosecuting attorney at the time of trial.

Through the years, there have been challenges to pornography laws. Additionally, supporters of the FIRST AMENDMENT argue that laws restricting one's right to possess and receive child pornography violate their constitutional rights. Moreover, there have been challenges to the portion of the Child Pornography Prevention Act of 1996 that makes it a crime to alter pornographic images to make them look like children.

In *Free Speech Coalition v. Reno* 198 F.3d 1083 (1999), the U.S. Court of Appeals for the Ninth Circuit held that the First Amendment prohibits Congress from enacting a statute that criminalizes the generation of computer images of fictitious children engaged in imaginary but explicit sexual conduct. The CPPA bans sexually explicit depictions that appear to be minors and visual depictions that are "advertised, promoted, presented, described, or distributed in such a manner that conveys the impression" that they contain sexually explicit depictions of minors. The court reasoned that the statute's failure to define the terms "appears to be" and "conveys the impression," makes it unconstitutional because the terms are so vague that a person of ordinary intelligence cannot understand what is prohibited. Regarding the remainder of the statute, however, the court found that it passed constitutional muster and added that the statute is enforceable if the computer images are of an identifiable child because there is potential harm to a real child.

The Ninth Circuit decision came on the heels of First Circuit and Eleventh Circuit decisions finding the opposite. In *United States v. Acheson*, 195 F.3d 645 (1999), and *United States v. Hilton*, 167 F.3d 61 (1st Cir.), the courts held that the law is not so vague that a consumer could not understand what type of pornography is illegal under the law. It seems that a Supreme Court decision is on the horizon, given the circuit courts' split in their decisions.

CROSS REFERENCES
First Amendment

PRIOR RESTRAINT

Government prohibition of speech in advance of publication.

Colorado's "Bubble Law" Contested

Some persons opposed to legalized abortion protest outside medical clinics that perform abortions. Some carry signs and march peacefully, while others are more vocal in their opposition. Many act as "sidewalk counselors," seeking to discourage women arriving at the clinic from going inside. At times, there have been confrontations between demonstrators and clinic staff. States and localities have responded by enacting laws that place limits on how close protesters may get to people entering or leaving clinic facilities. In the absence of these laws, judges have issued INJUNCTIONS that accomplish the same objectives. ABORTION opponents have challenged these laws and injunctions, claiming they serve as a prior restraint on speech and therefore violate the FIRST AMENDMENT. Defenders of these actions have argued that the PRIVACY rights of patients and staff members must be protected.

The U.S. Supreme Court, in *Schenck v. Pro-Choice Network of Western New York*, 519 U.S. 357, 117 S.Ct. 855, 137 L.Ed.2d 1 (1997), clarified what types of restrictions a judge can impose on abortion clinic protests. The Court upheld an injunction provision that imposed a "fixed buffer zone" around abortion clinics, but ruled unconstitutional "floating buffer zones," which prohibited demonstrations within fifteen feet of any person or vehicle seeking access to or leaving abortion facilities. However, the Court left open the constitutionality of state laws restricting abortion clinic protests. In *Hill v. Colorado*, ___ U.S. ___, ___ S.Ct. ___, ___ L.Ed.2d ___ 2000 WL 826733 (2000), the Court resolved the issue by upholding a Colorado law that requires anti-abortion demonstrators to stay at least eight feet away from anyone entering or leaving medical facilities. The Court concluded that restrictions on speech-related conduct did not violate the First Amendment because states had strong justifications for the policy.

Colorado enacted the law, Colorado Revised Statute § 18–9–122(3) in 1993. The statute makes it unlawful for any person within one-hundred feet of a health care facility's entrance to "knowingly approach" within eight feet of another person, without that person's consent, in order to pass "a leaflet or handbill to, display a sign to, or engage in oral protest, education, or

Protesters must stay more than one-hundred feet away from clinics and eight feet from patients, according to Colorado's contested "bubble law."
ANDRIESKI/AP/WIDE WORLD PHOTOS

counseling with that person." Legislators sought to balance a person's right to protest with that of another person's right to obtain or provide medical services.

After the enactment of the law, a group of anti-abortion sidewalk counselors sued in state court, alleging that the law was unconstitutional on its face, as it violated the First and FOURTEENTH AMENDMENTS. The counselors lost at the trial and appellate levels, but got a second chance in 1997, when the Supreme Court asked the Colorado Supreme Court to review the case in light of the *Schenck* decision. The Colorado Supreme Court upheld the law as constitutional, but the protesters won the right to appeal to the High Court.

On a 6–3 vote, the Supreme Court upheld the constitutionality of the statute. Justice JOHN PAUL STEVENS, writing for the majority, acknowledged that both sides had legitimate and important concerns. The protesters' First Amendment rights were countered by the state's police powers that seek to protect the health and safety of its citizens. Stevens also noted that the law in question, which is focused on medical facilities, provided "specific guidance" to law enforcement officers and helped serve the even-handed application of the law. Finally, Stevens pointed out that the law did not restrict a speaker's right to address a willing audience. Instead, the law protected listeners from unwanted communications.

In analyzing First Amendment issues, the Court examines whether the law is content neutral. If the law endorses or favors a particular point of view, it is not content neutral and therefore violates the First Amendment. Justice Stevens found the law content neutral for three reasons: (1) it regulated spaces where speech took place, not speech itself; (2) the law was not adopted because the government disagreed with the message of any speech; and, (3) the state's interests were unrelated to the content of the demonstrators' speech. Justice Stevens minimized the threat to free speech, stating that the law "merely places a minor place restriction on an extremely broad category of communications with unwilling listeners."

The majority also justified the law as a valid time, place, and manner regulation. Colorado had "narrowly tailored" the statute to accomplish its goal of providing unobstructed access to medical facilities. Justice Stevens concluded that the demonstrators had other ways to communicate their message, such as displaying a sign that could be seen eight feet away from the person entering or leaving the clinic. Stevens also ruled that the statute was not overbroad or unconstitutionally vague. In his view, it was "unlikely that anyone would not understand the common words used in the statute."

Finally, Stevens rejected the idea that the law served as a prior restraint on speech. He pointed out that in *Schenck*, the Court had rejected the prior restraint argument. In addition, prior restraint related to restrictions "imposed by official censorship." The Colorado law only applied if the "pedestrian does not consent to the approach."

Justices ANTONIN SCALIA, ANTHONY M. KENNEDY, and CLARENCE THOMAS dissented. Scalia, in an opinion joined by Thomas, argued that the majority had expanded its assault on the individual rights of abortion opponents who sought "to persuade women contemplating abortion that what they are doing is wrong." Scalia contended that the law was not content neutral, as its focus was on anti-abortion demonstrators.

CROSS REFERENCES
Abortion; First Amendment

PRISON

A public building used for the confinement of people convicted of serious crimes.

Miller v. French

Beginning in the 1970s, federal courts have ordered changes that remedy inadequate and unsafe living conditions in state prison systems. Prisoner lawsuits led to the federal courts issuing injunctive orders, based on the courts' equitable powers, which placed state prisons under judicial oversight. These orders have typically had no termination date, and many state prison systems remain bound by these orders.

Congress responded to complaints from the states by enacting the Prison Litigation Reform Act of 1996 (PLRA), which contains provisions (18 U.S.C.A. § 3626(b)(2) et seq) that limit the ability of federal judges to order changes in prison conditions. Under these provisions, state prison officials may file a motion with the court to terminate the federal oversight order. Once the motion is filed, the order will be stayed, or suspended, within ninety days, unless the court issues an order upholding its original order. The federal court, in reviewing its original order, must order changes in conditions of confinement "no further than necessary to correct the violation of the federal right of a particular plaintiff or plaintiffs."

In *Miller v. French*, ___ U.S. ___, ___ S.Ct. ___, ___ L.Ed.2d ___ 2000 WL 775572 (2000), the Supreme Court reviewed the constitutionality of the ninety-day stay provision. The Court held that Congress had the power to enact such legislation and that the federal courts had no power to "stay the stay" by issuing an order denying the stay. The Court sent a strong message to the lower federal courts that they must abide by the limitations placed on their power to remedy prison conditions.

Following the enactment of the PLRA, Indiana correctional officials filed a motion in 1997 with the federal court seeking to terminate an order that had governed prison conditions at the Pendleton Correctional Facility since 1982. The order mandated how many prisoners could be housed in one cell, set standards for food and medical services, and directed the state on how to staff the facility. After the filing of the motion, the inmates filed a motion asking that the court refuse to grant the stay that the PLRA imposed on the court. The court agreed and filed an order enjoining the automatic stay provision. On appeal, the Seventh Circuit Court of Appeals held the PLRA provisions unconstitutional on SEPARATION OF POWERS grounds. The court concluded that Congress did not have the power to restrict the equitable powers of the courts and suspend a court order.

The Supreme Court, in a 5–4 decision, reversed the lower courts. Justice SANDRA DAY O'CONNOR, writing for the majority, acknowledged that the circuit courts of appeal had been divided on this issue. She examined the statutory and constitutional questions surrounding the stay provision and found that Congress had not unconstitutionally intruded upon the judiciary's turf. In addition, she ruled that the courts did not have the power to nullify the stay provision by issuing an order.

As to the statutory issues, Justice O'Connor noted that the plain meaning of the statute demonstrated that the stay was mandatory. Once the state filed the motion asking for an end to the court order, the federal court had ninety days to rule on the motion. If it failed to rule in that period, the order was automatically suspended and the court had no power to prevent this from happening. Congress wanted to force federal judges to make prompt decisions on these motions, and it therefore imposed the ninety-day rule. Justice O'Connor concluded that it would "have been odd" for Congress to subvert this intention by allowing the courts to impose their own discretion on these matters.

Turning to the separation of powers issue, Justice O'Connor ruled that Congress had not overstepped its bounds. The inmates had argued that the law violated the Constitution because the legislative branch sought to suspend final judgments of the courts. O'Connor rejected this argument, as the type of orders involved in prison oversight cases were not final judgments. The relief ordered by the court "under a continuing, executory decree remains subject to alteration due to changes in the underlying law." In the majority's view, the PLRA did not tell judges "when, how or what to do, but reflects the change in the law" that established new standards for relief. The Court concluded that because the court order governing the Indiana prison was subject to the court's supervisory jurisdiction, it had to conform to the changes in the law.

Justice STEPHEN G. BREYER, in a dissenting opinion joined by Justice JOHN PAUL STEVENS, argued that the law should be read to allow an exception to the ninety-day time limit "where circumstances make it necessary to do so." As so read, the statute would neither displace the courts' traditional equitable authority nor raise significant constitutional difficulties.

CROSS REFERENCES
Equity; Separation of Powers

PRIVACY

In constitutional law, the right of people to make personal decisions regarding intimate matters; under the COMMON LAW, the right of people to lead their lives in a manner that is reasonably secluded from public scrutiny, whether such scrutiny comes from a neighbor's prying eyes, an investigator's eavesdropping ears, or a news photographer's intrusive camera; and in statutory law, the right of people to be free from unwarranted drug testing and ELECTRONIC SURVEILLANCE.

President's Disclosure of Willey's E-mail Judged in Violation of Privacy Act

In March 2000 in a case about the "Filegate" scandal, federal district Judge Royce C. Lamberth said President BILL CLINTON violated the Privacy Act while defending himself in an unrelated scandal by giving the press letters written to him by Kathleen Willey, a former

What Have Lawmakers Done to Regulate Human Cloning Research?

On February 23, 1997, Scottish scientists Ian Wilmut of the Roslin Institute and Keith Campbell of PPL Therapeutics announced that they had cloned a lamb—whom they named Dolly—starting with a single cell from its "parent." It represented the first time that a mammal had been cloned from an adult cell. Later that year an American physicist announced his intentions to begin cloning humans, starting with himself. These announcements sparked a flurry of state and federal legislation proposing to regulate human cloning in the United States. They also sparked an international debate over the propriety of cloning organisms, especially humans.

Cloning is a process by which cells are isolated from an organism through a biopsy and cultured under laboratory conditions. They grow and divide, producing new cells identical to the original cells. With the exception of sperm and egg cells, cloning from even a single cell of a mammal is possible because every cell in the organism contains a complete set of genes necessary to make an identical copy. Unlike artificial fertilization and other modern methods of conception, cloning requires just one parent.

Dolly was cloned through a process known as "electrofusion." A cell with a full set of chromosomes was removed from the udder of an adult sheep and transferred into another ewe's egg, from which the nucleus had been removed. The embryo was then placed in the womb of a surrogate sheep that gave birth to Dolly. Postnatal tests revealed that 99 percent of Dolly's genes came from the udder cell, while the balance came from the ewe's egg. The scientists failed as many as 400 times before succeeding with Dolly.

Ten months after the revelations from the Scottish scientists, Illinois physicist Richard Seed pronounced he was ready, willing, and able to start cloning human beings as soon as he procured the necessary funding. He said that he intended to use himself as his first subject. Twenty-five states responded to these developments by proposing bills to regulate human cloning, each seeking to regulate the procedure in a slightly different way. Only in California, Michigan, Rhode Island, and Missouri did the bills become law.

Missouri's statute bans state funding for human-cloning research, but does not ban the research itself. V.A.M.S. 1.217. Michigan's law makes it criminal for anyone to intentionally engage in the act of cloning or to attempt to engage in it. M.C.L.A. 750.430A. Violators are subject to maximum penalties of ten years imprisonment and a $10 million fine. California's law makes it a crime to clone a human being or buy fetal cells to do so. West's California Health and Safety Code 24185. Violators may be fined up to $1 million and compelled to forfeit their professional license. Rhode Island's provisions against human cloning closely mirror those enacted by California. Rhode Island General Laws 23–16.4–1. Michigan's law exempts scientific research for certain cell-based therapies from its provisions, while Rhode Island's law exempts in vitro fertilization from its provisions. Enacted in 1998, both California's and Rhode Island's laws contain clauses that allow them to expire in 2003.

Proposed legislation was tabled by some states in anticipation of federal regulations that once appeared imminent. In March 1997 President BILL CLINTON issued a directive barring the use of federal funding for research leading to human cloning. Three months later the National Bioethics Advisory Commission (NBAC) released a report stating it was "morally unacceptable" for anyone to attempt to create a child through cloning technology and urged Congress to draft legislation banning experiments aimed at cloning a human being. The eighteen-member panel consists of doctors, scientists, theologians, and psychologists appointed by the president to study bio-ethical issues.

Over the next two years more than a dozen federal bills were introduced to regulate human cloning and research relating to it. President Clinton introduced the first such bill. Known as the "Cloning Prohibition Act of 1997," the bill proposes to implement a number of recommendations made by the NBAC, including a comprehensive ban against human cloning by individuals and businesses. Violators could be fined up to $250,000. The bill would also authorize federal law enforcement agents to confiscate any property derived from the commission of an offense. The bill is careful, however, not to restrict research relating to the cloning of human molecules, cells, tissues, or deoxyribonucleic acid (DNA).

---

volunteer in the White House Social Office. President Clinton's lawyers filed an emergency appeal of the ruling, but in May 2000, the U.S. Court of Appeals refused to intervene, saying it could review the issue when the case is over. At the same time, the Court of Appeals criticized Judge Lamberth's ruling about the unrelated scandal as "unnecessary" and "inappropriate."

The Willey letters incident occurred in 1998, when President Clinton faced a sexual harassment lawsuit by Paula Jones and allegations that he had sexual relations with White House intern Monica Lewinsky. In a deposition in the Jones case, Kathleen Willey testified that on November 29, 1993, she went to the Oval Office to ask President Clinton for a paying job.

Congressional Democrats and Republicans submitted competing bills. The Democratic bills would have allowed scientists to clone human embryos to facilitate their research for better treatments of disease and illness. Democrats would have made it illegal, however, to implant a cloned embryo into a woman's uterus for the purpose of carrying the fetus to term. Republicans sought to prohibit cloning of human embryos for any purpose, whether it might lead to pregnancy or not.

By 1998 all proposed federal anti-cloning legislation had become mired in the ABORTION debate. Right-to-life forces argued that human cloning research should be outlawed because it cheapened the sanctity of life. Their adversaries maintained that banning such research would encroach upon constitutionally protected reproductive rights. These bills have not received serious attention from Congress in more than a year.

Debate over human cloning continues outside of Capitol Hill. In 1998 nineteen European nations signed an agreement to prohibit the cloning of humans. Professional organizations representing more than 64,000 scientists voluntarily imposed upon themselves a five-year moratorium on human cloning. Catholic officials at Vatican City issued a stinging condemnation of human cloning, stating that it "represents a grave attack on the dignity of conception and on the right to an unrepeatable, unpredetermined set of genes."

Ethicists have compared human cloning research to the eugenics programs in Nazi Germany, which sought to reproduce a master race of superior individuals who were thought to carry "pure" Aryan blood. Ethicists worry that parents might begin creating "designer offspring" by choosing to clone only the genes of highly accomplished individuals or "super humans." Even successful cloning of human cells and tissue for medical treatment, ethicists argue, uses people as a means and not as an end in themselves. Human beings have intrinsic value, they contend, independent of their ability to contribute to successful scientific experiments.

Opinion polls in the United States seem to oppose human cloning overwhelmingly as well. As many as eighty percent of Americans participating in a given poll have stated that human cloning for any reason is morally wrong and should be criminalized. Many Americans have indicated that they would treat cloned humans as "freaks." Others have expressed concern over a cloned child's psychological well-being and their potential risk for genetic abnormalities.

Despite their apparent minority status, proponents of human-cloning research remain adamant that scientists must be free to conduct experiments in this area. They argue that human cloning may provide another way for couples to overcome infertility. They contend that human-cloning research could provide a vital source for tissue and organ transplants, allowing parents with an ill child to clone that child to create a donor. Proponents point out that most of the important research comes within the first week after an embryo is formed, and that nearly all scientists presently conducting human-embryo-cloning research destroy the embryo within ten days after fertilization, thus avoiding some of the thorny ethical problems relating to terminating a more developed fetus.

Some scientists are interested in more than just the research and medical treatment aspects of human cloning. Clonaid, a Nevada-based company founded by former sports journalist Claude Vorilhon, is touting itself as the first firm to offer human cloning. For $200,000 Clonaid promises to deliver a human being cloned from the cells of the donor. The company says it should be ready to do business by the end of the year 2000.

The FOOD AND DRUG ADMINISTRATION (FDA) says that Clonaid will need to get its approval before beginning any human cloning experiments in the United States. Commissioner Michael Friedman announced in January 1998 that the FDA was asserting jurisdiction over "clinical research using cloning technology to create a human being." Friedman said the agency had authority to do this under its power to regulate research on biological products that are "more than minimally manipulated." Thus, Friedman concluded, Clonaid or any other U.S. company planning to conduct human-cloning experiments would first have to file with the FDA an Investigational New Drug Application and meet FDA licensing requirements.

The FDA was soon flooded with objections to their assertion of jurisdiction over human cloning. Several objections noted that in vitro fertilization and other analogous fertility techniques are not presently regulated by the FDA. Enough objections were raised to force the FDA to reconsider its position. By the end of 1998 the FDA appointed a panel of experts to examine the objections before human cloning became a reality. The panel has yet to publicly issue any response to the objections.

Willey said that during the encounter, President Clinton kissed her, groped her, and placed her hand on his genitals. On March 15, 1998, Willey made the allegation public in an appearance on CBS's *60 Minutes*.

President Clinton denied Willey's charge. On the Monday after the *60 Minutes* broadcast, the president's lawyers gave the press fifteen letters that Willey wrote to him, many after the alleged harassment. In the letters, Willey described herself as the president's "number one fan" and continued to seek a paid job in his administration. President Clinton hoped Willey's friendly tone would impeach the credibility of her accusation.

Kathleen Willey, shown leaving federal court after testifying in 1998.
WALSH/AP/WIDE WORLD PHOTOS

In his ruling on March 29, 2000, Judge Lamberth said that by releasing the letters to the press, President Clinton committed a criminal violation of the Privacy Act of 1974. The Act makes it illegal for federal agencies to release private records concerning federal personnel without their consent.

Judge Lamberth's ruling came in a case that involves Filegate, a scandal in which the FEDERAL BUREAU OF INVESTIGATION improperly gave the Clinton White House files concerning former political appointees and governmental employees from the REAGAN and BUSH administrations. Judicial Watch, a conservative watchdog group, filed the lawsuit against the FBI and the Executive Office of the President on behalf of plaintiffs who say the government violated their privacy rights during Filegate. Early in that lawsuit, Judge Lamberth ruled that the plaintiffs were allowed to learn about the Willey letters incident to establish a pattern of Privacy Act violations by the Clinton administration.

When the plaintiffs asked for information from White House Deputy Counsel Bruce Lindsey about the decision to release the Willey letters to the public, Clinton's lawyers said that that information was protected by the ATTORNEY-CLIENT PRIVILEGE. That privilege protects confidential communications between an attorney and his client, in this case between Lindsey and President Clinton. In his ruling on March 29, 2000, Judge Lamberth said the attorney-client privilege did not apply because there was no proof that Lindsey was trying to protect communications that he had with the president.

Judge Lamberth did not stop there. He went on to say that even if the attorney-client privilege applied, this case fell under the crime-fraud exception to the privilege. Under that exception, the attorney-client privilege does not apply when the communication is for the purpose of committing a crime, fraud, or other misconduct. In this instance, Judge Lamberth said any communication between President Clinton and Lindsey about releasing the Willey letters was for the purpose of violating the Privacy Act. That meant the attorney-client privilege did not apply, and Lindsey would have to give the plaintiffs any information he had about the decision to release those letters.

In a news conference the same day, President Clinton disagreed with Judge Lamberth's decision. A few days later his lawyers filed an emergency appeal to the U.S. Court of Appeals for the District of Columbia. Normally such appeals must wait until a case is over. In this case, Clinton's lawyers said they needed a quick decision for two reasons. First, they disagreed that the Privacy Act even applies to the president or the executive office. They said complying with the Privacy Act in the future would hamper the president's ability to do his job.

Second, they wanted the Court of Appeals to reverse the finding that President Clinton had committed a criminal violation of the Privacy Act. Clinton's lawyers said that he did not intend to violate the Act because the U.S. JUSTICE DEPARTMENT told him the Act did not apply to his conduct. Indeed, during the news conference after Judge Lamberth's decision, President Clinton said he never discussed the Privacy Act with anyone, including his lawyers, when he decided to give Willey's letters to the public.

On May 26, 2000, the Court of Appeals refused to give President Clinton emergency relief. It said that after Judge Lamberth makes a final decision in the case, the parties can take normal appeals to the Court of Appeals. At that time, the Court can decide whether the Privacy Act applies to the president and whether President Clinton committed a criminal violation of the Act.

As for Judge Lamberth's decision, the Court of Appeals said, "[I]t was inappropriate for the District Court gratuitously to invoke sweeping pronouncements on alleged criminal activity that extended well beyond what was necessary to decide the matters at hand." In other words, once Judge Lamberth decided that the attorney-client privilege did not apply, there was no need to go one step further by applying the crime-fraud exception. The Court of Appeals went on to suggest that outside the context of this case, President Clinton was free to follow the Justice Department's advice that the Privacy Act does not apply to him until a Court of Appeals ruled otherwise.

A White House spokesman said White House lawyers were disappointed by having to make Lindsey answer questions about the Willey letters but were pleased with other aspects of the decision. Court watchers had to wonder how politics affected the pair of rulings. Judge Lamberth, a Ronald Reagan appointee, often has been accused of being hostile to the Clinton administration. In contrast, two of the three appellate judges who criticized Judge Lamberth's decision were appointed by Democratic presidents, one by Clinton and the other by JIMMY CARTER. As of July 2000, it was uncertain whether President Clinton would face formal criminal Privacy Act charges for releasing Willey's letters to the public.

Todd v. Rush County Schools

As of early 2000, no high court has ever upheld routine or random drug testing of *all* public school students without cause or suspicion for doing so. Most attempts to implement such policies have failed to meet the protections against unreasonable search and seizure guaranteed by the FOURTH AMENDMENT. Notwithstanding, several important exceptions have been carved into law by appellate courts. In 1995, the U.S. Supreme Court ruled that random drug testing of school athletes did not violate their Fourth Amendment rights. (*Vernonia School District 473 v. Acton*, 515 U.S. 646, 115 S. Ct. 2386 [1995]). Again in 1998, two more cases came before the High Court, each with a different slant on the drug-testing rule. The Supreme Court denied CERTIORARI in both cases, therefore letting stand, as good law, the 7th Circuit decisions. While the denial of review meant that no national precedent was set, it nonetheless paved the way for other states to fashion drug testing programs similar to those that had been unsuccessfully challenged in the 7th Circuit.

In the first of these two cases, *Todd v. Rush County Schools*, cert denied, 525 U.S. 824 (1998), the quintessential issue was whether the Supreme Court's ruling in *Vernonia*, could be expanded to apply to *all* extracurricular school activities, and not just athletics. The Rush County, Indiana, school board had approved a program measure to prohibit student participation in any extracurricular activities—including driving to and from school—unless the students consented to random, unannounced urinalysis examinations for drugs, alcohol, and tobacco. The measure further defined extracurricular activities to include athletics, Student Council, Library Club, Foreign Language Clubs, and Future Farmers of America Officers. The $30 fee for each test was paid by a grant.

Under the program, if a test result came back positive, the student and family were privately informed and given the opportunity to explain the positive result—for example, that the student was taking a medication that would influence the result. If a positive result was not explained, the student was barred from extracurricular activities at school and not permitted to drive to and from school. Importantly, an unexplained positive result from a suspicionless, random test could not be used against the student for school disciplinary proceedings. Instead, the student and his family were provided with names of agencies that might assist the student. Requests for retesting were accommodated. Tests based upon a reasonable suspicion, however, subjected a student to school discipline.

There were 950 students in the Rush County High School for the 1996–1997 school year. By far, the majority of students (728) agreed to sign the consent form for the drug-testing program. Plaintiff William P. Todd, however, and his parents refused. This resulted in his being barred from the extracurricular activity of videotaping the football team. Likewise, three other students were barred from participating in Future Farmers of America and the Library Club when their parents refused to sign consent forms. The two sets of parents filed suit on behalf of their minor children. A trial court judgment in favor of Rush County Schools and its superintendent was entered. The parents then appealed.

On appeal, the 7th Circuit Court of Appeals ruled that the outcome of this case was governed by the U.S. Supreme Court's holding in *Vernonia*, as well as an earlier 7th Circuit case, *Schaill v. Tippecanoe County School Corp.*, 864 F.2d 1309 (1988). Both cases upheld the random urinalysis requirements for students participating in interscholastic athletics. Clearly the only difference between those cases and the present one was the expansion of urinalysis testing to other extracurricular activities in addition to athletics.

One of the key factors focused upon by the district judge at the trial court level was that involvement in extracurricular activities was a privilege and not a requirement for school attendance or credit. Therefore, Rush County's drug testing program applied only to those who voluntarily chose to participate. The 7th Circuit favored this reasoning, quoting it in its own opinion.

The challengers argued that historically, students engaged in extracurricular activities were the least likely to engage in drug use. The Court of Appeals noted that the purpose of a drug testing program was to protect the health of the students involved and concluded that:

> [p]articipation in [extracurricular activities] is a benefit carrying with it enhanced prestige and status in the student community... [thus]... [i]t is not unreasonable to couple these benefits with an obligation to undergo drug testing....

The 7th Circuit then concluded that the Rush County Schools' drug testing program was sufficiently structured so as "to pass muster under the Fourth and Fourteenth Amendments." The Court expressly noted that it was rendering no opinion on the constitutionality of the drug-testing program as applied to students driving to and from school. Since the appellants in this case were students who wished to engage in extracurricular activities, there was no need to reach that issue.

CROSS REFERENCES
Fourth Amendment; Probable Cause

PRODUCT LIABILITY

The responsibility of a manufacturer or vendor of GOODS to compensate for injury caused by a defective good that it has provided for sale.

Geier v. American Honda Motor Company, Inc.

Product liability lawsuits against automobile manufacturers for alleged defects in their vehicles have been common since the 1960s. Increased public demands for auto safety led Congress to enact the National Traffic and Motor Vehicle Safety Act of 1966, 15 U.S.C.A. § 1381 et seq. Since then, the federal government has used this statutory authority to enact regulations that impose motor vehicle safety standards on auto manufacturers. Beginning in 1989, the Department of TRANSPORTATION has phased in seat belt and air bag requirements for new vehicles. From 1989 to 1997, carmakers had to provide the driver with either an airbag or automatic seat belt. Since 1997, cars must have air bags for the driver and the front-seat passenger.

Despite these federal regulations, plaintiffs' attorneys have sued car manufacturers under state product-liability laws for failure to provide air bags in cars produced before 1989. Several state supreme courts and the federal circuit courts of appeal have barred these lawsuits, concluding that federal laws and regulations preempt "no airbag" lawsuits. A few states, however, have permitted the lawsuits. The Supreme Court resolved the issue in *Geier v. American Honda Motor Company, Inc.*, ___ U.S. ___, 120 S.Ct. 1913, ___ L.Ed.2d ___ (2000). The Court ruled that persons injured while riding in cars built before 1989 cannot sue carmakers for failing to include an airbag.

In 1992 Alexis Geier drove her 1987 Honda Accord into a tree and was seriously injured. The accident took place in the District of Columbia. Geier's car was equipped with manual shoulder and lap belts, which she had buckled at the time of the accident. Geier sued American Honda Motor alleging that it had designed its car negligently and defectively because it failed to provide a driver's side airbag. The federal district court dismissed her lawsuit, noting that federal regulation in 1987 had given Honda the choice to install either airbags or seatbelts. The court ruled that Geier's lawsuit sought to establish a different safety standard—an airbag requirement—than was provided by federal law and regulations. The court specifically found that the 1966 Safety Act had expressly preempted any safety standard that was not identical to federal safety standards. On appeal, the Court of Appeals for the District of Columbia affirmed the decision.

The Supreme Court, in a 5–4 decision, upheld the lower courts. Justice STEPHEN G. BREYER, writing for the majority, reached three subsidiary conclusions in arriving at its decision. The 1966 act did not expressly preempt airbag lawsuits such as Geier's; ordinary preemption principles applied to the case; and the lawsuit conflicted with federal safety regulations and therefore the 1966 act.

Justice Breyer noted that one provision of the 1966 Safety Act prohibits states from imposing different safety standards. A TORT action is a private lawsuit, though. Breyer concluded that Congress had sought to prevent states from enacting statutes but had not expressly contemplated barring COMMON-LAW ACTIONS. He also pointed to a different provision of the law, which stated that compliance with a federal safety standard did not exempt a person from any liability under COMMON LAW. Thus, in some circumstances, product liability lawsuits against a car manufacturer are permitted.

Justice Breyer found that this did not end the analysis. This provision appeared to "simply bar a defense that compliance with a federal safety standard automatically exempts a defendant from state law." The important question to be answered was whether the airbag lawsuits would "upset the careful regulatory scheme established by federal law." Breyer ruled that the lawsuit conflicted with federal regulations and the 1966 Safety Act. The regulations on seat belts and air bags were not minimum standards but ways of giving manufacturers a variety of choices among passive restraint systems during the phase-in period. In reviewing the history of passive restraint regulations, Breyer found that public resistance to the installation and use of such restraint systems played a part in the Department of Transportation's approach. The department had rejected an "all airbag" standard because of public resistance. In addition, the phase-in period allowed manufacturers to develop alternative, cheaper systems. In light of these facts, Justice Breyer concluded that allowing airbag lawsuits would frustrate the department's comprehensive regulatory scheme. Therefore, federal law preempts this type of product liability lawsuit.

Justice JOHN PAUL STEVENS, in a dissenting opinion joined by Justices DAVID H. SOUTER, CLARENCE THOMAS, and RUTH BADER GINSBURG, contended that the PREEMPTION doctrine should have been applied to airbag lawsuits. He argued that the states should have the power to determine whether such lawsuits should be permitted.

CROSS REFERENCES
Preemption; Torts

RACKETEER INFLUENCED AND CORRUPT ORGANIZATIONS ACT

A set of federal laws (18 U.S.C.A. § 1961 et seq. [1970]) specifically designed to punish criminal activity by business enterprises.

Beck v. Prupis

In 1970 Congress enacted the Racketeer Influenced and Corrupt Organizations Act (RICO) as a way to help eradicate organized crime in the United States. RICO attempts to accomplish these goals by providing severe criminal penalties for violations and also by means of a civil cause of action for any person "injured in his business or property by reason of a violation of section 1962." Section 1962 consists of four subsections that make it unlawful for persons to control business enterprises and use business income that is derived from racketeering activities. Subsection (c) makes it "unlawful for any person employed by or associated with any enterprise engaged in, or the activities of which affect interstate or foreign commerce, to conduct or participate, directly or indirectly, in the conduct of such enterprise's affairs through a pattern of racketeering activity or collection of unlawful debt." Subsection (d) makes it unlawful "for any person to conspire to violate any of the provisions of subsection (a), (b), or (c) of this section."

Beginning in 1989, the federal circuit courts of appeal divided over whether a person injured by an overt act in furtherance of a CONSPIRACY may assert a civil RICO conspiracy claim under § 1964(c) for a violation of § 1962(d), even if the overt act does not constitute "racketeering activity." The Supreme Court, in *Beck v. Prupis*, ___ U.S. ___, 120 S.Ct. 1608, ___ L.Ed.2d ___ (2000), finally resolved this issue, ruling that a plaintiff cannot assert a civil RICO claim unless the overt act involves racketeering activity. In *Beck*, this meant that a corporate executive who had been fired by corrupt members of the corporation could not sue them under RICO for damages, as the act of firing him was not a corrupt or racketeering activity.

Robert A. Beck II was the president, CEO, director, and shareholder of Southeastern Insurance Group (SIG). Until 1990, when it declared BANKRUPTCY, SIG was a Florida insurance holding company with three operating subsidiaries, each of which was engaged in the business of writing surety bonds for construction contractors. Beginning in 1987 a group of directors and officers of SIG began engaging in acts of racketeering. They created an entity called Construction Performance Corporation, which demanded fees from contractors in exchange for qualifying them for SIG surety bonds. The group also diverted corporate funds to personal uses and submitted false financial statements to regulators, shareholders, and creditors. In early 1988 Beck discovered the unlawful conduct and contacted insurance regulators concerning the financial statements. The corrupt executives then orchestrated Beck's firing by the board of directors by hiring an insurance consultant to write a false report suggesting that Beck had failed to perform his duties.

Beck filed a federal civil lawsuit against seven of the executives and officers, alleging that they had violated § 1962 of RICO. He argued that the executives had conspired to terminate his employment as a way to further their conspiracy, thereby violating § § 1962 (c) and (d). The executives asked the court to dismiss the lawsuit. They contended that employees who are terminated for refusing to participate in RICO activities, or who threaten to report RICO activities, do not have STANDING to sue under RICO for damages from their loss of employment. The district court agreed and dismissed Beck's RICO conspiracy claim. The Eleventh Circuit Court of Appeals affirmed the district court. It held that a cause of action under § 1964(c) for a violation of § 1962(d) is not available to a person injured by an overt act in furtherance of a RICO conspiracy unless the overt act is an act of racketeering. Since the overt act that allegedly caused Beck's injury was not an act of racketeering, it could not support a civil cause of action. The court held that "RICO was enacted with an express target—racketeering activity—and only those injuries that are proximately caused by racketeering activity should be actionable under the statute."

The Supreme Court, in a 7—2 decision, agreed with the Eleventh Circuit and four other circuit courts of appeal on this interpretation of RICO. Justice CLARENCE THOMAS, in his majority opinion, held that a person may not bring suit under RICO for injuries caused by an overt act that is not an act of racketeering or otherwise unlawful under the statute. Justice Thomas based his analysis on past rulings in common-law civil conspiracy cases. He found that these cases "support the notion that liability cannot be imposed unless the overt act that furthered the conspiracy and harmed the plaintiff was a particular kind of overt act."

Justice JOHN PAUL STEVENS, in a dissenting opinion joined by DAVID H. SOUTER, argued that the plain language of the RICO statute gave Beck the right to sue, whether or not the overt act was a listed racketeering activity.

CROSS REFERENCES
Conspiracy; Whistleblowing

RECUSE

To disqualify or remove oneself as a JUDGE over a particular proceeding because of one's CONFLICT OF INTEREST. Recusal, or the judge's act of disqualifying himself or herself from presiding over a proceeding, is based on the maxim that judges are charged with a duty of impartiality in administering justice.

New Hampshire Supreme Court Ethics Scandal

According to the U.S. Constitution, the opinion of the U.S. Supreme Court is "the law of the land." So also does the opinion of the highest court in each state represent the law of that state, and no power shall overrule those opinions, save the U.S. Supreme Court. Hence, when the integrity of a state supreme court or its members is questioned, a serious threat to public confidence in the judicial system is created, and must be addressed with the utmost care.

In early 2000 four of five New Hampshire state Supreme Court justices faced IMPEACHMENT investigations for ETHICS violations under what many have deemed to be New Hampshire's "old boy" legal system. In the wake of a damaging twenty-five-page report released by the state's Attorney General, Philip McLaughlin, Justice Stephen Thayer did not wait to be prosecuted, and resigned in return for IMMUNITY. On April 13, 2000, the state House of Representatives voted 343–7 to conduct an impeachment inquiry into the conduct of three other high court justices: Chief Justice David Brock, and Justices Sherman Horton and John Broderick. A fourth justice was not named, having been newly appointed and not part of the alleged violations. Thayer resigned two weeks prior to the vote, but one week after the release of the report. The House vote now affects only the remaining justices.

The most serious allegation against the remaining justices involves what Maclaughlin concluded was an "institutional practice" of participation in formulating court opinions for cases from which they had recused themselves due to a clear conflict of interest. The report revealed a long-standing manner of case management in which judges who had recused themselves from a case because of a conflict were nonetheless allowed to view draft opinions and comment on them. This, of course, serves to defeat the whole purpose of recusal, which is to avoid influencing a case because of inside knowledge or conflict of interest.

The entire controversy began when Court Clerk Howard Zibel privately and anonymously wrote a letter to the Attorney General, complaining of Thayer's unethical conduct. Thayer allegedly attempted to influence the court's handling of his wife's appeal of their divorce case. This is a criminal and an ethical violation. Judicial ethics rules require judges to recuse themselves from making decisions or offering input on any case in which they may be personally

NH justices respond to the Attorney General's report that lead to Justice Stephen Thayer's resignation.
COLE/AP/WIDE WORLD PHOTOS

vested. Moreover, rules require that judges and lawyers report instances of such misconduct.

Because Chief Justice Brock and Justice Sherman Horton listened to Thayer, without reporting the incident, they also violated ethics codes and rules, and the entire court became tainted with scandal. Moreover, the investigation disclosed that Thayer had previously and vociferously rendered his opinion in another 1999 matter from which he was officially recused. None of the justices had reported him at that time either. In fact, the report revealed that Chief Justice Brock had once previously persuaded since-retired Justice William Johnson not to report Thayer to the court committee that disciplined judges.

In all fairness, Justice Brock did not simply sit back and do nothing about Thayer's conduct. The justices had recommended that the court appoint a special counsel to consider options in dealing with Thayer. Apparently the justices were planning to report Thayer to the Judicial Conduct Committee, but wanted it to be handled internally without public scrutiny.

In any event, McLaughlin's twenty-five-page report disclosed more than just the misconduct of Thayer. McLaughlin also released 119 pages of investigative documents, including interviews with several past and present judges. Although many of the justices admitted that they read and commented on cases, they insisted that their comments were benign and usually addressed only grammar or spelling. Justice Horton advised the investigators, however, that a recused judge would often offer opinions "about why, as a matter of law, [he] disagrees with the results." Justice Horton went on to say that, although it probably was not right, such things were done to improve the outcome of the case.

McLaughlin's report was tendered to the House of Representatives, who then took the matter to a vote. It was the first time in 210 years that New Hampshire would conduct an impeachment probe of one of its judges. Under New Hampshire's law, impeachable offenses include "bribery, corruption, malpractice or maladministration in office." Judges may also be removed for other offenses through a "bill of address." The House Judiciary Committee may consider evidence for both impeachable and non-impeachable, lesser offenses. The Committee has full subpoena power over potential witnesses, and has its own attorney for legal assistance.

The House Judiciary Committee finished investigating the allegations in July 2000. On July 5 it voted 17–5 to let the state Senate decide if Chief Justice Brock committed PERJURY to obstruct the investigations into how his court operated. Two other indictments were issued against Brock for his alleged influence of a lower court to aid a senator. They decided not to pursue impeachment against Justices Horton and Broderick, however. The state House of

HAVE THREE-STRIKES LAWS WORKED TO REDUCE RECIDIVISM?

Most state and federal laws impose stiffer sentences for repeat offenders, but they do not impose punishments as harsh as "Three Strikes and You're Out" (TSAYO) laws. TSAYO laws mandate that a heavy sentence be imposed on persons who are convicted of a third FELONY. The minimum prison sentence required by such laws is typically between twenty-five years and life. The federal government and more than two dozen states have passed TSAYO legislation since 1992.

TSAYO legislation is designed to protect society from dangerous individuals who show a pattern of lawlessness, incapacitate repeat felony offenders by keeping them behind bars, and deter others from committing similar criminal offenses. National criminal justice statistics show that the number of violent crimes has precipitously dropped over the last eight years. TSAYO legislation is not without its critics, however. In 1998 several studies called into doubt the effectiveness of three-strikes laws. Constitutional challenges have been leveled against TSAYO laws at both the state and federal levels, but courts and legislatures have resisted overturning them.

In 1994 Congress passed the Violent Crime Control and Law Enforcement Act (VCCLEA). Public Law 103–322, September 13, 1994, 108 Stat 1796. It imposes a mandatory sentence of life imprisonment without parole on defendants who are convicted of a serious violent federal felony when they have two or more prior serious violent felonies or one or more serious violent felonies and one or more serious drug offenses. The first two convictions may be for state or federal offenses, but the third conviction must be for a federal offense before the VCCLEA three-strikes provision applies.

VCCLEA defines "serious violent felony" to include MURDER, voluntary MANSLAUGHTER, ASSAULT with intent to commit murder or RAPE, aggravated SEXUAL ABUSE, KIDNAPPING, aircraft PIRACY, ROBBERY, CARJACKING, EXTORTION, ARSON, and firearms use or possession, among others. 18 U.S.C.A. 3559. Offenses committed at the state level need not be deemed a felony by the state to trigger the VCCLEA three-strikes provision, as long as the state offense is "seriously violent," meaning the offense is similar to those specified by the VCCLEA. "Serious drug offense" is defined by the VCCLEA as knowingly or intentionally manufacturing, distributing, dispensing, or possessing with intent to manufacture, distribute, or dispense enumerated controlled substances. Drug offenses committed at the state level are considered "serious" under VCCLEA if they would be punishable by the federal controlled substances laws.

The impetus behind TSAYO laws came from a string of highly publicized cases in which a crime victim was viciously attacked by a repeat offender on PAROLE. One of the most publicized cases was that of 12-year-old Polly Klaas from California. In 1993 she was kidnapped, molested, and murdered by Richard Allen Davis, a sex offender with a long history of criminal convictions. Polly's father, Marc, appeared on a number of national television programs to attack the criminal justice system's lenient treatment of repeat felony offenders and to advocate the enactment of three-strikes laws. Relatives of other victims, concerned citizens, prosecutors, and politicians followed suit.

Washington state's legislature was the first to respond, passing TSAYO legislation in 1993. West's RCWA 9.94A.392 et seq. The law mandates life in prison after conviction on any three of about forty felonies, ranging from murder to robbery and vehicular assault. Defendants convicted under this law are not eligible for parole, nor may their sentence be suspended or shortened. California and eleven other states passed similar laws in 1994. Nine more states were added to the list a year later. By the year 2000 more than two dozen states had adopted TSAYO laws of their own. Georgia took matters a step further, enacting a "Two Strikes and You're Out" law. Ga. Code Ann. S 17–10–6.1(b). Felons convicted of the state's most serious crimes only twice are sentenced to life in prison without parole. Known as "the seven deadly sins," these crimes include murder, armed robbery, rape, kidnapping, aggravated SODOMY, aggravated child molestation, and aggravated sexual BATTERY.

Despite their popularity in the early 1990s, TSAYO laws have come under severe attack over the last three years. In 1998 several studies were released that questioned the effectiveness of such laws. Four studies were largely responsible for driving the debate: one by the Rand Institute, one by the National Institute of Justice, one by the Justice Policy Institute, and one by the Campaign for Effective Crime Policy,

---

Representatives was to vote on the recommendations by the end of the month. If they agree that impeachment hearings should proceed, then the Senate would take over as jury.

Some legislators believe that this behavior does not equate with corruption, but simply a mistake of presenting the wrong impression considering current attitudes toward government institutions. They believe that, unless further investigation reveals other forms of more serious misconduct, Brock and the others probably will receive only censure at most. Nonetheless, the court took the controversy to heart, expressly articulating a new policy of prohibiting

a nonpartisan group comprised of wardens, prosecutors, and law enforcement officials.

The studies revealed two kinds of results. In most states, little had changed. Washington had convicted only sixty-six people under its TSAYO law. Arkansas had twelve convictions and Alaska, Connecticut, Louisiana, Maryland, North Carolina, Pennsylvania, Vermont, and New Jersey had no more than six. Wisconsin had invoked its law only once, while no one in Utah, Virginia, Montana, Tennessee, New Mexico, or Colorado had ever been prosecuted for a third strike offense. Instead, the states that let their TSAYO laws lay idle were still seeking harsh punishments for dangerous recidivists, but under repeat-offender statutes that had been on the books for decades. In other words, for these states the TSAYO laws represented a symbolic measure that neither improved nor diminished a prosecutor's ability to keep dangerous recidivists off the streets. Similarly, the studies showed that only thirty-five offenders had been convicted of a third strike at the federal level through 1997.

The results were vastly different in California and Georgia. California had imprisoned more than 4,800 criminals for twenty-five years to life on third strikes; the state also identified more than 40,000 second-strike offenders who would await such a sentence were they subsequently convicted for any one of roughly 500 crimes. Georgia had sent approximately 1,000 defendants to prison for life without parole under its two strikes law and identified another 1,000 offenders eligible for that fate were they to subsequently commit one of the "seven deadly sins."

These studies did more than arm opponents of TSAYO laws with evidence of disparate results. They suggested that the laws had been enforced more often against minority offenders than against white offenders. In California only 1,237 of the more than 4,800 defendants sentenced for a third strike were white; 2,138 were African American, 1,262 were Latino, and 201 were classified as "other." The studies further indicated that these minority offenders were mostly being punished for nonviolent third strikes. Statistics demonstrated that more than twice as many defendants' third-strike offenses were for drug possession or petty theft as for murder, rape, or kidnapping. Some of these nonviolent third strikes included seemingly innocuous offenses, such as shoplifting, stealing packages of steak, and drinking alcohol at a liquor store without paying for it.

Proponents of TSAYO laws have not been dissuaded by these results. Prosecutors say that these laws remain a vital tool for them to hang over the heads of first- and second-time offenders. They contend that seemingly "harmless" third-strike offenses are often isolated from the first and second strikes that place the defendant in a less sympathetic context. For example, an individual who was prosecuted for a third strike after he stole a bottle of vitamins had eight prior convictions, one of which was for robbery. Another individual who was prosecuted for BIGAMY under California's TSAYO law had prior convictions for armed robbery. Prosecutors also point to statistics reflecting a dramatic decline in violent crime over the last eight years as conclusive proof of TSAYO laws' effectiveness.

Opponents of TSAYO laws acknowledge that prison populations have drastically increased in some states due in part to incarceration of third-strike offenders, but they question whether this result is entirely good. Reports indicate that prisons in California and Georgia are severely overcrowded. The Georgia Department of Corrections estimates that it needs nearly 14,000 more beds and a budget increase of twenty-five percent to accommodate the overflowing prison population. In the meantime, state prisons have erected tents as cell blocks, moved bunks into common areas, and housed three inmates in cells designed for two.

California officials have predicted that its prisons will experience a shortage of 70,000 beds from convictions under the state's TSAYO laws. They also predict that the number of inmates age fifty to sixty-four will increase eighty percent by 2013, and the number of prisoners sixty-five and older will increase by 144 percent. They agonize over booming medical costs spent to treat geriatric prisoners, and worry that the money being spent on them comes from funds designated for schools, roads, and neighborhood programs. According to one study, California spends about $1,000 on medical expenses for the average inmate, but more than $6,000 a year for inmates older than fifty.

While these figures have caused concern among even the staunchest proponents of three-strikes legislation, no TSAYO law has been repealed at the state or federal level, and no court has declared one unconstitutional. In 1999 the U.S. Supreme Court rejected the appeal from a defendant challenging the constitutionality of California's TSAYO law. *Riggs v. California*, ___ U.S.___, 119 S.Ct. 890, 142 L.Ed.2d 789, (1999). Even legislative proposals to study the law's impact have been rejected in California, being vetoed first by a Republican governor and then by a Democratic one. The fact that California's TSAYO law is regularly used by state prosecutors and universally hated by defendants, the governors said, speaks for itself.

---

recused judges from attending conferences, receiving draft opinions, and commenting on them.

Another area of fallout from the Thayer controversy was the joining of several ex-wives of judges who believe they have all been treated unfairly in their own divorce cases, based upon who their husbands were, or whom their husbands knew. Moreover, State Representative Fran Wendelboe has been approached by former wives of several prominent lawyers who have complained to her about unfair treatment in their divorce cases as well. Wendelboe has requested the House to investigate these additional accusations against the state's high court justices. Such cases are difficult to prove, however. As Albert Scherr, an associate dean at Franklin Pierce Law Center in Concord, told the Associated Press, "I doubt they'll be able to get any judge to say, 'I helped my fellow justice out because he's a buddy of mine.'"

CROSS REFERENCES
Ethics; Separation of Powers

RELIGION

Bear Lodge Multiple Use Association v. Babbitt

Controversies over the alleged state sanctioning of religion have been a staple of contemporary U.S. society. One of the most interesting fact situations came in *Bear Lodge Multiple Use Association v. Babbitt*, 175 F.3d 814 (10th Cir. 1999), where rock climbers challenged the National Park Service's (NPS) plan to limit access to the Devils Tower National Monument in Wyoming. The climbers disputed the legality of the plan because the goal of the NPS was to reduce the harmful effects on the spiritual practices of Native Americans who gathered at the foot of the butte each June. This, the climbers contended, violated the FIRST AMENDMENT's Establishment Clause.

The Devils Tower National Monument, which Native Americans call Bear Lodge, is a 600-foot butte located in northeastern Wyoming. Bear Lodge is a sacred site to Native Americans living in the northern plains. Lakota people inhabited the Bear Lodge area as early as 1000 A.D. and ancestors of the Shoshone people lived in the area in the 1500s. The tower is a prominent feature in many Sioux stories as well as in the cosmology of other northern plains tribes. Bear Lodge also is a pilgrimage site where important religious ceremonies are performed. In 1906 President THEODORE ROOSEVELT established the Devils Tower National Monument, encompassing the butte and the 1,300-acre area surrounding it. Since 1916 the NPS has managed the monument.

For rock climbers, Bear Lodge offers different attractions. Although the NPS has recognized climbing on the butte as a legitimate recreational activity, the growing popularity of the site for climbers has created problems. Climbers numbered little more than 300 in 1973, but that number had risen above 6,000 by the 1990s. This in turn has led to ecological damage. Native Americans also objected to climbers yelling out commands, taking photographs of sacred ceremonies, removing prayer bundles, and disturbing the natural solitude. These problems became most acute in the month of June, which is the most popular month for climbing Bear Lodge and the most culturally significant month for Native Americans to perform their ceremonies at the foot of the butte.

The NPS proposed a plan for the use of Bear Lodge that sought to promote ecological stability and to encourage climbers to refrain voluntarily from climbing during June. The original plan also prohibited commercial enterprises from organizing climbs during June, though that ban was soon revoked. Nevertheless, a number of parties, including a commercial rock climbing guide and individual rock climbers, filed a lawsuit in Wyoming federal district court alleging that the plan violated the First Amendment's Establishment Clause. The court dismissed the case, and the plaintiffs appealed to the Tenth Circuit Court of Appeals.

The Tenth Circuit upheld the dismissal. Judge John C. Porfolio, writing for a unanimous three-judge panel, recounted in detail the historical and cultural significance of Bear Lodge to Native American peoples. Turning to the legal arguments, he noted that the NPS had only proposed a *voluntary* program to reduce climbing during June. The NPS proposed to comply with its June closure by not allowing NPS staff on the butte in June except to enforce laws and regulations or to perform emergency operations.

The climbers argued that although the ban on commercial climbing in June had been rescinded, the Secretary of the INTERIOR DEPARTMENT, who oversees the NPS, contended that he had the power to impose the rule in the future. In addition to the voluntary ban on climbing in June, the plaintiffs objected to an interpretive education program intended to explain the monument's significance to some Native Americans and to the placement of signs that encourage people to remain on the trail surrounding Bear Lodge. In its totality, they felt the NPS program recognized the religious and spiritual needs of Native American peoples.

Judge Porfolio concluded that the court could not address these substantive issues because the plaintiffs did not have STANDING to sue. Standing is a central legal concept in the U.S. adversarial process. A plaintiff must have suffered an injury before bringing a lawsuit, otherwise they will not have a personal stake in the outcome. The fact that a person is merely interested as a member of the general public in the resolution of a dispute is not enough to confer standing.

The court pointed out that they remained free to climb the mountain any time, including the month of June, and that five of the plaintiffs had continued to climb in June. Although the climbers argued that mandatory closure of Bear Lodge in June was possible in the future, Judge Porfolio called this a remote and speculative possibility that did not confer standing. Because the climbers could not show that they had suffered any personal injury as a consequence of the NPS's plan, the court dismissed the case.

Indiana Allows Display of Ten Commandments in Public Buildings

On March 14, 2000, Indiana Governor Frank O'Bannon signed a bill that allows public schools and other government offices to post the Ten Commandments in their buildings. Some lawmakers and citizens hailed the bill as an effort to combat drugs, guns, and violence with morality, civility, and virtuosity. Civil libertarians, including the Indiana Civil Liberties Union (ICLU), called the bill unconstitutional.

The legal issue, which may reach the U.S. Supreme Court, is whether the government violates the Establishment Clause of the FIRST AMENDMENT when it posts the Ten Commandments. The Establishment Clause creates a so-called wall of separation between church and state by preventing the government from supporting one or more religions over others. In 1980 in *Stone v. Graham*, the U.S. Supreme Court said Kentucky violated the Establishment Clause by requiring public schools to post the Ten Commandments. The Court said Kentucky's law was "plainly religious."

Indiana's new law, which becomes effective on July 1, 2000, is slightly different. First, it allows but does not *require* public schools and other government offices to post the Ten Commandments. Second, it requires schools and offices that do post the Ten Commandments to display other documents to help emphasize the historical value of the Ten Commandments over the religious value.

In a written statement, Governor O'Bannon announced that Indiana's statehouse grounds would get a new monument in the summer of 2000 featuring the Ten Commandments, the preamble to the U.S. Constitution, and the Bill of Rights. Referring to the Ten Commandments, O'Bannon said, "Soon those words will stand alongside the abiding principles of our form of government, especially its protections of individual rights. They're ideals we all need to be reminded of from time to time."

The ICLU planned to file a lawsuit once the new monument went up. It rejected Indiana's effort to focus on the historical importance of the Ten Commandments. In a position paper on its website, the ICLU said, "The first four Commandments are purely religious in nature. There is no other way to view the Ten Commandments as anything other than a religious document." The ICLU said that when government supports one religion, it makes people who follow other religions feel like "second class citizens."

Indiana's bill followed other Ten Commandments controversies in the state. In December 1999 a federal judge ruled that Elkhart, Indiana, did not violate the First Amendment by placing a six-foot high granite tablet with the Ten Commandments in front of the town's courthouse. Judge Allen Sharp said the display had cultural and historical significance, just like the ram's head over the courthouse entrance and the Revolutionary War plaque on the opposite side of the courthouse. The ICLU, which handled the litigation for a group called American Atheists, said it would appeal the ruling to the U.S. Court of Appeals for the Seventh Circuit.

That same month, the school board in Scottsburg, Indiana, decided to post its own Eleven Common Precepts, which resembles the Ten Commandments. The Eleven Precepts include admonitions such as "Treat your classmates, teachers and school staff with respect" and "Resolve conflicts without using violence." The first precept was going to be "Trust in God" until the ICLU threatened to sue the school board. Instead, the board decided to mark each precept with a photograph of a penny, which is stamped with "In God We Trust."

Meanwhile, the Kentucky Senate passed a Ten Commandments bill that is similar to Indiana's, and legislatures are considering such legislation in Colorado, Florida, Georgia, Illinois, Indiana, Mississippi, Missouri, Oklahoma, and South Dakota. The Colorado and Georgia bills are stricter than Indiana's new law. Called America's Moral Heritage Act, Colorado's bill would require public schools to post the Ten Commandments and hold a moment of silent prayer at the beginning of each day. Georgia's bill would cut off public funding to any public school that did not post the Ten Commandments.

The drive to post the Ten Commandments began after April 1999, when two students at Columbine High School in Colorado shot and killed twelve classmates, a teacher, and themselves. Following that tragedy, the U.S. House of Representatives passed both a bill and a constitutional amendment to allow public schools to post the Ten Commandments. As of May 2000 the U.S. Senate has not voted on either measure. Nonetheless, in October 1999, forty-one Congressmen joined the Family Research Council's "Hang Ten" campaign by agreeing to post the Ten Commandments in their offices in Washington, D.C.

Mitchell v. Helms

The FIRST AMENDMENT's Establishment Clause prohibits federal and state governments from advancing the cause of any religion. The Supreme Court, in *Everson v. Board of Ed. of Ewing Tp.*, 330 U.S. 1, 67 S.Ct. 504, 91 L.Ed. 711 (1947) upheld the local public school board's decision to reimburse parents for the money spent transporting their children to and from Catholic schools. The Court concluded that the payments furthered the state's legitimate interest in transporting children to and from school. The Court also has upheld state laws requiring public school districts to lend textbooks on secular subjects to students in private and parochial schools.

The Supreme Court has been less receptive to state laws that provide direct financial assistance to parochial schools. The Court struck down laws that provided public funds as salary supplements to teachers in parochial schools. Court disapproval of other forms of direct financial aid to parochial schools continued through the 1980s, striking down programs that provided funds to supplement salaries of public school teachers who taught remedial courses on the premises of religious schools. The more conservative Court of the 1990s, however, began to rethink the issue. In 1997 the Court held constitutional a federal law that provides all educationally and economically disadvantaged children with publicly funded remedial education services, regardless of whether they attend public or private schools. In *Mitchell v. Helms*, 527 U.S. 1002, 119 S.Ct. 2336, 144 L.Ed.2d 234 (2000), the Court went further, approving the use of taxpayer money to buy computers and other instructional materials for parochial schools.

In 1985 Mary Helms and a group of parents of public-school children in Jefferson Parish, Louisiana, sued to prevent federal aid authorized by the Elementary and Secondary Education Act of 1965 from going to Catholic schools in the parish. The schools used the aid to pay for textbooks, overhead projectors, and school supplies. The parents contended that the law violated the Establishment Clause. A federal court agreed, which led Guy Mitchell and other Catholic parents to ask another federal judge to review the case. The judge ruled the law constitutional, but the case dragged on for thirteen years before it reached the Fifth Circuit Court of Appeals in 1998. The appeals court ruled that the parochial aid violated the Establishment Clause and rested its decision on Supreme Court cases from the 1970s.

The Supreme Court, in a 6–3 vote, reversed the Fifth Circuit. Four members of the Court—Chief Justice WILLIAM H. REHNQUIST and Justices ANTONIN SCALIA, ANTHONY M. KENNEDY, and CLARENCE THOMAS—expressed the desire to wipe the slate clean and allow almost any government aid to parochial schools. Justice Clarence Thomas wrote the main opinion for the majority, but Justice SANDRA DAY O'CONNOR, joined by Justice STEPHEN G. BREYER, wrote an opinion that placed some limitations on aid to religious schools.

Justice Thomas concluded that the federal law did not entangle the government with religion and did not have the effect of advancing religion. Moreover, the fact that the program was neutral was enough by itself to end the inquiry and uphold its constitutionality. Because the school aid had a secular purpose, this was sufficient to rebut an Establishment Clause violation. In addition, the Court overruled the two cases that the Fifth Circuit relied upon in its decision.

Justice O'Connor wrote separately because she found the Thomas opinion's "expansive scope . . . troubling." She agreed that the issue of neutrality was important, but it is only one of several factors to be considered. In addition, she rejected the plurality's approval of actual diversion of government aid to religious indoctrination. O'Connor limited her review to the aid program in question. She found six factors that supported the constitutionality of the program: (1) the aid had been allocated on the basis of neutral, secular criteria; (2) the aid was supplemental and did not supplant non-federal funds; (3) the funds were never deposited in school bank accounts; (4) the aid was secular; (5) the evidence of any diversion of funds was minimal; and (6) the program had adequate safeguards to prevent the diversion of funds to religious purposes. Based on these findings, O'Connor concluded that the aid program did not have "the impermissible effect of advancing religion."

Justice DAVID H. SOUTER wrote a dissenting opinion, which was joined by Justices JOHN PAUL STEVENS and RUTH BADER GINSBURG. Souter expressed concern that the Thomas opinion signaled the elevation of a new concept of neutrality that would ignore the effects of aid to religious schools. If the plurality someday becomes the majority, there "would be the end of the principle of no aid to the schools' religious mission."

Ohio's State Motto Ruled Unconstitutional

In 1956 the U.S. Congress enacted a law declaring the national motto of the United States to be "In God We Trust." Although the motto had existed *de facto* for more than one-hundred years, it had never been officially codified into law. The motto is now codified at 36 U.S.C. 302. The U.S. Supreme Court has never expressly ruled on the constitutionality of our national motto. When asked to rule on the issue, it has let stand the decisions of the several U.S. Circuit Courts of Appeal—one level down from the Supreme Court—which upheld the constitutionality of the motto.

On April 25, 2000, a three-member panel of the U.S. Circuit Court of Appeals for the 6th Circuit ruled 2–1 that the official motto of Ohio was unconstitutional. The motto, "With God All Things Are Possible," which was unanimously adopted by the state in 1959 (Ohio Rev.Code, Section 5.06), existed for years without ado, along with the state wildflower, the state animal, the state coat of arms, and the state song. The AMERICAN CIVIL LIBERTIES UNION (ACLU), representing a single plaintiff, challenged the motto in 1997. The ACLU, in behalf of Reverend Matthew Peterson, filed suit in U.S. District Court for the Southern District of Ohio at Columbus (No. 97–00863, reported at 20 F. Supp. 2d 1176, S.D. Ohio, 1998).

The case arose over an adopted proposal for the state seal and the words of the Ohio motto to appear on a granite plaza at the west end of the State House, located in Capitol Square Plaza. The ACLU and Reverend Peterson requested an injunction against the marker, challenging the constitutionality of the motto under the Establishment Clause.

U.S. District Court Judge James L. Graham found that the motto was compatible with the Establishment Clause, in that it advanced no particular religion, and denied plaintiffs' relief. He enjoined Ohio from attributing the words of the motto to the text of the New Testament, however, where ostensibly the words originate. ACLU appealed the ruling to the U.S. Circuit Court of Appeals for the Sixth Circuit.

The 6th Circuit characterized the issues presented on appeal as follows. Plaintiffs' position was that the words of the motto, attributable to Jesus in the Christian Bible, have no secular purpose. The words constituting the motto are not of longstanding or ubiquitous practice—as is prayer at the opening of a legislative session—and thus, the words have not become part of the fabric of our society. Therefore, the use of them in a state motto constitutes an impermissible advancement of the Christian religion and entangles government in religious affairs. To support their arguments, plaintiffs drew from language found in *Lemon v. Kurtzman*, 403 U.S. 602 (1971) and *Marsh v. Chambers*, 463 U.S. 783 (1983).

Ohio, in turn, argued that previous Supreme Court interpretations of the Establishment Clause have expressly allowed for nonsectarian references to god in government symbols and practice. Thus, the U.S. motto "In God We Trust," the approval of legislative prayer, and the support of military chaplains are all examples of permissible, generalized references to a higher power. The state cited *Chaudhuri v. Tennessee*, 130 F.3d 232 (6th Cir. 1997), as a more modern understanding of the Establishment Clause.

On April 25, 2000, the 6th Circuit reversed the District Court. In its thirty-six-page opinion, the two-judge majority ruled that the motto violated the Establishment Clause of the FIRST AMENDMENT. The third panel member, Circuit Judge David A. Nelson, submitted a two-page dissent in which he argued that there was no meaningful distinction between "With God All Is Possible" and the nation's motto, which also appears on all U.S. coins (4 U.S.C. Section 4). Moreover, he argued, a hypothetical "reasonable observer" would not take Ohio's motto to be an official endorsement of Christianity.

Ohio has appealed the decision, asking for rehearing before a full thirteen judge *en banc* panel of the 6th Circuit Court of Appeals. Additionally, on May 2, 2000, the Ohio Senate voted 29–4 in favor of endorsing the motto and requesting a full appeal. One week later, on May 11, 2000, the Ohio House of Representatives voted 89–2 on the same issues.

Santa Fe Independent School District v. Doe

The FIRST AMENDMENT's Establishment Clause prohibits government from enacting laws or adopting policies that aid any religion or establish an official state religion. Prior to 1962, many states required public schools to begin the school day with a prayer or a Bible reading. For example, the state of New York developed a nondenominational prayer and made student participation voluntary. Nevertheless, the Supreme Court struck the prayer down as a violation of the Establishment Clause in *Engel v. Vitale*, 370 U.S. 421, 82 S.Ct. 1261, 8 L.Ed. 2d 601 (1962). In *Abington School District v. Schempp*, 374 U.S. 203, 83 S.Ct. 1560, 10 L.Ed.2d 844 (1963), in the following year, the Court struck down voluntary Bible readings or recitations of the Lord's Prayer in public schools. In both cases, the Court found that these practices served religious rather than secular purposes, and therefore violated the Establishment Clause because they breached state neutrality requirements.

These decisions ignited enormous controversy, which has never disappeared. The issue reached the Supreme Court again in *Santa Fe Independent School District v. Doe*, __U.S.__, __ S.Ct. __, __ L.Ed.2d __ 2000 WL 775587 (2000). In this case, the Court ruled that a Texas public school district could not let its students lead prayers over the public address system before its high school football games. In so ruling, the Court reaffirmed its prior decisions on the separation of church and state. The school district's sponsorship of public prayers by elected student representatives was impermissible because the schools could not coerce anyone to support or participate in religion.

Until 1995 the Santa Fe High school student who had been elected student council chaplain delivered a prayer over the public address system before each varsity football game. Two sets of former students and their mothers filed a federal lawsuit in 1995, claiming that the public prayer violated their rights under the Establishment Clause. One family was Mormon, and the other was Catholic. They also alleged other offensive school practices, such as promoting attendance at Baptist revival meetings and distributing Gideon Bibles on school grounds. These allegations, however, were not part of the Supreme Court case. The district court permitted the families to litigate anonymously to protect them from intimidation or harassment from members of the small south Texas community.

While the lawsuit was pending, the school district modified its football prayer practices. The school district allowed elected student representatives, no longer called chaplains, to give a "message or invocation" before the games. The students were free to say whatever they chose, as long as it promoted good sportsmanship. The policy did not require that the invocations be nonsectarian. The federal district court ruled that this new policy was unconstitutional, as it violated the Establishment Clause. The Fifth Circuit Court of Appeals agreed, finding that no matter how the invocation process had been structured, school officials were present at these school-sponsored events and had the authority to stop the prayers.

The Supreme Court, on a 6–3 vote, affirmed the court of appeals. Justice JOHN PAUL STEVENS, writing for the majority, stated that "school sponsorship of a religious message is impermissible because it sends an ancillary message to members of the audience who are nonadherents that they are outsiders, not full members of the political community." Stevens concluded that banning the prayers did not stifle private expression. The facts of the case indicated that the prayer had been sanctioned by school policy, delivered over a school microphone by a student, and supervised by a school faculty member. Taken together, Stevens ruled that the prayer was public speech and subject to the Establishment Clause.

Marian Ward leads Santa Fe High School in a prayer after a district court ruled the school could not punish her for doing so.
COOMER/AP/WIDE WORLD PHOTOS

Justice Stevens acknowledged the importance of public worship and the desire of many people to include public prayer as part of various occasions. Nevertheless, he added that "such religious activity in public schools, as elsewhere, must comport with the First Amendment." The school district had argued that no student was compelled to attend the football games and therefore there was no coercion. Stevens rejected this argument, noting that some students, such as cheerleaders, football players, and members of the band had to attend. He concluded that the "Constitution demands that schools not force on students the difficult choice between whether to attend these games or to risk facing a personally offensive religious ritual."

Chief Justice WILLIAM H. REHNQUIST, in a sharply worded dissenting opinion joined by Justices ANTONIN SCALIA and CLARENCE THOMAS, disagreed with the majority's analysis. Rehnquist concluded that the school district policy did not impose state sponsorship of religious beliefs on all students. He also found the tone of the court's opinion disturbing, contending that it "bristles with hostility to all things religious in public life."

On July 7, 2000, the policy was officially voted out of existence by the Santa Fe school board. The board's president told the *Galveston County Daily News*, "Although we, along with most of the people across the nation are disappointed with the ruling, in keeping with the district's pattern, we will comply with the ruling."

CROSS REFERENCES
First Amendment; Jurisdiction; Schools and School Districts; Standing

REPARATION

COMPENSATION for an injury; REDRESS for a wrong inflicted.

Tulsa Race Riot of 1921

Just prior to the deadline that authorized its two-year investigation, the Oklahoma Tulsa Race Riot Commission released a report on February 4, 2000, recommending that reparations be paid to black survivors and descendants of victims in the city's infamous 1921 race RIOT. The state legislature had authorized and funded the eleven member commission in 1997, hoping to shed light on what has remained a dark story in Tulsa's history. Incentive for the measure came by way of example from the state of Florida. In 1994 Florida set a national precedent by acknowledging the loss of lives and valuables during the race riots that destroyed much of Rosewood, Florida, on New Year's Day in 1923. That riot started over the alleged RAPE of a white woman. The Florida legislature vicariously accepted responsibility for the state government's failure to protect the residents of Rosewood during the riots. It then authorized reparation payments to known survivors in varying amounts no greater than $150,000.

The little community of Greenwood, a black neighborhood in Tulsa, Oklahoma, was looted and burned in May 1921 after a white mob came looking for a black man accused of assaulting a white elevator worker. The two-day melee that followed left the thirty-five block wide, prosperous black business district virtually destroyed. Whites burned houses, churches, and businesses to the ground. Some historians have estimated the death toll to be as high as 300, mostly blacks. There are between seventy and eighty known survivors of the incident, many of whom have been able to offer personal accounts to the incident. Even so, the facts remain unclear, and panel members themselves acknowledge that it may be impossible to know what happened during those two days.

Some of the EVIDENCE is compelling, nonetheless. An elderly white man, who was ten-years old at the time, remembers seeing wooden crates full of black bodies near the town's Oaklawn graveyard. His TESTIMONY resulted in the commission's plan for limited excavation, and possible exhumation, of an area at Oaklawn to determine whether a mass grave exists there. State archaeologist Bob Brooks, using ground-penetrating radar, discovered what seemed to be a fifteen-foot square pit in one unmarked area of the cemetery. He proposed excavating a portion of the area and dating any bones found in it to determine if they are from the time of the riot. Excavation began in the Spring of 2000.

Meanwhile, facing the two-year deadline, the commission's six black and five white members approved a resolution stating that the riot was "the violent consequence of racial hatred institutionalized and tolerated by official, federal, state, county and city policy." It then recommended a reparation package of $33 million in the form of direct payments, scholarships, and a memorial. The commission's chairman, Bob Blackburn, insists that the commission's decisions and recommendations be based on historical fact and not emotion. If necessary, proposed legislation would allow the commission to continue until its work is completed.

Black Tulsans are taken to the Convention Hall for detainment after the 1921 riot.
TULSA HISTORICAL SOCIETY/AP/WIDE WORLD PHOTOS

Reparation remains a sensitive issue, though, and not one divided along racial lines. Both blacks and whites have discounted the notion of creating substitute victims and substitute payers, which could "shower the undeserving with tax-funded cash." Many feel that the healing process cannot be completed if people continue to live in the past. Others dismiss reparation as wholly impracticable. State Senator Robert Milacek, a commission member, told reporters that making the city pay for the 1921 riot would lead to future payments for injustices against other people. He claimed, "With the Native Americans, you could go on forever."

CROSS REFERENCES
Restitution; Riot

RICHARDSON, ELLIOT LEE

Obituary notice

Born on July 20, 1920, in Boston, Massachusetts; died on December 31, 1999, in Boston. Richardson was Attorney General under President RICHARD NIXON at the time of the WATERGATE scandal. He gained national notoriety by resigning instead of following Nixon's order to fire the special Watergate prosecutor. This was only a small fraction of Richardson's distinguished career in government service: he served as ambassador to Great Britain, became ambassador at large, and was the first person to hold four different cabinet positions.

Elliot Lee Richardson
CORBIS CORP.

RIOT

A DISTURBANCE OF THE PEACE by several persons, assembled and acting with a common intent in executing a lawful or unlawful enterprise in a violent and turbulent manner.

World Trade Organization Summits and Protests of Them

The World Trade Organization (WTO) was established by a 1994 TREATY representing the cumulative efforts of the eight-year long Uruguay Round of International Trade Negotiations. WTO became effective on January 1, 1995, and replaced the prior General Agreement on Tariffs and Trade (GATT), which had 125 signatory countries. Headquartered in Geneva, the WTO had 135 members as of 2000, following the controversial admission of China. The WTO's mandate is to work toward the continued expansion and liberalization of world commerce by eliminating tariffs and other impediments to free trade. It differs from the efforts begun by GATT in that its purview includes a wider range of responsibilities, including INTELLECTUAL PROPERTY rights and TELECOMMUNICATIONS to name just two. WTO policy is set at a meeting of council ministers every two years. Members agree to abide by WTO regulations and decisions, but the organization has no enforcement power. Disputes are resolved by settlement panels and general problems are solved by consensus of members.

Seattle police used pepper spray and gas bombs in an attempt to deter unruly WTO protests.
KEISER/AP/WIDE WORLD PHOTOS

The most recent scheduled two-year Ministerial meeting of the WTO was held in Seattle, Washington, from November 30–December 4, 1999. Days before the meeting officially opened, city officials received telephone calls and visits from various organizations, warning that protests against trade organization policies would be staged outside the Washington State Convention Center. The FEDERAL BUREAU OF INVESTIGATION (FBI) also had warned of violent or destructive activity more than two weeks earlier, but it appears that no organization accurately anticipated the extent of violence and destruction.

Starting with a volatile opening day on November 30th, an estimated 45,000 protesters ultimately took to the streets, first by marching into the downtown area and blocking ingress and egress to the meeting. When police arrived to hold the crowds back, anarchists—wearing fatigues and black masks and carrying M-80 firecrackers and hammers—began smashing windows of retail establishments and spray-painting their logo on walls. Looting and general VANDALISM rapidly escalated. On the streets near the conference, pushing and shoving erupted, and several delegates were bullied while trying to gain entrance to the conference. Police in riot gear attempted to disperse the crowds with tear gas, rubber bullets, and pepper spray, but were quickly overwhelmed. About 200 National Guardsmen and more than 600 state troopers were needed to restore order. Before it ended, 500 people were arrested and the city suffered about $9.3 million in overall damage, mostly incurred by the police department. There were no serious injuries or deaths, however.

What exactly was being protested appeared as diverse as all the interests proximally or distally affected by a global economy. Among WTO's current list of policy priorities are issues involving labor standards, environmental standards, competition law, cultural matters, financial stability and instability, development policy, investment, intellectual property law, and electronic commerce. Likewise, the protesters' causes included animal rights, child labor, organized labor issues, environmentalism, human rights, and opportunistic ANARCHISM. Students dressed as monarch butterflies protested genetically-engineered corn, which affects the butterflies' reproductive genes. Local Laotian refugees protested the presence of Laotian Communist leaders who came to the conference. Unionists comprised the biggest organized group of activists, protesting anything that potentially threatened their jobs or pay: multinational corporations were favored targets. The WTO was generally blamed for helping timber companies to clear out endangered rain forests, helping to kill sea turtles, and helping shoe companies to exploit Asian workers. Even U.S. President BILL CLINTON was treated with suspicion for his organized labor sentiments. An estimated eighty percent of member countries have poor or developing economies and resent being overseen by larger interest groups and controlling economies. Notwithstanding the specific causes, it was clear that domestic protests had taken on a new sophistication not previously seen in the quiet street protests of Seattle's past. With the aid of the INTERNET, cell phones, and walkie-talkies, protesters could achieve a "rapid marshaling of forces from all directions nearly simultaneously," as reported by Seattle's police department.

The trade meeting had intended to articulate issues up for negotiation over the next two years. Agricultural exporters, including the United States, want Europe and Japan to cut agriculture subsidies and import more products. Japan and Brazil want the United States to remove anti-dumping laws and to import more foreign steel. Europe and the United States want developing economies to control rampant PIRACY of intellectual properties by strictly enforcing the laws prohibiting it. The meeting ended without achieving consensus on any of the issues, except that the negotiators would try again in Geneva.

The repercussions and fallout from the WTO fiasco continued well into the new year. In March 2000, the AMERICAN CIVIL LIBERTIES UNION (ACLU) filed suit in federal district court (*Menotti v. City of Seattle* C00–0372) alleging that the city's creation of a "no protest zone" in a fifty-block area—following extensive vandalism and looting in the downtown area—was unconstitutional as not "reasonably related to security needs." A few days later, protesters threatened to shut down a World Bank-International Monetary Fund (IMF) meeting in Washington, though only peaceful protests followed. In June 2000 hundreds of anti-free trade demonstrators launched a protest outside a Windsor, Ontario, meeting of the Organization of American States (OAS), resulting in forty-one arrests. When more than 2,500 delegates from eighty-seven countries attended the June 2000 World Petroleum Congress held in Calgary, they were met with hundreds of protesters, mostly chanting slogans and waiving bright posters and puppets. These demonstrators called out for more development of renewable energy sources such as wind and solar power and for continued efforts to reduce reliance on pollution-causing fossil fuels.

ROBINSON, SPOTTSWOOD WILLIAM, III

Obituary notice

Born on July 26, 1916, in Richmond, Virginia; died October 11, 1998, in Richmond, Virginia. Robinson became a professor of law at Howard University, but soon was active in the civil rights movement. He worked tirelessly with the NATIONAL ASSOCIATION FOR THE ADVANCEMENT OF COLORED PEOPLE (NAACP) to end the "separate-but-equal doctrine" and played a key role in the Supreme Court decision BROWN V. BOARD OF EDUCATION OF TOPEKA, KANSAS. After careers in his own law practice, as member of the U.S. COMMISSION ON CIVIL RIGHTS, and as vice president and general counsel of Consolidated Bank and Trust Company, Robinson was appointed in 1964 to the U.S. District Court for the District of Columbia. In November 1966 he was appointed to the U.S. Court of Appeals for the District of Columbia Circuit. He was chief judge of the Court from May 1981 to July 1986. Robinson took full retirement in 1992.

SCHECK, BARRY

Barry Scheck emerged as a national figure during the 1995 California murder trial of O. J. SIMPSON, but the New York attorney and law professor was already known within legal circles for his innovative use of DNA EVIDENCE. In 1992, Scheck, along with his colleague Peter Neufeld, established the Innocence Project, which represents or assists inmates in reversing their convictions using DNA evidence. Since the O. J. Simpson trial, Scheck has continued to maintain a high profile, representing defendants accused of heinous crimes.

Scheck was born on September 19, 1949, in Queens, New York, and lived on Long Island until he was ten. Following a house fire in 1959 that killed Scheck's younger sister, the family moved to Manhattan. He attended Yale University and graduated in 1971. He then attended law school at the University of California at Berkeley, earning a law degree in 1974. Scheck returned to New York, gained admission to the New York bar, and took a position with a legal aid organization in the Bronx.

In 1979, Scheck joined the law faculty at Yeshiva University's Benjamin M. Cardoza School of Law in Manhattan, but he continued to try cases on the side. It was at Cardoza that Scheck became acquainted with law professor Peter Neufeld. The professional lives of the two lawyers changed in 1987 when they agreed to assist in the defense of Joseph Castro, who was accused of stabbing to death a pregnant woman and her two-year-old daughter. Prosecutors had sent a bloodstain found by police on Castro's watch to a Connecticut laboratory, which had begun to use the new and revolutionary technique of DNA testing. The lab reported that the DNA test confirmed the blood on the watch was from one of the victims.

Scheck and Neufeld immersed themselves in the forensic use of DNA, interviewing scientific experts and reviewing lab procedures. Based on their review of the Castro DNA evidence, they succeeded in having the murder charges dismissed by the trial judge. Their essential argument was that the lab had been careless with the blood sample. Other evidence later came forward that led Castro to confess to the murders. Nevertheless, Scheck and his colleague began to develop expertise in the emerging field of DNA law.

In 1992, Neufeld and Scheck established the Innocence Project at the Cardoza School of Law. With the assistance of law students, the project investigates claims by inmates that DNA evidence would exonerate them of their crimes. By 1999, the Innocence Project was handling more than 200 cases, with a waiting list in excess of 1,000. As of 1999, the project has represented or assisted in 33 of the 54 cases where U.S. courts have overturned convictions.

The defense attorneys for O. J. Simpson, nicknamed the "Dream Team," called on Scheck and Neufeld in 1994 after prosecutors had charged the retired professional football player with the murders of Nicole Brown Simpson—his ex-wife—and her friend. The two victims had been stabbed to death outside Nicole Simpson's condominium, so there was extensive blood evidence. Moreover, Los Angeles police

Barry Scheck
CHILD/AP/WIDE WORLD PHOTOS

BARRY SCHECK

- 1949 Born in Queens, New York
- 1974 Earned law degree from University of California at Berkeley
- 1992 Co-founded Innocence Project with Peter Neufeld
- 1995 O. J. Simpson Murder Trial

detectives found a bloody glove on O. J. Simpson's estate.

Though Simpson had many lawyers on his team, Scheck emerged as one of the most important. His cross-examination of those members of the police department who collected the blood samples at the crime scene was devastating. Scheck sought to show the jury the sloppy methods used to collect and store the blood and the unreliability of the DNA tests that showed Simpson's blood at the crime scene. He also alleged that a small portion of a blood sample that Simpson gave police had disappeared, raising the suggestion that police had used it to "plant" evidence.

After the jury acquitted Simpson of the murders, many members of the press and legal community lauded Scheck for his meticulous preparation and for his aggressive courtroom tactics. Others, however, criticized him, believing that he had gone too far in his cross-examination and in his objections to the court as prosecutors made their final arguments. These critics, including Simpson prosecutor MARCIA CLARK, contended that his courtroom behavior was obnoxious and that his DNA arguments were not intellectually honest. Other observers believed that the antagonism Scheck generated was based on a clash between East Coast and West Coast legal styles.

Scheck has continued to appear on the national stage. He assisted prosecutors in the investigation of the JonBenet Ramsey murder case in Colorado and served on the defense team representing Louise Woodward, an English *au pair* charged with murdering a young child in her care. Scheck has devoted most of his time, however, to the broader legal issues surrounding DNA testing. He serves as a commissioner on New York's Forensic Science Review Board, which regulates all of the state's crime and forensic DNA laboratories. He also serves on the board of directors of the National Association of Criminal Defense Lawyers and on the National Institute of Justice's Commission on the Future of DNA Evidence.

CROSS REFERENCES
DNA Evidence; Simpson, O. J.

SCHOOLS AND SCHOOL DISTRICTS

Illinois High School Accused of Racial Bias in Suspensions

Several Decatur, Illinois, high school students were expelled from school for two years after a fight during a football game on September 17, 1999. The students were first suspended for ten days, but after a Decatur board of education meeting on October 1, 1999, the board voted 3–1 to expel the students in accordance with its "no-tolerance position" toward violence. Of the board members voting for the expulsion, one stated that the fight put several people at risk because it was in a highly public place. Further, the students showed no regard for the other people in the stands and were punished accordingly. The one dissenting voter found that although the students should be punished, the penalty was too severe.

Before the board voted, the local Rainbow/PUSH Coalition spoke to the board and offered an alternative plan. The Coalition is a CIVIL RIGHTS organization geared toward effecting social change and headed by the Reverend JESSE JACKSON. The Coalition suggested that the students be suspended for thirty days, complete course work at Homework Hangout during that time, and complete twelve hours of community service per week for the entire school year. The school board rejected the coalition's suggestion and implemented the two-year suspension.

Many in the African American community were outraged at the stiff penalties. The community was further incensed at the media's characterization of the students as "mob-like," "thugs," and "gang-like." After an eight-hour meeting with representatives of the Coalition and Governor George Ryan, the school board reduced the expulsions to the remainder of the 1999–2000 school year. The students were also given the immediate opportunity to attend an alternative education program.

On November 30, 1999, the students filed an amended complaint against the Decatur

Six of the "Decatur Seven," stand at a rally in support of the expelled students.
KEISER/AP/WIDE WORLD PHOTOS

school board and its members pursuant to 42 U.S.C. § 1983. The students sought declaratory and injunctive relief, essentially asking to be reinstated in school. Declaratory relief establishes the rights of the parties without ordering anything be done. Injunctive relief is more coercive than declaratory relief and is a preventative measure that guards against future injuries by requiring a person to refrain from doing or continuing to do an activity or act.

At trial in late December 1999, the students argued that the zero-tolerance policy denied their constitutional rights and that their expulsions were racially motivated. The students further claimed that their expulsions were not warranted because the fight was of short duration and because no weapons or drugs were involved.

The court was not persuaded by the students' argument and found that the fight was significant and harmed innocent bystanders despite the fact that no weapons were used. *Fuller v. Decatur Public School Board of Education*, 78 F. Supp. 2d 812 (C.D.Ill.2000). The court found it important to show the school board's authority in controlling conduct in the schools. The court cited the Seventh Circuit Court of Appeals, which noted that the Supreme Court "has repeatedly emphasized the need for affirming the comprehensive authority of the States and of school officials, consistent with fundamental constitutional safeguards, to prescribe and control conduct in the schools."

Regarding the constitutional claims, the court found that the students received DUE PROCESS. Each student received notice of the hearing, and each student received a separate hearing and had an opportunity to appear and present witnesses before a hearing officer. Further, each student had a hearing before the school board.

The court also denied the students' claim that the expulsions were racially motivated. The court found that the evidence presented by the students showed that race was not an issue in the decision to expel.

Further, the court found that the students did not prove that the school board had a zero-tolerance policy. Rather, the evidence showed that the "school board adopted a resolution which declared a 'no-tolerance position on school violence'" and "that this resolution had no impact on student disciplinary cases."

Finally, the court did not find the provision "gang-like activity" void for vagueness. The court found that two weeks prior to the September 17 fight, members of two rival GANGS were involved in an "incident" and that the September 17 fight was a continuation of the conflict between members of the two rival gangs. The court stated that, notwithstanding the violation of the "gang-like activity" rule, the students could have been expelled for violating two other rules: the rule prohibiting physical confrontation or violence and the rule prohibiting acts that endanger the well-being of students, teachers, or other school employees.

The court found that the students failed to meet their burden of proof and that, accordingly, they were not entitled to a permanent injunction. Therefore, the students remained expelled for the balance of the 1999–2000 school year and were allowed to be readmitted beginning with summer school in June 2000.

During the expulsion debate, a research study revealed that zero-tolerance policies are racially biased, and that wide racial disparities exist in school suspension rates across the country. After Jackson's focus on the issue, school districts across the country as well as the U.S. Department of EDUCATION began to review how these policies were being administered nationwide.

Voucher Programs Continue to Face Legal Questioning

The very first Supreme Court case on the merits of the FIRST AMENDMENT's Establishment Clause in a school setting was *Everson v. Board of Education of Ewing Township*, 330 U.S. 1 (1947). In that case, the Court upheld a statute from New Jersey permitting local boards of education to reimburse parents of children who attended religiously affiliated nonpublic schools for the cost of transportation. In 1968 the Supreme Court decided *Board of Education of Central School District No. 1 v. Allen* 392 U.S. 236 (1968), which upheld a New York law requiring local public schools to lend secular textbooks, free of charge, to children attending religiously affiliated nonpublic schools. Most recently, *Mitchell v. Helms*, 119 S.Ct. 2336 (1999), upheld federal and Louisiana statutes that allow loans of computers, library books, and other instructional materials to religious schools. Notwithstanding the Court's willingness to hear these important cases, the Supreme Court has refused to hear important cases involving school vouchers.

Though school voucher programs differ from state to state, the basic concept is the same. Parents may enroll their children in private schools—sometimes religiously affiliated—and the state will provide a voucher for a specified amount of money to be received periodically. This tax-funded voucher allows parents to retain more control over where and how their children are educated.

Advocates of school vouchers argue that they save disadvantaged students from failing or poorly-run public schools and that the competition for students forces public schools to improve. Organizations such as Christian Legal Society, Union of Orthodox Jewish Congregations, and National Association of Evangelicals support the use of vouchers for religious schools. They contend that prohibiting students from using vouchers for religious schools violates the

Michigan's "Kids First! Yes!" group gathered almost 500,000 signatures in support of having a statewide school voucher ballot initiative.
ATKINS/AP/WIDE WORLD PHOTOS

free exercise of RELIGION also afforded by the First Amendment.

Opponents contend that vouchers take resources from public schools. They also argue that allowing vouchers for religious schools violates the constitutionally required separation of church and state. Such opponents of school vouchers include Americans United for Separation of Church and State, National Education Association, People for the American Way, and the AMERICAN CIVIL LIBERTIES UNION.

Research on the issue of whether school vouchers are successful is inconclusive. One study conducted by a Harvard University political science professor revealed that voucher students score higher than their public school peers. State-sponsored studies in Wisconsin and Ohio, however, indicated no significant differences in the test scores of the two groups.

On December 20, 1999, U.S. District Judge Solomon Oliver ruled that Ohio's school voucher program was unconstitutional. The judge stated, "the program has the effect of advancing religion through government-supported religious indoctrination." The judge did allow students already enrolled under the plan to receive another semester's worth of support from the state or until all appeals are decided. Ohio's Republican Governor Bob Taft expressed his dissatisfaction with the ruling because he feels that a valuable option has been taken away from parents and students.

Earlier in December 1999, the Supreme Court denied CERTIORARI for a case involving school vouchers from Vermont. Therefore, students in Vermont who attend some private schools may continue receiving funding while those attending religious schools are denied tuition help. The Vermont Supreme Court found the vouchers in violation of the Establishment Clause. In November 1999 the Supreme Court rejected a similar appeal from parents of religious-school students in Maine.

The cases in Ohio and Vermont represent a conservative trend. In 1998, however, the Wisconsin Supreme Court determined that the vouchers do not violate separation of church and state. That court reasoned that the funds are channeled to students—not to schools—and that one religion is not favored over another. Opponents promised to appeal to the U.S. Supreme Court.

The Supreme Court's refusal to hear the issue thus far leaves it unresolved on a national level. Until the Court grants *certiorari* and issues its opinion, each state may rule on school vouchers differently. Given the split among the states, it is probable that the Supreme Court will hear the issue in the near future.

CROSS REFERENCES
First Amendment; Religion: Establishment Clause

SEARCH AND SEIZURE

A hunt by law enforcement officials for property or communications believed to be evidence of crime, and the act of taking possession of this property.

Bond v. United States

The FOURTH AMENDMENT's prohibition on unreasonable searches has led the Supreme Court to define the parameters of various police tactics. In *Bond v. U.S.*, ___ U.S. ___, 120 S.Ct. 1346, 142 L.Ed.2d 624 (2000), the Court ruled that police cannot squeeze the luggage of bus passengers to try to find illegal drugs. The ruling forces law enforcement to modify the way they inspect luggage and packages that are carried by, or in the custody of, an individual.

Steven Bond was a passenger on a Greyhound bus that left California bound for Little Rock, Arkansas. The bus made a required stop at the Border Patrol checkpoint in Sierra Blanca, Texas, near El Paso. A Border Patrol agent boarded the bus to check the immigration status of its passengers. After reaching the back of the bus, the agent began walking toward the front. Along the way, he squeezed the soft luggage which passengers had placed in the overhead storage space above the seats. Bond was seated four or five rows from the back of the bus. As the agent inspected the luggage in the compartment above Bond's seat, he squeezed a green canvas bag and noticed that it contained a "brick-like" object. Bond admitted that the bag was his and allowed the agent to open it. Upon opening the bag, the agent discovered a "brick" of methamphetamine. The brick had been wrapped in duct tape until it was oval-shaped and then rolled in a pair of pants.

Bond was indicted for conspiracy to possess and possession with intent to distribute methamphetamine in violation of federal drug laws. He asked the trial court to suppress the drugs, forbidding their introduction as evidence at his criminal trial. He produced evidence showing that squeezing carry-on bags had been a standard Border Patrol procedure, arguing that the agent conducted an illegal search of his bag. The federal district court denied his motion and found him guilty on both counts. Bond was sentenced to fifty-seven months in prison. On appeal, Bond admitted that other passengers had access to his bag but contended that the agent manipulated the bag in a way that other passengers would not. The Fifth Circuit Court of Appeals rejected this argument, finding that the agent's manipulation of the bag was not a search within the meaning of the Fourth Amendment.

The Supreme Court, in a 7–2 decision, reversed the lower courts. Chief Justice WILLIAM H. REHNQUIST, writing for the majority, noted that the Fourth Amendment provides that a person's "effects" are protected from unreasonable searches and seizures. A traveler's piece of luggage was clearly an "effect" protected by the amendment. Therefore, the Court had to analyze the case based on two Fourth Amendment issues: Did Bond exhibit "an actual expectation of privacy," and, if so, was Bond's expectation of privacy "one that society is prepared to recognize as reasonable"?

As to the first question, Rehnquist concluded that Bond had sought to protect his PRIVACY by using an opaque bag and placing the bag directly above his seat. As to the second issue, Rehnquist stated, "A bus passenger clearly expects that his bag may be handled. He does not expect that other passengers or bus employees will, as a matter of course, feel the bag in an exploratory manner." Because the agent did manipulate the bag, he violated the Fourth Amendment.

The Court rejected the government's argument that Bond had lost a reasonable expectation that his bag would not be physically manipulated by exposing his bag to the public. The government relied on prior court decisions where police observations of a backyard from a plane or helicopter did not violate the Fourth Amendment. In those cases the Supreme Court found that any member of the public could have observed the backyards by flying overhead, thereby negating the landowner's expectation of privacy. Chief Justice Rehnquist distinguished these cases, ruling that they involved visual inspection, not tactile inspection. He concluded, "Physically invasive inspection is simply more intrusive than purely visual inspection."

Justice STEPHEN G. BREYER, in a dissenting opinion joined by Justice ANTONIN SCALIA, contended that a traveler placing a soft-sided bag in the shared overhead storage compartment of a bus, where strangers will push, pull, prod, and squeeze the bag, does not have a reasonable expectation of privacy. Justice Breyer found no difference between the squeezing that a bag is likely to receive from a stranger than from a law enforcement officer, as the world of travel "is somewhat less gentle that it used to be." It is an expectation of today's travelers that their overhead baggage will receive "minimally intrusive touching" by police or security personnel. Breyer agreed with the district court's conclusion that there was nothing unusual, unforeseeable, or special about this particular agent's squeeze. Therefore, in his opinion, the search was reasonable.

CROSS REFERENCES
Exclusionary Rule; Fourth Amendment

SELF-INCRIMINATION

Giving TESTIMONY in a trial or other legal proceeding that could subject one to criminal prosecution.

Dickerson v. United States

The U.S. Supreme Court's decision in *Miranda v. Arizona*, 384 U.S. 436, 86 S.Ct. 1602, 16 L.Ed. 694 (1966) has proved to be one of the most controversial in the history of the High Court. Under *Miranda*, police must inform suspects in their custody that they have the right to remain silent and to consult with an attorney. If the police fail to give these *Miranda* warnings before interrogating a suspect, any information they obtain will be barred from evidence at trial. Congressional anger at the decision led to the passage in 1968 of a law, 18 U.S.C.A. § 3501 (1968), that restored voluntariness as the test for admitting confessions in federal court. The U.S. JUSTICE DEPARTMENT, however, under attorneys general of both major political parties, has refused to enforce the provision, believing the law to be unconstitutional.

The law lay dormant until the Fourth Circuit Court of Appeals ruled in 1999 that Congress had the constitutional authority to pass the law. *U.S. v. Dickerson*, 166 F.3d 667 (1999). The Supreme Court, however, reversed the Fourth Circuit in *Dickerson v. United States*, __ U.S. __, __ S.Ct. __, __ L.Ed.2d __ 2000 WL 807223 (2000). The Court concluded that the *Miranda* decision was based on constitutional principles and therefore could not be overturned legislatively.

Charles T. Dickerson confessed to robbing a series of banks in Maryland and Virginia and was indicted by a federal grand jury on a variety of federal criminal charges. Before trial, however, Dickerson moved to suppress his CONFESSION. Although the district court specifically found that Dickerson's confession was voluntary for purposes of the FIFTH AMENDMENT, it nevertheless suppressed the confession because it believed that police had not read Dickerson his *Miranda* warnings before he confessed.

On appeal, the Fourth Circuit reacted negatively to the Department of Justice's refusal to argue that § 3501 was both constitutional and applicable in this case. In a rare display, the court examined § 3501 on its own, concluding that Congress enacted it with the express purpose of legislatively overruling *Miranda* and restoring voluntariness as the test for admitting confessions in federal court. The appellate court found that the *Miranda* opinion did not specifically state "the basis for its holding that a statement obtained from a suspect without the warnings would be presumed involuntary." Moreover, the appeals court noted that the *Miranda* decision did not refer to the warnings as constitutional rights. The Fourth Circuit concluded that the Supreme Court had no illusions that it was creating a constitutional right that Congress could not overrule.

The Supreme Court, in a 7–2 decision, disagreed, ruling that *Miranda* had been based on the Fifth and FOURTEENTH AMENDMENTS. Therefore, Congress did not have the authority to overturn the *Miranda* decision. In addition, the Court refused to overrule *Miranda*. Chief Justice WILLIAM H. REHNQUIST, writing for the majority, noted that the *Miranda* decision and two companion cases "applied to proceedings in state court." The federal courts have no supervisory power over state court proceedings except "to correct wrongs of constitutional dimension." Rehnquist also pointed to passages in the majority opinion that indicated the justices believed they were announcing a constitutional rule. Based on these factors, *Miranda*'s constitutional foundation was clear. Because of this authority, Congress lost the constitutional power to overturn it. Congress may only overrule court rulings based on the interpretation of statutes or rules.

The larger question concerned the continuing acceptance of *Miranda* by the Court. Chief Justice Rehnquist, a frequent critic of the decision, nevertheless joined the majority in upholding the decision. Though members of the Court might not agree with the reasoning and the rule of *Miranda*, Rehnquist acknowledged the essential place *Miranda* has in U.S. law and society. He pointed out the importance the judicial system places on STARE DECISIS, a concept that counsels courts to honor judicial precedents to insure stability and predictability in decision making. A court should only overrule its case precedents if there is, in Rehnquist's words, "special justification."

In this case, the majority found no such justification. Chief Justice Rehnquist concluded that the *Miranda* decision "has become embedded in routine police practice to the point where the warnings have become part of our national culture." Though the Supreme Court had in the past thirty-five years reduced *Miranda*'s impact on "legitimate law enforcement," the Court had continued to reaffirm the decision's "core ruling." Though the rule sometimes allows guilty defendant's to go free, Rehnquist characterized these cases as rare.

Justice ANTONIN SCALIA, in an angry dissenting opinion joined by Justice CLARENCE THOMAS, declared that the majority's decision "converts *Miranda* from a milestone of judicial overreaching into the very Cheops' Pyramid (or perhaps the Sphinx would be a better analogue) of judicial arrogance." Scalia argued that the court in *Miranda* had no constitutional authority to impose constraints on federal and state governments to manage their criminal justice systems.

United States v. Hubbell

The FIFTH AMENDMENT protects a person from being "compelled in any criminal case to be a witness against himself." Popular understanding about "taking the Fifth" revolves around the idea that a person cannot be compelled to testify in court about his or her criminal activity. The protection against self-incrimination, however, can be applied in some circumstances to documents possessed by the accused. Finally, the government can compel testimony from an accused person if the government gives the person IMMUNITY from prosecution. These issues came together in *United States v. Hubbell*, ___ U.S. ___, ___ S.Ct. ___, ___ L.Ed.2d ___ 2000 WL 712810 (2000), which involved a prominent Arkansas attorney targeted by Whitewater Independent Counsel KENNETH STARR. The Supreme Court ruled that Starr could not prosecute Webster Hubbell after he forced Hubbell to produce financial documents under a limited grant of immunity from prosecution.

Hubbell had been a close friend and colleague of President BILL CLINTON and his wife HILLARY RODHAM CLINTON in the 1970s and 1980s. Hubbell had served as chief justice of the Arkansas Supreme Court and had practiced in

Webster Hubbell and his wife pleaded "not guilty" along with their lawyer and accountants in May 1998.
COOK/AP/WIDE WORLD PHOTOS

the same law firm with Hillary Clinton after he left office. Following Bill Clinton's election in 1992, he appointed Hubbell to the third highest position in the U.S. Department of JUSTICE. The Whitewater scandal soon proved Hubbell's undoing, however. After Starr's investigation discovered incriminating evidence, Hubbell pleaded guilty in 1994 to charges of mail FRAUD and tax evasion based on his law firm billing practices. In his plea agreement, Hubbell promised to provide Starr with information about Whitewater matters.

Starr soon concluded that Hubbell would not provide truthful information. In 1996, Starr served Hubbell with a subpoena calling for the production of eleven categories of documents before a grand jury. Hubbell, who was still in prison, was called before the grand jury, where he invoked his Fifth Amendment right against self-incrimination when asked about the types of documents he possessed. Starr immediately produced an order granting Hubbell immunity "to the extent allowed by law." Hubbell then delivered more than 13,000 pages of documents and records. Starr used this information to indict Hubbell on various tax-related crimes and mail and wire fraud. The federal district court dismissed the charges, though, because all of Starr's evidence was based on the documents Hubbell gave under the grant of immunity.

The Court of Appeals for the District of Columbia vacated the ruling and sent it back to the district court. The appeals court stated that Starr had to convince the trial judge that he had independent knowledge of Hubbell's documents when he issued his subpoena. Starr acknowledged he could not meet this burden and entered into a conditional plea agreement with Hubbell. Hubbell agreed to plead guilty on the condition that the plea would be dismissed if the Supreme Court ruled in his favor.

The Supreme Court did just that in an 8–1 decision. Justice JOHN PAUL STEVENS, writing for the majority, held that the use of the documents that Hubbell was forced to produce violated his Fifth Amendment right against self-incrimination. Stevens noted that the documents "did not magically appear in the prosecutor's office like manna from heaven." Instead, they arrived only after Hubbell asserted his constitutional privilege, received a grant of immunity, and produced the documents.

A key issue was whether Starr knew about the documents before he asked for them. If he did, Hubbell could have been forced to turn them over without immunity. If he did not, Hubbell was not compelled to give the documents without immunity, as their production would confirm their existence and authenticity. In essence, the government is not permitted to go on a "fishing expedition," asking for documents it imagines the accused might possess.

Starr had argued that he should be allowed to use the contents of the documents as long as he did not try to show the information came from Hubbell. In addition, he claimed that Hubbell had no Fifth Amendment right against producing the documents. Hubbell argued that the grant of immunity meant that the documents were tainted and could not be used as evidence.

Justice Stevens rejected Starr's arguments. When Hubbell turned over the documents, it was the "first step" in a chain of evidence that led to his prosecution. He concluded that Starr had failed to show any prior knowledge of either the existence or the location of documents that Hubbell eventually produced. Stevens pointed out that the documents sought by one grand jury to see if Hubbell had violated a plea agreement had been used by a second grand jury to indict Hubbell for offenses "apparently unrelated to that agreement." Therefore, the immunity agreement prevented Starr from prosecuting Hubbell on the new charges.

CROSS REFERENCES
Fifth Amendment; Immunity; Stare Decisis

SEX DISCRIMINATION

Discrimination on the basis of gender.

$500 Million Dollar Sex Discrimination Settlement

In March 2000 the U.S. government settled a CLASS ACTION lawsuit brought against the U.S. Information Agency (USIA) by more than 1,100 women alleging sex discrimination by the agency in hiring and promotion. The award, which is the largest of its kind in U.S. legal history, came after twenty-three years of litigation. The women will receive an average before-tax settlement of $500,000. The settlement drew national attention both for its size and for the fact it took the government so long to agree to terms.

The U.S. Circuit Court of Appeals for the District of Columbia in *Hartman v. Duffey*, 88 F.2d 1232 (1996), presented a good summary of the tortuous route the litigation took. In November 1977 Carolee Brady Hartman, now Carolee Brady, filed a sex discrimination class action against the USIA, and in April 1978 the district court conditionally certified a class of women to join her lawsuit. After the parties agreed to separate the trial into LIABILITY and REMEDY stages, the district court held a BENCH TRIAL on class liability and found that plaintiffs had failed to establish a PRIMA FACIE case of sex discrimination. On the first appeal in 1982, the Circuit Court of Appeals reversed the dismissal of the hiring discrimination claim because it found error in the court's treatment of the statistical evidence. On remand, the district court in 1984 found that the USIA had discriminated against women in hiring for six occupational categories.

In 1988 the district court laid out the framework for relief, ruling that unless the parties agreed otherwise, class members who applied for civil service positions were to be given hearings to determine relief on an individual basis. At these hearings, each plaintiff had to show by a preponderance of the evidence that she applied for a job during the relevant period and was rejected. The burden then shifted to the USIA to show that there was a legitimate reason for not hiring the applicant. If the USIA met that burden, the plaintiff could offer evidence indicating that the proffered reason was simply a pretext for discrimination.

The class of women who sued included women who sought work as writers, editors, broadcasters, broadcast and electronic technicians, and production specialists between 1974 and 1984. The USIA and its broadcasting subsidiary, the Voice of America, transmitted public information about the United States around the world, with special emphasis directed at the then-Communist Soviet Union and Eastern Europe. These agencies rarely hired women for technical jobs and relegated women to low-ranking broadcasting positions. Carolee Brady sued after applying for a job as a USIA magazine

Plaintiffs who reached a $500 million settlement with the U.S. government listen to their lawyer address the National Press Club.

PAJIC/AP/WIDE WORLD PHOTOS

Cruel and Unusual Punishment?

Judges, by court rule and statutory law, are often granted great discretion in fashioning punishments and sentences to fit the facts of the case at hand. Such latitude is, of course, tempered by the prohibition against "cruel and unusual punishment" under the EIGHTH and FOURTEENTH AMENDMENTS to the U.S. Constitution. Generally, a punishment that is extremely disproportionate to the crime will be found to be PRIMA FACIE unconstitutional. Punishments or sentences that are merely uncommon or not customary are often suspect—under the same constitutional provisions—but not unconstitutional *per se*.

Many judges are clearly dissatisfied with the high rate of RECIDIVISM for crimes—in the ninety percent range—and a generalized failure of the judicial system to rehabilitate criminals through conventional incarceration or treatment. Increasingly they have sought to exercise their SENTENCING discretion by meting out innovative punishments intended to address the specific criminal conviction or the conviction history of the specific criminal. The intent of their narrowly-tailored sentences is a more lasting effect on criminals than traditional penalties.

A common example of a narrowly fashioned punishment is one directed at "deadbeat parents" who are delinquent in child support payments. High administrative costs in tracking them down, in addition to frequent evidence showing their continued comfortable lifestyles *vis-à-vis* that of their ex-spouses and children, resulted in court incentive to find new ways to force them to pay. Virginia was the first state to address the problem statewide. In January 2000 it implemented a new program that immobilizes vehicles owned by parents delinquent in their custody payments. The state attaches pink or blue car boots to the vehicles and affixes a sticker to their windshields that states, "This vehicle has been seized by the sheriff for unpaid child support." Many states are considering similar programs and several county jurisdictions already have such programs in force, including Wayne County, Michigan, and Cape May County, New Jersey.

Another seemingly "popular" alternative among judges is to order convicted persons to literally wear signs, exposing their guilt to the public. In Wilkesboro, North Carolina, Judge Todd Burke sentenced a drunk driver who pleaded guilty to FELONY death by vehicle to wear a sign once a month that reads, "I am a convicted drunk driver and as a result I took a life." The convicted woman, a first-time offender, was ordered to spend ninety days in jail, relinquish her driving license indefinitely, and physically maintain the crash site where there are eulogies, poems, and a photo of the victim placed in memoriam. Because she was a first-time offender, the judge was limited to a maximum one-year jail sentence by state sentencing guidelines. He believed this was inadequate for the taking of a life and also wanted to afford the convicted an alternative to the reality of a prison

---

editor and being told that only men would be considered for the position. Yet another member of the class applied to be a broadcaster. Although she had a graduate degree and five years of experience, the Voice of America chose a 21-year-old man, a former waiter.

In 1984 the district court found that the agencies had committed sex discrimination in employment. As the years unfolded, hearings disclosed that the agencies had rigged the selection process, including altering the test scores of some candidates. The district court appointed a special master to conduct the individual hearings. Out of forty-eight hearings that the special master had conducted by 1996, he awarded damages to forty-six of the women. The total amount of damages was $23 million.

At that point, the JUSTICE DEPARTMENT reexamined the case. Negotiations began in 1999 to resolve the claims of all 1,100 women. These settlement talks also reflected the decline and fall of the defendant agencies. The USIA and the Voice of America went out of existence in 1999, with the STATE DEPARTMENT absorbing their functions. The State Department made clear its desire to settle the matter as soon as possible.

Although the settlement did not become final until June 27, 2000, following a hearing before U.S. District Judge James Robertson, the judge's preliminary approval suggested that the settlement would pass judicial muster. The government will pay the settlement from the TREASURY DEPARTMENT's "judgment fund," which comes from reserves in the government's general fund budget. Bruce Fredrickson and Susan Bradshaw, lead attorneys for the women, will bill the government for 90,000 hours of legal work over the twenty-three years. It is estimated that these fees will exceed $12 million. The government will also pay an additional $23 million to the forty-six women who already received compensation from the special master. Therefore, the total amount of the settlement may exceed $550 million.

term for a less-than-intended death. Similarly, a Houston, Texas judge ordered a man to walk the perimeter of the Public Safety Building carrying a sign that read, "I killed two people while I was driving drunk on Westheimer."

A judge in Wilmington, North Carolina, gave a shoplifter the option of either serving a prison term or standing outside J.C. Penney carrying a sign that advised passersby of her transgression. In Seattle, a youthful car thief was sentenced to ninety days in detention, a monetary fine, and sixteen months of supervision, during which time he is required to wear a sign saying, "I'm a car thief." A Michigan judge ordered a man who pleaded guilty to health-care FRAUD to take out a full-page ad in the newspaper, saying "Health Care Fraud Does Not Pay." A teenage graffiti artist was made to apologize to the student bodies of thirteen schools he had defaced. In Montana, a judge ordered a drug-addicted mother to abstain from pregnancy for ten years. Several states have taken away the driver's licenses of minors caught using tobacco products or alcohol. Courts have almost overwhelmingly affirmed such suspensions in alcohol cases, holding that driving is not a right but a privilege. Wyoming is the exception, where that state's Supreme Court struck down a statute permitting such forfeitures as violating EQUAL PROTECTION and unusual punishment constitutional provisions. The West Virginia Supreme Court, however, upheld a law permitting license forfeiture for dropping out of high school. A man convicted of DOMESTIC VIOLENCE was ordered to apologize to his wife on the courthouse steps, where approximately 450 persons and several television cameras were present to witness the event.

The use of public humiliation and embarrassment as punishment for convicted crimes is not new, to either this country or the world. Several Asian cultures required a convicted person to be publicly shamed while his family, friends, neighbors, and strangers paraded past him, hurling criticisms, insults, and often spittle. In colonial days, early Americans resorted to dunking, public stocks, and public lashings.

More recently, tailored punishments often are directed at youthful or first-time offenders, based on the assumption that they are more capable of rehabilitation. However, they are also employed to address jaded repeat offenders who do not seem to respond to other corrective measures.

Critics, including the AMERICAN CIVIL LIBERTIES UNION (ACLU) deplore the punishments as inappropriate forms of public humiliation. In some instances, such as the Montana nonpregnancy order, or more commonly, where statutes require public SEX OFFENDER registration and notice, other constitutional interests are invoked, particularly, the right to PRIVACY. The U.S. Supreme Court has ruled favorably on the constitutionality of sex offender registration and notice laws, though.

Notwithstanding, the punishments are generally viewed as being responsive to the public's frustration with the perceived leniency or inefficacy of conventional criminal law and procedure. Ultimately, if and where any creative punishments are challenged, an appellate review may include a query as to whether the punishment is narrowly tailored to fit the protection of the state's interest—on behalf of the people of the state—while imposing the least interference upon the convicted person's retained rights.

CROSS REFERENCES
Class Action; Employment Law

SEX OFFENSES

A class of sexual conduct prohibited by law.

Pennsylvania v. Williams

All fifty states have some form of sex offender law that requires persons convicted of sexual offenses to register their names and addresses with local authorities for a period of years following release from prison. These laws are based on New Jersey's "Megan's Law," named for a young girl who had been kidnapped, raped, and murdered by a released convict. Most of these laws have survived challenge on constitutional grounds. In the 1999 case of *Cutshall v. Sundquist*, the U.S. Supreme Court let stand the 1995 version of Tennessee's sex offender law that requires potential lifetime registration and monitoring of sex offenders. Tennessee's law also applies retroactively to offenders convicted of certain sex offenses prior to the enactment of the law. The high court also has upheld the constitutionality of similar laws in New York and New Jersey.

Provisions in Pennsylvania's 1995 Registration of Sexual Offenders law (the "Act") required those convicted of certain sex crimes to register with police for ten years after release from prison. Other provisions of that same law created a legal presumption that criminals convicted of particular sex crimes were "sexually violent predators." The sex offender then carried the burden to rebut this designation, by clear and convincing evidence, to the court. It was this second part of Pennsylvania's law that came under challenge, in *Pennsylvania v. Williams*.

The initial challenge was from Donald Francis Williams. A jury found Williams guilty of numerous sexual offenses against a minor on July 15, 1997. As a convicted sex offender under Section 9793(a) of the Act, Williams was required to register with local authorities for ten years after release from prison. Additionally, un-

Databases of sex offenders such as this California one are constitutional; Pennsylvania's sex offender registration law placed an unconstitutional burden on offenders.
STERNER/AP/WIDE WORLD PHOTOS

der Section 9794(a) of the Act, the trial court was required to order a state board assessment of Williams pursuant to the subject law. If the board found that Williams had committed one of the predicate enumerated sex offenses, he would be classified as a "sexually violent predator" and subjected to a potential lifetime of required registration with local police. His obligation to register would not end unless and until a court no longer considered him a predator. Moreover, once designated a predator, the law mandated that "the offender's maximum term of confinement for any offenses or convictions specified . . . shall be increased to the offender's lifetime, notwithstanding lesser statutory maximum penalties for these offenses."

In the brief filed on behalf of Williams by his attorneys, counsel argued that the second provision of the law violated his procedural DUE PROCESS rights under the FIFTH and FOURTEENTH AMENDMENTS to the U.S. Constitution, as well as Article I, Section 9 of the Pennsylvania Constitution. Specifically, they argued that by establishing a presumption at law that the sex offender was a sexually violent predator, the law wrongfully shifted the burden of persuasion to the accused. They argued that it was unconstitutional to require the sex offender to rebut the presumption by clear and convincing evidence.

The crux of the argument was that being a sex offender did not necessarily mean that one was specifically a "sexually violent predator." Such a stigma or designation presumes criminal activity or intent beyond the present conviction. That is to say, because offenders had been convicted once of a sexual offense, they were automatically also a "sexually violent predator" seeking victims for future harm. This, the appeal argued, was contrary to basic constitutional protections that guarantee that a person is innocent unless proven otherwise. In fact, the appeal further argued, it was the *state's* burden to prove by clear and convincing evidence that the classification or designation should apply to that offender.

The trial court agreed and refused to order the state board's assessment of Williams. To appeal that decision under Pennsylvania law, state prosecutors were permitted to bypass the state court of appeals and go directly to the Pennsylvania Supreme Court. Meanwhile, the case was joined on appeal with similar cases of three other defendants: Douglas Loomis, Jose Luis Collazo, and Neil Edward Larson.

The Pennsylvania Supreme Court also agreed with Williams's counsel. It characterized the issue as one that involved "the constitutionality of the method by which offenders are designated sexually violent predators." After a lengthy, multi-page analysis, the state supreme court concluded that it was the state, and not the offender, who must bear the burden of demonstrating that a person was a sexually violent predator. Because the court found those provisions of the Act in violation of the procedural due process requirements of the Fourteenth Amendment, it did not address the remaining constitutional challenges that were raised. Nor did it determine whether the challenged provisions also violated state constitutional due process provisions and protections. On June 30, 1999, the Court struck down the second provision of the law, calling the legal presumption of sexually violent predators "constitutionally repugnant."

The state again appealed. By declining review of the state's appeal of the Pennsylvania Supreme Court's decision on January 10, 2000, the U.S. Supreme Court let stand the state decision that the offending second provision of Pennsylvania's law was unconstitutional.

SEXUAL HARASSMENT

Unwelcome sexual advances, requests for sexual favors, and other verbal or physical conduct of a sexual nature that tends to create a hostile or offensive work environment.

The Seinfeld Case

America's beloved NBC sitcom *Seinfeld* was central to the disposition of two Wisconsin sexual harassment cases filed in the mid-1990s by a secretary and her boss. The related cases involved a particular episode of the sitcom, in which Seinfeld's friends attempted to help him figure out the name of a woman he was dating. The only thing Seinfeld knew was that her name rhymed with a female body part. After the woman ended their relationship, Seinfeld realized that her name was Delores.

In the first lawsuit, plaintiff Patricia Best alleged that on the day following the airing of that episode, she was approached at work by her supervisor, Jerold MacKenzie, who asked if she had watched the show. She responded in the negative, and he told her the story line. When she failed to understand the punch line, MacKenzie admittedly photocopied a dictionary page that contained a word referencing female genitalia and gave it to her. She complained to management, and MacKenzie was fired.

Patricia Best proceeded to file suit against MacKenzie and their mutual employer, the Miller Brewing Company. She alleged sexual harassment and a "hostile work environment," for which a jury awarded her $6 million. The legal battles did not end there, however.

MacKenzie subsequently filed his own lawsuit against the Miller Brewing Company and Best, alleging that Miller merely used the *Seinfeld* incident as a ruse to wrongfully terminate his employment. MacKenzie further alleged that Miller interfered with his chances for promotion by failing to advise him of a downgrade in his job classification following a 1987 reorganization. Miller countered that the 54-year-old MacKenzie was fired due to a change in his job classification, inadequate performance, and an "inappropriate pattern of behavior" which included the *Seinfeld* incident and a similar claim in 1989.

The jury, after deliberating for six hours, agreed with MacKenzie and awarded him $26.6 million, roughly three times the $9.2 million in damages he had asked for. (The court later reduced the verdict to $9 million.) The jury award included $1.5 million assessed against Patricia Best. Members of the jury panel later told media reporters that in their minds, the facts of the case did not rise to the level of actionable sexual harassment. They explained that real sexual harassment had to be "more important" than what allegedly had occurred to Patricia Best. The jury panel, which included ten women, further indicated that they "didn't buy" the notion that women are helpless victims of men in the workplace. If Best had been so offended, one female juror told reporters, she should have told MacKenzie to stop the story before it got to the point where he was explaining the punch line. Hence, the award against Best. Moreover, as jurors thought little of the alleged harassment, they believed that the company had in fact used the *Seinfeld* incident as an excuse to dismiss MacKenzie.

Title VII of the CIVIL RIGHTS ACT of 1964 makes no specific reference to sexual harassment. The concept owes its origin to the 1986 U.S. Supreme Court case of *Meritor Savings Bank, FSB v. Vinson*. In that case, the high court ruled that a hostile environment "created by sexual harassment on the job . . . may constitute sex discrimination under Title VII." The Court further held that in order for sexual harassment to be actionable, it must be "sufficiently severe or pervasive to alter the conditions of the victim's employment and create an abusive working environment." The plaintiff-employee need not suffer severe emotional or psychological injury. Each case requires the trier of fact to view the totality of circumstances giving rise to the claim.

The viability of harassment claims often hinges on an understanding of statutory yet elusive terms such as "unwelcome" and "pervasive." According to the language of the act and Supreme Court interpretation thereof, intent has little to do with defining harassment. Instead, how the victim sees and understands the action is what counts. In the 1998 case of *Oncale v. Sundowner Offshore Services, Inc.*, the U.S. Supreme Court extended the concept of sexual harassment to same-sex conduct.

By the late 1990s, more than 15,000 cases alleging sexual harassment were being filed per year, compared with 6,900 cases in 1991. However, the trend had slowly declined from 1997 to 2000. In a 1998 *Time*/CNN poll, fifty-seven percent of men and fifty-two percent of women polled agreed that "we have gone too far in making common interactions between employees into cases of sexual harassment." With women now constituting at least fifty percent of the labor force, and work trends indicating ten percent longer hours worked than in 1969, some legal scholars have argued that the *Seinfeld* case indicates a backlash against the trend. Still others simply dismiss jury verdicts like that in the *Seinfeld* case as "flukes." In any event, such cases have created a new twist in workplace harassment litigation: the perpetrator becomes the "victim" and subsequent plaintiff.

In truth, proven sexual harassment still commands substantial jury verdicts and still wins the sympathy of jurors. Increasingly sophisticated and savvy jurors tend to sort out the evidence, however, discounting plaintiffs' cases when evidence shows that the plaintiffs themselves have engaged in offensive, vulgar, or crude "shop talk" or conduct. Juries also want to be convinced that the accused was given full opportunity to explain. Human Resources consultants and employee relations law experts continue to advise employers to allow the alleged perpetrator to explain their side; to sift through conflicting stories in order to make an educated decision; and to consider the options available beyond merely terminating the employee in question.

SHEPPARD, SAMUEL H.

Sam Reese Sheppard's Lawsuit Fails

In 1954 Marilyn Sheppard was raped and slain in bed in her suburban home in Cleveland, Ohio. In a case that inspired the television series and movie *The Fugitive*, a jury convicted Marilyn's husband, osteopath Dr. Sam Sheppard, of the gruesome murder.

Ten years later, Ohio released Dr. Sheppard from prison after a federal court determined that his jury had been influenced unfairly by pretrial publicity, a decision the U.S. Supreme Court affirmed in 1966. A jury acquitted Dr. Sheppard of MURDER in a retrial that year. Four years later, after a brief career as a professional wrestler named "Killer Sheppard," a despondent Sheppard died from liver complications caused by heavy drinking.

Since then, Sheppard's son, Sam Reese Sheppard, has been on a crusade to prove that his father was innocent. Dr. Sheppard maintained that he was asleep on a couch when his wife's screams awakened him on the night of the murder. When Dr. Sheppard tried to chase a "bushy-haired intruder," the intruder knocked him out. Sheppard awoke and chased the intruder out to a lakeside dock, only to be knocked out again.

With help from Dr. Mohammed Tahir, the younger Sheppard exhumed his father's remains in 1997 to conduct DNA tests. According to Tahir, neither Dr. Sheppard's nor Marilyn's DNA matched that in blood collected at the crime scene in 1954. According to Sam Reese Sheppard, that proves there was a third person who murdered his mother.

That person might have been Richard Eberling, a window washer for the Sheppards who was found with one of Marilyn's rings five years after the murder. In 1998 Eberling died in prison, where he was serving a life sentence for murdering an elderly woman. Eberling reportedly confessed to Marilyn's murder to both a fellow inmate and Kathleen Dyal, who once worked with Eberling. Some of his reported confessions, however, were unreliable, and he died maintaining his innocence.

In 1995 Sam Reese Sheppard had his father's estate file a lawsuit against Ohio for wrongful imprisonment of his father. To win the case, Sheppard had to prove that his father was innocent, a more difficult standard than for the acquittal Dr. Sheppard was granted at his retrial. Sheppard hoped to prove his father's innocence using the new DNA EVIDENCE. Although he said his sole intention was to clear his father's name, Sheppard stood to receive as much as $2 million in damages for the ten years his father spent in jail.

The wrongful imprisonment trial commenced in February 2000. Led by William Mason, Ohio prosecutors maintained their position that Dr. Sheppard killed his wife. They challenged Tahir's DNA results, saying Tahir used contaminated DNA samples. Prominent trial lawyer F. LEE BAILEY, who defended Dr. Sheppard during his retrial in 1966, was the first witness. Bailey testified that the 1954 trial was a conspiracy between police, prosecutors, the court, and newspapers to convict an innocent man.

The younger Sheppard, now a 52-year-old dental technician from California, testified about the night of the murder. He said there was no tension between his parents when his mother tucked him into bed that night. In the early morning hours, his uncle and a neighbor woke him to tell him "something terrible had happened." Anticipating the defense's case, Sheppard admitted that his father had extramarital sexual relations while Marilyn recovered from sexual problems.

While Sheppard testified, the prosecutors had a surprise for the jury. Although Sheppard always said he was more interested in clearing his father's name than making money, prosecutor William Mason disclosed in open court that Sheppard once asked for $3.2 million to settle the case out of court. The judge described Mason's disclosure as "improper" because the offer had been confidential. Mason's tactic worked, however, as jurors got to hear damaging evidence they should not have heard.

When it came time for the prosecutors' case, they belittled Tahir's DNA evidence as "mumbo jumbo." They said Dr. Sheppard was a playboy who had an affair with his lab technician and then killed his pregnant wife to get out of the marriage. Dr. Robert White used medical records to testify that Dr. Sheppard's story of being knocked out by an intruder was shaky. In closing arguments, Prosecutor William Mason said to the jury, "It may just be that you are being asked to award the killer's son for the killer bludgeoning his wife."

After listening to testimony for two months, the jury deliberated for less than three hours on April 12, 2000, before finding in favor of the Ohio prosecutors. In a short statement after his loss, Sam Reese Sheppard said, "The Sheppard family may be bloodied, but we are unbowed. We've been unbowed for 45 years. We'll be unbowed for all time."

CROSS REFERENCES
Murder

SIXTH AMENDMENT

Martinez v. Court of Appeal of California, Fourth Appellate District

Most persons accused of a crime want the assistance of an attorney to defend them at trial, as criminal attorneys know the intricacies of law and procedure. Some defendants, however, wish to represent themselves. The U.S. Supreme Court, in *Faretta v. California*, 422 U.S. 806, 95 S.Ct. 2525, 45 L.Ed.2d 562 (1975), ruled that a defendant "has a constitutional right to proceed *without* counsel when he voluntarily and intelligently elects to do so." Twenty-five years later, another California defendant argued that he should be allowed to conduct his own appeal of his criminal conviction, just as Faretta implied that it was his constitutional right under the Sixth Amendment.

The Supreme Court, in *Martinez v. Court of Appeal of California, Fourth Appellate District*, ___ U.S. ___, 120 S.Ct. 684, 145 L.Ed.2d 597 (2000), declined to accept this argument, holding that *Faretta* did not apply and that the state appeals court could require that an attorney be appointed to conduct the criminal appeal. In so ruling, the Court made clear that the Sixth Amendment does not apply to appellate proceedings.

Salvador Martinez described himself as a self-taught paralegal with twenty-five years of experience at twelve different law firms. While working as an office assistant at a Santa Ana, California, law firm, Martinez was accused of stealing $6,000 of a client's money. He was charged with grand THEFT and the fraudulent appropriation of the property of another. He

Sam Reese Sheppard (right) is in court hoping to prove his father's innocence in February 2000.
ANDERSEN/AP/WIDE WORLD PHOTOS

elected to represent himself at trial before a jury, because he claimed "'there wasn't an attorney on earth who'd believe me once he saw my past [criminal record].'" The jury acquitted him on grand theft, but convicted him of EMBEZZLEMENT. The jury also found that he had two prior convictions in Texas. Under California's "three strikes" law, the court imposed a mandatory sentence of twenty-five years to life in prison.

Martinez then filed a notice of appeal, a motion to represent himself, and a waiver of counsel, citing *Faretta* as binding on the appeals court. The California Court of Appeal denied his motion, stating that there was no constitutional right to self-representation on the initial appeal. The court held that the right to counsel on appeal was based on the DUE PROCESS and EQUAL PROTECTION Clauses of the Fourteenth Amendment, not the Sixth Amendment. *Faretta*, therefore, did not apply. The court then concluded that the denial of self-representation at the appellate level did not violate due process or equal protection guarantees. The California Supreme Court also denied Martinez's application for a WRIT of MANDAMUS to allow him to conduct his own defense.

Martinez then appealed to the U.S. Supreme Court. In a unanimous decision, the court upheld the California courts. Justice JOHN PAUL STEVENS, writing for the court, stated that neither the holding or the reasoning in *Faretta* requires a state to recognize a constitutional right to self-representation on direct appeal from a criminal conviction. Justice Stevens did acknowledge that some of the reasons given in *Faretta* to support the right of self-representation at the trial level appeared to apply at the appellate level. Nevertheless, he concluded that there were significant distinctions.

Stevens first dismissed the historical evidence referred to in *Faretta* as no longer useful. In that instance, the court had cited a case from the 1940s to justify self-representation. Justice Stevens stated that the evidence was "not always useful because it pertained to times when lawyers were scarce, often mistrusted, and not readily available to the average person accused of crime." Since the 1960s, it has been recognized that every indigent defendant in a criminal trial has a constitutional right to the assistance of appointed counsel. Therefore, a person's decision to represent himself "is no longer compelled by the necessity of choosing self-representation over incompetent or nonexistent representation." Instead, the decision more likely reflects a "genuine desire" to conduct the defense in one's own words.

Though there was some historical evidence justifying self-representation at the trial level, the Supreme Court found little to support it at the appellate level, concluding that it was "not aware of any historical consensus" establishing this right on appeal. Justice Stevens noted that the appeal of right—the absolute right to have a court hear an appeal—in the federal courts did not exist until the later part of the nineteenth century. Furthermore, appellate review of any kind rarely was allowed. State courts also did not generally recognize an appeal of right until almost 1900.

Turning to the Sixth Amendment, Justice Stevens found that it only applied to criminal prosecutions at the trial level. He stated conclusively that the Sixth Amendment "does not include any right to appeal." Therefore, it followed that the amendment itself did not provide a basis for finding a right to self-representation on appeal. Justice Stevens also concluded that the Fourteenth Amendment's Due Process Clause did not provide a basis for Martinez to represent himself on appeal. States have a strong interest in the fair and efficient administration of justice, and this interest outweighs the convicted defendant's interest in self-representation.

Therefore, the Court concluded, state courts are within their discretion to deny self-representation on appeal. This decision, however, does not preclude states from recognizing a right to self-representation at the appellate stage under their own constitutions.

Roe v. Flores-Ortega

The Sixth Amendment provides that a criminal defendant must be given adequate legal help to prepare a defense. The Supreme Court has had to decide what standards should apply to measure whether a defendant received adequate legal representation. In *Roe v. Flores-Ortega*, 528 U.S. ___, 120 S.Ct. 1029, 145 L.Ed.2d 985 (2000), the Court considered whether a defense lawyer must always consult with a defendant regarding an appeal of his or her conviction. The Court rejected a bright-line rule that would have mandated such a consultation, ruling that each case must be analyzed using a set of standards.

California authorities charged Lucio Flores-Ortega with a 1993 MURDER and ASSAULT. He appeared in court with Nancy Kops, a court-appointed public defender, as well as a Spanish language interpreter. He pleaded guilty to second-degree murder. Under California case law, he was allowed to deny committing the crime and to admit that there was sufficient evidence to convict him. After the judge sentenced Flores-Ortega to fifteen years to life in state prison, the judge informed him that he had sixty days from that day to file an appeal. The judge also said that the court would appoint an attorney to represent him. Although Kops wrote "bring appeal papers" in her file, she did not file a notice of appeal within the sixty days.

During the first ninety days after sentencing, Flores-Ortega underwent evaluation and could not communicate with Kops. About 120 days after sentencing, Flores-Ortega tried to file a notice of appeal, but it was rejected as untimely. He filed a HABEAS CORPUS petition in federal court alleging constitutionally ineffective assistance of counsel, based on Kops's failure to file a notice of appeal on his behalf after promising to do so. The district rejected his petition, concluding that Flores-Ortega had not proved that Kops had agreed to file the appeal.

The Ninth Circuit Court of Appeals reversed. It applied its precedent in *United States v. Stearns*, 68 F.3d 328 (1995), where it held that a defendant need only show that he did not consent to the attorney's failure to file a notice of appeal to be entitled to relief. Because Flores-Ortega had not consented to the failure to file a notice of appeal, the appeals court directed that he be allowed to appeal his conviction in state court.

The Supreme Court disagreed, reversing the Ninth Circuit in a 6–3 decision. Justice SANDRA DAY O'CONNOR, writing for the majority, noted that the lower federal courts were divided over this issue. The Court did not see merit in the Ninth Circuit approach. Instead, O'Connor ruled that the test set out in *Strickland v. Washington*, 466 U.S. 668, 104 S.Ct. 2052, 80 L.Ed.2d 674 (1984), should be employed to determine if Flores-Ortega's attorney was constitutionally ineffective for failing to file a notice of appeal. In *Strickland*, the Court held that criminal defendants have a Sixth Amendment right to "reasonably effective" legal assistance. A defendant claiming ineffective assistance of counsel must show that the attorney's representation "fell below an objective standard of reasonableness" and that the attorney's deficient performance prejudiced the defendant.

Justice O'Connor stated that the courts must judge the reasonableness of the attorney's conduct on the facts of the particular case, viewed as of the time of the attorney's conduct. Courts should be "highly deferential" in scrutinizing an attorney's performance, but they cannot ignore blatant conduct prejudicial to the client. For example, if a lawyer disregards a defendant's specific instruction to file a notice of appeal, the lawyer has acted in a professionally unreasonable manner. If the defendant tells his attorney not to file an appeal, however, the defendant cannot complain that his attorney performed deficiently by failing to file one. The Ninth Circuit's bright-line rule for cases where the defendant had not conveyed his wishes one way or the other adjudged the lawyer's failure to appeal without the defendant's consent *per se* deficient. This *per se* rule made it unnecessary to inquire into the facts and circumstances of the lawyer's conduct. Justice O'Connor found this approach inconsistent with *Strickland*'s specific reasonableness requirement.

The Court directed that an inquiry into a case like Flores-Ortega's should begin by asking whether the attorney in fact consulted with the defendant about the appeal. Such a consultation meant advising the defendant on the pros and cons of taking an appeal and making a reasonable effort to discover the defendant's wishes. Justice O'Connor agreed that the wisest course for an attorney is to consult with the defendant about the appeal. The attorney only has a constitutionally imposed duty to consult, however, if a "rational defendant would want to appeal" or if the defendant "reasonably demonstrated to the attorney that he was not interested in appealing."

The second part of the *Strickland* test requires the defendant to show PREJUDICE from the attorney's deficient performance. Justice O'Connor agreed with Flores-Ortega that if his attorney's deficient conduct prevented him from appealing his case, then "prejudice must be presumed." Flores-Ortega, however, would need to show that there was a reasonable probability that he would have filed a timely appeal if it had not been for his attorney's conduct. Because the lower courts did not apply the *Strickland* test, the Court remanded the case so the court could make a full inquiry to determine whether Kops rendered constitutionally inadequate assistance.

Justice DAVID H. SOUTER, in a dissenting opinion joined by Justices JOHN PAUL STEVENS and RUTH BADER GINSBURG, argued that under the *Strickland* test it was clear that Flores-Ortega had been denied his Sixth Amendment rights. Justice Souter stated that it is "unreasonable for a lawyer with a client like respondent Flores-Ortega to walk away from her representation after trial or after sentencing without at the very least acting affirmatively to ensure that the client understands the right to appeal."

Smith v. Robbins

The U.S. Supreme Court has made clear that the Sixth Amendment guarantees that an indigent criminal defendant is entitled to a court-appointed attorney, who is paid by the government. The Court has also recognized, however, that those persons convicted of crimes cannot compel a court-appointed attorney to file an appeal that the attorney believes is frivolous. In *Anders v. California*, 386 U.S. 738, 87 S.Ct. 1396, 18 L.Ed.2d 493 (1967), the Supreme Court set out a procedure that an attorney must follow, to request either withdrawing from the case or having the court dispose of the case without a full legal review.

The Supreme Court reconsidered this procedure in *Smith v. Robbins*, __ U.S. __, 120 S.Ct. 746, 145 L.Ed.2d 756 (2000), when it reviewed a California State Supreme Court decision that set out a procedure different from that announced in *Anders*. The U.S. Supreme Court concluded that its thirty-year precedent was not a "straitjacket" and that states were free to come up with procedures that protected both the criminal client and his or her attorney.

The case arose out of the 1990 conviction of Lee Robbins for second-degree MURDER and THEFT of an automobile. Following his conviction, Robbins was sentenced to seventeen years to life. Though Robbins had represented himself at trial, he asked for and received a court-appointed attorney for his appeal. After the attorney concluded that the appeal would be frivolous, as there were no substantive legal issues in dispute, the attorney refused to file an appeal and asked the California Court of Appeals to allow him to withdraw from the case.

The procedures for withdrawal in California differed from those described in the 1967 *Anders* decision. The Supreme Court in *Anders* found that in order to protect the defendant's constitutional rights to appellate counsel, courts must safeguard against the risk of granting such requests where an appeal is not actually frivolous. Therefore, the filing of a letter by the attorney stating that there were no legal issues worthy of consideration by the appeals court was not sufficient. Instead, a request to withdraw must be accompanied by a brief that refers to anything in the trial record that might "arguably support the appeal." Moreover, a copy of this brief must be given to the client, who may raise any additional points. Following these submissions, the appellate court decides whether the case is frivolous after a full examination of all trial proceedings. If the court decides the appeal is frivolous, it may allow the attorney to withdraw, and it may decide to dismiss the case or decide it on its merits. If, however, the court finds "any of the legal points arguable on their merits," it must provide the defendant with an appellate attorney.

California departed from these procedures in *People v. Wende*, 25 Cal.3d 436, 600 P.2d 1071 (1979). The California Supreme Court established that an attorney, upon concluding that an appeal would be frivolous, must file a brief with the appellate court that summarizes the procedural and factual history of the case, with citations to the trial record. The attorney also must attest that he or she has reviewed the record, explained the evaluation of the case to the client, provided the client with a copy of the brief, and informed the client of the right to file his or her own supplementary brief. The attorney must request the appellate court to examine the record for arguable issues independently. Unlike *Anders*, the attorney does not explicitly state that the appeal is frivolous or request to withdraw. Instead, the attorney is silent on the merits of the case. The appellate court then conducts a review of the entire record. If it concludes the appeal is frivolous, it affirms the trial verdict. If it finds issues worthy of examination, it orders the attorney to brief these issues.

In Robbins's case, the California Court of Appeals and the California Supreme Court found his appeal frivolous and affirmed his conviction. Robbins then appealed to the federal courts, arguing that he had received ineffective assistance of appellate counsel because the California courts had not complied with the procedures set forth in *Anders*. The federal district court agreed that by failing to follow *Anders*, the attorney had failed to include two issues in his brief that would not have been characterized as frivolous. The Ninth Circuit Court of Appeals also agreed with Robbins, ruling that states are obliged to follow the *Anders* procedures to the letter.

The U.S. Supreme Court disagreed, overruling the Ninth Circuit. On a 5–4 vote, the Court upheld the California procedure. Justice CLARENCE THOMAS, writing for the majority, stated that "any view of the procedure we described in [*Anders*] that converted it from a suggestion into a straitjacket would contravene our established practice rooted in federalism, of allowing the states wide discretion ... to experiment with solutions to difficult problems of policy." Justice Thomas characterized the *Anders* procedure as only one method of satisfying the constitutional requirements for indigent criminal appeals. States, therefore, are free to adopt different procedures so long as these procedures "adequately safeguard" a defendant's right to appellate counsel.

The Court remanded the case to the Ninth Circuit to evaluate more carefully Robbins's claim that there were two arguable issues that justified representation by an attorney.

Justice DAVID SOUTER filed a dissenting opinion that was joined by Justices JOHN PAUL STEVENS, RUTH BADER GINSBURG, and STEPHEN G. BREYER. Justice Souter contended that the California procedures allowed court-appointed lawyers "to remain too passive." He worried that the procedures did not "assure, or even promote, the partisan attention that the Constitution requires."

CROSS REFERENCES
Appeal; Criminal Procedure

STATEHOOD

Puerto Rican Sovereignty

Located forty miles east of the Virgin Islands in the Caribbean, Puerto Rico is a mountainous tropical island with an area of 3,515 square miles. Christopher Columbus was the first European to discover Puerto Rico in 1493, and the island remained under Spanish authority until 1898 when the Spanish ceded it to the United States following the Spanish-American War.

Between 1898 and 1900, the U.S. military worked to police Puerto Rico and improve its sanitation systems, highways, and public education. In May 1900 the United States passed the Foraker Act, instituting a civil, rather than military, government system, but still within complete control of the United States. Puerto Ricans objected to their exclusion from their own governing system, and Congress responded in 1909 with the Olmstead Act, which formed an executive department, designated by the U.S. president, to supervise Puerto Rican affairs. This did little to appease the Puerto Ricans, who wanted U.S. citizenship and local governmental control. So on March 2, 1917, Congress passed the Jones Act. This act made Puerto Rico an organized but unincorporated territory of the United States and conferred U.S. citizenship status to all Puerto Ricans.

The Jones Act slightly modified Puerto Rico's local civil government, but the U.S. president still appointed key local officials such as the governor, and Puerto Ricans still lacked governmental control. Early Puerto Rican governors worked to Americanize the residents, their language, and their business operations. The local economy, included in U.S. tariff borders, benefitted initially as Puerto Rican agricultural products—sugar in particular—found a demanding market in the United States. Puerto Ricans quickly became dependent on sugar as their major commercial resource. The introduction by the United States of better sanitation methods and advanced medical knowledge led to a population boom on the small island. Independent farmers sold their valuable land, and the island's limited agricultural properties became increasingly controlled by large corporations, resulting in a widening gap between the wealthy residents and the poor. Puerto Rican exports declined, and hurricane after hurricane rocked the island. U.S. officials, distracted by the Depression, had little time to notice Puerto Rico's growing economic distress.

Puerto Rican political parties focused on the island's relationship with the United States. The Union Party sought greater autonomy, while the Republican Party sought Puerto Rican statehood. In the 1920s, the National Party hoped to secure immediate independence from the United States. Puerto Ricans were focused on their island's political status, but divided on what that status should be in relation to the United States.

U.S. President FRANKLIN DELANO ROOSEVELT included Puerto Rico in his 1930s New Deal policies. The Puerto Rican Reconstruction Administration (PRRA) attempted to level the economic power on the island by limiting sugar production with quotas, and by enforcing a law that limited corporate agricultural ownership to 500 acres, thus returning Puerto Rican farmers to their small farms. Adopting the goals of the PRRA, a new political party called the Popular Democratic Party (PDP) reached Puerto Ricans with its slogan, "Bread, land, and liberty." The island's political status and relationship with the United States took a back seat to the growing concern over internal economic and social problems in the 1940s. In 1946, U.S. President HARRY S TRUMAN for the first time named a Puerto Rican, Jesus T. Pinero, as governor of that ter-

WHY DO ATHLETES' LEGAL PROBLEMS ATTRACT ATTENTION?

Professional athletes in the United States are revered as heroes by millions of Americans, but the athlete-as-hero image has taken a beating over the last decade as many high-profile sports figures have been arrested and convicted for a host of crimes. Pro athletes' legal problems attract national attention for several reasons, the two most important of which are the celebrity status of the suspect and the severity of the alleged offense. Sociologists generally disagree over the primary cause of athletes' legal problems, with some experts blaming athletes' problems on their being coddled as amateurs and other experts blaming some athletes' problems on their rough childhoods.

For many Americans, professional athletes represent a kind of modern-day group of Greek gods, divinely blessed creatures who transcend society with their physical talents and material wealth. Pro athletes are typically bigger, stronger, faster, and richer than the average person. Throngs of adulating children seek their autographs, and idolizing adults pay top-dollar to see them perform. The emotional life and psychological well-being of the communities in which pro athletes play are often bound up with the success or failure of the athletes themselves and the teams they play for. The profitability of businesses located near pro sports arenas depends in large part on a local franchise's ability to maintain a reasonable, steady fanbase.

When professional athletes run afoul of the law, it is not surprising that the story attracts national attention. It is tempting to lump these stories into a single category. The media often portrays a story about an athlete's legal problems as a tragedy involving a hero fallen from grace. Others see athletes' legal problems as representative of larger problems plaguing society as a whole. The reasons that such stories are publicly scrutinized, however, vary with the circumstances of each case.

Sometimes a story grabs national attention solely because a famous athlete is accused of committing the crime, no matter how minor the offense might be. A 1989 story about a driver who failed to pay a speeding ticket on time in Kentucky probably would not have attracted national attention except for the fact that the offender happened to be Michael Jordan. Sometimes a story attracts national attention more for the severity of the criminal offense than for the celebrity status of the alleged offender. Carolina Panthers wide receiver Rae Carruth was not a household name until the National Football League (NFL) player was charged with conspiring to murder his pregnant girlfriend in a 1999 drive-by shooting.

In those rare instances when the criminal offense is severe and the suspected athlete's notoriety is great, national attention becomes white hot. For example, intense international attention was generated during 1992 by the prosecution of former heavyweight boxing champion Mike Tyson, who was charged with raping a Miss Black America contestant in Indiana. The best example of this type of intense public scrutiny was the O.J. SIMPSON double-murder trial in 1995. The American public watched with almost obsessive fascination as the NFL hall-of-fame inductee, movie actor, and television personality was prosecuted for the brutal slaying of his ex-wife Nicole Brown Simpson and her friend Ronald Goldman. Simpson was acquitted of the murder charges, while Tyson was convicted and sentenced to six years in prison.

An increasing number of professional athletes generate national attention because of their frequent encounters with the law. National Basketball Association (NBA) player Charles Barkley has been arrested three times for off-court incidents usually involving a violent encounter with a fan. Another NBA player, J.R. Rider, was arrested three times in one month for various misdemeanor charges during the 1996 season. In 1999 New York Yankees outfielder Darryl Strawberry pleaded no contest to charges of cocaine possession and soliciting a prostitute after he had already been banned from baseball twice for drug use and convicted once for tax evasion. He was banned from baseball again in the year 2000, when he tested positive for cocaine. Since Lawrence Taylor retired from professional football in 1993, he has been arrested three times on drug charges, found guilty of filing false income tax returns, and was taken into custody during a deadbeat-parent sweep. Taylor was eventually released after paying $4,500 in overdue child support.

Sociologists disagree over the primary cause of professional athletes' legal problems. Many sociologists point to a culture in which amateur athletes are insulated from reality as the main reason for their legal problems later in life. According to University of Calgary sociologist Michael Atkinson, most profes-

---

ritory, and in 1947, Congress allowed Puerto Ricans to elect their own governor. They did so in 1948, electing Munoz Marin, leader of the PDP.

The PDP governed Puerto Rico from 1948 until 1968. During that time, the island's economy became less agricultural and more industrial. Rural workers moved to the cities, taking jobs in the electronic or pharmaceutical industries. Many Puerto Ricans also moved to New York City and other urban centers in the United States.

sional athletes are coddled from the time they are little until the time they retire from sports. In junior high and high school, he says, top athletes are taught that the rules do not apply to them. Coaches sweep academic problems under the rug and teachers are encouraged to ignore poor class performance and award them a passing grade.

By the time these athletes reach college, the best are anointed "Big Man on Campus" and given free run at major universities, Atkinson maintains. So-called "handlers" cover up college players' scholastic shortcomings and legal run-ins. As a result, Atkinson contends, athletes typically feel invincible once they hit the pros and have no idea how to handle problems on their own or comport themselves with the ordinary social rules that everyone else lives by. Atkinson says that athletes' problems are compounded when they are handed million-dollar paychecks by professional franchises and tempted by everything dangerous that money attracts. Many professional athletes are led to believe that they can buy their way out of trouble.

Other sociologists paint a different picture. They argue that a large number of athletes' legal problems can be traced to rough childhoods. Thousands of professional athletes were raised in abusive homes or tough inner city neighborhoods and had to fend for themselves to survive. Some teenage athletes are taught to communicate with their fists and others with weapons. Many join gangs, sell drugs, and commit violent crimes at the same time they are attracting national attention with their athletic prowess.

After running with an unsavory crowd for most of their lives, certain athletes find it difficult to disassociate themselves from such elements once they turn professional. For example, when NFL linebacker Ray Lewis was charged with murder in the stabbing deaths of two individuals outside an Atlanta nightclub hours after the Super Bowl, two of the men he was arrested with were old friends possessing criminal records. Philadelphia 76ers guard Allen Iverson has been questioned on several occasions in connection with the legal problems of his long-time friends, individuals who have been arrested on drug and gun charges. Iverson himself has been convicted of two misdemeanors for offenses he committed with those friends.

Some sociologists downplay the significance of athletes' legal problems. They claim that the crime rate for professional athletes is no higher than the crime rate for the rest of society. Instead, they argue that professional sports are simply a microcosm of society, with the same factors contributing to legal problems in this sector of society as they do in others. They cite statistics indicating that the number of violent crimes reported nationally dropped from 1997 to 1999; at the same time, the number of violent crimes committed by NFL players dropped from fifty-five to thirty-seven.

According to these sociologists, it often seems like pro athletes have more encounters with the law only because they are in the media spotlight. Many fans still hang on to the romantic idea that professional sports should be a sacred refuge from the daily travails of life, and think of athletes as superhumans who are not flawed by the same imperfections as the rest of their species. Those images are disturbed by media stories about athletes being arrested or sentenced to prison for serious crimes. Thus, some sociologists conclude that fans tend to remember stories about professional athletes' legal problems more vividly than they do stories about other criminal activity.

A few observers have suggested that the media's coverage of professional athletes' legal problems is tainted by a racial bias against minorities. They state that the media covers legal problems of black athletes more regularly than it covers the legal problems of white athletes, thereby creating the impression that race is a significant factor contributing to the crime rate in professional sports. An article from the April 2000 edition of *Emerge* magazine noted that in 1999 "[a]ll of the off-the-field arrests attracting national attention were of black players, and all of those players seemed to fit the growing stereotype these days of the menacing black man." The same article cited a National Opinion Research Center Survey showing that fifty-six percent of whites think African Americans are more violent.

Members of the media have taken issue with the suggestion that their coverage of athletes' legal problems is racially slanted. They point to the litany of media stories that feature the legal problems of miscellaneous white athletes. For example, National Hockey League (NHL) player Marty McSorley was in the news almost daily after he was charged with criminally assaulting another player with his stick during a game on February 21, 2000. Pete Rose is an example of another white athlete whose legal problems are constantly covered by the media. Baseball's all-time hit leader was banished from the game in 1989 for gambling and in 1990 he was convicted of federal tax evasion. The media revisits Rose's past legal woes each year when he gets passed over for the hall of fame and each time he threatens legal action to end his ban from the sport. Media members also note that news coverage of Darryl Strawberry's struggles with drug addiction often includes comparisons to the plight of Steve Howe, a white professional baseball player whose cocaine addiction resulted in him being suspended from the sport seven times during the 1980s.

In 1950 Congress allowed Puerto Ricans to help draft a document establishing the Commonwealth of Puerto Rico, proclaimed on July 25, 1952. This constitution set up a judicial system and a legislative branch in Puerto Rico, in addition to the previously established post of elected governor. Most Puerto Ricans supported U.S. efforts toward an autonomous commonwealth. Still, extremists in support of an independent Puerto Rico attempted to assassinate

Ruben Martinez, president of the Puerto Rican Independence Party, leads a protest of U.S. military exercises on the island of Vieques.
FIGUEROA/AP/WIDE WORLD PHOTOS

President Truman on November 1, 1950, and attacked the U.S. Capitol on March 1, 1954, wounding five congressmen.

By the 1960s Puerto Ricans were growing dependent on federal programs that helped the unemployed, retired citizens, and veterans of both the Korean and Vietnam wars. Alaska and Hawai'i had become states recently, and many island residents wanted Puerto Rican statehood as well. A plebiscite in 1967 resolved the issue in favor of continuing commonwealth status, however.

Commonwealth status for Puerto Ricans means that internal affairs are controlled by Puerto Rico's government, which includes its House of Representatives with fifty-one seats, its Senate with twenty-seven seats, and its elected governor. The U.S. federal government has authority over areas typically reserved for it: interstate trade, foreign relations and commerce, customs administration, immigration, nationality, citizenship, currency, maritime laws, control of air space, military, postal system, social security, and legal systems are some examples. Unlike citizens in the fifty states, Puerto Ricans are exempt from federal taxes. They cannot vote in U.S. presidential elections, and they are not directly represented in Congress. Instead, Puerto Rico has a resident commissioner who participates in congressional activities but, unlike senators and representatives, cannot vote on legislation. For non-federal issues, Puerto Rico has its own judicial system that includes a supreme court, a court of appeals, superior court, district court, and municipal court. A federal district court, located in San Juan, has jurisdiction over federal legal issues. Puerto Ricans can serve in the U.S. armed forces.

Throughout the 1970s, 1980s, and 1990s, Puerto Ricans came to be almost evenly divided between those in favor of statehood and those in favor of continuing commonwealth status. A smaller faction, ten to fifteen percent of the population, favors complete independence from the United States. In addition to the plebiscite in 1967, Puerto Ricans participated in plebiscites in 1993 and 1998 to vote on the question of pursuing U.S. statehood. Each time, continuing commonwealth status has defeated statehood by a narrow margin.

CROSS REFERENCES
Sovereignty

STOP AND FRISK

The situations where a police officer who is suspicious of an individual detains the person and runs his hands lightly over the suspect's outer garments to determine if the person is carrying a concealed weapon.

Florida v. J.L.

Beginning in the 1980s the U.S. Supreme Court has shown a willingness to side with police and law enforcement over FOURTH AMENDMENT issues. In this context the case of *Florida v. J.L.*, ___ U.S. ___, 120 S.Ct. 1375, 146 L.Ed.2d 254 (2000) was a surprising departure. The Court ruled in this case that an anonymous tip by itself does not give police officers the authority to stop and frisk a person for a weapon. In so ruling the Court declined to adopt a "weapons exception" advocated by the Department of JUSTICE and many police groups. The Court indicated that such an exception would give police too much authority to stop and frisk individuals for firearms.

The case arose in Miami, Florida. In 1995 an anonymous caller reported to the Miami-Dade Police that a young black male standing at a particular bus stop and wearing a plaid shirt was carrying a gun. Two officers responded to the call by driving to the bus stop. They saw three black males standing there. One of the three was J.L., a 15-year-old wearing a plaid shirt. Apart from the tip, the officers had no reason to suspect any of the three of illegal conduct. The officers did not see a firearm, and J.L. made no threatening or otherwise unusual movements. One of the officers approached J.L., told him to put his hands up on the bus stop, frisked him, and seized a gun from his pocket. The second officer frisked the other two individuals, against whom no allegations had been made, and found nothing.

J.L. was charged under state law with carrying a concealed firearm without a license and possessing a firearm while under the age of eighteen. He moved to suppress the gun as the fruit of an unlawful search, and the trial court granted his motion. The intermediate appellate court reversed, but the Supreme Court of Florida overturned that decision and held the search invalid under the Fourth Amendment. The court found that anonymous tips are less reliable than tips from known informants and can form the basis for reasonable suspicion only if there are other indicators of reliability. The tip in J.L.'s case lacked any indicators of reliability.

The U.S. Supreme Court agreed to hear Florida's appeal because two federal circuit courts of appeal had upheld the use of anonymous tips. In a unanimous decision, the Court upheld the Florida Supreme Court's interpretation of the Fourth Amendment. Justice RUTH BADER GINSBURG, writing for the Court, noted that a police officer may stop and frisk a person for a firearm if the officer reasonably concludes that criminal activity may be contemplated and that the person may be armed and dangerous.

In J.L.'s case, however, the officers' suspicion that J.L. was carrying a weapon did not arise from any observations of their own. The only basis for the suspicion came from a call made "from an unknown location by an unknown caller." Justice Ginsburg echoed the Florida Supreme Court in her belief that anonymous tips alone do not demonstrate the informant's veracity or basis of knowledge. She acknowledged that the Court, in *Alabama v. White*, 496 U.S. 325, 110 S.Ct. 2412, 110 L.Ed.2d 301 (1990), had found an anonymous tip sufficient to justify a stop, but noted that the tip had been corroborated by the informant's prediction of the suspect's movements. Moreover, Justice Ginsburg characterized this decision as a "close case."

The tip in J.L.'s case, however, lacked any supporting indicators of reliability. The police had no means to test the informant's knowledge or credibility. Although the allegation turned out to be true, the officers did not have a reasonable basis for suspecting J.L. of engaging in unlawful conduct. Justice Ginsburg pointed out that the "reasonableness of official suspicion must be measured by what the officers knew before they conducted their search." All the police had to go on was a "bare report" of an unknown informant. Florida contended that the tip was reliable because its description of the suspect's visible attributes proved accurate: a young black male wearing a plaid shirt at the bus stop. Justice Ginsburg admitted the information was reliable in the sense of identifying the person, but concluded that the tip did not show that the tipster had actual knowledge of "concealed criminal activity." A reasonable suspicion requires that a tip be reliable in its assertion of illegality.

Justice Ginsburg also forcefully rejected the idea that the Court should adopt a "firearm exception" to its stop and frisk rule. Under this proposed exception, "a tip alleging an illegal gun would justify a stop and frisk even if the accusation would fail standard pre-search reliability testing." Justice Ginsburg said such an exception would go too far, enabling "any person seeking to harass another to set in motion an intrusive, embarrassing police search of the targeted person simply by placing an anonymous call falsely reporting the target's unlawful carriage of a gun." Moreover, this exception would likely be extended to searches for illegal drugs. Therefore, the Court rejected the weapons exception.

CROSS REFERENCES
Fourth Amendment; Search and Seizure

STOUT, JUANITA KIDD

Obituary notice

Born on March 7, 1919, in Wewoka, Oklahoma; died August 21, 1998, in Philadelphia, Pennsylvania. Stout became the first African American woman elected to a judgeship in the United States after being elected to the position on the Philadelphia municipal court to which she had originally been appointed by Governor David L. Lawrence in 1959. She went on to be elected, then reelected, to the Philadelphia Court of Common Pleas. In 1988 Stout was appointed to the Pennsylvania Supreme Court, but her tenure was cut short by a state constitution-mandated age limit. She returned as a senior judge to the Philadelphia Court of Common Pleas. In addition to court work, Stout was a writer of numerous articles and a lecturer.

Juanita Kidd Stout
AP/WIDE WORLD PHOTOS

TELECOMMUNICATIONS

The transmission of words, sounds, images, or data in the form of electronic or electromagnetic signals or impulses.

United States v. Playboy Entertainment Group, Inc.

The clash over FIRST AMENDMENT rights and the rights of parents to protect their children from sexually-explicit material reached the Supreme Court in *United States v. Playboy Entertainment Group, Inc.*, __ U.S. __, 120 S.Ct. 1878, __ L.Ed.2d __ (2000). The Court ruled that Congress had acted unconstitutionally when it passed § 505 of the Telecommunications Act of 1996, 47 U.S.C.A. § 561, which required cable TELEVISION systems to restrict sexually-oriented channels to overnight hours if they did not fully scramble their signal to non-subscribers. In so ruling, the Court found that another provision of the act, which permits cable customers to request complete channel blocking, was a better and legal alternative.

Congress did not give much consideration to § 505 before its enactment. This provision, unlike most of the others in the 1996 act, was added by a floor amendment. Congress acted because of technological shortcomings in cable scrambling. Even before the enactment of § 505, cable TV operators scrambled the signals of their programming so non-subscribers could not view the channels. In addition, "premium" channels are scrambled so only those cable subscribers who pay an additional fee will gain access to the programming. Scrambling technology is imperfect, however. A phenomenon known as "signal bleed" allows audio and video portions of scrambled programs to be heard and seen for brief periods. Section 505 sought to prevent children from hearing or seeing sexually-explicit content because of signal bleed. If a cable operator could not completely scramble the signal, it could only transmit sexually explicit programming between 10 P.M. and 6 A.M.

Playboy Entertainment Group owns and prepares programming for adult television networks, including Playboy Television and Spice. Playboy transmits its sexually-explicit programs to cable TV operators, who then scramble the signal before retransmitting it to subscribers who pay a monthly subscription or who access it on a "pay per view" basis. After Congress enacted § 505, Playboy sought a preliminary injunction to prevent the law from going into effect. The courts refused this request, which led cable operators to restrict Playboy programming to the time period mandated by the law.

A three-judge federal district court panel heard Playboy's challenge of the statute. In 1998, the panel ruled that the restrictions violated the First Amendment. In addition, it held that a scheme in which viewers can request signal blocking on a household-by-household basis presented an effective, less restrictive alternative to § 505.

The Supreme Court, on a 5–4 vote, upheld the ruling. Justice ANTHONY M. KENNEDY, writing for the majority, noted that many adults would find the material "highly offensive," yet Playboy's programming is protected by the First Amendment because it is indecent but not OB-

SCENE. Adults have a constitutional right to view the programming.

Because § 505 is a content-based speech restriction, restricting signal bleed to only sexually-explicit programming, Justice Kennedy applied STRICT SCRUTINY review. Strict scrutiny is a standard of judicial review for a challenged policy in which the court presumes the policy to be invalid unless the government can demonstrate a compelling interest to justify the policy and the policy is narrowly tailored to accomplish its purpose. If there is a less restrictive alternative, the government must use that alternative. Justice Kennedy looked to prior court decisions for a rule on content-based speech restrictions designed to "shield the sensibilities of listeners." The "general rule is that the right of expression prevails, even where no less restrictive alternative exists."

Based on strict scrutiny, Justice Kennedy found that the government had a compelling interest to restrict sexually-explicit material from children. Section 505, however, unduly restricted the rights of subscribers who wished to view Playboy's programming. A less restrictive means of accomplishing the goal of the legislation lay in targeted blocking. Households that do not want to view the Playboy Channel may contact their cable operator and request that the channel be blocked from their cable lines completely.

Section 504 of the 1996 act provided this mechanism, but the three-judge panel believed that it would work only with adequate publicity. The government argued that few persons took advantage of individual blocking. Justice Kennedy agreed with the lower court panel that more publicity would generate more blocking requests. In addition, he agreed that the government had little hard evidence to show how widespread or how serious the signal problem actually was. Faced with lack of evidence, Kennedy ruled that the government had failed to justify a nationwide daytime speech ban. Therefore, he held § 505 unconstitutional.

Justice STEPHEN G. BREYER, in a dissenting opinion joined by Chief Justice WILLIAM H. REHNQUIST and Justices SANDRA DAY O'CONNOR and ANTONIN SCALIA, argued that the majority had failed to make a "realistic assessment of the alternatives. It thereby threatens to leave Congress without power to help the millions of parents who do not want to expose their children to commercial PORNOGRAPHY."

U S West Communications, Inc. v. FCC

The telecommunications industry has emerged as an important sector of the U.S. economy. It has undergone dramatic changes since American Telephone and Telegraph's (AT&T) MONOPOLY over virtually all aspects of the telephone business was broken in the early 1980s. AT&T settled an ANTITRUST lawsuit in 1982 by divesting itself of its local operating companies, while retaining control of its long distance activities. Seven regional telephone companies, known as Baby Bells, were given responsibility for local telephone service. Other companies then entered the long-distance service market to compete with AT&T.

Congress enacted the Telecommunications Act of 1996, Pub. L. No. 104–104, to increase competition within the industry and end state-sanctioned monopolies. The act allowed the Baby Bells to compete in the long-distance telephone market, but more importantly, it permitted AT&T and other long-distance carriers, as well as cable companies, to sell local telephone service. The Baby Bells cannot compete in the long-distance service until they prove to the FEDERAL COMMUNICATIONS COMMISSION (FCC) that they have opened their local markets to the long-distance carriers.

Since 1996 the Baby Bells have been slow to open their local markets to competition, thereby restricting their ability to market long-distance services. U S West and Ameritech, two of the Baby Bells, sought a way around this restriction by signing agreements in May 1998 with Qwest Communications Corporation to market Qwest's long-distance services to their local-service customers. Each company used a special label for the resulting package—"Buyer's Advantage" for U S WEST, "CompleteAccess" for Ameritech. These packages offered the customer "one-stop shopping" for both local and long distance, with all customer support, including sign-up and servicing, through U S West and Ameritech's own toll-free numbers. Qwest was to compensate each company with a fixed fee for every customer they obtained.

Competitors of Qwest in the long distance market filed administrative complaints with the FCC, arguing that the agreements violated § 271 of the Telecommunications Act. The FCC agreed that the deals with Qwest violated the statute and issued an order barring the arrangement. U S West, Ameritech, and Qwest then petitioned the District of Columbia Circuit Court of Appeals, asking the appellate court to overturn the FCC order. In *U S West Communi-*

cations, Inc. v. FCC, 177 F.3d 1057 (1999), the court upheld the FCC decision.

Judge Stephen F. Williams, writing for a unanimous three-judge panel, noted that § 271(a) states that the Baby Bells cannot "provide" long-distance service. However, the word "provide" appeared to be "somewhat ambiguous in the present context." Despite this ambiguity, the court concluded that the FCC had a reasonable belief that the arrangement with Qwest would give U S West and Ameritech a great advantage "once they became explicitly entitled to provide long distance service." Thus, the FCC's interpretation of the statute was permissible.

Judge Williams pointed out that the two Baby Bells had not yet received permission from the FCC to enter the long distance market themselves. The Baby Bells agreed but contended that their arrangements with Qwest did not violate this prohibition. They argued that the ban clearly did not apply to any marketing arrangements they cared to make with long-distance companies. They noted that the statute only prevented them from marketing or selling long distance service through their own affiliates. It said nothing about such marketing arrangements. Thus, the statute clearly implied that the agreements with Qwest were permissible.

The Court of Appeals disagreed. Judge Williams concluded that the FCC's reading of the statute had not led it into any "logical contradictions." He could find no reasons to suppose Congress intended such a narrow interpretation of the provisions. The word "provide" could not be read to allow the arrangements because such a reading would "tempt" the Baby Bells to "defer conduct that Congress hoped to accelerate—acts facilitating the development of competition" in the local-service market.

The FCC's reading of the word "provide" was reasonable because § 271 gives the Baby Bells the opportunity to enter the long-distance market and conditions that opportunity on their own actions in opening up their local markets. The arrangements with Qwest would have given U S West and Ameritech a "first mover's advantage" over any non-Baby Bell company "hoping to secure a position in the anticipated full-service market." By offering one-stop shopping for local and long distance under their own brand name and with their own customer care, U S West and Ameritech could have built up goodwill as full-service providers, positioning themselves in these markets before § 271 actually allowed them to enter. The Baby Bells argued that their marketing materials clearly stated that Qwest was the long-distance provider. The court rejected this argument, concluding that the materials would lead consumers to link long-distance service to U S West and Ameritech.

CROSS REFERENCES
Federal Communications Commission; Pornography; Strict Scrutiny

TERRORISM

The unlawful use of force or violence against persons or property in order to coerce or intimidate a government or the civilian population in furtherance of political or social objectives.

The Lockerbie Trial

Just after 7:00 P.M. on December 21, 1988, Pan Am Flight 103 from London's Heathrow Airport suddenly exploded in mid-air and fell upon the town of Lockerbie, Scotland. A total of 270 persons were killed, including eleven residents of Lockerbie. One-hundred eighty-nine passengers on board were Americans returning home for the Christmas holidays.

A massive, international investigation concluded that the explosion was the result of terrorist activity stemming from Libya. As a result, the name of Libya's leader, Moammar Khadhafi (or Qadhafi or Gadhafi), became a household word in the United States, and diplomatic relations with the country were altered forever.

Twelve years later, the trial has begun against two members of the Libyan Intelligence Service who are ultimately charged with the incident. Abdel Basset Ali Mohmed al-Megrahi and Al-Amin (Lamen) Khalifa Fhimah are both charged with MURDER and CONSPIRACY to commit murder in the international criminal case. They are also charged with violating the Aviation Security Act of 1982. To date, there is insufficient evidence to directly charge Khadhafi himself, deemed by many to be the real wrongdoer.

For years Libya refused to release the defendants to any jurisdiction outside of Libya. Later, Libya insisted that any trial be held outside of Scotland, the United Kingdom, and the United States. After countless negotiations and compromises, Khadhafi and the United Nations agreed to a trial conducted at Camp Zeist, a former NATO air base in the Netherlands, east of Utrecht and about thirty miles from Amsterdam. For purposes of the trial, the base has been temporarily declared a Scottish territory. An old school building on the air base is being used as the courtroom.

Part of the negotiations with Libya also resulted in a non-jury trial: three Scottish judges are hearing the case. Under Scottish law, a majority of two judges will be sufficient for a verdict. The case is being tried under both substantive and procedural Scottish law, which affects not only the presentation of evidence but also the burden of proof and the nature of permissible defenses to the charges.

Prosecution has charged that the demise of Flight 103 was the work of a conspiracy between Megrahi, the security chief for Libyan Airlines, and Fhimah, the airline's Malta station chief. They are accused of retaining a Swiss company to make electronic timers, one of which was attached to a plastic explosive hidden inside the case of a Toshiba radio-cassette player. This was packed with clothing bought in Malta, concealed in a Samsonite case with stolen tags, and boarded on a Malta Air Flight to Frankfurt, Germany. There, the case was moved to Pan Am's Frankfurt-London-New York flight.

Going into trial, the prosecution faced the unexpected change in testimony of one of its most important witnesses. Edwin Bollier, owner of a TELECOMMUNICATIONS company in Zurich, told FEDERAL BUREAU OF INVESTIGATION (FBI) agents in 1990 that a photograph of an electronic timer fragment found in a shirt in the wreckage was similar to twenty prototype timers he had made for the Libyan Army in 1985 and 1986. As trial approached, Bollier was shown the actual fragment and decided that it was not the same fragment as what he believes he was shown in the original FBI photograph. Moreover, his company submitted a report to the prosecutors, which opined that the fragment must have been attached to the inner wall of the plane, and not from a suitcase that had been linked to the defendants. Independent investigators had previously concluded that the suitcase was located twenty-five inches from the aircraft skin. Bollier stated that from such a distance, it would be impossible to create a hole in the aircraft the size of the one that brought the plane down. It is known that Bollier's company has engaged in business with Libya for decades, a factor which prosecution may emphasize in order to counteract his revised opinions.

Once trial began, the defense motioned to have conspiracy charges dismissed because no conspiracy occurred in Scotland. Presiding Judge Ranald Sutherland ruled that he was satisfied that Scottish courts had jurisdiction, however, and dismissed the motion. Scottish jurisdiction for the murder charges stems from the deaths of eleven Scottish residents when debris, fuel, and bodies fell upon them.

Another defense allowed under Scottish law is that of "incrimination," or pointing a finger at other potential defendants in order to create a reasonable doubt in the minds of the judges. This parallels the American trial tactic often referred to as the "empty-chair defendant." Scottish law requires that a court be notified in advance of any intent to employ such a defense. Accordingly, the Libyans' lawyers have advised the court that they may implicate members of the Palestinian Popular Struggle front, one of whom was an original suspect in the Lockerbie case. That person is currently serving time in Sweden for other terrorist activity. Libya also notified the court that it may implicate the Syria-based Popular Front for the Liberation of Palestine-General Command. German police had disintegrated the nucleus of that group just two months before the crash of Pan Am 103. During the raid and break-up, police found Toshiba cassette players modified to hold bombs in a fashion similar to that found in the Pan Am wreckage.

Importantly, and parallel to American criminal law and procedure, the defense does not have to prove anything, including the involvement or implication of anyone else. It simply needs to create, by direct or indirect evidence, a reasonable doubt as to the defendants' guilt.

Trial began on May 3, 2000, with actual witness testimony rather than with opening statements, per Scottish procedure. The trial is expected to continue for more than a year, and prosecution expects to call at least 1,125 witnesses.

TOBACCO

FDA v. Brown & Williamson

Since 1965 Congress has enacted six separate statutes that deal with tobacco use and human health. These statutes require, among other things, health warning labels on all packaging and in all print and outdoor advertisements. In addition, tobacco products may not be advertised on television and radio. Nevertheless, many public health advocates urged legislation that would place strict regulations on the manufacture and sale of all products that contain nicotine. Congress did not act, and in 1996, the

FOOD AND DRUG ADMINISTRATION (FDA) issued regulations based on current law. The tobacco companies challenged the regulations in court. The U.S. Supreme Court, in *Food and Drug Administration v. Brown & Williamson Tobacco Corp.*, ___ U.S. ___, ___ S.Ct. ___, ___ L.Ed.2d ___ 2000 WL 289576 (2000), ruled that the FDA had exceeded its statutory authority and struck down the regulations.

The Food, Drug, and Cosmetic Act (FDCA), 21 U.S.C. §301 et seq., gives the FDA the authority to regulate, among other items, "drugs" and "devices." In 1996 the FDA asserted jurisdiction to regulate tobacco products, concluding that, under the FDCA, nicotine is a "drug" and cigarettes and smokeless tobacco are "devices" that deliver nicotine to the body. Based on this authority, the FDA promulgated regulations governing tobacco products' promotion, labeling, and accessibility to children and adolescents. The FDA found that tobacco use is the leading cause of premature death, resulting in more than 400,000 deaths annually, and that most adult smokers begin when they are minors. Therefore, the regulations sought to reduce tobacco use by minors.

Tobacco manufacturing companies challenged the regulations in federal court. They argued that the FDA lacked the statutory authority to impose the regulations. The district court upheld the FDA's authority, but the Fourth Circuit Court of Appeals reversed. The appeals court concluded that construing the FDCA to include tobacco products would lead to several internal inconsistencies in the act. It also found that the FDA consistently stated before 1995 that it lacked jurisdiction over tobacco. In addition, Congress had considered and rejected many bills that would have given the agency such authority to issue the regulations.

The Supreme Court, on a 5–4 vote, agreed with the Fourth Circuit. Justice SANDRA DAY O'CONNOR, writing for the majority, held that the FDCA, read as a whole, along with Congress's recent tobacco legislation, clearly showed that Congress had not given the FDA the authority to regulate tobacco products. In her first sentence, she acknowledged that the case involved "one of the most troubling public health problems facing our Nation today: the thousands of premature deaths that occur each year because of tobacco use." Nevertheless, Justice O'Connor pointed out that a "fundamental precept" of the FDCA was that any product regulated by the FDA that remained on the market must be safe and effective for its intended use.

During the rule-making process, the FDA had documented that tobacco products were "unsafe, dangerous, and cause great pain and suffering from illness." Therefore, these findings logically implied that, if tobacco products were "devices" under the FDCA, the FDA would be required to remove them from the market.

Justice O'Connor found a major problem with this logic: Congress had foregone banning tobacco products by "choosing to create a distinct regulatory scheme focusing on the labeling and advertising of cigarettes and smokeless tobacco." This express policy was designed "to protect commerce and the national economy while informing consumers about any adverse health effects." Because a ban would contradict congressional intent, the FDA sought to get around this by calling tobacco products "safe" under the FDCA; banning them would cause a greater harm to public health than leaving them on the market. Justice O'Connor rejected this approach because a safety determination based on relative harms could not be substituted for those required by the FDCA. Applying the FDCA to tobacco would lead, in the Court's view, to the conclusion that "there is no room for tobacco products within the FDCA's regulatory scheme."

The Supreme Court also agreed with the Fourth Circuit that the history of tobacco legislation spoke directly to the FDA's authority to regulate tobacco products. Since 1965, Con-

Billboards such as this one near Brunson Elementary in North Carolina were in violation of the since-overturned FDA regulations.
HARRIS/AP/WIDE WORLD PHOTOS

gress had enacted a series of laws that restricted tobacco advertising, placed warning labels on tobacco-product packages, and authorized scientific research into the addictive qualities of tobacco. Moreover, Congress had considered and rejected bills that would have given the FDA the authority to do what it had done on its own with its regulations. Justice O'Connor read this legislative history to mean that Congress had "evidenced a clear intent to preclude a meaningful policymaking role for any administrative agency."

A final piece of evidence against the FDA's regulations came from the FDA itself. Justice O'Connor pointed out that from the FDA's inception to 1995, it had not asserted jurisdiction to regulate an "industry constituting a significant portion of the American economy." Now the FDA claimed authority over cigarettes and smokeless tobacco if it found that they were not safe. It was highly unlikely that Congress would have permitted such a delegation of authority to the FDA in any less than a clear and forthright way. Because there was no evidence of this, Justice O'Connor interpreted Congress's actions as demonstrating a "consistent judgment to deny the FDA this power."

Following the decision, members of Congress indicated a desire to change the law to permit the FDA to regulate tobacco. Some of the tobacco companies expressed a willingness to discuss "reasonable" regulation, but there appeared little political will to take up the issue right away.

Minnesota v. Philip Morris Incorporated

Many states have subjected the tobacco industry to civil litigation. Although the industry negotiated settlements without trials in a number of states, the state of Minnesota and a nonprofit health organization forced the major tobacco companies into a trial in St. Paul in 1998. In the years leading up to the trial, the defendants fought vigorously to prevent the state from gaining access to various types of internal documents. The trial judge ordered many of these documents released, but only after the tobacco companies appealed the orders all the way to the U.S. Supreme Court. Just before the case went to the jury, however, the parties agreed to a massive financial settlement. Though the parties settled, the tobacco companies sought to prevent public access to the documents given to the plaintiffs after the trial court ordered them released.

The Minnesota Court of Appeals, in *State of Minnesota v. Philip Morris Incorporated*, 606 N.W.2d 676 (Minn.App.2000), ruled that the trial court had properly examined the issues and that the documents could be released to the public. The ruling cleared the way for a massive release of internal documents and indices that would aid other plaintiffs in their pending lawsuits against tobacco companies. The court of appeals made clear in its decision that many of the documents had already been disseminated publicly.

The documents at issue had been the subject of intense litigation in the four years leading up to trial. In 1995 the state district court issued a protective order allowing the parties to designate DISCOVERY documents as confidential, based on a good-faith determination that they constituted a trade secret or confidential, private, or similarly protected information under applicable statutory or COMMON LAW. The court also ordered the parties to maintain a document depository, into which all documents produced in the action would be placed. The court warned that the protective order did not create a presumption that the designated documents were confidential and also stated that the order could be modified by the court on its own or on motion by the parties for good cause. Finally, the order stated that these provisions would remain in effect after the conclusion of the action, and that the court would issue an order addressing the use of confidential materials during the trial or at the conclusion of the trial.

A number of types of documents soon came into dispute. The court ordered the release of indices—litigation databases designed and prepared by the tobacco company attorneys in preparation and in response to lawsuits all over the United States. The court limited the release of information to only objective information, however. Any information protected by the ATTORNEY-CLIENT PRIVILEGE did not have to be included. The tobacco companies contested this order to the U.S. Supreme Court and lost.

Another significant issue was the plaintiff's request for more than 33 million pages of documents. The tobacco companies claimed that most of these pages were privileged and not subject to discovery. The trial judge appointed as special master an experienced lawyer to examine these documents based on fourteen categories. Because it was impossible to review each document, the special master reviewed a random sample of documents in each category. After review, he issued a 165-page report and a set of recommendations. He recommended that the tobacco companies did not have to release documents in ten of the fourten categories. Nevertheless, the four other categories yielded 39,000 documents for release. Again the tobacco companies unsuccessfully pursued appeals to the U.S. Supreme Court. The judge released several other categories of documents before and during the early part of the trial.

Following the settlement, Congress subpoenaed most of these documents and placed all but a few on the INTERNET. Nevertheless, the tobacco companies appealed the trial court's order releasing all of the documents to the public. The Minnesota Court of Appeals affirmed the trial court, ruling that the judge had not abused his discretion in releasing the documents. Chief Judge Edward Toussaint, writing for a unanimous court, methodically examined each category of document. Judge Toussaint noted that the appeals court would only overturn the trial court if the judge had abused his discretion. This is a very difficult standard of review for an appellant to meet.

In reviewing the various types of documents, the court concluded that there would be no injury to the tobacco companies. None of the documents contained confidential attorney-client work product. As to the more than 30,000 documents released on the Internet, the court found the legal issues moot, as they were now public information.

Other documents released by Congress were also deemed public, and thus the tobacco companies could not challenge their release. In addition, the court of appeals agreed with the trial court that the release of the documents met a "compelling public interest." The release of the indices would "assist the government and others researching the content of the millions of documents produced in this case." Government agencies could use the information to research and analyze tobacco-related health issues. Moreover, the information would "address the addictive nature of nicotine, research by the tobacco industry into nicotine addiction, and advertising tobacco products to minors." Therefore, the Minnesota Court of Appeals upheld the release of these sensitive and important documents.

CROSS REFERENCES
Civil Procedure; Discovery; Food and Drug Administration

TRADEMARKS

Distinctive symbols of authenticity through which the produts of particular manufacturers or the salable commodities of particular merchants can be distinguished from those of others.

Wal-Mart Stores v. Samara Brothers

U.S. trademark law seeks to promote competition by allowing companies to make their products distinctive from those made by other companies. In addition, trademark law is designed to protect consumers from confusion. Courts face many challenges, however, in determining whether a company has infringed on another company's trademark and whether similar products, only one of which has a trademark, will confuse consumers. The U.S. Supreme Court took a major step in limiting the trademark protection given to a product's design in *Wal-Mart Stores, Inc. v. Samara Brothers, Inc.*, ___ U.S. ___, 120 S.Ct. 1339, ___ L.Ed.2d ___ (2000). The Court ruled that a product's distinctive design, known as "trade dress," is only defensible if the design identifies a particular brand of product. In the context of clothing, the Court's decision made it easier for manufacturers of "knockoffs" to avoid trademark LIABILITY.

Samara Brothers, Inc., accused Wal-Mart Stores, Inc., one of the largest and best known U.S. retailers, of trademark infringement. Samara Brothers designs and manufactures children's clothing. Its primary product is a line of spring and summer one-piece seersucker outfits decorated with appliques of hearts, flowers, fruits, and similar motifs. A number of chain stores sold this line of clothing under contract with Samara.

In 1995 Wal-Mart contracted with one of its suppliers to manufacture a line of children's outfits for sale in the 1996 spring and summer season. Wal-Mart sent the manufacturer photographs of a number of garments from Samara's line and instructed the manufacturer to copy the designs. The manufacturer supplied copies, with only minor modifications, of sixteen Samara garments, many of which contained copyrighted elements. In 1996 Wal-Mart sold the knockoffs, generating more than $1.15 million in gross profits. During the summer of 1996, Samara launched an investigation after receiving complaints from the retailers that sold its product line. The investigation revealed that the clothing manufacturer had produced Samara knockoffs for Wal-Mart, Kmart, and several other retailers.

Samara sued in New York federal district court against all of these retailers, alleging infringement of unregistered trade dress under § 43(a) of the LANHAM ACT, 15 U.S.C.A. § 1125(a). All of the defendants except Wal-Mart settled before trial. Samara prevailed at trial and the court ordered Wal-Mart to pay DAMAGES, interests, costs, and fees totaling $1.6 million. The Second Circuit Court of Appeals upheld most of the award and found that Wal-Mart's selling of the knockoffs was "willful PIRACY with an intent to deceive consumer as to the source."

The U.S. Supreme Court, in a unanimous decision, reversed the lower courts. Justice ANTONIN SCALIA, writing for the Court, noted that the Lanham Act gives producers a cause of action against anyone who uses a symbol or device that is likely to cause confusion as to the origin of the product. Confusion-producing elements include words and symbols that are similar to trademarked words and symbols. Another element is "trade dress," which originally included a product's packaging or "dressing" of a product. Trade dress had been expanded in recent years by many of the circuit courts of appeal to include the product's design. Justice Scalia stated that to cause confusion, the trade dress had to be "distinctive."

In 1995 the Court had ruled that a product's colors qualify for trademark protection when they serve to identify a particular brand. It made clear that color could never be inherently distinctive for trademark purposes, but can be protected if it can be shown that color has a "secondary meaning." Justice Scalia stated that "design, like color, is not inherently distinctive." Attributing inherent distinctiveness to certain categories of word marks and product packaging "derives from the fact that the very purpose of attaching a particular word to a product, or encasing it in a distinctive package, is most often to identify the product's source." Justice Scalia went on to analyze consumer behavior. He concluded that consumers do not "equate the feature with the source." Consumers are aware of the reality that "even the most unusual of product designs—such as a cocktail shaker shaped like a penguin—is intended not to identify the source but to render the product itself more useful or more appealing."

Justice Scalia also found that other consumer interests were at stake besides confusion. Consumers should not be deprived of the benefits of competition "with regard to the utilitarian and esthetic purposes that product design ordinarily serves." Allowing Samara Brothers to prevail would mean other designers could threaten lawsuits against "new entrants based upon alleged inherent distinctiveness." Consumers benefitted by purchasing the knockoff dresses at lower prices than those charged by retailers selling the original Samara creations. They had no illusion they were buying the Samara brand. They bought dresses that were similar in design to those made by Samara because they found the design appealing.

CROSS REFERENCES
Lanham Act

TREATY

A compact made between two or more independent nations with a view to the public welfare.

Panama Canal Treaty Expires

Built by the United States and completed in 1914, the fifty-mile long Panama Canal crosses Panama, joins the Pacific and Atlantic Oceans, and cuts travel time for ships between New York and San Francisco in half. The canal was the dream of President TEDDY ROOSEVELT, an avid proponent of sea travel who orchestrated Panama's independence from Colombia in 1903 so the canal could be constructed. U.S. forces continued to protect Panama against Colombian repossession during the canal's construction, so Panamanians had little choice but to ratify a treaty granting the United States sovereign rights over the canal and the ten-mile strip bordering it.

Despite efforts over the years to regain control of the canal that runs through the heart of their country, Panamanians were unsuccessful until 1977. That year, President JIMMY CARTER signed an agreement with then Panamanian leader Omar Torrijos to return the waterway to Panama's control by December 31, 1999. The twenty-year preparation for the canal's handover also required the closing of U.S. military bases in Panama and the replacement of 8,000 U.S. canal workers with Panamanians. At the November 1999 handover ceremonies in Panama, U.S. Army Col. Edward D. Schumann handed a symbolic key to Panama's President Mireya Moscoso, and the Panamanian flag replaced the U.S. flag at the last of fourteen U.S. Army bases to be closed there. At noon on December 31, 1999, the Panama Canal officially became the property of Panama.

Close to 14,000 ships pass through the Panama Canal each year. Revenue from tolls paid by shipping companies amounts to $540 million annually. The canal is positioned along the narrowest strip of land that separates the Atlantic and Pacific Oceans and operates with a consecutive series of locks that fill with water, lifting boats up and over the land and depositing them on the other side. Panama's Canal Authority, created by agreement by all of Panama's political parties, now controls the waterway.

With the opening of the Panama Canal in 1914 came the Canal Zone, a fenced off ten-mile-wide strip of land that flanked the waterway and was run like a U.S. colony. Inhabitants of the Canal Zone were mostly Americans. Those born in the Canal Zone became U.S. citizens. The zone had its own police force and schools, and even in the heart of the Spanish-speaking country, the use of English was common. Panama's economy benefitted by millions of dollars a year thanks to the canal and the U.S. military bases controlling it.

Over the years, Panamanians appreciated the economic boost but resented the U.S. control of Panama's affairs. Violent protests erupted in the 1960s, and by 1978 the U.S. Senate reluctantly—by one vote—ratified Carter's treaty to ensure the canal's security by handing it over to the Panamanians. Opponents of the treaty complained that Panama was a strategic control point in the war against COMMUNISM.

Those concerns dissipated but did not die during the twenty years of preparation for the release of the canal to Panama. Following the 1999 handover, a Hong Kong company assumed leasing rights to operate the ports at each end of the canal. The end of the Cold War notwithstanding, some U.S. conservatives feared that communist China would take over the canal and block U.S. ships or even wage a nuclear attack on the United States. Panama responded, insisting that the Hong Kong company, Hutchison Whampoa, was a publicly traded company that operated seventeen port facilities around the globe and had no Chinese employees in Panama. Panamanian authorities insisted that control of the canal's waterways and the boats that navigate them remained in Panamanian hands despite the foreign presence operating its two ports.

Another worry was the loss of U.S. military bases. The first U.S. troops arrived in 1911 on permanent assignments to guard the canal's construction. During World War II, U.S. troops there numbered 65,000, and more than 10,000 U.S. soldiers were stationed in Panama at any given time until the mid 1990s. By the end of 1999, the American military presence in Panama had ended, even though polls showed that Panamanians favored a continued presence because of the millions of dollars and 18,000 jobs the military bases brought to Panama each year.

Bases in Panama also served as headquarters for U.S. drug fighting efforts in the region, with about 2,000 planes taking off each year in search of drug labs and drug trafficking airstrips in Central America, South America, and the Caribbean. The planes still take off from Ecuador, Aruba, and Curaçao, and eventually a new permanent headquarters for the effort will be located. Still, drug authorities in the United States worry that Panama will become an easier conduit for Colombian cocaine smugglers with the absence of U.S. military operations there.

The U.S. military will be leaving Panama with an environmental blight of munitions testing and target practice. Since the 1920s, troops have used the jungle along the banks of the canal as firing ranges and have left hundreds or possibly even thousands of unexploded munitions and chemical weapons. Efforts at cleaning up the 7,000 acre region were not totally successful. A complete clean up would require clear cutting the jungle terrain, which would in turn increase erosion into the canal. Instead, U.S. troops fenced off the dangerous areas and posted warning signs.

CROSS REFERENCES
International Waterways

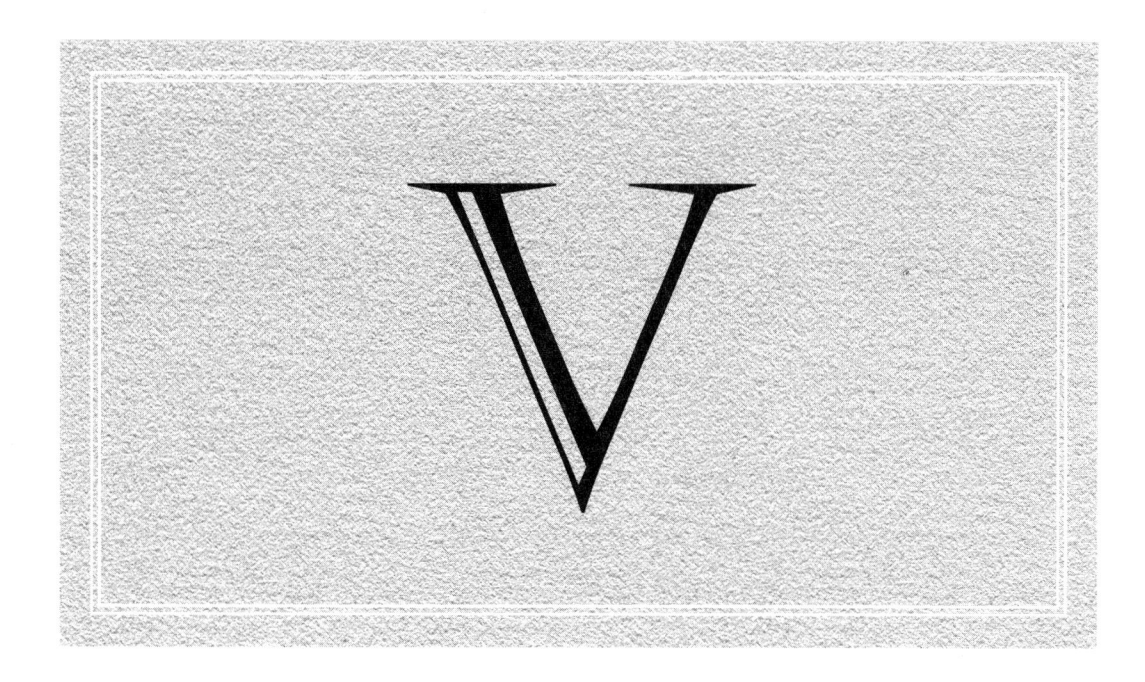

VOTING

Rice v. Cayetano

In 1978, exactly 200 years after Europeans first landed on the Hawai'ian Islands, Hawai'i voters passed a state constitutional amendment that established the Office of Hawai'ian Affairs. This office administers a $300 million trust fund that provides economic, social, health and education aid to about 200,000 Hawai'ians who claim native ancestry dating before 1778. The fund was established to compensate for past wrongs suffered by the native people. The amendment also created an elected nine-member board of trustees to oversee the office and mandated that only persons with Hawai'ian blood could vote for the trustees. This restriction went uncontested until 1996, when a white Hawai'i rancher filed suit in federal court, alleging that the restriction violated the FIFTEENTH AMENDMENT. The Supreme Court, in *Rice v. Cayetano*, 528 U.S. ___, 120 S.Ct. 1044, 145 L.Ed.2d 1007 (2000), agreed with the rancher, ruling that the trustee election must be open to all Hawai'ians, regardless of their ancestry.

The end of slavery led to the Fifteenth Amendment, adopted in 1870, which prohibits state and federal governments from denying a person the right to vote because of race, color, or condition of prior servitude. Harold Rice, a white rancher living in Hawai'i, argued that he was entitled to vote in the 1996 trustee election because race should not enter into voter qualifications. Those qualified to vote were "Native Hawai'ians," defined under the 1978 amendment as those with fifty percent Hawai'ian ancestry, and "Hawai'ians," defined as those with any degree of descent from the original residents. The federal district court rejected his lawsuit and this decision was upheld by the Ninth Circuit Court of Appeals. The appeals court justified the eligibility requirements as being "rooted in historical concern for the Hawaiian race."

The Supreme Court, in a 7–2 decision, reversed the Ninth Circuit. The Court concluded that the eligibility requirements violated the Fifteenth Amendment. Justice ANTHONY M. KENNEDY, writing for the majority, noted that the Fifteenth Amendment's purpose and command were set forth in "explicit and comprehensive language," prohibiting race as a voter qualification. Kennedy pointed out that the Court had used the amendment to strike down discriminatory voting practices targeted against African Americans. The practices ruled unconstitutional were often subtle and indirect, yet the Court had no trouble in seeing their discriminatory purpose.

In this case the voting structure was not indirect or subtle. The state amendment specifically granted the power to vote only to persons of the defined ancestry. Justice Kennedy acknowledged that the state sought to preserve native Hawai'ian physical characteristics, as well as native culture and community. Nevertheless, the state's definitions of who could claim Hawai'ian descent demonstrated that the state had used ancestry "as a racial definition and for a racial purpose." Kennedy concluded that the "ancestral inquiry mandated by the state implicates the same grave concerns as a classification specifying a particular race by name." In addi-

Harold Rice outside the Supreme Court after it heard arguments in his case.
COOK/AP/WIDE WORLD PHOTOS

tion, the use of racial classifications was "corruptive of the whole legal order democratic elections seek to preserve."

The state of Hawai'i presented three justifications for the voting requirements. First, it argued that the Supreme Court had endorsed similar restrictions on voting for Indian tribes. Justice Kennedy rejected this claim, finding that Indian tribes are "quasi-sovereign" entities that are not covered by the Fifteenth Amendment. Kennedy also rejected the idea that the limitation fit within prior Court decisions that allowed special purpose voting districts for water or irrigation issues. Finally, Hawai'i argued that the voting restrictions made practical sense, as they ensured the alignment of interests between the people administering the fund and those enjoying its benefits. Justice Kennedy replied in caustic terms, stating that this argument rested "on the demeaning premise that citizens of a particular race are somehow more qualified than others to vote on certain matters. There is no room under the [Fifteenth] Amendment for the concept that the right to vote in a particular election can be allocated based on race."

Justice JOHN PAUL STEVENS, in a dissenting opinion joined by Justice RUTH BADER GINSBURG, argued that the Court's holding "rests largely on the repetition of glittering generalities that have little, if any, application to the compelling history of the State of Hawaii." Stevens contended that the federal government must be given "wide latitude" in exercising its obligations to aboriginal people and that the state of Hawai'i had a proper responsibility to administer the trust funds wisely. In addition, Stevens saw no invidious discrimination in Hawai'i's efforts to "see that indigenous peoples are compensated for past wrongs, and to preserve a distinct and vibrant culture that is as much a part of this Nation's heritage as any."

In the wake of the decision, the state of Hawai'i had three options to consider. It could open the elections to everyone, make the agency's board appointed rather than elected, or transform the Office of Hawai'ian Affairs from a state to a private agency.

CROSS REFERENCES
Fifteenth Amendment

VOTING RIGHTS ACT OF 1965

An enactment by Congress in 1965 (42 U.S.C.A. § 1973 et seq.) that prohibits the states and their political subdivisions from imposing VOTING qualifications or prerequisites to voting, or standards, practices, or procedures that deny or curtail the right of a U.S. citizen to vote because of race, color, or membership in a language minority group.

Reno v. Bossier Parish School Board

The Supreme Court has continued to define the scope of the Voting Rights Act of 1965 (VRA). The VRA, which was extended in 1970 and again in 1982, seeks to prevent voting discrimination based on race, color, or membership in a language minority group. It was enacted at the high watermark of the CIVIL RIGHTS MOVEMENT to end a century of racial DISCRIMINATION in voting in seven southern states. Section 5 of the VRA, which now applies to all or part of sixteen states with histories of voter discrimination, prevents these states from changing their election laws without the prior approval of the Department of JUSTICE (DOJ) and a three-judge federal district court panel in Washington, D.C. To obtain "preclearance," state and local units of government in these states have the burden of proving that the proposed changes do not have the purpose or "effect of denying or abridging the right to vote on account of race or color."

In *Reno v. Bossier Parish School Board* ___ U.S. ___, 120 S.Ct. 866, 145 L.Ed.2d 845 the Supreme Court reversed twenty-five years of federal policy by limiting the power of the DOJ to block proposed redistricting changes for state and local elections that might dilute the voting power of African Americans and other racial minorities. As long as the proposed election plan does not leave racial minorities worse off than they were before, the federal government cannot reject the proposal.

The school board of Bossier Parish, Louisiana, proposed a redistricting plan following the 1990 census. The board redrew the election districts to equalize the population distribution. It chose to follow a municipal government redistricting plan which had been precleared by the DOJ under Section 5.

In selecting this plan, the board rejected a proposal by the local chapter of the National Association for the Advancement of Colored People (NAACP). The NAACP noted that none of the twelve districts in the board's existing or proposed plan contained a majority of black residents and that no African American had ever sat on the school board. It proposed a plan that created two districts each containing a majority of black voters.

Even though the municipal government had obtained preclearance, Attorney General Janet Reno objected to the school board's plan. She objected on the basis of the NAACP's proposal, which provided new information that demonstrated black residents were sufficiently numerous and geographically compact so as to constitute a majority in two districts. In the objection letter, the attorney general asserted that the plan violated Section 2 of the VRA because it "unnecessarily limit[ed] the opportunity for minority voters to elect their candidates of choice," as compared to the NAACP alternative.

Section 2 applies to all fifty states and their political subdivisions. It was designed as a way of eradicating voting practices that minimize or cancel out the voting strengths and political effectiveness of minority groups. Section 2 bars state and local governments from maintaining any voting "standard, practice, or procedure" that "results in a denial or abridgment of the right . . . to vote on account of race or color."

The school board filed suit in the district court of the District of Columbia, seeking preclearance for the plan from the three-judge panel. The panel granted the board's request for preclearance, concluding that a political subdivision that does not violate the effect or purpose of Section 5 cannot be denied preclearance because of an alleged Section 2 violation. On appeal, the Supreme Court essentially agreed with the lower court reasoning but vacated its decision and remanded the case to the panel with instructions to consider evidence of a Section 2 violation as evidence of discriminatory purpose under Section 5. *Reno v. Bossier Parish School Board*, 520 U.S. 471, 117 S.Ct. 1491, 137 L.Ed.2d 730, (1997). On remand, the panel again granted preclearance, finding no discriminatory purpose on the part of the school board. It could find no evidence of a "retrogressive intent" to make African American voters worse off than they were at the time the plan was proposed.

On a second appeal by the attorney general, the Supreme Court, on a 5–4 vote, upheld the decision of the three-judge panel. Justice ANTONIN SCALIA, writing for the majority, stated that Section 5 was intended by Congress to prevent "backsliding" by states that had a history of past voter discrimination. He based his analysis on *Beer v. United States*, 425 U.S. 130, 96 S.Ct. 1357, 47 L.Ed.2d 629 (1976). In *Beer*, the Court held that under Section 5, a redistricting plan would not be precleared if it "would lead to a retrogression in the position of racial minorities with respect to their effective exercise of the electoral franchise." Under this "retrogression" measurement, the proposed school board plan could only be compared to the existing districting plan. As long as the new plan did not increase the degree of discrimination, it was not retrogressive, and therefore was entitled to Section 5 preclearance. In addition, Justice Scalia expressed concern about the federal government intervening in local matters. Nevertheless, he pointed out that the DOJ could file a challenge under Section 2 of the VRA if it still believed the school board plan was discriminatory.

The four dissenting justices expressed dismay at the decision. Justice DAVID H. SOUTER worried that the decision would force the attorney general and the three-judge panel to "preclear illegal and unconstitutional voting schemes patently intended to perpetuate discrimination." He noted acidly that Congress had not intended to let state and local governments "pour old poison into new bottles."

As a footnote to this lengthy litigation, two African American candidates were elected to the school board in 1994. They were reelected in 1998 along with a third African American candidate.

CROSS REFERENCES
Voting

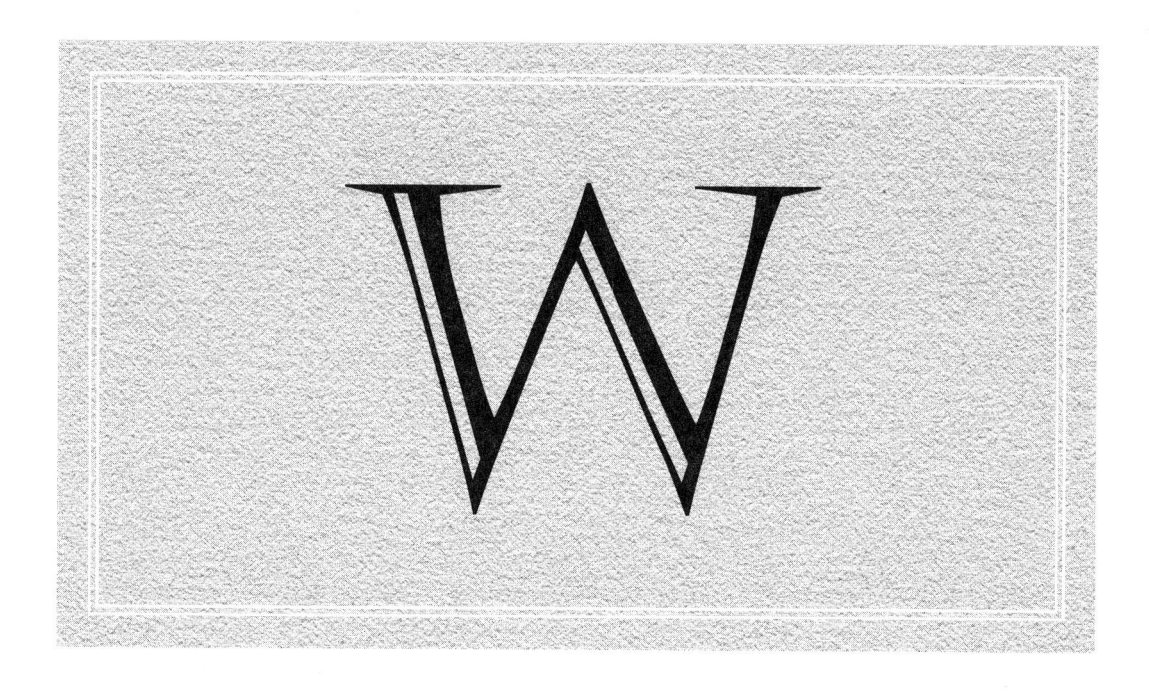

WELFARE

Government benefits distributed to impoverished persons to enable them to maintain a minimum standard of well-being.

City of Chicago v. Shalala

Congress radically changed the U.S. welfare system when it enacted the Personal Responsibility and Work Opportunity Reconciliation Act of 1996, Pub.L. No. 104–193, 110 Stat. 2105 (1996), popularly known as the Welfare Reform Act. The overriding goal of the act was to move people off the welfare rolls and enable them to gain economic self-sufficiency. With certain exceptions, this complex statute also prohibited legal immigrants from obtaining government benefits, including food stamps and SOCIAL SECURITY. The City of Chicago and a group of legal immigrants sued the federal government, arguing that this limitation on benefits denied legal immigrants EQUAL PROTECTION of the laws as guaranteed by the FIFTH AMENDMENT. The Seventh Circuit Court of Appeals, however, in *City of Chicago v. Shalala*, 189 F.3d 598 (1999), upheld the constitutionality of the provision, concluding that Congress had a rational basis for making the changes in eligibility requirements.

The 1996 Welfare Reform Act provides that, with some exceptions, "qualified alien[s]" are not eligible to receive SSI or Food Stamp benefits. Qualified ALIENS include permanent resident aliens, refugees, aliens who are paroled into the United States, aliens whose deportation is being withheld, aliens who have been granted conditional entry, certain Cuban and Haitian entrants, and certain other aliens. SSI provides supplemental security income to low-income individuals who are blind, disabled, or 65 or older. The Food Stamp program provides food-purchasing assistance to households with low income and few resources.

The City of Chicago sued the federal government, seeking a declaratory judgment that these provisions of the act were unconstitutional. The city argued that denying benefits to legal noncitizen immigrants violated the equal protection component of the Fifth Amendment's DUE PROCESS Clause. Soon after filing, a group of legal permanent residents of the United States joined Chicago in the lawsuit. The federal district court granted the government's motion to dismiss the cases, finding that Congress had a rational basis for the legislation. The court concluded that the provisions of the Welfare Reform Act bore a rational relationship to several of Congress's stated goals. These goals included encouraging self-sufficiency among immigrants, preventing public benefits from serving as an incentive to immigrate, and easing the burden on the public welfare system.

The plaintiffs then appealed to the Seventh Circuit Court of Appeals. In a unanimous decision, the three-judge panel upheld the district court's dismissal of the case. Judge Kenneth F. Ripple, writing for the appeals court, acknowledged that the key issue was the standard of constitutional review employed by the district court. The district court had used the RATIONAL BASIS TEST. Under this standard, a law that touches on a constitutionally protected interest must be rationally related to furthering a legitimate government interest. In applying the rational basis test, courts begin with a strong presumption that the law or policy under review is valid. The burden of proof is on the party making the challenge to show that the law or policy is unconstitutional. To meet this burden, the party must demonstrate that there is not a rational basis for the law or policy. In addition, courts do not require a legislature to articulate its reasons for enacting a statute, finding it irrelevant for constitutional purposes whether the conceived reason for the challenged distinction actually motivated the legislature. In short, plaintiffs usually have a difficult time prevailing under the rational basis standard.

Chicago and the other plaintiffs argued that the court should have employed the STRICT SCRUTINY standard of constitutional review. Under strict scrutiny, the court presumes the law to be invalid unless the government can demonstrate a compelling interest to justify the law and show that it has been narrowly tailored to address the issue in question. Plaintiffs have a much better chance of prevailing under the strict scrutiny standard.

Judge Ripple ruled that the district court properly used the rational basis standard. The appeals court concluded that when immigration laws are involved, the judicial review of decisions by Congress must be narrow. Although the Supreme Court had not explicitly endorsed the rational basis standard for reviewing immigration law, Judge Ripple read previous decisions to imply such a choice.

Having endorsed the rational basis standard, Judge Ripple proceeded to analyze whether Congress met this standard in enacting the Welfare Reform Act. He noted that Congress had stated in the act that the provisions in question were intended to foster the legitimate governmental purpose of encouraging aliens' self-sufficiency. Congress also stated that it did not want the availability of public benefits to serve as an incentive for immigration to the United States. In addition, Congress declared that it wanted to reduce the rising costs of operating benefit programs. Finally, the government argued in its brief to the court that the act's provisions were rationally related to the legitimate government purpose of encouraging naturalization. The act gave resident aliens in need of welfare benefits an incentive to become citizens. Judge Ripple concluded that all of these purposes were legitimate and gave Congress a rational basis for enacting the provisions restricting benefits.

CROSS REFERENCES
Equal Protection; Fifth Amendment

WOMEN'S RIGHTS

The efforts to secure equal rights for women and to remove gender discrimination from laws, institutions, and behavioral patterns.

Montana v. Sprinkle

In *State of Montana v. Dawn Sprinkle*, District Court Judge Dorothy McCarter sentenced defendant Dawn Marie Sprinkle to ten years' abstention from pregnancy. As part of the sentence, defendant Sprinkle is to have a pregnancy test taken every two months. If the results are positive, Sprinkle will be jailed.

The controversial February 2000 sentence followed Sprinkle's earlier conviction for endangering the life of her unborn child through drug abuse. During the course of the prosecution for repeated drug abuse in 1998, Sprinkle, then 27-years old, gave birth to a boy. Although the newborn infant tested positive for amphetamines, Judge McCarter showed deference to the new mother in the original 1999 sentencing. She gave Sprinkle a three-year deferred jail sentence, with several other conditions attached, so that Sprinkle could tend to the newborn and turn her life around. The conditions included payment of a fine in lieu of jail, completing chemical dependency treatment, and undergoing periodic drug testing. If Sprinkle had abided by these conditions, the conviction would have been removed from her record after three years.

Sprinkle failed to pay the fine and never completed the chemical dependency treatment. Worse yet, she again tested positive for drugs. When brought before the judge again on SENTENCING violations, Judge McCarter showed no more deference. As she later related to Associated Press reporters, "I don't want another damaged baby born because we didn't do enough to supervise that woman. . . . [W]e can't have her taking drugs when she's pregnant."

The revised sentence includes ten years under the supervision of the Montana Department of Corrections. Five of the ten years are suspended, but Sprinkle will ultimately have to serve part of that time in boot camp at the correctional facility. During the portion of the suspended sentence, she must take pregnancy tests. If she tests positive, she will be taken into state custody. On April 14, 2000, an appeal was filed in her behalf with the Montana Supreme Court (Case No. ADC 99–55). A decision was not expected until late summer of 2000.

At issue is the balancing between a state's interest in protecting an unborn child and a woman's self-interest to procreate. Under general circumstances, a woman's right of PRIVACY in her reproductive choices would prevail up until the point where state intervention was warranted in order to protect the unborn child's interest. This assumes a moving continuum from case to case.

Convicted persons, however, are deemed to have waived their rights to certain fundamental interests, for example, as where liberty interests are compromised by incarceration. In circumstances where there has been repeated abuse of a retained right, to the detriment of the state's interest, the state may intervene.

Notwithstanding, the fundamental right to procreate is one of the most basic and protected of all, and the highest scrutiny must attach to any state interference with that right. On the other hand, giving birth to a child who has been irreparably deformed or permanently harmed by the drug abuse of its mother seems to warrant state intervention. Ultimately, an appellate review may include a query as to whether the punishment in Sprinkle's case is tailored narrowly enough to fit the protection of the state's interest, while imposing the least interference upon the mother's rights. Less restrictive alternatives to the meted punishment may be argued by her counsel, while the state may argue that she had already violated less-restrictive measures, and no chances can again be taken.

United States v. Morrison

In 1994 Congress responded to the national problem of sexual assault and domestic abuse by enacting the Violence Against Women Act (VWA). Under one provision of the act, 42 U.S.C.A. § 13981, Congress gave women who have been sexually assaulted the ability to sue their attackers for damages in federal court for violating their CIVIL RIGHTS. This civil remedy provision drew immediate controversy, as it gave the federal courts jurisdiction over lawsuits previously thought to be within the sole jurisdiction of the states. In *Brzonkala v. Morrison*, ___ U.S. ___, 120 S.Ct. 1740, 146 L.Ed.2d 658 (2000), the Supreme Court settled the issue, ruling that § 13981 was unconstitutional. The Court found that neither the COMMERCE CLAUSE nor the FOURTEENTH AMENDMENT gave Congress the authority to enact the civil remedy provision.

Christy Brzonkala brought a § 13981 action against Antonio Morrison and James Crawford,

Christy Brzonkala speaks to the press about the case before the Supreme Court on January 7, 2000.
AP/WIDE WORLD PHOTOS

who were students and varsity football players at Virginia Polytechnic Institute (Virginia Tech). Brzonkala enrolled at Virginia Tech in the fall of 1994 and within a few weeks she alleged that Morrison and Crawford had assaulted and repeatedly raped her. Following the alleged attack, Brzonkala became severely depressed, saw a psychiatrist, took antidepressant medications, and dropped out of college. In early 1995 she filed a complaint against the men with Virginia Tech. After a series of hearings, appeals, and rehearings, the university found insufficient evidence to punish Crawford and found that Morrison's offense was not sexual assault but the use of abusive language.

In early December 1995, Brzonkala filed a civil lawsuit against Morrison and Crawford in federal court using § 13981. The district court, while acknowledging that Brzonkala had stated a legal claim under the statute, ruled that Congress did not have the authority to enact the section under either the Commerce Clause or the Fourteenth Amendment. On appeal, the Fourth Circuit Court of Appeals agreed with the district court that the provision was unconstitutional.

The Supreme Court, on a 5–4 vote, upheld the lower courts. Chief Justice WILLIAM H. REHNQUIST, writing for the majority, concluded that Congress had overstepped its constitutional authority. In looking at the Commerce Clause justification for the provision, he cited the Court's ruling in *United States v. Lopez*, 514

U.S. 549, 115 S.Ct. 1624, 131 L.Ed.2d 626 (1995). In that case the Court struck down a federal law that sought to make it a federal crime to possess a firearm in a school zone. Rehnquist applied the framework of the *Lopez* analysis to the civil remedy provision of the VWA. As in the firearm law, the VWA provision had nothing to do with commerce or any type of economic enterprise. Congress can invoke the Commerce Clause only if the economic activity in question substantially affects interstate commerce. Noneconomic activity, whether the possession of a gun or a sexual assault, did not by itself create that substantial effect.

Rehnquist did, however, note a difference between *Lopez* and the VWA provision. In *Lopez*, Congress had not provided factual findings that showed a link between gun possession and a substantial effect on interstate commerce. With the VWA, Congress produced a voluminous record that demonstrated the serious impact of gender-motivated violence on victims and their families. Yet despite these findings, the Court ruled that Congress had improperly reasoned from these facts that the aggregate impact of this type of crime had a substantial effect on employment, production, transportation, and consumption. Rehnquist expressed concern that if the VWA was found to be constitutional based on the effect argument, it would give Congress the ability to regulate all areas of family, including marriage, divorce, and child rearing. He concluded that the Constitution "requires a distinction between what is truly national and what is truly local." The suppression of violent crime and the "vindication of its victims" had, in the Court's view, always been the responsibility of state governments. Therefore, Rehnquist held that Congress "may not regulate non-economic, violent criminal conduct based solely on the conduct's aggregate effect on interstate commerce."

The Court also found no justification for the civil remedy provision in the Fourteenth Amendment. Section 5 of the amendment permits Congress to enforce through legislation the DUE PROCESS, EQUAL PROTECTION, and PRIVILEGES AND IMMUNITIES rights guaranteed individuals. The Amendment, however, is directed against the actions of state governments. Proponents of the civil remedy provision contended that state justice systems exhibited bias against victims of gender-motivated violence. Rehnquist rejected this argument, pointing out that the law attempted to deal with the private conduct of the attackers, not the bias of state justice systems. Therefore, victims of sexual assault could seek justice by filing civil lawsuits in state courts.

Justice DAVID H. SOUTER, in a dissenting opinion joined by Justices JOHN PAUL STEVENS, RUTH BADER GINSBURG, and STEPHEN G. BREYER, contended that Congress had a rational basis for enacting the civil remedy provision. The Court's rejection of the link between sexual violence and interstate commerce was shortsighted and appeared reminiscent of the period leading up to the 1930s, when the Supreme Court struck down economic regulation laws because it disagreed with Congress about how the economy should be managed. Souter suggested that the majority's approach would not be "enduring law."

CROSS REFERENCES
Commerce Clause; Fourteenth Amendment; Parent and Child; Reproduction; Sentencing

WRONGFUL DEATH

The taking of the life of an individual resulting from the willful or negligent act of another person or persons.

Waco Victims' Family Members Sue Federal Government

On February 18, 1993, federal ALCOHOL, TOBACCO, AND FIREARMS (ATF) officials, along with several local and state public safety officers, approached the Branch Davidian residential compound known as "Mount Carmel" in Waco, Texas. They demanded surrender of the occupants for weapons violations and other illegal activities. After Davidian religious leader David Koresh and his followers inside the compound shot and killed four ATF agents, a state of emergency "stand-off" between the parties dragged on for the next fifty-one days.

The crisis ended on April 19, 1993, when agents and officials from several state and federal organizations surrounded the compound and again demanded surrender. When their request was ignored, they began firing tear gas canisters into the compound, while deploying military tanks to move forward and crush the surrounding walls. No one exited the building, and it burst into flames. Officials later discovered the bodies of Koresh and at least eighty of his followers inside the ruins. They had died either of self-inflicted gunshot wounds or from the fire. Although they initially denied it, FEDERAL BUREAU OF INVESTIGATION (FBI) officials later acknowledged that isolated pyrotechnic tear gas devices were fired into the compound. This reversal of positions caused Attorney General JANET RENO to appoint John Danforth as Special Counsel to conduct a full investigation into the siege.

A multi-million dollar wrongful death suit was filed against the government by Branch Davidian survivors and family members of the deceased. In addition to the government, one individual was named as a defendant. FBI sharpshooter Lon Horiuchi was accused of firing shots at the Branch Davidians "with excessive force"—that is, without justification. (Coincidentally, Horiuchi was the agent who fired the shots that killed Vicki Weaver and her infant during the 1992 government siege at Ruby Ridge, Idaho.) U.S. District Court Judge Walter Smith, Jr., later ordered the dismissal of Horiuchi from the suit for lack of evidence.

Houston attorneys Michael Caddell and Jim Brannon represented the plaintiffs. U.S. Attorney Mike Bradford was key defense counsel representing the government. Under federal law, Judge Smith would hear the case instead of a jury, because the defendant was the U.S. government.

The two central issues at trial are (1) whether anyone under government control shot at the compound during the fiery ending of the standoff, which the plaintiffs allege constitutes use of "excessive force" under the circumstances and (2) whether government officials were negligent in withholding fire control efforts once flames broke out in the compound. As to the second issue, the plaintiffs have alleged that on-site FBI commanders deviated from the Reno-approved assault plan and failed to contain the fire that broke out. In fact, FBI commander Jeffrey Jamar testified in his deposition that he held fire trucks back from the blaze, for fear that firefighters might be shot.

The government has always maintained that the Davidians died by their own hand, whether by suicidal gunshot or fire. Government ARSON investigators had previously concluded that Davidians deliberately set the fire. This finding may undermine the plaintiffs' ability to establish that the alleged wrongful conduct was the PROXIMATE CAUSE of the injuries suffered. The plaintiffs have countered, however, that even if the fire was set by Davidians, the government was negligent in its failure to control the situation. Furthermore, they claim, the government's forces kept Davidians from escaping the blaze by firing upon them when they attempted to exit.

These three children, along with other survivors of Waco victims, sued the federal government for the 1997 disaster.
GAY/AP/WIDE WORLD PHOTOS

Of key evidentiary importance in the trial are several FBI infrared video tapes that were shot on April 19, 1993, showing repeated rhythmic flashes coming from government positions. Experts for the plaintiffs argued that the tapes supported their theory that the federal government fired upon the Davidians from the remote side of the compound, away from television and media cameras. The government argued that the airborne cameras were too far away to record heat signatures from gunfire and offered expert opinion that the flashes were caused by sunshine reflections.

In March 2000 Judge Smith, at the request of independent counsel John Danforth, ordered a field-test simulation of the last hours at Waco to be conducted at Fort Hood. The data from the simulation would be used by independent scientific experts to determine whether federal officials had fired upon sect members during the final hours of the siege. The British company of Vector Data Systems was retained by Danforth to offer neutral expertise in analyzing both the reenactment data and the original FBI infrared tapes.

One month later Vector Data Systems provided a 65-page written report to Judge Smith, concluding that government agents did not fire upon Branch Davidians during the 1993 siege. Vector found that sunlight reflections from area debris were responsible for causing the flashes captured on the infrared film. Vector justified its opinion by producing evidence that sunlight flashes reflecting from debris were considerably longer in duration than flashes produced by gunfire. When assessing the reenactment data, Vector concluded that any gunfire images picked up by the simulation infrared tapes also picked up the weapons shooters. No such shooters, or for that matter, no government persons, are seen in the actual 1993 tapes. Further, Vector concluded that no Davidians were seen attempting to escape from the compound, excepting one person seen on the roof of the complex—an image that was televised nationally. Judge Smith reminded both sides that Vector's conclusions and opinions constituted "expert opinion," which would be subject to CROSS-EXAMINATION at trial.

Accordingly, the plaintiffs' counsel intended to proceed at trial with retained experts who would testify that the infrared images *were* from government weapons. Defense counsel retained its own experts to coincide with the independent experts' conclusions. Importantly, counsel for the plaintiffs admitted that their experts could not prove that any particular Branch Davidian died from a government bullet. Legally, this may render the entire infrared issue moot at the close of evidence. In order to prevail at trial, the plaintiffs must prove that the alleged wrongful conduct on the part of the government was the proximate cause of death or injury to the Branch Davidians.

Trial of this case began in June 2000.

Appendix

NEBRASKA STATUTE § 28-328

This Nebraska law, one of nearly thirty passed in the United States, made partial birth abortion procedures illegal. The Supreme Court held the law to be unconstitutional in *Stenberg v. Carhart*.

Partial-birth abortion; prohibition; violation; penalties.

(1) No partial-birth abortion shall be performed in this state, unless such procedure is necessary to save the life of the mother whose life is endangered by a physical disorder, physical illness, or physical injury, including a life-endangering physical condition caused by or arising from the pregnancy itself.

(2) The intentional and knowing performance of an unlawful partial-birth abortion in violation of subsection (1) of this section is a Class III felony.

(3) No woman upon whom an unlawful partial-birth abortion is performed shall be prosecuted under this section or for conspiracy to violate this section.

(4) The intentional and knowing performance of an unlawful partial-birth abortion shall result in the automatic suspension and revocation of an attending physician's license to practice medicine in Nebraska by the Director of Regulation and Licensure pursuant to sections 71–147 to 71–161.20.

(5) Upon the filing of criminal charges under this section by the Attorney General or a county attorney, the Attorney General shall also file a petition to suspend and revoke the attending physician's license to practice medicine pursuant to section 71–150. A hearing on such administrative petition shall be set in accordance with section 71–153. At such hearing, the attending physician shall have the opportunity to present evidence that the physician's conduct was necessary to save the life of a mother whose life was endangered by a physical disorder, physical illness, or physical injury, including a life-endangering physical condition caused by or arising from the pregnancy itself. A defendant against whom criminal charges are brought under this section may bring a motion to delay the beginning of the trial until after the entry of an order by the Director of Regulation and Licensure pursuant to section 71–155. The findings of the Director of Regulation and Licensure as to whether the attending physician's conduct was necessary to save the life of a mother whose life was endangered by a physical disorder, physical illness, or physical injury, including a life-endangering physical condition caused by or arising from the pregnancy itself, shall be admissible in the criminal proceedings brought pursuant to this section. . . .

(9) Partial-birth abortion means an abortion procedure in which the person performing the abortion partially delivers vaginally a living unborn child before killing the unborn child and completing the delivery. For purposes of this subdivision, the term partially delivers vaginally a living unborn child before killing the unborn child means deliberately and intentionally delivering into the vagina a living unborn child, or a substantial portion thereof, for the purpose of performing a procedure that the person performing such procedure knows will kill the unborn child and does kill the unborn child.

Utah Child Welfare Amendments

HB 103

Be it enacted by the Legislature of the state of Utah:

78-30-1. Who may adopt—Adoption of minor—Adoption of adult.

(1) Any minor child may be adopted by an adult person, in accordance with the provisions and requirements of this section and this chapter.

(2) Any adult may be adopted by [any other] another adult. However, all provisions of this chapter apply to the adoption of an adult just as though the person being adopted were a minor, except that consent of the parents of an adult person being adopted is not required.

(3) (a) A child may be adopted by:

(i) adults who are legally married to each other in accordance with the laws of this state, including adoption by a stepparent; or

(ii) any single adult, except as provided in Subsection (3)(b).

(b) A child may not be adopted by a person who is cohabiting in a relationship that is not a legally valid and binding marriage under the laws of this state. For purposes of this Subsection (3)(b), "cohabiting" means residing with another person and being involved in a sexual relationship with that person.

Section 6. Section 78-30-1.5 is amended to read:

78-30-1.5. Legislative intent—Best interest of child.

(1) It is the intent and desire of the Legislature that in every adoption the best interest of the child should govern and be of foremost concern in the court's determination.

(2) The court shall make a specific finding regarding the best interest of the child, in accordance with Section 78-30-9 and the provisions of this chapter.

Section 7. Section 78-30-9 is amended to read:

78-30-9. Decree of adoption—Best interest of child—Legislative findings.

(1) The court shall examine each person appearing before it in accordance with this chapter, separately, and, if satisfied that the interests of the child will be promoted by the adoption, it shall enter a final decree of adoption declaring that the child is adopted by the adoptive parent or parents and shall be regarded and treated in all respects as the child of the adoptive parent or parents.

(2) The court shall make a specific finding regarding the best interest of the child, taking into consideration information provided to the court pursuant to the requirements of this chapter relating to the health, safety, and welfare of the child and the moral climate of the potential adoptive placement.

(3) (a) The Legislature specifically finds that it is not in a child's best interest to be adopted by a person or persons who are cohabiting in a relationship that is not a legally valid and binding marriage under the laws of this state. Nothing in this section limits or prohibits the court's placement of a child with a single adult who is not cohabiting as defined in Subsection (3)(b).

(b) For purposes of this section, "cohabiting" means residing with another person and being involved in a sexual relationship with that person.

Section 8. Effective date.

This act takes effect on May 1, 2000, except that Section 78-3g-103 takes effect on July 1, 2000.

FCC Ruling Is "Most Significant Action Since ADA"

Promotes Independence in the New Millennium

Today the FCC adopted rules and policies to implement Section 255 of the Telecommunications Act of 1996 and Section 251(a)(2) of the Communications Act of 1934, that require manufacturers of telecommunications equipment and providers of telecommunications services to ensure that such equipment and services are accessible to and useable by persons with disabilities, if readily achievable. These rules will give people with disabilities access to a broad range of products and services—such as telephones, cell phones, pagers, call-waiting, and operator services, that they cannot use today.

Today's action represents the most significant opportunity for people with disabilities since the passage of the Americans with Disabilities Act in 1990. The rules adopted today require manufacturers and service providers to design telecommunications equipment and services with the needs of people with disabilities in mind. In developing these rules, the FCC relied heavily on the Access Board guidelines for equipment developed pursuant to section 255, months of productive discussions with interested parties from the disability community and industry, and a careful analysis of the appropriate precedent under the ADA and other statutes designed to remove access barriers.

Our nation has an estimated 54 million Americans with disabilities. Persons with disabilities are the largest minority group in the United States, yet despite their numbers, they do not experience equal participation in society.

Access to telecommunications can bring independence. The disability community has told the FCC of the frustration of not being able to check the balance of a checking account using telecommunications relay service, or not being able to tell if a wireless phone is turned on, or not being able to use a calling card because of inadequate time to enter in the appropriate numbers. The FCC has received numerous reports from relatives of senior citizens saying that their elderly parents could live on their own, if only they had telecommunications equipment that they could use.

The benefits of increased accessibility to telecommunications are not limited to people with disabilities. Just as people without disabilities benefit from the universal design principles in the ADA and the Architectural Barriers Act (for example a parent pushing a stroller over a curbcut), many people without disabilities will also benefit from accessible telecommunications equipment and services.

Indeed, many of us already benefit from accessibility features in telecommunications today: vibrating pagers do not disrupt meetings; speaker phones enable us to use our hands for other activities; increased volume control on public pay phones allows us to talk in noisy environments.

The FCC expects many similar results from the rules adopted today. More importantly, we all benefit when people with disabilities become more active in our communities and in society as a whole.

Statistically, most Americans will have a disability, or experience a limitation, at some point in their lives. While 5.3% of persons 15–24 years of age have some kind of functional limitation, 23% of persons in the 45–54 age range experience functional limitation. The percentage of those affected by functional limitations increases with age: 34.2% of those aged 55–64; 45.4% of those aged 65–69; 55.3% for those aged 70–74 and 72.5% for those aged 75 and older. The number of persons with functional limitations will also increase with time. Today, only about 20% of Americans are over age 55, but by the 2050, 35% of our population will be over age 55.

Today, most Americans rely on telecommunications for routine daily activities, for example, to make doctors' appointments, call home when they are late for dinner, participate in conference calls at work, and make an airline reservation. Moreover, diverse telecommunications tools such as distance learning, telemedicine, telecommuting, and video conferencing enable Americans to interface anytime from anywhere. Understanding that communications is now an essential component of American life, Congress intended the 1996 Act to provide people with disabilities access to employment, independence, emergency services, education, and other opportunities.

More specifically, telecommunications is a critical tool for employment. If telecommunications technologies are not accessible to and usable by persons with disabilities, many qualified individuals will not be able to work or achieve their full potential in the workplace. Congress recognized the importance of creating employment opportunities for people with disabilities with Title I of the ADA, which addresses the employer's responsibilities in making the workplace accessible to employees with disabilities.

At a time when Americans are experiencing the lowest unemployment rate in years, unemployment among people with severe disabilities is roughly 73%, and when employed they earn only one-third of people without disabilities. The rules the FCC adopted today give employers expanded tools with which to employ and accommodate persons with disabilities.

Action by the Commission July 14, 1999, by Report and Order (FCC 99–181). Chairman Kennard, Commissioners Ness, and Tristani, with Commissioners Furchtgott-Roth and Powell approving in part and dissenting in part and all five issuing separate statements. Commissioner Furchtgott-Roth statement will be issued at a later date.

Report No. WT-22

Docket WT 96-198

Executive Order 13145

To Prohibit Discrimination in Federal Employment Based on Genetic Information

By the authority vested in me as President of the United States by the Constitution and the laws of the United States of America, it is ordered as follows:

Section 1. Nondiscrimination in Federal Employment on the Basis of Protected Genetic Information.

1–101. It is the policy of the Government of the United States to provide equal employment opportunity in Federal employment for all qualified persons and to prohibit discrimination against employees based on protected genetic information, or information about a request for or the receipt of genetic services. This policy of equal opportunity applies to every aspect of Federal employment.

1–102. The head of each Executive department and agency shall extend the policy set forth in section 1–101 to all its employees covered by section 717 of Title VII of the Civil Rights Act of 1964, as amended (42 U.S.C. 2000e-16).

1–103. Executive departments and agencies shall carry out the provisions of this order to the extent permitted by law and consistent with their statutory and regulatory authorities, and their enforcement mechanisms. The Equal Employment Opportunity Commission shall be responsible for coordinating the policy of the Government of the United States to prohibit discrimination against employees in Federal employment based on protected genetic information, or information about a request for or the receipt of genetic services.

Sec. 2. Requirements Applicable to Employing Departments and Agencies.

1–201. Definitions.

(a) The term "employee" shall include an employee, applicant for employment, or former employee covered by section 717 of the Civil Rights Act of 1964, as amended (42 U.S.C. 2000e-16).

(b) Genetic monitoring means the periodic examination of employees to evaluate acquired modifications to their genetic material, such as chromosomal damage or evidence of increased occurrence of mutations, that may have developed in the course of employment due to exposure to toxic substances in the workplace, in order to identify, evaluate, respond to the effects of, or control adverse environmental exposures in the workplace.

(c) Genetic services means health services, including genetic tests, provided to obtain, assess, or interpret genetic information for diagnostic or therapeutic purposes, or for genetic education or counseling.

(d) Genetic test means the analysis of human DNA, RNA, chromosomes, proteins, or certain metabolites in order to detect disease-related genotypes or mutations. Tests for metabolites fall within the definition of "genetic tests" when an excess or deficiency of the metabolites indicates the presence of a mutation or mutations. The conducting of metabolic tests by a department or agency that are not intended to reveal the presence of a mutation shall not be considered a violation of this order, regardless of the results of the tests. Test results revealing a mutation shall, however, be subject to the provisions of this order.

(e) Protected genetic information.

(1) In general, protected genetic information means:

(A) information about an individual's genetic tests;

(B) information about the genetic tests of an individual's family members; or

(C) information about the occurrence of a disease, or medical condition or disorder in family members of the individual.

(2) Information about an individual's current health status (including information about sex, age, physical exams, and chemical, blood, or urine analyses) is not protected genetic information unless it is described in subparagraph (1).

1–202. In discharging their responsibilities under this order, departments and agencies shall implement the following nondiscrimination requirements.

(a) The employing department or agency shall not discharge, fail or refuse to hire, or otherwise discriminate against any employee with respect to the compensation, terms, conditions, or privileges of employment of that employee, because of protected genetic information with respect to the employee, or because of information about a request for or the receipt of genetic services by such employee.

(b) The employing department or agency shall not limit, segregate, or classify employees in any way that would deprive or tend to deprive any employee of employment opportunities or otherwise adversely affect that employee's status, because of protected genetic information with respect to the employee or because of information about a request for or the receipt of genetic services by such employee.

(c) The employing department or agency shall not request, require, collect, or purchase protected genetic information with respect to an employee, or information about a request for or the receipt of genetic services by such employee.

(d) The employing department or agency shall not disclose protected genetic information with respect to an employee, or information about a request for or the receipt of genetic services by an employee except:

(1) to the employee who is the subject of the information, at his or her request;

(2) to an occupational or other health researcher, if the research conducted complies with the regulations and protections provided for under part 46 of title 45, of the Code of Federal Regulations;

(3) if required by a Federal statute, congressional subpoena, or an order issued by a court of competent jurisdiction, except that if the subpoena or court order was secured without the knowledge of the individual to whom the information refers, the employer shall provide the individual with adequate notice to challenge the subpoena or court order, unless the subpoena or court order also imposes confidentiality requirements; or

(4) to executive branch officials investigating compliance with this order, if the information is relevant to the investigation.

(e) The employing department or agency shall not maintain protected genetic information or information about a request for or the receipt of genetic services in general personnel files; such information shall be treated as confidential medical records and kept separate from personnel files.

Sec. 3. Exceptions.

1–301. The following exceptions shall apply to the nondiscrimination requirements set forth in section 1–202.

(a) The employing department or agency may request or require information defined in section 1–201(e)(1)(C) with respect to an applicant who has been given a conditional offer of employment or to an employee if:

(1) the request or requirement is consistent with the Rehabilitation Act and other applicable law;

(2) the information obtained is to be used exclusively to assess whether further medical evaluation is needed to diagnose a current disease, or medical condition or disorder, or under the terms of section 1–301(b) of this order;

(3) such current disease, or medical condition or disorder could prevent the applicant or employee from performing the essential functions of the position held or desired; and

(4) the information defined in section 1–201(e)(1)(C) of this order will not be disclosed to persons other than medical personnel involved in or responsible for assessing whether further medical evaluation is needed to diagnose a current disease, or medical condition or disorder, or under the terms of section 1–301(b) of this order.

(b) The employing department or agency may request, collect, or purchase protected genetic information with respect to an employee, or any information about a request for or receipt of genetic services by such employee if:

(1) the employee uses genetic or health care services provided by the employer (other than use pursuant to section 1–301(a) of this order);

(2) the employee who uses the genetic or health care services has provided prior knowing, voluntary, and written authorization to the employer to collect protected genetic information;

(3) the person who performs the genetic or health care services does not disclose protected genetic information to anyone except to the employee who uses the services for treatment of the individual; pursuant to section 1–202(d) of this order; for program evaluation or assessment; for compiling and analyzing information in anticipation of or for use in a civil or criminal legal proceeding; or, for payment or accounting purposes, to verify that the service was performed (but in such cases the genetic information itself cannot be disclosed);

(4) such information is not used in violation of sections 1–202(a) or 1–202(b) of this order.

(c) The employing department or agency may collect protected genetic information with respect to an employee if the requirements of part 46 of title 45 of the Code of Federal Regulations are met.

(d) Genetic monitoring of biological effects of toxic substances in the workplace shall be permitted if all of the following conditions are met:

(1) the employee has provided prior, knowing, voluntary, and written authorization;

(2) the employee is notified when the results of the monitoring are available and, at that time, the employer makes any protected genetic information that may have been acquired during the monitoring available to the employee and informs the employee how to obtain such information;

(3) the monitoring conforms to any genetic monitoring regulations that may be promulgated by the Secretary of Labor; and

(4) the employer, excluding any licensed health care professionals that are involved in the genetic monitoring program, receives results of the monitoring only in aggregate terms that do not disclose the identity of specific employees.

(e) This order does not limit the statutory authority of a Federal department or agency to:

(1) promulgate or enforce workplace safety and health laws and regulations;

(2) conduct or sponsor occupational or other health research that is conducted in compliance with regulations at part 46 of title 45, of the Code of Federal Regulations; or

(3) collect protected genetic information as a part of a lawful program, the primary purpose of which is to carry out identification purposes.

Sec. 4. Miscellaneous.

1–401. The head of each department and agency shall take appropriate action to disseminate this policy and, to this end, shall designate a high level official responsible for carrying out its responsibilities under this order.

1–402. Nothing in this order shall be construed to:

(a) limit the rights or protections of an individual under the Rehabilitation Act of 1973 (29 U.S.C. 701, et seq.), the Privacy Act of 1974 (5 U.S.C. 552a), or other applicable law; or

(b) require specific benefits for an employee or dependent under the Federal Employees Health Benefits Program or similar program.

1–403. This order clarifies and makes uniform Administration policy and does not create any right or benefit, substantive or procedural, enforceable at law by a party against the United States, its officers or employees, or any other person.

THE WHITE HOUSE,
February 8, 2000.

Weatherhead Letter

George W. Proctor Esq.

Director

US Department of Justice

Office of International Affairs

Criminal Division

Bond Building, Room 5100

1400 New York Avenue, NW

Washington, DC 20005

28 July 1994

Dear Mr. Proctor:

EXTRADITION OF SUSAN HAGAN AND SALLY CROFT TO THE UNITED STATES

Following the return of Susan Hagan and Sally Croft to the United States yesterday, there are a number of aspects of the case about which we have undertaken to write to you.

For the record, and as I believe your office is already aware, there is no English equivalent of the US offense of interstate transportation of firearms which appears in the US indictment. Thus by virtue of Article XII of the UK/US Extradition Treaty Ms. Hagan and Ms. Croft cannot be detained or proceeded against in the United States in respect of that offense.

As you will know Ms. Hagan and Ms. Croft and others, including prominent members of both Houses of Parliament, have expressed fears that they will not receive a fair trial in Oregon because of the age of the alleged offense, the nature of the evidence against them (obtained, so it appears, from plea bargains), and alleged continuing prejudice against members or former members of the Rajneesh community. Ms. Hagan and Ms. Croft had asked the Home Secretary to seek an undertaking with the United States Government that the place of trial be moved to another, neutral, state. The Home Secretary declined to do so because the place of trial is, of course, for U.S. authorities to decide. However, he did undertake to pass these concerns on to the U.S. authorities, and this letter fulfills that commitment.

Although judgment went strongly against Ms. Hagan and Ms. Croft on 27 July (we shall send you a copy as soon as a transcript is available), we would wish to stress the Home Secretary's concern that questions of local prejudice are examined most carefully by all those concerned with the trial process. This case has attracted an unprecedented degree of Parliamentary, public and media attention in this country. There will inevitably continue to be a great deal of concern expressed about the case by supporters of Ms. Hagan and Ms. Croft, both inside and outside Parliament. There are highly likely to be Parliamentary debates about it in October or November, after the summer Recess, possibly resulting in votes condemning the Home Secretary's actions. The British Cosul in Seattle will be taking a close interest in the progress of the trial. But particularly in view of the almost inevitable Parliamentary debate, I would be most grateful if you would ensure that we are kept in very close touch with developments.

Yours Sincerely,

Alison Rutherford

Driver's Privacy Protection Act of 1994

Public Law 103-322, Chapter 123

Prohibition on Release and Use of Certain Personal Information from State Motor Vehicle Records

Sec. 2721. Prohibition on release and use of certain personal information from State motor vehicle records

(a) IN GENERAL—Except as provided in subsection (b), a State department of motor vehicles, and any officer, employee, or contractor, thereof, shall not knowingly disclose or otherwise make available to any person or entity personal information about any individual obtained by the department in connection with a motor vehicle record.

(b) PERMISSIBLE USES—Personal information referred to in subsection (a) shall be disclosed for use in connection with matters of motor vehicle or driver safety and theft, motor vehicle emissions, motor vehicle product alterations, recalls, or advisories, performance monitoring of motor vehicles and dealers by motor vehicle manufacturers, and removal of non-owner records from the original owner records of motor vehicle manufacturers to carry out the purposes of the Automobile Information Disclosure Act, the Motor Vehicle Information and Cost Saving Act, the National Traffic and Motor Vehicle Safety Act of 1966, the Anti-Car Theft Act of 1992, and the Clean Air Act, and may be disclosed as follows:

(1) For use by any government agency, including any court or law enforcement agency, in carrying out its functions, or any private person or entity acting on behalf of a Federal, State, or local agency in carrying out its functions.

(2) For use in connection with matters of motor vehicle or driver safety and theft; motor vehicle emissions; motor vehicle product alterations, recalls, or advisories; performance monitoring of motor vehicles, motor vehicle parts and dealers; motor vehicle market research activities, including survey research; and removal of non-owner records from the original owner records of motor vehicle manufacturers.

(3) For use in the normal course of business by a legitimate business or its agents, employees, or contractors, but only—

(A) to verify the accuracy of personal information submitted by the individual to the business or its agents, employees, or contractors; and

(B) if such information as so submitted is not correct or is no longer correct, to obtain the correct information, but only for the purposes of preventing fraud by, pursuing legal remedies against, or recovering on a debt or security interest against, the individual.

(4) For use in connection with any civil, criminal, administrative, or arbitral proceeding in any Federal, State, or local court or agency or before any self-regulatory body, including the service of process, investigation in anticipation of litigation, and the execution or enforcement of judgments and orders, or pursuant to an order of a Federal, State, or local court.

(5) For use in research activities, and for use in producing statistical reports, so long as the personal information is not published, redisclosed, or used to contact individuals.

(6) For use by any insurer or insurance support organization, or by a self-insured entity, or its agents, employees, or contractors, in connection with claims investigation activities, anti-fraud activities, rating or underwriting.

(7) For use in providing notice to the owners of towed or impounded vehicles.

(8) For use by any licensed private investigative agency or licensed security service for any purpose permitted under this subsection.

(9) For use by an employer or its agent or insurer to obtain or verify information relating to a holder of a commercial driver's license that is required under the Commercial Motor Vehicle Safety Act of 1986 (49 U.S.C. App. 2710 et seq.).

(10) For use in connection with the operation of private toll transportation facilities.

(11) For any other use in response to requests for individual motor vehicle records if the motor vehicle department has provided in a clear and conspicuous manner on forms for issuance or renewal of operator's permits, titles, registrations, or identification cards, notice that personal information collected by the department may be disclosed to any business or person, and has provided in a clear and conspicuous manner on such forms an opportunity to prohibit such disclosures.

(12) For bulk distribution for surveys, marketing or solicitations if the motor vehicle department has implemented methods and procedures to ensure that—

(A) individuals are provided an opportunity, in a clear and conspicuous manner, to prohibit such uses; and

(B) the information will be used, rented, or sold solely for bulk distribution for surveys, marketing, and solicitations, and that surveys, marketing, and solicitations will not be directed at those individuals who have requested in a timely fashion that they not be directed at them.

(13) For use by any requester, if the requester demonstrates it has obtained the written consent of the individual to whom the information pertains.

(14) For any other use specifically authorized under the law of the State that holds the record, if such use is related to the operation of a motor vehicle or public safety.

(c) RESALE OR REDISCLOSURE—An authorized recipient of personal information (except a recipient under subsection (b)(11) or (12)) may resell or redisclose the information only for a use permitted under subsection (b) (but not for uses under subsection (b) (11) or (12)). An authorized recipient under subsection (b)(11) may resell or redisclose personal information for any purpose. An authorized recipient under subsection (b)(12) may resell or redisclose personal information pursuant to subsection (b)(12). Any authorized recipient (except a recipient under subsection (b)(11)) that resells or rediscloses personal information covered by this title must keep for a period of 5 years records identifying each person or entity that receives information and the permitted purpose for which the information will be used and must make such records available to the motor vehicle department upon request.

(d) WAIVER PROCEDURES—A State motor vehicle department may establish and carry out procedures under which the department or its agents, upon receiving a request for personal information that does not fall within one of the exceptions in subsection (b), may mail a copy of the request to the individual about whom the information was requested, informing such individual of the request, together with a statement to the effect that the information will not be released unless the individual waives such individual's right to privacy under this section.

Sec. 2722. Additional unlawful acts

(a) PROCUREMENT FOR UNLAWFUL PURPOSE—It shall be unlawful for any person knowingly to obtain or disclose personal information, from a motor vehicle record, for any use not permitted under section 2721(b) of this title.

(b) FALSE REPRESENTATION—It shall be unlawful for any person to make false representation to obtain any personal information from an individual's motor vehicle record.

Sec. 2723. Penalties

(a) CRIMINAL FINE—A person who knowingly violates this chapter shall be fined under this title.

(b) VIOLATIONS BY STATE DEPARTMENT OF MOTOR VEHICLES—Any State department of motor vehicles that has a policy or practice of substantial noncompliance with this chapter shall be subject to a civil penalty imposed by the Attorney General of not more than $5,000 a day for each day of substantial noncompliance.

Sec. 2724. Civil action

(a) CAUSE OF ACTION—A person who knowingly obtains, discloses or uses personal information, from a motor vehicle record, for a purpose not permitted under this chapter shall be liable to the individual to whom the information pertains, who may bring a civil action in a United States district court.

(b) REMEDIES—The court may award—

(1) actual damages, but not less than liquidated damages in the amount of $2,500;

(2) punitive damages upon proof of willful or reckless disregard of the law;

(3) reasonable attorneys' fees and other litigation costs reasonably incurred; and

(4) such other preliminary and equitable relief as the court determines to be appropriate.

Sec. 2725. Definitions

In this chapter—

(1) 'motor vehicle record' means any record that pertains to a motor vehicle operator's permit, motor vehicle title, motor vehicle registration, or identification card issued by a department of motor vehicles;

(2) 'person' means an individual, organization or entity, but does not include a State or agency thereof; and

(3) 'personal information' means information that identifies an individual, including an individual's photograph, social security number, driver identification number, name, address (but not the 5-digit zip code), telephone number, and medical or disability information, but does not include information on vehicular accidents, driving violations, and driver's status.'.

(b) CLERICAL AMENDMENT—The table of parts at the beginning of part I of title 18, United States Code, is amended by adding at the end the following new item: 2271

SEC. 300003. EFFECTIVE DATE.

The amendments made by section 300002 shall become effective on the date that is 3 years after the date of enactment of this Act. After the effective date, if a State has implemented a procedure under section 2721(b) (11) and (12) of title 18, United States Code, as added by section 2902, for prohibiting disclosures or uses of personal information, and the procedure otherwise meets the requirements of subsection (b) (11) and (12), the State shall be in compliance with subsection (b) (11) and (12) even if the procedure is not available to individuals until they renew their license, title, registration or identification card, so long as the State provides some other procedure for individuals to contact the State on their own initiative to prohibit such uses or disclosures. Prior to the effective date, personal information covered by the amendment made by section 300002 may be released consistent with State law or practice.

MICHIGAN PENAL CODE, ACT 328 OF 1931

750.337 Women and children; improper language in presence.

[M.S.A. 28.569]

Sec. 337. Indecent, etc., language in presence of women or children—Any person who shall use any indecent, immoral, obscene, vulgar or insulting language in the presence or hearing of any woman or child shall be guilty of a misdemeanor.

History: 1931, Act 328, Eff. Sept. 18, 1931;—CL 1948, 750.337.

Former Law: See section 1 of Act 219 of 1897, being CL 1897, § 11737; CL 1915, § 15533; and CL 1929, § 16888.

OHIO'S ANTI-PORNOGRAPHY LAW

Under provisions of this law, an Ohio mother was prosecuted in 1999 for taking nude and allegedly provocative photos of her child. She was reported to law enforcement authorities by the processing lab. A similar case involving a grandmother occurred in New Jersey in March 2000.

Section 2907.322

General Assembly: 121.

Bill Number: Amended Sub. S.B. 2

Effective Date: 07/01/96

(A) No person, with knowledge of the character of the material or performance involved, shall do any of the following:

(1) Create, record, photograph, film, develop, reproduce, or publish any material that shows a minor participating or engaging in sexual activity, masturbation, or bestiality;

(2) Advertise for sale or dissemination, sell, distribute, transport, disseminate, exhibit, or display any material that shows a minor participating or engaging in sexual activity, masturbation, or bestiality;

(3) Create, direct, or produce a performance that shows a minor participating or engaging in sexual activity, masturbation, or bestiality;

(4) Advertise for presentation, present, or participate in presenting a performance that shows a minor participating or engaging in sexual activity, masturbation, or bestiality;

(5) Solicit, receive, purchase, exchange, possess or control any material that shows a minor participating or engaging in sexual activity, masturbation, or bestiality;

(6) Bring or cause to be brought into this state any material that shows a minor participating or engaging in sexual activity, masturbation, or bestiality, or bring, cause to be brought, or finance the bringing of any minor into or across this state with the intent that the minor engage in sexual activity, masturbation, or bestiality in a performance or for the purpose of producing material containing a visual representation depicting the minor engaged in sexual activity, masturbation, or bestiality.

(B)(1) This section does not apply to any material or performance that is sold, disseminated, displayed, possessed, controlled, brought or caused to be brought into this state, or presented for a bona fide medical, scientific, educational, religious, governmental, judicial, or other proper purpose, by or to a physician, psychologist, sociologist, scientist, teacher, person pursuing bona fide studies or research, librarian, clergyman, prosecutor, judge, or other person having a proper interest in the material or performance.

(2) Mistake of age is not a defense to a charge under this section.

(3) In a prosecution under this section, the trier of fact may infer that a person in the material or performance involved is a minor if the material or performance, through its title, text, visual representation, or otherwise, represents or depicts the person as a minor.

(C) Whoever violates this section is guilty of pandering sexually oriented matter involving a minor. Violation of division (A)(1), (2), (3), (4), or (6) of this section is a felony of the second degree. Violation of division (A)(5) of this section is a felony of the fifth degree. If the offender previously has been convicted of or pleaded guilty to a violation of this section or section 2907.321 or 2907.323 of the Revised Code, pandering sexually oriented matter involving a minor in violation of division (A)(5) of this section is a felony of the fourth degree.

Section 2907.323

General Assembly: 121.

Bill Number: Amended Sub. S.B. 2

Effective Date: 07/01/96

(A) No person shall do any of the following:

(1) Photograph any minor who is not the person's child or ward in a state of nudity, or create, direct, produce, or transfer any material or performance that shows the minor in a state of nudity, unless both of the following apply:

(a) The material or performance is, or is to be, sold, disseminated, displayed, possessed, controlled, brought or caused to be brought into this state, or presented for a bona fide artistic, medical, scientific, educational, religious, governmental, judicial, or other proper purpose, by or to a physician, psychologist, sociologist, scientist, teacher, person pursuing bona fide studies or research, librarian, clergyman, prosecutor, judge, or other person having a proper interest in the material or performance;

(b) The minor's parents, guardian, or custodian consents in writing to the photographing of the minor, to the use of the minor in the material or performance, or to the transfer of the material and to the specific manner in which the material or performance is to be used.

(2) Consent to the photographing of the person's minor child or ward, or photograph the person's minor child or ward, in a state of nudity or consent to the use of the person's minor child or ward in a state of nudity in any material or performance, or use or transfer a material or performance of that nature, unless the material or performance is sold, disseminated, displayed, possessed, controlled, brought or caused to be brought into this state, or presented for a bona fide artistic, medical, scientific, educational, religious, governmental, judicial, or other proper purpose, by or to a physician, psychologist, sociologist, scientist, teacher, person pursuing bona fide studies or research, librarian, clergyman, prosecutor, judge, or other person having a proper interest in the material or performance;

(3) Possess or view any material or performance that shows a minor who is not the person's child or ward in a state of nudity, unless one of the following applies:

(a) The material or performance is sold, disseminated, displayed, possessed, controlled, brought or caused to be brought into this state, or presented for a bona fide artistic, medical, scientific, educational, religious, governmental, judicial, or other proper purpose, by or to a physician, psychologist, sociologist, scientist, teacher, person pursuing bona fide studies or research, librarian, clergyman, prosecutor, judge, or other person having a proper interest in the material or performance.

(b) The person knows that the parents, guardian, or custodian has consented in writing to the photographing or use of the minor in a state of nudity and to the manner in which the material or performance is used or transferred.

(B) Whoever violates this section is guilty of illegal use of a minor in a nudity-oriented material or performance. Whoever violates division (A)(1) or (2) of this section is guilty of a felony of the second degree. Whoever violates division (A)(3) of this section is guilty of a felony of the fifth degree. If the offender previously has been convicted of or pleaded guilty to a violation of this section or section 2907.321 or 2907.322 of the Revised Code, illegal use of a minor in a nudity-oriented material or performance in violation of division (A)(3) of this section is a felony of the fourth degree.

Colorado's "Bubble" Law

This Colorado law sought to provide staff and patients entering abortion clinics with an area of space that could not be knowingly entered by protesters to put forth their arguments or otherwise engage the individual within the space, as well as a safety zone for the clinic itself. The law was challenged by abortion foes, but the Supreme Court upheld the law by a 6–3 vote.

18-9-122.

Preventing passage to and from a health care facility—engaging in prohibited activities near facility.

(1) The general assembly recognizes that access to health care facilities for the purpose of obtaining medical counseling and treatment is imperative for the citizens of this state; that the exercise of a person's right to protest or counsel against certain medical procedures must be balanced against another person's right to obtain medical counseling and treatment in an unobstructed manner; and that preventing the willful obstruction of a person's access to medical counseling and treatment at a health care facility is a matter of statewide concern. The general assembly therefore declares that it is appropriate to enact legislation that prohibits a person from knowingly obstructing another person's entry to or exit from a health care facility.

(2) A person commits a class 3 misdemeanor if such person knowingly obstructs, detains, hinders, impedes, or blocks another person's entry to or exit from a health care facility.

(3) No person shall knowingly approach another person within eight feet of such person, unless such other person consents, for the purpose of passing a leaflet or handbill to, displaying a sign to, or engaging in oral protest, education, or counseling with such other person in the public way or sidewalk area within a radius of one hundred feet from any entrance door to a health care facility. Any person who violates this subsection (3) commits a class 3 misdemeanor.

(4) For the purposes of this section, "health care facility" means any entity that is licensed, certified, or otherwise authorized or permitted by law to administer medical treatment in this state.

(5) Nothing in this section shall be construed to prohibit a statutory or home rule city or county or city and county from adopting a law for the control of access to health care facilities that is no less restrictive than the provisions of this section.

(6) In addition to, and not in lieu of, the penalties set forth in this section, a person who violates the provisions of this section shall be subject to civil liability, as provided in section 13–21–106.7, C.R.S.

Remarks by Former President Jimmy Carter at a Ceremony Marking the Transfer of the Panama Canal

Panama City, Panama

December 14, 1999

I am honored to represent the United States of America and to head a distinguished delegation sent here to represent the people of my country and our government. This is indeed an historic occasion, perhaps one of the most significant that has ever occurred in this hemisphere. It is important to understand what has happened in the past in order to understand the present, in which we've just delivered officially the Canal to Panama and to lay the groundwork for the future.

I think it's appropriate to congratulate some of the heroes of the past. Our own President Theodore Roosevelt, who had the vision to encompass this enormous undertaking and George Goethals, a great engineer who could see how to accomplish an unprecedented achievement in his field and who had the foresight to design a Panama Canal control system that does not cause us any concern about the Y2K bug in the next few days.

Thousands of people—representing 97 countries on earth—died in this construction job. Most of them, of course, were from Panama and the Caribbean. And it was William Gorgas who developed a health program that benefitted not only the completion of this project, but also benefitted the world.

From the first, the 1903 Panama Canal Treaty created controversy. The text of the treaty before it was signed was never seen by the citizens of Panama. There were phrases in it, drafted in the United States, that were designed to be clear, but were never completely understood. One phrase was "control" of the Panama Canal Zone, as though the United States had sovereign rights. This did not give sovereignty to the United States, though many of my countrymen interpret it in that fashion. What we accomplished here was a source of great pride in my country from the time I was a child until I became President of the United States and even now. But we didn't understand clearly enough the feeling of many Panamanians that the arrangements implied an element of colonialism and subjugation and was not an equal representation of leaders from two sovereign countries. This created a controversy that later presidents needed to address.

Under President Eisenhower, as far back as 1953, there was a discussion about sovereignty and the flying of the U.S. flag in certain places in what was known as the Canal Zone. Then in 1964, when President Lyndon B. Johnson was president, there was a violent confrontation over the flying of the flag. Twenty-four people were killed. Panama broke diplomatic relations with the United States and many other Latin American countries threatened to follow suit. President Johnson wisely told the Panamanians, "we will begin to negotiate a new, responsible, and fair treaty." He failed to do so and that task and obligation was inherited by Richard Nixon and then by Gerald Ford. When I came into office early in 1977, we had lost the delicate balance and sense of mutual respect and cooperation that was important for the safety and proper operation of the Panama Canal.

I turned to some distinguished Americans to represent me, one of whom is here today, Sol Linowitz, and the assistant Ellsworth Bunker, and on the Panamanian side, Ambassadors Royo and Escobar (Rómulo). Also, I worked very closely with Omar Torrijos.

In my country and in Panama, there were then demagogues who made false statements, exaggerated problems, or predicted catastrophes to upset and disturb the people of my country. Unfortunately, in my nation today, there are still a few of those who are planting improper, incorrect, and false stories about the security of the canal and how well it is being operated.

We turned to a bipartisan phalanx of supporters for a new, fair, and mutually conducted treaty that would bind our countries together. I had good supporters on the democratic party side and good bipartisan support: Richard Nixon helped me; Gerald Ford helped me; Henry Kissinger helped me; Howard Baker, Republican leader in the Senate, helped me; David Rockefeller helped me; and perhaps the best support I had from the conservative side of the political picture was John Wayne.

Finally, the issue came to a vote in the U.S. Senate. Under our Constitution, a two-thirds majority is required to ratify a treaty. Finally, we had a vote: 52 Democrats voted in favor of the treaty—82% of the total Democrats; 16 Republicans voted for the treaty—42% of the total Republicans. Showing, I believe, one of the finest examples of political courage ever seen in the history of my nation.

This was not a popular treaty, particularly for those who felt most fervently about it. For instance, of the 20 senators who voted for the treaty, who also ran for re-election the next November, only seven came back the following January to serve in the Senate.

After the treaty was ratified by the Senate, I went to Panama. Hundreds of thousands of people were there for a ceremony to exchange the documents. I had a private meeting then with Omar Torrijos because I was concerned about some other things in this country. We talked about enhancement of human rights. We talked about the return of those who were in political exile, including presidential candidates on three or four occasions. We talked about the need for a free press in Panama and for the organization of elections that would be conducted by independent political parties.

Omar Torrijos agreed with me that these things should be done. Following this, 20 years ago, the Panama Canal Zone was abolished and there was no longer any dividing line between the two parts of Panama, which in reality always had been only one.

Today, we come together, as you have just witnessed, with a spirit of mutual respect, acknowledging without question, the complete sovereignty of Panama over this region—with the Canal operated superbly; with its organization in the hands of those who have even improved the quality of its operation in recent days; and with real democracy in Panama, with an honest election and then another freely conceded by those who were defeated and served well by those who succeeded.

Panama has done some interesting things already. The United States had something like state socialism here in that the government operated everything. Panama has decided to go a different, very interesting route—to establish free enterprise with private investors coming into what was the canal zone area to operate on a competitive basis. They are already doing this. Panama also has set up an International Advisory Commission made up of important leaders from nations that use the canal services.

A second treaty will go into effect at the beginning of the next millennium, the next century. It gives the United States the right and the obligation to defend the canal from any external threat. But it always has been understood that this would be done only in conjunction with, in cooperation with, and at the request of Panama, if that is forthcoming. Our ships also have a right to go to the head of the line in case there is an emergency that threatens the security of my country.

Let me conclude by saying that Panama not only has inherited the canal, but has inherited some challenges. There is always some threat to security. I think it is much less now than it has been in the past. There is always the threat of drug trafficking. That was here when we were in control; it's here today. There is a serious threat to the environment. The watershed behind me has to continue to provide adequate fresh water. So that the ships can go through this Canal, it takes fifty-two million gallons of water, fresh water that goes into the sea to transit one ship. And there is still some question of unexploded ordnance. The United States used some areas for target practice. When President Clinton met with President Moscoso, they discussed this, and there is a pledge to address this adequately in the future.

Well, I think it is a wonderful opportunity for the United States to realize the great potential of this canal, not only for Panama, but for the rest of the world. We want to be part of the economic development of the canal area, to see Panama become, in effect, the Singapore of this hemisphere in leadership, experimentation, commerce, education, and tourism.

We must honor the past. I tried to do that this morning. But we must pledge the United States of America to be a full partner, a harmonious partner, an equal partner, in answering any request that comes from Panama to make the operations of the Canal even greater in the next millennium. Thank you very much.

ABBREVIATIONS

A.	Atlantic Reporter
A. 2d	Atlantic Reporter, Second Series
AA	Alcoholics Anonymous
AAA	American Arbitration Association; Agricultural Adjustment Act of 1933
AALS	Association of American Law Schools
AAPRP	All African People's Revolutionary Party
AARP	American Association of Retired Persons
AAS	American Anti-Slavery Society
ABA	American Bar Association; Architectural Barriers Act of 1968; American Bankers Association
ABM Treaty	Anti-Ballistic Missile Treaty of 1972; antiballistic missile
ABVP	Anti-Biased Violence Project
A/C	account
AC.	appeal cases
ACAA	Air Carrier Access Act
ACF	Administration for Children and Families
ACLU	American Civil Liberties Union
ACRS	Accelerated Cost Recovery System
ACS	Agricultural Cooperative Service
ACT	American College Test
Act'g Legal Adv.	Acting Legal Advisor
ACUS	Administrative Conference of the United States
ACYF	Administration on Children, Youth, and Families
A.D. 2d	Appellate Division, Second Series, N.Y.
ADA	Americans with Disabilities Act of 1990
ADAMHA	Alcohol, Drug Abuse, and Mental Health Administration
ADC	Aid to Dependent Children
ADD	Administration on Developmental Disabilities
ADEA	Age Discrimination in Employment Act of 1967
ADL	Anti-Defamation League
ADR	alternative dispute resolution
AEC	Atomic Energy Commission
AECB	Arms Export Control Board
AEDPA	Antiterrorism and Effective Death Penalty Act
A.E.R.	All England Law Reports
AFA	American Family Association; Alabama Freethought Association

AFB	American Farm Bureau
AFBF	American Farm Bureau Federation
AFDC	Aid to Families with Dependent Children
aff'd per cur.	affirmed by the court
AFIS	automated fingerprint identification system
AFL	American Federation of Labor
AFL-CIO	American Federation of Labor and Congress of Industrial Organizations
AFRes	Air Force Reserve
AFSC	American Friends Service Committee
AFSCME	American Federation of State, County, and Municipal Employees
AGRICOLA	Agricultural Online Access
AIA	Association of Insurance Attorneys
AIB	American Institute for Banking
AID	artificial insemination using a third-party donor's sperm; Agency for International Development
AIDS	acquired immune deficiency syndrome
AIH	artificial insemination using the husband's sperm
AIM	American Indian Movement
AIPAC	American Israel Public Affairs Committee
AIUSA	Amnesty International, U.S.A. Affiliate
AJS	American Judicature Society
Alcoa	Aluminum Company of America
ALEC	American Legislative Exchange Council
ALF	Animal Liberation Front
ALI	American Law Institute
ALJ	administrative law judge
All E.R.	All England Law Reports
ALO	Agency Liaison
A.L.R.	American Law Reports
AMA	American Medical Association
AMAA	Agricultural Marketing Agreement Act
Am. Dec.	American Decisions
amdt.	amendment
Amer. St. Papers, For. Rels.	American State Papers, Legislative and Executive Documents of the Congress of the U.S., Class I, Foreign Relations, 1832-1859
AMS	Agricultural Marketing Service
AMVETS	American Veterans of World War II
ANA	Administration for Native Americans
Ann. Dig.	Annual Digest of Public International Law Cases
ANRA	American Newspaper Publishers Association
ANSCA	Alaska Native Claims Act
ANZUS	Australia-New Zealand-United States Security Treaty Organization
AOA	Administration on Aging
AOE	Arizonans for Official English
AOL	America Online
APA	Administrative Procedure Act of 1946
APHIS	Animal and Plant Health Inspection Service
App. Div.	Appellate Division Reports, N.Y. Supreme Court
Arb. Trib., U.S.-British	Arbitration Tribunal, Claim Convention of 1853, United States and Great Britain Convention of 1853
Ardcor	American Roller Die Corporation
ARPA	Advanced Research Projects Agency
ARPANET	Advanced Research Projects Agency Network
ARS	Advanced Record System
Art.	article
ARU	American Railway Union

ASCME	American Federation of State, County, and Municipal Employees
ASCS	Agriculture Stabilization and Conservation Service
ASM	Available Seatmile
ASPCA	American Society for the Prevention of Cruelty to Animals
Asst. Att. Gen.	Assistant Attorney General
AT&T	American Telephone and Telegraph
ATFD	Alcohol, Tobacco and Firearms Division
ATLA	Association of Trial Lawyers of America
ATO	Alpha Tau Omega
ATTD	Alcohol and Tobacco Tax Division
ATU	Alcohol Tax Unit
AUAM	American Union against Militarism
AUM	Animal Unit Month
AZT	azidothymidine
BALSA	Black-American Law Student Association
BATF	Bureau of Alcohol, Tobacco and Firearms
BBS	Bulletin Board System
BCCI	Bank of Credit and Commerce International
BEA	Bureau of Economic Analysis
Bell's Cr. C.	Bell's English Crown Cases
Bevans	United States Treaties, etc. *Treaties and Other International Agreements of the United States of America, 1776-1949* (compiled under the direction of Charles I. Bevans, 1968-76)
BFOQ	bona fide occupational qualification
BI	Bureau of Investigation
BIA	Bureau of Indian Affairs; Board of Immigration Appeals
BJS	Bureau of Justice Statistics
Black.	Black's United States Supreme Court Reports
Blatchf.	Blatchford's United States Circuit Court Reports
BLM	Bureau of Land Management
BLS	Bureau of Labor Statistics
BMD	ballistic missile defense
BNA	Bureau of National Affairs
BOCA	Building Officials and Code Administrators International
BOP	Bureau of Prisons
BPP	Black Panther Party for Self-defense
Brit. and For.	British and Foreign State Papers
BSA	Boy Scouts of America
BTP	Beta Theta Pi
Burr.	James Burrows, *Report of Cases Argued and Determined in the Court of King's Bench during the Time of Lord Mansfield* (1766-1780)
BVA	Board of Veterans Appeals
c.	chapter
C^3I	Command, Control, Communications, and Intelligence
C.A.	Court of Appeals
CAA	Clean Air Act
CAB	Civil Aeronautics Board; Corporation for American Banking
CAFE	corporate average fuel economy
Cal. 2d	California Reports, Second Series
Cal. 3d	California Reports, Third Series
CALR	computer-assisted legal research
Cal. Rptr.	California Reporter
CAP	Common Agricultural Policy
CARA	Classification and Ratings Administration
CATV	community antenna television
CBO	Congressional Budget Office
CCC	Commodity Credit Corporation

CCDBG	Child Care and Development Block Grant of 1990
C.C.D. Pa.	Circuit Court Decisions, Pennsylvania
C.C.D. Va.	Circuit Court Decisions, Virginia
CCEA	Cabinet Council on Economic Affairs
CCP	Chinese Communist Party
CCR	Center for Constitutional Rights
C.C.R.I.	Circuit Court, Rhode Island
CD	certificate of deposit; compact disc
CDA	Communications Decency Act
CDBG	Community Development Block Grant Program
CDC	Centers for Disease Control and Prevention; Community Development Corporation
CDF	Children's Defense Fund
CDL	Citizens for Decency through Law
CD-ROM	compact disc read-only memory
CDS	Community Dispute Services
CDW	collision damage waiver
CENTO	Central Treaty Organization
CEQ	Council on Environmental Quality
CERCLA	Comprehensive Environmental Response, Compensation, and Liability Act of 1980
cert.	*certiorari*
CETA	Comprehensive Employment and Training Act
C & F	cost and freight
CFC	chlorofluorocarbon
CFE Treaty	Conventional Forces in Europe Treaty of 1990
C.F. & I.	Cost, Freight, and Insurance
CI NP	Community Food and Nutrition Program
C.F.R.	Code of Federal Regulations
CFTA	Canadian Free Trade Agreement
CFTC	Commodity Futures Trading Commission
Ch.	Chancery Division, English Law Reports
CHAMPVA	Civilian Health and Medical Program at the Veterans Administration
CHEP	Cuban/Haitian Entrant Program
CHINS	children in need of supervision
CHIPS	child in need of protective services
Ch N.Y.	Chancery Reports, New York
Chr. Rob.	Christopher Robinson, *Reports of Cases Argued and Determined in the High Court of Admiralty* (1801-1808)
CIA	Central Intelligence Agency
CID	Commercial Item Descriptions
C.I.F.	cost, insurance, and freight
CINCNORAD	Commander in Chief, North American Air Defense Command
CIO	Committee for Industrial Organizations; Congress of Industrial Organizations
CIPE	Center for International Private Enterprise
CJ	chief justice
CJIS	Criminal Justice Information Services
CJ.S.	Corpus Juris Secundum
Claims Arb. under Spec. Conv., Nielsen's Rept.	Frederick Kenelm Nielsen, *American and British Claims Arbitration under the Special Agreement Concluded between the United States and Great Britain, August 18, 1910* (1926)
CLASP	Center for Law and Social Policy
CLE	Center for Law and Education; Continuing Legal Education
CLEO	Council on Legal Education Opportunity; Chief Law Enforcement Officer
CLP	Communist Labor Party of America

CLS	Christian Legal Society; critical legal studies (movement), Critical Legal Studies (membership organization)
C.M.A.	Court of Military Appeals
CMEA	Council for Mutual Economic Assistance
CMHS	Center for Mental Health Services
C.M.R.	Court of Military Review
CNN	Cable News Network
CNO	Chief of Naval Operations
CNR	Chicago and Northwestern Railway
CO	Conscientious Objector
C.O.D.	cash on delivery
COGP	Commission on Government Procurement
COINTELPRO	Counterintelligence Program
Coke Rep.	Coke's English King's Bench Reports
COLA	cost-of-living adjustment
COMCEN	Federal Communications Center
Comp.	Compilation
Conn.	Connecticut Reports
CONTU	National Commission on New Technological Uses of Copyrighted Works
Conv.	Convention
COPA	Child Online Protection Act (1998)
COPS	Community Oriented Policing Services
Corbin	Arthur L. Corbin, *Corbin on Contracts: A Comprehensive Treatise on the Rules of Contract Law* (1950)
CORE	Congress on Racial Equality
Cox's Crim. Cases	Cox's Criminal Cases (England)
COYOTE	Call Off Your Old Tired Ethics
CPA	certified public accountant
CPB	Corporation for Public Broadcasting, the
CPI	Consumer Price Index
CPPA	Child Pornography Prevention Act
CPSC	Consumer Product Safety Commission
Cranch	Cranch's United States Supreme Court Reports
CRF	Constitutional Rights Foundation
CRR	Center for Constitutional Rights
CRS	Congressional Research Service; Community Relations Service
CRT	critical race theory
CSA	Community Services Administration
CSAP	Center for Substance Abuse Prevention
CSAT	Center for Substance Abuse Treatment
CSC	Civil Service Commission
CSCE	Conference on Security and Cooperation in Europe
CSG	Council of State Governments
CSO	Community Service Organization
CSP	Center for the Study of the Presidency
C-SPAN	Cable-Satellite Public Affairs Network
CSRS	Cooperative State Research Service
CSWPL	Center on Social Welfare Policy and Law
CTA	*cum testamento annexo* (with the will attached)
Ct. Ap. D.C.	Court of Appeals, District of Columbia
Ct. App. No. Ireland	Court of Appeals, Northern Ireland
Ct. Cl.	Court of Claims, United States
Ct. Crim. Apps.	Court of Criminal Appeals (England)
Ct. of Sess., Scot.	Court of Sessions, Scotland
CU	credit union
CUNY	City University of New York

Cush.	Cushing's Massachusetts Reports
CWA	Civil Works Administration; Clean Water Act
DACORB	Department of the Army Conscientious Objector Review Board
Dall.	Dallas' Pennsylvania and United States Reports
DAR	Daughters of the American Revolution
DARPA	Defense Advanced Research Projects Agency
DAVA	Defense Audiovisual Agency
D.C.	United States District Court; District of Columbia
D.C. Del.	United States District Court, Delaware
D.C. Mass.	United States District Court, Massachusetts
D.C. Md.	United States District Court, Maryland
D.C.N.D.Cal.	United States District Court, Northern District, California
D.C.N.Y.	United States District Court, New York
D.C.Pa.	United States District Court, Pennsylvania
DC-S	Deputy Chiefs of Staff
DCZ	District of the Canal Zone
DDT	dichlorodiphenyltricloroethane
DEA	Drug Enforcement Administration
Decl. Lond.	Declaration of London, February 26, 1909
Dev. & B.	Devereux & Battle's North Carolina Reports
DFL	Minnesota Democratic-Farmer-Labor
DFTA	Department for the Aging
Dig. U.S. Practice in Intl. Law	Digest of U.S. Practice in International Law
Dist. Ct.	D.C. United States District Court, District of Columbia
D.L.R.	Dominion Law Reports (Canada)
DMCA	Digital Millennium Copyright Act
DNA	deoxyribonucleic acid
Dnase	deoxyribonuclease
DNC	Democratic National Committee
DOC	Department of Commerce
DOD	Department of Defense
DODEA	Department of Defense Education Activity
Dodson	Dodson's Reports, English Admiralty Courts
DOE	Department of Energy
DOER	Department of Employee Relations
DOJ	Department of Justice
DOL	Department of Labor
DOMA	Defense of Marriage Act of 1996
DOS	disk operating system
DOT	Department of Transportation
DPT	diphtheria, pertussis, and tetanus
DRI	Defense Research Institute
DSAA	Defense Security Assistance Agency
DUI	driving under the influence; driving under intoxication
DWI	driving while intoxicated
EAHCA	Education for All Handicapped Children Act of 1975
EBT	examination before trial
E.coli	Escherichia coli
ECPA	Electronic Communications Privacy Act of 1986
ECSC	Treaty of the European Coal and Steel Community
EDA	Economic Development Administration
EDF	Environmental Defense Fund
E.D.N.Y.	Eastern District, New York
EDP	electronic data processing
E.D.	Pa. Eastern-District, Pennsylvania
EDSC	Eastern District, South Carolina

E.D.	Va. Eastern District, Virginia
EEC	European Economic Community; European Economic Community Treaty
EEOC	Equal Employment Opportunity Commission
EFF	Electronic Frontier Foundation
EFT	electronic funds transfer
Eliz.	Queen Elizabeth (Great Britain)
Em. App.	Temporary Emergency Court of Appeals
ENE	early neutral evaluation
Eng. Rep.	English Reports
EOP	Executive Office of the President
EPA	Environmental Protection Agency; Equal Pay Act of 1963
ERA	Equal Rights Amendment
ERDC	Energy Research and Development Commission
ERISA	Employee Retirement Income Security Act of 1974
ERS	Economic Research Service
ERTA	Economic Recovery Tax Act of 1981
ESA	Endangered Species Act of 1973
ESF	emergency support function; Economic Support Fund
ESRD	End-Stage Renal Disease Program
ETA	Employment and Training Administration
ETS	environmental tobacco smoke
et seq.	*et sequentes* or *et sequentia* (and the following)
EU	European Union
Euratom	European Atomic Energy Community
Eur. Ct. H.R.	European Court of Human Rights
Ex.	English Exchequer Reports, Welsby, Hurlstone & Gordon
Exch.	Exchequer Reports (Welsby, Hurlstone & Gordon)
Ex Com	Executive Committee of the National Security Council
Eximbank	Export-Import Bank of the United States
F.	Federal Reporter
F. 2d	Federal Reporter, Second Series
FAA	Federal Aviation Administration; Federal Arbitration Act
FAAA	Federal Alcohol Administration Act
FACE	Freedom of Access to Clinic Entrances Act of 1994
FACT	Feminist Anti-Censorship Task Force
FAMLA	Family and Medical Leave Act of 1993
Fannie Mae	Federal National Mortgage Association
FAO	Food and Agriculture Organization of the United Nations
FAR	Federal Acquisition Regulations
FAS	Foreign Agricultural Service
FBA	Federal Bar Association
FBI	Federal Bureau of Investigation
FCA	Farm Credit Administration
F. Cas.	Federal Cases
FCC	Federal Communications Commission
FCIA	Foreign Credit Insurance Association
FCIC	Federal Crop Insurance Corporation
FCRA	Fair Credit Reporting Act
FCU	federal credit unions
FCUA	Federal Credit Union Act
FCZ	Fishery Conservation Zone
FDA	Food and Drug Administration
FDIC	Federal Deposit Insurance Corporation
FDPC	Federal Data Processing Center
FEC	Federal Election Commission
FECA	Federal Election Campaign Act of 1971

Fed. Cas.	Federal Cases
FEMA	Federal Emergency Management Agency
FFB	Federal Financing Bank
FFDC	Federal Food, Drug, and Cosmetics Act
FGIS	Federal Grain Inspection Service
FHA	Federal Housing Administration
FHWA	Federal Highway Administration
FIA	Federal Insurance Administration
FIC	Federal Information Centers; Federation of Insurance Counsel
FICA	Federal Insurance Contributions Act
FIFRA	Federal Insecticide, Fungicide, and Rodenticide Act
FIP	Forestry Incentives Program
FIRREA	Financial Institutions Reform, Recovery, and Enforcement Act of 1989
FISA	Foreign Intelligence Surveillance Act of 1978
FJC	Federal Judicial Center
FLSA	Fair Labor Standards Act
FMC	Federal Maritime Commission
FMCS	Federal Mediation and Conciliation Service
FmHA	Farmers Home Administration
FMLA	Family and Medical Leave Act of 1993
FNMA	Federal National Mortgage Association, "Fannie Mae"
F.O.B.	free on board
FOIA	Freedom of Information Act
FOMC	Federal Open Market Committee
FPC	Federal Power Commission
FPMR	Federal Property Management Regulations
FPRS	Federal Property Resources Service
FR	Federal Register
FRA	Federal Railroad Administration
FRB	Federal Reserve Board
FRC	Federal Radio Commission
F.R.D.	Federal Rules Decisions
FSA	Family Support Act
FSLIC	Federal Savings and Loan Insurance Corporation
FSQS	Food Safety and Quality Service
FSS	Federal Supply Service
F. Supp.	Federal Supplement
FTA	U.S.-Canada Free Trade Agreement of 1988
FTC	Federal Trade Commission
FTCA	Federal Tort Claims Act
FTS	Federal Telecommunications System
FTS2000	Federal Telecommunications System 2000
FUCA	Federal Unemployment Compensation Act of 1988
FUTA	Federal Unemployment Tax Act
FWPCA	Federal Water Pollution Control Act of 1948
FWS	Fish and Wildlife Service
GAL	guardian ad litem
GAO	General Accounting Office; Governmental Affairs Office
GAOR	General Assembly Official Records, United Nations
GA Res.	General Assembly Resolution (United Nations)
GATT	General Agreement on Tariffs and Trade
GCA	Gun Control Act
Gen. Cls. Comm.	General Claims Commission, United States and Panama; General Claims United States and Mexico
Geo. II	King George II (Great Britain)
Geo. III	King George III (Great Britain)

GI	Government Issue
GID	General Intelligence Division
GM	General Motors
GNMA	Government National Mortgage Association, "Ginnie Mae"
GNP	gross national product
GOP	Grand Old Party (Republican)
GOPAC	Grand Old Party Action Committee
GPA	Office of Governmental and Public Affairs
GPO	Government Printing Office
GRAS	generally recognized as safe
Gr. Br., Crim. Ct. App.	Great Britain, Court of Criminal Appeals
GRNL	Gay Rights-National Lobby
GSA	General Services Administration
Hackworth	Green Haywood Hackworth, *Digest of International Law* (1940-44)
Hay and Marriott	Great Britain. High Court of Admiralty, *Decisions in the High Court of Admiralty during the Time of Sir George Hay and of Sir James Marriott, Late Judges of That Court* (1801)
HBO	Home Box Office
HCFA	Health Care Financing Administration
H.Ct.	High Court
HDS	Office of Human Development Services
Hen. & M.	Hening & Munford's Virginia Reports
HEW	Department of Health, Education, and Welfare
HFCA	Health Care Financing Administration
HGI	Handgun Control, Incorporated
HHS	Department of Health and Human Services
Hill	Hill's New York Reports
HIRE	Help through Industry Retraining and Employment
HIV	human immunodeficiency virus
H.L.	House of Lords Cases (England)
H. Lords	House of Lords (England)
HNIS	Human Nutrition Information Service
Hong Kong L.R.	Hong Kong Law Reports
How.	Howard's United States Supreme Court Reports
How. St. Trials	Howell's English State Trials
HUAC	House Un-American Activities Committee
HUD	Department of Housing and Urban Development
Hudson, Internatl. Legis.	Manley Ottmer Hudson, ed., *International Legislation: A Collection of the Texts of Multipartite International Instruments of General Interest Beginning with the Covenant of the League of Nations* (1931)
Hudson, World Court Reps.	Manley Ottmer Hudson, ea., *World Court Reports* (1934-)
Hun	Hun's New York Supreme Court Reports
Hunt's Rept.	Bert L. Hunt, *Report of the American and Panamanian General Claims Arbitration* (1934)
IAEA	International Atomic Energy Agency
IALL	International Association of Law Libraries
IBA	International Bar Association
IBM	International Business Machines
ICBM	intercontinental ballistic missile
ICC	Interstate Commerce Commission
ICJ	International Court of Justice
ICM	Institute for Court Management
IDEA	Individuals with Disabilities Education Act of 1975
IDOP	International Dolphin Conservation Program
IEP	individualized educational program
IFC	International Finance Corporation

IGRA	Indian Gaming Regulatory Act of 1988
IJA	Institute of Judicial Administration
IJC	International Joint Commission
ILC	International Law Commission
ILD	International Labor Defense
Ill. Dec.	Illinois Decisions
ILO	International Labor Organization
IMF	International Monetary Fund
INA	Immigration and Nationality Act
IND	investigational new drug
INF Treaty	Intermediate-Range Nuclear Forces Treaty of 1987
INS	Immigration and Naturalization Service
INTELSAT	International Telecommunications Satellite Organization
Interpol	International Criminal Police Organization
Int'l. Law Reps.	International Law Reports
Intl. Legal Mats.	International Legal Materials
IPDC	International Program for the Development of Communication
IPO	Intellectual Property Owners
IPP	independent power producer
IQ	intelligence quotient
I.R.	Irish Reports
IRA	individual retirement account; Irish Republican Army
IRCA	Immigration Reform and Control Act of 1986
IRS	Internal Revenue Service
ISO	independent service organization
ISP	Internet service provider
ISSN	International Standard Serial Numbers
ITA	International Trade Administration
ITI	Information Technology Integration
ITO	International Trade Organization
ITS	Information Technology Service
ITT	International Telephone and Telegraph Corporation
ITU	International Telecommunication Union
IUD	intrauterine device
IWC	International Whaling Commission
IWW	Industrial Workers of the World
JAGC	Judge Advocate General's Corps
JCS	Joint Chiefs of Staff
JDL	Jewish Defense League
JNOV	Judgment *non obstante veredicto* (judgment "nothing to recommend it") or (judgment "notwithstanding the verdict")
JOBS	Jobs Opportunity and Basic Skills
John. Ch.	Johnson's New York Chancery Reports
Johns.	Johnson's Reports (New York)
JP	justice of the peace
K.B.	King's Bench Reports (England)
KGB	Komitet Gosudarstvennoi Bezopasnosti (the State Security Committee for countries in the former Soviet Union)
KKK	Ku Klux Klan
KMT	Kuomintang
LAD	Law Against Discrimination
LAPD	Los Angeles Police Department
LC	Library of Congress
LCHA	Longshoremen's and Harbor Workers Compensation Act of 1927
LD50	lethal dose 50
LDEF	Legal Defense and Education Fund (NOW)

LDF	Legal Defense Fund, Legal Defense and Educational Fund of the NAACP
LEAA	Law Enforcement Assistance Administration
L.Ed.	Lawyers' Edition Supreme Court Reports
LLC	Limited Liability Company
LLP	Limited Liability Partnership
LMSA	Labor-Management Services Administration
LNTS	League of Nations Treaty Series
Lofft's Rep.	Lofft's English King's Bench Reports
L.R.	Law Reports (English)
LSAC	Law School Admission Council
LSAS	Law School Admission Service
LSAT	Law School Aptitude Test
LSC	Legal Services Corporation; Legal Services for Children
LSD	lysergic acid diethylamide
LSDAS	Law School Data Assembly Service
LTBT	Limited Test Ban Treaty
LTC	Long Term Care
MAD	mutual assured destruction
MADD	Mothers against Drunk Driving
MALDEF	Mexican American Legal Defense and Educational Fund
Malloy	William M. Malloy, ed., *Treaties, Conventions International Acts, Protocols, and Agreements between the United States of America and Other Powers* (1910-38)
Martens	Georg Friedrich von Martens, ea., *Noveau recueil ge'neral de traites et autres act es relatifs azlx rapports de droit international* (Series I, 20 vols. [1843-75]; Series II, 35 vols. [1876-1908]; Series III [1909-])
Mass.	Massachusetts Reports
MCC	Metropolitan Correctional Center
MCH	Maternal and Child Health Bureau
Md. App.	Maryland, Appeal Cases
M.D. Ga.	Middle District, Georgia
Mercy	Movement Ensuring the Right to Choose for Yourself
Metc.	Metcalf's Massachusetts Reports
MFDP	Mississippi Freedom Democratic party
MGT	management
MHSS	Military Health Services System
Miller	David Hunter Miller, ea., *Treaties and Other International Acts of the United States of America* (1931-1948)
Minn.	Minnesota Reports
MINS	minors in need of supervision
MIRV	multiple independently targetable reentry vehicle
MIRVed ICBM	multiple independently targetable reentry vehicled intercontinental ballistic missile
Misc.	Miscellaneous Reports, New York
Mixed Claims Comm., Report of Decs	Mixed Claims Commission, United States and Germany, Report of Decisions
MJ.	Military Justice Reporter
MLAP	Migrant Legal Action Program
MLB	Major League Baseball
MLDP	Mississippi Loyalist Democratic Party
MMI	Moslem Mosque, Incorporated
MMPA	Marine Mammal Protection Act of 1972
Mo.	Missouri Reports
MOD	Masters of Deception
Mod.	Modern Reports, English King's Bench, etc.
Moore, Dig. Intl. Law	John Bassett Moore, *A Digest of International Law*, 8 vols. (1906)

Moore, Intl. Arbs.	John Bassett Moore, *History and Digest of the International Arbitrations to Which United States Has Been a Party*, 6 vols. (1898)
Morison	William Maxwell Morison, *The Scots Revised Report: Morison's Dictionary of Decisions* (1908-09)
M.P.	member of Parliament
MPAA	Motion Picture Association of America
MPAS	Michigan Protection and Advocacy Service
mpg	miles per gallon
MPPDA	Motion Picture Producers and Distributors of America
MPRSA	Marine Protection, Research, and Sanctuaries Act of 1972
M.R.	Master of the Rolls
MS-DOS	Microsoft Disk Operating System
MSHA	Mine Safety and Health Administration
MSSA	Military Selective Service Act
N/A	Not Available
NAACP	National Association for the Advancement of Colored People
NAAQS	National Ambient Air Quality Standards
NAB	National Association of Broadcasters
NABSW	National Association of Black Social Workers
NAFTA	North American Free Trade Agreement of 1993
NALA	National Association of Legal Assistants
NAM	National Association of Manufacturers
NAR	National Association of Realtors
NARAL	National Abortion and Reproductive Rights Action League
NARF	Native American Rights Fund
NARS	National Archives and Record Service
NASA	National Aeronautics and Space Administration
NASD	National Association of Securities Dealers
NATO	North Atlantic Treaty Organization
NAVINFO	Navy Information Offices
NAWSA	National American Woman's Suffrage Association
NBA	National Bar Association; National Basketball Association
NBC	National Broadcasting Company
NBLSA	National Black Law Student Association
NBS	National Bureau of Standards
NCA	Noise Control Act; National Command Authorities
NCAA	National Collegiate Athletic Association
NCAC	National Coalition against Censorship
NCCB	National Consumer Cooperative Bank
NCE	Northwest Community Exchange
NCF	National Chamber Foundation
NCIP	National Crime Insurance Program
NCJA	National Criminal Justice Association
NCLB	National Civil Liberties Bureau
NCP	national contingency plan
NCSC	National Center for State Courts
NCUA	National Credit Union Administration
NDA	new drug application
N.D. Ill.	Northern District, Illinois
NDU	National Defense University
N.D. Wash.	Northern District, Washington
N.E.	North Eastern Reporter
N.E. 2d	North Eastern Reporter, Second Series
NEA	National Endowment for the Arts; National Education Association
NEH	National Endowment for the Humanities
NEPA	National Environmental Protection Act; National Endowment Policy Act

NET Act	No Electronic Theft Act
NFIB	National Federation of Independent Businesses
NFIP	National Flood Insurance Program
NFPA	National Federation of Paralegal Associations
NGLTF	National Gay and Lesbian Task Force
NHRA	Nursing Home Reform Act of 1987
NHTSA	National Highway Traffic Safety Administration
Nielsen's Rept.	Frederick Kenelm Nielsen, *American and British Claims Arbitration under the Special Agreement Concluded between the United States and Great Britain, August 18, 1910* (1926)
NIEO	New International Economic Order
NIGC	National Indian Gaming Commission
NIH	National Institutes of Health
NIJ	National Institute of Justice
NIRA	National Industrial Recovery Act of 1933; National Industrial Recovery Administration
NIST	National Institute of Standards and Technology
NITA	National Telecommunications and Information Administration
NJ.	New Jersey Reports
N.J. Super.	New Jersey Superior Court Reports
NLRA	National Labor Relations Act
NLRB	National Labor Relations Board
NMFS	National Marine Fisheries Service
No.	Number
NOAA	National Oceanic and Atmospheric Administration
NOI	Nation of Islam
NORML	National Organization for the Reform of Marijuana Laws
North Carolina A&T	North Carolina Agricultural and Technical College
NOW	National Organization for Women
NOW LDEF	National Organization for Women Legal Defense and Education Fund
NOW/PAC	National Organization for Women Political Action Committee
NPDES	National Pollutant Discharge Elimination System
NPL	national priorities list
NPR	National Public Radio
NPT	Nuclear Non-Proliferation Treaty of 1970
NRA	National Rifle Association; National Recovery Act
NRC	Nuclear Regulatory Commission
NRLC	National Right to Life Committee
NRTA	National Retired Teachers Association
NSI	Network Solutions, Inc.
NSC	National Security Council
NSCLC	National Senior Citizens Law Center
NSF	National Science Foundation
NSFNET	National Science Foundation Network
NTIA	National Telecommunications and Information Administration
NTID	National Technical Institute for the Deaf
NTIS	National Technical Information Service
NTS	Naval Telecommunications System
NTSB	National Transportation Safety Board
NVRA	National Voter Registration Act
N.W.	North Western Reporter
N.W. 2d	North Western Reporter, Second Series
NWSA	National Woman Suffrage Association
N.Y.	New York Court of Appeals Reports
N.Y. 2d	New York Court of Appeals Reports, Second Series
N.Y.S.	New York Supplement Reporter

N.Y.S. 2d	New York Supplement Reporter, Second Series
NYSE	New York Stock Exchange
NYSLA	New York State Liquor Authority
N.Y. Sup.	New York Supreme Court Reports
NYU	New York University
OAAU	Organization of Afro American Unity
OAP	Office of Administrative Procedure
OAS	Organization of American States
OASDI	Old-age, Survivors, and Disability Insurance Benefits
OASHDS	Office of the Assistant Secretary for Human Development Services
OCC	Office of Comptroller of the Currency
OCED	Office of Comprehensive Employment Development
OCHAMPUS	Office of Civilian Health and Medical Program of the Uniformed Services
OCSE	Office of Child Support Enforcement
OEA	Organizaci;aaon de los Estados Americanos
OEM	Original Equipment Manufacturer
OFCCP	Office of Federal Contract Compliance Programs
OFPP	Office of Federal Procurement Policy
OICD	Office of International Cooperation and Development
OIG	Office of the Inspector General
OJARS	Office of Justice Assistance, Research, and Statistics
OMB	Office of Management and Budget
OMPC	Office of Management, Planning, and Communications
ONP	Office of National Programs
OPD	Office of Policy Development
OPEC	Organization of Petroleum Exporting Countries
OPIC	Overseas Private Investment Corporation
Ops. Atts. Gen.	Opinions of the Attorneys-General of the United States
Ops. Comms.	Opinions of the Commissioners
OPSP	Office of Product Standards Policy
O.R.	Ontario Reports
OR	Official Records
OSHA	Occupational Safety and Health Act
OSHRC	Occupational Safety and Health Review Commission
OSM	Office of Surface Mining
OSS	Office of Strategic Services
OST	Office of the Secretary
OT	Office of Transportation
OTA	Office of Technology Assessment
OTC	over-the-counter
OTS	Office of Thrift Supervisors
OUI	operating under the influence
OWBPA	Older Workers Benefit Protection Act
OWRT	Office of Water Research and Technology
P.	Pacific Reporter
P. 2d	Pacific Reporter, Second Series
PAC	political action committee
Pa. Oyer and Terminer	Pennsylvania Oyer and Terminer Reports
PATCO	Professional Air Traffic Controllers Organization
PBGC	Pension Benefit Guaranty Corporation
PBS	Public Broadcasting Service; Public Buildings Service
P.C.	Privy Council (English Law Reports)
PC	personal computer; politically correct
PCBs	polychlorinated biphenyls
PCIJ	Permanent Court of International Justice Series A-Judgments and Orders (1922-30)

	Series B-Advisory Opinions (1922-30)
	Series A/B-Judgments, Orders, and Advisory Opinions (1931-40)
	Series C-Pleadings, Oral Statements, and Documents relating to Judgments and Advisory Opinions (1923-42)
	Series D-Acts and Documents concerning the Organization of the World Court (1922-47)
	Series E-Annual Reports (1925-45)
PCP	Phencyclidine
P.D.	Probate Division, English Law Reports (1876-1890)
PDA	Pregnancy Discrimination Act of 1978
PD & R	Policy Development and Research
Pepco	Potomac Electric Power Company
Perm. Ct. of Arb.	Permanent Court of Arbitration
PES	Post-Enumeration Survey
Pet.	Peters' United States Supreme Court Reports
PETA	People for the Ethical Treatment of Animals
PGA	Professional Golfers Association
PGM	Program
PHA	Public Housing Agency
Phila. Ct. of Oyer and Terminer	Philadelphia Court of Oyer and Terminer
PHS	Public Health Service
PIC	Private Industry Council
PICJ	Permanent International Court of Justice
Pick.	Pickering's Massachusetts Reports
PIK	Payment in Kind
PINS	persons in need of supervision
PIRG	Public Interest Research Group
P.L.	Public Laws
PLAN	Pro-Life Action Network
PLI	Practicing Law Institute
PLLP	Professional Limited Liability Partnership
PLO	Palestine Liberation Organization
PLRA	Prison Litigation Reform Act of 1995
PNET	Peaceful Nuclear Explosions Treaty
PONY	Prostitutes of New York
POW-MIA	prisoner of war-missing in action
Pratt	Frederic Thomas Pratt, *Law of Contraband of War, with a Selection of Cases from Papers of the Right Honourable Sir George Lee* (1856)
PRIDE	Prostitution to Independence, Dignity, and Equality
Proc.	Proceedings
PRP	potentially responsible party
PSRO	Professional Standards Review Organization
PTO	Patents and Trademark Office
PURPA	Public Utilities Regulatory Policies Act
PUSH	People United to Serve Humanity
PUSH-Excel	PUSH for Excellence
PWA	Public Works Administration
PWSA	Ports and Waterways Safety Act of 1972
Q.B.	Queen's Bench (England)
QTIP	Qualified Terminable Interest Property
Ralston's Rept.	Jackson Harvey Ralston, ed., *Venezuelan Arbitrations of 1903* (1904)
RC	Regional Commissioner
RCRA	Resource Conservation and Recovery Act
RCWP	Rural Clean Water Program
RDA	Rural Development Administration
REA	Rural Electrification Administration

Rec. des Decs. des Trib. Arb. Mixtes	G. Gidel, ed., *Recueil des decisions des tribunaux arbitraux mixtes, institu;aaes par les trait;aaes de paix* (1922-30)
Redmond	Vol. 3 of Charles I. Bevans, *Treaties and Other International Agreements of the United States of America, 1776-1949* (compiled by C. F. Redmond) (1969)
RESPA	Real Estate Settlement Procedure Act of 1974
RFC	Reconstruction Finance Corporation
RFRA	Religious Freedom Restoration Act of 1993
RICO	Racketeer Influenced and Corrupt Organizations
RNC	Republican National Committee
Roscoe	Edward Stanley Roscoe, ed., *Reports of Prize Cases Determined in the High Court Admiralty before the Lords Commissioners of Appeals in Prize Causes and before the judicial Committee of the Privy Council from 1745 to 1859* (1905)
ROTC	Reserve Officers' Training Corps
RPP	Representative Payee Program
R.S.	Revised Statutes
RTC	Resolution Trust Corp.
RUDs	reservations, understandings, and declarations
Ryan White CARE Act	Ryan White Comprehensive AIDS Research Emergency Act of 1990
SAC	Strategic Air Command
SACB	Subversive Activities Control Board
SADD	Students against Drunk Driving
SAF	Student Activities Fund
SAIF	Savings Association Insurance Fund
SALT	Strategic Arms Limitation Talks
SALT I	Strategic Arms Limitation Talks of 1969-72
SAMHSA	Substance Abuse and Mental Health Services Administration
Sandf.	Sandford's New York Superior Court Reports
S and L	savings and loan
SARA	Superfund Amendment and Reauthorization Act
SAT	Scholastic Aptitude Test
Sawy.	Sawyer's United States Circuit Court Reports
SBA	Small Business Administration
SBI	Small Business Institute
SCCC	South Central Correctional Center
SCLC	Southern Christian Leadership Conference
Scott's Repts.	James Brown Scott, ed., *The Hague Court Reports*, 2 vols. (1916-32)
SCS	Soil Conservation Service; Social Conservative Service
SCSEP	Senior Community Service Employment Program
S.Ct.	Supreme Court Reporter
S.D. Cal.	Southern District, California
S.D. Fla.	Southern District, Florida
S.D. Ga.	Southern District, Georgia
SDI	Strategic Defense Initiative
S.D. Me.	Southern District, Maine
S.D.N.Y.	Southern District, New York
SDS	Students for a Democratic Society
S.E.	South Eastern Reporter
S.E. 2d	South Eastern Reporter, Second Series
SEA	Science and Education Administration
SEATO	Southeast Asia Treaty Organization
SEC	Securities and Exchange Commission
Sec.	Section
SEEK	Search for Elevation, Education and Knowledge
SEOO	State Economic Opportunity Office
SEP	simplified employee pension plan

Ser.	Series
Sess.	Session
SGLI	Servicemen's Group Life Insurance
SIP	state implementation plan
SLA	Symbionese Liberation Army
SLAPPs	Strategic Lawsuits Against Public Participation
SLBM	submarine-launched ballistic missile
SNCC	Student Nonviolent Coordinating Committee
So.	Southern Reporter
So. 2d	Southern Reporter, Second Series
SPA	Software Publisher's Association
Spec. Sess.	Special Session
SRA	Sentencing Reform Act of 1984
SS	Schutzstaffel (German for Protection Echelon)
SSA	Social Security Administration
SSI	Supplemental Security Income
START I	Strategic Arms Reduction Treaty of 1991
START II	Strategic Arms Reduction Treaty of 1993
Seat.	United States Statutes at Large
STS	Space Transportation Systems
St. Tr.	State Trials, English
STURAA	Surface Transportation and Uniform Relocation Assistance Act of 1987
Sup. Ct. of Justice, Mexico	Supreme Court of Justice, Mexico
Supp.	Supplement
S.W.	South Western Reporter
S.W. 2d	South Western Reporter, Second Series
SWAPO	South-West Africa People's Organization
SWAT	Special Weapons and Tactics
SWP	Socialist Workers party
TDP	Trade and Development Program
Tex. Sup.	Texas Supreme Court Reports
THAAD	Theater High-Altitude Area Defense System
THC	tetrahydrocannabinol
TI	Tobacco Institute
TIA	Trust Indenture Act of 1939
TIAS	Treaties and Other International Acts Series (United States)
TNT	trinitrotoluene
TOP	Targeted Outreach Program
TPUS	Transportation and Public Utilities Service
TQM	Total Quality Management
Tripartite Claims Comm.,Decs. And Ops.	Tripartite Claims Commission (United States, Austria, and Hungary), Decisions and Opinions
TRI-TAC	Joint Tactical Communications
TRO	temporary restraining order
TS	Treaty Series, United States
TSCA	Toxic Substance Control Act
TSDs	transporters, storers, and disposers
TSU	Texas Southern University
TTBT	Threshold Test Ban Treaty
TV	Television
TVA	Tennessee Valley Authority
TWA	Trans World Airlines
UAW	United Auto Workers; United Automobile, Aerospace, and Agricultural Implements Workers of America

U.C.C.	Uniform Commercial Code; Universal Copyright Convention
U.C.C.C.	Uniform Consumer Credit Code
UCCJA	Uniform Child Custody Jurisdiction Act
UCMJ	Uniform Code of Military Justice
UCPP	Urban Crime Prevention Program
UCS	United Counseling Service
UDC	United Daughters of the Confederacy
UFW	United Farm Workers
UHF	ultrahigh frequency
UIFSA	Uniform Interstate Family Support Act
UIS	Unemployment Insurance Service
UMDA	Uniform Marriage and Divorce Act
UMTA	Urban Mass Transportation Administration
U.N.	United Nations
UNCITRAL	United Nations Commission on International Trade Law
UNCTAD	United Nations Conference on Trade and Development
UN Doc.	United Nations Documents
UNDP	United Nations Development Program
UNEF	United Nations Emergency Force
UNESCO	United Nations Educational, Scientific, and Cultural Organization
UNICEF	United Nations Children's Fund
UNIDO	United Nations Industrial and Development Organization
Unif. L. Ann.	Uniform Laws Annotated
UN Repts. Intl. Arb. Awards	United Nations Reports of International Arbitral Awards
UNTS	United Nations Treaty Series
UPI	United Press International
URESA	Uniform Reciprocal Enforcement of Support Act
U.S.A.	United States of America
USAF	United States Air Force
USF	U.S. Forestry Service
U.S. App. D.C.	United States Court of Appeals for the District of Columbia
U.S.C.	United States Code; University of Southern California
U.S.C.A.	United States Code Annotated
U.S.C.C.A.N.	United States Code Congressional and Administrative News
USCMA	United States Court of Military Appeals
USDA	U.S. Department of Agriculture
USES	United States Employment Service
USFA	United States Fire Administration
USICA	International Communication Agency, United States
USMS	U.S. Marshals Service
USSC	U.S. Sentencing Commission
U.S.S.R.	Union of Soviet Socialist Republics
UST	United States Treaties
USTS	United States Travel Service
v.	versus
VA	Veterans Administration
VAR	Veterans Affairs and Rehabilitation Commission
VAWA	Violence Against Women Act
VFW	Veterans of Foreign Wars
VGLI	Veterans Group Life Insurance
Vict.	Queen Victoria (Great Britain)
VIN	vehicle identification number
VISTA	Volunteers in Service to America
VJRA	Veterans Judicial Review Act of 1988
V.L.A.	Volunteer Lawyers for the Arts
VMI	Virginia Military Institute

VMLI	Veterans Mortgage Life Insurance
VOCAL	Victims of Child Abuse Laws
VRA	Voting Rights Act
WAC	Women's Army Corps
Wall.	Wallace's United States Supreme Court Reports
Wash. 2d	Washington Reports, Second Series
WAVES	Women Accepted for Volunteer Service
WCTU	Women's Christian Temperance Union
W.D. Wash.	Western District, Washington
W.D. Wis.	Western District, Wisconsin
WEAL	*West's Encyclopedia of American Law*, Women's Equity Action League
Wend.	Wendell's New York Reports
WFSE	Washington Federation of State Employees
Wheat.	Wheaton's United States Supreme Court Reports
Wheel. Cr. Cases	Wheeler's New York Criminal Cases
WHISPER	Women Hurt in Systems of Prostitution Engaged in Revolt
Whiteman	Marjorie Millace Whiteman, *Digest of International Law*, 15 vols. (1963-73)
WHO	World Health Organization
WIC	Women, Infants, and Children program
Will. and Mar.	King William and Queen Mary (Great Britain)
WIN	WESTLAW Is Natural; Whip Inflation Now; Work Incentive Program
WIPO	World Intellectual Property Organization
WIU	Workers' Industrial Union
W.L.R.	Weekly Law Reports, England
WPA	Works Progress Administration
WPPDA	Welfare and Pension Plans Disclosure Act
WTO	World Trade Organization
WWI	World War I
WWII	World War II
Yates Sel. Cas.	Yates' New York Select Cases
YWCA	Young Women's Christian Association

INDEX
APPENDIX AND MILESTONES IN THE LAW FROM WEST'S ENCYCLOPEDIA OF AMERICAN LAW

Ain't I a Woman? **11:** 381
Articles of Confederation **11:** 95
Bill of Rights **11:** 123
Bradwell v. Illinois **11:** 382
Brown v. Board of Education of Topeka **2:** 351
"The Causes of the Popular Dissatisfaction with the Administration of Justice" **11:** 498
Civil Rights Act of 1964 **11:** 331
Civil Rights Cases **11:** 278
Common Sense **11:** 81
Compromise of 1850 **11:** 146
Constitution of the United States **11:** 109
Contracts **11:** 473
Declaration of the Causes and Necessity of Taking up Arms **11:** 77
Declaration of Independence **11:** 84
Dred Scott v. Sandford **11:** 165
English Bill of Rights **11:** 12
Farewell Address **11:** 439
Federalist, Number 10 **11:** 125
Federalist, Number 78 **11:** 128
Fourteen Points **11:** 450
Frame of Government **11:** 48
Frankfurter, Felix, "Some Reflections on the Reading of Statutes" **11:** 507
Gettysburg Address **11:** 447
Hamilton, Alexander, Federalist, Number 10 **11:** 125
Hamilton, Alexander, Federalist, Number 78 **11:** 128
Holmes, Oliver Wendell, Jr., *The Path of the Law* **11:** 475

Johnson, Lyndon B., Voting Rights Act Address **11:** 457
Kansas-Nebraska Act **11:** 157
Kennedy, John F., Inaugural Address **11:** 455
King, Martin Luther, Jr., Letter from Birmingham City Jail **11:** 321
Langdell, Christopher C., Contracts **11:** 473
The Laws and Liberties of Massachusetts **11:** 46
Lawyers and Judges **11:** 467
Lee v. Weisman **8:** 401
Lincoln, Abraham, Gettysburg Address **11:** 447
Lincoln, Abraham, Second Inaugural Address **11:** 448
Magna Charta **11:** 3
Mayflower Compact **11:** 45
"Mechanical Jurisprudence" **11:** 490
Miranda v. Arizona **3:** 335
Missouri Compromise **11:** 141
Monroe Doctrine **11:** 134
Muller v. Oregon, brief for the defendant in error **11:** 487
My Son, Stop Your Ears **11:** 432
National Organization for Women Statement of Purpose **11:** 387
The New Jersey Plan **11:** 108
New York Times v. Sullivan **8:** 251
Northwest Ordinance **11:** 101
The Path of the Law **11:** 475
The Patterson Plan **11:** 108
Plessy v. Ferguson **11:** 310

Pound, Roscoe, "Mechanical Jurisprudence" **11:** 490

Pound, Roscoe, "The Causes of Popular Dissatisfaction with the Administration of Justice" **11:** 498

The Randolph Plan **11:** 105

Reagan, Ronald W., First Inaugural Address **11:** 459

Roe v. Wade **1:** 313

Roosevelt, Franklin D., First Inaugural Address **11:** 452

Second Treatise on Government **11:** 16

Seneca Falls Declaration of Sentiments **11:** 379

Some Reflections on the Reading of Statutes **11:** 507

South Carolina Slave Code **11:** 49

Stamp Act **11:** 57

Surrender Speech **11:** 427

Townshend Acts **11:** 68

Treaty of Paris **11:** 87

Treaty with Sioux Nation **11:** 428

Virginia Declaration of Rights **11:** 82

The Virginia and Kentucky Resolves **11:** 131

The Virginia Plan **11:** 105

Voting Rights Act of 1965 **11:** 364

Washington, George, Farewell Address **11:** 439

What Shall Be Done with the Practice of the Courts? **11:** 471

Wilmot Proviso **11:** 145

Wilson, Woodrow, Fourteen Points **11:** 450

Worcester v. Georgia **11:** 395

TABLE OF CASES CITED BY NAME

A

Abington School District v. Schempp, 200
Acheson, United States v., 181
Akins v. Snow, 169
Alabama v. White, 227
Albertson's, Inc. v. Kirkingburg, 52–54
Alden v. Maine, 82–83
American Civil Liberties Union v. Capitol Square Review and Advisory Board, 199
American Farm Bureau Federation v. Babbitt, 68–69
Amgen Inc. v. Chugai Pharmaceutical Co., 172, 173
Anders v. California, 222
Apprendi v. New Jersey, 113–114

B

Baehr v. Lewin, 99
Baehr v. Miike, 99–100
Bailey v. United States, 170
Baker v. Vermont, 100–101
Bear Lodge Multiple Use Association v. Babbitt, 196–197
Beck v. Prupis, 191–192
Beer v. United States, 241
Board of Education of Central School District No. 1 v. Allen, 208
Board of Regents of the University of Wisconsin System v. Southworth, 88–89
Bond v. United States, 209–210
Boy Scouts of America v. Dale, 101–103
Brady v. Maryland, 39
Brzonkala v. Morrison, 245–246
Buckley v. Valeo, 64, 65

C

Calder v. Bull, 76
California Department of Corrections v. Morales, 169
Callahan v. Carey, 120
Carmell v. Texas, 76–77
Carter v. Rafferty, 38
Central Hudson Gas & Elec. Corp. v. Public Serv. Comm'n of N.Y., 91
Chapinsky v. New Hampshire, 96
Chaudhuri v. Tennessee, 199
Chisholm v. Georgia, 83
City of Chicago v. Shalala, 243–244
City of Cleburne v. Cleburne Living Center, 55
City of Erie v. Pap's A.M. tdba "Kandyland", 89–90
Cohen v. California, 96
College Savings Bank v. Florida Prepaid Postsecondary Education Expense Board, 83–84
Commonwealth of Massachusetts v. Woodward, 155
Cruikshank, United States v., 106
CSX Transportation, Inc. v. Easterwood, 85
Curtis Publishing v. Butts, 148
Cutshall v. Sundquist, 215

D

Dale v. Boy Scouts of America, 101–103
Diamond v. Chakrabarty, 172, 173
Dickerson, United States v., 210
Dickerson v. United States, 210–211
Doe v. Mutual of Omaha Insurance Co., 118–119
Doe v. Sundquist, 6–8

285

E

Edwards v. Carpenter, 111–112
Emerson, United States v., 40
Engel v. Vitale, 200
E.N.O. v. L.M.M., 103–105
Equality Foundation of Greater Cincinnati, Inc. v. City of Cincinnati, 98
Equality Foundation of Greater Cincinnati v. Cincinnati, 98
Everson v. Board of Ed. of Ewing Tp., 198, 208

F

Faretta v. California, 219, 220
Federal Baseball Club of Baltimore, Inc. v. National League of Prof'l Baseball Clubs, Inc., 25, 27
Fischer v. United States, 156–157
Flood v. Kuhn, 26, 27
Florida Prepaid Postsecondary Education Expense Board v. College Savings Bank, 83–84
Florida v. J.L., 226–228
Food and Drug Administration v. Brown & Williamson Tobacco Corp., 232–234
44 Liquormart, Inc. v. Rhode Island, 90
Free Speech Coalition v. Reno, 181
Fuller v. Decatur Public School Board of Education, 207
Funk Brothers Seed Co. v. Kalo Inoculant Co., 172, 173

G

Garner v. Jones, 169–171
Geier v. American Honda Motor Company, Inc., 188–189
Gigante, United States v., 106
Gillespie v. City of Indianapolis, 106, 107
Gonzalez v. Reno, 19
Greater New Orleans Broadcasting Association, Inc. v. United States, 90–92
Griffin v. California, 87
Gutierrez v. Ada, 63–64

H

Hamilton v. Accu-tek, 40
Hammer v. INS, 51–52
Hanousek v. United States, 48
Harris v. Thigpen, 4
Hartman v. Duffey, 213
Hill v. Colorado, 181–182
Hilton, United States v., 181
Hubbell, United States v., 211–212
Hunt-Wesson v. Franchise Tax Board of California, 41–42

Hurley v. Irish-American Gay, Lesbian and Bisexual Group of Boston, 103

I

Illinois v. Wardlow, 93–94
Innes v. Kansas State University, 23–24
In re Abraham, 138, 139
In re Kemmler, 33

J

Jewell v. Cox Enterprises Inc., 147
Johnson v. United States, 170–171

K

Kimel v. Florida Board of Regents, 10–11
Kolstad v. American Dental Association, 66–67

L

LaLonde v. County of Riverside, 124–125
Lemon v. Kurtzman, 199
Lettman v. Reno, 124
Liddy v. Wells, 149–150
Lilly v. Virginia, 45–47
L.M.M. v. E.N.O., 103–105
Locke, United States v., 69–70
Lopez, United States v., 245
Los Angeles Police Department v. United Reporting Publishing Corporation, 92–93

M

Marsh v. Chambers, 199
Martinez-Salazar, United States v., 137–139
Martinez v. Court of Appeal of California, Fourth Appellate District, 219–220
McDonnell Douglas v. Green, 11
Menotti v. City of Seattle, 204
Meritor Savings Bank, FSB v. Vinson, 217
Merrill v. Navegar, Inc., 39
Microsoft, United States v., 19–21
Miller v. French, 182–183
Minnesota Twins Partnership v. State of Minnesota, 25–27
Miranda v. Arizona, 210–211
Mitchell v. Helms, 198–199, 208
Morrison, United States v., 245–246
Murphy v. United Parcel Service, Inc., 55–56

N

New Hampshire v. Maine (1999), 28–29
New Jersey v. New York, 29
New York Times v. Sullivan, 147, 148

New York v. Hill, 48–50
Nixon v. Shrink Missouri Government PAC, 64–65
Norfolk Southern Railway Co. v. Shanklin, 84–86

O

O'Brien, United States v., 90
Ohler v. United States, 74–76
Olmstead v. L.C., 56–57
Oncale v. Sundowner Offshore Services, Inc., 218
Onishea v. Hopper, 4

P

Pegram v. Herdrich, 117–118
Pennsylvania v. Williams, 215–217
People v. Prak, 96
People v. Wende, 222
Piazza v. Major League Baseball, 26, 27
Playboy Entertainment Group, Inc., United States v., 229–230
Portuondo v. Agard, 87–88

R

Ray v. Atlantic Richfield Co., 69, 70
Reeves v. Sanderson Plumbing Products, Inc., 11–12
Reno v. American-Arab Anti-Discrimination Committee, 123
Reno v. Bossier Parish School Board, 240–241
Reno v. Condon, 86–87
Rice v. Cayetano, 239–240
Richardson v. Reno, 123–124
Riggs v. California, 194, 195
Roberts v. United States Jaycees, 103
Roe v. Flores-Ortega, 220–222
Roe v. Wade, 2
Romer v. Evans, 97
Ross v. Oklahoma, 139
Roth v. United States, 96

S

Santa Fe Independent School District v. Doe, 199–201
Schaill v. Tippecanoe County School Corp., 187
Schenck v. Pro-Choice Network of Western New York, 181
School Board of Nassau County, Fla. v. Arline, 4
Seminole Tribe of Fla. v. Florida, 83, 84
Slack v. McDaniel, 112–113
Smith v. Robbins, 222–223
Sony Corporation of America v. Universal City Studios, Inc., 128
Spielberg v. American Airlines Inc., 15–16
Spruill, United States v., 107
State of Michigan v. Abraham, 141
State of Minnesota v. Philip Morris Incorporated, 234–235
State of Montana v. Dawn Sprinkle, 244–245
State of North Carolina v. Thomas Richard Jones, 35–36
State v. Schmakel, 179
State v. Sudderth, 36
Stearns, United States v., 221
Stenberg v. Carhart, 2–4
Stone v. Graham, 197
Strickland v. Washington, 221
Studley, United States v., 180
Sutton v. United Airlines, Inc., 55, 57, 58

T

Tarver v. Hopper, 34
Terry v. Ohio, 94
Texas Beef Group v. Winfrey, 150–151
Thomas v. Network Solutions, 132, 133
Todd v. Rush County Schools, 187–188
Toolson v. New York Yankees, Inc., 25
Troxel v. Granville, 81–82

U

U S West Communications, Inc. v. FCC, 230–231
Utah Children v. Utah Division of Child and Family Services, 8

V

Vernonia School District 473 v. Acton, 187
Village of Willowbrook v. Olech, 71–72

W

Wal-Mart Stores, Inc. v. Samara Brothers, Inc., 235–236
Weatherhead v. United States, 78–79

INDEX
BY NAME AND SUBJECT

A

Abandonment
   of newborns, 1–2
ABC television
   libel case against, 148–149
Abortion
   and cloning legislation, 184–185
   and Colorado's "bubble law," 181–182
   Colorado's "bubble law" (Appendix), 259
   Nebraska partial-birth statute (Appendix), 249
   partial-birth, 2–4
Abraham, Nathaniel, 139–141
Acquired Immune Deficiency Syndrome (AIDS)
   health insurance benefits for, 118–119
   segregation of prisoners with, 4–5
Ada, Joseph F.
   and Guam election procedure, 63–64
Adoption, 5–8
   access to records, 6–8
   annulment of, 5–6
   and gay and lesbian rights, 98
   rights of unmarried adults, 8
   Utah Child Welfare Amendments (Appendix), 250
Affirmative action
   and One Florida Initiative, 8–10
Aftergood, Steven, 94
Agard, Ray
   and Fifth Amendment, 87–88
Age discrimination, 10–12
   in private employment, 11–12
   in state employment, 10–11
Age Discrimination in Employment Act (1967), 10–12

Agricultural law
   and Rally for Rural America, 12–13
Agriculture Competition Enhancement Act, 13
AIDS. *See* Acquired Immune Deficiency Syndrome
Air bags product liability, 188–189
Airlines, 13–16
   American Airlines Flight 58 lawsuit, 15–16
   and bombing of Pan Am Flight 103, 231–232
   Death on the High Seas Act, 13–15
   Spielberg v. American Airlines Inc., 15–16
   TWA Flight 800, 13–15
   ValuJet Flight 592 crash, 47–48
Alabama Department of Corrections
   segregation by HIV status, 4
Albert, Carl Bert, 16–17
Albertson's, Inc.
   disability case against, 52–54
Alcohol, Tobacco, and Firearms, Bureau of
   and Waco disaster, 246
Aliens
   Cuban immigration, 17–19
   and incarceration of immigrants, 123–124
al-Qadhafi, Mu'ammar. *See* Khadafi, Moammar
Amendment 2 (to Col. Constitution)
   and gay and lesbian rights, 97
American Airlines
   lawsuits against, 15–16
American Civil Liberties Union (ACLU)
   defense of Cynthia Stewart, 179
   defense of Timothy Boomer, 96
   and humiliation as punishment, 214–215
   and Ohio's state motto, 199
   and Seattle's "no protest" zone, 204

American Dental Association
    discrimination case against, 66–67
American Farm Bureau (AFB), 68–69
American Honda Motor Company, Inc.
    and product liability, 188–189
Americans with Disabilities Act (ADA), 54
    and health insurance, 118–119
    high blood pressure, 55–56
    public services, 56–57
    vision impairment, 52–54, 57–58
Ameritech
    and long-distance telephone services, 230
Amestoy, Jeffrey
    gay and lesbian rights, 101
Anderson, Terry, 128–130
Anticybersquatting Consumer Protection Act (1999), 130–131
Anti-Drug Abuse Act (1988), 60
Anti-gay and lesbian legislation, 97–99
Antiterrorism and Effective Death Penalty Act (1996), 36–37, 129
    and habeas corpus appeals, 112–113
Antitrust law
    and baseball, 25–27
    and Internet domain name sales, 132–133
    and Microsoft Corporation, 19–21
Appeals
    and effective counsel, 220–222
    frivolous, 222–223
    and habeas corpus, 111–112
    right to self-representation on, 219–220
Apprendi, Charles C., Jr.
    and hate crime, 113–114
Army Corps of Engineers
    and wetlands development rules, 70–71
Artis, John, 38–39
Asatru Folk Assembly
    and Kennewick Man, 162–163
AT&T
    break-up of, 230
Athletes, professional
    and legal troubles, 224–225
Atkinson, Michael
    and athletes' legal problems, 224–225
Atlanta Journal-Constitution, 146–148
Atlas Corporation
    and Native American land claims, 161
Attorney-client privilege
    and "Filegate," 186
Attorneys general
    Kleindienst, Richard (obituary), 144
    Richardson, Elliot Lee (obituary), 202
Automated teller machines (ATMs), 25
Aviation Security Act (1982), 231

B
Baby Bells
    and long-distance telephone services, 230–231
Bailey, F. Lee
    and Sam Sheppard case, 219
Banking Act of 1933. *See* Glass-Steagall Act
Bankruptcy
    filed by Edward Mezvinsky, 158
    and Mark and Genevieve Innes, 23
    and student loans, 23–24
Banks and banking
    and modernization of Glass-Steagall Act, 24–25
Barkley, Charles, 224–225
Baseball
    and antitrust law, 25–27
Bates, Daisy
    obituary, 27
Bear Lodge (Devils Tower National Monument)
    use of during Native American rituals, 196–197
Beck, Robert A., II
    and whistleblowing, 191–192
Best, Patricia
    and the "*Seinfeld* Case," 217–218
Binion, Ted, 158–159
Bird, Rose Elizabeth, 27–28
Bollier, Edwin
    and bombing of Pan Am Flight 103, 232
Bond, Steven, 209
Boomer, Timothy (aka "Cussing Canoeist"), 95–96
Bordallo, Madeleine Z.
    and Guam election procedure, 63–64
Boundaries, state
    and Portsmouth Naval Shipyard, 28–29
Boy Scouts of America
    and discrimination against homosexuals, 101–103
Brady, Carolee
    and sex discrimination suit against USIA, 213
Brady Handgun Violence Prevention Act ("Brady Bill"), 106–107
    and school shootings, 108
Brady, James
    and Brady Bill, 106
Branch Davidians
    and Waco disaster, 246–248
Brennan, William Joseph, Jr.
    obituary, 29
Breyer, Stephen Gerald
    abortion, 3
    age discrimination, 11
    Commerce Clause, 41–42

disabled persons, 56, 58
federalism, 84
Fifth Amendment, 88
First Amendment, 89
Fourth Amendment, 94
frivolous appeals, 223
habeas corpus, 112
hate crime, 114
litigation against states by their employees, 83
prison, 183
product liability, 188–189
public funds for private schools, 198
public railroad safety standards, 85
rules of evidence, 75
search and seizure, 210
sexually-explicit programming restrictions, 230
women's rights, 246

Bribery
as a federal crime, 156–157
trial of Al Lipscomb for, 29–31

British Foreign Office
and the Weatherhead letter, 78

Broadcasting
and sexually-explicit programming restrictions, 229–230

Brock, David
and N.H. Supreme Court ethics scandal, 192–194

Broderick, John
and N.H. Supreme Court ethics scandal, 192–193

Brzonkala, Christy
and women's rights, 245–246

Buculei, Catalin
and child pornography, 180–181

Buergenthal, Thomas, 31–32
Bush, Jeb, 8–10

Business disparagement laws
and slander suit against Oprah Winfrey, 150–151

C

Cable television
and sexually-explicit programming restrictions, 229–230

Camacho, Felix P.
and Guam election procedure, 63–64

Campaign finance reform
in Missouri, 64–65

Capital Cities/ABC, Inc.
libel case against, 148–149

Capital punishment, 33–37
as cruel and unusual punishment, 33–34
for drug-related offenses, 60–61
for drunk drivers, 35–36
and habeas corpus, 36–37
Illinois's moratorium on, 34–35

Carhart, Dr. Leroy, 3
Carmell, Scott, 76–77

Carmichael, Stokely
obituary, 37

Carpenter, Robert
and habeas corpus, 111–112

Carruth, Rae, 224–225

Carter, James Earl (Jimmy)
and Panama Canal speech (Appendix), 259–261
and Panama Canal Treaty, 236

Carter, Rubin "Hurricane," 38–39

Cayuga Indian Nation
land claim, 161–162

Center to Prevent Handgun Violence, 39–41

Central Intelligence Agency (CIA)
disclosure of budget under FOIA, 94–95

Chalek, Michael
and annulment of adoption, 5–6

Challenges, peremptory, 137–139

Child pornography
and family photographs, 178–180
Ohio anti-pornography law (Appendix), 257–259
and rape, 180–181

Child Pornography Prevention Act (1996), 180

Children's Online Privacy Protection Act (1998), 131–132

Children's rights
and abandonment, 1–2
and the Internet, 131–132

Child Sexual Abuse and Pornography Act (1986), 180

Chinese Americans
accused of espionage, 72–73

Christensen, John, 126

Citizenship, U.S.
and war crimes, 51–52

Civil rights
discrimination against homosexuals, 101–103

Civil rights abuses
and torture of Abner Louima, 176–177

Civil Rights Act (1964)
and sexual harassment, 217
Title VII of, 66–67

Civil Rights Movement
John R. Lewis, 145–146

Class action
against U.S. Information Agency, 213–215

Clifford, Clark McAdams
obituary, 41

Clinton, William Jefferson (Bill), 166

Clinton, William Jefferson (Bill) *(cont'd)*
and "Filegate," 183–188
and genetic discrimination, 65
and pardon of Preston King, 166–167
Clonaid (company), 184–185
Cloning
regulation of research, 184–185
Cloning Prohibition Act (1997), 184–185
College Savings Bank
and patents & trademarks, 83–84
Colorado's "bubble law," 181–182
Colorado's "bubble law" (Appendix), 259
Columbine High School shooting, 108–109
and public posting of Ten Commandments, 198
Commerce Clause
and baseball, 25–27
and federalism, 87
and taxation, 41–42
and Violence Against Women Act, 245–246
Commerce, electronic, 42–43
Commonwealth of Puerto Rico
political status of, 223–226
Communications
and disabled persons' access, 54–55
Communications Act (1934), 54–55
Community Resources Against Street Hoodlums (CRASH), 174–176
Compensation
and Tulsa race riot of 1921, 201–202
Competence
Kenneth Curtis trials, 43–44
Computer crime
denial of service attacks, 44–45
via the Internet, 133–135
Confrontation Clause
and hearsay evidence, 45–47
Congressional representatives
Albert, Carl (biography), 16–17
Mezvinsky, Edward (biography), 157–158
Conspiracy
trial of Al Lipscomb for, 29–31
ValuJet Flight 592 crash, 47–48
Construction Performance Corporation
and racketeering, 191
Copyright
and electronic media, 126–128
Counsel, effective
and timely appeals, 220–222
Court of Appeals, New York, 49
CRASH. *See* Community Resources Against Street Hoodlums (CRASH)
Crawford, James
and women's rights, 245–246
Credibility
and Fifth Amendment, 87–88

Criminal procedure
federal rule 24, 138
speedy trial, 48–50
Croft, Sally, 78
Cross-examination
introduction of prior convictions, 74–76
Cruel and unusual punishment
capital punishment as, 33–34
humiliation as punishment, 214–215
Cuban Americans
accused of espionage, 73–74
Cuban immigration, 17–19
Cuban Readjustment Act (1966), 17
Curtis, Kenneth, 43–44
Cussing Canoeist. *See* Boomer, Timothy

D

Dale, James
and gay and lesbian rights, 101–103
Deadbeat parents
sentencing of, 214–215
Death on the High Seas Act, 13–15
Death penalty. *See* Capital punishment
Decatur Seven
suspension of, 206–208
Defenders of Wildlife, 68–69
Defense of Marriage Act, 100
and gay and lesbian rights, 98
Deportation
Hammer, Ferdinand, 51–52
Deutch, John, 73
Devils Tower National Monument. *See* Bear Lodge
Diallo, Ahmed Amadou, 177–178
Dickerson, Charles T.
and Miranda warning, 210–211
Digital Millennium Copyright Act, 127
Disability
in communications, 54–55
new FCC rules (Appendix), 250–251
Disabled persons, 52–59
FCC rules changes, 54–55
high blood pressure, 55–56
public services, 56–57
vision impairment, 52–54, 57–58
Discovery
and tobacco litigation, 234–235
Discrimination
and anti-gay and lesbian legislation, 97–99
in employment, 52–54, 57–58
genetic, 65–66
sex-based, 66–67, 213, 215
in voting practices, 239–240
DNA
and patent law, 172–173

DNA evidence
    and Kennewick Man tests, 162–164
    and rape suspects, 59–60
    in Sam Sheppard case, 218
Draft evasion
    and pardon of Preston King, 166–167
Driver's Privacy Protection Act (1994), 86–87
Driver's Privacy Protection Act (1994) (Appendix), 255–257
Drugs and narcotics, 60–62
    in Central America, 237
    execution of Juan Raul Garza, 60–61
    and lawful searches, 209
    and Sammy "The Bull" Gravano, 61–62
Drug testing, 187–188
Drunk driving
    capital punishment for, 35–36
    sentencing for, 214–215

E

Eberling, Richard, 218
Education law
    and funding of college organizations, 88–89
Education, U.S. Department of, 23–24
Elections
    campaign finance reform, 64–65
    Guam, 63–64
Electrocution
    as cruel and unusual punishment, 33–34
Electronic commerce, 42–43
Electronic Freedom of Information Act, 95
Elementary and Secondary Education Act (1965), 198
Eleventh Amendment
    and bankruptcy, 23–24
Employee Retirement Income Security Act (1974), 117–118
Employment law, 65–67
    age discrimination, 10–12
    discrimination, 52–54, 57–58
    Executive Order 13145 (Appendix), 252–254
    genetic discrimination, 65–66
    high blood pressure as disability, 55–56
    litigation against states by their employees, 82–83
    sex discrimination, 66–67, 213, 215
Endangered Species Act (ESA), 68–69
Environmental law, 68–71
    endangered species, 68–69
    oil spills, 69–70
    wetlands development rules, 70–71
Equal protection
    and anti-gay and lesbian legislation, 97–99
    and private property, 71–72
    and welfare reform, 243–244
Erie, PA
    anti-nudity ordinance in, 89–90
Espionage, 72–74
    alleged against Cubans, 73–74
    alleged against Wen Ho Lee, 72–73
Establishment Clause, 196–201
    and access to Bear Lodge (Devils Tower National Monument), 196–197
    and Ohio's state motto, 199
    and prayer in public schools, 199–201
    and public funds for private schools, 198–199
    and school voucher programs, 208–209
    and Ten Commandments in public buildings, 197–198
Ethics
    and human cloning, 184–185
    and patenting human DNA, 172–173
Evans, Terrance T., 119
Evidence
    ex post facto laws, 76–77
    and self-incrimination, 74–76
Executive Order 12958
    and the Weatherhead letter, 79
Executive Order 13145
    and genetic discrimination, 65–66
Executive Order 13145 (Appendix), 252–254
Ex post facto laws
    and parole hearings, 169–171
    rules of evidence, 76–77
    and supervised release, 170
Extradition, 77–79
    of Augusto Pinochet, 77–78
    of Sally Croft and Susan Hagan, 78–79
Exxon *Valdez* oil spill, 69

F

Fagan, Stephen, 143–144
Faget, Mariano, 74
Fair Labor Standards Act (1938), 83
Family law
    grandparents' visitation rights, 81–82
    parental kidnapping, 143–144
Farmer, James, 145
Farmers and Ranchers Fair Competition Act, 13
Farming law
    and Rally for Rural America, 12–13
FDA. *See* Food and Drug Administration
Federal Aviation Administration (FAA), 47
Federal Bureau of Investigation (FBI)
    and computer crime, 45
    and Waco disaster, 246–247
    and Wen Ho Lee, 72–73

Federal Communications Act
    and advertising, 91
Federal Communications Commission (FCC)
    and disabled persons, 54–55
    and long-distance telephone services, 230–231
    new rules for handicap access (Appendix), 250–251
Federalism, 82–87
    and bankruptcy, 23–24
    litigation against states by their employees, 82–83
    and patents & trademarks, 83–84
    and privacy, 86–87
    and public railroad safety standards, 84–86
Federal Railroad Safety Act, 85
Federal Trade and Intercourse Act (1790), 161
Federal Trade Commission
    and Internet fraud, 135
    and Internet privacy, 131–132
Federation of American Scientists
    and disclosure of CIA budget, 94–95
Fhimah, Al-Amin Khalifa, 231
Fieger, Geoffrey, 140
Fifteenth Amendment
    and discrimination based on heritage, 239–240
Fifth Amendment
    and self-incrimination, 87–88
    and welfare reform, 243–244
Fighting
    in schools, 206–208
Filegate
    and Privacy Act (1974), 183–188
Financial Services Modernization Act, 24–25
First Amendment, 88–93
    and access to Bear Lodge (Devils Tower National Monument), 196–197
    and campaign contributions, 64–65
    and child pornography, 180–181
    and Colorado's "bubble law," 181–182
    and commercial speech, 90–93
    Establishment Clause of the, 196–201
    and freedom of speech, 95–96
    and funding of college organizations, 88–89
    and nude dancing, 89–90
    and nude photographs of children, 178–180
    and Ohio's state motto, 199
    and prayer in public schools, 199–201
    and public funds for private schools, 198–199
    and school voucher programs, 208–209
    and sexually-explicit programming restrictions, 229–230
    and television, 148–149
    and Ten Commandments in public buildings, 197–198
Fischer, Jeffrey, 156–157
Fisher, Justin R.
    and hate crime, 114–115
Florence, Eugene
    and ValuJet crash, 47
Flores-Ortega, Lucio
    and effective counsel, 220–222
Florida Board of Regents, 10–11
Florida Prepaid Postsecondary Ed. Expense Bd.
    and patents & trademarks, 83–84
Food and Drug Administration (FDA)
    and gene therapy, 171–174
    and human cloning, 184–185
    and tobacco regulation, 232–234
Food disparagement laws
    and slander suit against Oprah Winfrey, 150–151
Food, Drug, and Cosmetic Act
    and regulation of nicotine, 233
Food stamp program
    and welfare reform, 243
Foraker Act
    and Puerto Rican sovereignty, 223
Fourth Amendment
    and reasonable suspicion, 93–94
Fraud
    Edward Mezvinsky lawsuit, 158
    as a federal crime, 156–157
Fredman, Zev David, 64–65
Freedom of association
    and gay and lesbian rights, 103
    and protests of World Trade Organization, 202–204
Freedom of Information Act (FOIA)
    and disclosure of CIA budget, 94–95
    and the Weatherhead letter, 78–79
Freedom of speech
    and "Cussing Canoeist" case, 95–96
Freedom Rides, 145
Freedom to Farm Act, 12
Frisk. *See* Stop and frisk

G

Gadhafi, Muammar. *See* Khadafi, Moammar
Gambino family (organized crime), 105
Gambling
    advertisement of, 90–92
Garza, Juan Raul, 60–61
Gates, Daryl, 168
Gay and lesbian rights, 97–105
    adoption, 8
    discrimination, 101–103

hate crimes against homosexuals, 114–115
  legislation against, 97–99
  same-sex marriage, 99–101
  visitation of children, 103–105
Geier, Alexis, 188–189
Gelsinger, Jesse, 171–174
Gender discrimination. *See* Sex discrimination
General Agreement on Tariffs and Trade (GATT), 202
Genetic discrimination, 65–66
Genetic research
  and patent law, 172–173
Genovese family (organized crime), 105
Georgia
  and two strikes law, 194–195
Gigante, Louis, 105
Gigante, Vincent "The Chin," 105–106
Gillespie, Gerald
  and Brady Bill, 106–107
Ginsburg, Ruth Bader
  age discrimination, 11
  disabled persons, 57
  effective counsel, 221
  ex post facto laws, 76
  federalism, 84
  Fifth Amendment, 88
  First Amendment, 90
  Fourth Amendment, 94
  frivolous appeals, 223
  litigation against states by their employees, 83
  parole, 170
  peremptory challenges, 138–139
  product liability, 189
  public funds for private schools, 199
  rules of evidence, 75
  stop and frisk, 227
  voting discrimination, 240
  women's rights, 246
Glass-Steagall Act
  modernization of, 24–25
Glendening, Parris
  and gun control, 109
Glover, Calvin N.
  and hate crime, 114–115
Gonzalez, Daniel (ValuJet employee), 47
Gonzalez, Elian, 17–19
Gotti, John J., 61, 105
Gramm-Leach Act, 24–25
Gramm, Phil, 24
Granville, Tommie
  and grandparents' visitation rights, 81–82
Gravano, Salvatore "Sammy the Bull," 61–62
Gun control, 106–110
  and Brady Bill cases, 106–107
  Center to Prevent Handgun Violence, 39–41
  and lawsuits against gun makers, 109–110
  and school shootings, 107–109
Gun-Free Schools Act (1994), 108
Guns
  and stop and frisk rules, 226–228
Gutierrez, Carl T.C.
  and Guam election procedure, 63–64

H

Habeas corpus, 111–113
  and appellate procedure, 111–112
  and capital punishment, 36–37
  and incarceration of immigrants, 123–124
Hackers. *See* Computer crime
Hagan, Susan, 78
Halushka, Lisa, 140
Hammer, Ferdinand, 51–52
Handgun Control, Inc. (HCI), 39–41
Hartman, Carolee Brady
  and sex discrimination suit against USIA, 213
Hate crime, 113–115
  against African Americans, 113–114
  in the military, 114–115
Hawai'i
  discriminatory voting practices, 239–240
Health care law, 115–118
  and HMOs, 117–118
  Patients' Bill of Rights, 115–117
Health insurance
  and AIDS benefits, 118–119
Health Maintenance Organizations. *See* HMOs
Hearsay evidence
  and Confrontation Clause, 45–47
Helms, Mary
  and public funds for private schools, 198
Herbert, Adam, 9
Herdrich, Cynthia, 117–118
Hernandez, Linda, 74
Hernandez, Nilo, 74
Hill, Michael, 49
Hinton, Kimberly, 57–58
HMOs
  lawsuits against, 117–118
  and patients' rights, 115–117
Hogan, Thomas
  and Freedom of Information Act, 95
  and the Internet, 133
Holocaust, 31
Holtzman Amendment, 51
Homeless persons
  and workfare jobs in New York, 120–121
Homicide
  Kenneth Curtis trials, 43–44
  of Ted Binion, 158–159

Homicide *(cont'd)*
    trial of Nathaniel Abraham, 139–141
Honda (American Honda Motor Company, Inc.)
    and product liability, 188–189
Horiuchi, Lon
    and Waco disaster, 247
Horton, Sherman
    and N.H. Supreme Court ethics scandal, 192–193
Howe, Steve, 224–225
Hubbell, Webster
    and Whitewater investigation, 211–212
Human cloning
    regulation of research, 184–185
Human Genome Project, 172–173
    and genetic discrimination, 65–66
Human rights
    abuses by Pinochet's government, 77
    and Inter-American Court, 32
    and Truth Commission on El Salvador, 32
Hunt-Wesson, Inc.
    and Commerce Clause, 41–42

I

Illegal Immigration Reform and Immigrant Responsibility Act (1996), 123–124
Immigration
    Cuban, 17–19
    and incarceration of immigrants, 123–124
    and war criminals, 51–52
Immigration and Naturalization Act, 123
Immigration and Naturalization Service (INS)
    and Elian Gonzalez, 18–19
    and incarceration of immigrants, 123
Immunity
    of police officers, 124–125
    and self-incrimination, 211–212
Imperatori, Jose, 74
Indiana Civil Liberties Union
    and Ten Commandments in Indiana's public buildings, 197
Information Agency, U.S.
    sex discrimination lawsuit against, 213–215
Inheritance
    by unmarried partner, 125–126
Innes, Mark and Genevieve
    and bankruptcy, 23
Innocence Project, 205
Insurance, health, 115–117
Intellectual property
    and electronic media, 126–128
    and genetic research, 172–173
    Internet domain names as, 130–131
Inter-American Court
    and human rights, 32

Interior, U.S. Department of the
    and access to Bear Lodge (Devils Tower National Monument), 196–197
    endangered species, 68
International Association of Independent Tank Owners (Intertanko), 69
International Court of Justice (World Court), 32
International law
    extradition of Augusto Pinochet, 77–78
    and terrorism, 128–130
International relations
    with China, 73
    with Iran, 128–130
    with Libya, 231
    and the Weatherhead letter, 78–79
International waterways
    and Panama Canal Treaty, 236–238
Internet, 130–135
    computer viruses, 133–134
    crime on the, 133–135
    denial of service attacks, 44–45
    domain name sales, 132–133
    fraud on the, 135
    and intellectual property, 126–128
    and privacy, 131–132
    and trademark, 130–131
Interstate Agreement on Detainers (IAD), 48–50
Iverson, Allen, 224–225

J

Jackson, Jesse
    and suspension of the "Decatur Seven," 206, 208
Jewell, Richard, 146–148
Johnson, Denise R., 101
Johnson, Frank Minis, Jr.
    obituary, 137
Johnson, Roy Lee
    and supervised release, 170–171
Jones Act
    and Puerto Rican sovereignty, 223
Jones, Paula, 184
Jones, Robert, 169–171
Jones, Thomas Richard
    and capital punishment, 35–36
Jordan, Michael, 224–225
Jury
    peremptory challenges, 137–139
Justice, U.S. Department of
    and health insurance, 119
    and juvenile crime, 138–139
    and LAPD scandal, 176
    and Microsoft antitrust case, 19–20

and sex discrimination in U.S. Information Agency, 214
and the Weatherhead letter, 78
Juvenile law
    trial of Nathaniel Abraham, 139–141
    trying juveniles as adults, 138–139
Juvenile Waiver Law (Mich.), 138–139

K

Kalson, Donna, 43
Kansas State University
    and student loans, 23–24
Kennedy, Anthony McLeod
    abortion, 4
    campaign finance reform, 65
    environmental law, 70
    ex post facto laws, 76
    First Amendment, 89, 93
    habeas corpus, 112–113
    hate crime, 114
    litigation against states by their employees, 83
    Medicare, 156
    parole, 169–170
    prior restraint, 182
    public funds for private schools, 198
    sexually-explicit programming restrictions, 229–230
    voting discrimination, 239–240
Kennewick Man, 162–164
Ketterer, Drew, 28
Khadafi, Moammar
    and bombing of Pan Am Flight 103, 231
Kidnapping
    perpetrated by parents, 143–144
Kimel, J. Daniel, Jr.
    and age discrimination, 10–11
King, Martin Luther, Jr., 145
King, Preston, 166–167
King, Rodney, 168
Kirkingburg, Hallie
    and disabilities, 52–54
Kleindienst, Richard Gordon
    obituary, 144
Kolstad, Carole, 66–67
Kuralt, Charles
    estate of, 125–126

L

Labbe, J. R.
    and pardon of Preston King, 167
Labor law
    litigation against states by their employees, 82–83

LaLonde, John (immunity case petitioner), 124–125
Lamberth, Royce C., 183, 186–187
Land claims
    of Native Americans, 161–162
Lanham Trademark Act (1946), 130, 236
LAPD. *See* Los Angeles Police Department
Law Against Discrimination (N.J.), 101–103
Leach, James, 24
Leavitt, Mike, 8
Lee, Wen Ho, 72–73
Legal Action Project, 39
Lesbian rights. *See* Gay and lesbian rights
Levan, Alan, 148–149
Lewis, John R., 145–146
Lewis, Ray, 224–225
Libel and slander, 146–151
    and disparagement laws, 150–151
    and Richard Jewell, 146–148
    suit against G. Gordon Liddy, 149–150
    television, 148–149
Licensing, software, 42–43
Liddy, G. Gordon
    libel suit against, 149–150
Lilly, Benjamin, 45–47
Lipscomb, Al, 29–31
Los Angeles Police Department
    chief of (biography), 167–169
    as First Amendment case petitioner, 92–93
    scandal in Rampart Division, 168, 174, 176
Louima, Abner, 176–177
Lyman, Howard
    and slander suit against Oprah Winfrey, 150

M

MacKenzie, Jerold
    and the "*Seinfeld* Case," 217–218
Mafia. *See* Organized crime
Major League Baseball, 25–27
Manslaughter
    dog attacks as, 153–154
    Kenneth Curtis trials, 43–44
March on Washington, 146
Margolies-Mezvinsky, Marjorie, 157–158
Maritime law
    oil spills, 69–70
Marriage
    same-sex, 98–101
Marshall, Margaret Hilary, 154–155
Marshall, Thurgood, 55
Martinez-Salazar, Abel
    and peremptory challenges, 137–139
Martinez, Salvador
    and right to self-representation, 219–220
Mather, John R., 147

McCarran-Ferguson Act (MFA), 119
McCarter, Dorothy
    and women's rights, 244
McCord, James
    and Watergate, 149
McSorley, Marty, 224–225
Medicare
    federalization of Medicare fraud, 156–157
Medicine
    regulation of, 171–174
Megan's Law, 215
Megrahi, Abdel Basset Ali Mohmed al-, 231
Mezvinsky, Edward Maurice, 157–158
Michigan Penal Code, Act 328 (1931)
        (Appendix), 257
Microsoft Corporation, 19–21
Military
    homosexuals in, 114–115
Miller Brewing Company
    and sexual harassment case, 217
Million Mom March, 108
Minnesota Supreme Court, 26–27
Minnesota Twins (baseball franchise)
    and antitrust law, 25–27
Miranda warning, 210–211
Mitchell, Guy
    and public funds for private schools, 198
Mitnick, Kevin, 134
Montgomery, Alabama, bus boycott, 145
Montgomery Improvement Association (MIA), 145
Montreal Accord, 15
Moore, Eugene, 140
Morrison, Antonio
    and women's rights, 245–246
MP3.com, 127
Murder
    Kenneth Curtis trials, 43–44
    of Ted Binion, 158–159
    trial of Nathaniel Abraham, 139–141
Murphy, Sandra
    and the death of Ted Binion, 158–159
Murphy, Vaughn
    and disabilities case, 55–56
Music publishing
    and intellectual property, 126–128

N

Napster, 127–128
National Association for the Advancement of
        Colored People (NAACP)
    and voting, 241
National Conference of Commissioners on
        Uniform State Laws (NCCUSL), 42
National Institutes of Health
    and gene therapy, 172

National Park Service
    and access to Bear Lodge (Devils Tower
        National Monument), 196–197
National Rifle Association (NRA)
    and gun control legislation, 108
National Science Foundation
    and Internet domain name sales, 132–133
National Traffic and Motor Vehicle Safety
        Act (1966), 188–189
National Transportation Safety Board
    American Airlines Flight 1420, 15
    TWA Flight 800, 13
    ValuJet Flight 592, 47
Nationwide Permit 26 (construction
        regulations), 70–71
Native American Graves Protection and
        Repatriation Act (NAGPRA), 162
Native American rights, 161–164
    and access to Bear Lodge (Devils Tower
        National Monument), 196–197
    land claims, 161–162
    and tribal remains, 162–164
Navegar, Inc., 39
Nebraska partial-birth abortion statute
        (Appendix), 249
Network Solutions, Inc., 132–133
Neufeld, Peter, 205
New York Police Department
    and shooting of Amadou Diallo, 177–178
    and torture of Abner Louima, 176–177
Norfolk Southern Railway Co.
    and public railroad safety standards, 84–86
Northern Utes
    land claim, 161
Nude dancing
    legality of, 89–90

O

O'Bannon, Frank, 197
Obituary notices
    Bates, Daisy, 27
    Brennan, William Joseph, Jr., 29
    Carmichael, Stokely, 37
    Clifford, Clark McAdams, 41
    Johnson, Frank Minis, Jr., 137
    Kleindienst, Richard Gordon, 144
    Richardson, Elliot Lee, 202
    Robinson, Spottswood, 204
    Stout, Juanita Kidd, 228
Obscenity
    and First Amendment, 89–90
    Mich. anti-cussing law (Appendix), 257
    verbal, 95–96
O'Connor, Sandra Day
    age discrimination, 10–12
    capital punishment, 37

disabled persons, 55–56, 58
effective counsel, 221
employment law, 67
ex post facto laws, 76
First Amendment, 90
grandparents' visitation rights, 81–82
hate crime, 114
prison, 183
public funds for private schools, 198
public railroad safety standards, 85
sexually-explicit programming restrictions, 230
tobacco regulation, 233–234
Ohio's anti-pornography law (Appendix), 257–259
Ohler, Maria (evidence case petitioner), 74–76
Oil Pollution Act (1990), 69–70
Olech, Grace, 71–72
Olmstead Act
  and Puerto Rican sovereignty, 223
One Florida Initiative
  and affirmative action, 8–10
Organic Act of Guam, 63
Organized crime
  and Sammy "The Bull" Gravano, 61–62
  and Vincent "The Chin" Gigante, 105–106
Owens, Bill
  and Columbine High shooting, 109

P

Page, Alan Cedric, 165–166
Page Education Foundation, 165
Panama Canal Treaty, 236–238
  speech by Jimmy Carter (Appendix), 259–261
Pan Am Flight 103, 231–232
Pardon
  of Preston King, 166–167
Parents
  and gay and lesbian rights, 103–105
Parks, Bernard C., 167–169
  and LAPD scandal, 175
Parole
  hearings, frequency of, 169–171
  supervised release, 170–171
Partial-birth abortion, 2–4
Patent Act (1952)
  and genetic research, 172–173
Patent and Plant Variety Protection Remedy Clarification Act (1992), 84
Patents
  and federalism, 83–84
  and genetic research, 172–173
Patients' Bill of Rights, 115–117

Patients' rights
  and gene therapy, 171–174
  and health insurance law, 115–117
Pegram, Dr. Lori
  and health care law, 117–118
Peremptory challenges, 137–139
Perez, Rafael
  and LAPD scandal, 175
Personal Responsibility and Work Opportunity Reconciliation Act (1996), 243–244
Peterson, Matthew
  and Ohio's state motto, 199
Pinochet, Augusto, 77–78
Playboy Entertainment Group, Inc., 229–230
Police
  immunity of, 124–125
  and LAPD scandal in Rampart Division, 174–176
  and protests of World Trade Organization, 202–204
Police brutality, 176–178
  shooting of Amadou Diallo, 177–178
  torture of Abner Louima, 176–177
Popular Democratic Party
  and Puerto Rican sovereignty, 223–224
Porfolio, John C.
  and Bear Lodge case, 196–197
Poritz, Deborah T., 103
Pornography, 178–181
  control of a minor and, 180–181
  and family photographs, 178–180
  Ohio anti-pornography law (Appendix), 257–259
  and sexually-explicit programming restrictions, 229–230
Port and Waterways Safety Act (1972), 69
Porter, Anthony, 34
Portsmouth Naval Shipyard, legal boundary of, 28–29
Posner, Richard, 118
Prayer
  in public schools, 199–201
Preemption
  and public railroad safety standards, 84–86
Pregnancy
  and women's rights, 244–245
Prior restraint
  and Colorado's "bubble law," 181–182
Prison
  and Prison Litigation Reform Act, 182–183
Prisoners' rights
  and habeas corpus, 111–112
  and parole hearings, 169–171
  and segregation by HIV status, 4–5
  and supervised release, 170–171
Prison Litigation Reform Act (1996), 182–183

Privacy, 183–188
    and children on the Internet, 131–132
    and cloning research, 184–185
    and drug testing, 187–188
    and federalism, 86–87
Privacy Act (1974), 183–188
Probable cause
    and reasonable suspicion, 93–94
Proctor, George, 78
Product liability
    and air bags, 188–189
Proposition 21 (Calif. juvenile law), 138–139
Puerto Rico
    political status of, 223–226

Q

Qadhafi, Moamar. *See* Khadafi, Moammar
Qwest
    and long-distance telephone services, 230–231

R

Racism
    alleged in suspension of the "Decatur Seven," 207
    in application of three strikes laws, 194–195
    in media coverage, 224–225
Racketeer Influenced and Corrupt Organizations Act (RICO), 191–192
Railroads
    safety standards for public, 84–86
Rainbow/PUSH Coalition
    and suspension of the "Decatur Seven," 206
Rally for Rural America, 12–13
Ramones, Reomel
    and computer viruses, 134
Randolph, A. Raymond, 133
Rape
    and child pornography, 180–181
    and DNA evidence, 59–60
    and Violence Against Women Act, 245–246
Rational basis test
    and Welfare Reform Act of 1996, 243
Recidivism
    and humiliation as punishment, 214–215
    of juveniles tried as adults, 138–139
    and three strikes laws, 194–195
Recording Industry Association of America (RIAA), 127
Recusal
    and N.H. Supreme Court ethics scandal, 192–196

Reeves, Roger
    age discrimination, 11–12
Registration of Sexual Offenders Act (Penn.), 215–217
Rehabilitation Act (1973), 4
Rehnquist, William Hubbs
    abortion, 4
    disabled persons, 57
    ex post facto laws, 76
    federalism, 84, 86–87
    First Amendment, 92
    Fourth Amendment, 94
    hate crime, 114
    prayer in public schools, 201
    public funds for private schools, 198
    rules of evidence, 75
    search and seizure, 210
    self-incrimination, 211
    sexually-explicit programming restrictions, 230
    women's rights, 245–246
Religion, 196–201
    and access to Bear Lodge (Devils Tower National Monument), 196–197
    and Ohio's state motto, 199
    and prayer in public schools, 199–201
    and public funds for private schools, 198–199
    and school voucher programs, 208–209
    and Ten Commandments in public buildings, 197–198
Reno, Janet
    and voting, 241
Reparation
    and Tulsa race riot of 1921, 201–202
Repeat offenders. *See* Recidivism
Reproduction
    and Colorado's "bubble law," 181–182
    and women's rights, 244–245
Restitution
    and Tulsa race riot of 1921, 201–202
Rice, Harold
    and Hawai'ian voting practices, 239
Richards, Floyd
    and bribery, 29–31
Richardson, Bill, 161
Richardson, Elliot Lee
    obituary, 202
Richardson, Ralph, 123–124
RICO. *See* Racketeer Influenced and Corrupt Organizations Act
Rider, J.R., 224–225
Riot
    and protests of World Trade Organization, 202–204
    race, 201–202

Ripple, Kenneth F.
and Welfare Reform Act of 1996, 243–244
Robbins, Lee
and frivolous appeals, 222–223
Robinson, Spottswood William, III
obituary, 204
Roosevelt, Franklin Delano
and Puerto Rican sovereignty, 223
Rose, Pete, 224–225
Rosewood, Fla.
1923 race riot in, 201
Rubin, Marian
and charges of child pornography, 179
Rush County School district
and drug testing, 187–188
Ryan, George
and capital punishment, 35
and suspension of the "Decatur Seven," 206

S

SabreTech
and ValuJet Flight 592 crash, 47–48
Safety
standards for public railroad crossings, 84–86
Samara Brothers, Inc.
and trademark infringement, 235–236
Sanderson Plumbing Products, 11–12
Scalia, Antonin
abortion, 4
campaign finance reform, 65
criminal procedure, 49
disabled persons, 57
federalism, 84
Fifth Amendment, 87–88
First Amendment, 90, 93
habeas corpus, 112–113
Medicare, 157
prayer in public schools, 201
prior restraint, 182
public funds for private schools, 198
self-incrimination, 211
sexually-explicit programming restrictions, 230
trademark infringement, 236
Voting Rights Act of 1965, 241
Scheck, Barry, 205–206
Schools and school districts, 206–209
and drug testing, 187–188
and Establishment Clause, 198–199
and gun control legislation, 107–109
prayer in public, 199–201
and suspensions, 206–208
vouchers for, 208–209
Schwarz, Charles, 176–177

Search and seizure
and luggage, 209–210
Second Amendment
and Brady Bill cases, 106–107
and lawsuits against gun makers, 109–110
and school shootings, 107–109
Segregation
in accommodations, 145
by HIV status, 4–5
in transportation, 145
Seinfeld (TV program), 217
Self-incrimination, 210–212
and immunity, 211–212
and Miranda rights, 210–211
Self-representation
in appellate proceedings, 219–220
Selma to Montgomery march, 145
Sentencing
humiliation as punishment, 214–215
of juveniles, 140
of juveniles as adults, 138–139
and reproductive rights, 244–245
and three strikes laws, 194–195
Sentencing Reform Act (1984), 170
Separation of powers
and Prison Litigation Reform Act, 183
Sex discrimination, 66–67
in U.S. Information Agency, 213–215
Sex offenses, 215–217
Sexual harassment
and the "*Seinfeld* Case," 217–218
Shaheen, Jeanne, 29
Shanklin, Dedra and Eddie
and public railroad safety standards, 84–86
Shannon, Patricia, 125–126
Sheppard, Samuel H.
murder case update, 218–219
Sheppard, Samuel Reese, 218–219
Shields, N. T., 39
Shrink Missouri Government PAC, 64–65
Simpson, O. J., 205–206, 224–225
Sit-ins, lunch counter, 145
Sixth Amendment, 219–223
Confrontation Clause of the, 45–47
and effective counsel, 220–222
and frivolous appeals, 222–223
and self-representation on appeal, 219–220
Slack, Antonio, 112–113
Slander. *See* Libel and slander
Smith and Wesson, 40
Smith, David L.
and computer viruses, 134
Smithfield Foods, 12
Social Security Insurance
and welfare reform, 243
Software licensing, 42–43

Sonders, David G.
    Edward Mezvinsky lawsuit, 158
Souter, David Hackett
    age discrimination, 11
    campaign finance reform, 64–65
    disabled persons, 53–54
    effective counsel, 221
    elections in Guam, 63–64
    federalism, 84
    Fifth Amendment, 88
    First Amendment, 89
    Fourth Amendment, 94
    frivolous appeals, 223
    health care law, 118
    litigation against states by their employees, 83
    parole, 170
    product liability, 189
    public funds for private schools, 199
    Racketeer Influenced and Corrupt Organizations Act, 192
    rules of evidence, 75
    Voting Rights Act of 1965, 241
    women's rights, 246
Southeastern Insurance Group
    and racketeering, 191–192
Sovereignty
    of Puerto Rico, 223–226
Speagle, Frank, 153–154
Sports law, 224–225
Sprinkle, Dawn Marie
    and reproductive rights, 244–245
Starr, Kenneth
    and Whitewater investigation, 211–212
State Department, U.S.
    Weatherhead letter, 79
Statehood
    of Puerto Rico, 223–226
States' rights
    and litigation against states by their employees, 82–83
    and oil spills, 69–70
    and patents & trademarks, 83–84
    and taxation, 41–42
Statute of limitations
    and DNA evidence, 59–60
Stevens, John Paul
    age discrimination, 11
    capital punishment, 37
    Confrontation Clause, 46–47
    disabled persons, 56, 58
    effective counsel, 221
    ex post facto laws, 76
    federalism, 84
    Fifth Amendment, 88
    First Amendment, 89–93
    Fourth Amendment, 94
    frivolous appeals, 223
    grandparents' visitation rights, 82
    habeas corpus, 112
    hate crime, 114
    litigation against states by their employees, 83
    parole, 170
    prayer in public schools, 200–201
    prior restraint, 182
    prison, 183
    product liability, 189
    public funds for private schools, 199
    Racketeer Influenced and Corrupt Organizations Act, 192
    rules of evidence, 75
    self-incrimination, 212
    self-representation, 220
    voting discrimination, 240
    women's rights, 246
Stewart, Cynthia
    and allegations of child pornography, 178–179
Stop and frisk
    and reasonable suspicion, 93–94
    resulting from anonymous tips, 226–228
Stout, Juanita Kidd
    obituary, 228
Strawberry, Darryl, 224–225
Straw, Jack, 78
Strict scrutiny standard
    and Welfare Reform Act of 1996, 244
Student loans
    and bankruptcy, 23–24
Student Non-violent Coordinating Committee (SNCC), 145–146
Supervised release, 170–171
Sutton, Karen
    and disability case, 57–58

T

Tabish, Rick
    and the death of Ted Binion, 158–159
Tarver, Robert Lee
    and capital punishment, 34
Taxation
    and Internet domain name sales, 132–133
    interstate, 41–42
    and state boundaries, 28–29
Taylor, Lawrence, 224–225
Telecommunications, 229–231
    and disabled persons' access, 54–55
    and long-distance telephone services, 230–231
    and sexually-explicit programming restrictions, 229–230
Telecommunications Act (1996), 54–55

and long-distance telephone services, 230–231
sexually-explicit programming restrictions of, 229–230
Television
and the Internet, 128
and sexually-explicit programming restrictions, 229–230
Ten Commandments
posted in public buildings, 197–198
Tennessee Supreme Court, 6–8
Terrorism, 231–232
bombing of Pan Am Flight 103, 231–232
punitive damages awarded for victims of, 128–130
Texas Beef Group
and suit against Oprah Winfrey, 150–151
Thayer, Stephen
and N.H. Supreme Court ethics scandal, 192–193
Thomas, Clarence
abortion, 4
campaign finance reform, 65
disabled persons, 57
First Amendment, 90, 93
frivolous appeals, 222
habeas corpus, 113
Medicare, 157
prayer in public schools, 201
prior restraint, 182
public funds for private schools, 198
Racketeer Influenced and Corrupt Organizations Act, 192
self-incrimination, 211
Three strikes laws, 194–195
Tjoflat, Gerald B., 149
Tobacco, 232–235
classified documents, 234–235
regulation of, 232–234
Todd, William P., 187–188
Torrey Canyon oil spill, 69
Torrijos, Omar
and Panama Canal Treaty, 236
Toussaint, Edward
and tobacco litigation, 235
Trademark Remedy Clarification Act (1992), 84
Trademarks
and clothing design, 235–236
and federalism, 83–84
and the Internet, 130–131
Transportation, U.S. Department of, 53, 55
Treasury, U.S. Department of the, 25
Treaty, 236–238
and Panama Canal, 236–238
Troxel, Jenifer and Gary
and grandparents' visitation rights, 81–82

Truman, Harry S, 223
Truth Commission on El Salvador
and human rights, 32
TWA Flight 800, 13–15
Tyson, Mike, 224–225

U

UCITA. *See* Uniform Computer Information Transactions Act
Umatilla (Native Americans)
and Kennewick Man, 162, 164
Uniform Commercial Code (UCC), 42
Uniform Computer Information Transactions Act (UCITA), 42–43
United Airlines, Inc., 57–58
United Parcel Service, 55–56
United Reporting Publishing Corp., 92–93
U S West Communications, Inc., 230–231
Utah Child Welfare Amendments (Appendix), 250
Utah House Bill 103, 8

V

ValuJet Flight 592 crash, 47–48
Violence Against Women Act
and rape, 245–246
Violent Crime Control and Law Enforcement Act, 194–195
Virginia Supreme Court, 46
Visitation rights
of grandparents, 81–82
Voice of America (radio broadcast)
class action against, 213
Volpe, Justin, 176–177
Voting
discriminatory practices in, 239–240
and redistricting, 240–241
Voting Rights Act (1965)
and redistricting, 240–241
Vouchers, school, 208–209

W

Waco disaster, 246–248
Wal-Mart Stores, Inc.
and trademark infringement, 235–236
War crimes
and immigration, 51–52
Wardlow, William, 93–94
Warsaw Convention, 15
Washington (state)
and three strikes laws, 194–195
Watergate
and Carl Albert, 17

Watergate *(cont'd)*
   and libel suit against G. Gordon Liddy, 149–150
Weatherhead, Leslie, 78–79
Weatherhead letter, 78–79
Weatherhead letter (Appendix), 254–255
Welfare
   reform of, 243–244
Welfare Reform Act (1996), 243–244
Wells, Ida Maxwell
   and libel suit against G. Gordon Liddy, 149–150
Wetlands protection, 70–71
Whistleblowing
   and Robert Beck, 191–192
Whitewater investigation
   and Webster Hubbell, 211–212
Willey, Kathleen, 183–188
Williams, Donald Francis
   and sex offenses, 215
Williams, Stephen F.
   long-distance telephone services, 231
Williams, Terry, 37
Williams, Willie, 168
Winchell, Barry
   and hate crime, 114–115
Winfrey, Oprah, 150–151
Witness Protection Program, 61
Women's rights, 244–246
   and rape, 245–246
   and reproductive rights, 244–245
World Court, 32
World Trade Organization (WTO)
   and protests of, 202–204
Wrongful death, 246–248
   Waco disaster lawsuit for, 246–248
WTO. *See* World Trade Organization (WTO)

Y

Yahoo.com
   and denial of service attacks, 44
Yarber, Michael Edward Higginbotham. *See* Chalek, Michael

Z

Zero-tolerance policies
   in high schools, 206–208

ISBN 0-7879-4788-8

STAFFORD LIBRARY
COLUMBIA COLLEGE
COLUMBIA, MO. 65216